Crime and Justice

Crime and Justice
A Review of Research

Edited by Michael Tonry

VOLUME 30

The University of Chicago Press, Chicago and London

This volume was prepared under Grant Number 92-IJ-CX-K044 awarded to the Castine Research Corporation by the National Institute of Justice, U.S. Department of Justice, under the Omnibus Crime Control and Safe Streets Act of 1968 as amended. Points of view or opinions expressed in this volume are those of the editors or authors and do not necessarily represent the official position or policies of the U.S. Department of Justice.

The University of Chicago Press, Chicago 60637
The University of Chicago Press, Ltd., London

© 2003 by The University of Chicago
All rights reserved. Published 2003
Printed in the United States of America

ISSN: 0192-3234

ISBN: 0-226-80862-9

LCN: 80-642217

Contents

Preface

No one but the two of us, happily, is likely much to remember the long line of *Crime and Justice* prefaces we have written. Some people probably read the freshly minted ones as they appear and find them useful or not, but few people are likely to remember anything about them for more than a few hours.

We, on the other hand, have put pen to paper or, more recently, fingers to keyboards, thirty times now. Thirty volumes is a lot of volumes, and the more than twenty-five years since Blair Ewing, then acting administrator of the National Institute of Justice, convened the organizational meeting for *Crime and Justice*, is a lot of years.

During those years, we have written prefaces to a fair number of volumes that felt like milestones—volume 10, volume 25, the 2002 volume appearing after a quarter century of work—each time with a mixed sense of delight that the series had survived and thrived so long; bewilderment that we had managed to continue to obtain substantial financial support for it, principally from the National Institute of Justice but also, occasionally, from others; and apprehension that our run of luck could not continue indefinitely.

Here we are with another preface to another volume whose number ends in "0," and is another milestone. The delight, bewilderment, and apprehension all continue but, at least for the present, *Crime and Justice* is in good shape. Following shortly behind this volume are thematic volumes on cross-national crime and punishment trends and on youth justice systems in Western countries, and several general volumes. This volume has a particularly happy mix of essays on a wide range of topics, reflecting a wide range of disciplines, written by veteran *Crime and Justice* writers and newcomers, established senior scholars and emerging younger ones, and a healthy mix of Americans, Canadians, and Europeans.

It may be surprising after thirty volumes and more than a quarter century that there remain topics on which *Crime and Justice* has not previously published essays. Those by Tom Tyler on procedural justice and Ron Clarke and Rick Brown on international trafficking of stolen vehicles refute that hypothesis.

Others of the essays in this volume, however, build on prior, generally influential essays published previously. Tony Doob and Cheryl Marie Webster's examination of the evidence on the question whether changes in penalties affect crime rates, for example, builds on Phil Cook's now-classic essay on deterrence research (volume 2) and Daniel Nagin's more recent review of research (volume 23) on the same subject. Manuel Eisner's survey of eight centuries' data on long-term trends in homicide and necessarily therefore violent crime in Western countries, builds on Ted Gurr's seminal 1981 essay (volume 3) on the same subject. Candace Kruttschnitt and Rosemary Gartner's essay on women's prison and imprisonment builds on earlier works by Nicole Hahn Rafter on the history of women's prisons in the United States (volume 5) and Lucia Zedner's essay on the history of women's prisons in nineteenth-century England (volume 14). James Jacobs and Ellen Peters' essay on labor racketeering builds on Jacobs' own earlier essay on organized crime (volume 25, with Lauryn Gouldin), and Peter Reuter's essay on labor racketeering in New York City (volume 18). Finally, the essay by Alex Piquero, David Farrington, and Al Blumstein, providing a comprehensive overview of research to date on criminal careers, builds on a long series of essays, some of them written by Blumstein and Farrington, and all building on Joan Petersilia's pathbreaking 1980 essay entitled "Criminal Career Research: A Review of Recent Evidence" (volume 2).

Topics new and old, writers young and not so young, a wide range of disciplines, a fair number of countries—all these things are as *Crime and Justice*, in our view, should be. We think this is one of the strongest "annual" volumes we have published. Readers will decide for themselves whether they agree.

Michael Tonry
Norval Morris
Cambridge, May 2003

Candace Kruttschnitt and Rosemary Gartner

Women's Imprisonment

ABSTRACT

Incarceration of women in the United States is at a historic high, but understanding of women's experiences in prison, their responses to treatment, their lives after prison, and how changing prison regimes have affected these things remains limited. Individual attributes, preprison experiences, and prison conditions are associated with how women respond to incarceration, but assessments of their joint and conditional influences are lacking. Needs assessments abound, but systematic evaluations of interventions based on these assessments are rare, as are studies of the long-term consequences of imprisonment. Understanding of ways women negotiate power and construct their lives in prison is greater than in the past; new theoretical frameworks have provided important insights, but fundamental questions remain unanswered.

Punishment of criminal women has historically been characterized by methods, goals, and justifications different in important respects from punishment of men. Reasons include the relatively smaller number of female felons, the generally less serious nature of their offending, beliefs about the greater reformability—or at least tractability—of women, assumptions about women's peculiar psyches, and conceptions of normative femininities. Research on women in prison and women's prisons has, perhaps inevitably, been shaped by many of the same facts and assumptions. Since the 1960s, when a growing number of academics began to turn their attention to female prisoners and women's prisons, a major theme has been the distinctiveness of female prisoners' needs, disadvantages, and ways of adapting or responding to imprisonment.

Candace Kruttschnitt is professor of sociology at the University of Minnesota. Rosemary Gartner is director, Centre of Criminology, University of Toronto.

As the research on women in prison expanded and diversified in the last third of the twentieth century, a parallel process occurred in women's imprisonment in the United States and elsewhere. The enormous growth in imprisonment that has occupied the attention of policy makers and politicians, the public, and scholars characterized the female prison population at least as much as the male prison population. In the United States, for example, between 1990 and 2000 the number of women in prison increased by 125 percent (Bureau of Justice Statistics 2001c), and at the start of the twenty-first century over 166,000 women were held in U.S. prisons and jails (Bureau of Justice Statistics 2002a). Although the size of the female prison population has not increased to such levels or so consistently in other Western countries, the female proportion of the imprisoned population appears to be on the rise in many nations. As a consequence, the experience of imprisonment is not nearly as rare among women as it was a generation earlier.

The heightened punitiveness responsible for these increases has targeted some types of women more than others. In the United States, imprisonment rates for African-American and, to a lesser extent, Hispanic women—who have traditionally been overrepresented in prisons—have increased faster than for other women, as have imprisonment rates for female drug offenders in the United States and in England and Wales. As in the past, however, female prisoners continue to be drawn from the most economically and socially disadvantaged segments of society. Indeed, some evidence suggests that relative to their male counterparts, female prisoners have more extensive histories of disability, disadvantage, and misfortune. Whether this is because male prisoners are drawn from a broader cross-section of the population, because offending is more normative for males than females, or because more attention has been paid to female prisoners' backgrounds and psyches remains unresolved. Despite these apparently greater disadvantages, however, female prisoners' criminal histories remain less extensive than men's.

It is reasonable to expect that the life experiences of women sent to prison, including their histories of abuse, economic dependency, addiction, and mental health problems, will affect how they respond. However, our understanding of women's adaptations to imprisonment has been limited by long-standing curiosity about their sexuality and interest in the extent to which their responses are similar to men's. While there is no question that women prisoners place greater emphasis on their intimate and primary group relations than men, and engage in individual as opposed to collective acts of opposition to staff, we have far less understanding of other indicators of adjustment and coping among women prisoners, such as depression and self-harm. This inattention to women's adaptations to incarceration, most notably in the United States, at least partially reflects the movement away from rehabilitation and treatment modalities. Feminist scholars have taken a different approach to documenting women's adjustment to prison by largely shunning research pertaining to general styles of adaptation in favor of work that examines the interplay between biographies and individual modes of resistance to particular institutional environments.

There is considerable documentation of the needs of incarcerated women and advocacy for particular sets of programs that would address prior victimization and domestic violence, parenting skills, chemical dependency, and more. What is known about the life experiences of women inmates, and the factors that predict their recidivism, bolsters these claims. Nevertheless, the argument for gender-specific services and programs has yet to be coupled with systematic evaluations demonstrating positive treatment effects. Another body of work raises a different set of questions focused not on how to make prisons better for women but on the gendered nature of punishment and the role of criminal punishment in the social control of women generally.

In this essay we review evidence relevant to some of these questions and draw attention to a range of issues about which much less is known. Our focus is on the imprisonment of women, but we provide comparative data on men when such information can shed light on how the patterns and experiences of imprisonment may be gendered. There are some issues, however, which we do not examine either because they deserve a separate review essay (e.g., juvenile institutions for girls) or because systematic scholarly data are largely unavailable (such as the sexual abuse of women in prison by staff and women housed in private prisons; Harding 1998; Amnesty International 2002).

This essay is comprised of five sections. We begin by outlining trends in and characteristics of women in prison in the United States, England and Wales, and Canada. Although our coverage spans much of the twentieth century, we focus on the past two decades in an effort to understand women's contribution to what Simon (2000) refers to as "the era of hyper-incarceration." In Section II we review work on women's adaptations to and experiences of imprisonment. This research ranges widely and draws from a variety of conceptual and analytical frameworks, including the templates developed in the classic sociology of the

prison of the 1940s and 1950s and more recent feminist analyses of
women and social control. In Section III we review what is known about
how imprisonment affects women's lives after prison, including their
chances of reoffending and the hurdles they face upon returning to their
families and communities. In Section IV, we briefly examine current
scholarly work in penology and on women's imprisonment that highlights and debates the significance of recent transformations in criminal
punishment. In the final section of the essay, we suggest some directions
for future research on women in prison and women's imprisonment.

I. Trends in and Characteristics of Women in Prison
There has been dramatic growth in women's imprisonment over the
last two decades of the twentieth century in many, but not all, Western
countries. Changes over time in criminal justice policies appear to account for the differences in these trends. In the United States and England and Wales, two countries where the female prison population
has increased, this growth has occurred disproportionately among
women convicted of drug law violations. In these and other countries,
however, the background characteristics of women sent to prison appear to have changed little over time and are similar across different
countries: economically and politically disadvantaged women are overrepresented among the prison population. Relatively little is known,
however, about whether and how the lives of women behind bars have
changed as their proportional representation in prisons in these countries has risen and as prison policies and practices have undergone what
many see as major transformations.

A. Trends in Female Incarceration Rates
    In this section we examine incarceration data from the United
States, England and Wales, and Canada on both females and males and
where available from the early twentieth century onward. Using more
recent data, we also consider race- and offense-specific trends.
    1. *United States.* Trends in adult female imprisonment between
1925 and 2000, expressed as absolute numbers and as rates per 100,000
females, are shown in figure 1 and table 1.[1] Until the 1980s, the female
imprisonment rate never exceeded ten per 100,000 female population,
but between 1980 and 2000 it increased over fivefold, to almost sixty.
While male rates also increased steadily between 1980 and 2000, the

[1] See notes to table 6.1 in Bureau of Justice Statistics (2000e) for a discussion of
changes in the measurement of these rates over time. In particular, it should be noted
that beginning in 1978 a distinction was made between prisoners "in custody" and those

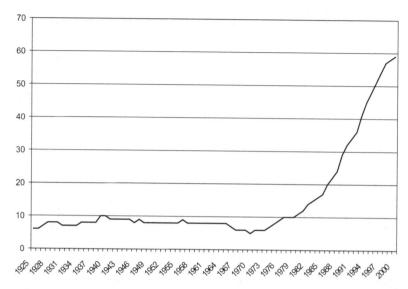

Fig. 1.—Rate per 100,000 female population of sentenced female prisoners under jurisdiction of U.S. state and federal correctional authorities on Dec. 31, 1925–2000. (See table 1 for data and sources.)

rate of growth was more dramatic for women (table 2).[2] As a consequence, the female proportion of the prison population increased from just under 4 percent in 1980 to almost 7 percent in 2001 (Bureau of Justice Statistics 2002a).[3]

The data in figure 1 and table 2 aggregate state and federal prisoners and exclude those incarcerated in jails. Because state prison populations account for over 60 percent of those in prison, the trends shown in the figure and table are driven by state prison populations (see, e.g., Bureau of Justice Statistics 2000c). Nonetheless, if we consider federal inmates and those in jails separately, we find patterns that parallel

---

"under jurisdiction"; data prior to 1978 include only prisoners in custody, whereas those from 1978 onward include prisoners under jurisdiction of state and federal correctional authorities. The difference in these figures for female prisoners is not large; for example, in 1977, 11,044 women were in custody, whereas 11,212 were under the jurisdiction of state and federal correctional authorities.

[2] We realize that percentage increases are inversely related to the size of the base numbers and therefore we urge caution in interpreting the relative growth patterns for women's imprisonment over time.

[3] At midyear 2001, 94,336 women were incarcerated in state and federal prisons in the United States, representing 6.7 percent of all prisoners.

TABLE 1

Data for Figure 1

Year	No. of Females	Rate	Year	No. of Females	Rate
1925	3,438	6	1963	7,745	8
1926	3,704	6	1964	7,704	8
1927	4,363	7	1965	7,568	8
1928	4,554	8	1966	6,951	7
1929	4,620	8	1967	6,235	6
1930	4,668	8	1968	5,812	6
1931	4,444	7	1969	6,594	6
1932	4,424	7	1970	5,635	5
1933	4,290	7	1971	6,329	6
1934	4,547	7	1972	6,269	6
1935	4,902	8	1973	6,004	6
1936	5,048	8	1974	7,389	7
1937	5,366	8	1975	8,675	8
1938	5,459	8	1976	10,039	9
1939	6,675	10	1977	11,044	10
1940	6,361	10	1978	11,583	10
1941	6,211	9	1979	12,005	10
1942	6,217	9	1980	12,331	11
1943	6,166	9	1981	14,227	12
1944	6,106	9	1982	16,329	14
1945	6,040	9	1983	17,426	15
1946	6,004	8	1984	19,205	16
1947	6,343	9	1985	21,296	17
1948	6,238	8	1986	24,544	20
1949	6,066	8	1987	26,822	22
1950	5,814	8	1988	30,145	24
1951	6,070	8	1989	37,264	29
1952	6,239	8	1990	40,564	32
1953	6,670	8	1991	43,802	34
1954	6,994	8	1992	46,501	36
1955	7,125	8	1993	54,037	41
1956	7,375	9	1994	60,125	45
1957	7,301	8	1995	63,900	48
1958	7,435	8	1996	69,464	51
1959	7,636	8	1997	73,835	54
1960	7,688	8	1998	78,706	57
1961	7,881	8	1999	90,530	58
1962	8,007	8	2000	91,612	59

Source.—Bureau of Statistics 2000e, fig. 6.2.

TABLE 2

Incarceration Rates in State and Federal Prisons by Gender, 1980, 1985, 1990, 1995, 2000

	No. of Prisoners per 100,000 Residents*		
	Total	Male	Female
1980	139	275	11
1985	202	397	17
1990	297	564	31
1995	411	781	47
2000	478	915	59

Source.—Bureau of Justice Statistics (1995, 1997a, 1998, 2000a, 2001c).

* Based on census estimates of the U.S. resident population on July 1 of each year and adjusted for census undercount. Sentenced prisoners are those with a sentence of more than one year.

those for women in state prisons (Bureau of Justice Statistics 1982, 1983, 2001c). Between 1980 and 2000, the female population of federal prisons increased over tenfold, to 10,245, and the female proportion of the federal prison population rose from 4 percent to 7 percent. Similarly, the female jail population increased by approximately 100 percent between 1980 and 2000, reaching almost 70,000, and the female proportion of the jail population rose from about 6 percent to over 11 percent. In other words, the growth rates for women in federal and state prisons, and in jails, exceeded those for men over this twenty-one-year period.

The increase in women in prison since 1980 occurred for all types of offenses, but was greatest for drug offenses. In the mid-1980s, women convicted of violent offenses and those convicted of property offenses each made up about 40 percent of the female state prison population, while less than 15 percent of this population was incarcerated for drug crimes (table 3). By the end of the 1990s, the largest proportion of the female state prison population—34 percent—was incarcerated for drugs, with violent offenders accounting for only 28 percent and property offenders only 21 percent. Males convicted of drug crimes were also being sent to prison at ever-increasing rates, but while the number of male inmates serving time for drug offenses increased by 55 percent between 1990 and 1996, the increase in drug offenders among female inmates was 100 percent (Bureau of Justice Statistics 1998). Thus, drug offenders made up only 20 percent of the male state prison population

TABLE 3

Most Serious Offense of State Prison Inmates by Gender,
1986, 1991, 1999

	Percent of Prison Inmates					
	1986		1991		1999	
	Female	Male	Female	Male	Female	Male
Violent	40.7	55.2	32.2	47.4	28.2	53.2
Property	41.2	30.5	28.7	24.6	20.7	13.1
Drugs	12.0	8.4	32.8	20.7	35.1	18.7
Public order	5.1	5.2	5.7	7.0	15.7	14.8

SOURCE.—Bureau of Justice Statistics 1994, table 2; 2000*b*, table 15; 2001*c*.
NOTE.—All columns do not add to 100 percent because they exclude "other/unspeci-fied" offenses (which include juvenile offenses and unspecified felonies) for 505 inmates in 1986, 7,462 inmates in 1991, and 2,700 inmates in 1991.

at the end of the 1990s, and violent offenders remained the predomi-nant group in men's prisons at about 50 percent of the population (Bu-reau of Justice Statistics 1994, 2001*c*).[4]

The increase in female incarceration has not occurred at the same rate across all ethnic and racial groups. Rates for nonwhite women grew faster than for white women during the 1990s. Black women's incarcera-tion rate almost doubled in the 1990s, from 117 per 100,000 in 1990 to 212 per 100,000 in 1999, and the rate for American Indian women more than doubled between 1990 and 1997, from thirty-five to eighty per 100,000. For Hispanic women, the increase was less (from fifty to eighty-seven per 100,000 over the past decade) but still well above the relatively moderate rate for white women, which was nineteen per 100,000 in 1990 and rose to twenty-seven per 100,000 by the end of the decade (Bureau of Justice Statistics 2000*a*, tables 1.9 and 1.10, 2000*d*).

There is some evidence that the differential growth rates by race are different for different types of offenses, but it is unclear how gender conditions these relationships. The Bureau of Justice Statistics partitions the total growth of sentenced prisoners under state jurisdiction by of-fense separately by gender and race. These data indicate that the growth

[4] Put another way, drug offenses accounted for 35 percent of the growth in female prison populations between 1990 and 1999, but only 19 percent of the growth in male prison populations. Conversely, violent offenses accounted for 53 percent of the growth in male prison populations between 1990 and 1999, compared to only 28 percent of the growth in female prison populations (Bureau of Justice Statistics 2001*c*).

in prison admissions for drug crimes occurred disproportionately for black offenders. Between 1990 and 1998, an increase in admissions of drug offenders accounted for 25 percent of the total growth rate among black prisoners, 18 percent among Hispanics, and only 12 percent among whites. By the end of the 1990s, black and Hispanic women were most likely to be imprisoned for drug crimes, whereas white women were most likely to be incarcerated for property or violent crimes (Bureau of Justice Statistics 2000a). Together this evidence suggests that the growth in female incarceration has occurred disproportionately among nonwhite women who are convicted of drug offenses.[5]

Generally, female incarceration rates were driven upward by many of the same factors responsible for the growth in male imprisonment. Government sources and academic researchers argue that the war on drugs, and federal and state sentencing reforms and sentencing guidelines, were major contributors to the growth in prison populations. The Bureau of Justice Statistics in their annual publications on the number of prisoners held in state prisons has drawn attention to three reasons for the growth in the state inmate populations: the increase in the number of arrests, especially for drug law violations, and the increased likelihood of incarceration following arrest, again, especially in the case of drug law violators, who had a fivefold increase in commitments (Bureau of Justice Statistics 1995); increasing time served (Bureau of Justice Statistics 1997a, 1999b); and an increase in the number of offenders returned to state prison for parole violations (Bureau of Justice Statistics 2000b; see also Petersilia 1999). In the case of federal prison inmates, they speculate that, following from the passage of the Sentencing Reform Act of 1984, increases in both the likelihood of incarceration following conviction and in time served contributed to a growth in the inmate population (Bureau of Justice Statistics 1995).

However, some factors may have had disproportionate effects on the growth in the female prison population. The war on drugs, for example, appears to have had a greater impact on the growth rate of women's, compared to men's, prison populations, at least at the state level.[6]

[5] Because comparable longitudinal data on other social and economic characteristics of incarcerated women are not available, it is not possible to determine the extent to which other characteristics of women in prison have changed over time. This is unfortunate in light of the changes that have occurred over the past few decades in the economic, domestic, and political lives of women in the general population (see, e.g., Goldberg and Kremen 1990; McLanahan and Booth 1995; Aube, Fleury, and Smetana 2000; Heimer 2000).

[6] At the federal level, women and men were about equally affected by the increase in committals for drug crimes. In 1980, just over 20 percent of both female and male fed-

Blumstein and Beck (1999, p. 26) partitioned the total growth in state prison population by crime type and gender for the years 1980–96. In so doing, they found that 43 percent of the growth rate in the female prison population was accounted for by drug offenders compared to only 28 percent of the growth rate in the male prison population.

Sentencing reforms and parole practices also may have made particularly substantial contributions to the growth of the female inmate population. Ostensibly gender-neutral mandatory minimum sentences for crimes such as conspiracy may affect women more than men (van Wormer 2001) and, as Hagan and Dinovitzer (1999, pp. 141–42) illustrate particularly well, the imposition of sentencing guidelines has had a disproportionate impact on women. In the preguideline era, judges could take family responsibilities of both women and men into account when deciding between probation and imprisonment. Yet, the effect of eliminating child-care responsibilities as a mitigating circumstance in sentencing decisions has had a greater effect on mothers than fathers since they are more likely than fathers to have dependent children living with them (Daly 1995; Raeder 1995). The contributions of parole practices to this increase in female incarceration may be more complex. For both men and women, the elimination or restriction of parole in many states has increased time served. But so also have parole violations. The rise in the state inmate population between 1990 and 1998 was fueled in part by a 54 percent increase in the number of offenders returned to prison for parole violations (Bureau of Justice Statistics 2000d), and women and drug offenders made up a growing proportion of parole violators in state prisons (Petersilia 1999; Bureau of Justice Statistics 2000b, 2000d, 2001d).

To place these trends in women's imprisonment in the United States into a larger context, we next consider evidence from England and Wales and from Canada. The United States is in a class by itself with regard to both the number of women it imprisons and their rate of imprisonment. Even so, the recent growth it has experienced is not unique.

2. *England and Wales.*[7] Trends in the female prison population in

---

eral inmates were incarcerated for drug crimes. By the end of the 1990s the majority of both female and male admissions were for drug offenses (66 percent and 57 percent, respectively) (Bureau of Justice Statistics 1982, 2000e).

[7] Unless otherwise noted, the data in this section are drawn from Home Office (1967–2001, 2001). In England and Wales, convicted adult males are incarcerated in either prisons (for those twenty-one or older) or young-offender institutions (for those aged fifteen to twenty). Those under twenty-one may be either exclusively in juvenile facilities or young-offender institutions. There are no young-offender institutions for females, but efforts have been made to separate younger women from other female offenders by des-

England and Wales from 1901 to 2000 (fig. 2) indicate that, unlike in the United States, women's risk of incarceration did not increase steadily over the twentieth century. The number of women in prison in 1901 was greater than in any subsequent year until the late 1990s; corresponding rates appear to follow a similar trend and indicate that the rate of female imprisonment at the turn of the twentieth century (eighteen per 100,000) exceeded that at the turn of the twenty-first century (twelve per 100,000).[8] Nevertheless, in the last third of the twentieth century, women's risks of imprisonment in England and Wales, as in the United States, rose, only marginally during the 1970s and 1980s, but much more sharply in the 1990s. Imprisonment rates for males also increased in the 1990s, but not as dramatically as for females. The number and the rate of females in custody increased more than 100 percent between 1990 and 2000, compared to a 40 percent increase in the male prison population. By 2002, the 4,032 females in prison made up 6 percent of the total prison population, substantially lower than their 16 percent share in 1901 but higher than at any point since the late 1940s.

As was the case in the United States, women convicted of some offenses contributed disproportionately to the doubling of the female prison population in England and Wales in the 1990s. As a consequence, the distribution of crimes for which women were sentenced to prison changed somewhat during the 1990s. The number of women serving time for drug crimes tripled (from 318 to 947) between 1990 and 2000 and accounted for 37 percent of women in prison in 2000, compared to only 29 percent in 1990.[9] The number of property offenders (i.e., burglary, theft and handling, and fraud and forgery) more than doubled, but accounted for a similar percentage (approximately

---

ignating one wing within a women's prison for young offenders (Liebling 2002). See Langan and Farrington (1998) for a detailed discussion of the comparability of prison statistics from England and Wales with those from the United States.

[8] Prior to World War I, a large proportion of women in prison in England and Wales were incarcerated for drunkenness or prostitution. Few of the women in English prisons in the 1990s were serving time for these offenses. Rates are available only for some of the years during this period and so are not presented in figure 2. Long-term trends in men's imprisonment followed a somewhat different pattern, with rates at the end of the 1990s (240 per 100,000) over twice those of the pre–World War I period.

[9] A similar pattern has been noted among women in prison in Scotland (Social Work Services and Prison Inspectorates for Scotland 1998). The number of males sentenced to prison for drug offenses also increased between 1990 and 2000, although at a lesser rate. They also made up a much smaller percentage (15 percent) of the male prison population compared to female drug offenders. The most common offense type for men was crime against the person (i.e., violent crimes, including sexual offenses and robbery), which accounted for 44 percent of the male prison population.

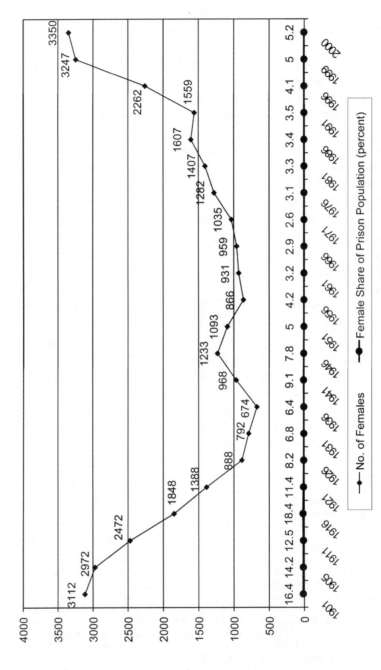

Fig. 2.—Average daily population in custody, adults and juveniles, remand and sentenced, in prisons in England and Wales, 1901–2000. (Source: Home Office 2001, table 1a.)

30 percent) of women in prison in 1990 and in 2000. The number of violent offenders also increased between 1990 and 2000, but their representation in the total female prison population remained stable at 24 percent.

The racial distribution of female prisoners in England and Wales did not change markedly over the 1990s. In 1991, whites accounted for at least 68 percent of female prisoners, blacks accounted for 23 percent, and South Asians and Chinese accounted for 6 percent.[10] In 2000, the proportion of whites had increased slightly, to 75 percent, and that for blacks had decreased, to 19 percent.[11] The proportion of foreign nationals—who, like racial minorities, are also overrepresented in English prison populations—remained largely stable during the 1990s.

A number of factors have been linked to the increase in the total prison population in England and Wales in the 1990s. The Home Office (2001) has identified a series of policy changes, such as the Criminal Justice Act of 1993 and the Crime (Sentences) Act of 1997, as well as some high-profile events, as important contributors to the overall growth. Academic researchers concur, noting the expansion of determinate sentencing, an increase in sentence lengths in Crown Courts, and pressure on judges to make greater use of custodial sentences beginning in 1993 (e.g., Langan and Farrington 1998; Bosworth 1999). Some argue that a "new punitiveness" in England and Wales has had a disproportionate impact on women in prison. Carlen (1998, see also 1995), for example, argues that young, single mothers—in and outside of the criminal justice system—have been targeted for failing to lead conventional family lives, with consequences for women's imprisonment that are not gender-neutral. Harsher policies toward drug offenders also may have contributed disproportionately (Howard League 2001).

3. *Canada.* Data on long-term trends in the female prison population in Canada are not available, nor are annual data on the average size of the female prison population for recent years regularly published. However, sex-specific annual data on sentenced admissions to provincial and federal institutions are available from the late 1970s.[12] Prisoner

[10] In 1991, racial background was not recorded for 3 percent of the female prison population.

[11] The racial distribution of male prisoners also changed little over the 1990s; compared to female prisoners, however, a smaller percentage of male prisoners in 2000 were black (12 percent).

[12] In Canada, offenders sentenced to two or more years are incarcerated in federal prisons, whereas those who receive custodial sentences of less than two years and those remanded to custody while awaiting trial are incarcerated in provincial or territorial in-

counts based on admissions data tend to be larger than those based on one-day counts of prison populations and include a larger proportion of persons with short sentences compared to one-day counts; conversely, one-day population counts overrepresent (compared to admissions data) more serious offenders with long-term sentences (Lynch 1995; Finn et al. 1999). As a consequence, Canadian female imprisonment rates based on admissions data are not comparable to those reported above for the United States and England and Wales. Moreover, the Canadian admissions data show a higher proportion of females than do the one-day count data. This is because women, who commit less serious offenses than men, tend to be given shorter sentences; as a consequence, women also tend to make up a larger proportion of the remand population (i.e., those held awaiting trial) than of the sentenced population.[13]

With these data limitations and comparability problems in mind, what can we say about trends in the imprisonment of women in Canada in the latter part of the twentieth century?[14] The admissions data in figure 3 show that the number and rate of female admissions to federal and provincial/territorial prisons peaked in 1993–94 after several years of uneven growth.[15] After 1994, female admissions declined, and by 1999–2000 were at their lowest level since the early 1980s. Male admissions for 1979/1980–1999/2000 follow a somewhat different trend, with both the number and rate of admissions peaking in 1982–83 and declining in most subsequent years to their lowest rate and number in 1999–2000. As a consequence of the greater decline in male admissions, the female percentage of the admissions population rose from a low of 6 percent in 1979–80 to 9 percent in the 1990s.

The admissions data, then, suggest that the use of imprisonment for

---

stitutions. Those under age eighteen are not incarcerated in these facilities and so are not included in these figures.

[13] Sex-specific admissions and count data are both available for 1996 and show that women made up 9 percent of those admitted to prison that year, but only 5 percent of the population in custody on any one day. In 1996, just over 10,000 of prison admittees were female, whereas on any one day only about 1,700 women were in custody.

[14] Unless otherwise noted, the source of the data in this section is "Adult Correctional Services in Canada," which was published annually beginning in 1981 by the Canadian Centre for Justice Statistics.

[15] This growth occurred at the provincial level, not at the federal level. While the number of women in federal prison increased during these years (to approximately 300), the growth was "proportionate to the population of women as a whole" (Shaw 1991, p. 47). Similarly, the subsequent decline occurred at the provincial level, with the number of women in federal prisons ranging between about 325 and 350 in the last half of the 1990s.

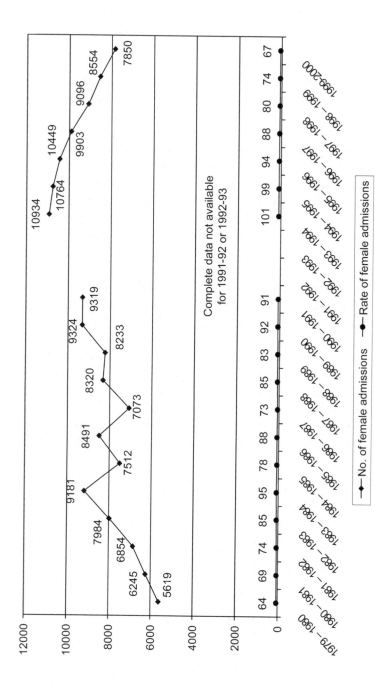

Fig. 3.—Number and rate of female sentenced admissions to provincial and federal institutions in Canada, 1979/80–1999/2000. (Source: Canadian Centre for Justice Statistics, "Adult Correctional Services in Canada" [various years].)

women declined beginning in the mid-1990s in Canada, after over a decade of moderate growth. Total (i.e., non-sex-specific) prison population counts support this conclusion: the number and rate of prisoners in custody showed gradual and uneven growth from 1979 until 1994 (when the rate reached 154 per 100,000 adult population) and decreased thereafter. Consequently Canada's total incarceration rate in 2000 (135 per 100,000 adult population) was only 5 percent higher than the rate in 1979 (128). We estimate the sex-specific rates of persons in custody on any one day at approximately fourteen per 100,000 adult females and 270 per 100,000 adult males.[16]

Why did female imprisonment in Canada in the 1990s not follow the upward trend observed in the United States and in England and Wales? A series of legislative and policy changes had complex effects on imprisonment in Canada beginning in the mid-1980s, with some pushing toward greater punitiveness and others working in the opposite direction (Roach 1999). Contributing to the decline in imprisonment after 1994 were several changes in sentencing policy and practice, of which the 1996 Sentencing Reform Bill (Bill C-41, An Act to amend the Criminal Code and other acts thereof, S.C. 1995, c. 22) was the most important. A major principle articulated in this bill was that judges were to consider "all available sanctions other than imprisonment that are reasonable under the circumstances" (subsection 718.2[e]). In rejecting numerical sentencing guidelines, establishing conditional sentences, and enabling jurisdictions to develop alternative (i.e., diversion) measures, the bill responded to concerns expressed by federal ministers of justice and the Canadian Sentencing Commission

[16] Comparing imprisonment rates in Canada, England and Wales, and the United States is not straightforward since published rates are often calculated in different ways across countries. Typically, U.S. rates, such as those shown in table 2, are calculated based only on those in state and federal prisons, so they do not take account of the jail population. They are also calculated based on the total population (or total sex-specific population for sex-specific rates), rather than an age-specific subgroup. To be comparable with data from England and Wales and Canada, the U.S. jail population should be added to the prison population. The Bureau of Justice Statistics (2001c) estimates the U.S. rate of imprisonment in state and federal prisons in 2000 at 435 per 100,000; the Home Office (2001) estimates the U.S. rate, including the jail population, at 702 in 2000. Published rates for England and Wales and for Canada may not be strictly comparable because the Home Office (2001) uses the total population to calculate the overall imprisonment rate in England and Wales, whereas the Canadian Centre for Justice Statistics calculates the overall imprisonment rate based on only the adult population (Lonmo 2001). This is because Canadian imprisonment data exclude those who are under age eighteen and hence housed separately from adults. For a more detailed discussion of comparing imprisonment cross-nationally, see Young and Brown 1993.

that Canada imprisons too many people.[17] The impact of these sentencing changes has not yet been systematically assessed, and so it is not known whether any effects have been gender-neutral. The establishment of conditional sentences could reduce the number of women in prison more than the number of men because women make up a larger proportion of those committing minor offenses (for which conditional sentences could be given) than of those committing serious offenses. But, as Martin (1999) argues, these and other apparently gender-neutral policies may also have disproportionately negative effects on women.[18]

The size of growth in the U.S. female prison population is remarkable. In 2001, 82,000 more women were serving time in U.S. state and federal prisons than in 1980. While the number and rate of women in prison in England and Wales are dramatically lower, the female prison population there also experienced steady growth beginning in the mid-1970s and accelerating in the 1990s. This expansion of women's imprisonment in the 1990s was not, however, common to all Western countries. In Canada, after peaking in 1994, the rate and number of women in prison in 2000 reached their lowest levels since the early 1980s. New Zealand's female prison population also appears not to have increased during the 1990s. It incarcerated fewer women between 1991 and 1997 than it had in 1990, though a 20 percent growth between 1996 and 1997 led some commentators to worry about whether that country was "starting to reflect the trend in women's imprisonment apparent in other Western jurisdictions" (Morris and Kingi 1999, p. 143). One of those other jurisdictions was Australia, where a tripling of the female imprisonment rate during the 1980s was followed by more restrained growth in the 1990s (Easteal 2001). Growth, then, has been the general—though not the exclusive—rule for women's imprisonment in English-speaking Western countries in the 1990s, and this extends to women's relative representation in the

---

[17] Conditional sentences allow offenders who would otherwise be jailed to serve their sentence in the community. Conditional sentences are different from probation and instead are essentially a peace bond for a period of up to two years (Roberts and Cole 1999).

[18] Data to determine whether the characteristics of women (e.g., race, offense of commitment) serving time in provincial and federal institutions have changed with the decline in female prison populations in Canada are not readily available. This means it is not possible to say whether some types of female offenders have benefited more from this decrease than others.

prison population. The female proportion of the prison population grew in the United States, England and Wales, and even in Canada during the 1990s. Thus, women's representation among the imprisoned populations of all three countries was increasing at the turn of the twenty-first century. The growth in female imprisonment appears to be linked, in part, to legislative changes that may have had differential effects on females and males. The growing punitiveness of the criminal justice system in the United States has had particular salience for women offenders because much of their offending is linked to drug consumption and trafficking and because efforts to hold offenders more accountable for their crimes have meant that judges increasingly ignore the mitigating factors that traditionally kept many women out of prison (e.g., child-care responsibilities, availability of jail space, degree of blameworthiness; Steffensmeier, Kramer, and Streifel 1993; Daly 1994).

B. Characteristics of Incarcerated Women

The characteristics that distinguish women in prison in Western countries from women in the general population appear to be very similar and to have changed little during the past few decades. As has been the case for as long as records have been kept, women in prison in the 1990s were disproportionately drawn from economically and politically disadvantaged populations. Official surveys and academic studies of jail and prison populations, although using different measures or criteria, consistently find un- and underemployed women, poorly educated women, and women receiving public assistance to be over-represented among incarcerated women in the United States, England and Wales, Canada, and elsewhere (Kline 1992; Shaw et al. 1992; Fletcher, Shaver, and Moon 1993; Shaw 1994*a*; Morris, Wilkinson, and Tisi 1995; Owen and Bloom 1995; Collins 1996; Prison Reform Trust 1996; Correctional Service Canada 1997; H.M. Chief Inspector of Prisons 1997; Carlen 1998, 1999; Bureau of Justice Statistics 1999*d*; Finn et al. 1999; General Accounting Office 1999; Morris and Kingi 1999; Owen 1999; Easteal 2001).[19]

Women from some racial and ethnic minority groups also are at greater risk of imprisonment than are white women. In the United States, nonhispanic black women are incarcerated at rates six times

---

[19] Unless otherwise noted, these are the sources for the subsequent discussion of characteristics of women in prison. Additional sources are cited where appropriate.

those for white women, and hispanic and American Indian women's rates are over twice those for white women (Bureau of Justice Statistics 2000e). In England and Wales, the disparity between black and white women's imprisonment rates is even greater: a black woman is about ten times more likely to be serving time in prison than is a white woman. Women of Chinese heritage living in England and Wales are serving time at a rate about four times that of white women (Home Office 2001; see also Smith 1997). In Canada, aboriginal women are greatly overrepresented in prison populations; they account for about 23 percent of women in provincial and federal facilities, but only 2 percent of the general female population (Finn et al. 1999; Correctional Service Canada 2000b).[20] In New Zealand and Australia, Maori women and aboriginal women (respectively) are also imprisoned in numbers disproportionate to their representation in the general population (Hampton 1993; Morris and Kingi 1999). The overrepresentation of some racial and ethnic minorities and of economically disadvantaged persons among incarcerated populations holds true for men as well. However, in England, though not in the United States or Canada, the disparity between black and white imprisonment rates is greater for women than men. In Canada, the disparity between aboriginal and nonaboriginal imprisonment rates is also greater for women than men (Finn et al. 1999; Correctional Service Canada 2000a).

Compared to women in the general population, women in prison are also more likely to be unmarried and to be mothers of dependent children. In the United States, for example, nearly half of the women in prison have never been married and seven out of ten have children under the age of eighteen. Single mothers are overrepresented among prison populations in England and Wales, Scotland, Canada, New Zealand, and Australia, and in all of these countries female prisoners are more likely than male prisoners to have lived with their children prior to their incarceration (Bureau of Justice Statistics 1993; Social Work Services and Prison Inspectorates for Scotland 1998; Howard League 2001). Scattered longitudinal data suggest that the proportion of single mothers in prison has been increasing over time, creating what some have called "a neglected class of young people whose lives

---

[20] Correctional population data disaggregated by other racial and ethnic groups are not readily available in Canada for provincially sentenced offenders. Among federally sentenced women—who make up about 20 percent of women in Canadian prisons—about 8 percent are black, compared to between 1 percent and 2 percent of the total female population in Canada (Correctional Service Canada 2000b).

are disrupted and damaged by their separation from imprisoned mothers," especially in the United States (Hagan and Dinovitzer 1999, p. 142; see also Bloom 1993).

Many argue that a history of physical or sexual abuse distinguishes women in prison from both women in the general population and from men in prison. Self-reported estimates of the lifetime prevalence of abuse among female prisoners are typically quite high, but range widely across studies, depending on their methodologies. In the United States, prevalence estimates range from 40 percent of women in federal prisons to 57 percent in state prisons (Bureau of Justice Statistics 1999*d*), but estimates also have been reported to be as high as 80 percent among women in California state prisons when emotional abuse is included (Owen and Bloom 1995). Comparable estimates for men in prison and jail in the United States are substantially lower, ranging from 7 percent of men in federal prisons to 16 percent of men in state prisons (Bureau of Justice Statistics 2000*e*). In the general population, men also report lower rates of child abuse (5–8 percent) than women (12–17 percent) (Bureau of Justice Statistics 1999*d*). In Canadian surveys, the prevalence of histories of physical or sexual abuse among women in provincial and federal prisons has been estimated at between 50 percent and 80 percent (Shaw 1994*a*, 1994*b*; National Crime Prevention Council of Canada 1995; Comack 1996). Estimates of female prisoners in England and Wales with abuse histories range more widely, from 25 percent to 80 percent (Home Office 1992; Morris, Wilkinson, and Tisi 1995; Howard League 2001; Reid-Howe Associates 2001). The variation in these prevalence estimates reflects, in part, how questions about abuse are asked and the range of experiences they tap (Loucks 1997).[21] To verify how much higher these rates in England and Wales and Canada are than those for nonimprisoned women, one would need data on the distribution of abuse in the general female population gathered using a similar methodology. Nevertheless, the higher range of the estimates noted above suggests that histories of abuse are more prevalent among women in prison than among women in the general population.

Government surveys and academic studies, particularly in the United States, point to a series of other disadvantages, disabilities, and misfortunes that appear to distinguish women in prison from women

---

[21] Some estimates include, in addition to physical and sexual abuse, emotional abuse and witnessing abuse.

in the general population as well as from men in prison.[22] These include histories of drug abuse (National Crime Prevention Council of Canada 1995; Owen and Bloom 1995; Bureau of Justice Statistics 2000e), which indicate more regular drug use by female inmates than male inmates (74 percent vs. 69 percent) prior to incarceration (Bureau of Justice Statistics 1999e); mental and physical health disorders (Teplin, Abraham, and McClelland 1996; Acoca 1998; Bureau of Justice Statistics 1999a; General Accounting Office 1999), with inmates generally having higher rates of physical disorders than the general population and incarcerated women reporting more physical impairments (14 percent vs. 12 percent) and more mental conditions than incarcerated men (16 percent vs. 10 percent) (Bureau of Justice Statistics 2001a); and HIV/AIDS (Bureau of Justice Statistics 1997b, 2001a; Brewer et al. 1998), with the AIDS rates being higher among inmates than among the general population and, again, with women inmates' HIV rates exceeding those of men (3.4 percent vs. 2.1 percent) (Bureau of Justice Statistics 2001d). The complex and overlapping nature of many of these problems almost certainly affects both women's risks of coming into conflict with the law as well as their ability to cope with imprisonment, which typically does not provide adequate treatment for most physical and psychological problems. This has encouraged some commentators on women in prison to depict them as more a "community of victims rather than a collection of victimizers" (Bosworth 1999, p. 56), and sometimes as more needy, deficient, and/or poorly adjusted than men in prison.

While recognizing the need to take account of female prisoners' histories of victimization, drug abuse, and mental health problems, some feminist scholars also warn of the potentially negative consequences of doing so. To the extent that such a portrayal encourages women's offending to be attributed to particular types of female pathology, some argue that it robs them of their agency (as well as their responsibility) and feeds into traditional gender stereotypes (Allen 1987; Shaw 1992). Others point to a slippage between the concepts of need and risk, such that "characteristics of the female offender that were previously considered needs (i.e., history of abuse, history of self-injury, single motherhood, mental health concerns and dependency on financial aid/welfare) are now defined as 'criminogenic factors' or risk factors that

---

[22] Unfortunately, data do not exist that would permit a comparison of incarcerated women with a demographically matched group of women in the general population.

can predict recidivism" (Hannah-Moffat 1999, p. 86). One consequence, given the influence of neoliberalism on criminal justice policies, may be the "responsibilization" (O'Malley 1992; see also O'Malley 1999) of female prisoners, whereby they are expected to treat these
needs/risks themselves. Another potential consequence is increased security and higher levels of coerced intervention for prisoners labeled
high need/high risk.

The portrayal of women in prison as particularly "high need" compared to men (see, e.g., Finn et al. 1999) and the linkage of some of
these needs (such as a history of abuse or of self-injury) to increased
risks of violent recidivism (Bonta, Pang, and Wallace-Capretta 1995;
Blanchette 1997a, 1997b) distract attention from the largely nonviolent
nature of female offending, both absolutely and relative to male offending. For example, in the United States, only 29 percent of women
in state prisons in 2000 were serving time for violent offenses, compared to 34 percent for drug offenses, 26 percent for property offenses,
and 11 percent for public order and other offenses (Bureau of Justice
Statistics 2001c). In contrast, 49 percent of men in state prisons in 2000
were serving time for violent offenses. Similar patterns exist in England and Wales, where only 24 percent of women in prison in 2000
were serving time for violent and sexual offenses compared to 44 percent of men in prison (Home Office 2001), and in Canada in 1996,
where violent offenders accounted for 32 percent of women in provincial and federal prisons compared to 51 percent of male prisoners (Finn
et al. 1999).

II. Women's Adaptations to and Experiences
of Imprisonment

Research on women's adaptation to incarceration was initially shaped
by the classic prison sociology of the 1950s and then by large-scale
studies of women's prisons in the 1960s. The attention these studies
gave to women's intimate and primary group relations, as well as to
the absence among women of traditional markers of men's prison adjustment (e.g., adherence to an inmate code of ethics), encouraged subsequent work in these areas. Important sources of variations in adjustment—institutional characteristics and characteristics of the prisoner
population—were left largely unexplored. Subsequent research on
women's adaptations to incarceration has focused on aggression, depression, self-harm, and suicide. Although abusive experiences and a
history of emotional disturbance appear as common correlates of all

four adaptations, the research is primarily descriptive and fails systematically to consider how the prison environment itself may compound preprison characteristics and experiences and contribute to poor adjustment.

Conceptual and methodological criticisms of the research on adjustment and coping have been articulated and responded to in recent research on women's experiences of imprisonment informed by feminist perspectives. This research has challenged some of the earlier interpretations and characterizations. It has also moved away from searching for ideal types or general styles of adaptation, instead looking at the complex ways in which women's identities and backgrounds shape how they negotiate power, resist depersonalization, and make sense of their time in prison. What women can tell us about the practices of imprisonment is an important theme in some of this work.

A. Early Studies of Prison Social Organization: The Theoretical Backdrop

Early studies of prison life examined the culture and social organization of men's institutions. Several important ethnographies of prison life emerged before the end of World War II (Reimer 1937; Hayner and Ash 1939; Schrag 1944), but it was Clemmer's (1958) study of Menard in the 1930s—the maximum-security prison for men in southern Illinois—that left a special mark on prison sociology. For Clemmer, the prison culture was comprised of "the habits, behavior systems, traditions, history, customs, folkways, codes, the laws and rules which guide inmates" (1958, p. 294). Inmates submerged in this culture were "prisonized"—a status that deepened their commitment to criminality and disrupted their reentry into society. Although his ethnography of prison life also included a description of the hierarchy of prisoners and their roles, it was Clemmer's concept of "prisonization" that became of particular importance.

By the late 1950s a new approach was emerging. The concepts of primary group and culture, so central to sociology at the University of Chicago during Clemmer's day, gave way to Talcott Parsons's (1951) *Social System*, and more generally his functionalist paradigm.[23] The prison was now conceived of as an adaptive miniature "social system," and interest emerged in relationships among and social roles of the actors in this system and ultimately their influence on the prison itself

---

[23] The functional theories explain phenomena such as behavior or social arrangements by their consequences.

(Irwin 1980, p. 32; Sykes 1995, p. 80). For example, Sykes (1958), in his classic study of the New Jersey State Prison, argued that inmate behavior was a conscious or unconscious attempt to deal with the deprivations of prison life. As Sykes recounts, "the behavior patterns of inmates sprang from a set of values, attitudes and beliefs that found expression in the so-called inmate code couched in prison argot. This code held forth a pattern of approved conduct . . . an ideal rather than a description of how inmates behaved" (1995, p. 82). Sykes's inmate code was intended only as an "ideal type" of inmate interactions, but its tenets—for example, "never rat on a con, be cool, do your own time, and don't exploit inmates"—became a central interest of functionalist studies of inmate behavior.

The prominence of the functional paradigm may not have been due so much to its empirical validity as to the fact that it generated both complementary and competing paradigms that significantly widened scholars' ability to understand inmate adaptations to incarceration. According to the situational version of the functionalist model, inmates' responses to imprisonment are not just a function of the fundamentally coercive character of total institutions but instead depend on specific institutional characteristics such as the nature of the disciplinary regime, size and physical layout of the institution, and its organizational objectives (Grusky 1959; Berk 1966; Street, Vinter, and Perrow 1966; Wilson 1968). What was typically posed as the competing paradigm, the importation model, argued that the prison is not a completely closed system. Consequently, inmates' responses and adaptations to incarceration were shaped by their preprison experiences, and originated in and were sustained by subcultures outside of the prison (Irwin and Cressey 1962; Cline and Wheeler 1968; Irwin 1970). Together these models dominated the literature on responses to imprisonment for the next several decades (see, e.g., Garbedian 1963, 1964; Wellford 1967; Jacobs 1974; Thomas 1977; Bukstel and Kilmann 1980), including the work on women in prison.

B. The Classic American Studies of Women's Adaptations to Imprisonment

The first large-scale study of women's imprisonment that was explicitly concerned with prisoners' adaptation was Ward and Kassebaum's (1965) study of the California Institution for Women (CIW) at Frontera. Looking for evidence of convict identities such as those described by Sykes, Ward and Kassebaum found that they were not only largely absent among the women at CIW but also that support for the tenets of the inmate code was relatively modest among this population. They concluded that while female prisoners, like their male counterparts, responded to the "pains of imprisonment" through withdrawal, rebellion, and institutionalization, women's intimate, often sexual, relationships were their major and most distinctive style of adaptation to prison life. Ward and Kassebaum saw the gender differences in responses to imprisonment as explicable by both the importation and the functional paradigms, whereby the formation of primary relationships was "rooted in social roles played in the free world" and emerged because of "psychological needs unsatisfied in the prison world" (Ward and Kassebaum 1965, p. 74). Although their research was criticized by contemporaries for providing both too much detail on the homosexual activity of prisoners (Elliott 1966) and a rather one-dimensional view of women's experiences of imprisonment (Messinger 1967), there is no question that it served as a template for much of the research on women in prison that followed.

Two other studies are particularly important in this early scholarly work on women's adaptations to imprisonment: Giallombardo's (1966) study of the Federal Reformatory for Women in Alderson, West Virginia, and Heffernan's (1972) research at Occoquan in Washington, D.C. Similar to Ward and Kassebaum, Giallombardo took the system of adaptations found in male correctional facilities as her point of comparison and the differences she found for women prisoners as her focus. Nevertheless, she also provided readers with a rich portrayal of women's carceral lives, including a consideration of the way prison architecture and iconography influenced group formations and the critical roles staff played in shaping inmate social relations and in integrating the conflicting goals of rehabilitation and custody. Her depiction of the prison experiences and adaptations of women at Alderson, as well as the sources of these adaptations, was largely consistent with that of Ward and Kassebaum. Female argot roles were numerous but revolved primarily around consensual sexual and prison-family relationships, and they were to be understood by employing deprivation and importation paradigms. Specifically, she argued that women attempt "to resist the destructive effects of imprisonment by creating a substitute universe within which the inmates may preserve an identity relevant to life outside the prison" (Giallombardo 1966, p. 129).

Heffernan (1972) initially intended to examine whether the concept of "prisonization" applied to female inmates. However, early in her research she rejected Clemmer's and Sykes's models of inmate adaptation and turned her attention to the propositions of Irwin and Cressey (1962), who assumed that preprison identities were critical to understanding how inmates "do time." Heffernan argued that women at Occoquan chose one of three ways of doing time: the "square," who adhered to conventional norms; the "cool," who were the more sophisticated criminals and who knew how to manipulate the prison environment to their advantage; and the "life," whose identities were influenced by their petty criminal activities (e.g., prostitution, theft) on the street. Although her research also contained a heavy dose of descriptive data on women's intimate relationships, it remains notable for its understanding of women's adaptations to prison life as only incompletely determined by their traditional gender role identities and the institutional context. Heffernan's analysis suggested that, despite these well-recognized influences, women exercised some autonomy in choosing particular adaptations and styles of doing time, and shaped these in an active, reflexive manner.

In identifying the ways in which women's responses to imprisonment differed from men's, these classic studies influenced much of the subsequent research on women in prison, particularly in North America. Two bodies of work followed directly from these studies: research concerned with women's intimate and primary group relationships, and research on the applicability of such traditional markers of male inmate adjustment as prisonization, inmate solidarity, and opposition to staff. A related area of research—that on coping—shares with these an interest in gender differences in adaptations to prison, but is less concerned with the social order of the prison and thus is further removed from the classic research on prison social organization and prison culture. We discuss each of these bodies of work in turn.

C. Research on Women's Intimate Relationships in Prison

Notwithstanding the previously noted as well as more recent criticisms of research documenting the nature and extent of intimate relationships among female prisoners, these relationships have continued to attract scholarly attention (e.g., Burkhart 1973; Norris 1974; Foster 1975; Climent et al. 1977; Propper 1982; Leger 1987; Jones 1993; Hawkins 1995; Owen 1998; Alarid 2000; Hensley, Tewksbury, and Kocheski 2001).[24] From its beginnings this work typically has linked

[24] The preoccupation with the sexual relationships of women in prison in the classic research of the 1960s has been criticized more recently for conflating lesbianism with aggressive criminality (Freedman 1996), for distracting attention from such important issues as the repressive and gendered nature of women's prison regimes (Dobash, Do-

women's sexual relations in prison to the deprivations of prison life and, more specifically, to the absence of opportunities for heterosexual sex and what have been seen as women's particular needs for emotional intimacy. The earliest work, which predated the studies by Ward and Kassebaum and by Giallombardo, explicitly pathologized both female prisoners' same-sex relations and prison-family structures while giving a nod to the causal role of deprivation in the formation of these relationships (see, e.g., Otis 1913; Ford 1929; Selling 1931; Halleck and Hersko 1962). More recent work assessing women's responses to incarceration has attempted to identify aspects of prison deprivation as well as personal characteristics that are related to women's sexual relations (see, e.g., Genders and Player 1990; Owen 1998).

In this line of research, only a few studies have addressed how, if at all, the extent of women's involvement in same-sex intimate relationships might vary across institutional contexts or over time. Here a continued, if at times implicit interest in comparing importation and situational functionalist perspectives can be seen. If the situational functionalist perspective has any validity, variations in institutional structures and processes should produce variations in adaptations, including involvement in same-sex intimate relations and prison families. And if the importation perspective is correct, changes in women's social roles and in the growing acceptability of same-sex relationships should have increased the prevalence of sexual relations among women in prison in recent years.[25] The results of this work are mixed. With regard to variations across institutions, some studies have found women's sexual relationships to be more common in treatment as opposed

---

bash, and Gutteridge 1986), and for failing to recognize that women's sexual relations could be expressions of resistance and autonomy (Bosworth 1999). The academic and popular concern with imprisoned women's same-sex relationships in the 1950s and 1960s has been attributed to the need to "help shore up white, marital heterosexuality" (Freedman 1996, p. 408) and to the prevalence of theories of female crime that stressed biopsychological and sexual causes (Dobash, Dobash, and Gutteridge 1986). Studies of consensual sexual relationships among male inmates have been notably rare until quite recently, with much more attention devoted to exploitative and coerced sex in men's prisons (Hensley, Struckman-Johnson, and Eigenberg 2000).

[25] For example, increases in divorce rates, female-headed households, and births to single mothers mean that more women are living without permanent male partners (Wilson 1987), have sole responsibility for their children, and have been raised by single mothers (Furstenberg 1990). If women going to prison are now more likely to be unattached and single mothers, this may affect the types of relationships they form and the deprivations they feel in prison. To the extent that attitudes toward homosexuality have become less intolerant over time, the willingness of women in prison to admit to sexual relations with each other should be greater as well, which would provide spurious support for the predictions of the importation model.

to custody facilities (Mitchell 1975) or to vary by the nature of staff behavior (Mahan 1984). However, others, when controlling for pre-prison sexual relations and considering a wide range of institutions, have found no significant institutional differences (Propper 1981; see also Giallombardo 1974). With regard to changes over time, Fox's (1984) study of Bedford Hills Reformatory revealed a decline in women's participation in kinship systems which he attributed to the impact of the feminist movement on the prison population. More recently, however, Greer (2000) has argued that such decreases are more likely due to the changing carceral environments in which women increasingly find themselves. In our own analysis of women in two prisons in California, we found that prisoners' estimates of the proportion of women involved in a consensual sexual relationship had increased over the past thirty years. We suspect that this reflects a number of things, including inmates' greater willingness to acknowledge same-sex relationships and changes in the types of women incarcerated in the 1990s as opposed to the 1960s. We also found no evidence that in the mid-1990s the prevalence of these relationships varied between the two prisons.

Whether it is due to cultural or institutional differences in prisoners' behaviors or to differences in prison researchers' orientations, some studies in England, Scotland, and Sweden suggest that homosexuality among women prisoners may be much less prevalent in other countries compared to the United States. Dobash, Dobash, and Gutteridge (1986), for example, maintained that there was no evidence of prison families or sexual relations among prisoners in Holloway or Cornton Vale. Other researchers in England and elsewhere, however, have noted these types of intimate and primary group relationships, albeit they vary in how central they see these relationships to be for prison life (cf. Mawby 1982; Mandaraka-Sheppard 1986; Bondeson 1989; Bosworth 1999; Dirsuweit 1999). What is noteworthy about some of these recent non-American studies of women in prison is the different analytic frameworks they bring to bear on, and the different questions they ask about, women's intimate relationships in prison as compared to earlier research. The concern has shifted from viewing these relationships as evidence of pathology or deprivation to viewing them as evidence of women inmates' active resistance to their carceral lives and the existing power relations within prison, or as efforts at identity construction in a depersonalizing environment (Bosworth 1999; Dirsuweit

1999). We return to some of this work below when we discuss recent scholarship on women's experiences of imprisonment.

D. Research on Prisonization and the Inmate Code of Ethics

A second line of research generated by the early studies of women in prison is concerned with the applicability of such traditional markers of male inmate adjustment as prisonization, inmate solidarity, and opposition to staff. Like the work on women's intimate relations in prison, this research has also been guided by an interest in how and why women adapt to prison differently from men. But the work on prisonization has made more explicit its comparisons of women to men, and has tended to treat men's responses as the norm from which women's responses often depart. Much of this work also frames its analysis within the traditional conceptual perspectives described earlier—that is, importation and functionalist or deprivation models—and attempts more rigorous evaluations of them.

In general, the results of this work suggest support for both models (see, e.g., Hartnagel and Gillan 1980) but also reveal some gender differences in the effects of prisoners' institutional careers on their adaptations. If the importation model is correct, a woman's background and attributes will predict her response to prison life. Here we find considerable consensus among studies of female prisoners about the characteristics associated with prisonization, opposition to staff, and misbehavior. Women who are young, who are nonwhite, who come from an urban background, who are single with no children, who have prior institutional experience, and who have been convicted of a violent crime or a drug law violation tend to score higher on these traditional indicators of male adaptation (Jensen and Jones 1976; Alpert, Noblit, and Wiorkowski 1977; Jensen 1977; Faily and Roundtree 1979; Zingraff and Zingraff 1980; Kruttschnitt 1981; Mandaraka-Sheppard 1986; Bondeson 1989). Many of these characteristics are also associated with male prisoners' misbehavior and prisonization (Adams 1992).

If the deprivation model is correct, variables such as sentence length, time served, and time left to serve should affect prisonization or identification with an inmate subculture and opposition to staff. The findings pertaining to female prisoners are not consistent across studies, suggesting that these relationships are complex and conditional. While some scholars find that acceptance of the inmate code is highest in the mid-career phase (Tittle 1969; Jensen and Jones 1976; Alpert, Noblit, and Wiorkowski 1977; Bondeson 1989), which is consistent with the research on men, others find no evidence that career phase affects inmate solidarity or prisonization (Kruttschnitt 1981; Mawby 1982; Mandaraka-Sheppard 1986; Craddock 1996). Further, there is also evidence that sentence length and prison crowding are positively related to defiance and misbehavior (Ruback and Carr 1984; Goetting and Howsen 1986; Singleton, Meltzer, and Gatward 1998), but the effects of type of institution (e.g., open vs. closed, training school vs. prison) remain unclear (Hartnagel and Gillan 1980; Larson and Nelson 1984; Mandaraka-Sheppard 1986; Bondeson 1989). Finally, studies on men suggest that the types of prisoners in a prison affect the level of conflict it experiences (Cline and Wheeler 1968). Fox (1982, 1984) uncovered a similar pattern in the women's prison he studied: an increase in young female prisoners coincided with higher levels of institutional conflict. Unfortunately, beyond Fox's research no attention has been given to this critical selection effect, even in the studies of women's imprisonment that have included multiple facilities in their research designs (Hartnagel and Gillan 1980; Larson and Nelson 1984; Mandarka-Sheppard 1986; Bondeson 1989). More generally, variations in institutions and prison populations have been ignored as possible explanations for variation in prisonization, support for the inmate code, or conflict among prisoners.

The attention given in this work to gender differences in such indicators of adaptation as prisonization or adoption of the inmate code has been criticized on several fronts, most commonly for evaluating women's responses to imprisonment with outdated male behavioral norms (Pollock-Byrne 1990, pp. 139–40). While there is no question that much of the early research relied on indicators that were not particularly relevant for female inmates, later research sought to rectify this by developing more gender-specific indicators (cf. Ward and Kassebaum 1965; Zingraff and Zingraff 1980). From a historical perspective, this body of research is perhaps more important for the attention it drew to a different aspect of women's adjustment to prison and one that did not involve gender roles or sexual behavior. In so doing, it began to shed light on the biographies and identities that shape women's responses to incarceration and moved away from viewing women in prison as a homogeneous group with a limited set of gender-specific ways of responding to prison.[26]

[26] An interesting example of the ways in which this work spawned new perspectives on gender differences in responses to incarceration is Ward's (1982) study of the social

E. Research on Individual Coping and Adjustment

Research on prisoner coping and adjustment continues in the classic tradition of the micro-sociology of imprisonment in one important respect: by examining the contribution of individual and environmental characteristics, and their interactions, to prisoners' adaptations.[27] However, because it typically is more psychological and less concerned with the social organization and daily life of the prison, research on coping signals a departure from the classic work on the prison community and growing interest in the individual prisoner as an isolated object of study and intervention, a point to which we return below.

Adams (1992) provides a thorough review of the research on prison adjustment and coping, noting that many of the central questions in the field have not been addressed for women (see also Wright 1991). The dominant work on prison adjustment flows from a stress-coping paradigm that has informed at least two recent studies on female prisoners. In one, Loucks and Zamble (2000) found only a small difference between the average coping efficacy scores of Canadian women and men beginning their prison sentences (Zamble and Porporino 1988); however, the scores for female prisoners were considerably lower than the average in a nonoffender population (Hughes and Zamble 1993). In addition, MacKenzie, Robinson, and Campbell (1989) found that women prisoners' anxiety and coping levels did not vary by the length of their sentences.[28]

It can be argued that the lack of recent research on coping among female inmates at a time when penal policies and practices are undergoing significant change is unfortunate. Given a growing concern in correctional practice with classification, risk assessment, and managerial control of female prison populations, it is important to understand

organization of a women's prison in England. Uncovering a high degree of "snitching" among the female inmates and relatively little evidence of inmate solidarity, Ward argues that the lack of solidarity had nothing to do with the fact that the inmates were women but instead was a product of their lack of power to determine their release dates and their institutional circumstances, which located this power in the hands of the staff with whom they interacted. "Snitching," then, was seen by these women as a commodity, something to be traded for a chance to influence staff, and ultimately their release dates.

[27] Liebling (1999, p. 312, n. 4) notes that coping refers to "a mixture of thoughts and actions; individuals' coping styles and abilities can vary over time, and coping can be seen as a mediator of emotion."

[28] Although Negy and colleagues (Negy, Woods, and Carlson 1997) also focused on female inmates' coping, their research examined the correlation between coping and adjustment among inmates. As the authors acknowledged, the findings are silent as to whether high levels of adjustment caused strong coping skills or the reverse, and the lack of a control group or any comparative data makes it unclear whether the inmates' adjustment reflects traits measured prior to or after incarceration.

how these elements of a certain type of organizational efficiency may affect women prisoners' psychological health and how these institutional concerns may interact with women's preprison attributes and experiences to have particularly marked effects on some types of women. Accordingly, we turn to the literature on a wider range of measures of adjustment to prison life (Adams 1992), focusing on aggression, depression, self-harm, and suicide.

1. *Misbehavior and Aggression.*   Most of the work on women's misbehavior in prison has focused on documenting gender differences in such behaviors.[29] Nonetheless, no consistent gender differences have been found in the prevalence of misbehavior or rule infractions. Some studies find that women have higher rates of rule violations while imprisoned than men (Lindquist 1980; McClellan 1994), whereas others report the opposite (Goetting and Howsen 1983; Craddock 1996; Harer and Langan 2001).

These discrepancies have raised questions about the degree to which correctional administrators' and staff perceptions, and gender stereotypes, of inmates' behaviors influence data on male and female prison infractions. There is some evidence that prison staff may respond differently to men's and women's behaviors by dealing with men through formal means, for example, with disciplinary hearings, in situations where women are dealt with informally (Poole and Regoli 1983; Sommers and Baskin 1990; McClellan 1994). Studies of correctional officers' (COs) perceptions of the supervision problems associated with female and male prisoners are rare, but paint a similar picture. Both Pollock (1986) and, more recently, Rasche (2001) found that COs' responses to male and female inmates were based on their attributions of sex-specific personality differences and behavior problems. Female prisoners were described as emotional, manipulative, impulsive, and resistant to taking orders. They were also viewed as less dangerous but more troublesome than male inmates. Similar types of attributional differences by staff have been noted in studies in English prisons and have been seen as responsible for more exacting, petty, and restrictive disciplinary practices—and hence higher rates of infractions—in the women's prisons there (Carlen 1998, p. 86; see also Carlen 1983, 1985).

[29] Misbehavior generally refers to any actions in prison for which an inmate can be disciplined. These acts range widely by institution but generally include failure to obey a direct order, violating posted/known rules, theft of property, damage of property, creating a disturbance, homosexuality, assaults on other inmates or staff, possession of a contraband substance or a weapon, and escape (see, e.g., McClellan 1994).

With regard to gender differences in the severity of misbehaviors, there is much more consistency across studies. Compared to female prisoners, male prisoners are more likely to commit serious infractions, including assaults on other inmates and staff (Bowker 1980; Lindquist 1980; Seear and Player 1986; McClellan 1994; Harer and Langan 2001). For example, in England and Wales in 2000, 1,652 male prisoners were restrained for violence or infractions, compared to only fifty-six female prisoners (Home Office 2001), a ratio of twenty-nine infractions by males for every one infraction by females. (The ratio of male to female prisoners in England and Wales is eighteen to one.) Further, when women are cited for rule breaking, they are more likely to be charged with stealing from other prisoners and verbal abuse than with violence (Mandaraka-Sheppard 1986).

Physical aggression by women in prison is, according to most studies, relatively rare, individualistic rather than collective, and often attributable to conflicts over intimate relationships (Bowker 1980; Loucks 1997).[30] One systematic analysis that attempted to link women's aggression to attributes of the prison and the prisoner found that levels of violence were low in the English prisons studied, and it occurred less often in open, as opposed to closed, institutions (Mandaraka-Sheppard 1986). Other institutional characteristics, such as method of punishment, extent of autonomy, and incentives for good behavior, accounted for almost two-thirds of the explained variance in physical violence.[31]

The limited work on predicting aggressive behavior among female prisoners indicates that early family experiences and childhood problem behaviors may be quite important. Aggressive female prisoners have been described as having family and personal backgrounds that

---

[30] Another form of violence in women's prisons that has until recently received little attention is the sexual victimization of prisoners by prison staff. In 1996, Human Rights Watch (1996) published a report charging that male guards in prisons in California, Illinois, Georgia, and Michigan were frequently sexually abusing women inmates (see also Hensley, Struckman-Johnson, and Eigenberg 2000; Stein 1996). Subsequent investigations in several Midwestern facilities revealed generally lower rates of sexual coercion reported by female inmates (6 percent to 19 percent) and the majority of these incidents were perpetrated by other prisoners, not by staff (Struckman-Johnson et al. 1996; Alarid 2000). However, as some scholars have noted, the generally low rates of reported sexual misconduct by staff are due at least in part to the requirement that inmates must prove the allegations they make against staff (Pogrebin and Dodge 2001).

[31] Qualitative research in a large urban county jail in the southern United States suggested that a different set of environmental conditions—large institutions with open dormitory-style housing and staff who ignore or encourage aggression among inmates—fuels incidents of sexual coercion and assault among female prisoners (Alarid 2000). These conclusions, however, were derived from only one informant.

include siblings with substance abuse problems, preadolescent sexual abuse, and an early age at first arrest (Loucks and Zamble 2000). There is also some evidence that among female prisoners, racial minorities, younger prisoners, and prisoners diagnosed with emotional problems are more likely than others to engage in violent behavior while they are incarcerated (Roundtree, Mohan, and Mahaffey 1980; Kruttschnitt and Krmpotich 1990; Loucks and Zamble 2000).

2. *Depression.* Relatively little systematic information is available on the prevalence of depression among incarcerated women. In part this reflects the lack of a consistent methodology to study depression among prisoners, and may also be related to the shift away from a treatment orientation in women's prisons, which has limited the extent of psychological testing of female inmates. The 1997 survey of inmates in U.S. state and federal correctional facilities provides self-reported data on the proportion of female and male prisoners with a mental or emotional condition that limits the kind or amount of work they can do (Bureau of Justice Statistics 2001*b*, table 2). While the results indicate that almost twice as many females as males (16 percent vs. 9.6 percent) report such a condition, the specific nature of the condition is not specified. Some researchers have sampled different prison populations for psychiatric disorders using self-report measures, behavioral observations, and the Beck Depression Index (Beck et al. 1961). While male prison populations are studied more often, when both sexes are included generally a larger proportion of females than males is diagnosed with depression or would meet the criteria for having severe, as opposed to mild or moderate, depression (Daniel et al. 1998; Singleton, Meltzer, and Gatward 1998; Boothby and Durham 1999).[32] One exception is Sheridan's (1996) study of eighty-one men and women serving sentences in two correctional institutions in the mid-Atlantic region in the United States. He reported that one-third of both the males and females had clinically significant problems with depression. However, because his respondents were voluntarily participating in substance abuse programs, they may not be representative of the larger prison populations from which they were drawn.

Given the paucity of information on the prevalence of depression among female prisoners, it is not surprising that relatively little is known about the penal environments and personal experiences of

---

[32] Females in the general population also appear to suffer from higher levels of depression than males.

those most likely to experience depression during their incarceration. There is some evidence that, regardless of gender, prisoners in close custody score higher on depression than their counterparts who experience less restrictive conditions (Boothby and Durham 1999). In addition, Hart (1995) has maintained that social support is particularly important to the psychological well-being of female prisoners. However, because his study compared males at a maximum-security prison with females at a medium-security prison, the observed effects for social support could be confounded with security level. More broadly based inquiries about psychological well-being and stress indicate that women who have more perceived control over their prison environment are less likely to be depressed (Ruback and Carr 1984).

Prisoners who score higher on measures of depression tend to be young, first-time offenders and those with a history of maltreatment (McClellan, Farabee, and Crouch 1997; Boothby and Durham 1999).[33] There is also some evidence that selected coping strategies (e.g., active coping, planning, restraint, acceptance) are negatively correlated with depression; however, it is unclear whether women's coping skills predict depression levels, depression predicts their coping strategies, or both (see also Sappington 1996). Finally, since preprison measures of depression are rarely available, research has not been able to determine systematically the extent to which imprisonment raises levels of depression above those experienced before coming to prison.[34]

3. *Self-Harm and Suicide.* In the United Kingdom and in Canada, concerns with self-harm and suicide among incarcerated women have grown as a result of the media's focus on selected incidents and scholarly research on what these acts indicate about women's prison environments (Heney 1990; Home Office 1990; Kershaw and Lasovich 1991; Wilkins and Coid 1991). In contrast, in the United States self-harm and suicide among prisoners have received much less attention.

Over twenty years ago, Fox (1975) documented sizable gender differences among prisoners in both self-injury and attempted suicide that are consistent with what is known about gendered patterns of self-injury in the general population and with recent studies conducted in

---

[33] The characteristics noted here as correlates of depression among female prisoners are often associated with depression in the general population as well.

[34] It is also not known to what extent gender differences in depression among prisoners might be a consequence of gender differences in the relationship between depression and crime. That is, if depression is more often linked with women's criminal behavior than with men's, depression should be higher among female, compared to male, prison populations.

prisons in England and Wales (Dooley 1990; Singleton, Meltzer, and Gatward 1998; Liebling 1999). Women in prison, like women in the general population, are more likely to self-injure or attempt suicide than are male prisoners, though estimates of the size of this gender difference vary.[35] In our own study of two women's prisons in California, 12 percent of the women in both institutions reported that they had intentionally hurt themselves before (but not during) their current sentences, 2 percent during their current incarceration (but not prior to it), and 3 percent both before and during their current incarceration. Between 8 and 9 percent also indicated that they had frequently felt suicidal since coming to prison. This self-reported rate of self-injury prior to incarceration is very similar to that (7.5 percent) documented for women in Holloway Prison in England (Liebling 1992); American estimates of self-harm during the current prison term are, however, about half that for the female sentenced population in England and Wales (10 percent) (Singleton, Meltzer, and Gatward 1998).

The correlates of self-harm among prisoners are generally similar to those found in the general population. Female prisoners who self-injure are more likely than other prisoners to have been convicted of violent crimes or property damage, to have received psychiatric treatment, to have been diagnosed with a personality disorder, and to have a history of alcohol abuse, family disruption, and/or physical and sexual abuse (Wilkins and Coid 1991; Liebling 1992, 1999). Whether aspects of women's current conditions of confinement, including sentence length or, in the United Kingdom or Canada, remand status, differentiate women who self-harm from other prisoners remains unclear (Cookson 1977; Singleton, Meltzer, and Gatward 1998). However, one attempt to distinguish among women who self-harm to relieve symptoms from those who do it as a response to an external event or as a suicide attempt revealed that the latter tended to be older, to have been older at their first court appearance, and to have had fewer priors than those who were relieving symptoms (Coid et al. 1992).

In contrast to patterns of suicide in the general population, suicide among prisoners does not appear to show strong or consistent gender differences. Indeed, research in England indicates that while suicide rates for men are just over three times those for women in the general

---

[35] Furthermore, surveys of males and females in England and Wales revealed that within the last week, sentenced women were twice as likely as sentenced men to report having had suicidal thoughts, and the same applies to suicide attempts both within the last week and the past year (Singleton, Meltzer, and Gatward 1998).

population, suicide rates among female prisoners appear to be as high as or higher than among male prisoners (Liebling 1994; Loucks 1997). Moreover, Liebling (1997, 1999) argues that prison suicides in England and Scotland involving women are increasing, although problems in the official documentation of this phenomenon obscure this trend.[36] Recent data from the Home Office (2001) support the conclusion that suicide among prisoners in England and Wales may not be the gendered phenomenon that it is in the general population. Between 1995 and 2000, 475 males and twenty-three females in prison are listed in official publications as dying from suicide. Females thus accounted for 4.6 percent of suicides in prison during years in which they accounted for a similar percentage of the prison population.

Data from the United States, where suicides by prisoners have received less attention, also suggest that the gender differential in suicides among prisoners is much smaller than it is in the general population.[37] The Bureau of Justice Statistics (2000e) reports that in 1997, female prisoners accounted for about 6.2 percent of the total state prison population. In the same year, female prisoners accounted for 3.8 percent of deaths classified as suicide and 5.6 percent of deaths classified as either suicide or accidental self-injury. This is consistent with Liebling's (1994, 1999) claim that when both suicide and accidental deaths due to self-injury are taken into account, women prisoners' rates are very close to men's rates.

Women prisoners thought to be at high risk for suicide share much in common with those who self-harm. These are women who have histories of psychiatric treatment, alcohol and drug abuse, and maltreatment, and often they are serving life sentences (Loucks 1997).[38] However, what may be as, if not more, important, but less well understood, is how the characteristics of the prison environment contribute to these attempted and completed suicides (Liebling 1995). Liebling (1997) has created a typology of suicide vulnerability that explicitly

[36] Liebling (1994, 1999) argues that suicides by women prisoners are often misclassified as due to accidental self-injury or undetermined causes.

[37] In the general population in United States, the suicide rate among men is about four times the rate among women.

[38] However, there is some evidence to suggest that the differences between inmates prone to suicide or self-harm and other inmates are greater for males than females. For example, Liebling (1992) found more significant differences between a subgroup of male suicide attempters and a group of male controls than between a subgroup of female suicide attempters and a group of female controls in her study of inmates in English prisons. For female inmates, histories of abuse and difficulties in coping did not distinguish as strongly between the two groups.

addresses the potential connections among individuals' backgrounds, their sentences, and "prison-induced stresses." Certainly the finding that women's suicide rates approach men's rates in prison suggests that prison itself is a particular contributor to women's risks of suicide.[39]

By considering how women's background experiences and personal characteristics affect their adjustment, this research also has continued the move away from viewing women in prison as having a common set of needs and similar backgrounds or a common set of gender-role constraints. As a consequence, it has encouraged the development of interventions aimed at previously neglected needs.

However, other work has pointed to the role that criminological and expert knowledge, especially that based in psychiatry and the behavioral sciences, can play in expanding and intensifying the disciplinary and punitive aspects of imprisonment in general, and women's imprisonment in particular (e.g., Dobash, Dobash, and Gutteridge 1986; Garland 1996; Rock 1996; Kendall 2000). This includes the development and application of assessment and diagnostic tools measuring adjustment that have been linked to the growth of risk-based technologies of governance in prisons (Feeley and Simon 1992; Hannah-Moffat 1999). Within such regimes, prisoners' adjustment scores may become the basis for determining their security levels or their risks of recidivism. As discussed above, a woman's difficulties in adjusting to prison may thus be translated not into a justification for providing her certain services or programs, but into a gendered set of criminogenic risk factors. And these, in turn, may affect the timing of her subsequent release or her conditions of parole. A related criticism is that compliant behavior, which is often taken as an indicator of good adjustment to imprisonment, may also indicate dependence and passivity. These in turn may be linked to an infantilization process that inhibits the development of abilities and attitudes important for successful reintegration upon release from prison.

There are other, more methodological criticisms of some of the quantitative research on adjustment, such as the use of scales developed in studies of male prisoners that have not been validated on females (cf., e.g., Harer and Langan 2001) and the inattention to the effects of institutional context on adjustment. Perhaps more fundamentally, this

---

[39] Of course, it may also be that women sent to prison have particularly elevated risks of suicide, and the higher rates for women in prison are the result of a selection effect. Nevertheless, the extent to which the imprisonment experience may contribute to women's suicide risks needs further examination.

work tends to treat women in prison as constellations of scores on a set of independent and dependent variables, which prevents considering how the interaction of their biographies and subjectivities shapes how they experience imprisonment. Recent qualitative and ethnographic research on women in prison is an antidote of sorts to this tendency, and provides a different set of concepts and analytic frameworks from within which to view imprisoned women's experiences.

F. Recent Scholarship on Women's Experiences of Imprisonment

The 1990s saw the beginning of a wave of scholarship on women in prison which in some respects harkens back to earlier work, especially the classic prison sociology of the 1940s and 1950s, and in other respects is heavily influenced by recent feminist scholarship within and outside of criminology. The work of inmate writers has again, as it was in the 1970s, been featured in several publications (e.g., Hampton 1993; Clark 1995; Cook and Davies 1999). Historical studies of women's imprisonment have drawn attention to the ways convict women in the past shaped their prison worlds as they in turn were shaped by them (e.g., Zedner 1991; Butler 1997; Damousi 1997; Daniels 1998). And a series of sociological studies has taken up issues about contemporary women's experiences of imprisonment in ways that have challenged earlier interpretations and highlighted both continuities and discontinuities in these experiences as women's lives and women's prisons have changed. It is to this recent sociological work, and its attention to women prisoners as active participants in constructing their lives in prison, that we turn now.[40]

In the tradition of the prison scholarship of Sykes, Schrag (1944), and others, Owen's (1998) quasi-ethnography of the Central California Women's Facility (CCWF)—then the largest prison for women in the world—describes the culture and social order of the prison, focusing on how women do time. Owen argues that women prisoners' histories of a "multiplicity of abuse," family relations, and economic marginality—which are often linked to their involvement in crime—are critical for understanding their experiences in prison. Implicitly, her analysis also shows how the effects of these histories are conditioned by the physical world of the prison and, in particular, crowding, which was a defining feature of life at CCWF. As in the classic studies of women

---

[40] We do not review here another important body of work that draws on interviews with incarcerated women not to describe their prison lives so much as to develop an understanding of their pathways into crime (e.g., Comack 1996; Richie 1996).

in prison, Owen sees women's affective relationships as a way they manage their sentences, as a source for conflicts among prisoners, and as a central element of the inmate culture. To describe this culture, Owen turns to Schrag's (1944) concept of the "axes of life" and portrays how women negotiate information and commodities, their commitment to the inmate code, and their involvement in "the mix" of trouble, hustles, and conflicts. She concludes, as much earlier research has, that both importation theory and "the indigenous theory of prison culture" (Owen 1998, p. 2) are relevant to understanding the social world of women's prisons.

Other work, including the recent historical analyses cited above, has explicitly challenged some of the long-standing assumptions about women prisoners, especially assumptions about their passivity, lack of activism, and sexuality. One example is Diaz-Cotto's (1996) analysis of the experiences of Latina and Latino prisoners in New York during the 1970s and 1980s. She shows how Latina prisoners' attempts to organize in the pursuit of prison reform were sufficiently threatening to cause the administration to develop strategies to block them. Nonetheless, the formation of a multiracial coalition and underground political activities exacted some concessions from the authorities. The decade lag in the implementation of these reforms in women's prisons highlights, however, the fundamental differences in responses to female and male prisoners during this post-Attica period. Another study that reinterprets what has been seen as a characteristically female behavior in prison is Dirsuweit's (1999) exploration of sexuality in a women's prison in South Africa. She views women's constructions of their sexual identities in prison as not simply shaped by the deprivations of prison life, but as forms of resistance and transgression; prison in this sense may provide women greater freedom to explore "alternative configurations of desire" (Dirsuweit 1999, p. 80) than does the outside world.

The ways in which women in prison construct identities to increase their capacities for resistance is a prominent theme in other work (e.g., McCorkle 1998). For example, in Bosworth's (1999) analysis of three women's prisons in England, the concepts of agency and resistance take center stage. For her, women's abilities to negotiate power in prison are shaped by the ways they construct, through the intersection of race, class, ethnicity, and sexuality, their identities.[41] Like others be-

---

[41] Another identity that appears to shape how women experience imprisonment is that of mother. Certainly separation from one's children is consistently cited as one of the major pains of imprisonment for women. There is a growing literature on imprisoned

fore her (e.g., Carlen 1983), Bosworth sees women's prison as both a material structure and a symbolic institution that is reflective of gender relations, and argues that the politics of femininity are enmeshed in women's lives in prison. Notably, Bosworth (1999) focuses on the same question as Owen: How do women do their time? But the answer she provides is quite different. The women she talked with engaged in efforts to subvert the mundane and alienating aspects of prison life on a private and individual level through their presentations of self. In the face of pressures toward compliance—through domestication, infantilization, and medicalization—and the homogenization of the prison population, women used their cultural and sexual identities to assert their agency and resist these demands. For Bosworth, femininity, as revealed in women's attention to their physical appearance and lesbian relationships with other prisoners, was not an accommodation to the deprivations of prison life, or a method of coping with a lengthy prison term, but a means of resisting the restrictions correctional authorities place on them. Although she acknowledges that lesbian relationships divided the inmate community, as some inmates were extremely critical of same-sex relationships, such division serves to reinforce the complexity of power relations in prison and the individual ways in which women respond to these power relations and, more generally, prison authority.

Despite the attention Bosworth draws to prisons as sites of constant negotiation in which both prisoners and the institution wield power, she does not consider how the penopolitical coordinates of her own sites—an open minimum-security prison, a remand center, and a high-security annex—shape the nature and outcomes of these negotiations. The question of whether and how women's experiences of imprisonment are shaped by the character of the regime in which they are incarcerated is addressed in other work. Rock (1996), for example, in tracing the redevelopment of Holloway Prison between 1968 and 1988, shows how the social order of the prisoners and their relations

---

women as mothers and on the children of imprisoned women that is too large for us to review here (see, e.g., Hagan and Dinovitzer 1999; Greene, Haney, and Hurtado 2000; Enos 2001). Moreover, much of this literature is primarily concerned with women as mothers and how imprisonment affects their ability to mother (see, e.g., Clark 1995), rather than with women as prisoners—the central concern of this essay. Enos's (2001) study is one exception to this in that it considers not only how women in prison construct and manage motherhood, but also how motherhood is a resource for them in dealing with prison life. We discuss some of her findings in a subsequent section on women's lives after prison.

with staff changed as Holloway was transformed from a radial structure focused on control, containment, and discipline into a therapeutic structure with vague and permeable boundaries. Each phase of this transformation was accompanied by different penal policies and priorities and by a different typification of the female criminal, and these too affected prisoners' lives. Rock's goal is not to offer a general theory of the relationship between prison regimes and the experiences of imprisoned women; instead, he shows how models of imprisonment at a specific institution, which were unstable and never exclusive, generated conflicting goals and responses from prisoners.

In another effort to document changes in a women's prison regime and its consequences for prisoners, Rierden (1997) recorded her observations of life at Niantic Correctional Institution in Connecticut from 1992 until 1995. Niantic opened in 1918 and for many decades remained a gendered embodiment of the rehabilitative model, where inmates performed farm work in a pastoral setting supervised by matrons. By 1992, however, the prison was overcrowded and its programs were inadequate for the changing prisoner population, which staff described as increasingly difficult to manage. The construction of a new maximum-security facility across the street alleviated the crowding problem while simultaneously ushering in a new confinement model that kept prisoners locked in their cells except while at school or work. According to Rierden, staff at the new facility firmly believed that their job was to ensure that prisoners learned personal responsibility. Consistent with this, discipline and classification of prisoners according to the seriousness of their crimes—not rehabilitation—was the central concern of the prison. However, because she was not allowed to conduct her research at the new prison as she had earlier, Rierden was not able to discover how prisoners reacted to these changes.

Our own research in two women's prisons in California focuses on what women's experiences in prison can tell us about the practices of imprisonment in different penal regimes and institutional environments. By combining the interviews and surveys we conducted with women at the California Institution for Women (CIW) and Valley State Prison for Women (VSPW) in the mid-1990s with the interviews and survey data Ward and Kassebaum collected at CIW in the early 1960s, we have been able to compare women's experiences at two critical times in the recent history of women's imprisonment: the height of the rehabilitative regime and the height of a neoliberal regime stressing custody and management. We have also been able to compare the

experiences of women serving time within the same increasingly punitive environment but at two different prisons. The California Institution for Women is the oldest prison for women in California and retains some of the physical and cultural features of its rehabilitative
heritage; VSPW is the newest prison for women in California and
epitomizes the preoccupation with danger, security, and efficient management.

In our comparison of CIW and VSPW in the 1990s we found that the
identities and experiences women brought to prison shaped how they
did their time, but in somewhat different ways at each prison. At CIW,
the older prison that retains elements of the maternal-rehabilitative
regime of the past, women's reactions to prison were more distinctly
patterned by their individual characteristics, but were also more likely
to include some positive evaluations of their time in prison. In contrast, at VSPW individual variations were blunted and women's ways
of doing time showed more homogeneity—in particular, women were
more uniformly distrustful of other inmates and staff, were more critical of the prison administration and operations, and consistently chose
to isolate themselves from others as the best way to do their time
(Kruttschnitt, Gartner, and Miller 2000; Gartner and Kruttschnitt
2002b). One implication of these institutional differences is that wom-
en's adaptations to prison may not be as fundamentally structured by
gender in many of the ways traditionally assumed. The adaptations described in so many other studies of women in prison therefore need to
be seen as shaped by the nature of women's imprisonment at a particular time and place rather than as simply products of the nature of
women themselves.

By comparing women's experiences at CIW over time, we found evidence that the practices of imprisonment in both the 1960s and the
1990s were partial, diverse, and contradictory (Gartner and Kruttschnitt 2002a). The stated goal of CIW in the 1960s was to provide
women with a therapeutically informed rehabilitative program. In the
1990s, the goal had shifted to providing women the time and space
to rehabilitate themselves. Women at CIW in both periods, however,
questioned the prison's ability to accomplish these goals and pointed
to fundamental characteristics of imprisonment that they felt would inevitably prevent rehabilitation, whether by the prison or by prisoners.
We also found continuity over time in many of the women's responses
to the problems of imprisonment: CIW experienced little serious violence, racial tension, or gang activity, and conflicts among women re-

mained largely interpersonal and relatively short-lived. Even so, women's experiences at CIW were altered by the more punitive climate of the 1990s. Women's distrust of and desire to keep their distance from others was greater in the 1990s than the 1960s, just as it was greater in the 1990s at VSPW than at CIW.

In summary, despite its efforts to consider how aspects of a woman's identity shape her experience of imprisonment, much of this research remains susceptible to a criticism also applicable to earlier work, that is, a tendency to universalize women's experiences in prison. Given the increasing diversity of women in prison—racial, ethnic, cultural, sexual, and more—greater attention is needed to how prisons' power to punish is greater for some women than others, with consequences for their lives not only in but also after prison.

III. The Consequences of Imprisonment for Women's Lives after Prison

There is widespread agreement among scholars and practitioners that incarcerated women have a set of needs that are not addressed with the traditional set of prison programs and that programs that have been designed to reduce men's recidivism may not be as effective for women. However, given the lack of systematic evaluations of women's prisons programs, the questions of "what works" for women prisoners and whether this varies based on women's cultural or other identities and experiences remain largely unanswered.

Recidivism data uniformly indicate that women are less likely to reoffend than men. Why might this be the case? Some criminal justice experiences and personal characteristics seem to be equally predictive of recidivism among male and female offenders. Prior record, age, substance abuse, and employment are notable in this regard. But the trajectories of women's postprison lives are complex and likely reflect the interactions of various experiences and the reactions of criminal justice agents and agencies. Qualitative work on the postrelease experiences of female offenders points to several components in the ability to remain crime free, including a sense of agency and the formation of attachments and bonds to conventional others (see also Shover 1996; Maruna 2001). What fosters this sense of agency among some women and not others is not well understood, however, despite the obvious implications it has for the types of pre- and postrelease programs that should be made available to incarcerated women (see also Carlen 1990).

*A. Treatment Programs in Prison and Their Effects
on Postprison Outcomes*

Traditionally, prisons have offered a limited range of programs and work opportunities, and this has been particularly true of women's prisons (Glick and Neto 1977; American Correctional Association 1990; Shover 1991). In response to this, in the 1970s first men and then women in prison launched a wave of litigation targeted at state correctional systems. In a series of class action suits, women prisoners claimed that their rights had been violated under the Fifth, Eighth, and especially the Fourteenth Amendments to the U.S. Constitution. These challenges centered on incarcerated women's access to basic education, vocational training, work, medical care, and legal assistance (Knight 1992; Morash, Haarr, and Rucker 1994). A series of favorable court rulings led to an initial expansion in the range of programming available to women in prison; subsequent cutbacks in spending on prison programs and services, however, have reversed many of these changes.

One of the most comprehensive examinations of prison program availability has been conducted in the United States by Morash and her colleagues (Morash, Haarr, and Rucker 1994; Morash, Bynum, and Koons 1998). Based on analyses of survey data collected from state and federal prisoners and from state prison administrators beginning in the mid-1980s, they concluded that there were sizable gender differences in the nature of and participation in education, work, medical and mental health, and legal assistance programs. With regard to levels of participation, women scored higher than men in many respects. For example, a larger proportion of women than men participated in all levels of educational programming (adult basic, secondary, and college) and had work assignments. However, the nature of prison work remained gender-typed (see also Glick and Neto 1977, p. 79; American Correctional Association 1990; Eaton 1993). Women were disproportionately involved in janitorial and kitchen work, whereas men were overrepresented in farm, forestry, maintenance, and repair. Pay levels also varied by gender, with men being paid more often than women for their prison work. The study also identified an important source of gender differences in work opportunities: vocational training is more widely available in maximum- and medium-security facilities, the types of facilities that are less likely to house women offenders.

With regard to access to and receipt of medical services, women were found to fare better than men. However, this was partly explained by the greater reliance on psychotropic drugs to deal with poor prison adjustment in women's prisons compared to men's prisons (Morash, Haarr, and Rucker 1994). The relationship between gender and drug treatment held when controlling for prior mental hospitalization and prior use of psychotropic drugs (see also Baskin et al. 1989).

Findings such as these have supported calls for innovative programs based on careful assessments of women offenders' needs. As Ross and Fabiano have argued, "there is very little evidence that policy or program development has been based on examination of program efficacy or systematic investigation of the female offender's needs. . . . The major current models are the 'equity model' or the 'forget-me-not' model. Actually, they are exhortations or pleas rather than models. It remains to be seen whether they lead to programs which actually fit the needs of female offenders or whether they only entrench the 'male model' more solidly" (1986, p. 12). Needs assessments calling for gender-specific services and programs have in fact increased dramatically in recent years (see, e.g., Yang 1990; Austin, Bloom, and Donahue 1992; Maden, Swinton, and Gunn 1994; Wellisch and Falkin 1994; Wellisch, Prendergast, and Anglin 1994; Barthwell et al. 1995; Gray, Mays, and Stohr 1995; Patterson 1995; Henderson 1998; Veysey 1998; Covington 2001; Reid-Howe Associates 2001). These assessments have consistently drawn attention to the characteristics, or needs, outlined earlier that are thought to distinguish women in prison both from women in the general population and, in many cases, from men in prison (e.g., histories of drug abuse, histories of physical and sexual abuse, limited vocational skills, physical and mental health problems, child-care responsibilities, and so on).[42] Most of the programs that address these needs are community based, designed to provide transitional or prerelease planning, alternatives to incarceration, or services for homeless women. Virtually none have been the subject of rigorous independent evaluations (Austin, Bloom, and Donahue 1992; Hawke 1994; Hawke and Natarajan 1994; Kilian 1994; Natarajan 1994; Wel-

---

[42] In addition to women inmates' histories of drug abuse, physical and sexual abuse, and health and child-care problems previously documented (Bureau of Justice Statistics 1997b, 1999a, 1999d, 1999e, 2000e, 2001a, 2001d), there is also evidence that women inmates have more limited job histories than male inmates. Only four in ten women in state prisons report having had full-time employment prior to arrest, relative to nearly six in ten men in prison. Female inmates also were more likely to have been receiving welfare than male inmates (30 percent vs. 8 percent), and over one-third of the females (37 percent) had incomes of less than $600 per month prior to arrest; the comparable figure for male inmates was closer to one-quarter (28 percent; Bureau of Justice Statistics, 1999a).

lisch and Falkin 1994; Wenger 1994; National Gains Center 1995; Wellisch, Prendergast, and Anglin 1996; Conly 1998).

Within prisons, innovative programming based on these needs assessments is less common and, according to some, almost nothing is known about its effectiveness. Nearly a decade after their first evaluation, Morash, Bynum, and Koons (1998) conducted a second survey of state correctional departments in which they sampled at least one prison in each state as well as jail administrators from fifty city and county jurisdictions. The vast majority of the surveyed institutions were for women only. Survey respondents were asked to identify innovative programs that they felt were meeting the needs of women offenders. A total of 242 programs were cited, but only three states reported a high level of innovation and thirty-four states indicated limited or no innovations.[43] The programs named included psychological programs addressing substance abuse, mental health, and domestic violence issues; work training programs; parenting programs focused on parental education and child visitation; and an assortment of other programs focused on transition, after-care, and life skills. However, evaluations of these programs are relatively rare, according to Morash and her colleagues (1998, p. 11). Their review of both published and unpublished reports uncovered "written reports on the outcomes of just sixty-eight programs, actual measurement of outcomes for twelve, and measurement of recidivism for six" (see also Koons et al. 1997).

Some researchers claim that data on the effectiveness of specific programs, including evidence about reductions in recidivism, are more widely available than was suggested by Morash and her colleagues. Andrews and Dowden (2000) use meta-analysis to summarize what is known about program effectiveness and to determine the applicability of human service principles (i.e., risk, need, and responsivity) to women offenders. Dowden and Andrews's (1999) analysis of the components of human services and treatment types in twenty-six studies of women offenders is the more revealing.[44] They found that the strongest predictor of treatment success was a set of family process variables, measured by the components of affection and supervision. Further, substance abuse treatment and basic educational skills training—identified in many needs assessments as important for reducing recidivism (Koons et al. 1997)—did not appear to be important predictors of

[43] The authors do not specify what proportion of these programs was housed in or adjacent to jails as opposed to prisons.

[44] The studies utilized in the Andrews and Dowden (2000) research were not listed.

treatment success.[45] However, these conclusions may be premature with regard to programs for adult women. Of the twenty-six studies examined, sixteen contained delinquent or status offenders; of the remaining, ten focused on adult offenders, and some included minor first-time offenders, women on probation, and women in community-based programs.

The results of a small number of other evaluations of programs designed to address women offenders' needs are available but need to be interpreted with caution. Some are based on very small samples of incarcerated women (twenty or fewer) with no information on sample representativeness. None followed their subjects longer than sixteen weeks or demonstrated a relationship between their outcomes (e.g., anger reduction, improved self-esteem) and lower rates of reoffending (Sultan and Long 1988; Smith, Smith, and Beckner 1994; Pomeroy, Kiam, and Abel 1998). An apparent exception is evaluations of the Women in Community Services (WICS) Life Skills Program that provides women a nine-to-twelve-week curriculum prior to their release from prison. According to Hale (2001), independent evaluations of this program find that rearrest rates for WICS graduates are significantly lower than for women in other programs (35 percent vs. 48 percent). However, Hale does not provide information about the length of the follow-up period and whether assignment to treatment and control groups was randomized.[46]

Evaluations of programs with randomized assignment and adequate follow-up periods are rare. In what has been referred to as "the most comprehensive and rigorous study of the effect of prison work and vocational training" (Gaes et al. 1999, p. 406), the Office of Research and Evaluation of the U.S. Federal Bureau of Prisons launched the Post-Release Employment Project (PREP). This project used a prospective longitudinal design to evaluate the effects of prison work and vocational training on a matched group of participants and controls. The most recent long-term follow-up of the recidivism rates of PREP participants—at a minimum of eight years postrelease—found a significant reduction in recidivism among both men who worked in prison

[45] None of the studies in the Dowden and Andrews (1999) analysis focused on factors such as past victimization or substance abuse, perhaps because the vast majority of the studies ($N = 19$) were over two decades old.

[46] There are also some ethnographic studies of programs tailored to treatment approaches for women offenders, but the findings of these studies are limited to discussions of how the various programs address women's drug use, criminal activity, and victimization (see, e.g., Welle, Falkin, and Jainchill 1998).

industry and men who participated in vocational or apprenticeship training relative to controls; there were no comparable effects, however, for the female federal inmates in this program (Saylor and Gaes 1997).

A similar set of findings also has been observed following the evaluation of CREST, the first program designed to integrate a therapeutic community with work release for drug offenders. CREST was designed to create a support network that assists with the transition from prison to employment. An initial evaluation examined both recidivism rates and drug relapses among a control group (assigned only to a work group) and a treatment group (work and participation in a therapeutic community) six and eighteen months after release from prison. Attrition rates were substantial by the eighteen-month follow-up, with only 58 percent of the CREST participants and 37 percent of the controls remaining. Nevertheless, the control group demonstrated significantly higher rates of recidivism and relapse than the CREST group (Nielsen, Scarpitti, and Inciardi 1996).[47] When women's experiences in the program were examined separately, no experimental effects were found. Women who participated in CREST did not have significantly lower recidivism rates or drug relapse rates relative to women in the working group at the eighteen-month follow-up (Farrell 2000).

An area of growing attention in the treatment literature is ethnocultural differences in responses to treatment programs and, relatedly, how to design programs sensitive to the diverse populations at which they are aimed. For example, Shearer, Myers, and Ogan (2001) note that resistance to drug treatment programs occurred across all ethnic groups they studied, but that it varied in its character and levels. They argue for training that sensitizes counselors to cultural, class, and linguistic differences among prisoners and the development of programs that take these differences into account. Implementing effective HIV/ AIDS prevention programs in prisons, according to West (2001), also requires attention to cultural distinctions. She found that Latina women, who are most at risk of entering prison with HIV infection, are least well served by existing educational programs because these ignore important cultural, linguistic, and religious distinctions among prisoners.

---

[47] It should also be noted that, relative to the CREST group, the control group had almost three times as many offenders who reported six or more prior periods of incarceration at the six-month follow-up and almost twice as many at the eighteen-month follow-up.

B. Predictors of Recidivism

One of the more important predictors of recidivism after prison is gender. Women appear from arrest and conviction data to reoffend at lower rates than do men. An early comprehensive study of 16,000 prisoners released in eleven U.S. states found that males were more likely than females to be rearrested (63 percent vs. 52 percent), reconvicted (47 percent vs. 39 percent), and reincarcerated (42 percent vs. 33 percent) within three years after their release from prison (Bureau of Justice Statistics 1989). Further, the number of prior arrests was a particularly strong predictor of recidivism for both males and females, but, except among prisoners with seven to ten prior arrests, men's rates of rearrest were consistly higher than women's regardless of prior arrest record. In 1994 a similar study was conducted of inmates released from prison in fifteen states in 1994. After three years, the rearrest and reincarceration rates of both males and females were higher than those found in the 1983 study, but they maintained the same gendered patterns; the reconviction rates of males and females, however, remained virtually unchanged (Bureau of Justice Statistics 2002b).

Other evidence suggesting that women recidivate at lower rates than men comes from data on the backgrounds of prisoners admitted to state prisons collected by the Bureau of Justice Statistics. Women generally have fewer prior arrests on admission, and this appears to have changed little over time. In 1991, for example, approximately 71 percent of women compared to 80 percent of men in prison had one or more prior incarcerations (Bureau of Justice Statistics 1994, table 5).[48] Women also violate parole at lower rates than men. In 1991, women comprised only 4 percent of the state parole violators, and this remained virtually unchanged throughout the 1990s (Bureau of Justice Statistics 2001d, table 20). Similar findings apply to the federal prison population, where women are less likely than men to be reincarcerated for a subsequent federal offense (Bureau of Justice Statistics 2000b).[49]

---

[48] Similarly, by the end of the 1990s, 65 percent of women and 77 percent of men in state prisons had a previous sentence to incarceration or probation (Bureau of Justice Statistics 1999a, table 22). The decrease in the proportions of male and female prisoners with prior incarcerations during the 1990s suggests that the criminal justice system has widened its net and is incarcerating a broader range of the population—especially more first offenders—than in the past.

[49] Since returns to prison are highest among violent offenders (especially those convicted of robbery) and considerably lower for drug offenders, the relationship between gender and return rate could be an artifact of offense. However, within each offense category, a higher percentage of men than women are returned to federal prison for a subsequent federal offense (Bureau of Justice Statistics 2000b).

1. *Predicting Recidivism among Women: Quantitative Analyses.* Methodological differences in recidivism studies—such as the use of different measures of recidivism or different follow-up periods—have greatly limited their comparability. Studies of recidivism among women are particularly problematic because samples tend to be small and are typically followed for quite limited time periods. An early but notable exception is the study of long-term parole outcome among California women parolees (Spencer and Berocochea 1979). In that study, 660 women released for the first time from the California Institution for Women in 1960 and 1961 were followed up eight years later. About 40 percent of the women had returned to prison during that time. Returnees differed from nonreturnees in having served more time during their original incarcerations. Perhaps of more interest was the finding that returns to prison were overwhelmingly the result of parole violations rather than new felonies. The variables most strongly associated with these violations were narcotics use and prior offenses. Women's racial background also appears to have affected their chances of being returned to prison for violating parole: Among women with the most extensive narcotics use and records of prior offending, black parolees were returned more frequently than white parolees, suggesting the possibility of racial discrimination in decisions to violate women on parole.

Subsequent studies of recidivism among women offenders encompass years in which there were significant changes in the social and economic lives of women and, one might expect, in societal responses to their criminal behavior (Harm and Phillips 2001). However, the predictors of women's recidivism appear to have changed little over time and are similar in the United States and Canada.[50] Recidivism rates tend to be higher for younger women (Simmons and Rogers 1970; Hoffman 1982; Belcourt, Nouwens, and Lefebvre 1993; Bonta, Pang, and Wallace-Capretta 1995) and for women with unstable family histories (Lambert and Madden 1975; Martin, Cloninger, and Guze 1978), substance abuse problems (Lambert and Madden 1975; Martin, Cloninger, and Guze 1978; Hoffman 1982; Mowbray 1982), emotional problems (Lambert and Madden 1975; Martin, Cloninger, and Guze

[50] There is one exception to this cross-national consistency. Native heritage appears to be a significant predictor of recidivism in Canadian studies (Lambert and Madden 1975; Belcourt, Nouwens, and Lefebvre 1993), but minority racial status rarely is a significant predictor of recidivism in studies of women in the United States (Spencer and Berocochea 1979).

1978; Washington and Diamond 1985; Belcourt, Nouwens, and Lefebvre 1993; Loucks and Zamble 2000), unstable employment (Lambert and Madden 1975; Martin, Cloninger, and Guze 1978; Hoffman
1982), and a history of offending (Lambert and Madden 1975; Spencer
and Berocochea 1979; Hoffman 1982; Curry and Pan 1991; Bonta,
Pang, and Wallace-Capretta 1995; Loucks and Zamble 2000).[51]

The possibility that recidivism also may be linked to particular institutional experiences has received relatively little attention in this research. Associations have been found between length of time served
(Simmons and Rogers 1970; Spencer and Berocochea 1979; Bonta,
Pang, and Wallace-Capretta 1995), type of correctional facility and administration within which sentences are served (Bondeson 1989; Curry
and Pan 1991), and women's recidivism. However, it is difficult to interpret these relationships because they could be due to selection effects or to the types of women housed in a particular facility. The previously noted study that followed 16,000 prisoners released from state
prisons found no association between time served and recidivism, controlling for the effects of prior record, age when released, age at first
adult arrest, and offense type (Bureau of Justice Statistics 1989). The
analysis, however, did not consider whether this effect was conditional
on gender.

Taken as a whole, the findings from recidivism studies suggest that
the sorts of individual characteristics and background experiences that
are associated with reoffending are similar for women and men. There
are, however, some notable exceptions to this conclusion that draw attention to the way in which gender conditions the effects of various
social locations and statuses, as well as the behaviors of legal agents
who are at least partially responsible for the production of recidivism
rates.[52] For example, Jurik (1983) analyzed data from the Transitional
Aid Released Prisoners (TARP) experiment to estimate the effects of
economic incentives on women's recidivism (Jurik 1983). This was a
randomized experiment designed to determine if newly released offenders who received transitional economic assistance were less likely

[51] Despite the attention given to abuse history as a need/risk factor for women in
prison, the limited findings regarding its relationship to recidivism are equivocal (cf.
Long et al. 1984; and Bonta, Pang, and Wallace-Capretta 1995).
[52] Although the findings from studies of female recidivism that examine the predictive
validity of recidivism scales developed for male offenders are relevant to inquiries about
the gendered nature of the correlates of recidivism (e.g., Bonta, Pang, and Wallace-
Capretta 1995), here we focus on the broader question of whether and how social control agents might influence our understanding of this phenomenon.

to reoffend than a control group. Jurik found that while each week of employment reduced the number of arrests for both women and men, the effects for women were considerably smaller than they were for men. In addition, a history of property convictions, which had no effect on reoffending among male TARP recipients, increased women's likelihood of rearrest for economic offenses. Jurik (1983, p. 618) argued that the smaller impact of employment on female recidivism relative to male recidivism may be due to the poorer earnings prospects of women ex-felons, and that women with extensive prior criminal histories are a qualitatively distinct group from men with extensive criminal histories.

More recently, Uggen and Kruttschnitt (1998) examined the predictors of both self-reported illegal behavior and arrest using data from the National Supported Work Demonstration Project. This project randomly assigned ex-offenders, ex-addicts, and young high school dropouts to a treatment or a control group.[53] Treatment consisted of subsidized jobs for up to eighteen months. Crime and arrest data were collected at nine-month intervals for up to three years. Only one factor had a significantly different effect on the self-reported illegal earnings of women and men: education decreased women's risks of illegal earnings but increased men's risks. Some factors had effects in the same direction for women and men, but the size of these effects was significantly different. Current drug use and prior crime increased arrest rates for both sexes, but the effects were twice as large for women. Among women, whites also had a higher risk of arrest than blacks. The authors interpret the findings as indicating that gender differences in desistance are at least partially a function of the ways in which legal officials respond to the social statuses and locations of women and men. Support for this interpretation comes from the long-term analysis of parole outcome in California in the 1960s noted earlier (Spencer and Berocochea 1979) which found that women were two to three times more likely than men to be returned to prison for a technical violation as opposed to a new criminal offense (see also Norland and Mann 1984; Erez 1992).

2. *Qualitative Studies of Recidivism.* Another, perhaps more subtle approach to understanding the ways in which women's reoffending is affected by their prior experiences and current situations has emerged

---

[53] The experiment also included welfare recipients, but data on their criminal behavior were not collected, so they were excluded from Uggen and Kruttschnitt's analysis.

in a group of qualitative studies of women released from prison. In these studies, recidivism, or the lack thereof, is a process that unfolds over time.

Eaton (1993) interviewed thirty-four female ex-prisoners who had served between six months and fifteen years in prison. At the time of the interviews, most of the women had been out of prison for over two years. Eaton concluded that the factors that impede recidivism and redirect women's lives are both individual and social. Despite the effects of imprisonment, which encourages passivity and mutes individual agency, women who succeeded afterward said that they had made the conscious decision to control their own lives. Especially important in this decision was ending an abusive and controlling relationship with a partner. Successful women also reported that they were willing to accept "normative" society and reestablish broken relationships with family and children.

Baskin and Sommers (1998) focused on the lives of thirty of the women in their study of violent female offenders who remained crime free for two years. These women claimed that aging had a dramatic effect on their behavior. "Aging" here referred not just to physical changes, but also to changing perceptions, such that the prospect of doing another prison term was viewed as particularly adverse. Similar to the women Eaton interviewed, these women reported that establishing a more conventional social network and forming ties that bound them to a more conventional life-style sustained and reinforced their "crime free" lives.

O'Brien (2001) interviewed eighteen women who had been out of prison for at least eighteen months about their incarceration and their return to free society. Similar to Eaton's focus on agency, for O'Brien "empowerment" is critical to understanding how women make a successful transition into society. Empowerment for these women meant gaining intrapersonal, interpersonal, and social power that enabled them to make efficacious choices for everyday life. In addition, the women's interpersonal experiences, such as support networks and their employment and economic resources upon release, were critical to establishing a crime-free life. In a nod to resources gained through contact with the criminal justice system, some of her respondents indicated that their employment and economic successes were facilitated by specific prison programs or community-based criminal justice contacts.

Harm and Phillips (2001) interviewed thirty-eight women who had served between two and six prison sentences. In contrast to the previous studies, their research looked at the obstacles that support networks and conventional society can present to women on their release from prison. For example, most of the women felt family ties made reintegration more difficult because they saw their families as either dysfunctional or controlling. Further, while employment was a positive experience for some women, for others it was stressful because of inadequate pay, a lack of child care, and the stigma they felt from their history of incarceration. Substance abuse problems and women's inability to exit deviant networks also contributed to events that preceded relapse and recidivism. The women's ability to recognize these patterns, however, underscores the importance of agency in individual decisions concerning subsequent involvement in crime.

These qualitative studies make an important contribution to our understanding of the complex influences on women's adjustment to society upon release from prison. These women are likely to be among the best sources of information on the constellation of factors that affect their postprison lives. Caution is needed, however, in drawing conclusions about recidivism based on interviews only with women who have avoided it. For example, knowing how many women who recidivate make conscious decisions not to do so would help us to evaluate how important such individual decisions are in explaining recidivism, compared to other influences on women's postprison lives, such as economic need. In addition, the emphasis in some of these studies on women's agency as a causal factor in avoiding recidivism needs to be balanced with an awareness of the limited range of choices available to most women released from prison.[54] Finally, seeing agency and empowerment as the most critical factors in reducing recidivism can lead to the conclusion that all that is required to stay crime free is to "just say no," thus making women solely responsible for their own success—or lack thereof—at avoiding reoffending.

C. Collateral Consequences of Imprisonment for Women

Imprisonment can have profound effects on women's relationships with their children, their families, their communities, and their economic opportunities in ways that are only beginning to be explored. In addition to the studies reviewed in the previous section, others have

---

[54] It should also be recognized that women who choose to recidivate exercise a certain agency, that is, agency should not be attributed only to normative choices.

considered some of these collateral consequences through interviews with women after their release. Relationships with children, which are a source of both stress and self-esteem while in prison (Enos 2001), can be difficult to reestablish for women upon their release. Some women are anxious to reestablish these relationships immediately, but face difficulties doing so because of their precarious economic circumstances or because they have lost custody (Dodge and Pogrebin 2001). Others assume responsibility for the care of their children while worrying about how they will be able to care for themselves, let alone others (Greene, Haney, and Hurtado 2000; Richie 2001). When family members provide a home for a woman's children while she is in prison, this may alleviate many of the stresses she experiences while inside, but it may also increase the conflicts with family over her resumption of parenting once she is released. Family members can feel stigmatized by a woman's imprisonment, which further strains these relationships.

Children and families, then, are a source of contradictory experiences for released women, and a woman's ethnocultural background, among other things, may shape these experiences in complex ways. In England the families of women of color who have spent time in prison, some claim, are more likely to feel disgraced by this, especially if they come from Asia, Africa, or South America (Chigwada-Bailey 1997).[55] Consistent with this, a study of female offenders in England found that almost 90 percent of white women, but only 40 percent of black women, reported receiving assistance from their families (Celnick 1993). In contrast, there is evidence that in the United States white women who have served time in prison are more likely to become estranged from their families than are black or hispanic women (Enos 2001). However, black and hispanic women released from prison are more often subject to requests for care and assistance from other family members at a time when their personal and economic resources are limited. As noted in the previous section, women's domestic and social networks can therefore have contradictory effects on the chances of resuming activities—such as drug use—that put them at risk of rearrest.

In considering the intersecting disadvantages that send many African-American women to prison, some analysts have concluded that prisons provide these women with a "safe haven" from the dangers they face in the outside world (Henriques and Jones-Brown 2000). "Thus,

---

[55] Over 15 percent of the women in prison in England and Wales in 2000 were foreign nationals (Home Office 2001).

making the break with incarceration is likely to be made more difficult for many because prison offers a 'safe' but temporary environment from the harsh realities of life outside" (Henriques and Manatu-Rupert 2001, p. 11). This can be compounded by the sense of dependence that prison life encourages. Henriques and her colleagues maintain that, as a consequence, African-American women may be at particularly high risk of entering what prison administrators call the revolving door of imprisonment. Our own research suggests that it is not only African-American women who feel prison is a respite from life on the streets and that judges may have this in mind when they sentence some homeless or particularly disadvantaged women to prison. The obvious question is why we should be resorting to prisons to provide women sustenance and safety.

In sum, studies of women's lives after prison highlight how they are often as difficult, if not more so, as before incarceration. Women released from prison typically return to families and communities plagued by economic disadvantages and offering few conventional op-portunites. Their time in prison may have provided them with some job skills and the opportunity to escape networks where drug abuse and physical violence were routine, but it may also have undermined their desire or ability to avoid these networks on their release. Prison's power to punish is apparent in its long-term consequences; its power to provide women with—or allow them to develop—the abilities and resources to avoid it is much less clear. Both of these aspects of impris-onment may have been particularly true at the end of the twentieth century.

IV. Women's Imprisonment and Changing Penal Regimes

As criminal punishment changed in the United States in the last de-cades of the twentieth century, so too did research on prisons and im-prisonment. Prison scholarship has moved away from its earlier inter-est in how prisoners organize their lives and the prison world in at least two very different directions. One of these is concerned with the effec-tive management and governance of prisons (e.g., DiIulio 1987).[56] The other, more critical line of work has raised a broader set of questions

[56] Simon (2000) provides a more detailed analysis of the changing nature of prison research. He compares the work of Sykes and Clemmer with that of DiIulio as represen-tatives of two models of "the relationship between expert knowledge, prison manage-ment, and the social order of prisons" (p. 285).

about the place of punishment in society today. This work has explored the crisis of self-definition and the refigurement and contradictions in official ideologies of criminal punishment over the last century in general, and the last two decades in particular (e.g., Garland 1990; Feeley and Simon 1992; O'Malley 1992; Christie 1993; Simon and Feeley 1995). Scholars of women's imprisonment have made important contributions to this second line of research, bringing to it a particular focus on the gendered nature of penal power. In this section we first briefly consider the more general debates that characterize recent critical scholarship on penality, and then some of the recent work on the contemporary politics of women's imprisonment.

A. Critical Scholarship on Penality

As prison populations soared in the United States, correctional and rehabilitative goals were largely supplanted in official and popular discourse by concerns with public safety and victims' rights. At the same time, penal policy became highly politicized, and public sentiment toward criminals hardened. In the 1990s punishment touched the lives of many more people, as prisoners, as employees of an expanding public and private prison industry, as investors in for-profit corporations providing "correctional services," as voters whose options were often restricted to candidates trying to outdo each other as "tough on crime," and as taxpayers paying the bill for the largest prison expansion in the nation's history.

The scholarly discourse on what has been referred to as the "get tough" or "penal harm" movement (Cullen, Fisher, and Applegate 2000) has been wide-ranging. Some scholars focus on politics, arguing that public opinion and values, which have been influenced by a moral panic, have crystallized in a political culture of intolerance of offenders and concomitant support for expanding imprisonment (Jacobs and Helms 1996; Caplow and Simon 1999). Others have focused on changes within the prison system itself, arguing that we have seen the emergence of the bureaucratic prison over the last quarter of the twentieth century. Prison authority has been centralized in various departments of corrections that emphasize classification of inmates, training of staff, and decreasing informal social control (Adler and Longhurst 1994; Irwin and Austin 1994). Still other commentators on these changes interpret them as signaling the rise of a postmodern or "new penology" which is evident in discourses of risk and probability, identification and management, and classification and control (Feeley and Simon 1992; Simon 1993). Although Simon and Feeley (1995) subsequently noted that this postmodern view of penality may not have been completely realized in practice, others continue to advance the notion that the "new punitiveness" is a postmodern one (e.g., Pratt 2000).

An uneasy fit between the current penal discourses, the strategies, techniques, and rationalities of punishment that accompany it, and the pragmatics of program implementation is suggested by recent research. For example, research on frontline criminal justice workers demonstrates that a new penology has not been fully embodied in practice, even in California (Haney 1996; Lynch 1998), which is often seen as the wellspring of this trend. Instead, the long-term tendency for penal discourses to be variably realized appears as applicable now as it has been in the past (Garland 1997; Riveland 1999). From this perspective, the penal sanctions of today are uneven and diverse, combining at once elements of discipline (e.g., in boot camps), rehabilitation (in prison industry/enterprise), and incapacitation (warehousing inmates) (O'Malley 1992, 1999). They also vary across different social contexts, reflecting criminal justice actors' abilities to absorb new technologies and ideologies about punishment (see, e.g., Harris and Jesilow 2000). As a consequence, criminal punishment continues to present "practical challenges and moral dilemmas for social organization" (Garland 1999, p. 5), many of which have been highlighted in work that takes issues and trends in women's imprisonment as relevant to a more general set of relations among social regulation and penal governance.

B. Critical Scholarship on Women and Penality

Critical, especially feminist, scholarship on the gendered nature of social control, discipline, and punishment stretches back thirty years and gained momentum in the 1990s with the expansion of women's imprisonment (e.g., Rafter 1990; Worrall 1990; Adelberg and Currie 1993; Faith 1993; Chesney-Lind 1995; Shaw 1996; Bertrand 1999; Hannah-Moffat and Shaw 2000). Pat Carlen's contributions to this scholarship, which began in the early 1980s, are among the most prolific, diverse, and well-known. Her early work explores the ways in which women prisoners are constituted by penal discourses and rendered knowable subjects, the place of prison in a larger disciplinary web of gendered social (and antisocial) control, and the autobiographies of women within and "without" the criminal justice system (Carlen 1983, 1985, 1988). While consistently arguing for alternatives to imprisonment (e.g., Carlen 1990), more recently she has framed this in an analysis of the prison's distinctive power to punish (Carlen 1994), and how this punitive power sharpened and deepened in England in the 1990s (Carlen 1998, 1999).

Other work has been less empirically based, less directly concerned with its policy implications, and more oriented toward theoretical development. A prime example is Howe's (1994) effort to develop a postmodern feminist approach to punishment. Like some of Carlen's work, Howe's interest is less in the prison than in what she sees as the wider domain of penality through which women's bodies are disciplined in myriad ways. In this sense, women in prison are seen to share with other women subjugation to a continuum of punishment, albeit at a different point along this continuum. While she notes that the relationship between "theorisation of penality and the lived experience of punishment regimes" is both significant and fraught with "hard political questions" (Howe 1994, p. 208), Howe leaves this relationship largely unexamined. And instead of considering how power in prison is expressed and negotiated in various ways by various actors, Howe's analysis implies that the logic of penal power renders it inevitably repressive, unidirectional, and coherent.

This sort of functionalist perspective on imprisonment contrasts with much of the current critical scholarship on penality briefly discussed above as well as with other work on women's imprisonment. Combining a theoretical and empirical analysis of women's imprisonment, Hannah-Moffat's (1995, 2001) case study of penal reform strategies in Canada is attentive to how different phases of women's imprisonment have contained particular legitimating ideologies and discourses, and allowed diverse expressions of power. These discourses are flexible and complex, however, combining contradictory themes such that efforts at progressive reform have been and continue to be undermined. In one of these recent efforts at reform, the report of a federal task force recommended that "women-centred prisons" be created where the focus would be on cooperation, challenge, agency, empowerment, and responsible choices. But, Hannah-Moffat argues, the notions of both "women-centred" prisons and empowerment ignore the reality of carceral relations in prison, a reality that cannot sustain a supportive environment (see also Shaw 1992). Women's imprisonment in Canada in the 1990s, then, is portrayed as a battleground where old disciplinary technologies uneasily coexist with new, and where the contested micro-politics of power are played out in prisoners' daily lives.

V. Directions for Future Research

Each of the topics reviewed in this essay is deserving of more research. The trends we have described in women's imprisonment will need to be updated almost as soon as this essay is published. There is some evidence that the rate of increase in imprisonment in the United States is slowing, but does this extend to women and will it occur in other countries where female prison populations are on the rise?[57] We have some limited information on the sorts of women who have been the primary targets of the imprisonment boom of the late twentieth century, but not enough to understand the extent to which ostensibly neutral policies may have had—and may continue to have—disproportionate effects on some segments of the female population. In those places—be they countries or states—where the female prison population has not increased, what alternatives, if any, to imprisonment have been tried and with what effects? Is imprisonment in these places being replaced to some extent by less expensive alternatives that have reduced prison populations while maintaining the size of the population under correctional supervision? And if so, have women—or some types of women—been the beneficiaries of noncarceral sanctions more than men?

With regard to the characteristics of women in prison, much is known and little appears to have changed over time. Yet we still do not know enough about the extent to which these characteristics shape the experiences of women in prison, including how they respond to treatment programs. There is evidence to indicate that, in some respects, the pains of imprisonment and the prison's ability to do other than exact pain vary by women's ethnocultural and class backgrounds and by the physical and mental health problems they bring into prison. This needs further study. Systematic evaluations of treatment programs, whether they be innovative or old-fashioned, are rare; these should become a required component of the initiation of such programs, and these evaluations should include attention to a range of outcomes in women's lives after prison. Given the size of the female prison population in the United States, there is no longer any excuse for scholars to neglect women's experiences in prison or afterward. The number of women in the general population who will have experi-

---

[57] To the extent that it is true that the U.S. rate of increase is slowing, it is not clear whether this is largely because the public is tired of the high costs of imprisonment or because of declining confidence in or support for imprisonment as a way to deal with crime.

enced imprisonment will continue to grow in the next few decades. What are the collateral consequences of imprisonment for their lives, their families, and their communities? If imprisonment is no longer a rare event for women in some communities, what effect will this have on girls growing up in those communities? As opportunities for employment of low-skill workers contract, how will female ex-convicts— who already face prospective employers who harbor doubts about them—sustain themselves economically?

Transformations in imprisonment regimes of the last two decades— which, we would argue, are likely to have had particularly profound effects on women's imprisonment—make these especially timely issues for scholars and for the public. There has been a radical and rapid shift away from the gendered rehabilitative and therapeutic approaches that gave women's "corrections" a certain coherence and distinctiveness for much of the twentieth century. In its place a neoliberal logic, which emphasizes individuals' responsibility for their own reform at the same time that it expresses pessimism over the possibilities for rehabilitation, began to penetrate women's imprisonment in the 1990s. How have such changes affected the daily lives of women in prison?[58] And, perhaps more importantly, what can women's experiences in prison tell us about the practices of imprisonment and their operations within very different penal eras? Asking this question treats women in prison not simply as subjects of our research, but as important sources of knowledge about prisons and imprisonment.

Asking these questions also implies the need for more comparative research—comparative in both a temporal and an institutional sense. The recent changes in penality that are preoccupying scholars occurred, to a large extent, at a very general and abstract level. There is still enormous variation both in the way imprisonment is practiced within different institutions and in the extent to which the "new penology" has permeated the daily routines of prisons. We need to know more about how these regimes and environments produce particular constellations of responses by prisoners. For example, is suicide or self-harm or violence more common in certain types of women's prisons,

[58] Historical work on women's imprisonment has made important contributions in this area. Daniels (1998), for example, has shown in her research on imprisonment in nineteenth-century Australia how the shift from punishments designed to hurt and humiliate to discipline meant to reform had different consequences for women and men in prison.

controlling for characteristics of the prisoners assigned to them?[59] And we need to know how changes in prison regimes alter the social order of prison life, especially if these changes have adverse effects on prisoners.

As this essay has demonstrated, research on women in prison is enormously diverse, and much of it has been less interested in imprisonment per se than in prison as an instance of a larger network of discipline or as a site in which a more general set of social relations and processes are played out. As such the research has contributed to our understandings of the processes of gender identity construction, of gendered social controls, and more; and it has explicitly or implicitly affirmed the importance of attending to women in prison in particular. While this has had value, we concur with others (e.g., Carlen 1994) who argue for research that is concerned with imprisonment as a site of state punishment and with questions about the pains of imprisonment asked in the classic prison sociology of the mid-twentieth century. The possibilities for such research, of course, may not only be small but diminishing, in part because such research "is virtually all political risk for prison administrators" (Simon 2000, p. 303).[60] And, to the extent that researchers refuse to "collude in the liberal myth that, 'We *all* want prisons to be more humane places'" (Carlen 1994, p. 137), their prospects for gaining access to prisons may be lowered even more. However, there may be advantages to such a stance—if it is not self-defeating—by broadening the range of questions that can be asked about the experiences, consequences, and justifications of imprisonment as punishment.

REFERENCES

Acoca, Leslie. 1998. "Defusing the Time Bomb: Understanding and Meeting the Growing Health Care Needs of Incarcerated Women in America." *Crime and Delinquency* 44:49–69.

[59] This question harkens back to the classic comparisons of deprivation and importation effects on prison life. Here the issue is whether prisons are painful because of the types of places they are or because they house people whose lives are generally painful.

[60] This may be somewhat less true for administrators of women's prisons, many of whom acknowledge that most of the women in their charge do not "really" belong in prison. This is a remarkably candid statement by people who might be expected to have a vested interest in preserving the institutions in which they work.

Adams, Kenneth. 1992. "Adjusting to Prison Life." In *Crime and Justice: An Annual Review of Research*, vol. 16, edited by Norval Morris and Michael Tonry. Chicago: University of Chicago Press.

Adelberg, Ellen, and Claudia Currie, eds. 1993. *In Conflict with the Law: Women and the Canadian Justice System*. Vancouver: Press Gang.

Adler, Michael, and Brian Longhurst. 1994. *Discourse, Power, and Justice: Toward a New Sociology of Imprisonment*. London: Routledge.

Alarid, Leanne Fiftal. 2000. "Sexual Assault and Coercion among Incarcerated Women Prisoners: Excerpts from Prison Letters." *Prison Journal* 80:391–406.

Allen, Hilary. 1987. *Justice Unbalanced: Gender, Psychiatry, and Judicial Decisions*. Philadelphia: Open University Press.

Alpert, Geoffrey P., George Noblit, and John J. Wiorkowski. 1977. "A Comparative Look at Prisonization: Sex and Prison Culture." *Quarterly Journal of Corrections* 1:29–34.

American Correctional Association. 1990. *The Female Offender: What Does the Future Hold?* Laurel, Md.: American Correctional Association.

Amnesty International. 2002. "Abuse of Women in Custody: Sexual Misconduct and Shackling of Pregnant Women." A state-by-state survey of policies and practices in the United States. Available at http://www.amnesty-usa.org/women/custody/abuseincustody.html. (Accessed May 5, 2002.)

Andrews, D. A., and Craig Dowden. 2000. "A Meta-Analytic Investigation into Effective Correctional Intervention for Female Offenders." *Forum on Corrections Research* 11:18–21.

Aube, Jennifer, Mosee Fleury, and Judith Smetana. 2000. "Changes in Women's Roles: Impact on and Social Policy Implications for the Mental Health of Women and Children." *Development and Psychopathology* 12:633–56.

Austin, James, Barbara Bloom, and Trish Donahue. 1992. *Female Offender in the Community: An Analysis of Innovative Strategies and Programs*. Washington, D.C.: U.S. Department of Justice, National Institute of Corrections.

Barthwell, A., P. L. Bokos, J. Bailey, M. Nisenbaum, J. Devereux, and E. Senay. 1995. "Interventions/Wilmer: A Continuum of Care for Substance Abusers in the Criminal Justice System." *Journal of Psychoactive Drugs* 27:39–47.

Baskin, Deborah R., and Ira B. Sommers. 1998. *Casualties of Community Disorder: Women's Careers in Violent Crime*. Boulder, Colo.: Westview.

Baskin, Deborah R., Ira B. Sommers, Richard Tessler, and Henry J. Steadman. 1989. "Role Incongruence and Gender Variation in the Provision of Prison Mental Health Services." *Journal of Health and Social Behavior* 30:305–14.

Beck, A. T., C. H. Word, M. Mendelson, J. Mock, and J. Erbaugh. 1961. "An Inventory for Measuring Depression." *Archives of General Psychiatry* 4:561–71.

Belcourt R., T. Nouwens, and L. Lefebvre. 1993. "Examining the Unexamined: Recidivism among Female Offenders." *Forum on Corrections Research* 5:10–14.

Berk, Bernard. 1966. "Organizational Goals and Inmate Organization." *American Journal of Sociology* 71:522–34.

Bertrand, M-A. 1999. "Incarceration as a Gendering Strategy." *Canadian Journal of Law and Society* 14:45–60.

Blanchette, K. 1997a. "Classifying Female Offenders for Correctional Interventions." *Forum on Corrections Research* 9(1):36–41.

———. 1997b. "Comparing Violent and Non-Violent Offenders on Risk and Need." *Forum on Corrections Research* 9(2):14–18.

Bloom, Barbara. 1993. "Why Punish the Children? A Reappraisal of the Children of Incarcerated Mothers in America." *IARCA Journal* 6:14–17.

Blumstein, Alfred, and Allen J. Beck. 1999. "Population Growth in U.S. Prisons, 1980–1996." In *Prisons*, edited by Michael Tonry and Joan Petersilia. Vol. 26 of *Crime and Justice: A Review of Research*, edited by Michael Tonry and Norval Morris. Chicago: University of Chicago Press.

Bondeson, Ulla v. 1989. *Prisoners in Prison Societies*. New Brunswick, N.J.: Transaction.

Bonta, J., B. Pang, and S. Wallace-Capretta. 1995. "Predictors of Recidivism among Incarcerated Female Offenders." *Prison Journal* 75:277–94.

Boothby, Jennifer L., and Thomas W. Durham. 1999. "Screening for Depression in Prisoners Using the Beck Depression Inventory." *Criminal Justice and Behavior* 26:107–24.

Bosworth, Mary. 1999. *Engendering Resistance: Agency and Power in Women's Prisons*. Aldershot: Ashgate.

Bowker, Lee H. 1980. "Variations on a Theme: Prisoner Violence among Females." In *Prison Victimization*, edited by Lee H. Bowker. New York: Elsevier.

Brewer, V. E., J. W. Marquart, J. L. Mullings, and B. M. Crouch. 1998. "AIDS-Related Risk Behavior among Female Prisoners with Histories of Mental Impairment." *Prison Journal* 78:101–18.

Bukstel, L., and P. Kilmann. 1980. "Psychological Effects of Imprisonment on Confined Individuals." *Psychological Bulletin* 88:469–93.

Bureau of Justice Statistics. 1982. *Sourcebook of Criminal Justice Statistics*. Washington, D.C.: U.S. Department of Justice, Bureau of Justice Statistics.

———. 1983. *Sourcebook of Criminal Justice Statistics*. Washington, D.C.: U.S. Department of Justice, Bureau of Justice Statistics.

———. 1989. *Recidivism of Prisoners Released in 1983*. NCJ-116261. Washington, D.C.: U.S. Department of Justice, Bureau of Justice Statistics.

———. 1993. *Survey of State Prison Inmates, 1991*. NCJ-136949. Washington, D.C.: U.S. Department of Justice, Bureau of Justice Statistics.

———. 1994. *Women in Prison*. NCJ-145321. Washington, D.C.: U.S. Department of Justice, Bureau of Justice Statistics.

———. 1995. *Prisoners in 1994*. NCJ-151654. Washington, D.C.: U.S. Department of Justice, Bureau of Justice Statistics.

———. 1997a. *Prisoners in 1996*. NCJ-164619. Washington, D.C.: U.S. Department of Justice, Bureau of Justice Statistics.

———. 1997b. *Survey of Inmates in State and Federal Correctional Facilities*. Washington, D.C.: Department of Justice, Bureau of Justice Statistics.

———. 1998. *Prisoners in 1997*. NJC-170014. Washington, D.C.: U.S. Department of Justice, Bureau of Justice Statistics.

————. 1999*a. Mental Health and Treatment of Inmates and Probationers.* NCJ-174463. Washington, D.C.: U.S. Department of Justice, Bureau of Justice Statistics.

————. 1999*b. Prior Abuse Reported by Inmates and Probationers.* NCJ-172879. Washington, D.C.: U.S. Department of Justice, Bureau of Justice Statistics.

————. 1999*c. Prisoners in 1998.* NCJ-175687. Washington, D.C.: U.S. Department of Justice, Bureau of Justice Statistics.

————. 1999*d. Special Report: Women Offenders.* NCJ-175688. Washington, D.C.: U.S. Department of Justice, Bureau of Justice Statistics.

————. 1999*e. Special Report: Substance Abuse and Treatment, State and Federal Prisoners, 1997.* NCJ-172871. Washington D.C.: U.S. Department of Justice, Bureau of Justice Statistics.

————. 2000*a. Correctional Populations in the U.S., 1997.* NCJ-177613. Washington, D.C.: U.S. Department of Justice, Bureau of Justice Statistics.

————. 2000*b. Offenders Returning to Federal Prison, 1986–97.* NCJ-182991. Washington, D.C.: U.S. Department of Justice, Bureau of Justice Statistics.

————. 2000*c. Prison and Jail Inmates at Mid Year 1999.* NCJ-181643. Washington, D.C.: U.S. Department of Justice, Bureau of Justice Statistics.

————. 2000*d. Prisoners in 1999.* NCJ-183476. Washington, D.C.: U.S. Department of Justice, Bureau of Justice Statistics.

————. 2000*e. Sourcebook of Criminal Justice Statistics.* Washington, D.C.: U.S. Department of Justice, Bureau of Justice Statistics.

————. 2001*a. HIV in Prisons and Jails, 1999.* NCJ-187456. Washington, D.C.: U.S. Department of Justice, Bureau of Justice Statistics.

————. 2001*b. Medical Problems of Inmates, 1997.* NCJ-181644. Washington, D.C.: U.S. Department of Justice, Bureau of Justice Statistics.

————. 2001*c. Prisoners in 2000.* NCJ-188207. Washington, D.C.: U.S. Department of Justice, Bureau of Justice Statistics.

————. 2001*d. Trends in State Parole, 1990–2000.* NCJ-184735. Washington, D.C.: U.S. Department of Justice, Bureau of Justice Statistics.

————. 2002*a. Prison and Jail Inmates at Midyear 2001.* NCJ-191702. Washington, D.C.: U.S. Department of Justice, Bureau of Justice Statistics.

————. 2002*b. Special Report: Recidivism of Prisoners Released in 1994.* NCJ-193427. Washington, D.C.: U.S. Department of Justice, Bureau of Justice Statistics.

Burkhart, Kathryn Watterson. 1973. *Women in Prison.* Garden City, N.Y.: Doubleday.

Butler, Anne M. 1997. *Gendered Justice in the American West: Women Prisoners in Men's Penitentiaries.* Urbana: University of Illinois Press.

Canadian Centre for Justice Statistics. Various years. *Adult Correctional Services in Canada.* Ottawa: Statistics Canada.

Caplow, Theodore, and Jonathan Simon. 1999. "Understanding Prison Policy and Population Trends." In *Prisons,* edited by Michael Tonry and Joan Petersilia. Vol. 26 of *Crime and Justice: A Review of Research,* edited by Michael Tonry and Norval Morris. Chicago: University of Chicago Press.

Carlen, Pat. 1983. *Women's Imprisonment: A Study in Social Control.* London: Routledge & Kegan Paul.

————, ed. 1985. *Criminal Women: Autobiographical Accounts.* Cambridge: Polity.

————. 1988. *Women, Crime, and Poverty.* Philadelphia: Open University Press.

————. 1990. *Alternatives to Women's Imprisonment.* Philadelphia: Open University Press.

————. 1994. "Why Study Women's Imprisonment? Or Anyone Else's?" In *Prisons in Context*, edited by Roy D. King and Mike Maguire. Oxford: Clarendon.

————. 1995. "Virginia, Criminology, and the Antisocial Control of Women." In *Punishment and Social Control*, edited by Thomas G. Blomberg and Stanley Cohen. New York: Aldine de Gruyter.

————. 1998. *Sledgehammer: Women's Imprisonment at the Millennium.* Houndsmills, Basingstoke: Macmillan.

————. 1999. "Women's Imprisonment in England, Current Issues." In *Harsh Punishment: International Experiences of Women's Imprisonment*, edited by Sandy Cook and Susanne Davies. Boston: Northeastern University Press.

Celnick, Anne. 1993. "Race and Rehabilitation." In *Minority Ethnic Groups in the Criminal Justice System: Papers Presented to the 21st Cropwood Roundtable Conference, 1992*, edited by Loraine R. Gelsthorpe. Cambridge: University of Cambridge, Institute of Criminology.

Chesney-Lind, Meda. 1995. "Rethinking Women's Imprisonment: A Critical Examination of Trends in Female Incarceration." In *The Criminal Justice System and Women: Offenders, Victims, and Workers*, 2d ed., edited and compiled by B. R. Price and N. J. Sokoloff. New York: McGraw-Hill.

Chigwada-Bailey, Ruth. 1997. *Black Women's Experiences of Criminal Justice: A Discourse on Disadvantage.* Winchester: Waterside.

Christie, Nils. 1993. *Crime Control as Industry: Towards GULAGS, Western Style.* London: Routledge.

Clark, Judith. 1995. "The Impact of the Prison Environment on Mothers." *Prison Journal* 75:306–29.

Clemmer, Donald. 1958. *The Prison Community.* New York: Holt, Rinehart & Winston.

Climent, Carlos E., Frank R. Ervin, Ann Rollins, Robert Plutchik, and Catello J. Batinelli. 1977. "Epidemiological Studies of Female Prisoners. IV. Homosexual Behavior." *Journal of Nervous and Mental Disease* 164:25–29.

Cline, Hugh, and Stanton Wheeler. 1968. "The Determinants of Normative Patterns in Correctional Institutions." *Scandinavian Studies in Criminology* 2: 173–84.

Coid, Jeremy, John Wilkins, Bina Coid, and Brian Everitt. 1992. "Self-Mutilation in Female Remand Prisoners. II. A Cluster Analytic Approach towards Identification of a Behavioral Syndrome." *Criminal Behavior and Mental Health* 2:1–14.

Collins, William C. 1996. *Women in Jail: Legal Issues.* Washington, D.C.: U.S. Department of Justice, National Institute of Corrections.

Comack, Elizabeth. 1996. *Women in Trouble: Connecting Women's Law Violations to Their Histories of Abuse.* Halifax: Fernwood.

Conly, Catherine. 1998. "The Women's Prison Association: Supporting Women Offenders and Their Families." In *Program Focus.* Washington, D.C.: U.S. Department of Justice, National Institute of Justice.

Cook, Sandy, and Susanne Davies. 1999. *Harsh Punishment: International Experiences of Women's Imprisonment.* Boston: Northeastern University Press.

Cookson, H. M. 1977. "A Survey of Self-Injury in a Closed Prison for Women." *British Journal of Criminology* 17:332–47.

Correctional Service Canada. 1997. *Risk and Need among Federally-Sentenced Female Offenders: A Comparison of Minimum-, Medium- and Maximum-Security Inmates.* Ottawa: Correctional Service Canada, Research Branch.

———. 2000a. *Basic Facts about Corrections.* Ottawa: Correctional Service Canada.

———. 2000b. *Profile of Incarcerated Women Offenders: September 1999.* Ottawa: Correctional Service Canada.

Covington, Stephanie S. 2001. "Creating Gender-Responsive Programs: The Next Step for Women's Services." *Corrections Today.* On-line publication of the American Correctional Association. (Available at http://www.corrections.com/aca/cortoday. Accessed August 7, 2001.)

Craddock, Amy. 1996. "A Comparative Study of Male and Female Prison Misconduct Careers." *Prison Journal* 76:60–80.

Cullen, Francis T., Bonnie S. Fisher, and Brandon K. Applegate. 2000. "Public Opinion about Punishment and Corrections." In *Crime and Justice: An Annual Review of Research,* vol. 27, edited by Norval Morris and Michael Tonry. Chicago: University of Chicago Press.

Curry, G. David, and Wei Qin Pan. 1991. "Correctional Administration and Recidivism among Female Inmates." Paper presented at the annual meeting of the American Society of Criminology, San Francisco, November 20.

Daly, Kathleen. 1994. *Gender, Crime and Punishment.* New Haven, Conn.: Yale University Press.

———. 1995. "Gender and Sentencing: What We Know and Don't Know from Empirical Research." *Federal Sentencing Reporter* 8:163–68.

Damousi, Joy. 1997. *Depraved and Disorderly: Female Convicts, Sexuality and Gender in Colonial Australia.* Cambridge: Cambridge University Press.

Daniel, A. E., A. J. Robins, J. C. Reed, and D. E. Wilfley. 1998. "Lifetime and Six-Month Prevalence of Psychiatric Disorders among Sentenced Female Offenders." *Bulletin of the American Academy of Psychiatry and the Law* 15:333–42.

Daniels, Kay. 1998. *Convict Women.* St. Leonards, N.S.W.: Allen & Unwin.

Díaz-Cotto, Juanita. 1996. *Gender, Ethnicity, and the State: Latina and Latino Prison Politics.* Albany: State University of New York Press.

DiIulio, John J. 1987. *Governing Prisons: A Comparative Study of Correctional Management.* New York: Free Press.

Dirsuweit, Teresa. 1999. "Carceral Spaces in South Africa: A Case Study of Institutional Power, Sexuality, and Transgression in a Women's Prison." *Geoforum* 30:71–83.

Dobash, Russell P., R. Emerson Dobash, and Sue Gutteridge. 1986. *The Imprisonment of Women.* New York: Basil Blackwell.

Dodge, Mary, and Mark R. Pogrebin. 2001. "Collateral Costs of Imprisonment for Women: Complications of Reintegration." *Prison Journal* 81:42–54.

Dooley, Edna. 1990. "Unnatural Deaths in Prison." *British Journal of Criminology* 30:229–34.

Dowden, Craig, and D. A. Andrews. 1999. "What Works for Female Offenders: A Meta-Analytic Review." *Crime and Delinquency* 45:438–52.

Easteal, Patricia. 2001. "Women in Australian Prisons: The Cycle of Abuse and Dysfunctional Environments." *Prison Journal* 81:87–112.

Eaton, Mary. 1993. *Women after Prison*. Philadelphia: Open University Press.

Elliott, Mabel A. 1966. "Review of David A. Ward and Gene G. Kassebaum, *Women's Prison: Sex and Social Structure*." *Annals of the American Academy of Political and Social Science* 368:232–33.

Enos, Sandra. 2001. *Mothering from the Inside: Parenting in a Women's Prison*. Albany: State University of New York Press.

Erez, Edna. 1992. "Dangerous Men, Evil Women: Gender and Parole Decision-Making." *Justice Quarterly* 9:105–26.

Faily, Anwar, and George A. Roundtree. 1979. "A Study of Aggression and Rule Violations in a Female Prison Population." *Journal of Offender Counseling, Services and Rehabilitation* 4:81–87.

Faith, Karlene. 1993. *Unruly Women: The Politics of Confinement and Resistance*. Vancouver: Press Gang.

Farrell, Amy. 2000. "Women, Crime and Drugs: Testing the Effect of Therapeutic Communities." *Women and Criminal Justice* 11:21–48.

Feeley, Malcolm M., and Jonathan Simon. 1992. "The New Penology: Notes on the Emerging Strategy of Corrections and Its Implications." *Criminology* 30:449–74.

Finn, Anne, Shelley Trevethan, Gisele Carriere, and Melanie Kowalski. 1999. "Female Inmates, Aboriginal Inmates, and Inmates Serving Life Sentences: A One Day Snapshot." *Juristat* 19:1–9.

Fletcher, Beverly R., Lynda Dixon Shaver, and Dreama G. Moon, eds. 1993. *Women Prisoners: A Forgotten Population*. Westport, Conn.: Praeger.

Ford, C. 1929. "Homosexual Practices of Institutionalized Females." *Journal of Abnormal and Social Psychology* 23:442–48.

Foster, Thomas. 1975. "Make-Believe Families: A Response of Women and Girls to the Deprivations of Imprisonment." *International Journal of Criminology and Penology* 3:71–78.

Fox, James. 1975. "Women in Crisis." In *Men in Crisis: Human Breakdowns in Prison*, edited by Hans Toch. Chicago: Aldine-Atherton.

———. 1982. "Women in Prison: A Study in the Social Reality of Stress." In *The Pains of Imprisonment*, edited by Robert Johnson and Hans Toch. Beverly Hills, Calif.: Sage.

———. 1984. "Women's Prison Policy, Prisoner Activism, and the Impact of the Contemporary Feminist Movement: A Case Study." *Prison Journal* 1:15–36.

Freedman, Estelle B. 1996. "The Prison Lesbian: Race, Class, and the Construction of the Aggressive Female Homosexual, 1915–1965." *Feminist Studies* 22:397–423.

Furstenberg, Frank F., Jr. 1990. "Divorce and the American Family." *Annual Review of Sociology* 16:379–403.

Gaes, Gerald G., Timothy J. Flanagan, Laurence L. Motiuk, and Lynn Stewart. 1999. "Adult Correctional Treatment." In *Prisons*, edited by Michael Tonry and Joan Petersilia. Vol. 26 of *Crime and Justice: A Review of Research*, edited by Michael Tonry and Norval Morris. Chicago: University of Chicago Press.

Garbedian, Peter. 1963. "Social Roles and Process of Socialization in the Prison Community." *Social Problems* 11:139–52.

———. 1964. "Social Roles in a Correctional Community." *Journal of Criminal Law, Criminology and Police Science* 55:235–47.

Garland, David. 1990. *Punishment and Modern Society: A Study in Social Theory.* Chicago: University of Chicago Press.

———. 1996. "The Limits of the Sovereign State: Strategies of Crime Control in Contemporary Society." *British Journal of Criminology* 36:445–71.

———. 1997. "'Governmentality' and the Problem of Crime: Foucault, Criminology, Sociology." *Theoretical Criminology* 1:173–214.

———. 1999. "Editorial: Punishment and Society Today." *Punishment and Society* 1:5–10.

Gartner, Rosemary, and Candace Kruttschnitt. 2002*a*. "A Brief History of Doing Time: The California Institution for Women in the 1960s and the 1990s." Unpublished manuscript, available from Rosemary Gartner, University of Toronto.

———. 2002*b*. "Women and Imprisonment: A Case Study of Two California Prisons." In *Punishment and Society*, edited by Thomas Blomberg and Stanley Cohen. New York: Aldine de Gruyter.

Genders, Elaine, and Elaine Player. 1990. "Women Lifers: Assessing the Experience." *Prison Journal* 80:46–57.

General Accounting Office. 1999. *Women in Prison: Issues and Challenges Confronting U.S. Correctional Systems.* Report to the Honorable Eleanor Holmes Norton, House of Representatives, December, 1999. Washington, D.C.: U.S. General Accounting Office.

Giallombardo, Rose. 1966. *Society of Women: A Study of a Women's Prison.* New York: Wiley.

———. 1974. *The Social World of Imprisoned Girls: A Comparative Study of Institutions for Juvenile Delinquents.* New York: Wiley.

Glick, Ruth M., and Virginia V. Neto. 1977. *National Study of Women's Correctional Programs.* Washington, D.C.: National Institute of Law Enforcement and Criminal Justice, Law Enforcement Assistance Administration, U.S. Department of Justice.

Goetting, Ann, and Roy Michael Howsen. 1983. "Women in Prison: A Profile." *Prison Journal* 63:27–46.

———. 1986. "Correlates of Prisoner Misconduct." *Journal of Quantitative Criminology* 2:49–67.

Goldberg, Gertrude S., and Eleanor Kremen, eds. 1990. *The Feminization of Poverty: Only in America?* New York: Greenwood.

Gray, Tora, G. Lorry Mays, and Mary K. Stohr. 1995. "Inmate Needs and Programming in Exclusively Women's Jails." *Prison Journal* 75:186–202.

Greene, Susan, Craig Haney, and Aida Hurtado. 2000. "Cycles of Pain: Risk Factors in the Lives of Incarcerated Mothers and Their Children." *Prison Journal* 80:3–23.

Greer, Kimberly R. 2000. "The Changing Nature of Interpersonal Relationships in a Woman's Prison." *Prison Journal* 80:442–68.

Grusky, Oscar. 1959. "Organizational Goals and the Behavior of Informal Leaders." *American Journal of Sociology* 65:59–67.

Hagan, John, and Ronit Dinovitzer. 1999. "Collateral Consequences of Imprisonment for Children, Communities, and Prisoners." In *Prisons*, edited by Michael Tonry and Joan Petersilia. Vol. 26 of *Crime and Justice: A Review of Research*, edited by Michael Tonry and Norval Morris. Chicago: University of Chicago Press.

Hale, Tessa. 2001. "Creating Visions and Achieving Goals: The Women in Community Service's Lifeskills Program." *Corrections Today*. On-line publication of the American Correctional Association. (Available at http://www.corrections.com/aca/cortoday. Accessed Aug. 7, 2001.)

Halleck, Seymour, and Marvin Hersko. 1962. "Homosexual Behavior in a Correctional Institution for Adolescent Girls." *American Journal of Orthopsychiatry* 32:911–17.

Hampton, Blanche. 1993. *Prisons and Women*. Sydney: University of New South Wales Press.

Haney, Lynn. 1996. "Homeboys, Babies, and Men in Suits: The State and the Reproduction of Male Dominance." *American Sociological Review* 61:759–78.

Hannah-Moffat, Kelly. 1995. "Feminine Fortresses: Women-Centered Prisons?" *Prison Journal* 75:135–64.

———. 1999. "Moral Agent or Actuarial Subject: Risk and Canadian Women's Imprisonment." *Theoretical Criminology* 3:71–94.

———. 2001. *Punishment in Disguise: Penal Governance and Federal Imprisonment of Women in Canada*. Toronto: University of Toronto Press.

Hannah-Moffat, Kelly, and Margaret Shaw, eds. 2000. *An Ideal Prison? Critical Essays on Women's Imprisonment in Canada*. Halifax: Fernwood.

Harding, Richard. 1998. "Private Prisons." In *The Handbook of Crime and Punishment*, edited by Michael Tonry. New York: Oxford University Press.

Harer, Miles D., and Neal P. Langan. 2001. "Gender Differences in Predictors of Prison Violence: Assessing the Predictive Validity of a Risk Classification System." *Crime and Delinquency* 47:513–36.

Harm, Nancy J., and Susan D. Phillips. 2001. "You Can't Go Home Again: Women and Criminal Recidivism." *Journal of Offender Rehabilitation* 32:3–21.

Harris, J. C., and P. Jesilow. 2000. "It's Not the Old Ball Game: Three Strikes and the Courtroom Workgroup." *Justice Quarterly* 17:185–203.

Hart, Cynthia Baroody. 1995. "Gender Differences in Social Support among Inmates." *Women and Criminal Justice* 6:67–88.

Hartnagel, Timothy F., and Mary Ellen Gillan. 1980. "Female Prisoners and the Inmate Code." *Pacific Sociological Review* 23:85–104.

Hawke, J. 1994. *Women's Opportunity Resource (WORC). Nassau County, New York*. Washington, D.C.: U.S. Department of Justice, National Institute of Justice.

Hawke, J., and M. Natarajan. 1994. *Substance Abuse Intervention Division: New York City Department of Corrections Drug Treatment Program for Women Offenders*. Washington, D.C.: U.S. Department of Justice, National Institute of Justice.

Hawkins, R. 1995. "Inmate Adjustments in Women's Prisons." In *The Dilemmas of Corrections: Contemporary Readings*, 3d ed., compiled by Kenneth C. Haas and Geoffrey P. Alpert. Prospect Heights, Ill.: Waveland.

Hayner, N., and E. Ash. 1939. *The Prison Community*. New York: Holt, Rinehart & Winston.

Heffernan, Esther. 1972. *Making It in Prison: The Square, the Cool and the Life*. New York: Wiley-Interscience.

Heimer, Karen. 2000. "Changes in the Gender Gap in Crime and Women's Economic Marginalization." In *The Nature of Crime: Continuity and Change*, vol. 1 of *Criminal Justice 2000*. NCJ 182408. Washington, D.C.: U.S. Department of Justice, Office of Justice Programs, National Institute of Justice.

Henderson, Dorothy. 1998. "Drug Abuse and Incarcerated Women: A Research Review." *Journal of Substance Abuse Treatment* 15:579–87.

Heney, Jan. 1990. *Report on Self-Injurious Behaviour in the Kingston Prison for Women*. Ottawa: Solicitor General.

Henriques, Z. W., and D. D. Jones-Brown. 2000. "Prisons as 'Safe Havens' for African-American Women." In *The System in Black and White: Exploring the Connections between Race, Crime, and Justice*, edited by M. Markowitz and D. D. Jones-Brown. Westport, Conn.: Praeger.

Henriques, Z. W., and N. Manatu-Rupert. 2001. "Living on the Outside: African-American Women Before, During and After Imprisonment." *Prison Journal* 81:6–19.

Hensley, Christopher, Cindy Struckman-Johnson, and Helen M. Eigenberg. 2000. "Introduction: The History of Prison Sex Research." *Prison Journal* 80:360–67.

Hensley, Christopher, Richard Tewksbury, and Mary Koscheski. 2001. "Masturbation Uncovered: Auto Eroticism in a Female Prison." *Prison Journal* 81:491–501.

H. M. Chief Inspector of Prisons. 1997. *Women in Prison: A Thematic Review*. London: Home Office.

Hoffman, Peter. 1982. "Females, Recidivism and Salient Factor Score: A Research Note." *Criminal Justice and Behavior* 9:121–25.

Home Office. 1967–2001. *Total Monthly Prison Population by Sex*. London: Research, Development, and Statistics Directorate, Offenders and Corrections Unit.

———. 1990. *Report on a Review by her Majesty's Chief Inspector of Prisons for England and Wales of Suicide and Self-Harm in Prison Service Establishments in England and Wales*. London: H.M. Stationery Office.

———. 1992. *Regimes for Women*. London: H.M. Stationery Office.

————. 2001. *Prison Statistics, England and Wales, 2000.* London: Research Development and Statistics Directorate, H.M. Stationery Office.

Howard League. 2001. *Women in Prison: Recent Trends and Developments.* London: Howard League Publications.

Howe, Adrian. 1994. *Punish and Critique: Towards a Feminist Analysis of Penality.* New York: Routledge.

Hughes, G., and Edward Zamble. 1993. "A Profile of Canadian Correctional Workers." *International Journal of Offender Therapy and Comparative Criminology* 37:99–113.

Human Rights Watch. 1996. *All Too Familiar: Sexual Abuse of Women in U.S. State Prisons.* New York: Human Rights Watch.

Irwin, John. 1970. *The Felon.* Englewood Cliffs, N.J.: Prentice-Hall.

————. 1980. *Prisons in Turmoil.* Boston: Little, Brown.

Irwin, John, and James Austin. 1994. *It's about Time: America's Imprisonment Binge.* Belmont, Calif.: Wadsworth.

Irwin, John, and Donald Cressey. 1962. "Thieves, Convicts, and the Inmate Culture." *Social Problems* 10:145–47.

Jacobs, David, and Ronald E. Helms. 1996. "Toward a Political Model of Incarceration: A Time-Series Examination of Multiple Explanations for Prison Admission Rates." *American Journal of Sociology* 102:323–57.

Jacobs, James. 1974. "Street Gangs behind Bars." *Social Problems* 21:395–409.

Jensen, Gary F. 1977. "Age and Rule-Breaking in Prison." *Criminology* 14: 555–68.

Jensen, Gary F., and Dorothy Jones. 1976. "Perspectives on Inmate Culture: A Study of Women in Prison." *Social Forces* 54:590–603.

Jones, Richard S. 1993. "Coping with Separation: Adaptive Responses of Women Prisoners." *Women and Criminal Justice* 5:71–97.

Jurik, Nancy C. 1983. "The Economics of Female Recidivism." *Criminology* 21:603–22.

Kendall, Kathleen. 2000. "Psy-ence Fiction: Inventing the Mentally-Disordered Female Prisoner." In *An Ideal Prison? Critical Essays on Women's Imprisonment in Canada,* edited by K. Hannah-Moffat and M. Shaw. Halifax: Fernwood.

Kershaw, Anne, and Mary Lasovich. 1991. *Rock-a-Bye Baby: A Death behind Bars.* Toronto: McClelland & Stewart.

Kilian, T. 1994. *Amethyst, Inc.* Washington, D.C.: U.S. Department of Justice, National Institute of Justice.

Kline, Sue. 1992. "A Profile of Female Offenders." *Federal Prisons Journal* 3: 33–36.

Knight, Barbara B. 1992. "Women in Prison as Litigants: Prospects for Post-Prison Futures." *Women and Criminal Justice* 4:91–116.

Koons, Barbara A., John D. Burrow, Merry Morash, and Tim Bynum. 1997. "Expert and Offender Perceptions of Program Elements Linked to Successful Outcomes for Incarcerated Women." *Crime and Delinquency* 43:512–32.

Kruttschnitt, Candace. 1981. "Prison Codes, Inmate Solidarity, and Women: A Re-examination." In *Comparing Female and Male Offenders,* edited by Marguerite Q. Warren. Beverly Hills, Calif.: Sage.

Kruttschnitt, Candace, Rosemary Gartner, and Amy Miller. 2000. "Doing Her Own Time? Women's Responses to Prison in the Context of the Old and the New Penology." *Criminology* 38:681–718.

Kruttschnitt, Candace, and Sharon Krmpotich. 1990. "Aggressive Behavior among Female Inmates: An Exploratory Study." *Justice Quarterly* 7:371–89.

Lambert, L. R., and P. G. Madden. 1975. *The Adult Female Offender: Before, During and After Incarceration.* Vanier Centre Research Report no. 3. Toronto: Ontario Ministry of Correctional Services.

Langan, Patrick A., and David P. Farrington. 1998. *Crime and Justice in the United States and in England and Wales, 1981–1996.* NCJ 169284. Washington, D.C.: Department of Justice, Office of Justice Programs, Bureau of Justice Statistics.

Larson, J. H., and Joey Nelson. 1984. "Women's Friendships and Adaptation to Prison." *Journal of Criminal Justice* 12:601–15.

Leger, Robert G. 1987. "Lesbianism among Women Prisoners: Participants and Nonparticipants." *Criminal Justice and Behavior* 14:448–67.

Liebling, Alison. 1992. *Suicides in Prison.* London: Routledge.

———. 1994. "Suicides amongst Women Prisoners." *Howard Journal* 33:1–9.

———. 1995. "Vulnerability and Prison Suicide." *British Journal of Criminology* 35:173–87.

———. 1997. "Risk and Prison Suicide." In *Good Practice in Risk Assessment and Risk Management 2: Protection, Rights, and Responsibilities,* edited H. Kemshall and J. Pritchard. London: Jessica Kingsley.

———. 1999. "Prisoner Suicide and Prisoner Coping." In *Prisons,* edited by Michael Tonry and Joan Petersilia. Vol. 26 of *Crime and Justice: A Review of Research,* edited by Michael Tonry and Norval Morris. Chicago: University of Chicago Press.

———. 2002. Personal correspondence with the author, Candace Kruttschnitt, April 22, 2002.

Lindquist, C. 1980. "Prison Discipline and the Female Offender." *Journal of Offender Counseling, Services and Rehabilitation* 4:305–19.

Long, G. T., F. E. Sultan, S. A. Kiefer, and D. M. Scrum. 1984. "The Psychological Profile of the Female First Offender and the Recidivist: A Comparison." *Journal of Offender Counseling, Services, and Rehabilitation* 9:119–23.

Lonmo, Charlene. 2001. "Adult Correctional Services in Canada, 1999–00." *Juristat* 21(5):1–15.

Loucks, Alexander D., and Edward Zamble. 2000. "Predictors of Criminal Behavior and Prison Misconduct in Serious Female Offenders." *Correctional Service Canada, Empirical and Applied Criminal Justice Review,* vol. 1, no. 1. (On-line journal of the Research on Criminal Justice Network. Available at http://qsilver.queensu.ca/rcjnet/journal. Accessed October 15, 2001.)

Loucks, Nancy. 1997. "HMPI Cornton Vale: Research into Drugs, Alcohol, Violence, and Bullying, Suicides and Self Injury, and Backgrounds of Abuse." ISBN 0-7480-5896-6. *Scottish Prison Service Occasional Papers.* Report no. 1/98. Edinburgh: Scottish Prison Service.

Lynch, James L. 1995. "Crime in International Perspective." In *Crime,* edited by James Q. Wilson and Joan Petersilia. San Francisco: ICS.

Lynch, Mona. 1998. "Waste Managers? The New Penology, Crime Fighting, and Parole Agent Identity." *Law and Society Review* 32:839–70.

MacKenzie, Doris Layton, James W. Robinson, and Carol S. Campbell. 1989. "Long-Term Incarceration of Female Offenders: Prison Adjustment and Coping." *Criminal Justice and Behavior* 16:223–38.

Maden, A., M. Swinton, and J. Gunn. 1994. "A Criminological and Psychiatric Survey of Women Serving a Prison Sentence." *British Journal of Criminology* 34:172–91.

Mahan, Sue. 1984. "Imposition of Despair: An Ethnography of Women in Prison." *Justice Quarterly* 1:357–84.

Mandaraka-Sheppard, Alexandra. 1986. *The Dynamics of Aggression in Women's Prisons in England*. Aldershot: Gower.

Martin, Dianne L. 1999. "Punishing Female Offenders and Perpetuating Gender Stereotypes." In *Making Sense of Sentencing*, edited by J. V. Roberts and D. P. Cole. Toronto: University of Toronto Press.

Martin, R. L., R. C. Cloninger, and S. B. Guze. 1978. "Female Criminality and the Prediction of Recidivism: A Prospective Six-Year Follow-up." *Archives of General Psychiatry* 35:207–14.

Maruna, Shadd. 2001. *Making Good: How Ex-convicts Reform and Rebuild Their Lives*. Washington, D.C.: American Psychological Association.

Mawby, R. I. 1982. "Women in Prison: A British Study." *Crime and Delinquency* 28:24–39.

McClellan, Dorothy Spektorov. 1994. "Disciplinarity in the Discipline of Male and Female Inmates in Texas Prisons." *Women and Criminal Justice* 5:71–79.

McClellan, Dorothy Spektorov, David Farabee, and Ben M. Crouch. 1997. "Early Victimization, Drug Use, and Criminality: A Comparison of Male and Female Prisoners." *Criminal Justice and Behavior* 24:455–76.

McCorkle, Jill A. 1998. "Going to the Crackhouse: Critical Space as a Form of Resistance in Total Institutions and Everyday Life." *Symbolic Interaction* 21:227–52.

McLanahan, Sara, and Karen Booth. 1995. "Mother-Only Families: Problems, Prospects and Politics." In *The Work and Family Interface: Toward a Contextual Effects Perspective*, edited by Gary L. Bowen and Joe F. Pittman. Minneapolis: National Council on Family Relations.

Messinger, Sheldon L. 1967. "Review of *Society of Women: A Study of a Women's Prison* by Rose Giallombardo and *Women's Prison: Sex and Social Structure* by David A. Word and Gene G. Kassebaum." *American Sociological Review* 32:143–46.

Mitchell, Arlene Edith. 1975. *Informal Inmate Social Structure in Prisons for Women: A Comparative Study*. San Francisco: R & E Research Associates.

Morash, Merry, Timothy S. Bynum, and Barbara A. Koons. 1998. "Women Offenders: Programming Needs and Promising Approaches." In *Research in Brief*. Washington, D.C.: U.S. Department of Justice, National Institute of Justice.

Morash, Merry, R. N. Haarr, and L. Rucker. 1994. "A Comparison of Programming for Women and Men in U.S. Prisons in the 1980s." *Crime and Delinquency* 40:197–221.

Morris, Allison, and Venezia Kingi. 1999. "Addressing Women's Needs or Empty Rhetoric? An Examination of New Zealand's Policy for Women in Prison." In *Harsh Punishment: International Experiences of Women's Imprisonment*, edited by Sandy Cook and Susanne Davies. Boston: Northeastern University Press.

Morris, Allison, Chris Wilkinson, and Andrea Tisi. 1995. *Managing the Needs of Female Prisoners.* London: Home Office.

Mowbray, Ellen J. 1982. "Parole Prediction and Gender." Paper presented at the annual meeting of the American Society of Criminology, Toronto, November.

Natarajan, M. 1994. *Crossroads: A Community-Based Outpatient and Alternative-to-Incarceration Program for Women Offenders in New York City.* Washington, D.C.: U.S. Department of Justice, National Institute of Justice.

National Crime Prevention Council of Canada. 1995. *Offender Profiles.* Ottawa: Prevention and Children Committee.

National Gains Center. 1995. *Women's Program Compendium.* Delmar, N.Y.: Gains Center.

Negy, Charles, Donald J. Woods, and Ralph Carlson. 1997. "The Relationship between Female Inmates Coping and Adjustment in a Minimum-Security Prison." *Criminal Justice and Behavior* 24:224–33.

Nielsen, Amie L., Frank R. Scarpitti, and James A. Inciardi. 1996. "Integrating the Therapeutic Community and Work Release for Drug-Involved Offenders: The CREST Program." *Journal of Substance Abuse Treatment* 13:349–58.

Norland, Stephen, and Priscilla J. Mann. 1984. "Being Troublesome—Women on Probation." *Criminal Justice and Behavior* 11:115–35.

Norris, Linda. 1974. "Comparison of Two Groups in a Southern State Women's Prison: Homosexual Behavior versus Nonhomosexual Behavior." *Psychological Reports* 34:75–78.

O'Brien, Patricia. 2001. *Making It in the "Free World: Women in Transition from Prison."* Albany: State University of New York Press.

O'Malley, Pat. 1992. "Risk, Power, and Crime Prevention." *Economy and Society* 21:252–75.

———. 1999. "Volatile and Contradictory Punishment." *Theoretical Criminology* 3:175–96.

Otis, M. 1913. "A Perversion Not Commonly Noted." *Journal of Abnormal Psychology* 8:113–16.

Owen, Barbara. 1998. *In the Mix: Struggle and Survival in a Women's Prison.* Albany: State University of New York Press.

———. 1999. "Women and Imprisonment in the United States: The Gendered Consequences of the U.S. Imprisonment Binge." In *Harsh Punishment: International Experiences of Women's Imprisonment*, edited by Sandy Cook and Suzanne Davies. Boston: Northeastern University Press.

Owen, Barbara, and Barbara Bloom. 1995. "Profiling Women Prisoners: Findings from National Surveys and a California Sample." *Prison Journal* 75:165–85.

Parsons, Talcott. 1951. *The Social System.* Glencoe, Ill.: Free Press.

Patterson, Richard L. 1995. "Criminality among Women: A Brief Review of the Literature." *Journal of Offender Rehabilitation* 22:33–53.

Petersilia, Joan. 1999. "Parole and Prisoner Reentry in the United States." In *Prisons*, edited by Michael Tonry and Joan Petersilia. Vol. 26 of *Crime and Justice: A Review of Research*, edited by Michael Tonry and Norval Morris. Chicago: University of Chicago Press.

Pogrebin, Mark R., and Mary Dodge. 2001. "Women's Accounts of Their Prison Experiences: A Retrospective View of Their Subjective Realities." *Journal of Criminal Justice* 29:531–41.

Pollock, Joycelyn M. 1986. *Sex and Supervision: Guarding Male and Female Inmates.* New York: Greenwood.

Pollock-Byrne, Joycelyn M. 1990. *Women, Prison, and Crime.* Pacific Grove, Calif.: Brooks/Cole.

Pomeroy, Elizabeth C., Risa Kiam, and Eileen Abel. 1998. "Meeting the Mental Health Needs of Incarcerated Women." *Health and Social Work* 23:71–75.

Poole, E. D., and R. M. Regoli. 1983. "Self-Reported and Observed Rule-breaking: A Look at Disciplinary Response." Paper presented at American Academy of Criminal Justice Sciences Meeting, San Antonio, Tex., March.

Pratt, John. 2000. "The Return of the Wheelbarrow Men; Or, the Arrival of Postmodern Penality?" *British Journal of Criminology* 40:127–45.

Prison Reform Trust. 1996. *Women in Prison: Recent Trends and Developments.* London: Penal Affairs Consortium.

Propper, Alice M. 1981. *Prison Homosexuality: Myth and Reality.* Lexington, Mass.: Lexington Books.

———. 1982. "Make-Believe Families and Homosexuality among Imprisoned Girls." *Criminology* 20:127–38.

Raeder, Myrna S. 1995. "The Forgotten Offender: The Effect of Sentencing Guidelines and Mandatory Minimums on Women and Their Children." *Federal Sentencing Reporter* 8:157–62.

Rafter, Nicole Hahn. 1990. *Partial Justice: Women, Prison and Social Control.* 2d ed. New Brunswick, N.J.: Transaction.

Rasche, Christine. 2001. "Cross-Sex Supervision of Female Inmates: An Unintended Consequence of Employment Law Cases Brought by Women Working in Corrections." Paper presented at the annual meeting of the American Society of Criminology, Atlanta, November 6–10.

Reid-Howe Associates. 2001. *Women Offenders: Effective Management and Intervention.* H.M. Institution Cornton Vale: Scottish Prison Service.

Reimer, Hans. 1937. "Socialization in Prison." Proceedings of the Sixty-Seventh Annual Congress of the American Prison Association.

Richie, Beth E. 1996. *Compelled to Crime: The Gender Entrapment of Battered Black Women.* New York: Routledge.

———. 2001. "Challenges Incarcerated Women Face as They Return to Their Communities: Findings from Life History Interviews." *Crime and Delinquency* 47:368–89.

Rierden, Andi. 1997. *The Farm: Life inside a Women's Prison.* Amherst: University of Massachusetts Press.

Riveland, Chase. 1999. "Prison Management Trends, 1975–2025." In *Prisons*, edited by Michael Tonry and Joan Petersilia. Vol. 26 of *Crime and Justice: A Review of Research*, edited by Michael Tonry and Norval Morris. Chicago: University of Chicago Press.

Roach, Kent. 1999. *Due Process and Victims' Rights: The New Law and Politics of Criminal Justice*. Toronto: University of Toronto Press.

Roberts, Julian, and David P. Cole, eds. 1999. *Making Sense of Sentencing*. Toronto: University of Toronto Press.

Rock, Paul. 1996. *Reconstructing a Women's Prison: The Holloway Redevelopment Project, 1968–1988*. Oxford: Clarendon.

Ross, R. R., and E. A. Fabiano. 1986. *Female Offenders: Correctional Afterthoughts*. Jefferson, N.C.: McFarlane.

Roundtree, George A., Brij Mohan, and Lisa W. Mahaffey. 1980. "Determinants of Female Aggression: A Study of a Prison Population." *International Journal of Offender Therapy and Comparative Criminology* 24:260–69.

Ruback, R. Barry, and Timothy B. Carr. 1984. "Crowding in a Women's Prison: Attitudes and Behavioral Effects." *Journal of Applied Social Psychology* 14:57–68.

Sappington, Andrew A. 1996. "Relationships among Prison Adjustment, Beliefs, and Cognitive Coping Styles." *International Journal of Offender Therapy and Comparative Criminology* 40:54–62.

Saylor, W. G., and G. G. Gaes. 1997. "Training Inmates through Industrial Work Participation and Vocational and Apprenticeship Instruction." *Corrections Management Quarterly* 1:32–43.

Schrag, Clarence. 1944. "Social Types in a Prison Community." Master's thesis, University of Washington.

Seear, N., and E. Player. 1986. *Women in the Penal System*. London: Howard League.

Selling, L. 1931. "The Pseudo-family." *American Journal of Sociology* 37:247–53.

Shaw, Margaret. 1991. *The Federal Female Offender: Report of a Preliminary Study*. Ottawa: Ministry of the Solicitor General.

———. 1992. "Issues of Power and Control: Women in Prison and Their Defenders." *British Journal of Criminology* 32:438–52.

———. 1994a. *Ontario Women in Conflict with the Law: A Survey of Women in Institutions and under Community Supervision in Ontario*. Ontario: Ministry of Correctional Services.

———. 1994b. "Women in Prison: A Literature Review." *Forum on Corrections* 6(1):13-21.

———. 1996. "Is There a Feminist Future for Women's Prisons?" In *Prisons 2000: An International Perspective on the Current State and Future of Imprisonment*, edited by Roger Matthews and Peter Francis. London: St. Martin's.

Shaw, Margaret, with K. Rodgers, J. Blanchette, T. Hattem, L. S. Thomas, and L. Tamarack. 1992. *Paying the Price: Federally Sentenced Women in Context*. Ottawa: Ministry of the Solicitor General.

Shearer, Robert A., Laura B. Myers, and Guy D. Ogan. 2001. "Treatment Resistance and Ethnicity among Female Offenders in Substance Abuse Treatment Programs." *Prison Journal* 81:55–72.

Sheridan, Michael J. 1996. "Comparison of the Life Experiences and Personal Functioning of Men and Women in Prison." *Families in Society* 77:423–34.

Shover, Neal. 1991. "Institutional Corrections: Jails and Prisons." In *Criminology: A Contemporary Handbook*, edited by J. F. Sheley. Belmont, Calif.: Wadsworth.

———. 1996. *Great Pretenders: Pursuits and Careers of Persistent Thieves.* Boulder, Colo.: Westview.

Simmons, Imogene L., and Joseph W. Rogers. 1970. "The Relationship between Type of Offense and Successful Post-institutional Adjustment of Female Offenders." *Criminologica* 7:68–76.

Simon, Jonathan. 1993. *Poor Discipline: Parole and the Social Control of the Underclass, 1890–1990.* Chicago: University of Chicago Press.

———. 2000. "The 'Society of Captives' in the Era of Hyper-incarceration." *Theoretical Criminology* 4:285–308.

Simon, Jonathan, and Malcolm Feeley. 1995. "True Crime: The New Penology and Public Discourse on Crime." In *Punishment and Social Control: Essays in Honor of Sheldon L. Messinger*, edited by Thomas G. Blomberg and Stanley Cohen. New York: Aldine de Gruyter.

Singleton, Nicola, Howard Meltzer, and Rebecca Gatward. 1998. "Psychiatric Morbidity among Prisoners in England and Wales." ISBN 011-6210-45. London: National Statistics Office.

Smith, David J. 1997. "Ethnic Origins, Crime, and Criminal Justice in England and Wales." In *Ethnicity, Crime and Immigration: Comparative and Cross-National Perspectives*, edited by Michael Tonry. Vol. 21 of *Crime and Justice: A Review of Research*, edited by Michael Tonry and Norval Morris. Chicago: University of Chicago Press.

Smith, Larry L., James N. Smith, Beryl M. Beckner. 1994. "An Anger Management Workshop for Women Inmates." *Families in Society: The Journal of Contemporary Human Services* 75:172–75.

Social Work Services and Prison Inspectorates for Scotland. 1998. *Women Offenders—a Safer Way: A Review of Community Disposals and the Use of Custody for Women Offenders in Scotland.* Edinburgh: Social Work Services Inspectorate.

Sommers, Ira, and Deborah R. Baskin. 1990. "The Prescription of Psychiatric Medications in Prison: Psychiatric versus Labeling Perspectives." *Justice Quarterly* 7:739–55.

Spencer, Carol, and John E. Berocochea. 1979. "Recidivism among Women Parolees: A Long Term Survey." In *The Criminology of Deviant Women*, edited by Freda Adler and Rita J. Simon. Boston: Houghton-Mifflin.

Steffensmeier, Darrell J., John Kramer, and Cathy Streifel. 1993. "Gender and Imprisonment Decisions." *Criminology* 31:411–46.

Stein, B. 1996. "Life in Prison: Sexual Abuse." *The Progressive* (July), pp. 23–24.

Street, David, Robert D. Vinter, and Charles Perrow. 1966. *Organization for Treatment: A Comparative Study of Institutions for Delinquents.* London: Collier-Macmillan.

Struckman-Johnson, C., D. Struckman-Johnson, L. Rucker, K. Bumby, and S. Donaldson. 1996. "Sexual Coercion Reported by Men and Women in Prison." *Journal of Sex Research* 33:67–76.

Sultan, Faye E., and Gary T. Long. 1988. "Treatment of the Sexually/ Physically Abused Female Inmate: Evaluation of an Intensive Short-Term Intervention Program." *Journal of Offender Counseling, Services, and Rehabilitation* 12:131–43.

Sykes, Gresham. 1958. *The Society of Captives: A Study of Maximum Security Prison.* Princeton, N.J.: Princeton University Press.

———. 1995. "The Structural-Functional Perspective on Imprisonment." In *Punishment and Social Control: Essays in Honor of Sheldon L. Messinger,* edited by Thomas G. Blomberg and Stanley Cohen. New York: Aldine De Gruyter.

Teplin, Linda, Karen Abraham, and Gary McClelland. 1996. "Prevalence of Psychiatric Disorders among Incarcerated Women." *Archives of General Psychiatry* 53:505–12.

Thomas, C. 1977. "Theoretical Perspectives on Prisonization: A Comparison of the Importation and Deprivation Models." *Journal of Criminal Law and Criminology* 68:135–45.

Tittle, Charles R. 1969. "Inmate Organization: Sex Differentiation and the Influence of Criminal Subcultures." *American Sociological Review* 34:492–505.

Uggen, Christopher, and Candace Kruttschnitt. 1998. "Crime in the Breaking: Gender Differences in Desistance." *Law and Society Review* 32:339–66.

van Wormer, Katherine S. 2001. *Counseling Female Offenders and Victims: A Strengths-Restorative Approach.* New York: Springer.

Veysey, Bonita M. 1998. "Specific Needs of Women Diagnosed with Mental Illness in U.S. Jails." In *Women's Mental Health Services: A Public Health Perspective,* edited by Bruce Lubotsky Levin, Andrea K. Blanch, and Ann Jennings. Thousand Oaks, Calif.: Sage.

Ward, David A., and Gene G. Kassebaum. 1965. *Women's Prison: Sex and Social Structure.* Chicago: Aldine.

Ward, Joyce. 1982. "Telling Tales in Prison." In *Custom and Conflict in British Society,* edited by Ronald Frankenberg. Manchester: Manchester University Press.

Washington, Pat, and R. J. Diamond. 1985. "Prevalence of Mental Illness among Women Incarcerated in Five California County Jails." *Research in Community and Mental Health* 5:33–41.

Welle, Dorinda, Gregory P. Falkin, and Nancy Jainchill. 1998. "Current Approaches to Drug Treatment for Women Offenders." *Journal of Substance Abuse Treatment* 15:151–63.

Wellford, Charles. 1967. "Factors Associated with Adoption of the Inmate Code: A Study of Normative Socialization." *Journal of Criminal Law, Criminology, and Police Science* 58:197–203.

Wellisch, Jean , and G. P. Falkin. 1994. *San Antonio Programs.* Washington, D.C.: U.S. Department of Justice, National Institute of Justice.

Wellisch, Jean, Michael L. Prendergast, and M. Douglas Anglin. 1994. *Drug-Abusing Women Offenders: Results of a National Survey.* Washington, D.C.: U. S. Department of Justice, Office of Justice Programs, National Institute of Justice.

———. 1996. "Needs Assessment and Services for Drug-Abusing Women Offenders: Results from a National Survey of Community-Based Treatment Programs." *Women and Criminal Justice* 8:27–60.

Wenger, P. 1994. *Profiles of Correctional Substance Abuse Treatment Programs: Women and Youthful Violent Offenders.* Washington, D.C.: National Institute of Corrections.

West, Angela D. 2001. "HIV/AIDS Education for Latina Inmates: The Delimiting Impact of Culture on Prevention Efforts." *Prison Journal* 81:20–41.

Wilkins, John, and Jeremy Coid. 1991. "Self-Mutilation in Female Remanded Prisoners. I. An Indicator of Severe Pathology." *Criminal Behavior and Mental Health* 1:247–67.

Wilson, Thomas P. 1968. "Patterns of Management and Adaptations to Organizational Roles: A Study of Prison Inmates." *American Journal of Sociology* 74:146–57.

Wilson, William Julius. 1987. *The Truly Disadvantaged: The Inner City, the Underclass, and Public Policy.* Chicago: University of Chicago Press.

Worrall, Anne. 1990. *Offending Women: Female Lawbreakers and the Criminal Justice System.* London: Routledge.

Wright, Kevin N. 1991. "A Study of Individual, Environmental, and Interactive Effects in Explaining Adjustment to Prison." *Justice Quarterly* 8:217–42.

Yang, S. 1990. "The Unique Treatment Needs of Female Substance Abusers in Correctional Institutions: The Obligation of the Criminal Justice System to Provide Parity of Services." *Medicine and Law* 9:1018–27.

Young, Warren, and Mark Brown. 1993. "Cross-National Comparisons of Imprisonment." In *Crime and Justice: An Annual Review of Research*, vol. 17, edited by Norval Morris and Michael Tonry. Chicago: University of Chicago Press.

Zamble, Edward, and F. J. Porporino. 1988. *Coping, Behavior, and Adaptation in Prison Inmates.* New York: Springer-Verlag.

Zedner, Lucia. 1991. *Women, Crime, and Custody in Victorian England.* Oxford: Clarendon.

Zingraff, Matthew T., and Rhonda Zingraff. 1980. "Adaptation Patterns of Incarcerated Female Delinquents." *Juvenile and Family Court Journal* (May), pp. 35–47.

Manuel Eisner

Long-Term Historical Trends in Violent Crime

ABSTRACT

Research on the history of crime from the thirteenth century until
the end of the twentieth has burgeoned and has greatly increased
understanding of historical trends in crime and crime control. Serious
interpersonal violence decreased remarkably in Europe between the
mid-sixteenth and the early twentieth centuries. Different long-term
trajectories in the decline of homicide can be distinguished between
various European regions. Age and sex patterns in serious violent
offending, however, have changed very little over several centuries.
The long-term decline in homicide rates seems to go along with a
disproportionate decline in elite homicide and a drop in male-to-male
conflicts in public space. A range of theoretical explanations for the long-
term decline have been offered, including the effects of the civilizing
process, strengthening state powers, the Protestant Reformation, and
modern individualism, but most theorizing has been post hoc.

"Symonet Spinelli, Agnes his mistress and Geoffrey Bereman were together in Geoffrey's house when a quarrel broke out among them; Symonet left the house and returned later the same day with Richard
Russel his Servant to the house of Godfrey le Gorger, where he found
Geoffrey; a quarrel arose and Richard and Symonet killed Geoffrey"
(Weinbaum 1976, p. 219). This is an entry in the plea roll of the eyre
court held in London in 1278. The eyre was a panel of royal justices
empowered to judge all felonies and required to inquire into all homicides that had occurred since the last eyre (Given 1977). The story is

Manuel Eisner is reader in sociological criminology at the Institute of Criminology,
University of Cambridge, England. The author thanks Michael Tonry, Kevin Reitz, and
the anonymous reviewers for their helpful comments.

typical of the situational structure of lethal violence in thirteenth-century London—a disagreement, a quarrel leading to a fight, and a fight resulting in a death. It could arise in different situations, often after drinking or over women, sometimes during a feast, but rarely premeditatedly. In two of the 145 instances of homicide recorded in the London eyre court rolls of 1278, the quarrel broke out after a game of chess.

For quantitatively minded historians, the completeness of the eyre court records, meticulously drawn up by the clerks of the justices, is a temptation to count. James Buchanan Given (1977) did this a quarter century ago, retrieving information on over 3,000 homicides recorded in twenty eyres in seven counties of thirteenth-century England. Beyond simple counts the data also include detailed information about the sex of offenders and victims, the personal relations between them, the number of cooffenders, the situations in which the events occurred, and the decisions taken by the judiciary.

The counts invite attempts at estimating a homicide rate. The 145 cases recorded in the 1278 London eyre court, for example, represent an average of about six cases per year, as twenty-five years had elapsed since the last convening of the court. And if the London population of the time was around 40,000 inhabitants, then the homicide rate—based on the cases reported to the eyre court—was around fifteen per 100,000.

Scientific enticements sometimes come in bunches, and Ted Robert Gurr (1981) took the issue one step further in an article in this series entitled "Historical Trends in Violent Crime: A Critical Review of the Evidence." Besides the cluster of twenty homicide rates provided by Given (1977), he reviewed two studies that offered estimates for a few counties in Elizabethan England (Samaha 1974; Cockburn 1977) and a series of homicide indictments in Surrey for the period 1663–1802 (Beattie 1974). Gurr plotted the some thirty estimates between about 1200 and 1800 on a graph, added the London homicide rates for the modern period, and fitted an elegant S-shaped trend curve to the data points (see fig. 1).

The curve suggested that typical rates may have been about twenty homicides per 100,000 population in the High and Late Middle Ages, dropping to ten around 1600, and ending after an extended downswing at about one per 100,000 in the twentieth century. Gurr interpreted this secular trend as "a manifestation of cultural change in Western society, especially the growing sensitization to violence and the devel-

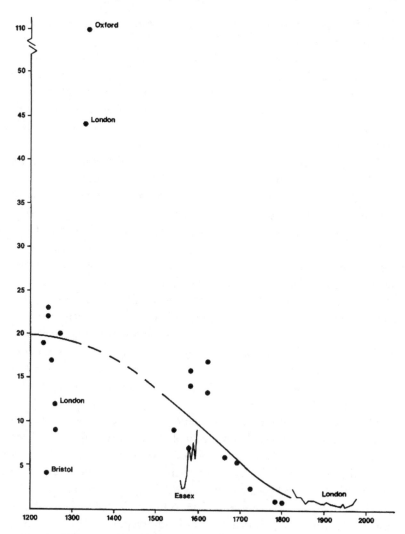

FIG. 1.—Indicators of homicides per 100,000 population in England, thirteenth to twentieth centuries. Note: Each dot represents the estimated homicide rate for a city or county for periods ranging from several years to several decades. Source: Gurr 1981, p. 313.

opment of increased internal and external control on aggressive behavior" (1981, p. 295; see also Gurr 1989). Gurr's essay easily qualifies as one of the most influential studies in the field of history of crime research, and the suggestive figure has been frequently reproduced (e.g., Daly and Wilson 1988, p. 276; Ylikangas 1998b, p. 10; Monkkonen

2001). But it also has raised a large number of questions, most of which fall into three broad categories.

For one, many historians have questioned whether counting homicides documented in premodern records and comparing respective rates over eight centuries is scientifically sound. This problem has a methodological side, including issues of how complete premodern records are, what the historical "dark figure" of homicide might look like, what the relationships among homicide and other forms of interpersonal violence are, what impact changing medical technologies have, and how accurate population estimates are. But some historians of crime also raise a more substantive problem since the comparison of numbers over time assumes some comparability of the underlying substantive phenomenon, namely, interpersonal physical violence. Controversy about this issue divides scholars of more cultural science inclinations from those with more behaviorist backgrounds. The former argue that violent acts are embedded in historically specific structures of meanings, values, and expectations and claim that considering the cultural context is essential to understanding historical manifestations of violence. From this viewpoint, the comparison of homicide rates is futile and misleading. Behaviorists, by contrast, argue that aggressive interpersonal behavior is a human universal and that counting the frequencies in manslaughter or murder gives some information about violence in everyday interactions.

The second set of questions concerns the degree to which Gurr's findings can be generalized and specified. Although extrapolation from a few counties in England to the Western world was probably inevitable at the time when the essay was written, it required a daring assumption. More recently, however, several historians of crime have put the hypothesis of a long-term decline in interpersonal violence to the test. Cockburn (1991) contributed an uninterrupted series of indicted homicide in Kent from 1560 to 1985. Possibly to his surprise, the data showed a more or less continuous tenfold fall from around three-to-six offenses per 100,000 to a rate of 0.3–0.7 over more than 400 years. During the 1970s, Ylikangas (1976) began to examine the long-term history of violence in Finland. His original findings were increasingly corroborated by a series of studies on Norway and Sweden, which suggested a coherent pattern in Scandinavia with a massive long-term decline of homicide rates during the early modern age (Naess 1982; Österberg and Lindström 1988; Österberg 1996). Finally, Spierenburg (1996) contributed evidence about the Netherlands, primarily focussing on Amsterdam and covering some 700 years. The findings again coincided with the long-term decline anticipated by Gurr, showing a drop from about fifty per 100,000 population in the fifteenth century to about one per 100,000 in the nineteenth century. Thus, at least for those captivated by transhistorical numbers, there remains little doubt about the empirical cogency of the broad picture Gurr painted. Supported by a growing flow of empirical findings, therefore, many have now started to ask new and more detailed questions (see, e.g., Karonen 2001; Monkkonen 2001; Roth 2001; Eisner 2002*b*). How can the quality of the data be ascertained? Can the beginning of the downturn be more narrowly identified? Does the timing and pace of the decline differ between large geographic areas? Can processes of pacification be attributed to specific social groups? Are there sustained periods of increasing levels of homicide rates, and how do they interact with the declining trend?

The empirical examination of these issues is intricately connected with the third group of questions: Why? Answering requires some macrolevel theory of social, cultural, and political developments that is not among the usual stock of criminological theorizing. Many criminologists, when theorizing about the effects of long-term social change, are primarily equipped to explain why urbanization and industrialization should lead to more crime (Shelley 1981). But they are at a loss when asked to explain declining trends. Historians of crime, however, found that their empirical observations fit surprisingly well with the work of the late German sociologist Norbert Elias. In his major work, *The Civilizing Process* (1978), Elias assumed that an interplay between the expansion of the state's monopoly of power and increasing economic interdependence would lead to the growth of pacified social spaces and restraint from violence through foresight or reflection (Elias 1978, p. 236). In an attempt to bridge sociological macrotheory and psychological insight, he suggested that the average level of self-control would increase to the degree that state institutions stabilize the flow of everyday interactions. Since these expectations match so well what crime historians have been finding, Elias has become the major theoretical reference for scholars who are working in the field and interested in theorizing about the long-term trend. But it is open to debate and the refinement of empirical findings precisely how far the theory of the civilizing process goes toward providing a causal framework for explaining the long-term decline in lethal violence.

Departing from these groups of questions, this essay is organized in three sections. Section I presents a reanalysis of quantitative estimates of homicide rates in Europe from the Middle Ages to the present day. It is based on a much larger set of historical studies than Gurr was able to examine and discusses the increasing degree to which we can distinguish different long-term trajectories in the decline of homicide in various European regions. Section II reviews evidence on various contextual factors. I examine historical evidence on sex, age, and class of violent offenders as well as studies that have examined historical patterns of the sex of homicide victims and their relationship with the offender. Section III explores theoretical approaches used in recent scholarship for explaining these secular trends, examining how theoretical arguments match the available data and in what ways future research might help to decide between alternative approaches.

I. The Secular Trend in Lethal Violence

What makes any assessment of our knowledge about the long-term trend in homicide rates relatively difficult is that relevant research has been published in many different languages, sometimes in difficult-to-find specialized historical journals, and with widely varying research questions forming the background of scholarly work. Therefore, this section builds on a systematic meta-analysis of more than ninety publications on premodern homicide rates in Europe as well as on a comprehensive collection of modern homicide time series in ten countries, based on national statistics and stretching over periods of more than 120 years. Taken together, these data first confirm the Europe-wide massive drop—roughly by a factor of 10:1 to 50:1 over the period from the fifteenth to the twentieth century—in lethal interpersonal violence first observed by Gurr on the basis of English data (1981). Second, the transition to declining homicide rates appears to have started earliest in the northwestern parts of Europe and then to have gradually diffused to the more peripheral regions of the continent. By the nineteenth century, therefore, homicide rates were lowest in the modernized, affluent, and urban regions of Europe, which were surrounded by a belt of high homicide rates in the periphery. By around 1950, most European countries experienced their lowest historically known levels of homicide rates. Since then, an increasing trend has prevailed.

A. Sources: History of Homicide Database

To examine long-term trajectories of lethal violence, I have assembled an extensive database of serial data on homicide in Europe. The resulting "History of Homicide Database" is an attempt at a comprehensive collection of available quantitative information on homicide over several centuries. The database incorporates two very different types of sources. National vital statistics providing annual counts of homicide victims probably constitute the most reliable source. In most European countries, data series start during the second half of the nineteenth century, although Swedish national death statistics were introduced in the middle of the eighteenth century (Verkko 1951). The second main source are statistics on homicides known to the police or persons accused of murder or manslaughter. Partly based on earlier research (Eisner 1995), the database for modern national homicide statistics includes ten European countries with series of annual data stretching over more than 100 years.

Prior to the introduction of national statistics, however, statistical data on homicides accrue from the painstaking archival work of historians who scrutinize large numbers of judicial sources produced for widely varying purposes and not originally intended for statistical analysis. Because of the fragmented judicial structure of premodern Europe, limitations on the amount of time researchers can spend in archives, and large gaps in surviving sources, we are left with a patchwork of local studies. Some of them aim at establishing long-term trends in serious violence. Many, however, are not primarily interested in estimating the frequency of homicide but aim at gaining insight, through judicial records, into the administration of justice, the mentalities of historical epochs, and the lives of ordinary people. However, departing from the elegant curve boldly drawn by Gurr through some thirty estimates of homicide rates, it is worthwhile to reassess the issue of long-term trends in violent crime by using the wealth of new research on the history of crime. Therefore, I systematically collected the results published in articles and monographs in several languages that present data on premodern homicide rates. A number of recent research reviews facilitated access to this literature (Johnson and Monkkonen 1996; Schüssler 1996; Rousseaux 1999a; Blauert and Schwerhoff 2000).

The History of Homicide Database at the time of writing includes approximately 390 estimates of premodern homicide rates based on more than ninety publications containing relevant data (Eisner 2001). Coded variables include information about the geographical area, the period, the counting units (offenders, victims, and offenses), the type of sources, the absolute number of homicide cases, the population estimates, and assessments of the quality of the data in the primary publication. When available, I also coded the percentages of female offenders and victims and the percentage of infanticides included in the data. Although the inclusion of infanticide is not wholly satisfying, it aims at improving comparability, since the majority of publications do not allow for separating infanticides and other killings. Three rules guided the coding process.

First, a threshold decision had to be made about whether to include a study. I excluded studies that are explicitly based on highly selective sources such as minor courts, that quote only approximate estimates without specifying the source, or that are based on extremely small samples. I included all studies, however, that at least present information on the respective territory covered, the type of source, and the time period covered. If it was sufficiently clear how the information had been gathered, I ignored occasional warnings by the original author against using homicide counts for computing rates. Schuster (2000), for example, extensively explains why he objects to computing homicide rates on the basis of medieval records. However, since he describes the origin of his data (judicial proceedings) and the territorial unit to which they refer, I decided to include his data on fifteenth-century Constance in the database.

Second, some publications present time series of counts for each single year or for short subperiods. This required a rule about how to aggregate these counts into larger units in order to reduce random variation. Generally, I summed up counts for single years and short subperiods and grouped them into ten-year periods. However, some flexibility was required to take varying sample sizes into account. Thus, series for small geographic units, providing low annual numbers, were aggregated to twenty-year intervals.

Third, whenever possible I used the population estimates quoted in a publication for computing the homicide rates. If a range of population estimates was given, the lower and upper bounds were coded separately, and the mean was used. Some publications cite counts of homicides without giving population estimates. In these cases I used demographic sourcebooks like Bairoch, Batou, and Chèvre (1988) and de Vries (1984) for population data.

Most data come from scholarship using one of three types of sources. A first type encompasses lists of coroners' inquests or body inspections of persons purportedly killed irrespective of whether the suspect was identified. Spierenburg (1996), for example, has used this kind of source in his analysis of homicide in Amsterdam. The second type of source is records on the offenders indicted and tried by a court and constitutes the basis for the vast majority of the data included here. A third type comprises records of suspected or proscribed homicide offenders registered by local authorities. An example here are the so-called medieval *Achtbücher* in German urban jurisdictions, which list persons banished from a city because of homicide, often after they have fled from the city (see, e.g., Simon-Muscheid 1991; Schüssler 1998).

Geographically, the data cluster in five large areas. Among those, England remains exceptional in respect of the wealth of sources that cover significant territorial units and the number of excellent studies (for syntheses, see Sharpe 1984, 1988; Emsley 1996), yielding 137 estimates. Historical estimates of homicide rates start in thirteenth-century England with the impressive analysis by Given (1977) on the coroners' rolls submitted to the eyre courts. Hanawalt (1979) then examined some 16,000 crimes recorded in the jail delivery rolls during the first half of the fourteenth century. These documents, in which the key information (e.g., the name and residence of the victim, the type of crime committed, and the jury's verdict) was recorded, include almost 3,000 homicide cases. From the mid-sixteenth century onward, comprehensive studies by Beattie (1974, 1986), Cockburn (1977, 1991), and Sharpe (1983, 1984) have traced the development of homicides indicted at the assize courts of several counties over extended periods of time.

A second area with a wealth of data and a rich tradition of criminal history research is the Netherlands and Belgium. Beginning with work by Berents (1976) on crime in fourteenth-century Utrecht, several studies now cover medieval cities such as Antwerp (Heyden 1983) and Amsterdam (Boomgaard 1992). Studies by Rousseaux (1986) and Spierenburg (1996) provide evidence for the early modern period until the beginning of the nineteenth century.

Since the 1980s, a large body of scholarship has emerged in Scandinavia, exploring the very homogenous judicial sources produced by a centralized and uniform judicial system in existence since the fifteenth century. Österberg and Lindström (1988) have examined judicial records in Stockholm and some smaller cities from 1450 to the mid-seventeenth century. Recent studies by Karonen (1995, 1999), Ylikangas (1998*a*, 1998*b*), and Ylikangas, Karonen, and Lehti (2001) have added impressive series of estimates for various regions in both Sweden and Finland, some of which cover more than 200 years.

Fourth, a significant number of studies provide information on long-term trends in Germany and Switzerland, although both the sources and the judicial structures are extremely complex. Some evidence comes from an old tradition of local studies on medieval crime and criminal justice (Buff 1877; Frauenstädt 1881; Cuénod 1891). Much recent scholarship has focused on the Middle Ages with detailed studies of Cologne (Schwerhoff 1991), Constance (Schuster 1995, 2000), Nuremberg (Schüssler 1991), Olmütz (Schüssler 1994), Kraków (Schüssler 1998), Basel (Hagemann 1981; Simon-Muscheid 1991), and Zurich (Burghartz 1990). The early modern period had received less attention, but there are now growing numbers of studies on various areas in the seventeenth and eighteenth centuries (Schormann 1974; Henry 1984; Dülmen 1985; Behringer 1990; Lacour 2000).

Although somewhat less thoroughly covered than the other areas, Italy is the fifth region with a series of studies that permit empirically based extrapolations. Studies of medieval and renaissance cities include Bologna (Blanshei 1981, 1982), Florence (Becker 1976), and Venice (Ruggiero 1978, 1980). Romani (1980) has examined court records in late sixteenth-century Mantova, and a fascinating study by Blastenbrei (1995) analyzes wounding reports by medical professionals and judicial records in late sixteenth-century Rome. Finally, a series of studies on Padova (Zorzi 1989), Citra (Panico 1991), Sardinia (Doneddu 1991), Tuscany (Sardi 1991), and Rome (Boschi 1998) yields another cluster of estimates for the late eighteenth and early nineteenth centuries before the onset of national statistics.

B. How Reliable Are Estimates of Premodern Homicide Rates?

Historians who analyze extensive criminal justice records usually resort to statistical counts in presenting their findings. But they disagree whether retrieved historical data should be used to compute homicide rates, whether such numbers provide any useful information about the real incidence of killings, and whether long-term historical comparison is scientifically justifiable (for the recent debate, see Spierenburg 2001; Schwerhoff 2002). There are five major issues with regard to reliability and validity.

The first is whether murder or manslaughter cases in premodern sources qualify as homicides in a modern legal sense, or whether the data are inflated by cases that would nowadays be regarded as negligent manslaughters or accidents (see, e.g., Aubusson de Cavarlay 2001, p. 27). Legally, homicide represented a felony throughout Europe since the High Middle Ages, and definitions invariably included some notion of intentional aggression. Philippe de Beaumanoir, officer of the French Crown in the thirteenth century, defined homicide in the following way: "Homicide: When one kills another in the heat of a fight, in which tension turns to insult and insult to fighting, by which one often dies" (cited in Rousseaux 1999a, p. 145). A reading of the case descriptions in historical sources suggests that, some exceptions notwithstanding, most cases would qualify as criminal acts. In this vein, DeWindt and DeWindt (1981, p. 54) conclude—based on a close examination of 111 presentments of homicide in the Huntingdonshire Eyre of 1286—that 90 percent were definite acts of aggression or violence.

Another important issue concerns the quality of the immensely varied judicial sources used in historical analyses. Spierenburg (1996), for example, has argued that homicide estimates based on court records may yield considerable underestimates because only a fraction of offenders were captured and brought to trial. His comparison between body inspection records and the judicial sources in late medieval and early modern Amsterdam suggests that possibly as few as 10 percent of all homicides may have resulted in a suspect being brought to court (see also Boomgaard 1992; Spierenburg 1996, p. 80). Even if this is an extreme estimate, it suggests that early court records constitute selective evidence. In order to examine this issue empirically, Monkkonen (2001) recently proposed the use of capture-recapture methods, which yield estimates of the size of the unknown underlying population of offenders based on comparisons between different types of sources (e.g., court records, coroners' inquests, proscriptions, reports in diaries, or printed sources). It remains to be seen whether such a strategy can clarify the issue of historical dark figures. Yet it is uncontroversial that the progressive shift toward more efficient prosecution has the effect of underestimating the long-term decline in lethal violence (Stone 1983, p. 23).

A related issue is whether homicide rates constitute a leading indicator of overall levels of violence through long historical periods (see, e.g., Schuster 2000). For present-day societies, homicide appears quite adequately to reflect variation in overall violence. In the United States and Great Britain, for example, trends in assault, as measured by the National Crime Victimization Survey, are highly correlated with fluctuations in homicide rates (Langan and Farrington 1998). Moreover, cross-national homicide rates are also significantly correlated with levels of robbery, assault, and sexual violence as measured by the International Crime Victimization Survey (Eisner 2002*a*). Yet until recently there seemed to be no way directly to address this question historically since alternative data for measuring historical levels of violence were not available. But recent research for several sixteenth- and seventeenth-century Swedish cities now suggests that time series of recorded assault and homicide are surprisingly parallel in both trends and fluctuations (Karonen 2001). However, since historical trends for other types of violence that differ from those for homicide cannot be ruled out, the subsequent analysis is based on the assumption that homicide may be cautiously construed as an indicator only of serious interpersonal violence.

A fourth, somewhat overemphasized, issue concerns the variability of homicide rate estimates because of the small sizes of geographic units, the small number of cases used for computing respective rates, or both (Aubusson de Cavarlay 2001). With only a handful of estimates based on a few killings each, this would be a serious issue. But with several hundred estimates, many based on large numbers of homicides, covering both urban and rural areas, and converging to coherent patterns despite heterogeneous sources, one may safely assume that the data are not random noise. Likewise, the low precision of population estimates, although important, should probably not be regarded as an insurmountable issue. Better population data are important for more accurate estimates. Fortunately, however, my interest is not to compare differences in the magnitude of 50 or 60 percent over time, but a ten- to possibly fifty-fold decline. Therefore, quite considerable inaccuracy in population estimates—especially if it is randomly distributed between the different studies—can be accepted.

Probably the most important "distorting" factor in comparisons of homicide across long periods is the interplay between changes in the technology of violence and growth in medical knowledge. The lives of a large proportion of those who died from the immediate or secondary consequences (e.g., internal bleeding, infections) of a wound in any society before the twentieth century could have been saved with modern medical technology. But until recently it seemed wholly impossible to estimate the size of this effect. Monkkonen (2001), however, has proposed to use information about the elapsed time from injury to death as a rough indicator of the potential impact of modern medical technology. He argues that most deaths occurring within the first one to two hours after the injury are probably not preventable even with modern medicine, while the vast majority of those occurring after twenty-four hours could be prevented by modern technology. A series of studies yields quite consistent results in regard to the typical time from assault to death before the twentieth century. In mid-nineteenth-century New York, about one-fourth of victims died immediately and another fourth within the first twenty-four hours (Monkkonen 2001). In seventeenth-century Castile, about 37 percent of the victims died immediately and another third within the first twenty-four hours (Chaulet 1997, p. 22); Spierenburg (1996) estimates that somewhat less than half of victims in seventeenth-century Amsterdam died immediately. Even if these estimates are far from precise, they give a rough idea about the order of magnitude, by which the lethal consequences of violence might have declined with late twentieth-century technology. Most authors agree, however, that changes in medical technology are unlikely to have had any major impact on the chances of surviving a wounding before the late nineteenth century.

C. Results

Figures 2–7 graphically display the estimates collected for the five areas. Figure 2 includes all local premodern estimates for the whole of

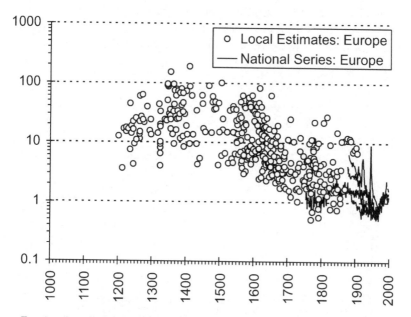

Fig. 2.—Overall trend in homicide rates, all premodern local estimates and four national series. Note: All 398 local estimates from the History of Homicide Database; national series for Sweden, England and Wales, Switzerland, and Italy.

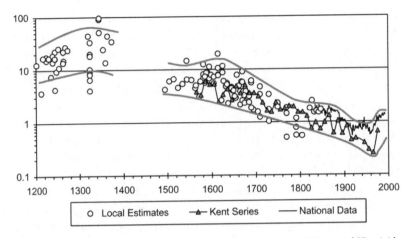

Fig. 3.—England: local estimates and national series. Source: History of Homicide Database; see text for details.

Europe along with national series for four countries. Figures 3–7 show trends for the five geographic areas over longer periods of time. In each figure, dots represent single local estimates based on the mean year of the investigated period and the mean homicide rate, if upper and lower bonds for the respective population were given. For the premodern period, lines show selected continuous series of estimates for one geographic subunit. During the modern period, lines show na-

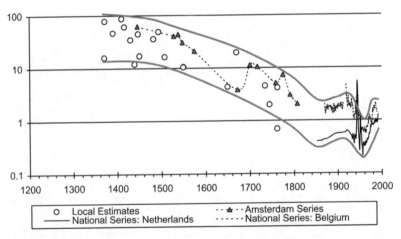

Fig. 4.—Netherlands and Belgium: local estimates and national series. Source: History of Homicide Database; see text for details.

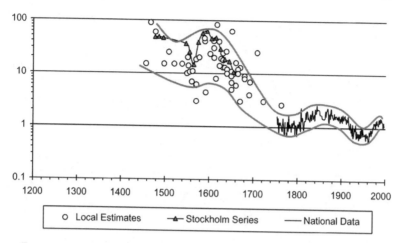

FIG. 5.—Scandinavia: local estimates and national series for Sweden. Source: History of Homicide Database; see text for details.

tional homicide rates based on vital statistics or police statistics. For two reasons, the graphs use a logarithmic scale for the vertical axis. First, estimated homicide rates range between over 100 and 0.3 per 100,000 population over the centuries. Hence, variation at lower absolute levels would become invisible with a linear scale. Second, a logarithmic scale has the advantage of making relative differences comparable across the whole range of absolute levels. In addition, table 1 shows

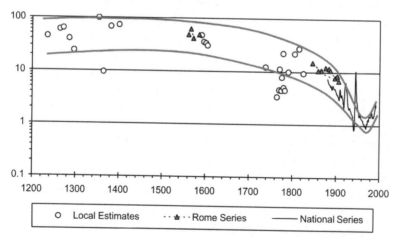

FIG. 6.—Italy: local estimates and national series. Source: History of Homicide Database; see text for details.

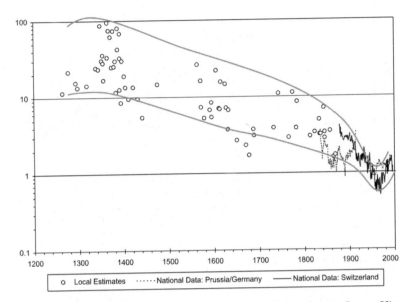

Fɪɢ. 7.—Germany and Switzerland: local estimates and national series. Source: History of Homicide Database; see text for details.

average estimates of homicide rates for specified subperiods. These estimates are based on the unweighted averages. It could be argued, though, that averages should be weighted for differences of population size and the length of the period on which the estimate is based. However, since the larger urban areas are more thoroughly covered anyway, it did not seem appropriate to increase their contribution to the overall mean even more. The results can be summarized in the following ways.

1. *Overall Secular Decline.*   The data displayed in figure 2 suggest a common trend in homicide rates across western Europe. Three main conclusions can be drawn. First, the total of all estimates is located in a band in which upper and lower limits gradually move toward lower levels from around 1500 until the mid-twentieth century. Taken together, the empirical evidence suggests a continent-wide gradual decline of serious interpersonal violence. Computing averages per century and including all estimates yields the series displayed in table 2. Comparing these estimates with the original curve plotted by Gurr shows impressive consistency. Adding new data, it appears, has little impact on the overall pattern.

Second, for each century, the estimates show a large degree of dis-

TABLE 1

Homicide Rates in Five European Regions

Period	England	Netherlands and Belgium	Scandinavia	Germany and Switzerland	Italy
Thirteenth–fourteenth centuries	23	47	...	37	(56)
Fifteenth century	...	45	46	16	(73)
Sixteenth century	7	25	21	11	47
Seventeenth century:					
First half	6	(6)	24	11	(32)
Second half	4	9	12	(3)	...
Eighteenth century:					
First half	2	7	3	(7)	(12)
Second half	1	4	.7	(8)	9
1800–1824	2	2	1.0	3	18
1825–49	1.7	...	1.4	4	15
1850–74	1.6	.9	1.2	2	12
1875–99	1.3	1.5	.9	2.2	5.5
1900–1924	.8	1.7	.8	2.0	3.9
1925–49	.8	1.3	.6	1.4	2.6
1950–74	.7	.6	.6	.9	1.3
1975–94	1.2	1.2	1.2	1.2	1.7

SOURCE.—History of Homicide Database.

NOTE.—Data are arithmetic means of all available estimates for a given period and region. Estimates based on local data are rounded to the next integer. Figures in parentheses are particularly unreliable because they are based on fewer than five estimates. Figures in italics are based on national statistics.

TABLE 2

Overall Homicide Rates in Europe, Thirteenth to Twentieth Centuries

Period	Average Homicide Rate	Number of Estimates
Thirteenth–fourteenth centuries	32	76
Fifteenth century	41	25
Sixteenth century	19	76
Seventeenth century	11	107
Eighteenth century	3.2	65 (excluding national series)
Nineteenth century	2.6	Mostly national series
Twentieth century	1.4	National series

SOURCE.—History of Homicide Database.

persion with a ratio between the lowest and the highest bundle of estimates typically being around 1:10. This variation may arise from a number of different sources. There may be measurement errors (systematic or random) influencing each estimate for all kinds of reasons (e.g., gaps in the sources, unrecorded homicides, or faulty population estimates). Variability may be the result of historically contingent conditions, such as food crises, local warfare, or banditry, that influence the local level of serious violence. Based on our knowledge of the large local variability of homicide rates in present societies, we should not expect anything else when working with historical data. Finally, variation in each period may reflect large-scale systematic differences between areas of the European continent. As I argue below, the evidence suggests that a large-scale pattern of geographic variation emerges from the sixteenth century onward and is due to different trajectories in the secular transition from high to low levels of lethal violence. Third, there appears to be a significant process of convergence between the mid-nineteenth and mid-twentieth centuries, when very little variation remains between various countries of western Europe.

2. *Relative Homogeneity in the Middle Ages.* Before 1500, the database includes about 100 different estimates of homicide rates. They come from a widely dispersed sample of areas, primarily larger cities (i.e., more than 5,000 inhabitants) but also some small towns and rural territories, and are based on a staggering variety of sources. However, the evidence suggests a startlingly homogeneous pattern throughout Europe. Evidence based on coroners' rolls in fourteenth-century Oxford and London result in estimates in the order of twenty-five to 110 homicides per 100,000 (Hanawalt 1976; Hammer 1978), while estimates for other areas of England typically vary between eight and twenty-five homicides per 100,000. In the south of Europe, data from judicial archives in Florence (Becker 1976; Cohn 1980), Venice (Ruggiero 1980), Bologna (Blanshei 1982), and Valencia (Garcia 1991) yield estimates between a low of ten and a high of 150 homicides per 100,000. And studies on an extensive sample of urban jurisdictions in what are now Belgium, the Netherlands, Germany, Switzerland, and northern France again result in estimates between a low of six and a high of about 100 homicides per 100,000 of the population. Overall, there is considerable haphazard variation between individual estimates, which may result from peculiarities of the surviving sources or reflect local economic and social conditions, political conflict, or the intensity of law enforcement. However, and more important, there appears to

be little systematic difference during this period when larger areas of Europe are compared.

3. *Increasing Geographic Differences from the Late Sixteenth Century Onward.* By the late sixteenth century, however, significant large-scale differences begin to emerge. They suggest that the secular trajectory from high to low levels of lethal violence may have had different shapes in different areas. More particularly, homicide rates, as estimated on the basis of indictments brought before the assize courts in Elizabethan and early Stuart England, typically range between three and ten per 100,000 (see fig. 3). Experts in the field seem to agree that these estimates indicate a real decline compared with the late Middle Ages (Sharpe 1996, p. 22). Yet because of the lack of records between the late fourteenth and the mid-sixteenth centuries, the precise period when the secular downturn started cannot be identified.

In the Low Countries, too, evidence indicates a marked shift from the high homicide pattern during the sixteenth century (see fig. 4). Studies by Boomgaard (1992) and Spierenburg (1996, pp. 80 ff.) based on body inspection reports suggest that homicide rates in Amsterdam may have declined from about forty to twenty per 100,000 during the sixteenth century. For Brussels, Vanhemelryck (1981) suggests that the rate of homicides recorded by the judiciary may have declined from about twenty per 100,000 in the fifteenth century to about ten per 100,000 in the sixteenth century. The pattern becomes even clearer by the end of the seventeenth century, when Spierenburg (1996, p. 86) calculates a homicide rate of about four per 100,000 for Amsterdam. The estimate for Brussels, based on the whole century, is four to five per 100,000 (depending on the population estimate). And another century later, a few scattered figures suggest that the homicide rate in late eighteenth-century Belgium or the Netherlands typically ranged between 0.7 and about three per 100,000.

The Scandinavian countries show similar trends but differences in timing. Figure 5 shows that homicide rates remained at very high levels until the first decades of the seventeenth century. Estimates based on the thorough work by Karonen (2001) yield homicide rates of thirty to sixty per 100,000 in Turku, Arboga, and Stockholm around the turn of that century. These rates, considerably higher than anything found in England or the Netherlands at this time, may have been the result of an upsurge from the mid-sixteenth century, when estimates tend to be considerably lower. From about 1620 onward, however, Scandinavian scholars observe a staggering decline in homicide rates. By the second half of the seventeenth century, rates had dropped to around eight to ten homicides per 100,000, while estimates for early eighteenth-century Sweden were in the region of about four per 100,000. By 1754, when national death statistics were initiated, the Swedish homicide rate had dwindled to a mere 1.3 per 100,000.

Although lethal interpersonal violence had declined to both historically and cross-culturally remarkably low levels by the late eighteenth century throughout northern Europe, a very different trend is found in southern Europe (see fig. 6). Admittedly, the data from Italy have large gaps, and we lack long-term continuous series similar to those available in England, the Netherlands, and Sweden. However, the contrast is so stark that there is no reason to doubt its main characteristics. Departing from the handful of estimates for late medieval and early Renaissance cities, studies by Blastenbrei (1995) on Rome and by Romani (1980) on the Duchy of Mantova give some idea of typical homicide rates around 1600. Blastenbrei shows that medical professionals in late sixteenth-century Rome were registering some twenty-five to thirty-five killings per year, which yields an estimated homicide rate of thirty to seventy per 100,000. In a similar vein, the criminal justice records in Mantova include some ten to fifteen cases of murder or manslaughter each year. Romani (1980) estimates the population at 30,000–40,000, which in turn suggests a homicide rate of between twenty-five and fifty-five per 100,000.

Another two centuries later a sample of figures suggests some decline. In this period, the rate of convicted homicide offenders in Tuscany or Padova can be estimated at between four and ten per 100,000 (Zorzi 1989; Sardi 1991). In the south of Italy as well as in Sardinia, however, late eighteenth-century homicide rates were still well above twenty per 100,000 (Doneddu 1991), and Boschi's figures for Rome around 1840 put the homicide rate at over ten per 100,000 (Boschi 1998).

It is hard to say whether Germany and Switzerland followed the northern European pattern of a sustained decline or whether the long-term trajectory resembles the Italian pattern of high homicide rates well into the beginning of the industrial revolution. Because of the heterogeneity of the sources and the political fragmentation of territories, but possibly also because of a lack of scholarly interest in examining quantitative long-term trends, the existing data make solid conclusions impossible.

As figure 7 shows, the data first suggest a dramatic drop in homicide rates at the beginning of the fifteenth century. However, this apparent trend probably reflects a shift in the sources used for historical research rather than any real change. Most estimates for the fourteenth century are based on banishment records. These documents include a large proportion of suspects, who had fled an urban jurisdiction after a crime and may never have been put to trial (Schüssler 1994). In the early fifteenth century, the practice of banishment without formal trial fell out of use, and studies for this period are mostly based on proceedings of the local judiciary. Yet many scholars argue that early modern judiciaries may have been able to deal with only a small fraction of actual crimes, including homicide. By around 1600, estimates for the cities of Cologne and Frankfurt range between six and sixteen homicides per 100,000, a figure similar to those in England or the Netherlands in this period (Dülmen 1985, p. 187). However, a series of estimates for several areas in southern Germany and Switzerland and primarily based on offenders tried by the judicial authorities typically hover between two and ten during the late eighteenth and early nineteenth centuries. These are consistently higher estimates than are found during this period in northern Europe, and they suggest that the frequency of serious violence in Switzerland and southern Germany may have been somewhere between the low rates found in the north and the high rates found in the south of Europe.

4. *Center-Periphery Structures in the Nineteenth Century.* By the beginning of the nineteenth century, the impact of different long-term trajectories in the evolution of serious interpersonal violence since the Middle Ages had created a pattern of large-scale regional differences within Europe. Since the late sixteenth century, England and the Netherlands had moved a long way in the transition from a high violence society to one characterized by a much more pacified mode of everyday behavior. In Sweden, the same process seems to have started later, occurred faster, and produced a similar result. In Italy, however, homicide rates appear to have moved little from their late medieval and early modern levels, especially so in the south and on the islands. The development in Germany and Switzerland is hard to track, but by the early nineteenth century a north-south divide may have come into existence, with higher levels characteristic of many areas in Switzerland and southern Germany.

Against this background, it seems worthwhile to summarize the large-scale ecology of lethal violence in Europe around 1900, originally described by Ferri (1925) and Durkheim (1973) but discernible

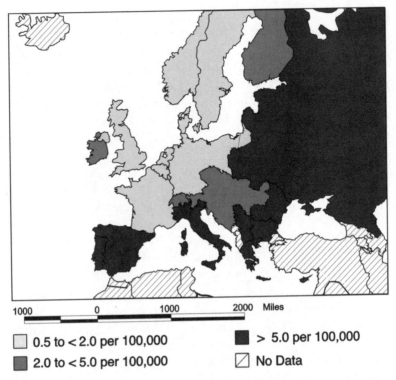

1000   0   1000   2000   Miles

☐ 0.5 to < 2.0 per 100,000   ■ > 5.0 per 100,000

■ 2.0 to < 5.0 per 100,000   ▨ No Data

Fɪɢ. 8.—Homicide rates around 1880. Sources: History of Homicide Database; Verkko 1951; Chesnais 1981.

in much greater detail now thanks to additional recent work (see, e.g., Chesnais 1981; Johnson 1995; Eisner 1997; Thome 2001). On the level of nations, the pattern resembles a trough with low homicide rates across the highly industrialized countries of northern Europe, including Germany and France. A rim of high-homicide countries surrounds the trough and includes Portugal, Spain, Italy, and Greece in the south, and all eastern European countries and Finland (see fig. 8). By the end of the twentieth century, this large-scale geographic pattern changed. While homicide levels in eastern Europe remained high, rates in southern European countries have converged to levels typically found in northern and western Europe (see fig. 9).

    Within countries, nineteenth-century regional differences appear to have followed a distinctly similar pattern. In Italy, homicide rates were higher in the rural south with its low literacy rates than in the more industrialized north. In 1880–84, for example, the homicide rate varied

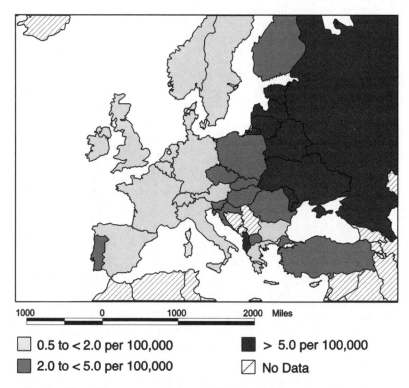

| ☐ 0.5 to < 2.0 per 100,000 | ■ > 5.0 per 100,000 |
| ■ 2.0 to < 5.0 per 100,000 | ▨ No Data |

Fig. 9.—Homicide rates around the end of the twentieth century. Note: Data refer to completed homicides known to the police, 1998–2000. Source: Interpol at http://www.interpol.int/Public/Statistics/ICS/downloadList.asp (last accessed February 2, 2003).

from a high of 45.1 in the district of Palermo to a low of 3.6 in the district of Milan (Chesnais 1981). French maps suggest higher levels of homicide in southern France than in the prosperous and urbanized north (Durkheim 1973). Within Germany, homicide and assault rates were generally higher in areas characterized by low urbanization, low proportions of professionals and public servants, and a high overall death rate (Johnson 1995). In late nineteenth-century Poland, homicide and assault were more common in the countryside than in cities; in Switzerland, too, homicide rates were negatively correlated with levels of urbanization and industrialization (Kaczynska 1995; Eisner 1997).

All in all, it seems, a center-periphery dimension characterized the geographic distribution of lethal violence across late nineteenth-century Europe. Homicide was low in the centers of modernization characterized by high urbanization, industrialization, literacy, and education. Elevated levels of violence, in turn, were found throughout the peripheral areas with high birth rates, high illiteracy rates, and a predominantly rural population. This pattern, I tentatively conjecture, was the result of differential long-term pathways, some of which can be traced back to the beginning of the early modern period.

5. *The Past 120 Years: The U-Shaped Pattern.* From about the 1880s onward, death statistics and police statistics cover the majority of western European countries. These data permit us quite accurately to trace main trends in homicide rates over the past 120 years. The main message can be summarized in three points. First, a comparison of the 1950s with the 1880s suggests that the frequency of lethal violence fell by at least another 50 percent even in northern European countries, and considerably more in the south. Indeed, as Gurr, Grabosky, and Hula (1977; see also Gurr 1989) had shown, declining trends were the predominating pattern for other types of violence (e.g., serious assault, robbery) as well as for property crime in many Western societies (Gatrell 1980). In a sense, therefore, homicide rates around 1950 may serve as a benchmark for the lowest level of interpersonal lethal violence as yet attained in any known Western society. It stands at about 0.4–0.6 deaths per year per 100,000 inhabitants. Second, the data demonstrate a rapid convergence of homicide rates between the late nineteenth century and the 1960s. By then, cross-national differences within western Europe had become inconsequential and have remained small since. Third, the data from 1950 until the early 1990s point to an upsurge of homicide rates throughout most of Europe accompanied by a much sharper rise in recorded levels of assault and robbery.

These increases occurred despite advances in medical technology throughout the twentieth century, which are likely significantly to have dampened this latest increase. The main trend over the past 150 years, therefore, corresponds to the U-shaped pattern identified earlier by Gurr and his collaborators (Gurr, Grabosky, and Hula 1977).

6. *Countertrends.* The well-documented increase in criminal violence between the 1950s and the early 1990s may well be just one of several periods in which violence rates increased over several decades. For obvious reasons, we know very little about earlier medium-term periods of increasing interpersonal violence. It might be interesting to know, for example, whether the upswing in lethal violence documented

for Sweden between the 1790s and the 1840s also occurred in other European areas. But there is too little evidence to address this question even tentatively. Recently, however, Roth (2001) offered a fascinating observation on trends between 1550 and 1800. Comparing time series for England, Scandinavia, and France, he found evidence of a similar trend of sharply increasing homicide rates between the 1580s and the 1610s, followed by a continuous drop thereafter. The coincidence between areas far apart from each other is remarkable. As for England, Roth suggests that demographic pressure, economic depression, crop failure, the militarization of culture, and military demobilization together may have caused homicide rates to soar in the late sixteenth and early seventeenth centuries. Yet the relative importance of those factors remains to be explored. Furthermore, one might wonder whether similar factors played a role in other areas during that time or if the parallel trends are coincidental.

7. *Some Evidence for Other Areas.*   Research in recent years has explored long-term trends for geographic areas that I have not discussed. For example, there is now good evidence for developments in Ireland from the beginning of the eighteenth century until 1914 (Garnham 1996; Finnane 1997). The data from indictments in two Irish counties through 1801 suggest homicide rates of around four to seven per 100,000 population in the 1740s and 1750s. These are considerably higher rates than those found in any of the English counties investigated by Beattie (1986) and Cockburn (1991). By around 1900, national homicide rates were down to below two per 100,000, and Finnane (1997) concludes that there is strong evidence of a declining trend in interpersonal violence during the nineteenth century.

Furthermore, Roth (2001) has recently presented data on European-American adult homicides in Connecticut, Massachusetts, Maine, and New Hampshire from 1630 to 1800. His work is particularly notable because it uses sophisticated capture-recapture methods in order more accurately to estimate homicide rates for European colonists. Before 1637, during the era of frontier violence, he finds that the homicide rate in colonial New England stood at over 100 per 100,000 adults. It then dropped to about seven to nine for the next four decades, which—assuming some underreporting in the English assize court data—may have been quite similar to the rate that probably prevailed in southeastern England. It fell again at the beginning of the eighteenth century and reached a low of about one per 100,000 adults at the end of the century. Examining the causes of this massive decline,

Roth argues that the sudden decline correlated with increased feelings of Protestant and racial solidarity among the colonists (2001, p. 55).

II. Contextual Trajectories

To this point I have primarily traced the long-term trajectory of overall levels of lethal interpersonal violence. But historians of crime have long underscored that these trends need to be embedded in an analysis of contextual change, including, for example, the cultural meaning of violence, the typical situations giving rise to conflict and aggression, the characteristics of offenders and victims, and the framework of legal and judicial reactions (Rousseaux 1999a). Similarly, criminologists increasingly have become interested in disaggregating violence trends by, for example, offender-victim configurations (Wikström 1992), offender age groups (Blumstein 2000), or weapons used in the offense (Wintemute 2000). And they found such distinctions highly valuable for understanding the determinants of change in overall crime levels.

As the consensus about the overall decline grows, therefore, establishing the long-term variation, and stability, of contextual characteristics of violent crime will become increasingly important. A better understanding of contextual dimensions may provide the decisive cues for more refined interpretations of the transition from high to low homicide levels during the process of modernization. The following analyses explore some relevant dimensions. They primarily stick to a statistical framework, presenting numerical evidence on factors that criminologists find relevant when describing the basic characteristics of violent crime. The evidence partly derives from the publications comprised in the History of Homicide Database. I also include data from a series of studies that have examined historic patterns of robbery or assault.

The available evidence suggests impressive historical stability in some respects. Most particularly, both the sex distribution and the age distribution of serious violent offenders appear to have remained within very narrow limits over several centuries. However, changes are apparent along other core dimensions. First, the overall decline in homicide rates regularly appears to coincide with a decline in the proportion of male-to-male killings. In a similar vein, the drop appears to be inversely related to a (relative) increase in family homicides. Finally, evidence suggests that the overall drop in homicide rates may have been accompanied by a gradual withdrawal of elites from interpersonal violence.

A. Sex of Offenders

Among contextual characteristics of violent crime, the sex distribution of offenders is the most obvious starting point. This information should be ascertainable from any historical source that provides offenders' first names. Unfortunately, however, many historical studies on crime do not present individual-level data, and only recently have historians of crime become interested in variability in gender ratios among offenders. In this respect, research by Feeley and Little (1991) and Feeley (1994) has exposed fascinating observations on historical variation in overall female participation rates. Feeley and Little (1991) first examined Old Bailey Sessions Papers from 1687 to 1912. They found that women constituted well over one-third of the caseload during the eighteenth century, after which the proportion steadily declined to about 10 percent around 1900. Feeley (1994) reviewed a number of studies that had examined female criminality in early modern Europe. He found a pattern that should be surprising for those who believe, with Gottfredson and Hirschi (1990, p. 45), that gender differences are invariant over time and space. Research on urban areas in the eighteenth-century Netherlands shows that women accounted for up to 75 percent of the criminal cases. And even after discounting the various types of "moral offenses," the figures remain high and striking. In Amsterdam, women comprise 50 percent of the persons accused of property offenses, and similar proportions were found in other northern European cities (van de Pol 1987; Diederiks 1990). Feeley (1994, p. 263) argues that the exceptionally high involvement of women in property crime—found in many eighteenth-century urban areas throughout northern Europe—reflects their high participation in the preindustrial mercantile economy. As production shifted away from the family to the factory, however, women were again relegated to the home, which in turn may explain their gradual retreat from property crime throughout the nineteenth century.

A series of estimates for the percentage of female offenders from 1200 to 2000 show that female involvement in violent crime has been much less susceptible to social change. Records across Europe over 800 years consistently show that the proportion of women committing homicide (excluding infanticide), assault, or robbery was hardly ever above 15 percent and typically ranged between 5 and 12 percent. Table 3 summarizes the major findings. Exceptions most probably result from problems in classifications (e.g., inclusion of verbal insult in assault) rather than real differences.

TABLE 3

Female Offenders as a Percentage of All Offenders in Various Historical Studies

Region	Assault	Robbery	Homicide	Property Crime	Source
Fourteenth–sixteenth centuries:					
England, 1202–76	...	...	8.6	...	Given (1977, p. 48)
England, various counties, 1300–1348	...	5.1	7.0	9.8	Hanawalt (1979, p. 118)
Cracau, 1361–1405	1.0	.0	1.0*	10.0	Schüssler (1998, p. 313)
Zurich, 1376–85	1.4	...	...	4.0	Burghartz (1990, p. 80)
Avignon, 1372	21.0†	...	...	23.7	Chiffoleau (1984, p. 250)
Arras, 1400–1436	13.7‡	...	...		Muchembled (1992, pp. 34, 89)
	4.6§				
Constance, 1430–60	4.7	...	.0*	17.2	Schuster (2000, p. 71)
Douai, 1496–1519	...	...	1.0	...	Fouret (1984)
Amsterdam, 1490–1552	14.0	...	3.0	15.0	Boomgaard (1992)
Arras, 1528–49	5.0	...	...	20.0	Muchembled (1992, pp. 34, 89)
Brussels, 1500–1600	8.2	...	...	7.4	Vanhemelryck (1981, p. 314)
Cologne, 1568–1612	4.4	4.7	5.7*	22.9	Schwerhoff (1995, p. 91)
Seventeenth and eighteenth centuries:					
Rural areas near Trier, late sixteenth to early eighteenth centuries	12.3	4.5	3.7*	5.2	Lacour (2000, p. 535)
Castile, 1623–99	...	...	1.4*	...	Chaulet (1997, p. 17)

Bavaria, 1600–1649	4.5	…	2.9*	12.4	Behringer (1995, p. 65)
Bavaria, 1685–89	5.0	.0	4.5*	13.2	Behringer (1995, p. 67)
Surrey, 1663–1802	18.2	7.9	13.0	23.9	Beattie (1975, p. 81)
Leiden, 1678–1794	7.8	41.0||	5.5*	47.3	Kloek (1990, p. 8)
Gent, 1700–1789	10.2	…	…	24.6	Roets (1982)
Stockholm, 1708–18	41.0	…	43.0	67.0	Andersson (1995)
Alençon, northern France, 1715–45	20.0	…	…	33.5	Champin (1972)
Armagh, Ireland, 1736–95	6.5	…	7.6	9.7	Garnham (1996)
Neuchatel, 1707–1806	6.2	…	…	14.7	Henry (1984, p. 660)
Nice, 1736–92	…	…	3.0	…	Eleuche-Santini (1979)
Rural northern Germany, 1680–1795	3.5	…	…	18.5	Frank (1995, p. 235)
Late nineteenth-century Germany	8.0	…	16.0	…	von Mayr (1917, p. 754)
Late twentieth century:					
England and Wales, 1997	14.7	8.5	11.9*	23.0	Home Office (1998)
Italy, 1998	16.0	6.9	5.2	15.2	Istituto Nazionale di Statistica (2000)
Germany, 1997	12.0	7.5	10.0*	23.0	Bundeskriminalamt (1998)
United States, 1997	15.0	8.0	10.0	32.0	Federal Bureau of Investigation (1998)

* Infanticide explicitly excluded.
† Includes insult.
‡ Minor assault only.
§ Serious assault only.
|| Includes pickpocketing.

This is not the place to discuss the causes of that apparent long-term stability. But accepting these data as reasonably valid estimates of involvement in violent crime probably means that sex is not a relevant variable in explaining the decline in overall levels of serious violence. Neither increasing economic prosperity, historical variation in female participation in the labor market, nor changing cultural models of the family and gender roles appear to have had a significant impact on male predominance in serious violent crime.

There is one major exception to this pattern. In early eighteenth-century Stockholm, women not only accounted for more than 60 percent of property crime offenders but also 45 percent of murder and manslaughter offenders and 41 percent of assault offenders (Andersson 1995). These are probably the highest female participation rates in serious violent crime found anywhere in the world. Scholars examining this phenomenon emphasize a combination of factors including—besides demographic imbalance—a highly specific cultural configuration, which embraced some kind of otherworldly calculus. More particularly, for fear of eternal punishment in hell, suicidal women appear often to have chosen to kill somebody else, usually their offspring, and then suffer the death penalty imposed on them by the judiciary (Jansson 1998). Homicide would bring them to purgatory for a limited period of time, after which they would enter heaven for eternity, which was definitely to be preferred to consignment to eternal hell because of suicide.

B. Age of Offenders

If sex differences have remained more or less constant over 800 years, variability in age patterns should attract scholarly curiosity. Hirschi and Gottfredson's seminal 1983 article precipitated a heated debate among criminologists (see, e.g., Baldwin 1985; Greenberg 1985, 1994; Steffensmeier and Streifel 1991). Hirschi and Gottfredson argued that the age curve of criminal offending is basically invariant across time and place, demographic groups, and social and cultural conditions. Various researchers have produced evidence with the intent of showing the contrary. The debate may be said to have resulted in a stalemate. Studies convincingly suggest that police-recorded offenders in the past two decades tend to be somewhat younger than, for example, in the 1950s (see, e.g., Steffensmeier et al. 1989; Junger-Tas 1991). However, the variability of the age-crime curve appears to remain within relatively narrow limits, and the overall shape does not appear fundamentally to differ between different subperiods of modernity.

It therefore is useful to explore age patterns in violent crime before the onset of criminal statistics. However, important limitations of such an effort should first be noted. Above all, age was not generally recorded before the seventeenth century, and most early sources offer no information whatsoever about offenders' ages. Second, historians of crime have not been particularly interested in the age variable (with the notable exception of King 2000, pp. 169 ff.). Hence, very few studies on crime in the seventeenth and the eighteenth centuries include relevant analyses, although the information is probably available in many primary sources. Third, even when historians have gathered data on age, the age structure of the underlying population is almost always unknown, thus making estimation of rates per population impossible.

These limitations notwithstanding, the existing evidence offers some necessarily crude but nevertheless noteworthy insights. The earliest evidence that I could find refers to early sixteenth-century Douai, a city located in the northeast of modern France close to the Belgian border (Fouret 1987). The archives include information on the ages of some 100 out of 623 indicted violent offenders and their victims. The average age of violent offenders in this sample was 26.6 years, while victims had a mean age of 29.6 years. If these figures represent the overall age structure of violent offenders in sixteenth-century Douai, their similarity with modern data is astonishing. In the United States in 1999, the average age of homicide offenders was 28.6 years, and the age of victims was 32.3 years. A study by Wikström (1985) on violent crime in Stockholm in the 1980s found a mean age of 31 years for offenders and 34 years for the victims. Thus, not only is the age difference between offenders and victims almost identical (three years), but there may also be little difference in the effective mean age, since we can safely assume that the average population was considerably younger in the sixteenth century.

This is corroborated by other evidence. I found four studies that include data on the distribution of violent offenders in the period before the onset of statistics. The earliest details the age of more than 85 percent of the 1,500 offenders delivered to jail in the Duchy of Mantova in northern Italy at the end of the sixteenth century (Romani 1980). These data include all offenders, but violent offenses constitute 40 percent of the total. A second age distribution is based on a small sample of eighty-three people publicly punished for wounding and attacking in the city of Amsterdam between 1651 and 1749 (Spierenburg 1984, p. 321). The third series, based on data presented in Ruff (1984, p. 90), concerns persons convicted for physical violence in two *sénéchaussées* in southwestern France near Bordeaux in the period 1696–1789. The fourth age distribution comes from a study by Champin (1972) of 230 violent offenders indicted in the rural community of Alençon in Britanny between 1715 and 1745.

Some of these studies use detailed age brackets. For comparative reasons, however, I recalculated all distributions for ten-year intervals. Figure 10 shows the average percentage of offenders per year of age in the respective age group. Overwhelmingly, the data show a very similar pattern, with roughly 35–45 percent of the offenders in the twenty-to-twenty-nine-year age group and a steady decline thereafter. Certainly, one should bear in mind that these data may be imprecise in themselves and that no correction for the age distribution of the population could be made. The extent to which these data support the notion of an "invariant" age curve of violent offending is open to debate. Future research may come up with more detailed data allowing for a more elaborate assessment of the age-violence relationship in

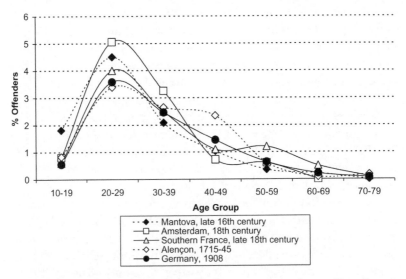

Fɪɢ. 10.—Age distribution of violent offenders across time and space. Note: Persons convicted of assault in 1908 in Germany added for comparative reasons. Sources: Mantova: Romani 1980; Amsterdam: Spierenburg 1984, p. 321; southern France: Ruff 1984, p. 90; Alençon: Champin 1972, p. 55; Germany: von Mayr 1917, p. 766.

early modern Europe. However, at present, one may cautiously conclude that evidence from six different areas in Europe and extending over a period of some 400 years shows a strikingly similar overall pattern. If this finding can be generalized, we may conclude that historical variation in overall levels in serious violence does not covary with differences in the age distribution of violent offenders. That would imply that changing cultural definitions of youth and young adulthood, changing marriage patterns, or varying economic prospects for young men did not result in major changes of the age distribution of serious violent offenders.

C. Social Status of Offenders

Class is the third primary variable used to describe demographic characteristics of violent offenders. Research in contemporary society consistently shows that serious violent offenders are heavily overrepresented among socially disadvantaged groups. Historical studies on the nineteenth century tell a very similar story, even if the official statistics of the time are likely to have a stronger class bias. About 50 percent of a sample of assailants indicted in Bedfordshire between 1750 and 1840 were recorded as laborers or servants (Emsley 1996, p. 45). Similarly, in late nineteenth-century German crime statistics, offenders from a working-class background were more strongly overrepresented for aggravated assault and homicide than for any other crime (Johnson 1995, p. 208).

Many contemporary historians of crime have been strongly interested in retrieving information about the social background of offenders recorded in the written sources. Examination of these studies yields a surprisingly consistent pattern. During the Middle Ages, interpersonal physical violence was not at all a class-specific phenomenon. Only to the degree that overall levels of violence fell throughout the early modern age did violence become correlated with class.

Ruggiero (1980) has done probably the most thorough analysis of the social status of premodern violent offenders. In a detailed study of violence in Venice between 1324 and 1406, he was able to identify the social standing of more than 1,600 offenders dealt with by the secular judicial authorities. He distinguishes four groups in Venetian society, for which he also provides estimates of their approximate share of the total population. The nobility, a group demarcated by its access to political power, accounted for about 4 percent of the population. Below it came a group of "important people," which included merchants,

TABLE 4

Social Status of Violent Offenders in Early Renaissance Venice,
1324–1406

	Type of Crime					
	Speech (%)	Assault (%)	Rape (%)	Murder (%)	Total (%)	Population (%)*
Nobles	35	22	20	4	18	4
Important people	8	11	8	9	9	10
Workers	52	61	65	70	63	75
Marginal people	5	5	7	16	9	8
Number of cases	223	566	416	424	1,629	

Source.—Data based on Ruggiero 1980.

* Clerics, who may have constituted 3 percent of the population, are not included in these figures. Therefore, population total is less than 100 percent. Clerics were not referred to the secular courts.

professionals, and civil officials, and which constituted some 10 percent of the population. Below them came the large group of workers and artisans, such as laborers in the textile industry, butchers, bakers, and marine workers, who may have totaled 75 percent of the population. At the bottom end came the marginal people, vagabonds and beggars, who may have been about 8 percent of the population. Ruggiero's data show the relative shares of these groups among the cases of recorded violence, which may be roughly compared with their respective share in the total population (see table 4). The data suggest that people of lower standing were not overrepresented among violent offenders and that nobles had a highly overproportionate share in all but homicide cases. As Ruggiero points out, these data may be considerably skewed since much violence among the lower classes may have gone unnoticed or have been handled with summary justice without leaving traces in the records (Ruggiero 1980, p. 96). Nonetheless, disregarding the evidence from nonlethal violence and assuming some unnoticed lower class murders still leaves the impression that the higher ranks of fourteenth-century Venetian society engaged in their fair share of violent behavior. In addition, upper-class people seemingly victimized people of lower standing more often than vice versa, which again contrasts strikingly with modern patterns. Nobles, it appears, did not scruple to assault, rape, or kill people of lower standing.

Although probably unparalleled in their detail, these figures do not seem to be unusual. Several historians of medieval crime have found similar patterns. In thirteenth-century Bologna, 10 percent of 521 banishment cases for major crimes were urban magistrates and nobles, who were aptly labeled by the *popolo* government as rapacious wolves (Blanshei 1982, p. 123). In fourteenth-century Lyon, Gonthier (1993) observes a recurrent involvement of nobles in violent behavior, including the organization of gangs to revenge failures to comply with their interests. Also, tax returns of offenders in fifteenth-century Constance reveal that wealthy groups were at least as likely to engage in violent offending as the poor (Schuster 2000, p. 137). Hanawalt (1979, p. 131) found that members of the oligarchy in a small fourteenth-century English rural area committed about one-third of all homicides recorded in the Gaol Delivery Rolls (Hanawalt 1979, p. 131). She concluded that members of the higher status groups committed at least as much violence as lower classes since they were likely to become involved in conflicts over rights and goods, which, in the absence of reliable state control, often escalated into violent conflicts.

No one has yet attempted to provide comparative data on the social status of offenders across longer periods. Yet some evidence suggests that upper classes in northern Europe may have become more pacified and less prone to physical aggression from the sixteenth century onward. Spierenburg (1998), for example, argues that homicide rates declined in Amsterdam after 1620 because wealthy, churchgoing citizens renounced violence, while lower-class violence in the form of knife fighting remained undiminished. Similarly, Sharpe (1984, p. 95) assumes a gradual decline in the involvement of the upper class in criminal violence in the century after 1550.

In the south of Europe the retreat of the nobility from aggressive behavior appears to have occurred later. In the French Auvergne, a mountainous and very poor area, the decisive shift occurred between the beginning and the end of the eighteenth century, when the upper classes increasingly withdrew from violent behavior. This transformation was paralleled by the increasing acceptance, among the nobility, of merit and competence as core social values, to the detriment of honor and the military ethic (Cameron 1981, p. 202). Further south, late eighteenth-century Sardinia offers striking evidence (Doneddu 1991). Ridden by chronic banditry as well as the vendetta, Sardinia had an overall homicide rate of thirty-five to forty per 100,000 in the years 1767–89. During that period, members of the nobility were recorded for committing fifty-one homicides. Since the island's nobility counted some 6,000 members at that time, this puts their homicide rate at thirty-seven per 100,000, the same as the approximate rate in the total population.

If this interpretation of upper-class involvement in violent behavior, based on a few scattered studies, withstands further scrutiny, it may lead to an important generalization. The transition to lower overall levels of interpersonal criminal violence, one might hypothesize, was accompanied by an overproportional withdrawal of the elite from the use of physical aggression to seize and defend their interests.

D. Sex of Victims

Few studies on premodern homicide tell us anything about the sex distribution of the victims, although most judicial and nonjudicial sources presumably include relevant information. Although female criminality has increasingly become a topic of historical scholarship, no study has as yet systematically examined female victimization. The premodern homicide database only includes some thirty estimates of the proportion of female victims (see table 5).

Most of these estimates are based on work by Given (1977), Hanawalt (1979), Schüssler (1991, 1998), and Spierenburg (1996). The period up to the sixteenth century is covered by a comprehensive sample of data, including various counties in England and cities scattered throughout Europe north of the Alps. The pattern revealed is concordant in suggesting that male victims considerably outnumbered female victims. The average proportion of female homicide victims during the period between the thirteenth and the sixteenth centuries is 7 percent

TABLE 5

Average Estimates of Gender-Specific Victimization Rates before the Nineteenth Century

	Female Victims (percent)	Male/Female Ratio	Approximate Homicide Rate
Thirteenth–sixteenth centuries	7	12.5 : 1	≈30 per 100,000
Seventeenth century	13	6.7 : 1	≈8 per 100,000
Eighteenth century	27	2.7 : 1	≈3 per 100,000

Source.—History of Homicide Database.
Note.—All estimates refer to various regions in England, the Netherlands, Germany, and France.

and has a range of between 0 and 20 percent. From a criminological perspective, this figure conveys an air of inevitability. At the beginning of the twentieth century, Verkko (1951, p. 52) examined the proportions of female victims in countries with high homicide rates (Finland, Serbia, Bulgaria, Italy, and Chile). The average proportion of female victims in these countries was 7 percent, the same as the medieval pattern.

Only a few relevant observations are available for the seventeenth and eighteenth centuries. Those suggest that the proportion of female homicide victims increased as the overall level of lethal violence declined throughout northern Europe. National death statistics for various countries corroborate these findings. Trends in overall homicide rates appear to concur with shifts in the male-to-female victim ratio, thus confirming the "dynamic law" put forth by Verkko (1951, p. 52), which holds that fluctuations in overall homicide rates primarily result from variation in male victimization rates. Generally, the shift toward lower homicide rates appears to have been primarily—but not exclusively—a drop in male-to-male violent encounters.

E. Personal Relationship between Offender and Victim

This finding can be further substantiated by examining another variable, the relationship between offender and victim. A number of studies have examined the proportions of homicides involving family members (spouses, offspring, and parents). Table 6 shows a series of estimates from the thirteenth through the twentieth centuries that can be fleshed out with qualitative evidence on circumstances likely to result in a (recorded) killing.

The data suggest that the proportion of family homicides was very low throughout the Middle Ages. Typically, the killing of family members made up less than 10 percent in medieval societies. In contrast, a large proportion of cases occurred in situations of conflict between (primarily male) acquaintances, with the offender and the victim often sharing a similar social background or being neighbors in a rural community. Not only in fourteenth-century Oxford, did "quick tempers, strong drink, and the ready availability of weapons" contribute to the great frequency of homicides among men (Hammer 1978, p. 20). In many urban areas, the tavern was the place where violence occurred. In sixteenth-century Arras, 45 percent of ninety recorded homicides were committed in or just outside taverns (Muchembled 1992, p. 94). Likewise, about half of all violent crimes in sixteenth-century Douai,

TABLE 6

Proportion of Homicides against Members of the Family in Various Historical Periods

	Period	Family Homicide (percent)	Homicide Rate	Source
Thirteenth–sixteenth centuries:				
England, various counties	Thirteenth century	5	22.0	Given (1977, p. 144)
England, various counties	1300–1348	2–8	35.0	Hanawalt (1979, p. 159)
Germany, Nurnberg	1285–1400	9	14.0	Schüssler (1991, p. 174)
England, Huntingdonshire	1286	5	20.0	DeWindt and DeWindt (1981, p. 54)
Seventeenth century:				
Essex	1620–80	15	6.0	Sharpe (1983, p. 126)
Amsterdam	1651–1700	11	3.9	Spierenburg (1994, p. 710)
Kent	Seventeenth century	26	4.5	Cockburn (1991)
Castile	1623–99	12	35.0	Chaulet (1997, p. 20)
Eighteenth century:				
Amsterdam	1701–50	14	10.0	Spierenburg (1994, p. 710)
Amsterdam	1751–1810	48	6.0	Spierenburg (1994, p. 710)
Kent	Eighteenth century	28	2.0	Cockburn (1991)
Surrey	1678–1774	36	4.0	Beattie (1986, p. 105)
Nineteenth century, England	1850s–1860s	55	1.0	Emsley (1996, p. 43)
Twentieth century:				
England and Wales	1998	39	1.4	Home Office (2000)
Germany	1996	30	1.4	Bundeskriminalamt (1997)

and probably an even greater proportion in Cologne, occurred in the context of alcohol drinking (Schwerhoff 1991). In a similar vein Sharpe argues, summarizing the English evidence, that "Stuart homicides were characteristically unplanned acts of violence arising spontaneously from quarrels, being simple assaults that went too far in most cases" (Sharpe 1983, p. 131).

However, many historians point out that what seems to have been impulsive and spontaneous violence often was more culturally guided than might first be suspected. Male honor seems to have played an important role here. Thus Liliequist (1999, p. 197) finds that boxing ears, issuing challenges, fighting and combat interrupted by temporary reconciliation, and drinking rituals constituted the pattern of a culture of fighting, which was the backdrop of the vast majority of homicide cases in early modern Scandinavia. Hence, insults constituted a serious affront and a large class of crimes dealt with by any court of medieval and early modern society; throughout Europe knife fighting appears to have been the appropriate reaction if efforts for reconciliation failed.

During the transition to lower overall homicide rates, however, the relative share of family killings appears to have increased continuously, which in turn suggests that overt public fights between men resulting in serious injury became progressively less frequent. Knife fighting, for example, became restricted to the lower classes in late seventeenth-century Amsterdam and all but disappeared as a distinct culture of violence by the late eighteenth century (Spierenburg 1998). In a similar vein, the decline of homicide in late nineteenth-century Italy, to a large extent, probably resulted from the disappearance of public fights between men over issues of honor. The decline of private revenge and the vendetta—an almost exclusively male prerogative, too—also appear to be associated with the overall drop in homicide rates. In countries such as England or Sweden, as a result, family homicide accounted for more than half of the killings by the end of the nineteenth century, when the overall level of homicide rates was at most one-tenth of that before the sixteenth century.

The patterns with respect to homicide victims' sex and the relation between offenders and victims suggest another far-reaching generalization. Declines in homicide rates primarily resulted from some degree of pacification of encounters in public space, a reluctance to engage in physical confrontation over conflicts, and the waning of honor as a cultural code regulating everyday behavior.

III. Theoretical Approaches

Gurr's (1981) original study, though innovative in its pathbreaking synthesis of empirical developments, has little to offer by way of theoretical interpretation. Stating that the long-term decline can be explained by "the rise of nonaggressive modes of behavior" (Gurr, p. 304) and a sensitization to violence amounts to little more than re-phrasing and describing the empirical pattern. Since then many historians of crime, nourished by the flow of empirical findings, have developed and debated theories that might explain the long-term trends.

The following discussion is based on two prior decisions: first, any theoretical discussion of the trend in violent crime must assume that it describes real changes in behavior rather than methodological artifacts or consequences of the operations of criminal justice systems. There is still debate about this, but many historians of crime accept the basic inferences drawn here from existing data. Second, there is debate over whether the observed patterns require local and specific interpretations of manifestations of violence or whether we may profitably attempt to develop general theories. A large part of the craft of historical research consists in meticulous analysis of specific historical sources resulting in rich and thick descriptions of some historical reality, sometimes at the detriment of theoretical generalization. One might argue, for example, that the declining trend in seventeenth-century Sweden requires a wholly different explanation from the drop observed in nineteenth-century Italy. The following discussion, however, starts from the premise that the existing evidence asks for a generalizing theory, which takes into account commonalities across large geographic spaces.

These general patterns, partly resting on admittedly shaky empirical evidence, may be summarized in five points. First, in the long run, there appears to have been little change in the sex and age structure of serious violent offenders. Second, serious interpersonal criminal violence has declined considerably over the past six centuries throughout Europe. The decline probably started as early as the fifteenth century, but it is well documented for the long period between the early seventeenth and the mid-twentieth centuries. Third, areas in Europe appear to differ in respect of the timing and pace of the drop in serious violence. The process may have started earliest in the Netherlands and England; in Sweden, the main transition may have occurred between the early seventeenth and mid-eighteenth centuries; and in Italy, homicide rates dropped dramatically only from the mid-nineteenth century onward. Fourth, historically, high overall levels of violence appear to be associated with high levels of elite involvement in physical violence. Drops in lethal violence were disproportionately related to a decline in elite violence. Fifth, in any high-homicide society, the majority of cases are male-to-male encounters, often between people of similar social status, arising out of situational conflicts involving clashes over honor, property, or other entitlements. Sustained declines in homicide rates, in turn, are accompanied by some degree of pacification of interactions in public space.

A. The Theory of the Civilizing Process

Theories may be suspected of being good theories if they predict something that is corroborated by ensuing empirical work. For this reason, the work of Elias (1976, 1983) provides the most prominent theoretical framework discussed by historians of crime who are interested in explaining the decline in homicide rates. Elias's theory of the civilizing process, developed in the 1930s and primarily introduced into the history of crime and punishment research by Spierenburg (1984, 1995), embraces long-term social dynamics at a macrolevel as well as changes in typical psychological traits and developments in characteristic modes of behavior at a psychological microlevel.

At the microlevel, the theory of the civilizing process holds that, over a period of several centuries, personality structures have become transformed in a distinct cumulative direction. The change is characterized by an increasing affect control, a greater emphasis on long-term planning, a rationalized manner of living, a higher reflexive sensitivity to inner psychological states and processes, and a decreasing impulsivity—in brief, higher levels of self-control. Higher levels of self-control imply, in turn, the gradual pacification of everyday interactions, which becomes manifest in lower levels of violent behavior. The idea that, on the personality level, criminal violence is the result of low self-control should be an attractive starting point to (many) criminologists. Many empirical studies now convincingly show that, in contemporary society, violent and serious offending strongly correlates with a tendency to seek immediate gratification, a tendency toward risk-seeking behavior, a high level of impulsivity, and an indifference to the needs of others (Gottfredson and Hirschi 1990, p. 90; Farrington 1998). For the historical past, a direct measurement of personality structures is obviously impossible. But assuming causal mechanisms at a microlevel that do not contradict current criminological knowledge certainly constitutes an advantage for theorizing about long-term macrolevel dynamics.

The overlap between the theory of the civilizing process and current criminological thinking ends, however, with the question of why and how levels of self-control may differ. Criminology has as yet offered pitifully little on this subject. Elias, by contrast, proposes a coherent sociological theory. This is partly because of a difference in focus. Elias was not interested in individual-level variation in self-control, found in every society, but, rather, in explaining historical variation in population averages. On the most general level, he argues that these changes result from the internalization of outer social control, which, in turn, results from the increasing interdependency between social actors. Higher interdependency in complex and extended chains of interaction—buttressed by stable social institutions—promotes self-control, since it creates advantages for those able to dampen affect and rationally plan their behavior (Elias 1978, p. 322).

Two interrelated macrolevel dynamics promote this long-term change since the Middle Ages: the expansion of the state with its monopoly on violence and the extension of the market economy resulting in increasing functional interdependency. In respect of the first factor, Elias argues that the elites of the knightly warrior societies of the Middle Ages gradually became transformed in the sixteenth and seventeenth centuries into relatively pacified court societies, where violence came to be monopolized by central authorities. The decisive factor was the rise of monarchic absolutism, in which the state monopoly of power over a large territorial unit was accomplished to a high degree (Elias 1976, p. 353). The nobility lost its bellicose functions, which in turn facilitated the rise of complex economic and social chains of interdependency. As a result, courtly manners became increasingly differentiated, refined, and civilized. This culture of the nobility then gradually diffused from its very center to other social groups and strata. In regard to the effects of functional interdependency, Elias basically relied on classical Enlightenment ideas. The view that increasing commercialized exchanges of goods and services creates incentives for restraint from violence was commonplace among liberal thinkers. Adam Smith, for example, assumed that "commerce and manufactures gradually introduced order and good government, and with them, the liberty and security of individuals, among the inhabitants of the country, who had before lived in a continual state of war with their neighbors, and of servile dependency upon their superiors" (quoted in Beattie 1986, p. 137).

Some historians of crime, such as Spierenburg (1996), accept Elias's wide-ranging theoretical model of the rise of European modernity. Others refute the model as insufficient (Schuster 2000). Many, however, view the theory of the civilizing process as a fruitful point of departure (Österberg 1996; Sharpe 1996). Thus, if nothing else, most historians of crime would probably agree that the long-term trajectory in homicide rates is an indicator of a wider dynamic that encompasses some sort of pacification of interaction in public space. Beattie, for example, when commenting on the decline of homicide in England between 1660 and 1800, notes that

> men and women would seem to have become more controlled, less likely to strike out when annoyed or challenged, less likely to settle an argument or assert their will by recourse to a knife or their fists, a pistol, or a sword. The court record suggests that other ways of resolving conflicts became increasingly favored and that men became more prepared to negotiate and to talk out their differences. This supposes a developing civility, expressed perhaps in a more highly developed politeness of manner and a concern not to offend or to take offense, and an enlarged sensitivity toward some forms of cruelty and pain. (1986, p. 112)

But the problem that divides scholars is the identification of the causal factors that have brought about sensitization to violence.

B. Social Control

Exploring the notion that there may be a link, however indirect and complex, between the rise of bureaucratic state structures and the decline of violence, several historians of crime have become interested in changing patterns of judicial and social control. Two strands of inquiry can be distinguished. First, scholars have paid progressively more attention to immediate patterns of official attitudes to homicide and violence, including prosecution and punishment. Second, changes in the wider context of social control over everyday behavior may constitute an important element for understanding the secular change in violent interpersonal behavior.

In regard to official attitudes toward homicide, a decisive shift occurs during the sixteenth century (Rousseaux 1999*a*). During the late Middle Ages, although official authorities had become increasingly involved in the regulation of lethal interpersonal violence, homicide was regarded with lenience if it was perceived as the result of passion or occurred in defense of honor. Only the most premeditated cases of murder invariably required the death penalty (see, e.g., Blanshei 1982, p. 125). However, when the peace between two families was broken because of a mortal aggression, retaliation by means of private vengeance was still regarded, in popular perception, as a legitimate pathway to reestablish order. Increasingly, however, the parties would be likely to resort to the courts, where peace treaties comprising a wergild payable to the victim's family could be accomplished. In England, because of early unification under the Normans, jurisdiction of homicide was the exclusive prerogative of the crown within the jurisdiction of the royal courts. This led to the normative distinction of three categories of homicide, namely, culpable homicide punishable by the death penalty; excusable homicide, which could be pardoned by the crown with a letter of pardon; and justifiable homicide, which was liable to be acquitted by a jury.

Between the sixteenth and the seventeenth centuries in continental Europe, settlement fell out of the hands of families and into the hands of judges and sovereigns whose aim was to deliver punishment rather than to reconcile factious families. Only then, Rousseaux (1999*a*, p. 154) argues, did homicide invariably become seen as a crime and the offender as a criminal; its perceived character shifted from an unfortunate accident to a rigorously repressed heinous crime. Manifestations of this change can been found throughout Europe. In Zurich, for example, the concept of honorable manslaughter, punishable by a penalty only, became the object of intensive judicial conflict and political negotiation between 1480 and 1530, when the primacy of "urban peace" finally won out over the notion of legitimate defense of honor (Pohl 1999). For the small city of Nivelles, the origins of a new model of social control can be traced to the period between 1520 and 1530, when "the aim is no more to re-establish peace between the citizens but to subordinate the subjects to the social order determined by the prince" (Rousseaux 1999*b*, p. 266). In Germany, too, evidence suggests that private reconciliation had become an unusual way of settling homicide by the end of the sixteenth century (Schwerhoff 1991, p. 280). Rousseaux argues that more rigorous repression may have played a role in the decline of homicide in early modern Europe: "Mortal aggression became the object of a campaign of 'moralization' and 'civilization' around the sixteenth and seventeenth centuries, between the religious wars and the Thirty Years War. This undertaking was visible mainly in the development of criminal law and in the growing sophistication of legal definitions as well as in the emergence of homicide as a matter for the gallows. This undertaking was relatively successful if we take into account the drop in the number of homicides and the virtual disappearance of private dispute settlements" (Rousseaux 1999*a*, p. 157).

However, the replacement of the primacy of private reconciliation by the dominance of state repression was embedded in a much wider pattern of increasing social control. From the mid-sixteenth century onward, social historians find a wave of intensified magisterial social control spreading throughout Europe that restructured the relationship between the state and its citizenry. It included the creation of more centralized administrative and judicial organizations, the greater continuity of bureaucratic intrusions into everyday life, and the construction and expansion of professional armies (Tilly 1992). Particularly, this period saw a flood of ordinances regarding feasts, child rearing, appropriate clothing, consumption of alcohol, and church attendance (Oestreich 1968, 1982). Together, these activities resulted in an acceleration of social disciplining, a process that can be seen as the result of complex interactions among different social, political, and economic forces (Dülmen 1993, 1996). The consolidation of state power is only one of them. Yet factors such as the increased religious zeal following the Reformation movements, the expansion of literacy and schooling, and early capitalist organization of work constitute independent sources of the disciplining process in the early modern age. Their similar effects on the structures of the self were both to enforce self-control rigidly and to provide the cultural and social resources needed for a more orderly conduct of life.

C. Limitations of the "State Control" Model

Strangely one-sided in respect to the role of the state as an internally pacifying institution, Elias almost exclusively emphasizes the state's coercive potential exercised through the subordination of other power holders and bureaucratic control. Echoing the old Hobbesian theme, the decline in interpersonal violence should thus develop out of increased state control. Although the long-term expansion of the state and the decline of lethal violence appear to correlate nicely on the surface, a closer look reveals several inconsistencies. Muchembled (1996), for example, points out that the decline of homicide rates in early modern Europe does not appear to correspond with the rise of the absolutist state. Rather, he argues, the example of the Low Countries shows that homicide rates declined in polities where centralized power structures never emerged and the political system much more resembled a loose association of largely independent units. Neither does intensified policing nor the harsh regime of public corporal punishment, both probably the most immediate manifestations of state power in any premodern society, seem to aid understanding of the trajectories into lower levels of homicide rates. Police forces in medieval and early modern Italian cities were surprisingly large—Schwerhoff (1991, p. 61) cites per capita figures of between 1 : 145 and 1 : 800—but they did not effectively suppress everyday violence. Furthermore, no historian seems to believe that the popularity of the scaffold and the garrote among sixteenth- and seventeenth-century European rulers decisively reduced crime.

Rather, the Italian case exemplifies a more general problem. For whatever the deficiencies of early modern Italian states may have been, they were certainly not characterized by a lesser overall level of state bureaucracy and judicial control than, for example, states in England or Sweden during the same period (see, e.g., Brackett 1992). England was not centralized in bureaucratic terms, and the physical means of coercion, in terms of armed forces, were slight (Sharpe 1996, p. 67). The mere rise of more bureaucratic and centralized state structures thus hardly seems to account for the increasingly divergent development of homicide rates in northern and southern Europe. Examining Rome, Blastenbrei (1995, p. 284) argues that the divergence may, rather, be related to the evolution of different models of the relationship between the state and civil society. While northern European societies were increasingly characterized by a gradually increasing legitimacy for the state as an overarching institution, the South was marked by a deep rupture between the population and the state authorities. In respect to state control, Roth emphasizes a similar point when examining the massive drop in homicide rates in New England from 1630 to 1800: "The sudden decline in homicide did not correlate with improved economic circumstances, stronger courts, or better policing. It did, however, correlate with the rise of intense feelings of Protestant and racial solidarity among the colonists, as two wars and a revolution united the formerly divided colonists against New England's native inhabitants, against the French, and against their own Catholic Monarch, James II" (2001, p. 55).

Both Roth and Blastenbrei emphasize, from different angles, a sociological dimension whose importance for understanding the long-term decline in serious violence has not yet been systematically explored, namely, mutual trust and the legitimacy of the state as foundations for the rise of civil society. Both are, of course, clearly to be distinguished from the coercive potential of the state—strong states in terms of coercion can be illegitimate, while seemingly weak states may enjoy high legitimacy. And on the level of macro-transhistorical comparison, the decline of homicide rates appears to correspond more with integration based on trust than with control based on coercion.

Intertwined with the rise of legitimate state structures and political integration, honor probably is an important concept to consider systematically. Much research emphasizes the crucial role of insults in triggering situational conflicts in medieval or early modern societies. Indeed, insult constituted a major class of criminal offenses, frequently brought to court and often resulting in severe fines to be paid to the victim. This is in accordance with a society in which "honor" constituted a highly important symbolic, and therefore also economic, resource to be legally protected and publicly regulated (Muchembled 1984; Burghartz 1990; Schwerhoff 1991; Schuster 1995). It required retributive violence as a potential and culturally accepted means for maintaining one's honor (Schmidt 1994). In late fourteenth-century Zurich, for example, the butcher Welti Oechen stabbed another butcher in a quarrel (Pohl 1999). The judges decided that the case had been an "honorable manslaughter," because the victim had insulted Oechen by alleging that the Oechen family were villains. The offender had to pay a fine to the victim's family and is known to have continued to live a respectable life thereafter. The example is similar to many others found in late medieval records.

Homicide here seems to originate in the necessity to react personally to any challenge to one's reputation or honor, which is persistently found in any high-violence society; the judicial reaction is based on accepting the legitimacy—not necessarily the legality—of the course of action taken by the offender. The long-term decline in violence, in turn, appears to have been consistently paralleled by the loss of the cultural significance of honor. From about the mid-seventeenth century in northern Europe, verbal violence—blasphemy, slander, and insult—began to cause much less alarm, and rashly spoken statements, formerly regarded as unwitting but inevitable revelations of nefarious purposes, lost their awful significance (Soman 1980). The gradual withdrawal of honor from constituting a symbolic resource to be defended, if necessary, by physical force may be related to the expansion of reliable state structures. But cultural change may also have played an important role.

D. Culture

Culture, it is true, is an elusive concept, and explaining the decline in violence by an increasing sensitization to violence is not likely to be very helpful. However, systems of values and ideas, when embedded in social institutions, do have the potential of changing everyday routines and interaction patterns. But if cultural explanations of the long-term decline in serious violence are to be kept from being tautological, they must start with possible causes outside the more narrow subject matter of attitudes toward violence. This might include, for example, culturally transmitted and widely shared views of the role of the individual in society or assumptions about adequate patterns of child raising in the family. These, in turn, would then have to be shown to impinge directly on variables that can plausibly be assumed to correlate with violence.

At least two broad cultural streams in Western society may have been associated with the decline in interpersonal violence, namely, Protestantism and modern individualism. Max Weber (1922) interpreted the Protestant ethic primarily as a gigantic disciplining project that emphasized fulfillment of one's duty, sobriety and frugality, and a methodic conduct of life. Also, inner-directedness and a conscientious life were among the principal commands of early Protestantism, making relentless introspection and the cultivation of shame and guilt pervasive cultural goals, especially among the Puritan and Pietist strands of the Reformation. Furthermore, both Reformation and Counter Reformation brought about an encompassing wave of church religiosity, legitimating the intrusion of clerics into the private sphere but also serving as a backbone of increasing literacy and education.

The rise of modern individualism from the sixteenth century onward is interrelated with Protestantism but clearly distinguished from it (Dülmen 1997). It embraces the cultural diffusion of a specifically modern ideal of the self, which is characterized by "disengagement" and "inwardness" as its preeminent qualities (Taylor 1989). It implies

a methodological reflexive distance from the immediate outer and inner world and an orientation toward guiding ideals such as autonomy,
self-responsibility, and authenticity. This development, while following its own cultural and philosophical logic, is at the same time linked
to mutually reinforcing religious, political, economic, and artistic practices (Taylor 1989, p. 206). Examples include the permanent self-scru-
tiny of the religious reformation movements; the sharper delineation
of an independent, private sphere; the rise of a market based on contractual guarantees; and the production of art aimed toward individual
uniqueness.

Emile Durkheim—forty years earlier than Elias—explicitly assumed
that the rise of modern individualism may constitute a crucial variable
for explaining the long-term decline in lethal violence. He argued that
individual violence should always be interpreted as the "product of a
specific moral culture," which regulates the relationship between the
individual and society (Durkheim 1991). Hence, he interpreted the decline of homicide rates primarily as resulting from the liberation of the
individual from collective bonds. High levels of lethal violence mirror
the intensity of "collective emotions," which bind the individual to
"groups of things that symbolically represent these groups" (my trans-
lation, see Durkheim 1991, p. 161). He explicitly refers to the tradition
of the vendetta as an example. Violence thus declines to the degree
that the person becomes liberated from his or her sacred obligation to
the group, and individualism brings about both subjective reflexivity
and emotional indifference in conflict situations (Thome 1995, 2001).

Many specialized historians, when interpreting the contextual circumstances of declining levels of violence, find that culture change
may have been at least as important as state control or the extension
of economic networks. Commenting on the downturn of interpersonal
violence in Swedish cities after about 1630, Jarrick and Söderberg
(1993) emphasize that there is no concomitant increase in state intervention that could explain the shift. Rather, the decline appears to have
coincided with an increased concern, disseminated by the Lutheran
church, about the expiation of sin and an intensified attention to issues
of human dignity and empathy for the weak. Likewise, the decline in
serious violence in seventeenth- and eighteenth-century England appears to have been embedded in a distinct cultural climate where principles of Protestantism combined with notions of individual responsibility (Gaskill 2000, pp. 203 ff.). A pervasive culture of Protestantism,
disseminated through cheap print, embedded violence in a dense rhet-

oric of providence, sin, and repentance. Pamphlets and ballads told an interested audience about how murderers—"troubled in conscience"—felt remorse for their acts, how dying victims piously forgave their assailants, and how the justice of heaven and earth would combine to punish the evildoer.

To criminologists, the rise of moral individualism should not be an implausible candidate for explaining the fall in criminal violence. Rather, a large number of recent survey studies find that violence is correlated with low autonomy, unstable self-esteem, a high dependence on recognition by others, and limited competence in coping with conflict, which together may well be interpreted as subdimensions of low moral individualism (Agnew 1994; Baron and Richardson 1994; Heitmeyer 1995). To this we might add the hypothesis that the secular decline of lethal violence occurred when institutional structures and educational practices supported the stabilization of that type of individualized identity that is shaped to meet the challenges of modern life.

E. Conclusions

Considering the vast field—temporally, geographically, and theoretically—covered in this essay, it may be wise not to attempt an even more condensing conclusion. Rather, I am tempted to speculate about elements of further research that may help to clarify some of the issues pertaining to the long-term development of serious interpersonal violence in Western society. These suggestions are premised on the idea that more sophisticated theories and comparison of theories only make scientific sense to the degree that we dispose of detailed empirical data, which permit the appraisal of alternative explanations. It therefore seems obvious to ask for more and better data. There are several dimensions to this aim. First, we can improve our understanding of the accuracy and comparability of historical estimates of homicide rates. Monkkonen (2001) and Roth (2001) have proposed promising strategies, and it remains to be seen how far capture-recapture methods, better population estimates, or more broadly based information on the effects of improved medical technology can improve estimates of homicide rates. Second, as our knowledge of overall levels of lethal violence increases, it may become more important to examine developments in subtypes such as family homicide, infanticide, or robbery-related killings. Third, existing research has not yet fully explored historical variation in contextual variables. Qualitative dimensions are obviously important here. However, examining to a fuller extent quantifiable information about offenders, victims, and situations—possibly using some degree of standardized tools across studies—may also significantly contribute to our knowledge. Finally, it would be useful to fill in some of the blank spots on the geo-historical map of homicide in Europe. France and Spain are conspicuously missing, and more information about trends in Italy and different areas in the German-speaking parts of Europe would enrich comparative analyses.

Further empirical research may particularly profit from a more coherent set of theoretically based questions. Thus far, attempts at explanation were primarily post hoc interpretations in the light of cultural, social, and political covariates of the secular trend in homicide rates. But it might be fruitful to adopt systematically comparative perspectives in future research. Findings from social history research may provide, for example, indicators of historical and geographic variation in patterns of formal social control, levels of literacy, political conflict, and the commercialization of the economy. By comparing regions that systematically differ in these respects, we might be able to learn more about what variables contribute to changing levels of homicide.

REFERENCES

Agnew, Robert. 1994. "The Techniques of Neutralization and Violence." *Criminology* 32:555–80.

Andersson, Hans. 1995. "Genus och Rättskultur: Kvinnlig Brottslighet i stormaktstidens Stockholm." *Historisk Tidskrift* (Sweden) 2:129–59.

Aubusson de Cavarlay, Bruno. 2001. "Les limites intrinsèques du calcul de taux d'homicide: À propos des nouveaux standards proposés par Eric Monkkonen." *Crime, Histoire et Société—Crime, History and Society* 5(2):27–32.

Bairoch, Paul, Jean Batou, and Pierre Chèvre. 1988. *La population des villes européennes: Banque de données et analyse sommaire des résultats, 800–1850.* Geneva: Droz.

Baldwin, John. 1985. "Thrill and Adventure Seeking and the Age Distribution of Crime: Comment on Hirschi and Gottfredson." *American Journal of Sociology* 90(6):1326–29.

Baron, Robert A., and Deborah R. Richardson. 1994. *Human Aggression.* 2d ed. New York: Plenum.

Beattie, John M. 1974. "The Pattern of Crime in England, 1660–1800." *Past and Present* 62:47–95.

———. 1975. "The Criminality of Women in Eighteenth-Century England." *Journal of Social History* 8:80–116.

————. 1986. *Crime and the Courts in England, 1660–1800*. Oxford: Clarendon.

Becker, Marvin. 1976. "Changing Patterns of Violence and Justice in Fourteenth- and Fifteenth-Century Florence." *Comparative Studies in Society and History* 18:281–96.

Behringer, Wolfgang. 1990. "Mörder, Diebe, Ehebrecher: Verbrechen und Strafen in Kurbayern vom 16. bis 18. Jahrhundert." In *Verbrechen, Strafen und soziale Kontrolle*, edited by Richard van Dülmen. Frankfurt am Main: Suhrkamp.

————. 1995. "Weibliche Kriminalität in Kurbayern in der Frühen Neuzeit." In *Von Huren und Rabenmüttern: Weibliche Kriminalität in der frühen Neuzeit*, edited by Otto Ulbricht. Cologne: Böhlau.

Berents, Dirk Arend. 1976. *Misdaad in de Middeleeuwen: Een onderzoek naar de criminaliteit in het Laat-middeleeuwse Utrecht*. Utrecht: Stichtse historische Reeks.

Blanshei, Sarah R. 1981. "Criminal Law and Politics in Medieval Bologna." *Criminal Justice History* 2:1–30.

————. 1982. "Crime and Law Enforcement in Medieval Bologna." *Journal of Social History* 16:121–38.

Blastenbrei, Peter. 1995. *Kriminalität in Rom, 1560–1585*. Tübingen: Niemeyer.

Blauert, Andreas, and Gerd Schwerhoff, eds. 2000. *Kriminalitätsgeschichte: Beiträge zur Sozial- und Kulturgeschichte der Vormoderne*. Constance: Universitätsverlag Konstanz.

Blumstein, Alfred. 2000. "Disaggregating the Violence Trends." In *The Crime Drop in America*, edited by Alfred Blumstein and Joel Wallman. Cambridge: Cambridge University Press.

Boomgaard, Johannes Everardus Antonius. 1992. *Misdaad en straf in Amsterdam: Een onderzoek naar de strafrechtspleging van de Amsterdams schepenbank, 1490–1552*. Zwolle: Waanders.

Boschi, Daniele. 1998. "Homicide and Knife Fighting in Rome, 1845–1914." In *Men and Violence: Gender, Honor, and Rituals in Modern Europe and America*, edited by Pieter Spierenburg. Columbus: Ohio State University Press.

Brackett, John K. 1992. *Criminal Justice and Crime in Late Renaissance Florence, 1537–1609*. Cambridge: Cambridge University Press.

Buff, Otto. 1877. "Verbrechen und Verbrecher zu Augsburg in der zweiten Hälfte des 14. Jahrhunderts." *Zeitschrift des Historischen Vereins für Schwaben und Neuburg* 4:160–231.

Bundeskriminalamt. 1997. *Polizeiliche Kriminalstatistik Bundesrepublik Deutschland*. Wiesbaden: Bundeskriminalamt.

————. 1998. *Polizeiliche Kriminalstatistik Bundesrepublik Deutschland*. Wiesbaden: Bundeskriminalamt.

Burghartz, Susanna. 1990. *Leib, Ehre und Gut: Delinquenz in Zürich Ende des 14. Jahrhunderts*. Zurich: Chronos.

Cameron, Iain A. 1981. *Crime and Repression in the Auvergne and the Guyenne, 1720–1790*. Cambridge: Cambridge University Press.

Champin, Marie-Madeleine. 1972. "Un cas typique de justice baillagère: La criminalité dans le baillage d'Alençon de 1715 à 1745." *Annales de Normandie* 22(1):47–84.

Chaulet, Rudy. 1997. "La violence en Castille au XVIIe siècle à travers les Indultos de Viernes Santo (1623–1699)." *Crime, Histoire et Société—Crime, History and Society* 1(2):5–27.

Chesnais, Jean-Claude. 1981. *Histoire de la violence en Occident de 1800 à nos jours.* Paris: Laffont.

Chiffoleau, Jacques. 1984. *Les justices du pape: Délinquance et criminalité dans la région d'Avignon au XIVe siècle.* Paris: Publications de la Sorbonne.

Cockburn, J. S. 1977. "The Nature and Incidence of Crime in England, 1559–1625: A Preliminary Survey." In *Crime in England, 1550–1800,* edited by J. S. Cockburn. London: Methuen.

———. 1991. "Patterns of Violence in English Society: Homicide in Kent, 1560–1985." *Past and Present* 130:70–106.

Cohn, Samuel. 1980. "Criminality and the State in Renaissance Florence, 1344–1466." *Journal of Social History* 14(2):211–33.

Cuénod, John. 1891. *La criminalité à Genéve au XIX Siècle.* Geneva: Aubert-Schuchardt.

Daly, Martin, and Margo Wilson. 1988. *Homicide.* New York: de Gruyter.

de Vries, Jan. 1984. *European Urbanization, 1500–1800.* London: Methuen.

DeWindt, Anne R., and Edwin B. DeWindt, eds. and trans. 1981. *Royal Justice and the Medieval English Countryside: The Huntingdonshire Eyre of 1286, the Ramsey Abbey Banlieu Court of 1287, and the Assizes of 1287–88.* Toronto: Pontifical Institute of Mediaeval Studies.

Diederiks, Herman A. 1990. "Quality and Quantity in Historical Research in Criminality and Criminal Justice: The Case of Leiden in the 17th and 18th Centuries." *Historical Social Research—Historische Sozialforschung* 15(4):57–76.

Doneddu, Giuseppe. 1991. "Criminalità e società nella sardegna del secondo settecento." In *Criminalità e società in età moderna,* edited by Luigi Berlinguer and Floriana Colao. Milan: Guiffrè.

Dülmen, Richard van. 1985. *Theater des Schreckens: Gerichtspraxis und Strafrituale in der frühen Neuzeit.* Munich: Beck'sche Verlagsbuchhandlung.

———. 1993. *Gesellschaft der frühen Neuzeit: Kulturelles Handeln und sozialer Prozess: Beiträge zur historischen Kulturforschung.* Vienna: Böhlau.

———. 1996. "Norbert Elias und der Prozess der Zivilisation: Die Zivilisationstheorie im Lichte der historischen Forschung." In *Norbert Elias und die Menschenwissenschaften: Studien zur Entstehung und Wirkungsgeschichte seines Werkes,* edited by Karl-Siegbert Rehberg. Frankfurt am Main: Suhrkamp.

———. 1997. *Die Entdeckung des Individuums, 1500–1800.* Frankfurt am Main: Fischer.

Durkheim, Emile. 1973. *Le suicide: Étude de sociologie.* Paris: Presses Universitaires de France.

———. 1991. *Physik der Sitten und des Rechts: Vorlesungen zur Soziologie der Moral.* Frankfurt am Main: Suhrkamp.

Eisner, Manuel. 1995. "The Effects of Economic Structures and Phases of Development on Crime." In *Crime and Economy*. Vol. 32, *Criminological Research*, edited by Council of Europe. Strasbourg: Council of Europe.

———. 1997. *Das Ende der zivilisierten Stadt? Die Auswirkungen von Individualisierung und urbaner Krise auf Gewaltdelinquenz*. Frankfurt am Main: Campus.

———. 2001. "Modernization, Self-Control and Lethal Violence: The Long-Term Dynamics of European Homicide Rates in Theoretical Perspective." *British Journal of Criminology* 41:618–38.

———. 2002a. "Crime, Problem Drinking, and Drug Use: Patterns of Problem-Behavior in Cross-National Perspective." *Annals of the American Academy of Political and Social Science* 580:201–25.

———. 2002b. "Long-Term Trends in Violence: Empirical Research and Theoretical Approaches." In *Handbook of Violence Research*, edited by John Hagan and Wilhelm Heitmeyer. New York: Westview (forthcoming).

Eleuche-Santini, V. 1979. "Violence dans le compté de Nice au XIIIe siècle." *Provence Historique* 29:362–78.

Elias, Norbert. 1976. *Über den Prozess der Zivilisation: Soziogenetische und psychogenetische Untersuchungen*. Frankfurt am Main: Suhrkamp.

———. 1978. *The Civilizing Process*. Vols. 1–2. Oxford: Oxford University Press.

———. 1983. *Die höfische Gesellschaft: Untersuchungen zu einer Soziologie des Königtums und der höfischen Aristokratie*. Frankfurt am Main: Suhrkamp.

Emsley, Clive. 1996. *Crime and Society in England, 1750–1900*. 2d ed. London: Longman.

Farrington, David P. 1998. "Predictors, Causes, and Correlates of Male Youth Violence." In *Youth Violence*, edited by Michael Tonry and Mark H. Moore. Vol. 24 of *Crime and Justice: A Review of Research*, edited by Michael Tonry. Chicago: University of Chicago Press.

Federal Bureau of Investigation. 1998. *Uniform Crime Reports: Crime in the United States—1997*. Washington, D.C.: U.S. Government Publishing Office.

Feeley, Malcolm. 1994. "The Decline of Women in the Criminal Process: A Comparative History." *Criminal Justice History* 15:235–74.

Feeley, Malcolm, and Deborah L. Little. 1991. "The Vanishing Female: The Decline of Women in the Criminal Process, 1687–1912." *Law and Society Review* 25:719–57.

Ferri, Enrico. 1925. *L'omicida nella psicologia e nella psicopatologia criminale*. Turin: Unione tipografico-editrice torinese.

Finnane, Mark. 1997. "A Decline in Violence in Ireland? Crime, Policing and Social Relations, 1860–1914." *Crime, Histoire et Société—Crime, History and Society* 1(1):51–70.

Fouret, Claude. 1984. *L'amour, la violence et le pouvoir: La criminalité à Douai de 1496 à 1520*. History thesis, Université de Lille III.

———. 1987. "Douai au XVIe siècle: Une sociabilité de l'aggression." *Revue d'Histoire Moderne et Contemporaine* 34:3–30.

Frank, Michael. 1995. *Dörfliche Gesellschaft und Kriminalität: Das Fallbeispiel Lippe, 1650–1800*. Paderborn: Schöningh.

Frauenstädt, Paul. 1881. *Blutrache und Totschlagsühne im deutschen Mittelalter.* Leipzig: Duncker & Humblot.

Garcia, Pablo Pérez. 1991. *La comparsa de los malhechores, Valencia, 1479–1518.* Valencia: Diputacio de València.

Garnham, Neal. 1996. *The Courts, Crime and the Criminal Law in Ireland, 1692–1760.* Dublin: Irish Academic Press.

Gaskill, Malkolm. 2000. *Crime and Mentalities in Early Modern England.* Cambridge: Cambridge University Press.

Gatrell, V. A. C. 1980. "The Decline of Theft and Violence in Victorian and Edwardian England." In *Crime and the Law: The Social History of Crime in Western Europe since 1500,* edited by V. A. C. Gatrell, Bruce Lenman, and Geoffrey Parker. London: Europa.

Given, James B. 1977. *Society and Homicide in Thirteenth-Century England.* Stanford, Calif.: Stanford University Press.

Gonthier, Nicole. 1993. *Délinquance, justice et société dans le Lyonnais médiéval de la fin du XIIIe siècle au début du XVIe siècle.* Paris: Arguments.

Gottfredson, Michael R., and Travis Hirschi. 1990. *A General Theory of Crime.* Stanford, Calif.: Stanford University Press.

Greenberg, David F. 1985. "Age, Crime, and Social Explanation." *American Journal of Sociology* 91(1):1–20.

———. 1994. "The Historical Variability of the Age-Crime Relationship." *Journal of Quantitative Criminology* 10(4):361–73.

Gurr, Ted Robert. 1981. "Historical Trends in Violent Crime: A Critical Review of the Evidence." In *Crime and Justice: An Annual Review of Research,* vol. 3, edited by Michael Tonry and Norval Morris. Chicago: University of Chicago Press.

———. 1989. "Historical Trends in Violent Crime: Europe and the United States." In *The History of Crime.* Vol. 1, *Violence in America,* edited by Ted Robert Gurr. Newbury Park, Calif.: Sage.

Gurr, Ted Robert, Peter N. Grabosky, and Richard C. Hula. 1977. *The Politics of Crime and Conflict: A Comparative History of Four Cities.* Beverly Hills, Calif.: Sage.

Hagemann, Hans-Rudolf. 1981. *Basler Rechtsleben im Mittelalter.* Basel: Helbling & Lichtenhahn.

Hammer, Carl I, Jr. 1978. "Patterns of Homicide in a Medieval University Town: Fourteenth-Century Oxford." *Past and Present* 78:3–23.

Hanawalt, Barbara A. 1976. "Violent Death in Fourteenth- and Early Fifteenth-Century England." *Comparative Studies in Society and History* 18:297–320.

———. 1979. *Crime and Conflict in English Communities, 1300–1348.* Cambridge, Mass.: Harvard University Press.

Heitmeyer, Wilhelm. 1995. *Gewalt: Schattenseiten der Individualisierung bei Jugendlichen aus unterschiedlichen Milieus.* Weinheim: Juventa.

Henry, Philippe. 1984. *Crime, Justice et Société dans la principauté de Neuchâtel au XVIIIe siècle (1707–1806).* Neuchâtel: Editions de la Baconnière.

Heyden, J. 1983. "Misdrijf in Antwerpen: Een onderzoek naar de kriminaliteit in de periode 1404–1429." *Acta Falconis* 83(3):223–40.

Hirschi, Travis, and Michael Gottfredson. 1983. "Age and the Explanation of Crime." *American Journal of Sociology* 89(3):552–84.

Home Office. 1998. *Criminal Statistics, England and Wales*. London: Home Office.

———. 2000. *Criminal Statistics, England and Wales*. London: Home Office.

Istituto Nazionale di Statistica. 2000. *Statistiche giudiziarie penali, Anno 1998*. Rome: ISTAT.

Jansson, Arne. 1998. *From Swords to Sorrow: Homicide and Suicide in Early Modern Stockholm*. Stockholm: Almqvist & Wiksell.

Jarrick, Arne, and Johan Söderberg. 1993. "Spontaneous Processes of Civilisation." *Ethnologia Europea* 23:5–26.

Johnson, Eric A. 1995. *Urbanization and Crime: Germany, 1871–1914*. Cambridge: Cambridge University Press.

Johnson, Eric A., and Eric H. Monkkonen, eds. 1996. *The Civilization of Crime: Violence in Town and Country since the Middle Ages*. Urbana: University of Illinois Press.

Junger-Tas, Josine. 1991. "Nature and Evolution of the Criminality of Young Adults." In *Tenth Criminological Colloquium on Young Adult Offenders and Crime Policy*, edited by Council of Europe. Strasbourg: Council of Europe.

Kaczynska, Elzbieta. 1995. "Town and Countryside in Penal Judicature and Criminality: Kingdom of Poland, 1815–1914." *Acta Poloniae Historica* 71: 197–210.

Karonen, Petri. 1995. "Trygg eller livsfarlig? Våldsbrottsligheten i Finlands stöder, 1540–1660." *Historisk Tidskrift för Finland* 80(1):1–11.

———. 1999. "In Search of Peace and Harmony? Capital Crimes in Late Mediaeval and Early Modern Swedish Realm (ca. 1450–1700)." In *Crime and Control in Europe from the Past to the Present*, edited by Mirkka Lappalainen and Pekka Hirvonen. Helsinki: Hakapaino.

———. 2001. "A Life for a Life versus Christian Reconciliation: Violence and the Process of Civilization in the Kingdom of Sweden, 1540–1700." In *Five Centuries of Violence in Finland and the Baltic Area*, by Heikki Ylikangas, Petri Karonen, and Martti Lehti. Columbus: Ohio State University Press.

King, Peter. 2000. *Crime, Justice, and Discretion in England, 1740–1820*. Oxford: Oxford University Press.

Kloek, Els. 1990. "Criminality and Gender in Leiden's Confessieboeken, 1678–1794." *Criminal Justice History* 11:1–29.

Lacour, Eva. 2000. "Kriminalität in den Grafschaften Manderscheid-Blankenheim und Manderscheid-Gerolstein." *Zeitschrift der Savigny-Stiftung für Rechtsgeschichte, Germanistische Abteilung* 117:518–49.

Langan, Patrick A., and David P. Farrington. 1998. *Crime and Justice in the United States and in England and Wales, 1981–1996*. Washington, D.C.: U.S. Department of Justice, Office of Justice Programs, Bureau of Justice Statistics.

Liliequist, Jonas. 1999. "Violence, Honour and Manliness in Early Modern Northern Sweden." In *Crime and Control in Europe from the Past to the Present*, edited by Mirkka Lappalainen and Pekka Hirvonen. Helsinki: Hakapaino.

Mayr, Georg von. 1917. *Statistik und Gesellschaftslehre, Dritter Band: Moral-statistik mit Einschluss der Kriminalstatistik.* Tübingen: Mohr.

Monkkonen, Eric. 2001. "New Standards for Historical Homicide Research." *Crime, Histoire et Société—Crime, History and Society* 5(2):7–26.

Muchembled, Robert. 1984. "Crime et société urbaine: Arras au temps de Charles Quint (1528–1549)." In *La France d'Ancien Régime: Etudes réunies en l'honneur de Pierre Goubert,* edited by Pierre Goubert. Toulouse: Société de démographie historique.

———. 1992. *Le temps des supplices; de l'obéissance sous les rois absolus. XVe–XVIIIe siécle.* Paris: Colin.

———. 1996. "Elias und die neuere historische Forschung in Frankreich." In *Norbert Elias und die Menschenwissenschaften,* edited by Karl-Siegvert Rehbert. Frankfurt am Main: Suhrkamp.

Naess, Hans Eyvind. 1982. *Trolldomsprosessene i Norge på 1500–1600–tallet: En retts- og sosialhistorisk undersökelse.* Oslo: Universiteits Forlaget.

Oestreich, Gerhard. 1968. "Strukturprobleme des europäischen Absolutis-mus." *Vierteljahreszeitschrift für Sozial- und Wirtschaftsgeschichte* 55:329–47.

———. 1982. *Neostoicism and the Early Modern State.* Cambridge: Cambridge University Press.

Österberg, Eva. 1996. "Criminality, Social Control, and the Early Modern State: Evidence and Interpretations in Scandinavian Historiography." In *The Civilization of Crime: Violence in Town and Country since the Middle Ages,* edited by Eric A. Johnson and Eric H. Monkkonen. Urbana: University of Illinois Press.

Österberg, Eva, and Dag Lindström. 1988. *Crime and Social Control in Medieval and Early Modern Swedish Towns.* Uppsala: Academia Upsaliensis.

Panico, G. 1991. "Criminali e peccatori in Principato Citra alla fine del Set-tecento (1770–1780)." In *Criminalità e società in età moderna,* edited by Luigi Berlinguer and Floriana Colao. Milan: Giuffrè.

Pohl, Susanne. 1999. "'Ehrlicher Totschlag'—'Rache'—'Notwehr.' Zwischen männlichem Ehrcode und dem Primat des Stadtfriedens (Zürich 1376–1600)." In *Kulturelle Reformation: Sinnformationen im Umbruch 1400–1600,* edited by Bernhard Jussen and Craig Koslofsky. Göttingen: Vandenhoeck & Ruprecht.

Roets, Anne-Marie. 1982. "Vrouwen en criminaliteit in Gent in de achttiende eeuw." *Tijdschrift voor Geschiedenis* 92:363–78.

Romani, Mario A. 1980. "Criminalità e Giustizia nel Ducato di Mantova alla fine del Cinquecento." *Rivista Storica Italiana* 92:679–706.

Roth, Randolph. 2001. "Homicide in Early Modern England, 1549–1800: The Need for a Quantitative Synthesis." *Crime, Histoire et Société—Crime, History and Society* 5(2):33–68.

Rousseaux, Xavier. 1986. "Ordre et violence: Criminalité et répression dans une ville brabançonne. Nivelles (1646–1695)." *Revue de Droit Pénal et de Criminologie* 66(7):649–92.

———. 1999a. "From Case to Crime: Homicide Regulation in Medieval and Modern Europe." In *Die Entstehung des öffentlichen Strafrechts: Bestandsauf-*

nahme eines europäischen Forschungsproblems, edited by Dietmar Willoweit. Cologne: Böhlau.

———. 1999*b*. "Sozialdisziplinierung, Civilisation des moeurs et monopolisation du pouvoir: Elements pour und histoire du contrôle social dans les Pays-Bas méridionaux, 1500–1815." In *Institutionen, Instrumente und Akteure sozialer Kontrolle und Disziplinierung im frühneuzeitlichen Europa*, edited by Heinz Schilling. Frankfurt am Main: Klostermann.

Ruff, Julius R. 1984. *Crime, Justice and Public Order in Old Regime France: The Sénéchaussées of Libourne and Bazas, 1696–1789*. London: Croom Helm.

Ruggiero, Guido. 1978. "Law and Punishment in Early Renaissance Venice." *Journal of Criminal Law and Criminology* 69(2):243–56.

———. 1980. *Violence in Early Renaissance Venice*. New Brunswick, N.J.: Rutgers University Press.

Samaha, Joel. 1974. *Law and Order in Historical Perspective: The Case of Elizabethan Essex*. New York: Academic Press.

Sardi, Laura Carli. 1991. "Analisi statistica sulla criminalita nel 1700 (reati e pene) con riguardo allo Stato senese." In *Criminalità e società in età moderna*, edited by Luigi Berlinguer and Floriana Colao. Milan: Giuffrè.

Schmidt, Axel. 1994. "'Wo die Männer sind, gibt es Streit': Ehre und Ehrgefühl im ländlichen Sardinien." In *Ehre: Archaische Momente in der Moderne*, edited by Ludgera Vogt and Arnold Zingerle. Frankfurt am Main: Suhrkamp.

Schormann, Gerhard. 1974. "Strafrechtspflege in Braunschweig-Wolfenbüttel." *Braunschweigisches Jahrbuch* 55:90–112.

Schüssler, Martin. 1991. "Statistische Untersuchung des Verbrechens in Nürnberg im Zeitraum von 1285 bis 1400." *Zeitschrift der Savigny-Siftung für Rechtsgeschichte, Germanistische Abteilung* 108:117–91.

———. 1994. "Verbrechen im spätmittelalterlichen Olmütz: Statistische Untersuchung der Kriminalität im Osten des Heiligen Römischen Reiches." *Zeitschrift der Savigny-Siftung für Rechtsgeschichte, Germanistische Abteilung* 111:149–269.

———. 1996. "Quantifizierung, Impressionismus und Rechtstheorie: Ein Bericht zur Geschichte und zum heutigen Stand der Forschung über Kriminalität im Europa des Spätmittelalters und der frühen Neuzeit." *Zeitschrift der Savigny-Siftung für Rechtsgeschichte, Germanistische Abteilung* 113:247–78.

———. 1998. "Verbrechen in Krakau (1361–1405) und seiner Beistadt Kasimir (1370–1402)." *Zeitschrift der Savigny-Stiftung für Rechtsgeschichte, Germanistische Abteilung* 115:198–338.

Schuster, Peter. 1995. *Der gelobte Frieden: Täter, Opfer und Herrschaft im spätmittelalterlichen Konstanz*. Constance: Universitätsverlag Konstanz.

———. 2000. *Eine Stadt vor Gericht: Recht und Alltag im spätmittelalterlichen Konstanz*. Paderborn: Schöningh.

Schwerhoff, Gerd. 1991. *Köln im Kreuzverhör: Kriminalität, Herrschaft und Gesellschaft in einer frühneuzeitlichen Stadt*. Bonn: Bouvier.

———. 1995. "Geschlechtsspezifische Kriminalität im frühneuzeitlichen Köln." In *Von Huren und Rabenmüttern, Weibliche Kriminalität in der frühen Neuzeit*, edited by Otto Ulbricht. Cologne: Böhlau.

———. 2002. "Criminalized Violence and the Civilizing Process—a Reappraisal." *Crime, Histoire et Sociétés—Crime, History and Societies* (forthcoming).

Sharpe, James A. 1983. *Crime in Seventeenth-Century England: A County Study.* Cambridge: Cambridge University Press.

———. 1984. *Crime in Early Modern England, 1550–1750.* London: Longman.

———. 1988. "The History of Crime in England c. 1300–1914." *British Journal of Criminology* 28:254–67.

———. 1996. "Crime in England: Long-Term Trends and the Problem of Modernization." In *The Civilization of Crime: Violence in Town and Country since the Middle Ages,* edited by Eric A. Johnson and Eric H. Monkkonen. Urbana: University of Illinois Press.

Shelley, Louise I. 1981. *Crime and Modernization: The Impact of Industrialization and Urbanization on Crime.* Carbondale: Southern Illinois University Press.

Simon-Muscheid, Katharina. 1991. "Gewalt und Ehre im spätmittelalterlichen Handwerk am Beispiel Basels." *Zeitschrift für historische Forschung* 18(1):1–31.

Soman, Alfred. 1980. "Deviance and Criminal Justice in Western Europe (1300–1800): An Essay in Structure." *Criminal Justice History* 1:3–28.

Spierenburg, Pieter. 1984. *The Spectacle of Suffering: Executions and the Evolution of Repression: From a Preindustrial Metropolis to the European Experience.* Cambridge: Cambridge University Press.

———. 1994. "Faces of Violence: Homicide Trends and Cultural Meanings, Amsterdam, 1431–1816." *Journal of Social History* 27:701–16.

———. 1995. "Elias and the History of Crime and Criminal Justice: A Brief Evaluation." *International Association for the History of Crime and Criminal Justice Bulletin* 20:17–30.

———. 1996. "Long-Term Trends in Homicide: Theoretical Reflections and Dutch Evidence, Fifteenth to Twentieth Centuries." In *The Civilization of Crime: Violence in Town and Country since the Middle Ages,* edited by Eric A. Johnson and Eric H. Monkkonen. Urbana: University of Illinois Press.

———. 2001. "Violence and the Civilizing Process: Does It Work?" *Crime, Histoire et Société—Crime, History and Society* 5(2):87–106.

Spierenburg, Pieter, ed. 1998. *Men and Violence: Gender, Honor, and Rituals in Modern Europe and America.* Columbus: Ohio State University Press.

Steffensmeier, Darrell J., Emilie Andersen Allan, Miles D. Harer, and Cathy Streifel. 1989. "Age and the Distribution of Crime." *American Journal of Sociology* 94(4):803–31.

Steffensmeier, Darrell, and Cathy Streifel. 1991. "Age, Gender, and Crime across Three Historical Periods." *Social Forces* 69(3):869–94.

Stone, Lawrence. 1983. "Interpersonal Violence in English Society, 1300–1980." *Past and Present* 101:22–33.

Taylor, Charles. 1989. *Sources of the Self: The Making of the Modern Identity.* Cambridge, Mass.: Harvard University Press.

Thome, Helmut. 1995. "Modernization and Crime: What Is the Explanation?" *IAHCCJ Bulletin* 20:31–47.

———. 2001. "Explaining Long Term Trends in Violent Crime." *Crime, Histoire et Société—Crime, History and Society* 5(2):69–87.

Tilly, Charles. 1992. *Coercion, Capital, and European States, A.D. 990–1992.* Rev. ed. Cambridge, Mass.: Blackwell.

van de Pol, Lotte C. 1987. "Vrouwencriminaliteit in Amsterdam in te tweede helft van de 17e eeuw." *Tijdschrift voor Criminologie* 5:148–55.

Vanhemelryck, Fernand. 1981. *De criminaliteit in de ammanie van Brussel van de Late Middeleeuwen, tot het einde het Ancien Régime (1404–1789).* Brüssel: Paleis der Academiën.

Verkko, Veli. 1951. *Homicides and Suicides in Finland and Their Dependence on National Character.* Vol. 3, *Scandinavian Studies in Sociology.* Copenhagen: Gads.

Weber, Max. 1922. "Die protestantische Ethik und der 'Geist' des Kapitalismus." In *Gesammelte Aufsätze zur Religionssoziologie,* vol. 1, edited by Max Weber. Tübingen: Mohr.

Weinbaum, Martin, ed. 1976. *The London Eyre of 1276.* London: London Record Society.

Wikström, Per-Olof H. 1985. *Everyday Violence in Contemporary Sweden: Situational and Ecological Aspects.* Stockholm: National Council for Crime Prevention, Sweden, Research Division.

———. 1992. "Context-Specific Trends for Criminal Homicide in Stockholm, 1951–1987." *Studies on Crime and Crime Prevention* 1:88–105.

Wintemute, Garen. 2000. "Guns and Gun Violence." In *The Crime Drop in America,* edited by Alfred Blumstein and Joel Wallman. Cambridge: Cambridge University Press.

Ylikangas, Heikki. 1976. "Major Fluctuations in Crimes of Violence in Finland: A Historical Analysis." *Scandinavian Journal of History* 1:81–103.

———. 1998a. "Die langfristigen Entwicklungstrends der Verbrechen wider das Leben in Finland." In *About Violence,* edited by Heikki Ylikangas. Helsinki: University of Helsinki.

———. 1998b. *What Happened to Violence? An Analysis of the Development of Violence from Medieval Times to the Early Modern Era Based on Finnish Source Material.* Helsinki: Suomen Akatemia.

Ylikangas, Heikki, Petri Karonen, and Martti Lehti. 2001. *Five Centuries of Violence in Finland and the Baltic Area.* Columbus: Ohio State University Press.

Zorzi, Domenico. 1989. "Sull'ammistrazione della Giustizia penale nell'età delle riforme: Il reato di omicidio nella Padova di fine settecento." In *Crimine, Giustizia e società veneta in età moderna,* edited by L. Berlinguer and F. Colao. Milan: Giuffrè.

Anthony N. Doob and Cheryl Marie Webster

Sentence Severity and Crime: Accepting the Null Hypothesis

> To every thing there is a season, a time to every purpose.
> (Ecclesiastes 3:1)

ABSTRACT

The literature on the effects of sentence severity on crime levels has been reviewed numerous times in the past twenty-five years. Most reviews conclude that there is little or no consistent evidence that harsher sanctions reduce crime rates in Western populations. Nevertheless, most reviewers have been reluctant to conclude that variation in the severity of sentence does not have differential deterrent impacts. A reasonable assessment of the research to date—with a particular focus on studies conducted in the past decade—is that sentence severity has no effect on the level of crime in society. It is time to accept the null hypothesis.

This essay examines one aspect of general deterrence—the effects of sentence severity on crime. In addressing this issue—and concluding that variation in the severity of sanctions is unrelated to levels of crime—we do not suggest that the justice system as a whole has no

Anthony N. Doob is a professor and Cheryl Marie Webster is a doctoral candidate at the Centre of Criminology, University of Toronto. The impetus for this essay originated with a request from defense counsel Sal Caramanna for a review of the deterrence literature for a case involving a woman found guilty of importing prohibited drugs. We thank him for his suggestion to challenge the sentence severity–crime nexus. We also thank Assistant Crown Attorney John North for helping us sharpen our arguments and encouraging us to consider research that otherwise might have gone uncriticized. Development of the paper was supported by Legal Aid Ontario, a Social Science and Humanities Research Council Grant to Anthony N. Doob, and a graduate fellowship to Cheryl Marie Webster from the Fundação para a Ciência e a Tecnologia. Finally, we thank Andrea Shier and Carla Cesaroni for bibliographic assistance.

deterrent effect. On the contrary, we agree with Nagin (1998), who concludes that substantial evidence exists that the overall system deters crime. This conclusion is similar to that drawn by others with respect to specific offenses. For instance, Cavanagh (1993) affirms that the criminal justice system adds "cost" to those involved in the drug trade and consequently affects the size of that industry. Therefore, while Cavanagh is not optimistic about the effects of harsher sentences on drug offending rates, he still argues that any system that criminalizes drugs can be expected to affect the quantity of illegal substances used. We expect that the same could be said for any crime.

Further, this essay does not focus directly on issues surrounding the certainty—or the perception of certainty—of apprehension. However, this is not to suggest that certainty of apprehension is unrelated to the effects of the severity of punishment. There are clearly some circumstances in which these issues may become intertwined. For example, a change in punishment severity can increase or decrease police activity and consequently alter the actual likelihood of apprehension. Conversely, a modification in penalty—or simply a great deal of public discussion about it—may alter the perceived likelihood of apprehension (for at least a short period). Indeed, it is important to recognize that it is not the actual probability of apprehension or the actual penalty that would be likely to affect a potential offender's behavior. Rather, it is the perceived likelihood of apprehension and the expected penalty. This distinction is crucial.

Notwithstanding these intersections between certainty and severity of punishment, these issues constitute conceptually distinct phenomena with their own distinct literatures. A similar argument may be made for distinctions between specific and general deterrence. While analogous entwinements may be found between these two issues, the (theoretical and practical) differences between them demand separate analyses. In this light, this essay addresses only the question of whether there is a reasonable likelihood that variation in the severity of a sentence—or of sentences being handed down for an identifiable "class" of offenses—will have differential impacts on the likelihood that other people will commit that type of offense. More simply, this essay examines the existence of an association between sentencing severity and levels of crime.

As any research-methods textbook in social science will suggest, a useful way of testing a particular supposition is by distinguishing between the "research hypothesis"—usually that a relationship between two variables exists—and the "null hypothesis"—that there is no association between these same factors. However, the problem with this approach is that one cannot logically prove the absence of a phenomenon. Indeed, a relationship may not be found for an infinite number of reasons (e.g., the effect is obscured by some other factor, one has been searching in the wrong place, measures are not sufficiently sensitive). In more mundane terms, that one cannot find something (i.e., a deterrent effect, or a missing sock) does not mean that it does not exist. It may or may not exist. In a technical sense, all that can be demonstrated is that the effect was not to be found with the methods that were employed at the particular time and space in which one looked.

It is perfectly reasonable—from a scientific perspective—to be cautious in drawing conclusions. This is especially so when one is considering the acceptance of the null hypothesis. Indeed, it was only after several decades of research producing consistent results in different periods and places and using multiple measures and methods that most social scientists abandoned the notion that capital punishment deters. This widespread acceptance of the null hypothesis is clearly suggested by a recent survey conducted by Radelet and Akers (1996). Groups that would be expected to differ (i.e., police chiefs and past/present presidents of U.S. criminology organizations) were generally in agreement that the death penalty does not significantly reduce the number of homicides. Further, a recent review of the literature by Bailey and Peterson (1999) corroborated this conclusion. Even when examining specific types of homicides (e.g., killings of police, first degree murder, felony murder) and using multiple sources of data, these reviewers found no consistent evidence that capital punishment "works."

In curious contrast, social scientists have been remarkably more cautious in accepting the null hypothesis that sentence severity, in general, does not reduce levels of crime. Despite similar circumstances (i.e., consistently negative findings over space and time), scholars continue to resist more definitive conclusions. Symptomatically, the 1999 review of the deterrence literature by von Hirsch, Bottoms, Burney, and Wikström quotes Sutherland and Cressey's 1960 edition of *Principles of Criminology* which suggested that the deterrent impact of penalty size had been "seriously challenged" (von Hirsch et al. 1999, p. 11) by modern criminology. Although these scholars do not present any strong evidence disputing this affirmation, their own conclusion—arrived at almost forty years later—is not much more definitive in nature. Rather, it simply states that the effect of sentence severity is "less impressive" than that of certainty (1999, p. 47). While noting that certain types of research "fail" to demonstrate an effect on crime of harsh sentences (1999, p. 47), these scholars continue to call for additional evidence before reaching more definite conclusions.

This assessment is similar to that reached by Daniel Nagin in his 1998 *Crime and Justice* review of the research on deterrence. Despite being confident "in asserting that our legal enforcement apparatus exerts a substantial deterrent effect" (1998, p. 36), Nagin was less certain about "what works in specific circumstances" (1998, p. 36). As a result, he preferred to identify areas in which research would help fill gaps in knowledge. Said differently, although Nagin did not appear to believe that specific criminal justice policies should be based on deterrence, he was not (yet) willing to throw in the towel and accept that variation in sentence severity does not affect crime levels. Once again, the quest for the missing sock continued.

While not disagreeing with these assessments, we believe that research produced in the past several years—some of which appeared after the Nagin (1998) essay and the von Hirsch et al. (1999) report were completed—warrants a stronger conclusion. Although it is tempting to extend the search for consistent relationships between sentence severity and crime rates "just one last time" in the belief that general deterrent effects may still be lurking at the end of the next regression equation, one must recognize that sentencing policies currently in place in many jurisdictions are still based on the assumption that harsh sentences deter. There is no plausible body of evidence that supports policies based on this premise. On the contrary, standard social scientific norms governing the acceptance of the null hypothesis justify the present (always rebuttable) conclusion that sentence severity does not affect levels of crime.[1]

This essay reviews the evidence that supports the conclusion that harsher sentences do not deter. We begin with a discussion of some of the more recent reviews of the deterrence literature, comparing and contrasting them with earlier summaries conducted on the topic (Sec.

---

[1] When we are discussing variation in sentence severity, we are clearly considering only those sanctions that fall within the range that is plausible in our present society. Said differently, we are not negating the possibility that the severity of punishments may, in fact, affect levels of crime if taken to the extreme (e.g., a one-dollar fine for murder or capital punishment for stealing a sock). We are simply restricting our analysis to the range of sentences that is currently acceptable in Western countries.

I). We subsequently examine some of the studies that have been cited as evidence for a deterrent impact of sentence severity, demonstrating why we consider their findings generally to be unreliable (Sec. II). Section III assesses the research that—we believe—justifies the conclusion that more severe sentences are no more effective in reducing crime than less severe sentences. Our primary but not exclusive focus is on studies conducted over the last decade, with special consideration to those that examine the dramatic changes in sentencing policy that occurred during the 1990s. In conclusion, we suggest that the continued belief of many people in the deterrent effect of harsh sanctions may be rooted in an imperfect or simplistic form of reasoning about deterrence. This position is contrasted with emerging trends in several countries toward the rejection of policies based on the notion that variation in sentencing severity has differential deterrent impacts (Sec. IV).

I. An Overview of Summaries of the Deterrence Literature

With a body of literature that extends over at least thirty years, it is not surprising that numerous reviews have been conducted on deterrence. The virtues of examining these summaries are twofold. They amass a large number of studies, permitting us to draw general conclusions about the deterrent effects of variations in sentence severity. We are also able to discern trends over time, providing insights into the stability of results. As we demonstrate in this section of the essay, the majority of the reviews examined do not support the claim that harsher sanctions deter. Further, there is a general consistency of this conclusion over time—if not, in fact, a trend toward increased skepticism.

The first era of deterrence summaries could easily be denoted as one of agnosticism. Largely associated with the review conducted for the U.S. Department of Justice by the National Academy of Sciences (Blumstein, Cohen, and Nagin 1978) and—albeit to a much lesser extent—the 1980 summary of deterrence by Cook, this initial period is characterized by an unwillingness to conclude that crime is reduced by harsh sentences. However, the reviewers were equally reluctant to draw the conclusion that sentence severity was not causally linked to levels of crime. Interestingly, Cook was not only more definite in his assessment of the overall impact of the criminal justice system on crime rates than was the National Academy of Science, but was also critical of the research that had been cited as evidence of the marginal deterrent impact of sentence severity. He suggested that studies of policy experiments—dramatic changes in law and practice—would be most useful in informing us about the deterrent process. This insight foreshadowed the pivotal role played by such sentencing experiments as the three-strikes legislation enacted during the 1990s that permits us to draw firmer conclusions about the differential deterrent effects of variation in sentence severity.

However, in terms of immediate effects, the uncertain conclusions of these initial reviews provided little direction for policy decisions. The Canadian and U.S. sentencing commissions adopted substantially different approaches to the issue of general deterrence. The U.S. commission decided that it was too difficult to choose between a "proportionality" model and a "crime control" model (deterrence or incapacitation) and concluded, in any case, that the results would be the same (see Doob [1995] for a discussion of this issue). By extension, this panel was willing to incorporate deterrence-type thinking in the determination of sentence severity within its guidelines, considering it unnecessary to examine the literature.

In sharp contrast, the Canadian Sentencing Commission concluded that "it can be questioned whether legal sanctions can be used beyond their overall effect to achieve particular results (e.g., deterring a particular category of offenders, such as impaired drivers)" (Canadian Sentencing Commission 1987, p. 138). Its assessment that the evidence did not support the deterrent impact of harsher sentences was one of the justifications for its proposal that sentences be proportionate to the harm done rather than based on deterrence. More specifically, this commission proposed that the "paramount principle" be that the sentence be proportionate to the gravity of the offense and the degree of responsibility of the offender for the offense. However, the court would still be permitted to give consideration to the issue of deterrence when applying this principle. In this way, deterrence could continue to be relevant in sentencing, but only within the range set by the proportionality principle. One interpretation of this proposal is that deterrence could determine the sanction but not the severity of the sentence.

At the same time as these commissions were considering how to address the issue of deterrence, Donald Lewis, an economist, published an unusual review of the research on deterrence in 1986. The selection of papers reviewed is interesting because it is limited to those studies in which the magnitude of the apparent deterrent effect is quantified.

Not surprisingly, the result of this approach is that his summary almost exclusively contains papers that were published in economics journals. This review of the deterrence literature could easily be characterized as "Ehrlich paradigm" research (including some papers by Ehrlich himself)—an expression employed by Cook to describe what he considered to be the "major false start" (1980, p. 269) of deterrence studies in the 1970s. Predictably, Cook (1980) is not referenced in Lewis's (1986) article.

Lewis's conclusion that there is a "substantial body of evidence which is largely consistent with the existence of a deterrent effect from longer sentences" (1986, p. 60) does not appear to have been taken seriously by many commentators on deterrence (see, e.g., von Hirsch et al. 1999). We suggest three possible explanations for this lack of attention. First, the review is based on a small and selective set of data, using largely, if not exclusively, one methodology. Second, Lewis's suggestion that harsher sentences for murder will deter is not consistent with the bulk of the evidence on that specific topic. Third, the manner in which some of the evidence is presented is not entirely consistent with the conclusions drawn by the original authors. For instance, one Canadian paper (Avio and Clark 1978) is summarized by Lewis (1986, p. 49, table 1) as showing "mixed (weak support [for robbery, burglary, and larceny], none for fraud)" in a column headed "evidence generally consistent with deterrent effect of longer sentences." However, Avio and Clark (1978) are considerably more cautious in their conclusions. More specifically, they point out that "the expected sentence length variable is insignificant for all crimes and has the wrong sign in the fraud equations" (1978, p. 13). Said differently, "A statistically significant inverse relationship between incarceration prospects and crime rates is not found for any of the variables examined" (1978, p. 14). Similar skepticism is raised by another study cited by Lewis (1986) which examined the impact of the sentence given to hijackers during the period 1961–76 on their offending rates (Landes 1978). It is hard to know what to make of this study given that two seemingly fundamental factors were not taken into account. More specifically, Landes (1978) did not control for the effects of either the security measures that were implemented during the study period or the agreement between the United States and Cuba to extradite or punish hijackers.

The second era of deterrence summaries could be designated as one of increasing skepticism. Characterized primarily by the reviews car-

ried out by Nagin (1998) and von Hirsch et al. (1999), this period reflects, to a large extent, the sheer accumulation of studies over the past
two to three decades that have not supported the notion that variation
in sentence severity affects crime rates. However, given the unwillingness of the reviewers of this era to (conditionally) accept the null hypothesis that harsher sanctions do not deter, their summaries tend to
be as much a discussion of other potential avenues of study (the pro-
verbial "further research is needed") as a rehashing of the increasingly
consistent body of literature that is generally unsupportive of a deterrent effect.

The principal conclusions of Daniel Nagin's 1998 summary of the
deterrence research were not substantively different from those drawn
in his review of the same issue two decades earlier (Nagin 1978).
Rather, he continued to be unable to find plausible support for the idea
that increased penalties would have a reliable impact on crime levels.
For instance, Nagin noted that although traditional utility-theory approaches to deterrence state that increased sanctions would lead to increased deterrent effects, some of the research that examined what individuals actually do suggests that "people do not perceive that costs
are proportional to potential punishment. Instead, it seems that they
perceive that there is a fixed cost associated with merely being convicted or even apprehended if it is public record" (1998, p. 21). The
reason for this phenomenon—in the situation that he describes (tax
evasion)—is simple: the criminal justice costs may not be as important
as the costs of criminal stigmatization. As Nagin points out, this interpretation is consistent with findings related to the "costs" of criminal
conviction (e.g., social and economic costs). He further suggests that
if a criminal justice policy "increases the proportion [of a population]
that is stigmatized, the deterrent effect [of that stigmatization process]
is less likely to be sustainable" (1998, p. 23).

Moreover, Nagin concludes—similar to his findings twenty years
earlier—that there is substantial evidence of the deterrent impact of
the justice system as a whole, and that evidence exists that the probability of being punished and crime rates are related in a direction consistent with deterrence theory. However, he also states that "this conclusion is of limited value in formulating policy" (including, one might
add, sentencing policy) because for policy makers (including judges in
interpreting sentencing policy) "the issue is not whether the criminal
justice system in its totality prevents crime but whether a specific pol-

icy, grafted onto the existing structure, will materially add to the preventive effect" (1998, p. 3). As an expert in deterrence, he was not optimistic about any generalizations concerning the impact of specific policies—even those in which one might reasonably expect to see an effect (i.e., the increased likelihood of criminal justice sanctions). It is worth noting that when addressing a specific offense—drugs—Nagin argues, "It is not likely that [the] drastic increases in penalties [during the latter part of the twentieth century] for drug dealing have had any material effect on the drug trade. . . . Indeed they may have actually increased the rate of other income-generating crime such as robbery, burglary, and larceny by making them comparatively more attractive than dealing" (1998, pp. 28–29).

Shortly after Nagin's review appeared, von Hirsch et al. (1999) published what is probably the most extensive recent report on the deterrent impact of variation in the harshness of sentences. Similar to Nagin (1998), von Hirsch et al. (1999) are not optimistic about the ability of increased sentences to deter crime. In fact, they note that "present association research, mirroring earlier studies fails . . . to disclose significant and consistent negative associations between severity levels (such as the likelihood or duration of imprisonment) and crime rates" (1999, p. 47). Further, they conclude their review by stating, "there is as yet no firm evidence regarding the extent to which raising severities of punishment would enhance deterrence of crime" (1999, p. 52). However, like Nagin (1998), they do not explicitly accept the null hypothesis that an increase in the size of criminal justice penalties would not reduce crime generally or any specific type of offense. Rather, they prefer to identify gaps in our knowledge of deterrence and speculate on the reasons for a lack of a "severity" effect on crime.

Von Hirsch et al. cite Nagin (1998) when noting that "the most serious deficiency of current deterrence research . . . is the absence of systematic inquiry into how much people know about changes in the . . . severity of punishment" (von Hirsch et al. 1999, p. 46). The studies they located did not address "the link between changes in . . . severity of punishment and potential offenders' awareness of the existence or extent of such changes" (1999, p. 46). Similarly, the research on offender decision making and its amenability to deterrence does not consider severity effects. Finally, there was a clear lack of knowledge surrounding the critical question of "the extent to which penalties would need to be increased in order to achieve a substantial reduction in crime rates" (1999, p. 47). Arguably, we may simply have not (yet) reached the threshold above (or under) which variation in sentence severity affects the crime rate.

Like the first era of deterrence reviews, this second period also includes a notable exception to the majority of the reviews of the deterrence literature that have failed to find evidence supporting the hypothesis that variation in sentence severity affects levels of crime. More specifically, Levitt (2002)—in a book entitled *Crime: Public Policies for Crime Control* and edited by James Q. Wilson and Joan Petersilia—concludes that harsh sentences do, in fact, deter. In a chapter that purports to focus on "assessing the existing empirical evidence on deterrence" (2002, p. 436), Levitt (an economist) has a relatively short (3.5-page) section on "expected punishment and crime rates." His conclusion that longer sentences have a deterrent effect is interesting, particularly in light of his selective assessment of the available evidence. Specifically, Levitt ignores the large bulk of literature—and the extensive review by von Hirsch et al. (1999)—which comes to a different conclusion. In addition, although this section is quite short, he cites certain research studies that he, himself, suggests can be explained more readily in terms of incapacitation. Indeed, he describes these studies in the end as "extremely weak tests of deterrence because of the potential incapacitation effects of prisons" (2002, p. 444).

Further, the evidence that Levitt cites on the impact of the three-strikes legislation in various states is selective (i.e., other contrary papers are not referred to) and peculiar. For example, he suggests—in support of the conclusion that harsh punishment deters—that the effect of three-strikes legislation in California "appears to be more consistent with the predictions of deterrence" than with incapacitation (2002, pp. 444–45). To support this affirmation, Levitt states that "between 1994 and 1998, California's prison population grew at a rate only slightly above the national average (29 percent vs. 23 percent) and California's violent crime rate per capita fell 30 percent, compared to 20 percent for the rest of the nation" (2002, p. 445). As far as we could deduce, he seems to be suggesting that these two sets of percentages would have to be equivalent in order to conclude that the three-strikes legislation had no impact on levels of crime. This implication is, of course, unusual for two reasons. First, it assumes that percent reductions in crime should be equivalent no matter what the "starting point" (e.g., that very low crime rates should decrease at the same "rate" as very high crime rates). Second, it implicitly supposes that there are no other influences on crime. Neither of these is a safe assumption, except perhaps to an economist.

Levitt's review focuses largely on only two studies—both his own (Kessler and Levitt 1999 and Levitt 1998)—as evidence "for a deterrent effect of increases in expected punishment" (2002, p. 445).[2] In addition, two other studies are cited in which offenders were interviewed. However, this latter research relates more to individual deterrence than to general deterrence. The fact that imprisoned offenders tell interviewers that being sent to prison has taught them a lesson and that they have given up criminal activity forever should not impress anyone (2002, p. 446). Another two-page section on capital punishment is equally void of data that conflict with the perspective that harsh sentences deter. In other words, as with other parts of this assessment of "existing empirical evidence on deterrence," Levitt is remarkably selective in the literature that he cites. This review is notable largely because it is so different—in the detail of its analysis, its selection of materials, and its conclusions—from other published reviews.

For the sake of completeness, it is worth noting that the focus of the reviews that we have addressed has been on crime generally rather than on specific offenses. However, other summaries of the deterrence literature have been produced that examine specific offenses (or offense groups) as well as particular legislation. Interestingly, these reviews not only continue to find little or no support for the notion that harsher sanctions reduce levels of crime, but—in many cases—are bolder in their conclusions than the more general summaries and, by extension, more closely approach our position of (conditional) acceptance of the null hypothesis.

More specifically, Cavanagh's (1993) review on deterrence and drug crimes for the U.S. Office of National Drug Control Policy is pessimistic about the usefulness of deterrence as an approach to reducing drug crimes. However, like much of the more general literature, it is,

[2] Within the context of this essay, we discuss only the first of these studies in any detail. The latter research (Levitt 1998), which examines the drop in offending as youths shift from the juvenile justice system to the adult system, is a complex paper that appears to us to have little relevance for the question at issue. The main focus—for deterrence purposes—is on the ratio of two quotients: (*a*) adult prisoners divided by adult violent crime, and (*b*) juvenile delinquents/juvenile violent crime. The ratio of *a*/*b* is said to be the "relative punitiveness" of the two systems (Levitt 1998, p. 1173). This ratio is subsequently said to relate to the crime rate of those over the age of majority. Aside from whether this ratio has anything to do with the relative severity of sentences, we do not appear to have independent measures of "crime" that are not, themselves, related to the relative punitiveness of the system.

in the end, agnostic in its conclusion: "Research on the effects of increased certainty, severity, and/or celerity of punishment upon levels of crime is inconclusive. . . . In short, current research provides little guidance for policy makers in this area" (1993, p. 46). In contrast, MacCoun and Reuter—in a chapter focusing on "drug control" in *The Handbook of Crime and Punishment*—concluded that "severity of sanctioning has little or no influence on offending" (1998, p. 213). Mauer and Young (1996) came to the same conclusion about deterrent sentencing more generally.

On occasion, one gets glimpses of the extent to which the notion that differential sentencing severity does not affect crime is widely accepted among criminologists. Greenwood et al. (1996) estimated the impact of California's three-strikes legislation. They noted in their analysis that "we assume no deterrent effect. That is, we assume that the various alternatives [provided for in the new sentencing legislation] reduce crime by removing criminals from the streets, not by deterring criminals on the street from committing further crimes. This assumption is consistent with recent research" (1996, p. 68). In a similar statement, Tonry notes that "the clear weight of the evidence on the deterrent effects of marginal manipulation of penalties demonstrates few or no effects" (1996, p. 137). Even James Q. Wilson—a man often identified with conservative views of crime—is not confident that harsher penalties will deter crime, or at least drug crimes. In the concluding chapter of a *Crime and Justice* volume on *Drugs and Crime*, Wilson notes that "every contributor to [the] volume agrees that significant reductions in drug abuse will come only from reducing the demand for those drugs" (1990, p. 534), and that he knows of "no serious law-enforcement executive who disagrees with this conclusion" (p. 534). Indeed, though noting that—in his view—supply reduction efforts must continue, Wilson states that the "marginal product of further investments in supply reduction is likely to be small, especially at the international level" (1990, p. 534). Further, he points out—albeit with neither enthusiasm nor endorsement—that "many (probably most) criminologists think we use prison too much and at too great a cost and that this excessive use has had little beneficial effect on the crime rate" (Wilson 1995, p. 499).

As is typically the case with social science, it is not surprising that the reviews of the research literature on deterrence are not entirely consistent. However, with the exception of the selective reviews by

Lewis (1986) and Levitt (2002), most summaries on the deterrence literature have not been optimistic about the ability of variations in the severity of sentences to affect levels of crime in the community. Indeed, the body of literature that does not support the research hypothesis that harsher sanctions deter continues to grow in size and consistency. Nonetheless, many would still like to see further research done before they are willing to throw in the towel—or throw out the sock—on deterrence. Said differently, while a great deal of effort has been spent looking for the missing sock whose whereabouts continues to elude us, reviewers continue to be reluctant in concluding that it does not exist in this particular place and time.

II. Evidence Used to Suggest Harsher Sentences Deter Crime

Any reviewer looking at an area of social science that has been extensively researched will almost certainly find contradictory evidence. The reason can be one of two possibilities. It is plausible that the relationship discovered by these studies is real or genuine. It is also possible that the association identified by this research is spurious or the result of random error whereby methodological, statistical, or conceptual problems within the study produce misleading findings. To resolve this conundrum, one must critically assess the evidence reported in the research and examine trends over time.

There are in the deterrence literature—not surprisingly—several studies that conclude that harsher sentences reduce crime rates. However, the majority of the findings produced by this research are unreliable and, by extension, should cautiously be dismissed. Indeed, these studies suffer from multiple problems that could clearly bias their findings. In particular, the conclusions drawn by some researchers can be more readily explained by mechanisms (e.g., incapacitation) other than deterrence. In addition, the ways in which the principal variables (severity of sentence or crime) are measured in some of the studies are problematic, casting doubt on their meaning and implications. Further, issues of questionable data selection raise skepticism surrounding the generalizability of a number of the findings. Similarly, several studies draw causal inferences that the nature of their data does not justify. Finally, no consistent patterns may be found for some of the results, suggesting the possibility of random fluctuation or chance occurrence.

A. Studies That Can Best Be Explained by Mechanisms Other than Deterrence

Many of the studies that relate "crime levels" to "punishment levels" suffer from a number of different problems (Nagin 1998). Aside from whether an apparent drop in crime has anything to do with changes in the criminal justice system, it is often virtually impossible to differentiate increased severity from other possible causes. An increase in severity is often associated (as it was in the United States) with increased numbers of police and modifications in the manner in which the police target crime. In this way, changes in severity are frequently related to changes in the probability of apprehension. Further, alterations in sentencing severity are frequently also associated with modifications in release procedures (e.g., abolition of parole or restrictions in it). Thus, these changes may relate to "incapacitation" effects. Looking at the "500 percent growth in prison population" (Nagin 1998, p. 28) that took place in the United States in the last two decades of the twentieth century, Nagin notes that "any effect on the crime rate of the increase in prison population reflects the effect of an amalgam of potentially interacting treatments" (1998, p. 28). Though relatively little is fully understood about the drop in violent crime that took place in the United States beginning in the early 1990s, there is no logical reason to attribute it to the general deterrent impact of increased imprisonment.

This affirmation takes on particular relevance when examining Levitt's 1996 study that was originally cited as evidence of the deterrent impact of punishment severity. This paper assessed the effects of prison overcrowding litigation on crime. In certain (largely southern) U.S. states, large numbers of inmates were freed before their scheduled release dates as a result of court orders to reduce overcrowding in prison. In effect, the total amount of punishment that sentenced offenders received was suddenly reduced on a once-only basis for those who were incarcerated at the time of the litigation. Levitt suggests that the apparent increase in crime that occurred in these states following this event was a result of a reduced deterrent impact (due to abbreviated prison terms).

Various other commentators (Nagin 1998; von Hirsch et al. 1999) have noted that the impact—if one actually exists—of the early release of a large number of prisoners is more plausibly related to the reduced incapacitation effect of suddenly freeing them. Levitt himself, in his 2002 review of deterrence, appears to agree that the results are explainable by incapacitation. More generally, though, Nagin points out that "Levitt's estimate [of crime increases caused by the unanticipated release of prisoners] is not likely to be informative about policies affecting prison sanctions for specific types of offenses" (1998, p. 29).

Beyond these obvious problems, Levitt also failed to control for other possible explanations. Knowing that something changes (in this case, crime rates) after some event occurs (release of prisoners from prison) does not identify that event as the only possible cause. The paper provides no evidence of the mechanism that would explain the increase in crime. For example, no data are reported that would suggest that anyone (least of all potential offenders) believed that time served in prison would be less than it had previously been (nor, of course, was there any evidence that it would be less in the future). One might suggest that a potential offender who was aware that large numbers of prisoners had been released before their scheduled dates might also be sufficiently informed to realize that this reduced punishment for one group of offenders had no necessary bearing on the penalty which he or she would experience if apprehended and convicted years (or even decades) later for a similar offense. That is, unless, of course, the offender had read Levitt's paper.

Another paper that inexplicably makes it into the deterrence literature as support for a deterrent effect of harsher sentences is one by Marvell and Moody (1994). The study is framed in terms of incapacitation and focuses largely on the problem of estimating the number of offenses that prisoners might have committed if they had been in the community. In a complex analysis, they suggest that changes in prison populations in the United States are associated with changes in crime rates for certain offenses. However, there are numerous difficulties involved in interpreting this article as evidence of deterrence. Among them, no attempt is made to estimate general deterrent effects independent of incapacitation effects or the effect of the changes in the likelihood of apprehension, either of which could plausibly account for their results.

One must be vigilant in separating the effects of certainty from those of severity. A study by Wright (1996) demands a careful reading of his results in order not to confuse these two issues. In responding to those who suggest that variations in harshness within the range that would be plausible in most societies would not add deterrent value, Wright cites evidence that a "summary of sophisticated studies of drunk driving penalties shows that tougher enforcement efforts and more certain punishments generally reduce drunk driving rates" (1996, p. 262). We do not take issue with either the cited finding or the specific statement that is made. Rather, we point out that a reader who was not careful in differentiating between severity of penalty and certainty of apprehension ("tougher enforcement efforts and more certain punishment") could easily have been misled to believe that this statement supports the idea that "prisons can achieve the objective of general deterrence"—the topic of this section (Wright 1996, p. 262).

Although not explicitly framed as a contribution to the deterrence literature, a study by Langan and Farrington (1998) has sometimes also been cited publicly as an example of the ways in which national sentencing policies affect crime. For example, the English *Sunday Times* concluded on the basis of this study that "the report appears to be a vindication of tough American policies such as 'zero tolerance' policing, 'three strikes and you're out,' which sends repeat offenders to jail for life, and frequent use of custodial sentences" (Rufford 1998, p. 2). This is clearly a more sophisticated study than many. However, several weaknesses deserve careful consideration.

First, this article could be seen to encourage the reader to mistakenly draw causal inferences about the relationship between criminal justice practices and crime levels. The study looks at crime and "punishment" trends in two countries (the United States, and England and Wales—"England" for short) and "shows" that increases in "punishment" are associated with decreased crime in one country (the United States) while decreases in "punishment" are associated with increased crime in another (England). The problem with studies of this kind as evidence of deterrence is obvious: an infinite number of explanations can be offered for any single trend. For instance, an increase in the homicide rate in Canada during the 1960s could just as easily be attributed to the end of executions in Canada in the early 1960s, the growth in the proportion of the population of young males that took place at that time, the increased popularity of the Rolling Stones, sun spots, or none of the above. Said differently, a rise in crime in a particular jurisdiction (or nation, as is the case here) might be caused by any number of factors: decreased social services, increased enforcement (or increased numbers of police officers to apprehend offenders), broad social changes in the community, or some other alteration in the operation of the criminal justice system. Therefore, studies such as this one may be useful in developing hypotheses, but they cannot be used as serious explanations for changes in crime levels.

Further, the Langan and Farrington (1998) report looks at crime (measured both by victimization surveys and police reports) and the operation of the justice system in the United States and England, and suggests that the trends in crime and those in "punishment" (or the reaction to crime) in the two countries are different. By juxtaposing these trends in both nations, Langan and Farrington are implicitly asking the question of whether trends in crime are affected by trends in punishment. Unfortunately, these are not the ideal data to answer this question, given the doubtful comparability of the two countries under study. Crime patterns and criminal justice policies have changed in the past two decades in England and in the United States. Moreover, they have changed in different directions. While the United States has tended to favor intensive criminal justice processing, England has preferred more selective prosecution of crime, diverting relatively minor offenders out of the system and attempting—somewhat inconsistently—to develop punishments in the community and thereby limit the use of imprisonment. Similarly, crime patterns have also varied in the two countries. Murder rates in England have been low and unchanged since 1981, whereas American rates look more like a roller coaster: going down in the early 1980s, up in the late 1980s, and then down again since 1991 (Langan and Farrington 1998, p. 4, fig. 5). Comparing other specific crime rates across countries is equally problematic. Looking at robbery as an example, police statistics suggest that firearms were used in 5 percent of English robberies and 41 percent of U.S. robberies (Langan and Farrington 1998, p. iii).

Despite these inherent problems, this report compares the crime levels in these two countries across time. The danger of this practice is illustrated by a news report that quoted one of the authors of the study—Patrick Langan—as saying, "With rising punitiveness in the U.S., crime rates are falling. In England, there is less punitiveness and crime rates are rising" (Johnston 1998, p. 2; Lardner 1998, p. 2). Though perhaps descriptive, the causal inference suggested by this statement between the severity of criminal justice practices and levels of crime is clearly not justified on methodological grounds given the nature of the data.

The second weakness of this study is its use of problematic measures. In the summary that the authors prepared on the "justice system's impact on crime," Langan and Farrington state, "Negative correlations in England between trends in punishment *risk* and crime trends offer the strongest support for the theory that links falling risk of punishment to rising crime. Specifically, since 1981 the conviction rate fell in England and English crime rates . . . rose. . . . Likewise, the incarceration rate fell, and English crime rates . . . rose" (1998, p. 38). While statements such as these might seem to imply that failure to incarcerate people caused crime to rise (see p. 28 for "graphic" evidence that "incarceration rates" fell in England while rising in the United States), they may be more a reflection of misleading measures than actual patterns in the data.

There is more to the term "incarceration rates" than meets the eye. This variable does not mean the rate at which convicted offenders are put in prison. Rather, this variable—explained in the notes associated with a set of figures—is "the number of incarcerated persons per 1,000 *alleged offenders* [which was] obtained by dividing the number of juveniles and adults sentenced to incarceration for the specified crime during the year . . . by the number of persons committing the crime [taken from police *reports* of crime, whether or not the offender was apprehended] . . . that year" (1998 p. 62, emphasis added). Langan and Farrington state that incarceration rates are going "down" in England. However, in order for a person to be incarcerated, the offender has to not only be apprehended and convicted but also sentenced to prison. Hence, while the rate at which convicted offenders go to prison could plausibly remain the same, a decrease in apprehension or conviction rates would mean that the "incarceration rate" will still go down. The authors present changes in "conviction" rate in England and, not surprisingly, they tend to go down (1998, p. 18). However, this decline does not necessarily reflect "failed" prosecutions. On the contrary, these data are "convictions per 1,000 offenders" (apprehended or not). Failure to apprehend can obviously lead to failure to convict. But so can criminal justice policy. If minor offenders are apprehended but not prosecuted in the courts—instead being dealt with in the community—there will be a decrease in "convictions" (and, consequently, a decline in both the "conviction rate" and the "incarceration rate"). Using this type of definition, a successful diversion program—in which many minor offenders are placed in programs that might even reduce recidivism—would lead to a "lower conviction rate" and a "lower incarceration rate."

Similar skepticism surrounding the meaning of their measures arises with another variable: "days of incarceration an offender risks serving." The figures presented by Langan and Farrington show that the values of this measure are generally going up in the United States while they are unchanged or going down in England. However, one needs to carefully examine the meaning attributed to this factor. As they explain, "'Days of incarceration an offender risks serving' were obtained by multiplying the probability of conviction given an offence . . . by the probability of incarceration given conviction and by the average number of days served per incarceration sentence" (Langan and Farrington 1998, p. 63). In other words, let us assume that there are 1,000 burglaries in England, that approximately 60 percent of them are reported to the police (see p. 8), and that the police "record" about 40 percent of them (p. 10). Not everyone gets apprehended. In fact, most do not, and some of those who are apprehended are found not guilty. Some are also diverted into community programs. The result is that there are about eight burglary convictions per 1,000 alleged burglars in England (p. 18). About 40 percent of those convicted (see p. 22) are incarcerated. The report suggests that there are only about two burglars incarcerated per 1,000 alleged burglars (p. 28). These two burglars who make it this far in the process are each sentenced to about twelve months (p. 30) and each serves about six months (p. 32). In other words, the authors argue that twelve person-months (365 days) are served for 1,000 burglaries. Hence, the "days of incarceration a burglar risks serving" is less than one, or roughly 365/1,000 days or 0.4 days (p. 36). This figure is meaningless since the "days of incarceration a burglar risks serving" largely reflects the fact that most burglars are not apprehended.

The third problematic area of this study is, ironically, its findings. Even if the measurement difficulties were put aside, several of the results do not support their general conclusion that punishment severity affects crime trends. In particular, the measures of changes in punitiveness (Langan and Farrington 1998, p. 22) show essentially no change in the likelihood that a convicted offender will be sentenced to incarceration. While they tend to show that for property offenses, the United States incarcerates more, the court-based incarceration rates—that is, the probability that a convicted offender will go to prison—are essentially unchanged. Further, if one is interested in the "average incarceration sentence imposed on convicted offenders," one finds that, if anything, they tended to go up in both countries (or they stayed the same) (1998, p. 30). Finally, the percent of time served "is generally about the same in the U.S. and England" (1998, p. 35), and the changes over time are small and inconsistent (see p. 34, figs. 61–66). In other words, the inferences about "crime going up as punishment risk goes down" have nothing to do with punishment as meted out by the courts.

The inference that "increased punitiveness" is associated with lower crime rates is challenged by referring to the authors' own words: "correlations [in the United States] between punishment *severity* and crime trends were mixed (table 2, p. 39). Approximately half were positive [more punitiveness, more crime] and half were negative [more punitiveness, less crime]. Moreover, in instances where there were negative correlations, they were often weak. Furthermore, . . . correlations between punishment severity and [victimization] survey crime rates often had a different sign than correlations between severity and police-recorded rates for the same crime. In short, trends in punishment severity had an inconsistent relationship with trends in crime in the U.S." (1998, p. 38). They subsequently point out that some consistency existed for burglary but provide no explanation as to the reasons for the "consistency" for this particular offense and not others. Furthermore, the authors show these same mixed findings for England as well, providing little consistent support for the relationship between punishment severity and crime.

B. *Problems of Measurement (Either of Severity or of Crime)*

As Langan and Farrington (1998) demonstrate, measures matter. Unfortunately, this study is not unique in its lack of measures appropriate for examining the effects of sentence severity. For instance, a study by Klepper and Nagin (1989) has been cited as evidence of a deterrent effect of sentence severity. This article uses a scenario-based methodology to ask questions concerning a hypothetical case of tax evasion by a plumber to 163 students enrolled in an evening master's program of public management, presumably at Carnegie Mellon University. The measure of perceived severity of sanctions was the estimate given by the student of the chances that a tax-evading plumber would face criminal prosecution.

A somewhat simplified summary of one aspect of the findings is that students who thought that the tax-evading plumber would face criminal prosecution indicated that they would be less likely to evade tax if they were in the plumber's position. While these results appear to be compatible with a "deterrent" interpretation, Klepper and Nagin (1989) suggest that they are also consistent with the hypothesis that "the perceived probability of criminal prosecution is also a function of the taxpayer's noncompliance behavior" (1989, p. 238). Said differently, the fact that a person breaks the law can affect that person's estimate of the likelihood of apprehension. A person who breaks the law and does not get caught may change his or her views of the likelihood of being caught. In other words, the person's perceived apprehension risk may be the result of offending, not the other way around. Von Hirsch et al. suggest that although Klepper and Nagin "treat risk of prosecution as a severity variable, in view of the collateral social consequences of prosecution for the middle class individuals potentially involved" (von Hirsch et al. 1999, p. 35 n.), risk of prosecution is probably best considered to be related to certainty.

Beyond these measurement problems, we would, generally speaking, agree with von Hirsch et al. (1999) in their general critique of this type of methodology: "Scenario studies, one must remember, do not measure subjects' *actual* behavior, but only how they say they would behave in a given hypothetical situation (i.e., 'armchair deterrence'). A great deal therefore depends on whether the researchers have been successful in developing hypothetical situations in a way that is likely to reflect respondents' real-life behavioral choices" (1999, pp. 34–35). As they further note, these studies explore the link from "respondents' perceptions of the certainty or severity of punishment to their potential criminal choices. They do not explore the link from criminal justice policy changes to changes in those perceptions" (1999, pp. 34–35). Cavanagh (1993) summarizes the problems of many scenario-based studies in his review (conducted for the U.S. Office of National Drug Control Policy) of the deterrence literature in relation to drug crime but which, we argue, is equally applicable to the study by Klepper and Nagin (1989): "the sample is upper-middle-class and not at all representative of persons who are most likely to consider indulging in felonious behavior. Second, the responses are descriptions of how respondents feel they would behave in hypothetical situations not actual behavior in those situations" (Cavanagh 1993, p. 41).

In other papers, additional difficulties emerge in knowing exactly what a measure means. In a study claiming a deterrent effect of punishment severity on crime, Reilly and Witt (1996) examined certain crime rates across time in forty-two English police jurisdictions. Though the study purports to find correlations between harsh punishment and levels of crime, its measure of severity—the length of prison stay, given conviction—is peculiar under the circumstances. Indeed, it uses only average sentence length as its measure of severity, ignoring the fact that the probability of going to prison was relatively low in many instances as well as variable across time. As such, it is unclear in this study what the "severity" variable is actually measuring.

C. Data-Selection Issues

While no study is perfect, it is important to be able to understand the logic involved when data are selected for inclusion in a study. Unfortunately, this selection process is not always clear, raising doubts about the validity of the findings. For instance, in a study cited by Levitt (2002) as evidence that harsher sentences deter, Kessler and Levitt (1998) attempt to separate the impact of variation in sentence severity on deterrence and incapacitation by examining a referendum-induced sentencing policy change that came into effect in California in 1982. This alteration increased the sentences for a set of crimes that were of particular concern to members of the public (i.e., willful homicide, rape, robbery, aggravated assault with a firearm, and residential burglary). Kessler and Levitt compared changes in rate of these offenses to those of six other crimes not affected by the referendum (i.e., non-residential burglary, motor vehicle theft, theft under $200, theft over $200, nonaggravated assault, and aggravated assault without a firearm).

The first problem is obvious: the two groups of offenses constitute considerably different sets of crimes, and there is no reason to expect that short-term changes in one set (e.g., the more serious first set) might normally be expected to parallel those in the other set (the less serious offenses). Furthermore, the second group is generally more prevalent than the first. Finally, we could find no clear and convincing rationale for comparing these two subsets of crimes.

However, the most important problem with the paper is the researchers' inexplicable choice of data points to examine. More specifically, Kessler and Levitt (1998) chose only two data points (1979 and 1981) before the change in sentencing policy and two points subsequent to it (1983 and 1985). The reason for restricting the time after the change in policy to 1985 was said to be to avoid contamination by incapacitation effects (i.e., crime reduction because potential offenders were in prison longer). While it was argued that this incapacitative impact would likely occur only after the sentence enhancements took effect (i.e., some number of years after sentencing), the deterrent impact of the change in sentencing policy was expected to be immediate. However, we are left wondering why the even-numbered years were not included. For statistical reasons, it would also have been advisable

TABLE 1

Trend in Residential Burglary, 1979–85

Year	No. of Crimes (in Thousands)
1979	328
1981	369
1982	Change in sentencing policy
1983	309
1985	301

SOURCE.—Kessler and Levitt 1998, p. 26, table 1.

to break this time period down into shorter intervals to obtain more data observations, thereby more accurately illustrating any trends.

Even more perplexing is the reason guiding the authors' decision to examine only two pre- and postintervention data points. Without additional observations, we have no idea of the overall pattern before the change in sentencing policy. While Kessler and Levitt claim that the rate for the serious crimes had been going up (on the basis of a comparison of 1979 vs. 1981 only) but was reversed by the alteration of policy (in 1983 and 1985), we have no way of verifying this interpretation. To illustrate this problem more clearly, potentially the easiest way is to look at (simplified) data presented for residential burglary—the crime which the authors suggest showed the largest deterrent effect. The data are presented in table 1.

Kessler and Levitt argue that the change in policy that took place in 1982 reversed an upward trend. The problem with the "trend" before 1982 is that it is based on only two observations. It is not difficult to find a consistent trend with two data points. However, the interpretation of their "trend" (and, by extension, the conclusions drawn concerning a deterrent impact of the change in sentencing policy) could be considerably different depending on the values of other preintervention observations. To demonstrate, we have constructed three sets of hypothetical data for odd-numbered years between 1965 and 1977. Kessler and Levitt's data for 1979–85 are also presented in table 2.

If the preintervention data had looked like Pattern A, no one would plausibly believe that the change in sentencing policy had any positive impact on crime. The aberrant years would be 1979 and 1981—the years before the changes in policy. The years after the change in policy would be simply viewed as "normal" years. Pattern B would illustrate

TABLE 2

Hypothetical and Actual Trends in Residential Burglary

Year	Pattern A	Pattern B	Pattern C
Hypothetical data:			
1965	300	450	210
1967	305	410	245
1969	304	425	255
1971	309	372	277
1973	305	355	289
1975	306	370	301
1977	302	330	315
Actual data:			
1979	328	328	328
1981	369	369	369
		Change in law	
1983	309	309	309
1985	301	301	301

a general downward trend that was not completely consistent but continued through the period of the law change. Again, the evidence would not support the conclusion of a treatment effect. Only Pattern C could possibly be argued as demonstrating an intervention effect. These data display a general increase over time that is followed by a decrease occurring after 1981. If this decline continued and was consistent over time, it could plausibly be interpreted as being related to some event happening in 1982. However, without additional data points following the change in law, it is equally impossible to assess the postintervention trend. Indeed, the point that we are making is a simple one. Crime trends are not always consistent across time. As such, two points simply cannot be used to describe a "trend." In our opinion, no conclusions should be drawn from this paper.

A similar paper (Kessler and Levitt 1999) extended the analysis to include one more odd-year data point (1977) before the change and two more observations after the change (1987 and 1989). Interestingly, the risk of contamination by incapacitation effects—used to justify their prior study's rejection of data beyond 1985—no longer seemed to be a concern. Further, their examination of only odd-numbered years still remains a mystery. Similarly, despite having added three more data points to their analysis, we continue to be surprised by the choice of statistical techniques employed by Kessler and Levitt. Their data (or extended versions of them from publicly available data sources) are virtually ideal for carrying out an interrupted time-series analysis. This statistical approach—often used in social science—not only constitutes a considerably more powerful test of their research hypothesis, but also has the additional virtue of being able to handle data from even-numbered years just about as easily as they can for those from odd-numbered years.

Beyond this continuing enigma regarding the limited number of (odd-numbered) data points, only four "noneligible" crimes were used as comparison in this paper. However, the authors included an additional comparison between California and the rest of the United States. Rates were reported rather than numbers of crimes as had been the case in the earlier study. The principal problems with the findings of this paper are twofold. Anomalies in the results are not adequately explained. For example, one of the four "noneligible crimes" (burglary of a nonresidence) appears to show a dramatic drop in rate after the intervention that, presumably, had no bearing on this offense. In addition, the findings of this research are not discussed adequately within the wider deterrence literature. More specifically, this study (as well as the one preceding it) examines the impact of a legal change that is similar to the three-strikes legislation or other harsh sentencing practices. Although their findings are not consistent with those presented in other published research, Kessler and Levitt do not—for the most part—address this difference.

D. Studies in Which the Effects Do Not Show a Consistent, Replicated Pattern

Given that there are no accepted theories that explain or predict when differential sentencing practices are expected to affect crime and when they will not, one has special concerns about research whose findings are inconsistent and, by extension, theoretically inexplicable. In particular, a study by McDowall, Loftin, and Wiersema (1992) needs to be considered in light of this concern. This research examined the effects of laws imposed in three American states (Michigan, Florida, and Pennsylvania) that created mandated minimum prison sentences for offenses that involved the commission of certain other offenses with a firearm. The researchers looked at data from six cities (three in Florida, two in Pennsylvania, and one in Michigan) for homicides, assaults, and robberies with and without a firearm. There was an overall effect on gun homicides, but not gun assaults, or gun robberies. Further, the gun homicide effect showed up in Detroit, Philadelphia, Pittsburgh, and Tampa, but not Jacksonville and Miami. Gun assaults went up in Tampa and down in Jacksonville. Armed robberies were unaffected by the law.

Attributing these findings to deterrence is clearly problematic in that there is no theoretical reason that would predict effects on gun homicides but not on the other two (considerably more common) offenses. Similar arguments can be made for the appearance of an impact in some cities but not in others. More particularly, it is difficult to understand, given the magnitude of homicide penalties, how the expectation of an additional few years to one's sentence in a homicide offense would deter someone from committing the crime while the homicide penalty (without the firearm penalty added) would not have the same deterrent effect. Presumably, these results would only be relevant in those homicides that occur while committing another offense and in cases in which the sentence was less than life in prison. While the authors attribute the discrepancy to differences in the quality of the data, they provide us with no hard evidence on which to evaluate this explanation.

Another study that should be included within this wider category of theoretically inexplicable findings is one by Grasmick and Bryjak (1980). This research constitutes one of the more thoughtful survey studies on the deterrent impact of perceived punishment. It was carried out by asking 400 ordinary city respondents to indicate which of eight "crimes" (e.g., theft, littering, using fireworks within city limits) they had committed in the past. They were also asked the likelihood of being arrested by the police if they did each of these acts. Finally, the authors used two measures of the severity of the punishment: the chances of being imprisoned if the respondents were arrested, and one that might be called a "subjective" measure of severity. More specifically, study participants were asked to imagine that they had been arrested and found guilty, and were handed down the punishment that they thought they would get. They were subsequently required to "indicate how big a problem that punishment would create for [their] life" (1980, p. 480).

Clearly, there is a problem with the design of the study: the "crime" measure is retrospective and reflects what the person did in the past. In contrast, the certainty and severity measures are "current." In deterrence theory, we are interested in the opposite temporal ordering.

Nevertheless, the data are worth examining. As we described, there are four relevant measures: involvement in crime, a composite measure of the certainty of being apprehended, severity measured by a composite measure of the likelihood of imprisonment, and severity measured by the respondent's estimate of the degree to which the expected punishment would be a problem for them.

The respondents were divided into four groups according to how likely—across the eight offenses—they thought it was that they would be apprehended if they committed each of the offenses. From data presented in table 1 of the report (Grasmick and Bryjak 1980, p. 479), we estimated that most or all of the respondents in the highest-certainty group answered (combined across the eight offense categories) that they "probably would be" or "definitely would be" arrested by the police if they committed these offenses. For these people—and these people only—the subjective measure of severity (how much of a problem it would be if the respondent received the punishment that he or she expected) made a difference: those who anticipated that the expected punishment would have a serious effect on their lives were less likely (in the past) to have committed these offenses. In other words, crime involvement and subjective measures of severity were correlated in the direction consistent with deterrence theory.

For the other three groups—who indicated lower likelihoods of being apprehended—there was no relationship between subjective severity and offending. In fact, rather mundane findings emerge when one uses this measure. More specifically, if you think that you are likely or certain to get caught, the subjective estimate of the effect of the penalty for you makes a difference. Inversely, if you think that the likelihood of apprehension is less than "likely or certain," the subjective severity of the penalty has no effect. The deterrence literature is full of findings that people do not commit serious criminal offenses when they think that they are going to get caught and they believe that the expected penalty would be devastating to them. The problem with many criminal offenses is that the objective—and subjective—likelihood of being apprehended is undoubtedly low. It is likely that few people commit offenses thinking that they probably or definitely would be caught. Hence, these data—although logical—are not particularly helpful in determining legislative or judicially created sentencing policy.

It is also noteworthy that the conventional measure of severity—whether the respondent thought that prison would be the ultimate result of arrest—showed a rather peculiar relationship to offending. Those who were most likely to think that they would be jailed if arrested were most likely to be those who had committed offenses. This result is clearly in the opposite direction from that predicted by deterrence theory. Indeed, whatever the reason for these findings, they do not support the notion that harsh sentences will deter.

E. Studies in Which the Conclusions Seem to Be at Odds with the Data

In an extensive analysis of the implementation and impact of three-strikes and truth-in-sentencing legislation in various American states, Chen (2000)—in a political science dissertation with James Q. Wilson as co-chair of the committee—provides a set of findings that is not always, in our assessment, consistent with her commentary on these findings.[3] Her main analysis of the impact of this type of legislation on crime rates consists of an assessment of crime data in fifty states over a twelve-year period. Each of these "state-years" appears to be considered a data point for her principal analyses. The best evidence that she could find of an impact of the sentencing legislation on crime appears to come from an analysis that, in effect, apparently compares the four post-three-strikes years (1994–97) for California with all other state-year combinations.

The findings are instructive for those interested in deterrence, even though the author suggests (2000, p. 58) that the effects (presumably for some of the less serious crimes, in particular) could be due to incapacitation rather than deterrence. The reason for this is that some offenders—under three-strikes legislation in California—would get a prison sentence under the new law but would not have been imprisoned prior to its enactment. In addition, some offenders would get dramatically longer sentences than they would have prior to the implementation of the three-strikes laws.

Chen (2000) presents the findings as supportive of deterrence. In summarizing the "trend in California after three strikes," she states that "most coefficients [in her analysis of the impact of the legislation on crime] [are] not significant, but they are large in magnitude and show a very clear pattern" (2000, p. 98). It must be remembered that

---

[3] This is an extensive dissertation addressing a number of questions related to the legislative choice to impose three-strikes and "truth in sentencing" laws as well as their effects. It uses several different sets of data and provides some interesting and useful findings. Our concerns are limited only to the inferences related to the general deterrent impact of the three-strikes legislation.

her analysis had 600 data points. Particularly with such a large N, it is our conservative view that findings that are "not significant" are best thought of as exactly that: not significant. "Not significant" in ordinary circumstances means that one does not reject the "null hypothesis" that there is no impact of the treatment variable—in this case the three-strikes legislation—on crime. Despite this traditional practice in social science, Chen concludes that "even when pre-existing trends in California and in other Three Strikes states are included as control variables, a consistent pattern of substantial declines was found in the growth rates of several types of crime, and these declines appeared to be temporally and spatially correlated with the adoption of Three Strikes and [Truth in Sentencing] in California. Large and statistically significant declines occurred in motor vehicle theft. These findings are consistent with the idea that deterrent effects are more likely to exist for property offenses, which are more likely to be 'calculated' than violent crimes" (2000, p. 236).

Social scientists generally accept as "statistically significant" something whose likelihood of being a "chance" event is less than 5 percent. In contrast to most traditional social scientific research, Chen uses the 10 percent level for her main analyses. As such, one would expect to see instances that she calls "significant" effects that are, in fact, random (chance) events more often in her findings than in most others in the social sciences. The results that she presents as showing an impact of three-strikes and truth in sentencing in California are shown in table 3 (2000, pp. 82–85).

It is worth repeating that she describes these findings—misleadingly, in our opinion—as supportive of the conclusion that the legislation had an effect in California. However, she clearly concludes that three-strikes legislation does not appear to have had an effect on crime nationwide.

In a later part of this same document, she presents a more detailed analysis of what is apparently part of the Zimring, Hawkins, and Kamin (2001) data described briefly elsewhere in this essay. This analysis examined the proportion of people with "strikes" who were arrested before and after the three-strikes law came into force. Her description of the findings is illuminating, particularly when juxtaposed with information provided in the footnotes. In the text, Chen states that "robbers, property offenders, and drug offenders with two strikes [or more] on their criminal records all represented a much smaller proportion of the post-three-strikes sample than they did in the pre-three-

TABLE 3

Summary of Findings, Chen (2000)

Crime Category	Statistical Significance
Overall violent crime	N.S.
Overall property crime	N.S. at the traditional 5 percent level, "significant" at $p < .10$
Murder	N.S.
Rape	N.S.
Aggravated assault	N.S.
Robbery	N.S.
Burglary	N.S.
Larceny	N.S.
Motor vehicle theft	N.S. at the traditional 5 percent level, "significant" at $p < .10$

SOURCE.—Chen 2000, pp. 82–85.
NOTE.—N.S. = not significant.

strikes sample, lending support to the idea that three-strikes had some impacts on the offenders in these categories who were most likely to receive the mandatory 'third strike' sentence of 25 years to life" (2000, pp. 173–74). However, she notes later in the text that these findings were not significant. Footnote 79 tells the careful reader that the statistical tests applied to these data demonstrate that the likelihood that each of these findings is a result of chance is 32 percent for robbers, 54 percent for property offenders, and 52 percent for drug offenders. Given that social scientists typically accept the 5 percent standard, we believe that these findings are best described as being "chance" or "random" events and not worthy of consideration. Indeed, these significance levels suggest that no differences exist between the pre- and postintervention periods for these particular offenses.

Finally, it is noteworthy that Chen found no significant effects (even at her impoverished definition of significance) for three-strikes legislation across the United States on any of her nine measures. She attributes this largely to the fact that these laws were not implemented as thoroughly elsewhere as they were in California. However, from a deterrence perspective, this is not of central importance: the legislation received a great deal of publicity, and it took careful studies such as her own—carried out years afterward—to discover that the laws were not being used as extensively as one might have thought. We doubt that many offenders were conducting complex multivariate analyses to determine if three-strikes legislation was being fully implemented.

III. Evidence Suggesting That Increased Severity of Sentences Will Not Deter

Philip Cook (1980) suggested—more than twenty years ago—that policy experiments would, in the end, provide the most useful evidence for assessing the effects of harsh sentences on crime. The three-strikes laws, and other dramatic changes in sentencing policy in the United States introduced in the last ten years, fulfill this prophecy, creating an almost ideal environment for testing deterrent effects. Deterrence is ultimately a perceptual theory: the potential offender must hold the belief that increased penalties will result from apprehension and conviction. Three-strikes legislation in various states of the United States was introduced during a flurry of publicity and, in California, as a result of a referendum vote. Hence, the opportunity for people to know about the increased penalty was much higher than would occur if high penalties were imposed simply through routine cases in a courtroom.

We suggest in this section that the continuing absence of firm evidence demonstrating the existence of crime-reduction patterns attributable to general deterrent effects of these dramatically harsher sentences is important. However, our examination of the literature is not limited to this type of research. Rather, we extend the perceptual element—central to the three-strikes avenue of inquiry—to studies that examine the offenders' thought processes. Particularly when combined with individual studies or programs of research focusing on specific types of offenses or criminal justice punishments, the consistency of findings provides the most convincing evidence yet that variation in sentence severity does not affect crime levels.

A. Simple Descriptive Data on Three-Strikes Laws

We begin our examination of the three-strikes laws and deterrence with several fairly simple descriptive studies. In our opinion they illustrate the importance of looking at the impact of sentencing reforms broadly rather than selectively. The starting point for a study by Zimring, Hawkins, and Kamin (2001) was a statement by the governor and attorney general of California implying that the three-strikes legislation was responsible for a 27 percent to 31 percent drop in crime. However, these researchers note that the rapid decline in these crime measures in California had started before the three-strikes laws came into force, and that the drop in crime in Los Angeles (the country's second largest city) was less than the drop in New York and Chicago (cities that did not have three-strikes legislation at the time). The only evidence that they could find that was possibly consistent with a deterrent impact of this type of law was that the proportion of felony arrest suspects (in a sample of large California cities) who were eligible for enhanced sentences under the three-strikes legislation decreased by 1.1 percent. However, this very small effect held only when one examined arrests of third-strike-eligible offenders, but not second-strike-eligible arrests. Given that these are arrest data (rather than crime data) and do not consistently meet normal standards of statistical significance across groups eligible for increased penalties, the conclusion that the authors drew appears to us to be reasonable: "The decline in crime observed after the effective date of the Three Strikes law was not the result of the statute" (2001, p. 101).

Nevertheless, Zimring, Hawkins, and Kamin (2001) are cautious about dismissing the possibility that there was an impact on third-strike-eligible offenders. Clearly, though, we should recall that the only data they have on this aspect of the impact of the law relate to arrests rather than offending by this group or to overall crime rates. Further, the impact on arrests—if due to the change in the law—is very small. As the authors point out in the context of noting that there may be a weak deterrence effect on arrests of the third strike, "The most obvious practical finding of this study is the tiny maximum impact of the new law on crime in California" (Zimring, Hawkins, and Kamin 2001, p. 105).

The concern one might have with this study is that other causes of the change in the pattern of arrests were not examined. In particular, the measure that is used is the proportion of second- and third-strike-eligible suspects in certain California cities. For some offenses, the rates of clearance by arrests are low. In addition, other possible explanations (e.g., changes in police targeting of potential offenders) were not considered. In addition, there is no evidence that the legislation had an overall impact on crime in California. Further, their use of only two data points before and after the implementation of the three-strikes laws as well as the absence of control variables undermine their findings. Indeed, one would not want to make much of the effect, especially given its size. For these reasons, studies that focus more directly on crime measures (rather than those of arrest) are of greater relevance.

A study by Schiraldi and Ambrosio (1997) provides valuable insights into the (lack of) deterrence effect of harsher sentences on crime rates. These authors compared thirteen states that brought in tough sentencing laws by 1993 with the thirty-seven that had not. This latter group was divided into those that introduced three-strikes laws after the first group and those that did not have three-strikes legislation at all during the study period. They found no evidence that violent crime (the apparent focus of three-strikes laws), or crime generally, had been affected by the legislation. Indeed, their findings are easy to describe: "From 1994–1995, violent crime in non-three-strikes states fell *nearly three times* more rapidly than in three-strikes states. In non-three-strikes states, violent crime fell by 4.6 percent. In states which have passed three-strikes laws, crime fell by only 1.7 percent" (1997, p. 2). Further, California—the state most often identified with the three-strikes model of sentencing—had an overall drop comparable to that in non-three-strikes states. Even when Schiraldi and Ambrosio (1997) examined the data for "total crime," the results were similar. In particular, they note that "from 1994–95, total crime decreased by an average of 0.4 percent in the three-strikes states and decreased by an average of 1.2 percent in states which have not implemented the three-strikes law" (1997, p. 4).

For our purposes, these simple comparisons are useful for a somewhat different reason. More specifically, the data clearly show the variability across jurisdictions. Indeed, crime rates in some states with three-strikes legislation went up while they went down in others. The data in table 4 show the difficulty in comparing individual states with one another. States (including the District of Columbia) were divided into those that had three-strikes legislation by the end of 1994, those that implemented three-strikes laws in 1995 or later, and those that did not have three-strikes legislation by the completion of the study.

If California (a three-strikes state) were to be compared to neighboring Arizona (a non-three-strikes state), three-strikes legislation would look promising as a deterrence policy. California's rate of overall crime decreased 5 percent and violent crime went down by 4.2 percent, while Arizona shows an increase in total crime of 7.3 percent and a rise in violent crime of 5.0 percent. On the other hand, a comparison of California with New York (a non-three-strikes state) would not be as favorable for three-strikes laws. In fact, total crime fell 10.2 percent and violent crime declined 13 percent in New York. Similarly, the total crime in Michigan (a non-three-strikes state) decreased by 4.3 percent

TABLE 4

Number of States Showing an Increase/Decrease in Total Crime
and Violent Crime as a Function of the Existence
of Three-Strikes Legislation

	Total Crime			Violent Crime		
	Three-Strikes States	"Late" Three-Strikes States	Non-Three-Strikes States	Three-Strikes States	"Late" Three-Strikes States	Non-Three-Strikes States
No. of states where crime decreased	4	2	13	5	7	15
No. of states where crime increased	9	9	14	8	4	12
Total	13	11	27	13	11	27

SOURCE.—Schiraldi and Ambrosio 1997, pp. 8–9, tables 1–3.

and its rate of violent crime fell by 9.7 percent. In brief, variability, more than consistency, appears to describe state patterns of crime during this period in the United States, illustrating the dangers of haphazardly constructed comparisons between jurisdictions.

This was one of the earlier studies, and as such the authors are correct in concluding that "it is entirely too early to conclude if three-strikes legislation is working or not" (Schiraldi and Ambrosio 1997, p. 4). Interestingly, one of the arguments proposed to justify such a cautious conclusion was that the deterrent effects of three-strikes laws are sometimes confused with their incapacitation potential. However, it is in the early stages that one would expect deterrence impacts to be greatest. This is when there is the most publicity surrounding the legislation. Incapacitation effects would be expected to show up later in time as the enhancement on sentence length began to be felt. Hence, the conclusion that the effects of the laws, overall, are "inconclusive" (1997, p. 6) is a sensible but conservative conclusion.

B. More Sophisticated Studies of Three-Strikes Laws

In a larger study of the impact of three-strikes legislation, Stolzenberg and D'Alessio (1997) examined the effects of the new law on felonies (which presumably should be deterred by the three-strikes legislation) using month-by-month data from California's ten largest cities. For comparison the authors looked at reported misdemeanor larcenies, which one would assume not to be affected by the three-strikes law.

The findings are easy to describe: "The results generally indicate that the three-strikes law did not decrease the California Crime Index [a crime rate based on the rate of reported "index" crimes] below that expected on the basis of preexisting trends" (1997, p. 464). This study correctly examines preexisting trends since crime in California—as elsewhere in North America—was going down before the three-strikes law came into force. As we demonstrated with the Kessler and Levitt (1998) paper, simple "before vs. after" comparisons when examining trends over time can be misleading. If crime were already going down before the three-strikes law was introduced, one cannot logically attribute the drop in crime to the new legislation. In one city (Anaheim), there was a significant decrease in the crime index not attributable to preexisting trends. However, there is no explanation linked to the three-strikes laws that might explain this isolated effect in comparison with that found in the other nine cities. The best guess is that something unrelated to the three-strikes legislation was responsible for the apparent drop in this one city.

This set of findings is very similar to those presented by Austin et al. (1999). They examined California crime data at a county level. As they affirm, in this case as in many other studies suggesting deterrent effects of interventions, it is important to look both at preexisting trends (measured with a reasonable number of data points) and trends elsewhere. The authors note that the implementation of the law was more complete (i.e., harsher) in some counties (San Diego, Los Angeles, and Sacramento) than in others (San Francisco and Alameda). Hence, they argued that the reduction should be larger in those counties in which the prosecutors and police were mostly likely to implement the harsh penalties mandated by the three-strikes law. The results demonstrate that crime trends (or violent crime trends) appeared to be unrelated to the aggressiveness with which the laws were enforced. They also compared three states that had three-strikes laws by 1993–94 with three others that did not. In this rather simple comparison, crime patterns were not consistent with the deterrence hypothesis. As they note in conclusion, "The bottom line is that California, which is the only state to aggressively implement a three-strikes law, has shown no superior reductions in crime rates. Furthermore, within Cal-

ifornia, counties that have vigorously implemented the law also show
no superior decreases in crime rates as compared to other counties"
(1999, p. 158).

C. Studies of the Impact of New Harsh Sentencing Regimes

Research has also examined the effects of other harsher sentencing
policies. For instance, a study by Wicharaya (1995) assesses changes in
sentencing law that took place in forty-five states from 1959 to 1987.
Using time-series techniques, Wicharaya (1995) examined the impact
of these alterations in sentencing structure across jurisdictions, rather
than concentrating on a single or a small number of states. These
changes generally fall into the category of "get tough on crime" (1995,
p. 161), and include such regimes as mandatory or presumptive sentences and mandatory minimum sentences. The premise of most of
these reforms was to make prison sentences more certain or longer.
Not surprisingly, many were undermined in the court process in various ways. Nevertheless, because they typically came into force as a result of high-profile political processes and appear—at least on the surface—to meet the criteria of increasing the perception that harsh
sentences would flow from a conviction for one of the relevant offenses, they can be seen as forming a reasonable basis for expecting
deterrence effects. These results show the importance of replication.
Indeed, a focus on a single state might have led to a conclusion that
would not describe the chaotic nature of the findings. Wicharaya examined data from forty-five states on four violent crimes. His findings
are summarized in table 5.

Wicharaya notes that the relationship between sentencing reform
and these offenses is mixed. Changes are as likely to be in one direction
as the other. One can hardly suggest that the data in table 5 support
the notion that increased severity of sentences is associated with a decline in crime. In his own words, "Sentencing reforms have not yet
proved to be efficacious anticrime measures" (1995, p. 161).

Wicharaya (1995) subsequently extends this analysis by employing a
more elaborate statistical approach to these same data—a "pooled time
series" technique—that allows a generalizable conclusion (across
states) on the effects of sentencing reforms. The author summarizes
these findings as again showing "no crime reduction effects of the reform on any crime type nationwide. Both murder and robbery rates
remain unaffected in some states, but increased significantly in the remaining part of the country. Similarly, both rape and aggravated as-

TABLE 5

Number of States in Which Changes in Their Crime Rates
(Following the Introduction of New Sentencing Regimes) Are
Consistent/Inconsistent with a Deterrent Effect of Harsher Sanctions

Crime Type	No. of States with a Change in the Direction Expected by Deterrence Theory (Decline in Crime)		No. of States with a Change in the Direction Opposite to That Expected by Deterrence Theory (Increase in Crime)		Total No. of States
	Significant Decline	Nonsignificant Decline	Significant Increase	Nonsignificant Increase	
Murder	4	14	7	20	45
Rape	4	10	6	25	45
Robbery	4	13	7	21	45
Assault	6	15	7	17	45

SOURCE.—Data adapted from Wicharaya 1995, p. 162, table 7.2.

sault rates increased significantly throughout the United States. The evidence of no deterrent effects is consistent across all crime types" (1995, pp. 150–51). The author is even more definitive in his conclusions later in the paper: "Violent crime rates were not deterred by the new sentencing policies" (1995, p. 164). It should be noted that another part of this study shows that harsh sentencing regimes were typically not successfully (or consistently) implemented. A true believer in deterrence could argue that this study does not constitute a fair test of deterrence. However, to argue this is to ignore one important fact: deterrence, by definition, is a perceptual theory. Hence, it is perception that counts. The publicized legal changes did not affect the crimes upon which the author focused.

Beyond the U.S. reality, mandatory sentences in the form of three-strikes legislation also found their way to Australia in the 1990s (Morgan 2000). Although mandatory (prison) sentences came under fire in early 2000 when the predictable types of cases occurred and were publicized (e.g., mandatory imprisonment for a yo-yo thief, a year in prison for an aboriginal man who stole a towel from a washing line to use as a blanket, and a prison sentence for a one-legged pensioner who damaged a hotel fence), the laws in western Australia and the Northern Territory were written broadly enough to ensure that these kinds of cases would result in a prison sentence.

The rationales given for mandatory sentencing laws in Australia (as elsewhere) have varied over time. General deterrence constituted one justification. However, the evidence as summarized by Morgan (2000) showed that crime rates were unaffected by mandatory minimums. Notwithstanding the fact that the laws unequivocally increased the likelihood of a prison sentence and received considerable publicity (providing optimal conditions for deterrence effects), there is "compelling evidence" that the laws did not achieve a deterrent effect (Morgan 2000, p. 172). The author notes that governments "have effectively conceded that mandatory sentences have no deterrent effect, and that there is a need for judicial discretion and for the more vigorous use of diversionary schemes and alternative strategies" (2000, p. 182).

Further evidence of a lack of deterrent effects of new harsh sentencing laws comes from a careful analysis by Kovandzic (1999) of the impact of Florida's habitual offender law. While often justified as an effective way of incapacitating high-rate offenders, this type of legislation is also sometimes justified in terms of deterrence. Kovandzic examined the deterrent effects of the additional amount of prison time imposed by the habitual offender law at a county level. His findings—using data from all Florida counties for a seventeen-year period (1981–97)—would not bring cheer to those who think that crime can easily be legislated away. As the author states, "The results suggest that incarcerating [habitual offenders] for extended periods of time has no significant impact on short or long-term crime rates" (1999, p. viii).

Notwithstanding this overall assessment, Kovandzic did find what he describes as "*weak* empirical support for the [habitual offender] law effectiveness hypothesis in high population counties, but the reasons for the significant results remain ambiguous" (1999, p. 69). In the face of these findings, this author recommends that these significant effects be seen in the context of the existence of other effects in the opposite direction from that which would be expected (1999, pp. 68–69). In addition, there is no theoretical reason to expect effects in one size county but not another. One may add another argument in favor of largely dismissing this particular finding. The problem with large studies such as this one (and others such as that by Chen, described earlier) in which numerous statistical tests are being carried out is that some of them are going to be "significant" simply by chance. Kovandzic concludes that the results of this study should not be used to support the view that there is a deterrent impact of the legislation: "Of the 720 crime [analyses performed], no [measures—habitual offender prison months, or the extra months that habitual offenders received in that county] show consistent effects across crime types, varying model specifications, or samples. The few lags that are significant and negative (48) [more imprisonment, less crime] are not consistent with any theory of deterrent or incapacitative effects and are usually balanced by positive, significant associations (24)" (1999, p. 72).

D. Offenders' Thought Processes

The reduction of crime through general deterrence is based on a perceptual theory: the behavior of a person is hypothesized to be related to the severity of sentences because he or she knows—or perceives—the sanctions to have a certain level of magnitude. Within this context, it is worthwhile to examine several studies in which offenders or potential offenders are asked about the importance of penalties. This approach is particularly relevant to consider after looking at the impact of sentencing law changes such as the three-strikes legislation. Indeed, the findings from this research naturally raise the intriguing question of why offenders do not understand (or do not accept or care) that they will be punished harshly. Asked differently, why it is that offenders do not appear to act as the economists say they should (i.e., calculating utility functions before deciding whether to commit an offense).

Like scenario-based research, these studies of offenders' post hoc explanations of their own thought processes need to be interpreted cautiously. In everyday life, we are often not particularly good at identifying the importance or relevance of factors that affect our behavior. Furthermore, the samples of those caught may not be representative of offenders, generally, or of potential offenders. Nevertheless, they are worth examining, in part because they may tell us something about offenders' thought processes in deciding whether or how to carry out an offense.

In a study of eighty largely middle-class former sellers of cocaine, Waldorf and Murphy (1995) were able to identify only two people for whom fear of rearrest or imprisonment had been one of the influences in their decision to stop selling cocaine. This is interesting for a number of reasons. It is not what we would have anticipated. On the contrary, one would have expected, at least, that the normal job stresses they experienced due to concerns about apprehension would have been a major factor in a decision to look for another profession. However, the subjects of this study were not impetuous street sellers of drugs. Rather, they were, for the most part, relatively well-educated, middle-aged men who were making a living or supplementing their income by selling cocaine, often to other middle-class people. That only two of the eighty appeared to have been stopped in part because of criminal justice concerns is notable. Concerns about customers, informants, and so on were more important than police investigations (let alone court decisions). "More than half reported that they felt no criminal justice pressures at all to stop sales. Of those who reported pressures there were near equal percentages of direct [e.g., police investigations] and indirect pressures. The most frequently mentioned indirect pressure to stop was an arrest of a member of a supply network" (1995, p. 31). The severity of the punishment that they might receive from the criminal justice system was not important in their decision to abandon the trade.

Similar findings were reported in a study of ordinary repetitive offenders by Tunnell (1996). This author interviewed sixty prisoners who had been in prison twice or more and at least once for armed robbery or burglary. Respondents were asked to describe their most recent crime, the context in which they made the decision to commit it, and their method of assessing the risk and rewards of committing the crime. The respondents were blunt in reporting that neither they nor other thieves whom they knew considered legal consequences when planning crimes. Thoughts about getting caught were put out of their minds. As one burglar responded to the question of whether "the crime or thinking about getting caught for the crime" came first, "The crime comes first because it's enough to worry about doing the actual crime itself without worrying about what's going to happen if you get caught" (1996, p. 43). Fifty-two of the sixty prisoners reported that they did not think that they would be caught and, as a result, punishment size was unimportant. Thirty-two of the same sixty inmates apparently did not know what the punishment would likely be. Most (fifty-one of the sixty) believed that they would not be arrested. Even with regard to those who had stopped offending at one point in their lives, the reasons reported were other than threats of punishment.

There was some evidence of short-term individual deterrence. In particular, some of those who had previously been threatened with being declared habitual criminals expressed concern about this possibility in the future. However, predicting the future is more risky than describing the past. Just as one would not want to put much faith in the view of a murderer that capital punishment would have deterred him, one would not want to build criminal justice policy on the views or predictions of repeat property offenders regarding what they would do in the future. Further, these findings should be interpreted, as the author points out, in the context of the sample: imprisoned offenders. While this study sheds some light on the decision-making processes of those who were caught, it does not necessarily inform us of the factors that may affect other groups of people.

Despite these limitations to the generalizability of the findings, it is interesting that the lack of thought given by offenders to criminal justice consequences is replicated by Benaquisto (1997) in an interview study of 152 inmates in three Canadian penitentiaries. Focusing on the 122 inmates whose own description of their offenses was corroborated by information in their prison files, she asked inmates to talk about the circumstances that led to their arrest. The goal was to try to understand whether the inmate had "anything in mind about whether they would be punished." As Benaquisto notes, "it was relatively rare for an inmate to offer a 'crime story' without referring to the potential risk of being caught or punished. A dominant theme in most such stories is why the deed was done in spite of the consequences, or why and how deterrence failed" (1997, p. 11).

Only 13 percent of her sample "explicitly spoke of their actions in terms of costs and benefits" (1997, pp. 17–18). These individuals tended, it seemed, to be accomplished "professional" offenders (e.g., high-level drug dealers with a great deal of experience) who felt that they could beat the system. In contrast, the largest group of offenders—the noncalculators—simply did not think about the possible consequences. More precisely, it is not that they calculated incorrectly. Rather, they did not calculate consequences at all. As Benaquisto affirms, "crime that results in incarceration is, much more often than not, action taken without any attention, much less reasoned attention to the possible incarceration as a consequence" (1997, pp. 31–32). Not surprisingly, her conclusion is pessimistic: "the vast majority of those already engaging in criminal activities, activities of the most serious nature (and who have, for the most part, experienced punishments prior to the one they are currently experiencing) are very bad candidates for an enhanced deterrence model" (1997, p. 31). Perhaps the only optimism resides with the small minority of federal prisoners whose consideration of utility functions of offending reassures economists that they are not alone in believing in deterrence.

Benaquisto's general conclusion is consistent with that drawn by von Hirsch et al. (1999). In discussing a study of active and persistent burglars (who were interviewed in the community rather than in prison), they note that most of the burglars "consciously refused to dwell on the possibility of getting caught" (1999, p. 36). Apprehension risk affected "*how* they committed the burglary . . . to a much greater extent than *whether* they offended" (1999, p. 36). As von Hirsch et al. (1999) point out, improving marginal deterrence would require that such people—currently inclined to offend—be persuaded not to offend because of the enhanced penalty. This practice is unlikely if the possible penalty is not part of their decision-making process.

One situation in which one might expect people to calculate utility functions of offending is a crime that people commit with calculators in their hands: tax evasion. In a Canadian survey carried out in 1990 (Varma and Doob 1998), 18.4 percent of respondents indicated that they had evaded tax. By interviewing both offenders and nonoffenders, this study has the advantage of being able to compare their views of punishment. The sample of offenders (tax evaders) involved, almost exclusively, those who had not been apprehended. Not surprisingly, those who thought that tax evaders (by way of either undeclared cash income, undeclared small business income, or falsified business deductions) would be likely to be caught were less likely to report that they had evaded tax in the previous three years than were those who thought that tax evaders would not be caught. As in other areas of crime, the perceived likelihood of apprehension for a crime is negatively related to involvement in the crime and consistent with deterrence theory.

To test the effect of severity, people were also asked what they thought the penalty would be for evading tax on one of three different amounts ($500, $5,000, and $100,000). Predictably, people thought that the sanction would increase with the size of the tax evasion. However, what is important is that the relationship between expected penalty and reported tax evasion was opposite to what would be predicted by deterrence theory. For example, 27 percent of those who thought that jail would be the likely penalty for evading $5,000 in tax had evaded tax in the previous three years. In contrast, the tax evasion rate for those who thought that a fine would be the result was 16 percent. Said differently, tax evaders do not appear to be controlled by the expected size of the criminal justice penalty.

E. More Specific Studies

Despite the apparent predominance of studies that examine general deterrent effects of sentence severity across (groups of) offenses, a growing body of literature focuses on more specific types of crime or criminal justice punishment. For example, deterrence has been studied extensively within the context of drinking and driving. This research was carried out largely by H. Lawrence Ross and summarized in his 1982 book that affirms that enforcement campaigns of drinking-driving laws act by increasing people's perceptions of the likelihood of punishment. In contrast, Ross concludes that, when examining the impact of penalties on drinking and driving, size does not matter: "It could not be demonstrated that the increase in the statutory severity of sanctions in Finland, the increase in the threat of judicial severity in Chicago, or the increase in actual judicial severity in Traffictown produced declines in indexes of the threatened behavior. However, conclusions about severity based on these cases must be qualified by the knowledge that the drinking-and-driving offense is one for which the general level of certainty of punishment is extremely low" (Ross 1982, p. 96). Based on these findings, Ross concludes that "the studies reviewed here in their cumulative impact justify the policy recommendation to avoid dependence on severe penalties in attempting to cope with drinking and driving, as least as long as the probability of an offender's being apprehended remains very low" (1982, p. 96).

In an interesting variation on the study of sentence severity, D'Alessio and Stolzenberg (1998) examined the relationships among crime measures, arrests, and pretrial jail incarceration. From a deterrence perspective, arrests are clearly relevant, though not relevant in terms of sentencing policies or decisions. However, from a "sentencing" perspective, it would be pertinent if pretrial detention appeared to reduce crime. Indeed, the effect of pretrial detention—if one, in fact, existed—could be through a mechanism of deterrence or incapacitation, or both. While these authors focus on the incapacitation possibility, we think that it is fair to suggest that deterrence is also relevant.

In any case, a sophisticated analysis produced findings that show that arrests were associated with decreases in criminal activity the day after they had taken place. However, when examining pretrial jail incarceration (a measure of severity of treatment by the justice system), "contrary to predictions derived from the incapacitation thesis, our findings do not lend credence to the importance of pretrial jail confinement as a factor in reducing crime" (D'Alessio and Stolzenberg 1998, p. 748). Neither pretrial nor total jail incarceration levels affected reported crime rates. Once again, evidence suggests that while apprehension of offenders may have a deterrent impact, punishment—in this case operationalized as pretrial jail confinement—did not have a similar effect. Clearly, pretrial detention is different from being sentenced to prison or penitentiary. Nevertheless, it is interesting that being caught makes a difference to crime levels, but the immediate consequences of this apprehension (detention or not) do not.

The ability of deterrence research to assess the independent effects of apprehension and sentence severity is fundamental in avoiding misleading findings. In a detailed analysis of crime and punishment across Illinois's 102 counties, Olson (1997) noted that the term "deterrence" is used in a number of different ways and that some of these methods almost certainly create artifactual effects that look consistent with deterrence. For example, in the case in which offense rates are measured as offenses per 100,000 in the population, and risk of imprisonment is operationalized as prison admissions per offense, the presence of measurement error in "offenses" will create a "deterrence-like" effect. Indeed, an error in the measurement of offenses (e.g., a campaign to increase reporting) will simultaneously increase the offense rate (more offenses reported per 100,000 in the population) and decrease the risk of imprisonment (by increasing the denominator of the index). This could erroneously lead to the conclusion that a decrease in risk of imprisonment "caused" an increase in offenses.

The related problem is clearly that "risk of imprisonment" measured in this way combines apprehension, conviction, and sentencing. Though the term "imprisonment" is used, what is actually being measured is all three criminal justice processes. As Olson (1997) points out, the correct way to proceed is to employ a model that examines the probability that an offense leads to an arrest, that an arrest leads to a conviction, and that a conviction leads to imprisonment. Measures that look at risk of punishment by combining apprehension, conviction, and sentence tell us nothing about the relative importance of severity and certainty.

Olson looked at the "risk of incarceration relative to conviction" operationalized as the number of prison sentences over the number of convictions (1997, p. 60). He examined data across 102 counties and over a ten-year period. He started by showing that the simple measure of punishment—incarceration relative to offenses—would appear to show a "deterrence" effect in its relationship to crime (1997, p. 86). However, this value dropped dramatically when he examined incarceration relative to conviction (i.e., number of incarcerations over the number of convictions in each county for each of the ten years) (1997,

p. 86). When Olson controlled for certain variables known to be related to crime, the "risk of incarceration relative to offenses" dropped below standard levels of significance, but could be described as showing a "marginal" effect of deterrence. It dropped even further when "risk of conviction" was entered into the equation (1997, p. 110).

The most relevant finding for those interested in the impact of sentencing decisions (i.e., likelihood of going to prison given conviction) is to be found in an analysis that controls for the likelihood of arrest as well as standard predictors of crime. When arrest is held constant, there is no hint of a significant effect of the risk of (adult) incarceration relative to conviction (Olson 1997, p. 113). Olson provides a sensible conclusion: "The most significant policy implication of the results is that risk of punishment has relatively little effect on crime rates. This conclusion, although not necessarily new, adds additional evidence to the fact that earlier assessments . . . may have led policy makers astray" (1997, p. 129). Said differently, simplistic approaches to deterrence— using measures that combine apprehension, conviction, and penalty size—may show deterrent impacts of "punishment." However, when sentence severity is looked at independent of these other factors, sentence severity has no significant effect.

IV. Conclusion

Can we conclude that variation in the severity of sentences would have differential (general) deterrent effects? Our reply is a resounding no. We could find no conclusive evidence that supports the hypothesis that harsher sentences reduce crime through the mechanism of general deterrence. Particularly given the significant body of literature from which this conclusion is based, the consistency of the findings over time and space, and the multiple measures and methods employed in the research conducted, we would suggest that a stronger conclusion is warranted. More specifically, the null hypothesis that variation in sentence severity does not cause variation in crime rates should be conditionally accepted. The condition is a simple one: If a "deterrent effect" of harsh sentences were to be consistently demonstrated under specified conditions at some point in the future, our broad conclusion would require revision.

We have not attempted in this essay to review every paper ever published on the topic of deterrence. Rather, we began with the published reviews of the deterrence literature and moved from there to the studies that are held out, occasionally, as evidence that harsher sentences would deter crime. We subsequently examined the research that does not find support for a deterrent effect on variation in sentence severity, focusing largely—albeit not exclusively—on those that assessed the general deterrent impact of the structural changes in sentencing laws that have occurred in the last decade in the United States. In brief, this essay looks not only at other reviews but also at research that purports to support as well as challenge the view that variation in sentence severity affects the levels of crime in society. Our findings can be summarized as follows.

With two exceptions, neither of which purports to be comprehensive, the reviews of the deterrence literature are pessimistic about the possibility that harsher sentences handed down in criminal courts would decrease crime. Indeed, our assessment of general deterrence is consistent with the views expressed by most criminologists who have reviewed the current body of literature and concluded that the evidence does not support the hypothesis that variation in sentence severity will differentially affect crime rates. Further, the summaries that challenge this conclusion not only constitute sporadic anomalies but also do not address most of the relevant research literature on the topic.

The studies that have found support for the notion that harsher sentences deter are relatively few in number. Additionally, they suffer from one or more serious methodological, statistical, or conceptual problems that render their findings problematic. In some cases, causal inferences between sentence severity and crime cannot be drawn because of the basic nature of the data under analysis (e.g., a simple comparison of crime and punishment in two locations). In other cases, alternative explanations (e.g., incapacitation) are more plausible than deterrence. In still others, data selection, measurement, or methodological questions raise sufficient doubt about the generality of the findings that inferences are dangerous. Finally, while some findings do seem to support a deterrent effect, they appear in unstable and inconsistent ways (e.g., for some offenses but not others, in some locations but not others). The data held out as supportive of the general deterrent impact of sentence severity are not strong enough to allow one to conclude that there is a relationship between the severity of sanctions and crime. A strong finding would be one that appears to be reliable across time, space, and, perhaps, offense. The research examined in this essay favorable to the conclusion that there is a deterrent impact of the severity of sentences clearly does not fulfill these criteria.

An impressive body of literature has appeared in the past ten years

that has taken advantage of dramatic sentencing changes that have occurred in the United States (e.g., three-strikes legislation). The studies
vary in their scope, but not in their findings.

There is no consistent and plausible evidence that harsher sentences
deter crime. Moreover, these studies were frequently conducted in almost ideal research conditions in which one would, in fact, expect to
find a deterrent effect. There was generally substantial publicity surrounding the introduction of these new sentencing laws. Hence, people would be likely to know (or at least believe) that harsh sentences
would follow conviction for the offenses covered by these laws. Further, these sentencing changes have been studied in different countries
and with different units of analysis (e.g., states, counties, cities, etc.).
Finally, some of these studies were able to break down "punishment"
into its various components (i.e., apprehension, conviction, sentencing), permitting an assessment of the separate or unique effects of sentence severity. Even under these conditions, sentencing levels do not
appear to be important in determining crime. The effects are consistent: the severity of sentence does not matter. The hypothesis that
harsher sentences would reduce crime through general deterrence—
which is to say that there are marginal effects of general deterrence—
is not supported by the research literature.

A. Accepting the Null Hypothesis

We started this essay by pointing out that we cannot logically
"prove" that harsher sentences do not deter. Strictly speaking, one
cannot prove the absence of a phenomenon. It may exist somewhere,
but research may not have (yet) identified where this is. However, no
consistent body of literature has developed over the last twenty-five to
thirty years indicating that harsh sanctions deter. While one must always reserve judgment for the possibility that in the future someone
may discover persons or situations in which the relative severity of sentences does have an impact on crime, it would not seem unreasonable
to conclude that at present in Western populations and with the current methods and measures available, variation in sentence severity
does not affect the levels of crime in society.

Our conclusion—and, for that matter, that of the majority of criminologists who have examined the hypothesis that variation in sentence
severity has a deterrent effect—defies an intuitive appeal inherent in
the logic of deterrence. Indeed, we seem to naturally (want to) accept
the notion that any reasonable person—like ourselves—would be de-

terred by the threat of a more severe sanction. This continued belief, however, is rooted, at least in part, in a simplistic form of reasoning about deterrence. We may not adequately separate the effects of certainty of apprehension and severity of punishment in our minds and, by extension, think of the latter largely within the context of a high likelihood of the former. As research has shown us (see Ross [1982] for a pertinent example), the assumption that the majority of offenses have a high probability of apprehension is clearly not a safe one.

We may also not adequately break down the actual process by which deterrence works. Indeed, many people may not be aware of the complex sequence of conditions that must be met if variation in sentence severity is potentially to affect levels of crime. As von Hirsch et al. (1999, p. 7) have outlined, for a harsher sanction to have an impact, individuals must first believe that there is a reasonable likelihood that they will be apprehended for the offense and receive the punishment that is imposed by a court. Second, they must know that the punishment has changed. It does no good to alter the sanction if potential offenders do not know that it has been modified. Consequences that are unknown to potential offenders cannot affect their behavior. Third, the individual must be a person who will consider the penal consequences in deciding whether to commit the offense. Finally, the potential offender—who knows about the change in punishment and perceives that there is a reasonable likelihood of apprehension—must calculate that it is "worth" offending for the lower level of punishment but not worth offending for the increased punishment. In other words, in arguing that a three-year sentence will deter more people than a two-year sentence, one is suggesting that a measurable number of people would commit the offense with a reasonable expectation of serving a two-year sentence who would not do so if they thought that they would serve a three-year sentence.

Viewed from this perspective, the lack of evidence in favor of a deterrent effect for variation in sentence severity may gain its own intuitive appeal. Clearly, the number of intervening processes that must take place between (a) the change in penalties for a crime and (b) the possible impact of that alteration on the population of potential offenders is considerably greater than most of us imagine. When one factors in the perceptual element at the root of deterrence, the complexity of the process only increases. The very logic upon which deterrence rests may break down. As Foglia (1997) found in her study of the perceived likelihood of arrest on the behavior of inner-city teenagers in a large U.S. northeastern city, "the threat of formal sanctions means little to young people from economically depressed urban neighborhoods. . . . The irrelevance of arrest is understandable considering these young people have less to lose if arrested; also, they perceive less of a connection between behavior and legal consequences because they see many commit crimes with impunity and view law enforcement as arbitrary" (1997, p. 433).

If penalty structures are irrelevant to potential offenders, it does not matter how severe they might be. Or, more broadly, the deterrence process—as a perceptual model—is not nearly as simple as one might assume or the economist might contemplate when employing utility functions to explain why the chicken crossed the road against the red light.

B. The Consequences of Accepting the Null Hypothesis

The time has come to conditionally accept the null hypothesis: severity of sentences does not affect crime levels. This analysis assumes variation in sentence severity within fixed limits. We do not suggest that a one-dollar fine for armed robbery would be the same as a three-year prison sentence. Rather, we propose acceptance of the null hypothesis that variation within the limits that are plausible in Western countries will not make a difference.

Potentially the most intriguing ramification of this conclusion is for sentencing objectives. Principled arguments against sentencing according to deterrence principles have been made by others (e.g., von Hirsch 1985). It is not our purpose to review those arguments here. We simply suggest that in addition to those more theoretically based discussions, we should add another of a more practical or pragmatic nature. Deterrence-based sentencing makes false promises to the community. As long as the public believes that crime can be deterred by legislatures or judges through harsh sentences, there is no need to consider other approaches to crime reduction.

It may be no coincidence that sentencing systems that do not subscribe to general deterrence—in part or in whole—already exist in several Western nations. Finland bases its sentencing provisions on a principle of "general prevention" (i.e., educating the public about the seriousness of offending) rather than general deterrence (Lappi-Seppälä 2000). Canada's new youth justice legislation focuses on imposing proportional sentences and avoids the notion that youths will be deterred by harsh sentences imposed on others (Doob and Sprott, forthcoming). Similarly, the Law Reform Commission of Ireland has suggested that general deterrence has no place in a modern sentencing structure in large part because there is no credible evidence of its effectiveness (Law Reform Commission 1996, p. 6). Finally, the Swedish Ministry of the Attorney General notes in a discussion of sanctions that prison is not a deterrent (National Council for Crime Prevention Sweden 1997, p. 22). In other words, it no longer appears to be a radical suggestion to accept that, like the missing sock, the general deterrent effects of harsher sentences do not exist.

REFERENCES

Austin, James, John Clark, Patricia Hardyman, and D. Alan Henry. 1999. "The Impact of 'Three Strikes and You're Out.'" *Punishment and Society* 1: 131–62.

Avio, Kenneth L., and C. Scott Clark. 1978. "The Supply of Property Offences in Ontario: Evidence on the Deterrent Effect of Punishment." *Canadian Journal of Economics* 11:1–19.

Bailey, William C., and Ruth D. Peterson. 1999. "Capital Punishment, Homicide and Deterrence: An Assessment of the Evidence." In *Studying and Preventing Homicide: Issues and Challenges*, edited by M. Dwayne Smith and Margaret A. Zahn. Thousand Oaks, Calif.: Sage.

Benaquisto, Lucia. 1997. "The Non-Calculating Criminal: Inattention to Consequences in Decisions to Commit Crime." Unpublished paper. Montreal: Department of Sociology, McGill University.

Blumstein, Alfred, Jacqueline Cohen, and Daniel Nagin, eds. 1978. *Deterrence and Incapacitation: Estimating the Effects of Criminal Sanctions on Crime Rates.* Washington, D.C.: National Academy of Sciences.

Canadian Sentencing Commission. 1987. *Sentencing Reform: A Canadian Approach.* Ottawa: Minister of Supply and Services, Canada.

Cavanagh, David P. 1993. "Relations between Increases in the Certainty, Severity, and Celerity of Punishment for Drug Crimes and Reductions in the Level of Crime, Drug Crime, and the Effects of Drug Abuse." Report conducted by Botec Analysis Corporation for the Office of National Drug Control Policy.

Chen, Elsa Yee-Fang. 2000. "'Three Strikes and You're Out' and 'Truth in Sentencing': Lessons in Policy Implementation and Impacts." Ph.D. dissertation, UCLA, Department of Political Science.

Cook, Philip J. 1980. "Research in Criminal Deterrence: Laying the Groundwork for the Second Decade." In *Crime and Justice: An Annual Review of Research*, vol. 2, edited by Norval Morris and Michael Tonry. Chicago: University of Chicago Press.

D'Alessio, Stewart J., and Lisa Stolzenberg. 1998. "Crime, Arrests, and Pretrial Jail Incarceration: An Examination of the Deterrence Thesis." *Criminology* 36:735–61.

Doob, Anthony N. 1995. "The United States Sentencing Commission Guidelines: If You Don't Know Where You Are Going, You May Not Get There." In *The Politics of Sentencing Reform*, edited by Chris Clarkson and Rod Morgan. Oxford: Clarendon.

Doob, Anthony N., and Jane B. Sprott. Forthcoming. "Youth Justice in Canada." In *Youth Crime and Youth Justice: Comparative and Cross-National Perspectives*, edited by Michael Tonry and Anthony N. Doob. Vol. 31 of *Crime and Justice: A Review of Research*, edited by Michael Tonry and Norval Morris. Chicago: University of Chicago Press.

Foglia, Wanda D. 1997. "Perceptual Deterrence and the Mediating Effect of Internalized Normals among Inner-City Teenagers." *Journal of Research in Crime and Delinquency* 34:414–42.

Grasmick, Harold G., and George J. Bryjak. 1980. "The Deterrent Effect of Perceived Severity of Punishment." *Social Forces* 59:471–91.

Greenwood, Peter, C. Peter Rydell, Allan F. Abrahamse, Jonathan P. Caulkins, James Chiesa, Karyn E. Model, and Stephen P. Klein. 1996. "Estimated Benefits and Costs of California's New Mandatory-Sentencing Law." In *Three Strikes and You're Out: Vengeance as Public Policy*, edited by David Shichor and Dale K. Sechrest. Thousand Oaks, Calif.: Sage.

Johnston, Philip. 1998. "English Crime Rates Set to 'Overtake America.'" *London Telegraph*, online (Oct. 12); downloaded from www.telegraph.co.uk: 80/et on Dec. 4, 1998.

Kessler, Daniel, and Steven D. Levitt. 1998. "Using Sentence Enhancements to Distinguish between Deterrence and Incapacitation." Working Paper no. 6484. Cambridge, Mass.: National Bureau of Economic Research.

———. 1999. "Using Sentence Enhancements to Distinguish between Deterrence and Incapacitation." *Journal of Law and Economics* 42:343–63.

Klepper, Steven, and Daniel Nagin. 1989. "Tax Compliance and Perceptions of the Risks of Detection and Criminal Prosecution." *Law and Society Review* 23:209–40.

Kovandzic, Tomislav Victor. 1999. "Crime Prevention through Selective Incapacitation: An Empirical Assessment of Florida's Habitual Offender Law." Ph.D. dissertation, School of Criminology and Criminal Justice, Florida State University.

Landes, W. 1978. "An Economic Study of U.S. Aircraft Hijacking 1961–1976." *Journal of Law and Economics* 21:1–31.

Langan, Patrick A., and David P. Farrington. 1998. *Crime and Justice in the United States and in England and Wales, 1981–96*. Washington, D.C.: U.S. Department of Justice, Office of Justice Programs, Bureau of Justice Statistics.

Lappi-Seppälä, Tapio. 2000. "The Fall in the Finnish Prison Population." *Journal of Scandinavian Studies in Criminology and Crime Prevention* 1:27–40.

Lardner, George, Jr. 1998. "Weighing Crime, Consequences: England's Rates Are Mostly Higher, Punishment Less than in U.S." *Washington Post* (Oct. 5), online; downloaded from proquest.umi.com on Dec. 3, 1998.

Law Reform Commission. 1996. *Report on Sentencing.* Dublin: Office of the Taoiseach.

Levitt, Steven D. 1996. "The Effect of Prison Population Size on Crime Rates: Evidence from Prison Overcrowding Litigation." *Quarterly Journal of Economics* 111:319–51.

———. 1998. "Juvenile Crime and Punishment." *Journal of Political Economy* 106:1156–185.

———. 2002. "Deterrence." In *Crime: Public Policies for Crime Control,* edited by James Q. Wilson and Joan Petersilia. Oakland, Calif.: Institute for Contemporary Studies Press.

Lewis, Donald E. 1986. "The General Deterrent Effect of Longer Sentences." *British Journal of Criminology* 26:47–62.

MacCoun, Robert, and Peter Reuter. 1998. "Drug Control." In *The Handbook of Crime and Punishment,* edited by Michael Tonry. New York: Oxford University Press.

Marvell, T. B., and E. E. Moody. 1994. "Prison Population Growth and Crime Reduction." *Journal of Quantitative Criminology* 10:109–40.

Mauer, Marc, and Malcolm C. Young. 1996. *Truths, Half-Truths, and Lies: Myths and Realities about Crime and Punishment.* Washington, D.C.: Sentencing Project.

McDowall, David, Colin Loftin, and Brian Wiersema. 1992. "A Comparative Study of the Preventive Effects of Mandatory Sentencing Laws for Gun Crimes." *Journal of Criminal Law and Criminology* 83:378–94.

Morgan, Neil. 2000. "Mandatory Sentences in Australia: Where Have We Been and Where Are We Going?" *Criminal Law Journal* 24:164–83.

Nagin, Daniel S. 1978. "General Deterrence: A Review of the Empirical Evidence." In *Deterrence and Incapacitation: Estimating the Effects of Criminal Sanctions on Crime Rates,* edited by Alfred Blumstein, Jacqueline Cohen, and Daniel Nagin. Washington, D.C.: National Academy of Sciences.

———. 1998. "Criminal Deterrence Research at the Outset of the Twenty-First Century." In *Crime and Justice: A Review of Research,* vol. 23, edited by Michael Tonry. Chicago: University of Chicago Press.

National Council for Crime Prevention Sweden. 1997. "Our Collective Responsibility: A National Programme for Crime Prevention." Available online from the Ministry of Justice, Sweden, at http://justitie.regeringen.se/inenglish/_issues/crimeprev.htm.

Olson, David E. 1997. "Testing Deterrence and Incapacitation as Crime Control Mechanisms: A Refinement of the Hypothesis." Ph.D. dissertation, Department of Public Policy Analysis—Political Science, University of Illinois at Chicago.

Radelet, Michael L., and Ronald L Akers. 1996. "Deterrence and the Death Penalty: The Views of Experts." *Journal of Criminal Law and Criminology* 87: 1–16.

Reilly, B., and R. Witt. 1996. "Crime, Deterrence, and Unemployment in England and Wales: An Empirical Analysis." *Bulletin of Economic Research* 48: 137–59.

Ross, H. Laurence. 1982. *Deterring the Drinking Driver: Legal Policy and Social Control*. Lexington, Mass.: Lexington Books.

Rufford, Nicholas. 1998. "Official: More Muggings in England than U.S." *Sunday Times* (London) (Oct. 11); available online at www.the-times.co.uk/news/pages/sti/98/10/11.

Schiraldi, Vincent, and Tara-Jen Ambrosio. 1997. *Striking Out: The Crime Control Impact of "Three-Strikes" Laws*. Washington, D.C.: Justice Policy Institute.

Stolzenberg, Lisa, and Stewart J. D'Alessio. 1997. "'Three Strikes and You're Out': The Impact of California's New Mandatory Sentencing Law on Serious Crime Rates." *Crime and Delinquency* 43:457–69.

Tonry, Michael. 1996. *Sentencing Matters*. New York: Oxford University Press.

Tunnell, Kenneth D. 1996. "Choosing Crime: Close Your Eyes and Take Your Chances." In *Criminal Justice in America: Theory, Practice, and Policy*, edited by Barry W. Hancock and Paul M. Sharp. Upper Saddle River, N.J.: Prentice-Hall.

Varma, Kimberly, and Anthony N. Doob. 1998. "Deterring Economic Crimes: The Case of Tax Evasion." *Canadian Journal of Criminology* 40(2): 165–84.

Von Hirsch, Andrew. 1985. *Past or Future Crimes: Deservedness and Dangerousness in the Sentencing of Criminals*. New Brunswick, N.J.: Rutgers University Press.

Von Hirsch, Andrew, Anthony E. Bottoms, Elizabeth Burney, and Per-Olof Wikström. 1999. *Criminal Deterrence and Sentence Severity: An Analysis of Recent Research*. Oxford: Hart.

Waldorf, Dan, and Sheilagh Murphy. 1995. "Perceived Risks and Criminal Justice Pressures on Middle Class Cocaine Sellers." *Journal of Drug Issues* 25:11–32.

Wicharaya, Tamasak. 1995. *Simple Theory, Hard Reality: The Impact of Sentencing Reforms on Courts, Prisons, and Crime*. Albany: State University of New York Press.

Wilson, James Q. 1990. "Drugs and Crime." In *Drugs and Crime*, edited by Michael Tonry and James Q. Wilson. Vol. 13 of *Crime and Justice: A Review of Research*, edited by Michael Tonry and Norval Morris. Chicago: University of Chicago Press.

———. 1995. "Crime and Public Policy." In *Crime: Public Policies for Crime Control*, edited by James Q. Wilson and Joan Petersilia. Oakland, Calif.: Institute for Contemporary Studies Press.

Wright, Richard A. 1996. "In Support of Prisons." In *Criminal Justice in America: Theory, Practice, and Policy*, edited by Barry W. Hancock and Paul M. Sharp. Upper Saddle River, N.J.: Prentice-Hall.

Zimring, Franklin E., Gordon Hawkins, and Sam Kamin. 2001. *Punishment and Democracy: Three Strikes and You're Out in California*. New York: Oxford University Press.

Ronald V. Clarke and Rick Brown

International Trafficking
in Stolen Vehicles

ABSTRACT

For many years, trafficking in stolen cars seemed largely to be confined to the Americas, with an estimated 200,000 cars per year flowing from the United States to Mexico and Central and South America. Trafficking in stolen cars is now a worldwide phenomenon. Perhaps half a million or more cars each year are transported from developed to less developed nations, hidden in containers or driven across national borders. Because vehicle trafficking causes less personal harm than other transnational crimes, governments have given it little priority. However, a recent spate of policy efforts has focused on identification and repatriation of stolen vehicles. Further development of policy would be assisted by a modest investment in research. This could produce detailed information about the methods used by criminals, provide more information about the involvement of immigrants, and yield improved measures of trafficking. The availability of comprehensive government and industry data makes this transnational crime a promising field of research.

Until recently, the export of stolen vehicles seemed to be confined largely to the Americas. During the 1980s, the U.S. Customs estimated

Ronald V. Clarke is university professor at Rutgers, The State University of New Jersey. Rick Brown is managing consultant with Evidence Led Solutions, a research consultancy. Many people assisted us in tracking down information. Gisela Bichler-Robertson helped with Web and Lexus-Nexis searches. Klaus van Lampe translated German materials. Phyllis Schultze found numerous pieces of fugitive literature archived in the NCCD/Criminal Justice Library at Rutgers and enlisted the help of the World Criminal Justice Library Network, of whom John Myrtle (Australian Institute of Criminology), Aniela Belina (University of Montreal), and Kirsi Nissala (HEUNI) were especially helpful. Elaine Hardy (International Car Distribution Programme Ltd.), Matti Joutsen (HEUNI), Joe Pierron (NICB), Joanna Sallybanks (Home Office), and Jaap de Waard (Dutch Ministry of Justice) sent us copies of articles and reports. Joe Pierron, David Lowe (National Criminal Information Service), and Kim Hazelbaker (Highway Loss Data Institute) all shared their knowledge of the topic.

that some 200,000 vehicles were stolen each year—an estimate that remained the same throughout the 1990s (General Accounting Office 1999; National Insurance Crime Bureau 1999). Many cars were exported to other countries in South America or the Caribbean using containers and roll-on/roll-off ferries (National Automobile Theft Bureau 1989). Others were simply driven across the border into Mexico (Miller 1987). In some cases, the thefts were organized on a massive scale, with criminal groups responsible for the theft and shipping of hundreds of vehicles. Other thefts were opportunistic, often committed by juvenile offenders who might steal a car in the afternoon and sell it that same evening in Mexico (Resindez 1998; Resindez and Neal 2000).

Trafficking in stolen cars is no longer a distinctively American phenomenon. Equal or greater numbers of cars are now being stolen in Western Europe and exported to Russia and other countries of Eastern Europe (United Nations 1997). The newly emerging market economies in these countries have created a demand for cars (especially luxury models) that cannot be met by domestic producers, and criminal entrepreneurs have moved in to fill this gap.[1] Increasing globalization has created similar conditions in other parts of the world with the result that many other countries have become markets for cars stolen abroad. The Middle East is now a destination for cars stolen in Europe, West Africa for cars stolen in the United States and the United Kingdom, and China for cars stolen in the United States and Japan. Regional theft markets have also developed. Bolivia is the destination for cars stolen in Brazil and Argentina, Nepal for ones stolen in northern India, Indonesia for ones stolen in Malaysia, Cambodia for cars stolen in Thailand, and other parts of Africa for cars stolen in South Africa. According to an Associated Press story that was widely picked up by the world's press (e.g., New York Times 2002; Taipei Times 2002), Japan has recently emerged as a major source of exported stolen vehicles to Indonesia, the Russian Far East, the United Arab Emirates, Nigeria, and even the United Kingdom.

No reliable figures exist for the scale of the problem, but combining current estimates from different countries suggests that half a million vehicles are stolen and sold abroad each year. These vehicles are

---

[1] Ruggiero quotes an article in the *Independent* stating that many Mercedes stolen in Germany are sold in Albania, where "the number of cars has soared since the collapse of communism, growing from 5,000 in the early 1990s to 50,000 in 1998. Yet, in the previous year only three new cars were officially registered" (2000, p. 207).

mostly cars, exported whole with false identities. There is also a small export trade in stolen commercial vehicles and motorcycles and a large, though poorly measured, trade in stolen vehicle parts.

Clear differences in preferred models exist among recipient countries. German-made cars (especially expensive makes such as BMW and Mercedes) are in heavy demand in Eastern Europe. African and South American countries seem to prefer jeeps and other 4 × 4 vehicles, which suit the local roads. In Mexico, the models most in demand are ones manufactured in the United States but also manufactured or marketed in Mexico (Miller 1987; Field, Clarke, and Harris 1991; Resindez and Neal 2000). In China, the opposite is true: the most popular stolen models are Lexus and other luxury Japanese makes that are not distributed there. According to Joe Pierron (personal communication, 1999) of the National Insurance Crime Bureau, Toyota is reputed to have sold $2 million worth of spare Lexus parts in China in 1998. In many former colonies of the United Kingdom, there seems to be a heavy demand for stolen Bedford parts—Bedfords being obsolete trucks produced in the United Kingdom that were once exported in large numbers (Brown 1995).

Whichever vehicles or countries are involved, the pattern is the same: the principal flow is from developed to less developed countries (Williams 1999).[2] This mirrors the wider global economy in which manufactured goods move from the developed to the less developed world but is contrary to most other forms of transnational crime, where the flow is in the other direction. Research into the reasons for this difference could help to clarify the relationship between organized transnational crime and patterns of immigration. However, more compelling reasons are needed for investing research resources in the problem because the human misery caused by trafficking in stolen cars is insignificant compared with other transnational crimes such as trafficking in drugs, in human organs, and in women and children.

There are two good reasons for giving research priority to vehicle trafficking. The first reason relates to the rich data readily available on vehicles and vehicle theft. Car thefts are more reliably reported to the police than most other crimes, and comprehensive data about stolen cars are published by insurance agencies. In all developed countries, detailed records are maintained of vehicles manufactured, imported,

---

[2] In a small reversal of this trend, some expensive cars are now being stolen in Mexico and exported for sale in California (Cearley 2001).

sold, and in use. Industry and governments also routinely produce data about the characteristics of the vehicle fleets in the various countries. For no other form of transnational crime would it be possible to draw on data of this quality.

The second reason for giving priority to research on trafficking in stolen cars is that this could be of real assistance in reducing the problem. Already, substantial law enforcement efforts are being made to improve procedures for recovering vehicles that have been stolen and exported. Research could assist these efforts by identifying the difficulties of this approach, seeking solutions, and evaluating the success of measures adopted. But it could perform two even more important roles. First, it could assist in the development of reliable, repeatable measures of the extent of vehicle trafficking. Existing ways of estimating the size of the problem are crude and cannot be used to measure the effect of policy interventions. Second, research could help explore other approaches to the problem than the primarily reactive one of identifying and recovering stolen vehicles. In particular, it could explore the scope for successfully intervening at earlier stages in the process of stealing cars, giving them new identities, and getting them out of the country.

The broad outline of what is known about trafficking in stolen cars has been reviewed above, relying largely on knowledge accumulated by various enforcement agencies and transmitted in newspaper reports or brief official statements. Unlike most essays in this series, very little of the information reviewed has been gathered through formal research studies. In Section I below, a more detailed examination is made of this information in several areas key to the development of a policy-oriented research agenda. In Section II, some specific ideas for research will be outlined. Section III is a brief conclusion.

I. Key Policy Questions

It may be true that deeper understanding of a problem leads to better solutions, but such understanding takes time to achieve, and policy makers cannot usually wait. They want information quickly, and it must be relevant to their immediate policy concerns. It can be difficult to predict what this information will be, but those seeking to control a particular form of crime would need, at a minimum, reliable measures of its extent and costs, information about the kinds of offenders involved, an understanding of the conditions facilitating its commission and of the means by which it is accomplished, and information about the practicality and likely effects of different interventions. This section summarizes the state of knowledge on these matters by offering answers to a number of specific questions about vehicle trafficking.

A. How Large a Problem, and How Costly?

According to current estimates, half a million or more cars are stolen and exported each year. This includes about 200,000 from the United States (General Accounting Office 1999; National Insurance Crime Bureau 1999), 20,000 from Canada (Corelli 1998), and perhaps 200,000–300,000 in Western Europe. According to one estimate, as many as 100,000 vehicles per year may be imported into Russia alone (figures from PlanEcon, Inc., quoted by Hardy 1998, p. 29). It is now widely believed that very large numbers of cars are stolen for export in South America, South Africa, Japan, and the rest of the world, though the bulk of the problem still lies in North America and Western Europe.

The method of estimating the size of the problem is the same everywhere. It relies on estimates made by police and other experts of the proportions of unrecovered stolen vehicles that are exported. In the United States, this proportion is thought to be around 30–35 percent, while in Britain it is usually estimated as being around 15–20 percent.[3] The number of cars stolen for export is estimated by applying these proportions to the numbers of stolen but unrecovered vehicles. In the United States around one-third of the annual total of about 1.5 million cars stolen were not recovered in 1997 (National Insurance Crime Bureau 1999); in Europe about 40 percent of 2 million cars stolen each year are not recovered (Liukkonen 1997; see Hardy 1998 for higher estimates).

These estimates are too crude to inform policy. They are based on the recovery rates of all models, when newspaper stories invariably mention that traffickers target only certain models (these vary with the region of the world). More generally, research has found that the tar-

---

[3] Apart from a small residual category of vehicles dumped and never recovered, the other principal categories of unrecovered stolen vehicles are those given a new identity and sold domestically (known as "ringing" in the United Kingdom), thought to comprise about 15–25 percent of unrecovered vehicles; those that are disassembled into their component parts (i.e., "chopped" in U.S. parlance), which are then sold separately (about 30–35 percent of unrecovered vehicles); and those that were never really stolen in the first place but that were the basis of fraudulent insurance claims (about 10–15 percent).

geted models vary with the nature of the thefts. Thus, an American study found that cars with the lowest recovery rates are high-priced luxury vehicles (Clarke and Harris 1992b), while several studies have shown that cars stolen in the United States and exported to Mexico are models also marketed or manufactured there (Miller 1987; Field, Clarke, and Harris 1991; Resindez and Neal 2000). In Section II, we estimate the number of cars stolen for export based on the models at most risk.

Estimates of the cost of trafficking in stolen cars are also deficient. Most of these are made simply by multiplying the estimated numbers of cars exported by their average value, sometimes inflated to reflect their presumed value in the destination countries. These inflated values take account of the huge import duties in countries such as China, which in 1995 was said to levy duties of around $120,000 on a vehicle costing $50,000 in the United States (Onishi 1995).

In any case, the value of the vehicles is only one component of the total cost of trafficking in stolen cars. Other costs include those involved in enforcement, in recovery and return of vehicles, in inconvenience to victims, and in costs to insurance companies.

Trafficking in stolen cars also has benefits that cannot be ignored in any full accounting of its costs. For instance, insurers can raise their premiums as a result of the losses sustained and thus increase their future profits, while shippers benefit from the increased use of their services. Manufacturers in the country of origin also profit by selling replacement vehicles to victims (though these profits need to be balanced against forgone sales of legally exported cars to the host countries [Porteous 1998]). One could also argue that vehicle thefts are a form of liquidating (someone else's) assets. A proportion of the profits from selling an exported vehicle will be used to consume goods and services in the donor country that may otherwise not have been consumed. In this sense, stolen vehicle exports are not only "invisible exports" that generate revenue, but they also stimulate the domestic market.

More sophisticated measures of costs taking account of these various considerations are needed for two important policy-related reasons. First, a realistic estimate of costs is needed in order to help determine the investment that should be made in reducing the problem. At present, governments have no idea whether the police and customs resources allocated to dealing with the problem are commensurate with its scale. Second, knowing where the costs fall, and who is hurt by the traffic in stolen cars, will help policy makers determine which of a range of possible interventions have the best chance of being implemented. For instance, if motor manufacturers profit from trafficking in stolen cars, it will be harder to enlist their support for preventive devices to be installed at manufacture. Similarly, if host countries are net beneficiaries of trafficking in stolen cars, it may be difficult to enlist their assistance in dealing with the problem.

The potential policy value of an economic analysis of the problem can be illustrated by an analysis of the costs of auto theft in the United States undertaken by Simon Field. These costs amounted to about $45 dollars per automobile per year and, on the basis of where these costs fell, he concluded that, "there is very little incentive for individual owners to prevent auto theft, since most of the costs fall in the form of insurance premiums and government expenditures rather than in the form of losses falling to individual owners . . . (Therefore) there should be government-mandated standards of design security applied to all automobiles, since the private market is inadequate to the task of providing an optimal level of theft security" (Field 1993, p. 69).

B. What Conditions Facilitate Trafficking in Stolen Cars?

At the most general level, the export trade in stolen cars relies upon a ready supply of attractive vehicles in one country or region, the demand for such vehicles in another, and a ready means of transporting them from origin to destination. These conditions have existed for many years in the Americas and have more recently arisen in Europe with the emergence of free markets in the former countries of the Soviet bloc. Some other specific conditions that facilitate trafficking in stolen cars should be noted because of their potential relevance to policy.

1. *Numbers.* Vast numbers of cars cross national borders every day. As a result of political change, trade agreements, and worldwide increases in tourism, many border controls have been eased or lifted in order to cope with the huge numbers of cars traversing national boundaries. Looking for stolen cars among this vast amount of legal traffic presents a formidable challenge to the authorities. Some idea of the magnitude of the task is provided by data on the numbers of vehicle crossings at the Hungarian borders with its seven immediate neighbors. The total number recorded at all border crossings in 1995 was 33,132,677 vehicles, of which 469 were detected as stolen.[4]

---

[4] Data were provided to an international meeting on "Organized Transborder Car Thefts" held at the Hungarian National Police Headquarters in Budapest, August 26–28, 1996.

2. *Containers.* Huge volumes of containers are shipped from many ports in developed countries. Stolen cars and auto parts are frequently shipped in sealed containers to other countries. As many as four cars can be put in one container. Many of the cars have been given new identities, but in some cases, they are shipped in sealed containers labeled as "kitchen equipment," "household goods," or something similar. Customs officials examine only about 1 percent of containers shipped from U.S. ports, partly because cargo ships work to tight turn-around times. They may be in port for less than twelve hours, and in that time they will have to be unloaded and loaded. This allows little time for bills of lading to be checked and suspicious containers to be examined. If there is any sign of increased vigilance at a particular port, criminals can move to another port to reduce the risk of detection.

3. *Legal Trade.* A substantial legal trade exists between countries in used cars. Large volumes of used cars are legally traded between developed countries and undeveloped countries. For example, Belgium exported 154,981 used cars in 1998 (Hardy 1999), while Russia imports about 900,000 used cars per year (figures from PlanEcon, Inc., quoted in Hardy 1998, p. 29). Criminals involved in trafficking in stolen cars can shelter behind this trade, masking their activities as legitimate business.

4. *Customs.* Customs controls are focused on arrivals, not departures. Of 6,500 U.S. Customs inspectors in 1995, only 230 were assigned to monitor exports (Onishi 1995). This pattern holds worldwide because customs officers are focused on goods arriving, not departing the country.[5] This is because they are responsible for keeping prohibited goods out of the country and for levying duties on certain goods entering. Thus, customs officials at the border with Mexico near San Diego make no attempt to respond to alarms from automatic license plate readers (Wright 2001), which go off "anywhere from four to eight times a day," indicating that a stolen car may be departing the United States (*New York Times* 2001, p. 15). This is because they do not have the resources to pursue and stop possibly stolen cars, which might number as many as 2,000 per year.

5. *Illegal Imports.* Many countries have difficulty in controlling the illegal import of cars that have not been stolen. Until countries can control illegal imports, they have little prospect of preventing the im-

---

[5] More scrutiny of goods leaving the ports in developed countries could result from concerns, expressed in the wake of the World Trade Center disaster, that weapons (or depleted uranium) bound for terrorist organizations are being exported from developed countries.

portation of stolen cars. In 1999, Mexico tried to control its problem of illegally imported cars by proposing that drivers of vehicles with American plates would be required to deposit a substantial sum equal to the import duty when entering the country. This deposit would be returnable when the car reentered the United States (Dillon 1999). However, the proposal was subsequently withdrawn in the face of protests from Mexicans living in the United States, who were accustomed to visiting Mexico in their own cars (Preston 1999). China has moved to tighten controls on car assembly businesses, which were suspected of evading import controls (Yu 1999).

6. *Documents.* International standards for vehicle documents do not exist. The lack of standardized vehicle registration and ownership documents makes it difficult for officials to detect forged or altered papers (Malinowski 1996). Language barriers make this task even more difficult.

7. *Registration.* Vehicle registration procedures vary greatly among countries, and their enforcement is frequently lax. These procedures vary considerably even among European Union (EU) countries (Hardy 1999). In some countries, such as the United Kingdom, it is not necessary for the registering officer to see the vehicle. In many less developed countries, vehicle registration requirements are poorly enforced.

8. *Corruption.* Corruption is widespread among officials in undeveloped countries. For many years, prior to the current agreements concerning the recovery of stolen cars, police officers in Mexico could routinely be seen driving around in stolen American cars, sometimes with their U.S. number plates still in place (Lepage and Romero 1990; Rotella 1994). In South Africa, corruption (and intimidation) of officials in vehicle registration offices is thought to be one method of obtaining a new identity for stolen vehicles, many of which are thought to be exported to neighboring countries, facilitated by bribing officials at border crossings (Ndhlovu 2002). Surely the most egregious case of corruption concerns the official in Panama responsible for negotiating a long-stalled treaty with the United States on the return of stolen cars. On being informed by the police that the Mercedes in her possession had been stolen from its owners in Miami and must be returned to them, she claimed it belonged to her husband, an ambassador to Panama from an Arabian state, and was therefore protected by diplomatic immunity (Ragavan et al. 1999).

9. *Priority.* Vehicle theft is not a high law enforcement priority. Developing countries are faced with many more serious crime problems than the import of stolen cars and cannot be expected to give this

high priority. Liukkonen (1997) reported many complaints from police in the thirty-two countries surveyed about slow responses to enquiries about the legal status of cars suspected to have been stolen abroad. At the same time, penalties for theft of cars are not generally high, and lower-level operatives have relatively little to fear if apprehended for this crime.

10. *Migration.* Substantial migration into developed countries has expanded the numbers of offenders with the necessary contacts to undertake vehicle trafficking. Though hard information is lacking, available evidence suggests that many of those involved in vehicle trafficking are immigrants, who discover and exploit the opportunities existing for this crime. They may already have the necessary contacts in their home countries, and they may avoid prosecution by working in their own language, which may be unfamiliar to the police. For example, law enforcement authorities in New York state were recently forced to hire a translator fluent in Mandarin so they could tap the phone conversations of a Chinese gang exporting stolen cars to Asia (Chen 2001).

C. How Is Trafficking in Stolen Cars Accomplished?

The methods used in the trafficking of stolen cars are known in broad outline, but detailed information is lacking. Such detail is needed for devising countermeasures, particularly of the situational, opportunity-reducing kind. These must be tailored to the modus operandi and the specific contexts in which target crimes occur (Savona 1998). Unfortunately, substantial difficulties are encountered in studying the methods used in vehicle trafficking. These arise from the complexity of the phenomenon, which has a number of sources.

Just like any other form of transnational crime, trafficking in stolen cars can take a variety of forms that differ in the organization and skills they demand. There are three main forms, each of which has to be understood in some detail. These forms are driving stolen cars across national borders or transporting them in ferries, shipping them overseas in sealed containers, and disassembling them and shipping them overseas for sale as spare parts. In addition, some cars are carried in trucks across borders or flown in aircraft.

All forms of trafficking in stolen cars involve a complex sequence of actions, including the following: preferred vehicles are identified and stolen, either to order or "on spec"; they may be moved to a safe place and their identities changed; they may be stored, awaiting pickup for transfer across the border; depending on the method of transfer, they may be placed in sealed containers and loaded onto ships, or they may be driven across the border. At the destinations, they may be handed over to a local contact or collected by such a person from the docks; they may be legally registered; and finally, they may be sold on the open market or to a private buyer.

Because of local conditions, considerable differences exist in methods employed, even for similar forms of trafficking. Thus, in South Africa, where stolen cars are mostly driven to neighboring countries, many criminals acquire the vehicles through "carjacking," that is, by robbery at gunpoint from their owners. This method is rarely used in other countries (van der Leest and Degen 1999). At the export stage, the many and varied routes used by traffickers suggest that a wide variety of methods are likely to be used. Liukkonen (1997) identified six distinct routes in Europe alone, which he labeled the Balkan Route, the Italian Route, the Middle-European route, the Sea Route, the Spanish Route, and the Northern Route. Some routes require cars to be driven through multiple border crossings, whereas others require only a single border crossing. Criminals stealing cars near the Mexican border sometimes drive them across the border before they are reported stolen, without any attempt to change the identity of the vehicle. Routes with many border crossings would require considerably more organization on the part of the criminals. Finally, variations among countries in the methods of registering vehicle ownership (Hardy 1999) again suggest that methods employed by criminals at this stage will also have to vary considerably.

The methods employed by traffickers, the routes they use, and the countries principally involved all undergo constant change as a consequence of law enforcement activities or the changing opportunity structure for this crime. For instance, in the early 1990s, there were many reports of cars being exported from Hong Kong and Japan to China. By the mid-1990s, the trade in illegal imports to China decreased, partly as a result of actions taken by the Chinese authorities, including banning the import of right-hand-drive vehicles (Dobson 1993).

Trafficking in stolen cars therefore consists of many different kinds of undertakings involving many different steps. Methods may change quite quickly in response to law enforcement initiatives and to changing opportunities. Unraveling this complexity and gaining a detailed understanding of the phenomenon is a considerable challenge for researchers and policy makers alike.

D. Who Is Involved?

According to an INTERPOL (1999) briefing note, well-organized criminal gangs, consisting of large numbers of people with specific, sometimes specialized, roles, are responsible for most of the trafficking in stolen vehicles. The note provides the following description of such organizations:

> Members of the group can have specific roles. Certain members will, for instance, have expertise in stealing and will be responsible for the initial theft. Others are trained mechanics who change the identity of the vehicle, either by simply replacing the number plate or going further and altering the vehicle identification number, the paintwork and, in some situations, cutting up the vehicle and resoldering it to parts of other vehicles. There are also specialists in the forgery of vehicle documentation who can create a registration certificate, a driver's licence and technical vehicle documents where necessary. Then there are the vehicle couriers who move the vehicles around from one country to the other. Often organizers behind the whole operation never have any contact with the other individuals or vehicles and operate through intermediaries so that it is difficult to implicate them in the operation. (INTERPOL 1999, p. 2)

This description reads more like a public information document than the distillation of intelligence reports. It could have been provided by anyone with a rudimentary knowledge of the steps in exporting stolen cars, who is also familiar with traditional writings on organized crime. It is also out of step with some recent research on groups currently involved in organized and transnational crimes.

In their study of thirty-nine drug-trafficking organizations prosecuted in New York City during the 1990s, Natarajan and Belanger (1998) identified some "corporations" (large formal hierarchies with well-defined divisions of labor) that fit the traditional conception of organized criminals, but they also identified three other groups: "freelancers" (small, nonhierarchical entrepreneurial groups), "family businesses" (cohesive groups with clear structure and authority derived from family ties), and "communal businesses" (flexible groups bound by a common tie such as ethnicity). They also reported that many groups specialized in only one or two steps of the trafficking process, such as import or regional distribution, rather than managing the whole enterprise.

Levi and Naylor (2000) have argued that the character of organized crime has changed. The groups now involved are quite different from the traditional "Mafia" of the textbooks. Many more small, loosely structured networks of criminal entrepreneurs have arisen, often with specialized knowledge, who come together to exploit specific opportunities for crime, such as credit card fraud or counterfeiting banknotes. The existence of these opportunities, which permit substantial illegal sums of money to be made, encourages the development of these networks.

Eck and Gersh have reached similar conclusions from studying drug trafficking in the Washington-Baltimore area during 1995–97. They argued that this consisted of a "cottage industry" of "many small groups of traffickers that form and break up easily," rather than a "concentrated industry" of a "relatively small set of large, hierarchically organized distribution networks" (2000, p. 241).

These studies suggest that much organized crime is now the province of small groups of entrepreneurs who exploit opportunities for crime discovered through their businesses or through their family and community contacts. It would not be surprising, therefore, if many people engaged in trafficking vehicles were employed in legitimate export businesses or in selling used cars and have discovered that they can exploit their knowledge and contacts to make large profits selling stolen cars overseas.

There are also hints in the literature that some vehicle trafficking is carried out on a much more disorganized, opportunistic basis. It is said, for example, that when seasonal migrant workers depart from Sweden after working in the fields in the summer, many leave their old and battered Eastern European models parked in the countryside and drive home in Volvos and Saabs stolen locally. It is also said that crewmen on Chinese and Vietnamese freighters commonly steal motorcycles in Japan and take them home as deck cargo (United Nations 1997). Finally, Resindez (1998) has reported how a group of Mexican-American youths developed a relationship with a fence in Mexico whom they regularly supplied with cars stolen in a border town in Texas where they lived. None of those interviewed considered themselves to be part of a criminal organization though they regularly stole cars together. They used crude methods to steal the cars and equally crude methods of getting cars across the border: if challenged by U.S officials at the bridge or by officials at the Mexican checkpoint, they simply drove through at high speed.

The lack of information about those involved in trafficking stolen cars makes it difficult to formulate a rational, comprehensive policy response and to anticipate the likely results of countermeasures. For instance, if organized criminals are heavily involved in trafficking in stolen cars, it will be much harder to control. If control efforts are successful, they will much more likely result in displacement to some other form of trafficking that could be harder to control and more harmful.

A particularly important question is the degree to which immigrants are involved in the trafficking of vehicles (Onishi 1995). Immigrants are known to be heavily involved in drug trafficking (Natarajan 1998; Reuter 2000), and their contacts in destination countries make it likely they would be similarly involved in vehicle trafficking. If this were the case, it could help explain patterns of car theft, at least in the United States, and might help in formulating preventive responses. As discussed in Section II, known trafficking routes provide a useful starting point for research on this topic.

E. How Is Trafficking in Stolen Cars Being Addressed?

Despite the generally low priority accorded to vehicle theft by law enforcement authorities, recent years have seen a spate of activity directed to trafficking. In much of this work, the United States has been the prime mover, though INTERPOL and the United Nations have also played important roles in stimulating international cooperation. A catalog of recent activity would include the following:

The United States has developed a model bilateral agreement for the repatriation of stolen vehicles (see United Nations 1997) and has signed agreements with numerous countries in Latin America.

United States agents have provided training to customs officials in these countries in ways to identify stolen cars.

The National Insurance Crime Bureau (which is supported by the American insurance industry) has assisted these efforts by stationing officials in Mexico and other South American countries to assist the process of repatriation.

X-ray machines and gamma ray technology (that produces an x-ray-like image of a container's contents) are being evaluated for use in inspecting sealed containers in ports in the United Kingdom and the United States (Cottrill 1999; General Accounting Office 1999; Interagency Commission on Crime and Security at U.S. Seaports 2000), and documentation relating to any car for export must now be presented at U.S. ports seventy-two hours prior to loading (General Accounting Office 1999).

The U.S. Motor Vehicle Theft and Law Enforcement Act 1984 required car manufacturers to mark the major body parts of high-risk models to deter their theft for chopping and for export (Clarke and Harris 1992*a*).

The stolen vehicle database maintained by the FBI is being opened to other countries (Davis 1999).

INTERPOL has developed a similar database of stolen vehicles for access by member states (Wegrzyn 1997).

EUCARIS, the European Car and Driving Licence Information System, was established in 1994 in response to increased international trafficking of cars in Europe. The system allows member countries, of which there are presently seven full members with several other countries making use of the system on a limited basis, to share data about vehicle and driver registrations.[6]

The United Nations hosted several international meetings during 1996–97 (Vetere 1996) and conducted a survey of member states with the object of identifying "measures for the prevention and suppression of illicit trafficking in motor vehicles" (United Nations 1997, p. 1).

The European Institute for Crime Prevention and Control (known as HEUNI), together with the Russian Ministry of the Interior, initiated a survey of all European countries focused on issues of international cooperation in dealing with trafficking in stolen cars (Liukkonen 1997).

Many countries have established committees or task forces to study auto theft and to make policy recommendations, including ways to curb the export of stolen vehicles (United Nations 1997).

Europol is currently developing a protocol for greater sharing of information about vehicles stolen in one member state and recovered in another.

The National Crime Intelligence Service (NCIS) has received EU funding to explore the nature of stolen vehicle exports across Europe and to identify ways of improving enforcement at European ports.

Much of this activity has been undertaken to assist the repatriation of stolen cars. Important as this is, it may play only a minor role in

---

[6] See on-line at www.eucaris.net.

deterrence, since very small numbers of trafficked cars are detected. Much greater attention should be devoted to the earlier stages of trafficking in an effort to prevent cars leaving the countries of origin. In particular, research should be focused on the conditions facilitating illegal exports at border crossings and the ports. It is here that stolen cars are funneled to their ultimate destinations and where they run the greatest risk of interception (Katona 1996). In addition, Liukkonen (1997) notes that countries responding to the HEUNI survey identified the need for the international harmonization of registration documents and much greater attention in general to the process of registering vehicles in all countries (including establishing ownership). These measures are essentially preventive in nature and should therefore be a priority for research.

Finally, it would be useful to know what effects on trafficking in stolen cars could be expected from recent improvements in vehicle security. Many of these improvements are designed to foil thieves less determined than those involved in trafficking. Persuasive data exist to show that the mandatory fitting of immobilizers to new cars in the United Kingdom since October 1998 has reduced overall car theft rates (Brown and Thomas, forthcoming). However, in analyzing unpublished data from the *Car Theft Index* (Home Office 2001), we found that for vehicles under three years old the rate of unrecovered thefts increased by 26 percent between 1998 and 2000. By contrast, the rate of unrecovered thefts of vehicles aged over three years declined by 16 percent. These findings indicate that immobilization may have had minimal impact on the risk of theft of new vehicles, which are the ones most likely to be stolen for export.

Clearly more information is needed about the methods employed by thieves in stealing a car for export. It would be helpful to know, for example, how many of these vehicles are stolen off the streets in the usual way, and how many by more sophisticated methods. These include the use of flatbed trucks to remove the car, making copies of keys, stealing keys in the course of burglary, entering into fraudulent rental or lease agreements to obtain vehicles, and even carjacking.

II. Meeting the Research Needs

If research is to assist policy, it must at a minimum provide better information on the extent of trafficking in stolen cars, its costs, the methods employed, and the groups responsible. It must also provide information to support the development of preventive measures—as distinct from enforcement—since these have been neglected to date.

In this section, we offer some suggestions for meeting these needs, though we avoid topics where we lack competence, such as economic analysis of trafficking in stolen cars. We avoid ambitious or complex studies because these could fail in the present undeveloped state of knowledge. In any case, research that takes a long time to complete runs the risk of providing yesterday's answers to today's questions. Cornish and Clarke have argued this point:

> Organized crimes are dynamic activities characterized by contingency and innovation, and these sources of instability and change apply even more to the fluid relationships and temporary dependencies that may exist amongst complex crimes. While research is being conducted, permutations and innovations are constantly occurring as opportunities and technologies change, and as crime-control agencies stimulate further change and complexity. . . . Thus, even though the complexities of criminal activity at one point in time might well be best described by lengthy and rigorous research, they might still shed little light on the complexities of ongoing forms of organized crimes at another point. Indeed, the results of such research may be counterproductive insofar as they misdirect policy makers as to the nature of the phenomena in question and the properties—dynamic rather than static—of the underlying processes involved. (Cornish and Clarke 2002, pp. 55–56)

The policy purpose of gaining improved insight into current organized crimes should be tackled instead using "rapid appraisal" research approaches (Beebe 1995).[7] These approaches might include studying police and prosecution case papers of detected cases of vehicle trafficking, studying the reports of undercover operations, interviewing experts and convicted offenders about methods of trafficking, interviewing those involved in the export of used cars in order to understand the means by which legal business is transacted and the loopholes available to offenders, and undertaking newspaper searches.

Such research could provide policy makers with more information about key topics such as the kinds of offenders involved, the ways they establish links with others in destination countries, how they evade

---

[7] Kelly and Regan (2000) followed essentially this approach in their study of trafficking of women for sexual exploitation in the United Kingdom.

customs controls at export and import, how they give stolen cars a new identity, and how they re-register and sell cars in the destination countries. It is only with this kind of information that policy can respond quickly to change and innovation in an area where illegal entrepreneurial expertise, opportunism, and responsiveness to changing market conditions combine to set the agenda. Tremblay, Talon, and Hurley (2001) describe in great detail how this process has led in Quebec to a large increase of thefts of cars for resale.

A. Measuring the Extent of the Problem

Better measures of trafficking in stolen cars are needed both for evaluating policy and for determining the appropriate level of policy intervention. This is the most urgent priority for research in this field.

Present estimates rely upon educated guesses about the percentage of unrecovered stolen cars that is exported. Thus the National Criminal Intelligence Service has recently stated in its newsletter for police that "it is estimated that 10–20 percent of permanently stolen U.K. vehicles are exported. This translates to 20,000–40,000 vehicles—a very significant number" (National Criminal Intelligence Service 2001, p. 2).

The NCIS estimate is much lower than that usually quoted for the United States, which is around 30–35 percent. The figure is likely to be lower for Britain because, unlike the United States (and Continental Europe), all cars stolen for export in Britain have to be transported on ships or must leave the country via the Channel Tunnel. This would reduce the profitability of this offense.

It seems highly improbable that 20,000–40,000 vehicles could be illegally exported from Britain through the ports without attracting the notice of police and customs officials, particularly in light of the volume of the legal export trade in used cars. According to Department of Trade and Industry figures, 24,259 used vehicles were exported from Britain in 2001—a figure not much different from the numbers stolen and exported.[8] This means that police and customs officials at the ports could expect nearly half the cars they encountered to be stolen.

Another reason why theft for export might be a smaller problem in Britain is that British vehicles are right-hand drive, whereas those in

[8] Compiled from HM Customs and Excise Data; available on-line at www.uktradeinfo. com.

most other countries are left-hand drive. The only nearby right-hand-drive countries are Ireland, Cyprus, and Malta, all of which are comparatively small and unlikely to be able to absorb large numbers of stolen vehicles from Britain. Nigeria and Ghana are generally thought to be the principal overseas destinations for stolen cars exported from Britain. These are both left-hand-drive countries, though they do not discriminate particularly between left- and right-hand-drive vehicles. Nigeria is second only to the United States as a destination for used cars legally exported from Britain (2,985 in 2001), and it turns out that more used cars are legally exported from Britain to left-hand-drive countries (77 percent of the total of 24,259) than to other countries. Altogether, these data suggest that right-hand drive is not as great a deterrent to theft for export as might appear at first sight—but this is yet another topic for detailed study.

Even though the U.K. estimate of vehicles stolen for export is lower than for other parts of the world, like all such estimates, it takes no account of the fact that only a few models are thought to be vulnerable to theft for export. Estimates of the numbers of cars stolen for export ought to be based on these models, not on all cars stolen, as at present.

As we found in an exploratory study, this produces very much smaller estimates of the size of the problem. From interviews with seventeen experts (Hardy and Clarke 2001), we obtained information about models believed to be at "high risk" of theft for export.[9] All seventeen experts identified luxury vehicles as being the most at risk, with sport-utility vehicles (SUVs) or off-road vehicles in second place. Between them, the experts identified twenty-one specific models, two of which we excluded from our analysis because they were light commercial vehicles, not cars.

Thirteen of the seventeen experts stated that cars stolen for export were generally less than three years old, while two others stated that they were less than four years old. Accordingly, we confined the study to vehicles three years old or less.

In case the experts had overlooked some high-risk models, we undertook an examination of police records of vehicles impounded between 1999 and 2001 at Tilbury, one of Britain's largest ports. (Unfor-

[9] Fourteen of these experts were police or customs officers in nine of the seventeen major ports covering the coastline of England and Wales, one was the head of the Metropolitan Police Stolen Vehicle Unit, one an analyst for the National Criminal Intelligence Service, and one was an investigator who specializes in the international recovery of vehicles stolen in the United Kingdom and exported.

tunately, these records did not distinguish between cars suspected of being stolen from those with outstanding loans that had to be paid before the vehicles could leave the country.) These records consisted of 146 cars comprising fifty-seven different models. Two of these models were excluded because they were light commercial vehicles, not cars, and a further thirty-one models were excluded because only one car had been recovered of each model. It would be dangerous to include these thefts, which might have been committed for unusual reasons, when seeking to arrive at a national estimate of the number of cars stolen for export.

This left twenty-four models of which at least two examples were recorded. This group of twenty-four models accounted for 76 percent of the cars impounded during the three-year period and included eleven of the nineteen identified by the experts. Most of the other models were small- or medium-sized sedans with only two or three cars impounded in each case. These were likely to be cars with outstanding loans rather than ones stolen for export. In fact, only two models not already identified by the seventeen experts seemed to fit the category of high-risk cars for export theft—the Volkswagen Golf (sixteen cars impounded) and the Mercedes M class (seven cars impounded). These two models were added to the nineteen models identified by the experts, for a total of twenty-one high-risk models (see appendix). The twenty-one models represented only 3 percent of the 697 models identified in the *Car Theft Index 2001* (Home Office 2001).

For each of these twenty-one models, unpublished data from the Home Office *Car Theft Index 2001* yielded the numbers of cars first registered in 1998–2000 that were stolen and not recovered in 2000. The percentage stolen and not recovered for each of the twenty-one models was compared with the average percentage not recovered for all other vehicles in the same market segment (e.g., sports cars)—a necessary step because recovery rates vary by market segment. In each case, the percentage not recovered of the twenty-one high-risk models was greater than for the other models in the segment. It was assumed that this difference reflected the cars stolen for export—on the further assumption that the twenty-one models at high risk of theft for export did not also differ consistently from other models in their risks of other forms of unrecovered theft (e.g., broken for spares or insurance frauds).

Table 1 shows the overall results of this exercise. The average rate of nonrecovery was four percentage points higher for the twenty-one

TABLE 1

Differences in Nonrecovery Rates between Twenty-One Models at High Risk of Theft for Export and Others in the Same Market Segments (All Models Aged Three Years or Less Stolen in England and Wales in 2000)

Market Segment	Average Nonrecovery Rate of 21 High-Risk Models	Average Nonrecovery Rate for Rest of Market Segment	Difference in Nonrecovery Rates
Small sedans	37.3	35.2	2.1
Medium sedans	41.0	32.3	8.7
Large sedans	37.7	29.2	8.5
Luxury sedans	28.6	27.0	1.6
Sports cars	33.0	29.3	3.7
SUVs and minivans	34.8	33.6	1.2
Total	37.0	33.0	4.0

NOTE.—SUV = sport-utility vehicle.

high-risk models than for the comparison models. An "export ratio" was then calculated, which reflected the proportion of high-risk vehicles estimated to be exported. Using the terminology in table 1, this ratio was expressed as the "difference in nonrecovery rates: average nonrecovery rate of twenty-one high-risk models." This yielded an export ratio of 4.0:37.0, or nearly 11 percent. This translates into a national export rate of 0.2 percent of unrecovered stolen cars, equating to about 140 cars.

These estimates fall so far short of the official ones (10–20 percent of stolen unrecovered cars exported, with a total of somewhere between 20,000 to 40,000 vehicles) that they run the risk of being dismissed out of hand on grounds of faulty methodology. We would readily concede some limitations of our method, including that the seventeen experts who were interviewed covered only nine of the largest twenty-seven ports in the country; records of cars seized by police and customs officials were examined at only one port; our group of twenty-one high-risk models did not include ones dismantled for spare parts before leaving the country, which therefore might not come to the attention of the authorities; we omitted cars that are more than three years old; we omitted 676 models that individually might be stolen in small numbers but collectively could yield a large total of cars stolen for export; and we assumed that the rates of other forms of unrecovered thefts for our twenty-one models were no different from cars not stolen for export.

Conceding these limitations and that our estimate is conservative, we still believe the true figure of cars stolen for export is much closer to our own estimate. The NCIS estimate greatly inflates the problem by including all unrecovered stolen cars, when the literature is widely agreed that the problem is mostly confined to a small group of new models. The NCIS estimate also leads to the unlikely conclusion that the number of used cars stolen for export is little different from the number legally exported.

Our selection of twenty-one high-risk models was based on the opinion of experts with firsthand experience of the problem. Even so, the recovery rates of this high-risk group were on average only four percentage points lower than for other comparable vehicles—suggesting that rather few of the cars in this high-risk group were exported. These facts cannot be reconciled with the NCIS estimate, and the issue of the number of vehicles stolen for export cannot be resolved without more detailed research. In fact, our purpose in undertaking this exploratory study was less to produce a firm estimate of the scale of the problem than to make the case for this research—a case made simply by the huge gap between the NCIS estimate and our own. Our study also underlines the need for hard information on the fate of unrecovered vehicles. Without this information, it is impossible to think clearly about preventive policy.[10]

The need for improved measures is not confined to Britain, and, in fact, our study could be repeated comparatively easily in the United States by comparing the theft and recovery rates of models at high risk of theft for export to South America with those of other models sold in the United States. As a refinement, the study could be repeated for U.S. cities with seaports and for the U.S. states sharing land borders with Mexico, both of which are thought to have higher rates of theft for export (National Insurance Crime Bureau 1999).

Three other methods of estimating the numbers of cars stolen for export in the United States are possible. First, U.S.-wide records of

---

[10] As an example of the confusion surrounding recovery rates, it is frequently claimed that because these have tended to decline over recent years, "professional" thefts are increasing. In fact, the official statistics show that the numbers of both recovered and unrecovered thefts have decreased markedly in recent years, though the drop is slightly greater for recovered ("nonprofessional") thefts. This makes it appear that professional thefts are increasing when they are decreasing.

the numbers of cars registered for use in year 1 could be compared with numbers registered for years 2, 3, and 4 for high-risk models and for all other models. Allowance should be made for cars legally exported and ones written-off in accidents. The difference in yearly attrition rates between the two groups could provide a measure of cars stolen for export. Second, statistically valid counts could be attempted of high-risk models using border crossings between the United States and Mexico. Comparisons of the numbers observed and numbers expected could provide estimates of the trade in stolen vehicles using this route. Third, representative samples of cars using border crossings and containers awaiting shipment at U.S. ports could be examined to determine the numbers of stolen vehicles.

While seemingly feasible, these approaches need to be more closely examined. They all depend upon obtaining access to data sources maintained by various federal and private agencies, the latter including the National Insurance Crime Bureau, the Highway Loss Data Institute, and R. L. Polk (commercial providers of statistical information for the motor industry). The last of the methods, while apparently straightforward, could involve considerable legal and logistical difficulties. It would also require extensive cooperation from port authorities and from U.S. Customs and immigration services.

B. Studying the Methods Used by Vehicle Traffickers

The difficulties of acquiring detailed information about vehicle trafficking methods needed for prevention have been discussed above. These relate to the many variant forms of this transnational crime and the many steps involved in each. A way of studying the sequential steps involved in the commission of any crime has been outlined by Cornish (1994). This depends on the concept of the crime "script," the uses of which he has described:

> By drawing attention to the way that events and episodes unfold, the script concept offers a useful analytic tool for looking at behavioral routines in the service of rational, purposive, goal-oriented action. A script-theoretic approach provides a way of generating, organizing and systematizing knowledge about the procedural aspects and procedural requirements of crime commission. It has the potential for eliciting more crime-specific, detailed and comprehensive offenders' accounts of crime commission, for extending analysis to all stages of

the crime-commission sequence and, hence, for helping to enhance situational crime prevention policies by drawing attention to a fuller range of possible intervention points. (P. 151)

To date, most applications of this concept involve relatively simple crimes such as breaking into parked cars. For the more complex process of trafficking in stolen cars, scripts would have to be developed for each stage of the specific variety of the crime being studied, with links between each stage in the sequence. This approach might assist in comparing variation among the methods used in the different kinds of trafficking and in synthesizing information from various studies.

A way to begin developing such scripts would be through interviews with two groups of knowledgeable persons: those arrested for the crime and law enforcement officials responsible for dealing with it. Examples of such studies already exist. Resindez (1998) interviewed ten offenders for her study of trafficking in stolen cars between Texas and Mexico. Liukkonen's (1997) study for HEUNI surveyed those involved in enforcement. Hinchcliffe's (1994) detailed account of methods used in ringing stolen vehicles was based on surveys completed by eighty-five British police officers with direct experience of dealing with professional vehicle theft. Sehr's (1995) account of police methods of dealing with auto theft in Germany includes a lengthy interview with an experienced insurance auto theft investigator in Eastern Europe, which sheds some light on fencing networks. Apart from focusing on the methods used at different stages of trafficking in stolen cars, future studies should obtain estimates of the financial rewards for those involved at each stage (see Stefancic 1996 for one set of estimates).

Another approach geared specifically to understanding the export stage would be to interview those involved in legally exporting used cars to developing countries. Such studies might focus on loopholes in procedures and regulations that criminals could exploit.

These interview studies should be complemented by what might be called "operational studies" of official systems and procedures relevant to various stages of the process involved in vehicle trafficking. Again, these studies would be intended to identify loopholes that could be blocked by situational measures (Clarke 1995). They would include studies of the vehicle registration systems in countries (both developed and undeveloped) involved in the international trade in stolen cars; studies of the customs, port, and other procedures for exporting and importing vehicles (Smith and Burrows [1986] report that changes made in the documentation necessary for importing cars into the United Kingdom were successful in reducing illegal imports); studies of existing methods for detecting stolen cars at border crossings and on ferries; and studies of barriers to repatriation in different countries (for discussions of these, see Liukkonen 1997; Hegstrom 1999).

C. Studying the Role of Immigrants

Immigrants are involved in other forms of transnational crime and are likely also to be involved in trafficking in stolen cars. This possibility could be studied by examining the known export routes for trafficking in stolen cars. The aim would be to examine ways immigration patterns do and do not correspond to vehicle trafficking patterns.

First, the fit between drug trafficking routes and routes used by those trafficking in stolen cars should be examined. The results might clarify the possible involvement in vehicle trafficking of immigrants from particular countries and might support speculations that cars are frequently used as a form of payment for drugs. This study would require vehicle trafficking routes in the Americas to be documented with equal precision to those in Europe.

Second, the fit between legal export routes and the routes used by those trafficking in stolen cars should be investigated. The results might clarify the possible involvement of those with legitimate export business in vehicle trafficking.

Third, the fit between patterns of immigrant settlement in the United States and the known routes used by those trafficking in stolen cars should be investigated. This study could also match preferred models in different destination countries with theft of these models in the immigrant areas in the United States.

These studies should be supplemented by interviews with law enforcement officials about the involvement of immigrants. Additional sources of relevant information may be newspaper accounts of trafficking in stolen cars and court records of vehicle trafficking cases (the latter comprising the source used by Natarajan and Belanger [1998] in studying drug trafficking organizations).

III. Conclusions

Whether because of improved security on new cars or generally falling crime rates, auto theft in developed countries is declining (personal communication, Jaap de Waard, Dutch Ministry of Justice, November 11, 1999; based on Home Office and Eurostat data). Trafficking in stolen cars will probably be immune to this trend because improvements in vehicle security provide little deterrent to professional thieves, and the demand for stolen cars in developing countries, fueled by increasing globalization, is unlikely to abate. Unlike rare animals and cultural artifacts catering to more refined tastes, cars are widely coveted and are constantly updated and improved. For all these reasons, they are likely to remain "hot products" on the world's theft markets for some considerable time to come (Clarke 1999).

Little hard information is available to guide the future development of policy in this field. At the most basic level, it is unclear whether trafficking in stolen cars resembles what Eck and Gersh (2000) call a "concentrated industry," dominated by a few large criminal organizations, or a "cottage industry" of many small groups of entrepreneurs that form to take advantage of the opportunities for this crime and that dissolve just as easily. Nor is the size of the problem known. Our study reported above indicates it could be much smaller than is claimed by law enforcement agencies and the media, both of which benefit from portraying vehicle trafficking as vast and highly organized—the police in terms of prestige and resources and the newspapers in terms of readership.

Research is urgently needed on these issues, but if it is to be helpful to policy, it must be completed quickly using rapid appraisal techniques (Beebe 1995) because those engaged in trafficking are constantly adapting to new restrictions. At the same time, new opportunities for trafficking are continually drawing in fresh recruits. If researchers do not move equally fast, the information they produce will be out of date before it can be put to use. Police agencies will have to play their part by streamlining procedures for giving researchers access to sensitive data.

Apart from more information about the scale and nature of the problem, the most urgent priority for research is to uncover the methods by which traffickers circumvent registration and licensing requirements, and avoid detection at customs and border checkpoints. Operational research of this kind should be complemented by studies of immigrant involvement in vehicle trafficking and by economic (and business) analyses of the crime. The latter will be assisted by the multiple databases that exist on vehicles and vehicle theft. While it may be a benign form of transnational crime, and not as large a problem as is usually portrayed, vehicle trafficking is a costly drain on law enforcement. The modest investment in the studies identified above should not be delayed.

APPENDIX

TABLE 1A

Numbers Stolen and Not Recovered of Twenty-One Models at
"High Risk" of Theft for Export (England and Wales 2000)

Market Segment	Make and Model	Stolen in 2000	Recovered in 2000	Not Recovered in 2000	Percent not Recovered
Small sedan	VW Golf	664	416	248	37.3
Medium sedan	BMW 3 series	672	399	273	40.6
	Mercedes C class	198	114	84	42.4
Large sedan	BMW 5 series	195	132	63	32.3
	Mercedes 200 series	83	44	39	47.0
	Mercedes 300 series	35	22	13	37.1
	Mercedes E class	234	143	91	38.9
	Honda Legend	5	3	2	40.0
	Peugeot 504 and 505	5	3	2	40.0
Luxury sedan	BMW 7 series	41	30	11	26.8
	Lexus GS300/LS400	50	35	15	30.0
Sports car	Mercedes CLK/SLK	260	181	79	30.4
	Porsche 911/944/968	89	53	36	40.4
Sport-utility vehicle	Jeep Cherokee	86	64	22	25.6
	Land Rover Discovery	204	109	95	46.6
	Mercedes M class	99	66	33	33.3
	Mitsubishi Shogun	186	153	33	17.7
	Nissan Terrano	44	27	17	38.6
	Toyota Landcruiser	80	47	33	41.3
	Isuzu Trooper	50	30	20	40.0
	Land Rover Range Rover	119	70	49	41.2
All market segments	All models identified	3,399	2,141	1,258	37.0

REFERENCES

Beebe, James. 1995. "Basic Concepts and Techniques of Rapid Appraisal." *Human Organization* 54(1):42–51.

Brown, Rick. 1995. *The Nature and Extent of Heavy Goods Vehicle Theft*. Crime Detection and Prevention Series, Paper no. 66. London: Home Office, Police Research Group.

Brown, Rick, and Nerys Thomas. Forthcoming. "Aging Vehicles: Evidence of the Effectiveness of New Car Security from the Home Office Car Theft Index." *Security Journal*.

Cearley, Anna. 2001. "Thieves Reverse the Trend, Bring Mexican Cars to U.S." *San Diego Union-Tribune* (March 5), p. A-1.

Chen, David W. 2001. "Eight Arrested in Smuggling of Luxury Cars." *New York Times* (March 2), p. B5.

Clarke, Ronald V. 1995. "Situational Crime Prevention." In *Building a Safer Society: Strategic Approaches to Crime Prevention,* edited by Michael Tonry and David P. Farrington. Vol. 19 of *Crime and Justice: A Review of Research,* edited by Michael Tonry. Chicago: University of Chicago Press.

———. 1999. *Hot Products: Understanding, Anticipating and Reducing the Demand for Stolen Goods.* Policing and Reducing Crime Unit, Paper no. 112. London: Home Office.

Clarke, Ronald V., and Patricia M. Harris. 1992a. "Auto Theft and Its Prevention." In *Crime and Justice: A Review of Research,* vol. 16, edited by Michael Tonry. Chicago: University of Chicago Press.

———. 1992b. "A Rational Choice Perspective on the Targets of Automobile Theft." *Criminal Behaviour and Mental Health* 2:25–42.

Corelli, Rae. 1998. "Car Theft for Export." *Maclean's* 111 (August 17): 36–39.

Cornish, Derek. 1994. "The Procedural Analysis of Offending and Its Relevance for Situational Crime Prevention." In *Crime Prevention Studies,* vol. 3, edited by Ronald V. Clarke. Monsey, N.Y.: Criminal Justice Press.

Cornish, Derek B., and Ronald V. Clarke. 2002. "Analyzing Organized Crimes." In *Rational Choice and Criminal Behavior: Recent Research and Future Challenges,* edited by Alex R. Piquero and Stephen G. Tibbetts. New York: Routledge.

Cottrill, Ken. 1999. "Port Security Fighting Back." *Traffic World* (May 31) 258:30–32.

Davis, Jessica. 1999. "FBI Relies on Web Interface to Bust Car Theft Rings." *InfoWorld* (May 10), p. 50.

Dillon, Sam. 1999. "To Keep Out Illegal Cars, Mexico Plans a Huge Fee." *New York Times* (October 30), pp. 1, A6.

Dobson, Chris. 1993. "Mainland Authorities Have Seized Five Luxury Boats Believed to Have Been Stolen from Hong Kong." *South China Morning Post* (December 5), p. 5.

Eck, John E., and Jeffrey G. Gersh. 2000. "Drug Trafficking as a Cottage Industry." In *Illegal Drug Markets: From Research to Prevention Policy,* edited by Mangai Natarajan and Mike Hough. Vol. 11 of *Crime Prevention Studies.* Monsey, N.Y.: Criminal Justice Press.

Field, Simon. 1993. "Crime Prevention and the Costs of Auto Theft: An Economic Analysis." In *Crime Prevention Studies,* vol. 1, edited by Ronald V. Clarke. Monsey, N.Y.: Criminal Justice Press.

Field, Simon, Ronald V. Clarke, and Patricia M. Harris. 1991. "The Mexican Vehicle Market and Auto Theft in Border Areas of the United States." *Security Journal* 2:205–10.

General Accounting Office. 1999. *Efforts to Curtail the Exportation of Stolen Vehicles.* Report to the Chairman, Permanent Subcommittee on Investigations, Committee on Governmental Affairs, U.S. Senate. GAO/OSI. Washington, D.C.: U.S. General Accounting Office.

Hardy, Elaine. 1998. *Vehicle Theft in Europe: The Unofficial Redistribution of Vehicles.* Solihull, England: International Car Distribution Programme Ltd.

———. 1999. *Cross Border Flows of Used Cars in Europe.* May 20. Solihull, England: International Car Distribution Programme Ltd.

Hardy, Elaine, and Ronald V. Clarke. 2001. "Estimating the Numbers of Cars Stolen for Export: A Feasibility Study." Unpublished report to the Policing and Reducing Crime Unit. London: Home Office.

Hegstrom, Edward. 1999. "A Pickup Stolen in Houston Stays Parked in Guatemala: Vehicles Illegally Taken South of the Border Rarely Return to U.S." *Houston Chronicle* (February 7), p. A1.

Hinchcliffe, Michael. 1994. *Professional Car Thieves: Their Knowledge and Social Structure.* Police Research Award Scheme. London: Home Office, Police Research Group.

Home Office. 2001. *Car Theft Index 2001.* Communications Directorate, November 1, CTI/01. London: Home Office.

Interagency Commission on Crime and Security in U.S. Seaports. 2000. *Report.* Fall 2000. Washington, D.C.: Interagency Commission on Crime and Security in U.S. Seaports.

INTERPOL. 1999. "Frequently Asked Questions about Vehicle Theft." Copy downloaded by the author on January 12, 1999. Web site no longer functional.

Katona, Geza. 1996. Summary of the Conference on "Organised Transborder Vehicle Theft," August 26–28, 1996. Budapest: Police College.

Kelly, Liz, and Linda Regan. 2000. *Stopping Traffic: Exploring the Extent of, and Responses to, Trafficking in Women for Sexual Exploitation in the U.K.* Police Research Series, Paper no. 125. London: Home Office.

Lepage, Andrew, and Fernando Romero. 1990. "Mexico Won't Tolerate Stolen-Vehicle Use." *San Diego Union-Tribune* (May 19), p. B-1.

Levi, Michael, and Tom Naylor. 2000. "Organised Crime: The Organisation of Crime, and the Organisation of Business." Research Paper, CD Annex, in *Turning the Corner: Crime 2020.* Foresight Panel. London: DTI.

Liukkonen, Markku. 1997. "Motor Vehicle Theft in Europe." Paper no. 9. Helsinki: European Institute for Crime Prevention and Control (HEUNI).

Malinowski, Sean. 1996. "Eastern Europe Battles Transnational Auto Theft Problems." *CJ Europe* 6:1, 4–5.

Miller, Michael V. 1987. "Vehicle Theft along the Texas–Mexico Border." *Journal of Borderland Studies* 2:12–32.

Natarajan, Mangai. 1998. "Drug Trafficking in the Metropolitan Area." In *Crime and Justice in New York City,* edited by Andrew Karmen. New York: McGraw-Hill.

Natarajan, Mangai, and Mathieu Belanger. 1998. "Varieties of Drug Trafficking Organizations: A Typology of Cases Prosecuted in New York City." *Journal of Drug Issues* 28:1005–26.

National Automobile Theft Bureau. 1989. *Annual Report.* Palos Hills, Ill.: National Automobile Theft Bureau.

National Criminal Intelligence Service. 2001. *Lynx Newsletter* (Summer). London: National Criminal Intelligence Service.

National Insurance Crime Bureau. 1999. "Thieves Target Vehicles in Coastal and Border Communities; More than 200,000 Vehicles Illegally Exported

Each Year." News release, March 22. Palos Hills, Ill.: National Automobile Theft Bureau.

Ndhlovu, Francis K. 2002. "Organized Crime: A Perspective from Zambia." In *Organized Crime: World Perspectives*, edited by Jay S. Albanese, Dilip K. Das, and Arvind Verma. Upper Saddle River, N.J.: Prentice Hall.

New York Times. 2001. "Customs Officials Spot Stolen Cars but Don't Try to Stop Them." (February 25), p. 15.

———. 2002. "Japan Battles an Alliance of Gangs That Trades in Stolen Cars." (January 6), p. 5.

Onishi, Norimitsu. 1995. "Stolen Cars Find a World of Welcome." *New York Times* (July 10), p. B1.

Porteous, Samuel D. 1998. *Organized Crime Impact Study: Highlights.* Ottawa: Public Works and Government Services of Canada, Ministry of the Solicitor General. Available on-line at www.sgc.gc.ca.

Preston, Julia. 1999. "Mexico Suspends Plan for Hefty Deposit on Cars." *New York Times* (December 4), p. A9.

Ragavan, Chitra, David E. Kaplan, Andrea Mandel-Campbell, and Linda Robinson. 1999. "Why Auto Theft Is Going Global." *U.S. News and World Report* (June 14), p. 16.

Resindez, Rosalva. 1998. "International Auto Theft: An Exploratory Research of Organization and Organized Crime on the U.S./Mexico Border." *Criminal Organizations* 12:25–30.

Resindez, Rosalva, and David M. Neal. 2000. "International Auto Theft: The Illegal Export of American Vehicles to Mexico." In *International Criminal Justice: Issues in a Global Perspective*, edited by Delbert Rounds. Boston: Allyn & Bacon.

Reuter, Peter. 2000. "Connecting Drug Policy and Research on Drug Markets." In *Illegal Drug Markets: From Research to Prevention Policy*, edited by Mangai Natarajan and Mike Hough. Vol. 11 of *Crime Prevention Studies*. Monsey, N.Y.: Criminal Justice Press.

Rotella, Sebastian. 1994. "Both Sides of Mexico Drug Wars Adore Stolen 4 × 4s." *Los Angeles Times* (May 22), p. A1.

Ruggiero, Vincenzo. 2000. "Criminal Franchising: Albanians and Illicit Drugs in Italy." In *Illegal Drug Markets: From Research to Prevention Policy*, edited by Mangai Natarajan and Mike Hough. Vol. 11 of *Crime Prevention Studies*. Monsey, N.Y.: Criminal Justice Press.

Savona, Ernesto U. 1998. *Illicit Trafficking in Arms, Nuclear Material, People and Motor Vehicles: The Most Important Things We Have Learnt and Priorities for Future Study and Research.* Transcrime Working Paper no. 23. Trento, Italy: University of Trento.

Sehr, Peter. 1995. *Internationale Kraftfahrzeug-Verschiebung: Das Millionending mit Gestohlenen Autos.* Lubeck: Schmidt-Romhild.

Smith, Lorna J. F., and John Burrows. 1986. "Nobbling the Fraudsters: Crime Prevention through Administrative Change." *Howard Journal* 25:13–24.

Stefancic, Martin. 1996. "Eastern European Black Markets: Car Theft." *Banka* (July). Available on-line at www.banka-mzb.tel.hr.

Taipei Times. 2002. "Auto Theft a Thriving Japanese Business." On-line edition (January 4) available at http://taipeitimes.com/news/2002/01/04.

Tremblay, Pierre, Bernard Talon, and Doug Hurley. 2001. "Body Switching and Related Adaptations in the Resale of Stolen Vehicles: Script Elaborations and Aggregate Crime Learning Curves." *British Journal of Criminology* 41:561–79.

van der Leest, Wouter, and Jos Degen. 1999. *Carjacking: A Literature Study.* Zoetermeer: National Police Agency, Netherlands.

Vetere, Eduardo. 1996. Address to "International Conference on Theft of and Illicit Trafficking in Motor Vehicles," Warsaw, Poland, December 2–3. Vienna: Crime Prevention and Criminal Justice Division, United Nations.

Wegrzyn, Jack. 1997. "Cross-Border Vehicle Crime." *Police Journal* 70:302–10.

Williams, P. 1999. "Emerging Issues: Transnational Crime and Its Control." In *Global Report on Crime and Justice,* edited by Graeme Newman. Published for the United Nations Office for Drug Control and Crime Prevention, Centre for International Crime Prevention. New York: Oxford University Press.

Wright, Jeanne. 2001. "Push Is On to Stem Flow of Stolen Cars Crossing Mexican Border." *Los Angeles Times* (April 11), p. G1.

United Nations. 1997. *International Cooperation in Combating Transnational Crime: Illicit Trafficking in Motor Vehicles.* Vienna: Commission on Crime Prevention and Criminal Justice, United Nations.

Yu, Xiao. 1997. "Car Smuggling Remains Rife." *South China Morning Post* (March 21), p. 9.

James B. Jacobs and Ellen Peters

Labor Racketeering: The Mafia and the Unions

ABSTRACT

The labor movement and its members have long suffered from extortion, thievery, and fraud. Corrupt labor officials have used union power to extort money from businesses. Labor racketeering has been a major source of the Cosa Nostra crime families' power and wealth since the 1930s. Nonetheless, combating labor racketeering did not become a federal law enforcement priority until Jimmy Hoffa's assassination in 1975. The U.S. Department of Justice, beginning in the early 1980s, brought or threatened civil racketeering lawsuits against numerous mobbed-up locals and four international unions. These lawsuits led to an unprecedented effort by court-appointed monitors and trustees to purge the corrupted unions of racketeers and racketeering and to reform the unions.

When John L. Lewis, former president of the United Mine Workers (1920–60), observed that "Labor, like Israel, has many sorrows" (*United States v. Local 560, IBT*, 581 F. Supp. 279 [1984], p. 279), he was referring to the long history (even then) of corruption and racketeering that has plagued the American labor movement. Likewise, the labor leader David Dubinsky called labor racketeering "a cancer that almost destroyed the American labor movement" (Dubinsky and Raskin 1977, p. 145). Robert F. Kennedy, who served as general counsel (1957–60) to the Senate Select Committee on Improper Activities in the Labor Management Field (McClellan Committee), warned that labor racketeering was a threat to society generally, and he made labor

James B. Jacobs is Warren E. Burger Professor of Law and director of the Center for Research in Crime and Justice, New York University School of Law. Ellen Peters is a 2002 graduate of the New York University School of Law. We are grateful to Robert Stewart and Herman Benson for comments and suggestions.

racketeering (especially Jimmy Hoffa) a top Justice Department priority when he became attorney general in 1961 (Kennedy 1960). No
other country has a history of union-related criminality approaching
what has been exposed in a century-long litany of scandals, articles
by investigative journalists, governmental hearings, prosecutions, and
lawsuits.[1]

"Labor corruption" refers to the misuse of union office and authority for unlawful personal gain. The immediate victim may be an employer or the union itself, but the ultimate victim is always the union
rank and file. "Labor racketeering" refers to labor corruption committed by, in alliance with, or under the auspices of organized crime
groups.[2] Labor racketeers include members or associates of organized
crime groups, some of whom hold union offices, as well as union officials who work on behalf of organized crime. Common criminal offenses subsumed by the term "labor racketeering" include extortion of
employers by threatening unlawful strikes, work stoppages, picketing,
and workplace sabotage; soliciting and receiving bribes from employers
in exchange for allowing the employer to ignore the terms of the collective bargaining agreement ("sweetheart deal") or for a guarantee
just to be left alone ("labor peace"); thefts and embezzlements from
the union and its pension and welfare funds; violence against rank-and-
file "dissidents"; and the maintenance of illegal employer cartels by
threatening to strike or sabotage businesses that are not cartel members (New York State Organized Crime Task Force 1990, pp. 131–43).

There has been sporadic recognition of labor racketeering as a crime
problem and a social problem since the beginning of the twentieth
century. Congressional hearings gave the matter unprecedented publicity in the late 1950s, but there was no concerted political or law enforcement commitment to attacking the problem until the late 1970s
and well into the 1980s. By then, the Federal Bureau of Investigation
(FBI) and the U.S. Department of Justice (DOJ) had come to see the

---

[1] It need hardly be added that focusing on labor racketeering as a crime problem is
no more an indictment of the vast majority of union officials and members than focusing
on corporate crime is an indictment of the vast majority of businessmen.

[2] In his classic *Organized Crime in Chicago* (1968), first published in 1929 (by the Illinois Association for Criminal Justice), John Landesco provided a great deal of information and commentary on labor racketeering. One of the earliest studies of labor racketeering is Harold Seidman's (1938) *Labor Czars: A History of Labor Racketeering.* Probably
the most famous early study was Daniel Bell's classic, "The Racket-Ridden Longshoremen," originally published in *Fortune Magazine* (1951) and then reprinted in *The End of
Ideology: On the Exhaustion of Political Ideas in the Fifties* (1962). See also Taft 1970;
Hutchinson 1970.

eradication of labor racketeering as the centerpiece of a comprehensive organized crime control strategy. The FBI devoted massive resources to investigating Cosa Nostra's control over a score of local unions and a number of major national/international unions.[3] The federal organized crime strike forces and the U.S. attorneys began bringing civil racketeering lawsuits against labor racketeers with the goal of having federal courts issue injunctions requiring wide-ranging union reforms, including the purge of racketeers and the restoration of union democracy (Goldberg 1989).

The most successful of these civil Racketeer Influenced and Corrupt Organizations Act (RICO) lawsuits have demonstrated the capacity of federal courts, when supported by courageous and creative former prosecutors serving as court-appointed trustees, to effectuate impressive institutional reform in thoroughly racketeer-dominated unions. Hundreds of criminals have been purged from union positions, fair election procedures have been instituted, and fundamental changes in union governance and operations have been adopted. But the path to reform has not been easy, and it has not been unidirectional. Many civil racketeering suits have failed to root out racketeering and to achieve fundamental union reform. Each lawsuit, and especially each trusteeship, has approached its challenge afresh. There has yet to emerge any systematic body of knowledge about what works and what does not work for trustees and monitors, operating under court auspices, charged with the task of rehabilitating unions that have been corrupted and devastated by decades of mob dominance. Thus, there is a crying need to document and analyze the efforts that have so far taken place in order to refine and improve anti-labor-racketeering and union reform strategies for the future.

This article has three goals. First, it seeks to make a case for taking labor racketeering seriously, indeed as an important form of systematic criminality that festers in one of society's key sociopolitical institutions. Second, this article begins to document and analyze the federal government's remedial efforts to purge organized crime from the four most corrupted international unions. Third, it attempts to find a theoretical place for labor racketeering in academic criminology.

---

[3] An international union has affiliated locals in Canada as well as the United States. National and international unions differ with respect to how centralized they are. Some unions permit their local affiliates wide-ranging independence while others seek to monitor and manage their locals. Most national and international unions are members of the AFL-CIO, a labor federation that lobbies on behalf of the labor movement.

Section I of this essay sketches the history of labor racketeering up until the early 1980s, when the President's Commission on Organized Crime (PCOC) took stock of the problem. Sections II–V present PCOC's assessment of labor racketeering in the International Brotherhood of Teamsters (IBT), International Longshoremen's Association (ILA), Hotel Employees and Restaurant Employees International Union (HEREIU), and Laborers International Union of North America (LIUNA) as of the early 1980s and then, in each case, document the extraordinary steps taken by the U.S. Department of Justice's Organized Crime and Racketeering Section (OCRS) and the U.S. attorneys to purge those unions and their locals of organized crime racketeering. Section VI begins to sketch out a criminology of labor racketeering.

I. History of Labor Racketeering

In the labor wars from the 1860s through the 1930s, both employers and unions reached out to gangsters to counteract the violence directed at them (Landesco 1968, pp. 132–47). Gangsters also served as a counterweight to communists and leftist elements in the labor movement (Kimeldorf 1988); the gangsters were simply less threatening than communists to some government officials, businessmen, and union leaders. In some cases, once the gangsters gained a foothold, they consolidated their power through intimidation and patronage.[4] Control over a union was immensely valuable to the organized crime bosses, who could steal from the union coffers and extort money from employers. In addition, they could barter union support to politicians in exchange for immunity from investigation and prosecution. Some labor racketeers wielded influence with local political party machines. With ties to the underworld and influence in legitimate society, the labor racketeers became major power brokers at the local level and even at the state and national levels.

In the 1920s and 1930s Arnold Rothstein, Louis Buchalter (aka Louis Lepke), and Jacob "Gurrah" Shapiro were the most powerful labor racketeers in New York City, where they dominated crucial union locals in the garment industry. Through his control of the Tailors and Cutters Union, Lepke extracted millions of dollars from the garment industry. Thomas Dewey, New York City's special prosecutor

---

[4] The best study of how organized crime achieved a foothold in a union is Howard Kimeldorf's (1988) *Reds or Rackets? The Making of Radical and Conservative Unions on the Waterfront.* See also Philip S. Foner's (1950) *The Fur and Leather Workers Union.*

for racketeering (and later Manhattan district attorney, New York governor, and twice Republican Party presidential candidate) referred to Lepke as "the foremost labor czar in the U.S." (Sifakis 1987, p. 186). Dewey concentrated a great deal of his prosecutorial attention on labor racketeering, especially in the restaurant sector where an organized-crime dominated union systematically extorted the restaurateurs (Hughes 1940; Dewey 1974; Stolberg 1995, chap. 8). A similar situation existed in Chicago, where Al Capone was the leading labor racketeer of the 1930s (Vaira and Roller 1978).

The repeal of national alcohol prohibition (1933) ended organized crime's monopoly over alcohol and thus made the labor unions more important as a source of revenue for organized crime groups. As early as 1933, the U.S. Senate (Copeland Committee) held hearings on "racketeering," including the role of mobsters within international and local labor organizations (United States Congress 1933). The committee heard testimony about workers who were forced to pay kickbacks to corrupt union officials. The attorney for the American Federation of Labor (AFL) Building Trade Unions Anti-Racketeering Committee explained that the committee had been formed two years earlier by union members concerned "that most of the unions in New York were saturated with rackets" (United States Congress 1933, p. 798). Employers recounted extortion by labor racketeers.

In January 1940, journalist Westbrook Pegler exposed the connection of organized crime figures, especially Dutch Schultz, to George Scalise, president of the Building Services Employees International Union (Witwer 2001). According to historian David Witwer, Scalise

used his connections with Arthur Flegenheimer, better known as Dutch Schultz, to gain a charter for a Brooklyn branch of Teamsters Local 272, a union of parking garage workers. Unions of parking garage employees attracted gangsters, because organization could most quickly be achieved through selective acts of violence. Damage to cars parked in non-union garages—ice pick punctures to the tires or slashed upholstery—could quickly force an employer to sign his employees into the union. And union organization in turn provided a cover for corralling the businessmen into an employers' organization, whose dues could be tapped by organized crime. In spite of the use of force against employers in such an organizing campaign, this was not a case of out and out extortion; employers enjoyed real benefits. This kind of collusive arrangement between a union and an employers' organization offered owners a way to manage competition. Employers' associations could set uniform rates and limit the entrance of new competitors. (Witwer 2001, p. 1)

Daniel Bell's article, "The Racket-Ridden Longshoremen" (first published in *Fortune Magazine* in 1951 and later as a chapter in *The End of Ideology*, 1962) provided a detailed picture and penetrating explanation of racketeering in the International Longshoremen's Association (ILA), where union bosses forced longshoremen to make payoffs in order to work, and shippers had to pay to have their cargo unloaded. This was brilliantly dramatized in Elia Kazan's classic 1954 film *On the Waterfront* (starring Marlon Brando, Eva Marie Saint, Karl Malden, Lee J. Cobb, and Rod Steiger), based on Budd Schulberg's screenplay and on Malcolm Johnson's 1949 Pulitzer Prize–winning *New York Sun* series, "Crime on the Labor Front" (Johnson 1950). In 1953, the AFL expelled the east coast ILA, citing organized crime domination, and formed a competing union, the International Brotherhood of Longshoremen. The effort failed. The AFL and the Congress of Industrial Organizations (CIO), which combined in 1955, admitted the ILA to membership in 1959. Also in 1953, Congress enacted an interstate compact that permitted New York and New Jersey to establish the Waterfront Commission of New York Harbor, which was authorized to regulate waterfront business activity and labor relations.[5] The Waterfront Commission replaced the infamous "shape up" (whereby the union bosses picked out who would work that day from the men assembled on the pier) with a hiring system that licensed longshoremen, assigned them to jobs, and guaranteed them an annual wage. It also ended the "public loading" racket, by which the ILA required truckers to make payoffs in order to have cargo loaded or unloaded from their vehicles at the piers, even if the service was not needed (Jensen 1974).

Since the 1940s, Italian-American Cosa Nostra organized crime families have dominated in labor racketeering and organized crime generally (Sifakis 1987; Fox 1989; Abadinsky 1990). Some Cosa Nostra labor racketeers achieved enormous local, regional, and even national prominence, including economic power and political clout—for example, Joseph "Socks" Lanza, Albert Anastasia, Anthony "Tony Pro"

---

[5] The Supreme Court upheld the constitutionality of the legislation creating the Waterfront Commission in De Veau v. Braisted, 363 U.S. 144 (1960).

Provenzano, Johnny (Dio) Dioguardi, Al Pilotto, Anthony Scotto, Ralph Scopo, and Vincent DiNapoli. The close links between some of the nation's most powerful labor leaders and the organized crime families are by now well documented through the prosecutions of labor officials like IBT's Bernard Adelstein, Frank Fitzsimmons, Roy Williams, and Jackie Presser; by prosecutions of mob figures who also held positions in labor unions like Vincent DiNapoli (United Brotherhood of Carpenters and Joiners), Ralph Scopo (LIUNA), and Thomas "Teddy" Gleason (ILA); and by prosecutions of organized crime bosses like Tony Salerno, Mathew Ianniello, and Carmine Romano of New York; Tony Accardo, Joseph Lombardo, Joseph Aiuppa, and Paul Ricca in Chicago; Nick Civella in Kansas City; Raymond Patriarcha in Boston; and Nicodemo Scarfo in Philadelphia.

Labor racketeering received national political attention in the U.S. Senate's 1950–51 Kefauver hearings. These nationally televised hearings introduced the citizenry to Frank Costello, Albert Anastasia, and other top mafia bosses (Kefauver 1951). Senator John McClellan, chairman of the Senate Select Committee on Improper Activities in the Labor or Management Field, held comprehensive hearings from 1957 to 1959 (Kennedy 1960; United States Congress 1960; McClellan 1962). (The creation of the committee was at least partly a result of the journalist Victor Reisel having been blinded with acid after publishing articles exposing labor racketeering; authorities believed Johnny Dio was behind the attack.) While the committee was frustrated by inadequate resources and the refusal of many witnesses to answer questions on Fifth Amendment grounds, its hearings illuminated and dramatized extensive labor corruption and racketeering and led directly to passage of the Labor Management Reporting and Disclosure (Landrum-Griffin) Act in 1959.

Landrum-Griffin sought to protect unions from organized crime penetration by banning persons with criminal records from union office, making embezzlement from a union a federal crime, prohibiting unions from issuing loans to their officers or paying their fines, strengthening the democratic rights of rank-and-file members (including fair elections), imposing reporting and disclosure requirements on unions and criminal penalties for false reporting, and providing union members access to federal courts to enforce their rights (29 USCA sec. 401, et seq.; Summers, Raub, and Benson 1986). Unfortunately, the law failed to achieve its aims because of weaknesses in the enforcement mechanisms, the hostility of the mainstream labor movement, and the

U.S. Department of Labor's (DOL) inability or unwillingness to enforce the law vigorously (Rauh 1971; Nelson 2000).

During the presidency of George Meany (1955–79), the AFL-CIO attempted to oppose racketeering in some of its affiliated unions. For example, the first AFL-CIO convention (1956) established a Committee for Ethical Practices to assist the executive council in keeping the federation free of corruption (Taft 1964, p. 696). The committee ultimately drafted six codes of ethical practices. The AFL-CIO was given the authority to investigate its affiliates' internal activities and to expel a union for failing to abide by the codes. In 1957, the federation expelled the Teamsters, and during the late 1950s it demanded reforms in several other unions, temporarily suspending their memberships until blatant corruption was addressed.[6] After the early 1960s, the ethical practices committee never met, and the AFL-CIO ceased playing any significant role in opposing corruption and racketeering in its affiliated unions.

When Robert F. Kennedy became U.S. attorney general in 1961, he made the prosecution of IBT president Jimmy Hoffa his number one priority (Kennedy 1960; Navasky 1971). He expanded the Department of Justice's Organized Crime and Racketeering Section and turned a spotlight on labor racketeering (Goldfarb 1995).

Hoffa was convicted of union pension fund fraud and jury tampering (1964) and was sent to prison in 1967, but he managed to obtain a pardon from President Richard Nixon in December 1971 (Brill 1978; Moldea 1978; Crowe 1993). Although the pardon banned him from union politics for fifteen years, Hoffa immediately began litigating and campaigning to reclaim the Teamsters' general presidency from his former protégé, Frank Fitzsimmons, whom Hoffa had selected as a caretaker. Cosa Nostra had become comfortable with Fitzsimmons and distrusted Hoffa, who now denounced Fitzsimmons as a mob puppet. On July 30, 1975, Hoffa disappeared. A mob "hit" was immediately presumed (and is now believed to have been orchestrated by Anthony Giacalone, a leader of the Detroit Cosa Nostra family, and Tony Provenzano, boss of the IBT Local 560 and a member of the Genovese crime family in New Jersey).

Hoffa's assassination mobilized government action against both organized crime and labor racketeering. Within three years, labor racke-

---

[6] The AFL-CIO took action against the Distillery Workers, United Textile Workers, Bakery and Confectionery Workers, the International Jewelry Workers, and the Laundry Workers International.

teering became the centerpiece of the FBI's organized crime control strategy (Jacobs, Panarella, and Worthington 1994). The most significant FBI investigations were "PENDORF," which focused on Cosa Nostra control over the IBT Central States Pension Fund and resulted in the conviction of IBT president Roy Williams (who succeeded Fitzsimmons), Joe Lombardo (member of the Chicago Outfit), and Allen Dorfman (the financial associate of the Chicago Outfit) for attempting to bribe U.S. Senator Howard Canon to vote against trucking deregulation; "STRAWMAN," which focused on a conspiracy by four Cosa Nostra families to use the IBT's Central States Pension Fund to secure interests in Las Vegas casinos and to skim profits from those businesses—and resulted in convictions of Joey Aiuppa and Jackie Cerone (boss and underboss of the Chicago Outfit), Angelo La Pietra and Joe Lombardo (Outfit capos), Frank Balistrieri (boss of the Milwaukee family), and Thomas and Milton Rockman (associates of the Cleveland family); "LILREX," which targeted racketeering in New York City's construction industry; and "LIUNA," which focused on Cosa Nostra racketeering in the Laborers International Union of North America. These FBI investigations led to a steady stream of prosecutions of labor racketeers, both organized crime figures and labor officials (Lynch 1987a, 1987b). Nevertheless, at a Senate hearing in 1978, Assistant U.S. Attorney General Benjamin Civiletti testified that more than 300 union locals remained controlled or heavily influenced by organized crime (United States Congress 1978, p. 77).

The Teamsters' Central States Pension Fund had been the target of allegations of mismanagement and organized crime influence since its establishment in 1955. In 1956 Senator Paul Douglas issued "The Douglas Report," which disclosed the results of congressional investigations that found numerous conflict-of-interest situations in which "insiders" had charged exorbitant fees and profited at the expense of benefit plans and their beneficiaries. Payments from individual union members were routinely skimmed off by plan administrators, and union employees secured positions as employees of the benefit plans while doing little work for high fees. Union officials also received kickbacks from persons or institutions to whom high-risk loans had been granted. In 1958 Congress passed the Welfare and Pension Plan Disclosure Act (WPPDA) in response to the abuses it uncovered. The WPPDA attempted to curb abuses of benefit plans by requiring publication of financial information by benefit plans. Congress believed that disclosure of benefit plan financial information would curb abuses and that plan beneficiaries could police the plans themselves. But later investigations found that widespread abuses continued unabated. In 1962 Congress strengthened the WPPDA by adding criminal provisions to address kickbacks and conflicts of interest, and gave the Department of Labor investigatory powers (Coleman 1989).

The 1964 prosecution of Jimmy Hoffa partly involved his receipt of kickbacks in exchange for making benefit fund loans. Organized crime associate Allen Dorfman (an employee of and later a service provider to the fund) was convicted in 1972 of conspiring to receive a kickback for influencing a fund loan. In his 1972 book, *The Fall and Rise of Jimmy Hoffa*, former Kennedy assistant Walter Sheridan charged that "there has been no meaningful monitoring of the Pension Fund by the federal government since Hoffa's conviction in Chicago. . . . Neither the Department of Justice nor the Labor Department followed up in an effective way to determine whether the plundering of the Fund continued" (p. 110).

Organized crime's plundering of union benefit funds was one of the factors leading Congress to pass ERISA (Employee Retirement Income Security Act) in 1974; ERISA gave the Department of Labor authority to investigate pension and welfare funds. A joint Labor and Justice Department investigation of the IBT Central States Fund began in the fall of 1975. The fund, more than 70 percent invested in (mostly Las Vegas) real estate and casinos, was notorious for lending money to organized crime figures and their associates. The IRS sought to revoke the fund's tax-exempt status, leading to a settlement in which twelve of the fund's sixteen trustees resigned, and the fund agreed to hire an independent fiduciary (Equitable Life Insurance Society) to handle investments (United States Congress 1977). While this was an improvement, the corruption and racketeering did not end.

In 1978 Congress established a system of independent inspectors general in all major federal agencies. The inspector general's mission was to combat fraud, waste, and abuse. The Office of Inspector General in the Department of Labor was charged with investigating labor racketeering; this office would play a key role in many of the most important investigations in the next two decades.

In 1980, the Senate Permanent Subcommittee on Investigations, now under the leadership of Senator Sam Nunn, held hearings on the Teamsters (IBT), Longshoremen (ILA), Laborers (LIUNA), and the Hotel and Restaurant Workers (HEREIU) (Nunn 1986). These hearings revealed widespread looting of pension and welfare funds by labor racketeers connected to organized crime. The subcommittee criticized the Department of Labor for having failed to investigate vigorously and prosecute this wrongdoing. It also proposed "The Labor-Management Racketeering Act," which required that pension and welfare plan officials be removed immediately from office on conviction of certain felonies rather than remaining in office until the exhaustion of appeals; the bill, which finally passed in 1984, authorized DOL to investigate and refer evidence of criminal activity to DOJ.

Although investment decisions had been taken out of the hands of the trustees of the IBT Central States Pension Fund by the 1975 settlement agreement, the trustees were still permitted to purchase goods and services for the fund, to administer pension benefits, and to handle money from the time it was paid into the fund each month to the time (approximately thirty days later) it was deposited with the institutional fiduciary. In 1982, DOL filed a lawsuit against all current and former trustees of the IBT Central States Pension Fund, alleging violations of fiduciary obligations imposed by ERISA. This lawsuit resulted in a consent decree that provided for a court-appointed fiduciary to manage the IBT's Central States Pension Fund and the IBT's Health and Welfare Fund (*Donovan v. Fitzsimmons*, consent decree, 90 F.R.D. 583 [N.D. Ill. 1981]). The funds were prohibited from employing or doing business with any person who had been convicted of a felony or misdemeanor involving a breach of fiduciary responsibility. The consent decree also required the appointment of independent special counsel to monitor the fund's operations. The agreement provided that this oversight would sunset in ten years, but it was later amended, so that the oversight extended until September 22, 2002. Today (mid 2002), virtually every Teamster-related pension and welfare fund is managed by professional money managers.

The famous Racketeer Influenced and Corrupt Organizations Act (RICO) (18 U.S.C. sec. 1961 et seq.) was enacted in 1970 as part of the Organized Crime Control Act. Not only did RICO make it a serious federal offense to participate in the affairs of an enterprise (e.g., a labor union) through a pattern of racketeering activity (defined as at least two of a long list of federal and state criminal offenses), it also gave the Department of Justice authority to sue civilly to enjoin a person's or organization's future RICO violations. By the early 1980s, some federal prosecutors realized that they could use such civil suits to purge the racketeering influence from mobbed-up unions.

The groundbreaking case, *United States v. Local 560, IBT*, filed in

March 1982, charged that the largest Teamsters local in New Jersey had been run by Tony Provenzano, a captain in the Gambino crime family, and his henchmen for more than a quarter century (Jacobs, Panarella, and Worthington 1994). Even while serving time for murder, "Tony Pro" ran the union through his brothers and other members of his clique for the benefit of organized crime. The government's suit asked for the removal of all union officers and the appointment of a trustee to run the union and purge it of organized crime influence so that it could be returned to the control of its rank and file. After a long trial, Judge Harold Ackerman granted the requested relief. The trusteeship would last for thirteen years (Goldberg 1989; Summers 1991; Jacobs and Santore 2001). Ackerman observed:

> This is not a pretty story. Beneath the relatively sterile language of a dry legal opinion is a harrowing tale of how evil men, sponsored by and part of organized criminal elements, infiltrated and ultimately captured Local 560 of the International Brotherhood of Teamsters, one of the largest local unions in the largest union in this country.
> This group of gangsters, aided and abetted by their relatives and sycophants, engaged in a multifaceted orgy of criminal activity. For those that enthusiastically followed these arrogant mobsters in their morally debased activity there were material rewards. For those who accepted the side benefits of this perverted interpretation of business unionism, there was presumably the rationalization of "I've got mine, why shouldn't he get his." For those who attempted to fight, the message was clear. Murder and other forms of intimidation would be utilized to insure silence. To get along, one had to go along, or else. (*United States v. Local 560, IBT*, p. 279)

In March 1983, Donald Wheeler, a Department of Labor investigator, told the Senate Permanent Subcommittee on Investigations that "it is estimated that within the jurisdiction of the Chicago Strike Force there are approximately eighty-five labor organizations affiliated with twenty separate international, national, or independent parent unions that are suspected of being associated with, influenced or controlled by organized crime and racketeering elements" (United States Congress 1983, p. 212). In July 1983, President Ronald Reagan (by Executive Orders 12435 and 12507) appointed a President's Commission on Organized Crime (PCOC) and charged it with making "a full and complete national and region-by-region analysis of organized crime as well as emerging organized crime groups . . . and mak[ing] recommendations concerning appropriate administrative and legislative improvement and improvements in the administration of justice" (E.O. 12435, 1983). The commission produced a number of reports, including *The Edge: Organized Crime, Business and Labor Unions* (President's Commission on Organized Crime 1986), which reviewed a half century of labor racketeering, highlighted governmental failures and missed opportunities, and recommended more effective countermeasures. *The Edge* provides a point of departure for assessing change in the state of labor racketeering since the early 1980s.

Sections II–V use the PCOC findings as a basis for assessing the state of labor racketeering circa the early 1980s in the four most notoriously racketeer-influenced international unions. The commission's focus on the IBT, LIUNA, ILA, and HEREIU is not surprising. For decades, these unions have been the subject of congressional hearings, public scandals, and occasional prosecutions. The PCOC volume, *The Edge* (1986), brought together information and allegations that had been in the public domain for many years. Each of the next four sections summarizes the findings for each of these unions and then analyzes the government's subsequent remedial efforts.

II. The Teamsters

The PCOC charged that "corruption and the Teamsters [are] synonymous," and that since the 1950s the Teamsters had been "firmly under the influence of organized crime" (PCOC 1986, pp. 89–90). John "Johnny Dio" Dioguardi, a capo in the Lucchese crime family, and a power broker with influence in many unions, was one of Jimmy Hoffa's key supporters in his quest for the IBT presidency. Dioguardi gave Hoffa several New York City IBT "paper locals" (i.e., a local without rank-and-file members), which allowed Hoffa to control the important New York area IBT Joint Council and thereby secure the presidency of the international union.[7] According to the PCOC, "organized crime has continued to maintain a firm grip on the IBT long after Hoffa's reign" (PCOC 1986, p. 92). Organized crime used threats

---

[7] The McClellan Committee focused on Johnny Dio, especially on his role in establishing the IBT local that had jurisdiction over trucking cargo into and out of JFK airport.

and occasional acts of violence "to quell all forms of dissent, criticism, and opposition" (PCOC 1986, p. 114).

According to the PCOC, the organized crime families converted their influence in the IBT into wealth, status, and power. Control over the IBT provided organized crime leverage over tens of thousands of businesses dependent upon truck deliveries; this leverage could be exercised through extortion, solicitation of bribes, and demands for no-show jobs (PCOC 1986, pp. 91–92). The mobsters enriched themselves by siphoning money directly from union coffers and by taking kickbacks for sweetheart service contracts and "loans" from IBT pension and benefit funds.

The PCOC traced organized crime's control over the Teamsters' international union to its control over key IBT locals. The commission found a documented relationship between Cosa Nostra families and thirty-six IBT locals, one joint council, and a conference (a regional association of joint councils) (PCOC 1986, p. 123).

According to the PCOC, general IBT presidents "[Jimmy] Hoffa and [Roy] Williams were indisputably direct instruments of organized crime," and [Frank] Fitzsimmons held his office by "establish[ing] a measure of détente whereby he was allowed to head the union, while organized crime stole the workers' benefit funds and used the union for numerous criminal ventures" (PCOC 1986, pp. 90–91). At the time of the commission's work, Williams was a federal cooperating witness, having been convicted of attempting to bribe Senator Howard Cannon. He testified that "every big [Teamster] local union . . . had some connection with organized crime" (PCOC 1986, p. 89). Williams admitted that he himself had been controlled by Kansas City Cosa Nostra boss Nick Civella who had quarterbacked Williams's campaign for the IBT presidency by obtaining necessary support from organized crime bosses around the country. The PCOC asserted that Jackie Presser (whose father, "Big Bill" Presser, was a major Cleveland organized crime figure and, until forced to resign in 1976, an IBT Central States Pension Fund Trustee), general president at the time of the PCOC report, depended upon organized crime support for his election to the IBT presidency (PCOC 1986, p. 90). This charge was later confirmed by government prosecutors (Neff 1989).

Mob-controlled locals elected mob-controlled officers, who chose mob-controlled convention delegates, who ratified the choice of mob-controlled international presidents, vice presidents, and general executive board (GEB) members. Because the rank and file did not vote directly for international officers, PCOC judged it "unlikely . . . that a reform-minded Teamster president can be elected in the near future" (PCOC 1986, p. 104).

The PCOC reviewed organized crime's longtime influence over the Teamsters' huge Central States Pension Fund. Organized crime associates like Allen Dorfman and Bill Presser managed the fund's investments, loans, and operations. While a typical pension fund invested 5–10 percent of its assets in real estate, the Central States Pension Fund invested more than 70 percent in real estate, much of it mobsponsored ventures (mostly casinos) in Las Vegas. Despite the 1976 agreement that put control over fund investments in the hands of an institutional fiduciary, organized crime continued to "plunder the Central States Pension Fund" (PCOC 1986, p. 99). Moreover, Dorfman continued to draw substantial fees for handling the fund's insurance business (PCOC 1986, p. 100). (Dorfman was murdered in 1983 while awaiting trial on charges arising out of the STRAWMAN investigation.)

The PCOC report concluded pessimistically that "no single remedy is likely to restore even a measure of true union democracy and independent leadership to the IBT" (PCOC 1986, p. 138). It urged the Department of Justice to make a commitment to purge corruption and racketeering from the IBT through criminal prosecutions, civil actions, administrative proceedings, and trusteeships. Even then, PCOC foresaw only a "modest hope of success" in wresting the IBT from the grip of organized crime (PCOC 1986, p. 120).

A. DOJ's Civil RICO Suit and the IBT Trusteeship

Almost immediately following the release of *The Edge* (PCOC 1986), rumors began to circulate that Rudy Giuliani, U.S. attorney for the Southern District of New York, was preparing a civil RICO complaint against the IBT general executive board. As a preemptive measure, IBT general president Jackie Presser launched an extensive lobbying and public relations campaign. More than two hundred senators and representatives were persuaded to petition the Justice Department not to file such a suit (Jacobs, Panarella, and Worthington 1994). Such an unprecedented intervention on behalf of a potential racketeering defendant illustrates the enormous political power of the nation's largest union, which provides politicians with endorsements, financial support, and even campaign manpower. Members of the U.S. House of Representatives have to face reelection every two years; few of them can afford to be indifferent to the support or opposition of a large Teamsters local in their district. Senatorial candidates, who seek to represent whole states, are less vulnerable to a particular union's opposition than House candidates. (It is not surprising that most congressional investigations into labor racketeering occurred in the Senate and that the chairmen of these investigating committees came from southern states where unions are not strong.)

On June 28, 1988, Giuliani filed a civil RICO complaint against the International Brotherhood of Teamsters, the Cosa Nostra "commission," twenty-six Cosa Nostra members and associates, the IBT's general executive board, and eighteen present and former members of IBT's general executive board (including president Jackie Presser and general secretary-treasurer Weldon Mathis) (*United States v. International Brotherhood of Teamsters*, complaint, 88 Civ. 4486 [S.D.N.Y. 1988]). The complaint charged that the organized crime defendants, aided and abetted by the union defendants, acquired and maintained control of the Teamsters through a pattern of racketeering activity; the defendants violated the members' rights to control over and information concerning the governance of their own union by creating a climate of intimidation and fear and by creating or tolerating pervasive corruption. Giuliani asked the court to remove the IBT general executive board members and to appoint a trustee to oversee the union's affairs and a monitor to supervise a fair election for international union officers (*United States v. International Brotherhood of Teamsters*, complaint, pp. 104–15).

On March 14, 1989, the IBT and the government settled the case with a consent decree (*United States v. International Brotherhood of Teamsters*, consent decree, 808 F. Supp. 279 [S.D.N.Y. 1988]). The union acknowledged "that there have been allegations, sworn testimony and judicial findings of past problems with La Cosa Nostra corruption of various elements of the IBT" and agreed that the IBT should be free of any criminal element and governed democratically "for the sole benefit of its membership without unlawful outside influence" (*United States v. International Brotherhood of Teamsters*, consent decree, p. 2; Lacey 1992, p. 1).

The consent decree provided for a permanent injunction barring the union defendants from any future involvement with the IBT, various changes to the IBT constitution, democratic elections for international officers, and, most important, the selection of three court-appointed officers—independent administrator, investigations officer, and elections officer—to oversee the union's reform. The independent administrator was given authority to remove or discipline any member or officer of the union and to impose trusteeships on locals. The consent decree empowered the independent administrator to veto any IBT decision that would further the interests of organized crime or labor racketeers.[8] The investigations officer was charged with investigating corruption at all levels of the Teamsters hierarchy and recommending disciplinary action to the independent administrator against individuals found to have violated the IBT constitution. The elections officer's role was to promote democracy in union locals and internationals, and to oversee direct rank-and-file secret-ballot elections for the union's top officers in 1991 and 1996. United States District Court (S.D.N.Y.) Judge David Edelstein appointed former federal judge Frederick Lacey as independent administrator, former Assistant United States Attorney Charles Carberry as investigations officer, and labor lawyer Michael Holland as elections officer.[9]

Initially, the consent decree was greeted by a great deal of IBT resistance. William McCarthy, who became general president following Jackie Presser's death in July 1988, encouraged IBT locals around the country to file lawsuits in order to paralyze the court-appointed officers (Lacey 1992, pp. 5–6). Judge Edelstein thwarted this strategy by combining all IBT/consent decree litigation in his court (*United States v. International Brotherhood of Teamsters*, 728 F. Supp. 1032, aff'd 907 F.2d 277 [2d Cir. 1990]).

The IBT refused, in violation of the consent decree, to reimburse many of the court-appointed officers' expenses. At its 1991 convention, the IBT refused to enact constitutional amendments to which it had committed itself by signing the consent decree. The IBT also resisted the court-appointed officers' efforts to inform the rank and file of the independent administrator's findings and sanctions against corrupt IBT officials. Ultimately, Judge Edelstein obtained compliance in all these matters.

Independent Administrator Lacey served as the trier of fact and sentencing authority on charges brought by the investigations officer

---

[8] Although the independent administrator had substantial authority over union management and discipline, he did not have the authority to make collective bargaining agreements—that power remained in the hands of the IBT general president and the general executive board.

[9] Over the following ten years, Judge Edelstein issued approximately 200 decisions and orders related to the remedial phase of the case.

against Teamsters members and officials. Typical charges included association with and membership in Cosa Nostra (*Investigations Officer v. Senese, et al.*, Decision of the Independent Administrator [July 12, 1990], aff'd *United States v. IBT*, 745 F. Supp. 908 [S.D.N.Y. 1990], aff'd 941 F.2d 1292 [2d Cir. 1991], cert. denied, *Senese v. United States*, 112 S.Ct. 1161 [1992]), failure to investigate corruption and refusal to testify at a disciplinary hearing (*Investigations Officer v. Calagna, Sr., et al.*, Decision of the Independent Administrator [June 14, 1991], aff'd *United States v. IBT*, 1991 WL 161084 [S.D.N.Y. 1991]), embezzlement (*Investigations Officer v. Salvatore*, Decision of the Independent Administrator [October 2, 1990], aff'd *United States v. IBT*, 754 F. Supp. 333 [S.D.N.Y. 1990]), and assault (*Investigations Officer v. Wilson, et al.*, Decision of the Independent Administrator [December 23, 1991], aff'd *United States v. IBT*, 787 F. Supp. 345 [S.D.N.Y. 1992], aff'd in part, vacated in part, 978 F.2d 68 [2d Cir. 1992]). Sentences ranged from reprimand to expulsion from the union. Judge Edelstein consistently upheld Independent Administrator Lacey's decisions.

Investigations Officer Carberry exercised broad authority to investigate corruption and racketeering by union members and officers. Carberry and his staff audited locals and interviewed their officers and members. He reviewed old criminal cases against IBT members and officials for leads on current corruption and racketeering (*United States v. International Brotherhood of Teamsters*, 803 F. Supp. 767 [S.D.N.Y. 1992], aff'd in part, rev'd in part, 998 F.2d 1101 [2d Cir. 1993]). The FBI provided a constant flow of information. Carberry set up a toll-free telephone number for IBT members to report wrongdoing in their locals. When he found sufficient evidence, he filed disciplinary charges.

Elections Officer Holland created a three-step process for the election of the IBT general president, general secretary, and general executive board. First, the IBT locals would hold secret-ballot elections for delegates to the IBT convention. Second, the delegates would nominate candidates for office. Third, the rank and file would vote in a secret-ballot election supervised by independent monitors. The IBT opposed these election reforms, arguing that the consent decree gave Holland authority only to monitor the electoral process for fraud and not to create new election rules. Ultimately, the court supported Holland's interpretation (*United States v. International Brotherhood of Teamsters*, 803 F. Supp. 267 [1992], p. 770).

The first direct election of international IBT officers took place in 1991. The election by mail-in ballots resulted in victory for Ron Carey who, as a candidate independent of the clique that had dominated the IBT for decades, enjoyed the support of the reformist group Teamsters for a Democratic Union (see La Botz 1990; Crowe 1993). Carey promised to eradicate all remnants of mob influence in the Teamsters. Upon assuming office, he eliminated many multiple salaries, trimmed the IBT budget, sold some of the union's more extravagant possessions, created an Ethical Practices Committee, and imposed trusteeships on a number of mob-controlled locals.

Pursuant to the 1989 consent decree, following the 1991 election, the independent administrator and investigations officer were replaced by a three-member Independent Review Board (IRB) that was responsible for continuing to investigate and purge corrupt influences. The U.S. attorney general appointed Lacey to the IRB, and the IBT appointed E. Harold Burke. When Lacey and Burke were unable to agree on the third member, the court appointed former FBI director William Webster. Between 1992 and 1998, the IRB recommended charges against 229 individuals. As of fall 2001, more than 120 individuals had been expelled from the union; a large number of others were suspended or retired. The IRB placed twenty-one corrupt locals and one joint council under trusteeship.

The 1996 election was vigorously contested. Carey, though benefited by his incumbency, was hampered by the rank and file's perception that the Teamsters' bargaining power was declining. Carey's opponent was James P. Hoffa, son of the hugely popular Jimmy R. Hoffa who was IBT president from 1957 to 1971. (Despite having been sent to prison in 1967 [pardoned in 1971] for jury tampering and corruption, the senior Hoffa's reputation only grew larger over the years, perhaps in part because of his spectacular disappearance in 1975.)

James P. Hoffa, a lawyer, had to contend with his own set of troubles. Lacey had ruled him ineligible to run for general president in 1991 because he was not a Teamster. To qualify for the 1996 election, Hoffa signed on as an assistant to an IBT local president.

The 1996 election was even closer than the 1991 election. Carey won a slim majority of votes, but the elections officer refused to certify the election because of campaign finance violations. Carey's campaign was found to have illegally funneled $885,000 to political action groups, which in turn arranged donations to the Carey campaign from wealthy individuals (*United States v. International Brotherhood of Team-*

sters, 988 F. Supp. 759 [S.D.N.Y. 1997]). In November 1997, the IRB
barred Carey from the rerun election; it later expelled him from the
union. Carey was then prosecuted for corruption but acquitted (October 12, 2001). Without a significant challenger, Hoffa won the 1998
rerun election by a wide margin, and, in 2001, he and the Hoffa Unity
slate of candidates for the general executive board overwhelmingly
won a five-year term. Also in 2001, former U.S. attorney Joseph Di
Genova replaced Harold Burke as the IBT's representative on the IRB,
and former U.S. Attorney General Benjamin Civiletti replaced Judge
Lacey as the government's representative; William Webster continued
to serve.

B. Project RISE

Immediately following the election, Hoffa announced the formation
of a new unit to cleanse the IBT of any remaining taint of corruption
and to persuade the court that it was time to terminate the IRB. To
head the initiative, named Project RISE (Respect, Integrity, Strength,
Ethics), Hoffa appointed Ed Stier, the ex-prosecutor who served for
thirteen years as the court-appointed trustee in the IBT Local 560 case
(Goldberg 1989; Summers 1991; Jacobs and Santore 2001).[10]

Stier appointed a former justice of the New Mexico Supreme Court
to lead an effort to draft an Ethical Practices Code. The code-drafting
committee consisted of a diverse group of rank-and-file members and
local officers from around the United States and Canada. The group
met over a period of eighteen months and produced an impressive
product that, if carried out, would be a model for the labor movement.
The code includes rules and procedures, and establishes several new
enforcement roles. It was endorsed at the 2001 IBT convention in
Phoenix, Arizona, but its implementation depends upon the termination or at least modification of the IRB.

The second Project RISE component was an investigation of organized crime influence in the IBT. For this job, Stier chose Jim Kossler,
the former organized crime coordinator in the New York City FBI office. Kossler, in turn, hired as consultants a number of former FBI colleagues from around the country. The Kossler team produced a comprehensive report on the current state of every IBT local that had ever
been proved or alleged to have been organized crime infiltrated or in-

[10] Stier also appointed an advisory board to monitor Project RISE's progress and to
make suggestions where appropriate. One of the authors of this article, Jacobs, served
as a member of that board.

fluenced. It found no indication of organized crime influence in the vast majority of these previously tainted locals. In several locals, where questionable influences still existed, investigations and disciplinary proceedings were already under way.

Project RISE also carried out a comprehensive history of corruption in the IBT. The principal writer was Howard Anderson, one of Ed Stier's law partners and a former congressional staffer. This history, released in October 2002, provides the most comprehensive study to date of labor racketeering in the IBT.[11] Since this document is an authorized self-study it may well force many Teamsters who never encountered racketeers to confront the truth of the government's allegations about the mob's role in the union's affairs.

C. Conclusions

For decades, the IBT, the nation's largest and most powerful union, was controlled by organized crime. Indeed, from the 1950s on, Cosa Nostra bosses chose the union's general president. Organized crime used its influence to loot the pension and welfare funds, extort employers, and place its own members and associates in high-paying jobs. Through their influence in the IBT, the organized crime families were able to exert political and economic influence at the local, state, and national levels. Whereas businessmen and politicians cannot justify meeting, working with, and befriending organized crime bosses, they can easily justify, indeed hardly refuse, meeting with the heads of international and local unions, even leaders reputedly connected to organized crime families. Likewise, positions as labor officials provide organized crime bosses with a legitimate public identity and a reason to function as political and economic power brokers.

In 1986, PCOC considered the situation nearly hopeless. But that prediction proved unduly pessimistic. The federal civil RICO suit against the IBT international and the court-imposed trusteeship that it produced, along with the government's relentless campaign against Cosa Nostra, has led to a major transformation of the IBT. None of the 1989 defendants are in positions of authority. The trusteeship and Independent Review Board have purged over 120 organized crime figures and associates from the union and produced three fair and com-

---

[11] See Stier, Anderson, and Malone (2002). Additional histories of Teamster corruption include Witwer (1994) and Crowe (1993).

petitive elections at the international level.[12] Separate court-appointed trusteeships in some of the most mobbed-up locals have also led to impressive results. The James P. Hoffa administration seems committed to routing out any vestiges of organized crime in order to persuade the government and the court to dissolve the trusteeship and return the union to its officials and members. Where they were once vilified, former FBI agents and federal prosecutors now have easy access to IBT headquarters, president Hoffa, and his top staff.

III. Hotel Employees and Restaurant Employees International Union

At least since Prohibition (1920–33), according to the PCOC, the Hotel Employees and Restaurant Employees International Union had been plagued by criminal infiltration and exploitation. The murder of a union member at HEREIU's 1936 national convention precipitated an investigation by Thomas Dewey's Special Commission on Crime. The commission found "a flourishing restaurant racketeering business in New York City"; subsequent prosecutions resulted in the criminal conviction of three union officials, the suspension of a local union, and the expulsion of several union members on account of their ties to organized crime (PCOC 1986, p. 72). The McClellan Committee's hearings (1957–59) revealed pervasive organized crime influence in Chicago's restaurant industry through control of three HEREIU locals. The PCOC charged that HEREIU has "a documented relationship with the Chicago 'Outfit' of La Cosa Nostra at the international level and [is] subject to the influence of the Gambino, Colombo, and Philadelphia La Cosa Nostra families at the local level" (PCOC 1986, p. 71).

Shortly before PCOC's investigation, the Senate Permanent Subcommittee on Investigations held hearings (1981–84) on HEREIU. Its final report concluded that "many of the officers of HEREIU have consistently accorded a higher priority to their own personal and financial interests than to the interests of the rank and file membership" (United States Congress 1984a, p. 9).

The PCOC described HEREIU as corrupt to the core. It charged that Tony "Joe Batters" Accardo, boss of the Chicago Outfit, handpicked Edward Hanley as HEREIU's international president (PCOC

---

[12] There are some critics of the independent review board's continuing role (see Dean 2000).

1986, p. 73). Control over Hanley assured Cosa Nostra control over union affairs because HEREIU's centralized governance empowered the international officers to dictate policy and personnel decisions to the locals. Under Hanley's regime, mob figures obtained union loans and jobs, and otherwise feasted on the union's assets. In short, "the union's assets have been used to enrich the top officers of HEREIU's hierarchy" through high salaries, expense accounts, allowances, and lifetime employment contracts (PCOC 1986, pp. 74–75). When asked by the Senate's Permanent Subcommittee on Investigations about HEREIU's ties to organized crime, Hanley asserted his Fifth Amendment right not to incriminate himself (PCOC 1986, p. 75).

The PCOC identified several HEREIU locals controlled or heavily influenced by the Chicago Outfit and other organized crime families. For example, since 1978, Local 54 (Atlantic City, New Jersey) had been dominated by different factions of Philadelphia's Bruno/Scarfo crime family.[13] Several of Local 54's officers had criminal records for murder, arson, extortion, drugs, bribes, kickbacks, and racketeering. The local's dental and welfare funds were controlled by organized crime (PCOC 1986, pp. 78–79). The local's corrupt influence infected both business and government in Atlantic City.[14] In 1982, the New Jersey Casino Control Commission prohibited Local 54 from collecting dues from casino employees because the influence of organized crime made the local unfit to represent the casino workers' interests (PCOC 1986, p. 80). Ultimately, this decision was upheld by the U.S. Supreme Court (*Brown v. HEREIU Local 54*, 468 U.S. 491 [1984]).

The PCOC found that HEREIU Locals 6 and 100 (New York City) had been chartered and governed in furtherance of the interests of the Colombo and Gambino families. What appeared to be a jurisdictional split between these two HEREIU locals in fact represented the division of New York's restaurant workers between the Colombo and Gambino crime families (PCOC 1986, p. 84). In an intercepted conversation, Paul Castellano, boss of the Gambino crime family, explained that the Chicago Outfit "own[ed] the international" and that

---

[13] The struggle for control of Local 54 led to a murder in 1980, when a leader of a rival union sought to take the bartenders away from Local 54 (PCOC 1986, pp. 76–77).

[14] The PCOC reported that Atlantic City mayor Michael Matthews solicited illegal campaign contributions from Local 54 officials. Matthews admitted that he approached Local 54 leaders in order to obtain money from Philadelphia's Bruno/Scarfo crime family. In return for the donation, Matthews agreed to assist the Scarfo family in its effort to obtain a piece of land owned by the city on which the Scarfo family wanted to build a casino.

the Colombo crime family controlled the other local (PCOC 1986, p. 83). The PCOC reported that "legitimate trade unionists are aware of the mob ties to HEREIU and await government action to oust the mob from the union" (PCOC 1986, p. 85).

A. Civil RICO Suit against Local 54

In December 1990, the United States filed a civil RICO suit against HEREIU Local 54 (Atlantic City) alleging a twenty-year pattern of racketeering orchestrated by the Philadelphia (Scarfo) organized crime family (*United States v. Hanley*, complaint, Civ. No. 90-5017 [D.N.J. 1990]). The complaint charged that Ralph Natale and other members of the Philadelphia Cosa Nostra crime family had prevented democratic elections within Local 54 by threatening to kill union members who challenged mob-backed candidates. In April 1991, Local 54 agreed to a consent decree in which eight officers and employees of the local were removed from office because of ties to organized crime (*United States v. Hanley*, 1992 U.S. Dist. LEXIS 22192 [D.N.J. 1992]). The U.S. District Court for the District of New Jersey in Trenton appointed James F. Flanagan (former deputy director of the New Jersey Division of Gaming Enforcement) to monitor the affairs of the local, and postponed Local 54's election until Flanagan could establish democratic procedures for the nomination and election of non-organized-crime-influenced candidates (*United States v. Hanley*). Under Flanagan's monitorship, Local 54 began holding quarterly membership meetings, providing education and training to union members, and revitalizing its handling of members' grievances (Seal 1997).

Local 54's 1993 election demonstrated increasing democracy and a decreasing organized crime influence; eight candidates were disqualified on account of their organized crime ties. In the 1996 election, 33 percent of Local 54's membership voted. None of the ninety candidates investigated by the monitor was found to be associated with organized crime. The election produced wholly new leadership. In February 1997, the monitorship was dissolved (Seal 1997).

B. Civil RICO Suit against HEREIU International

On September 5, 1995, the Department of Justice filed a civil RICO complaint against the HEREIU international union, alleging that members of its executive board had conspired with organized crime figures since the 1970s to accept illegal payments from employers, embezzle union assets, and control the union membership through intimidation. Along with the complaint, HEREIU and DOJ filed a consensual settlement decree (*United States v. HEREIU*, Civ. No. 95-4569 [D.N.J. 1995]) whose object was to make "HEREIU and all its locals be free from the direct or indirect influence of organized crime, now and in the future" (Muellenberg 1998, p. 2). Toward that end, the defendants agreed to be enjoined from committing any crimes listed in Title 18 U.S.C. 1961 (1) (RICO), associating with organized crime members and associates, permitting a barred person from exercising any control or influence in HEREIU affairs, and obstructing efforts to implement the consent decree.

Judge Garrett E. Brown appointed Kurt Muellenberg (former head of DOJ's Organized Crime and Racketeering Section) as monitor over HEREIU for a term of at least eighteen months. The monitorship was later extended until March 5, 1998. The consent decree gave Muellenberg authority to remove union officials at all levels for violating any provision of the settlement, committing any crime involving running a union or overseeing an employee benefit plan, or furthering the influence of any organized crime group. Muellenberg's authority also extended to disapproving collective bargaining agreements and to appointing or discharging union employees and candidates for union office. Additionally, the court ordered that at its 1996 convention HEREIU adopt an Ethical Practices Code that would define and prohibit conflicts of interest by union officers. Muellenberg appointed Daniel F. Sullivan as chief investigator and former New York City Police Department commissioner Howard E. O'Leary as investigations officer. Rank-and-file HEREIU members were encouraged to use a toll-free telephone number to report corruption and racketeering in the union (Muellenberg 1998, pp. 2–5).

Muellenberg found that many HEREIU locals with a history of organized crime infiltration did not obey their own bylaws; gave inadequate notice of membership meetings; failed to document expenses, bonuses, and raises to the membership for approval; failed to train officers, business agents, and organizers; and failed to promulgate or maintain standards for personnel, pay scales, job descriptions, and performance (Muellenberg 1998, pp. 5–6). According to Muellenberg, the international union "suffered from a management deficit and did not subscribe to generally accepted business practices" (Muellenberg 1998, p. 14). He described HEREIU's international union as an agglomeration of employees and officers without any clear rules or procedures. "There is no budget, no organizational chart, no job descriptions for employees, and no manual" (Muellenberg 1998, p. 15). General President Hanley hired friends and family members to union positions and consultancies, remunerated them generously, and ran the union as his personal fiefdom. There was a pattern of highly questionable union donations to charitable organizations and events.[15] Officials' business expenses were reimbursed without submission of receipts and explanations and without prior approval.[16]

Muellenberg lifted trusteeships that had been imposed on eleven locals for no good reason or, worse, to provide jobs to organized crime friends and relatives. He placed five locals under trusteeship because federal prosecutors had charged those locals' leaders with organized crime associations, embezzlement, and filing false reports to the Department of Labor.[17]

During the course of his monitorship, Muellenberg permanently barred twenty-three individuals from participating in union affairs because of organized crime associations or failure to cooperate with the monitor, barred two individuals from participation in union affairs for thirteen years, and barred two individuals from holding a position of trust in the union for three years.[18]

Muellenberg devoted much time to investigating Edward T. Hanley, who served as general president from 1973 to 1998. Muellenberg charged Hanley with using HEREIU automobiles and an airplane for personal purposes, receiving unearned salary and pension contributions, associating with organized crime members, and setting up a paper local near his Wisconsin vacation home so that the local's presi-

---

[15] The HEREIU donated $94,000 to the Catholic Church, $25,000 to the All-American Collegiate Golf Foundation, and $450,000 to the Irish American Sports Foundation. Each of these organizations, while having little if anything to do with the hotel and restaurant business, was valued by HEREIU's general president Edward Hanley (Muellenberg 1998, p. 31).

[16] In one particularly egregious example, a union official left an $80 tip for a meal costing $5.80. The same official commonly left tips in amounts substantially greater than the cost of the meal (Muellenberg 1998, p. 18).

[17] The five locals placed in trusteeship by Muellenberg were Local 122 in Milwaukee, Wisconsin; Local 69 in Secaucus, New Jersey; Local 4 in Buffalo, New York; Local 57 in Pittsburgh, Pennsylvania; and AFL-CIO Nursing Home Council in Buffalo, New York. Two (Local 122 and Local 69) held elections and were removed from trusteeship by the end of Muellenberg's term as monitor (Muellenberg 1998, pp. 52–53). These actions in tabular form can be found at http://www.ipsn.org/HEREIU_Table.htm.

[18] Daniel Rostenkowski, a consultant, and Robert L. Hickman, Sr., a consultant and business agent for Chicago Local 1, were barred for thirteen years. Nancy Ross (secretary-treasurer of Local 57 and international vice-president) and Vince Fera (executive board member) were prohibited from holding positions of trust for three years beginning April 23, 1998 (Muellenberg 1998, p. 58).

dent could do favors for Hanley and his friends. On February 19, 1998, the Office of the Monitor and Hanley entered into an agreement. Hanley agreed to retire, pay HEREIU $13,944 relating to his purchase of HEREIU-leased automobiles, and assume payment of life insurance premiums on a policy purchased for him by the union (Muellenberg 1998, p. 59). In return, Muellenberg agreed to terminate his investigation of Hanley's actions during his tenure as HEREIU's general president; Hanley was permitted to retain a $350,000 a year salary for life (Hanley's son, Thomas W., agreed to resign for one year and to reimburse HEREIU $25,000 in order to end an investigation into his abuse of expense accounts) (Muellenberg 1998, p. 60).

Muellenberg released his final report on August 25, 1998. On September 1, 1998, HEREIU's general executive board voted to implement all of his many recommendations on structure, governance, and operations of the international and locals (United States Congress 1999).

When the monitorship expired, it was replaced by a public review board (PRB) responsible for overseeing implementation of the Ethical Practices Code. In addition, the PRB has authority to review member complaints and to conduct hearings to insure ethical standards in the union's operations. The PRB has power to suspend or expel members found to have violated the code. Muellenberg, Archbishop James P. Keleher of Kansas City, and former Illinois governor James R. Thompson were appointed to this board. Hanley was replaced as general president by John W. Wilhelm, a longtime union official (who graduated from and then represented workers at Yale University and who has never been alleged to be associated with or influenced by organized crime).

C. Conclusions

General President Edward Hanley ran HEREIU in dictatorial fashion and in cooperation with organized crime, especially the Chicago Outfit. Many union locals were also controlled by organized crime. The 1995 civil RICO suit and settlement established a monitorship that expelled some of the most notorious members from the union and finally managed to secure Hanley's resignation. While the deal with Ed Hanley might seem to some like letting a labor racketeer off too easily, it is well to remember that it is one thing to allege organizational criminality and another thing to prove it. Corruption by high-level officials is almost always difficult to prove because powerful officials have the resources and capacity to cover their tracks and give colorable legitimacy to their exploitative conduct. Furthermore, it might take the government years to prosecute successfully a corrupt labor official. Thus, on balance, prosecutors and court-appointed trustees have sometimes concluded that a settlement that allows union reform to proceed expeditiously justifies forgoing a possible prosecution. A further obstacle to punishing wrongdoing is posed by ERISA, which prevents pension forfeiture, even against an official who has stolen money from his union (see Jacobs, Friel, and O'Callaghan 1997).

The monitor's recommendations for improving the union's management were adopted by the new administration, untainted by the long history of organized crime influence in the union. The union adopted a progressive Ethical Practices Code to its constitution and a public review board to enforce it. Hanley's successor has not been tied to organized crime, but neither has he been a sharp Hanley critic. The extent and depth of HEREIU's commitment to reform remains to be seen.

Reform of an international union is a necessary, but not necessarily sufficient, condition for reform of its racketeer-influenced locals. The HEREIU monitor, whose office lasted only two-and-a-half years, expressed concern about locals operating without accountability. Some of these locals have had a long history of organized crime domination. In April 2002, for example, the New Jersey U.S. attorney's office brought a civil RICO suit against HEREIU Local 69 charging that associates of the Genovese crime family had used fear and extortion to control Local 69 for the previous fifteen years. The federal prosecutors alleged that the local, among other things, had made $524,000 in "severance payments" to a former official who had been removed on account of organized crime ties. The district court appointed Kurt Muellenberg to serve as monitor over the local.

IV. Laborer's International Union of North America

The PCOC found that "organized crime has a documented relationship with at least twenty-six Laborer's International Union of North America (LIUNA) locals, three district councils, as well as the International Union" (PCOC 1986, p. 146). The mob profited from this relationship by defrauding the union's benefits funds, extracting no-show jobs from LIUNA employers, drawing reimbursement for fictitious and padded business expenses, manipulating the construction industry, and obtaining access to powerful government officials (PCOC 1986,

p. 153). The commission complained that the federal government had not seriously addressed this situation (PCOC 1986, p. 160).

According to the PCOC, "organized crime exerts its influence [in LIUNA] principally through top officers who are associates of organized crime" (PCOC 1986, p. 146). General President Angelo Fosco (whose father, Peter Fosco, was LIUNA general president from 1968 to 1975 and an associate of Al Capone) was closely associated with members of the Chicago Outfit. The PCOC charged that Fosco owed his presidency to his willingness to award jobs to organized crime members and associates, and to authorize whatever expenditures his organized crime associates requested (PCOC 1986, pp. 146–47). In 1982, he and Tony Accardo, boss of the Outfit, were tried (and acquitted) of labor racketeering charges.

The PCOC asserted that Vice President John Serpico was also controlled by organized crime. "Serpico admitted that he is a friend or personal acquaintance of virtually every important organized crime leader in Chicago" (PCOC 1986, p. 147). According to the PCOC, the Outfit used LIUNA's international officers to gain access to important political figures like Chicago Mayors Daley and Byrne and Illinois Governors Walker and Thompson (PCOC 1986, pp. 148–49). For example, Vice President John Serpico received successive gubernatorial appointments to serve as chairman of the Illinois International Port District.

Questioned about John Fecarotta's duties as a LIUNA business agent and organizer, Vice President Serpico could not specify a single contribution by Fecarotta to Local 8. For his part, Fecarotta could not remember having done anything for the union at any time, did not know any of the terms of the union's collective bargaining agreements or of its pension plans, did not know what information was on union membership cards he supposedly distributed, and did not know the names of management employees or union officers with whom he supposedly worked. The PCOC branded Fecarotta a ghost employee who used his union position as a legitimate cover for his criminal career (PCOC 1986, p. 148).

The PCOC charged that organized crime thoroughly controlled LIUNA's Chicago Locals 1, 5, and 8. Local 1's president, Vincent Solano, territorial boss for the Outfit's north side clique, used union headquarters as a "contact point for his criminal organization" (PCOC 1986, p. 150). Local 5's president was also an Outfit boss (PCOC 1986, p. 151). The PCOC called Local 8, Vice President John Serpico's home local, "ground zero for an organized crime-led LIUNA benefit plan scam" (PCOC 1986, pp. 153–55). Organized crime members and their associates siphoned money from LIUNA's Central States Joint Board Health and Welfare Trust Fund. The dental plan was egregiously corrupt; 68 percent of its budget went to "administrative costs" rather than to services (PCOC 1986, pp. 153–55).[19] The LIUNA's treasury paid lawyers' fees on behalf of officials charged with looting the union as well as fees to private investigators for monitoring the federal government's investigation of LIUNA (PCOC 1986, pp. 156–57).

According to the PCOC, LIUNA's organization and procedures reinforced its relationship with organized crime. It was nearly impossible for an opposition candidate to be elected to a union office because LIUNA's executive board members were elected as a unified at-large slate (PCOC 1986, p. 157). The executive board filled union vacancies (PCOC 1986, p. 158).

The PCOC found that organized crime used violence and intimidation to keep union members from running for office in opposition to the ruling clique. It charged General President Angelo Fosco with personally threatening to kill a potential challenger for his office (PCOC 1986, p. 158). In an intercepted conversation, LIUNA's International Secretary-Treasurer Arthur E. Coia told a colleague that LIUNA was controlled by the "Italians" (i.e., organized crime families) who would never relinquish their power (PCOC 1986, pp. 158–59). At the 1981 LIUNA convention, when a candidate opposing the incumbent regime tried to speak, he was beaten up on the spot (PCOC 1986, pp. 159–60). The PCOC pessimistically concluded that there was "little chance that the LIUNA membership will be able to eliminate organized crime's influence, or control over their union, if the current leadership or governance structure remains intact. The commission believes that federal law enforcement agencies should give high priority to investigations of LIUNA and its locals" (PCOC 1986, pp. 162–63).

The decade after the PCOC report provided little reason to be optimistic about reform in LIUNA. For example, in 1989, Arthur A. Coia, son of longtime mob-affiliated LIUNA General Secretary-Treasurer Arthur E. Coia (who retired in 1987), reportedly made pilgrimages to

---

[19] These grossly inflated service fees were shocking even to the Teamsters Central States Pension Fund officials, who were embarrassed to admit that their administrative costs had in the past gone as high as 8 percent. George Lehr, executive director of the Teamsters Central States Pension Fund, described the 68 percent rate as "outrageous" and "a ripoff on its face" (United States Congress 1985, p. 600).

Chicago to request permission from the Chicago Outfit to run for LIUNA general secretary-treasurer (Mulligan and Starkman 1996). Having obtained the mob's approval, he served as secretary-treasurer until 1993, when Angelo Fosco died. With mob approval, Coia was elected general president. During this period, LIUNA made substantial political contributions to the Democratic Party and to President Clinton with whom Coia enjoyed a personal relationship. Critics charged that, on account of these political ties, the Clinton administration backed off in its investigation and reform efforts (Mulligan and Starkman 1996; United States Congress 1997; Isaac 1998; Mencimer 1998; Methvin 1998).

A. DOJ Takes Action against LIUNA

In late 1994, the DOJ presented LIUNA officials with a draft civil RICO complaint, alleging that organized crime dominated the international union and many locals.[20] The complaint named as defendants twenty-five individuals plus the individual members of the LIUNA general executive board, General President Arthur A. Coia, General Secretary-Treasurer Rollin P. "Bud" Vinall, all ten of the union's vice presidents, and the union's general counsel. The complaint alleged that the defendants violated the rights of union members through intimidation, violence, and economic coercion, and violated their fiduciary duty to the membership by corrupting the union and by refusing and failing to prevent or remedy the corruption.[21]

As a remedy, the government sought the expulsion of Coia and other union leaders. It requested the appointment of one or more court liaison officers to carry out the duties of the general president and general executive board and to prevent any GEB action that would violate union members' rights or perpetuate criminal influence. The draft complaint also demanded that the union's constitution be amended to reform discriminatory hiring-hall procedures and to pro-

---

[20] The draft complaint, although never filed, is available on-line at http://www.laborers.org/complaint.html.

[21] The 1990 New York State (NYS) Organized Crime Task Force's final report, "Corruption and Racketeering in the NYC Construction Industry," identified ten New York City LIUNA locals that were controlled or heavily influenced by organized crime. For example, the report charged that "Housewreckers Union Local 95 is controlled by Vincent 'Chin' Gigante, boss of the Genovese Crime Family" (New York State Organized Crime Task Force 1990, p. 81), and that Cement and Concrete Workers Local 6A "had for years been controlled by Ralph Scopo, a soldier in the Colombo Crime Family" (New York State Organized Crime Task Force 1990, p. 79).

vide for direct rank-and-file election of officers. The court was also asked to appoint an elections officer.

After three months of negotiations, LIUNA and the DOJ announced a unique settlement. The DOJ agreed to forgo filing the civil RICO complaint if LIUNA established its own internal anticorruption program and signed a consent decree stipulating to the requested relief. The settlement provided that the consent decree could be filed at DOJ's option until February 1, 1998, if the DOJ found that LIUNA failed to clean up the union. The agreement was later extended to 2001 and then, with certain election reforms added, to 2006.

B. The LIUNA's Internal Reform Program

The LIUNA instituted radical changes in its governing structure and constitution and adopted an Ethical Practices Code. To enforce the provisions of the Ethical Practices Code, LIUNA adopted a set of Ethics and Disciplinary Procedures and established four new positions: GEB attorney, filled by Robert Luskin, formerly a member of DOJ's Organized Crime and Racketeering Section, to investigate and prosecute violations of the Ethical Practices Code; inspector general, filled by Douglas Gow, retired FBI agent, to investigate violations of the Ethical Practices Code; independent hearing officer, Peter Vaira, former chief of the Chicago Organized Crime Strike Force and former U.S. attorney in Philadelphia, to serve as judge and arbitrator in all disciplinary actions; and appellate officer, Neil Eggleston, former federal prosecutor, to hear appeals of disciplinary cases.

These newly appointed officers initiated an aggressive program of corruption control. They established a confidential toll-free telephone number and a confidential post office box to solicit complaints from the LIUNA membership. By mid-1996, the reform officers had begun over 345 investigations, removed twenty-five union officers and members for violations of the Ethical Practices Code, removed all of Buffalo Local 210's officers on account of corruption, placed Chicago Local 8 under emergency trusteeship, actively assisted the United States government with its efforts to clean up the New York City Mason Tenders by hiring the former chief of the organized crime unit in the Southern District of New York to investigate the Mason Tenders, and announced an investigation of Arthur A. Coia (United States Congress 1996).

The LIUNA's election procedures were also reformed. Direct rank-and-file secret-ballot election of general president and general secretary-treasurer was added to the constitution. Additionally, LIUNA expanded its general executive board from ten to thirteen members and required that nine of the thirteen be elected by nine regions, making the GEB less accountable to the general president and more accountable to the membership. The LIUNA modified its procedures for the selection of delegates to union conventions and merged several locals that appeared to exist only to provide convention votes to organized crime. The LIUNA also hired an independent elections officer and two deputy election officers—jointly selected by the government and union—to monitor union elections. The union adopted a uniform set of job referral rules to prevent discriminatory hiring-hall practices. An independent accounting firm was hired to audit LIUNA's finances (United States Congress 1996).

In November 1997, GEB attorney Robert Luskin filed disciplinary charges against Arthur A. Coia, alleging that Coia associated with organized crime, permitted organized crime to influence union affairs from 1986 to 1993, and accepted illegal payoffs from a LIUNA service provider. The hearing, which lasted from April 14, 1998, until June 23, 1998, included over 500 exhibits and testimony that filled thousands of transcript pages. Independent Hearing Officer Vaira found that GEB attorney Luskin failed to prove the allegations of organized crime association and influence but did prove that Coia had violated the Ethical Practices Code by accepting illegal benefits from a LIUNA service provider. Vaira fined Coia $100,000 but permitted him to retain his office (Office of the Independent Hearing Officer 1999).

In December 1999, Coia retired as general president, acceding to the position of general president emeritus for life at an annual salary of $335,516 (Mulligan 1999). The GEB appointed Terrence O'Sullivan, Coia's chief of staff, to succeed Coia. The union agreed to continue to support the internal reform program and, until the completion of its 2006 general election, not to make any material changes to its governing structure without the government's prior approval. The DOJ officially ended its oversight. In January 2000, Arthur A. Coia pled guilty to defrauding the State of Rhode Island and the Town of Barrington, Rhode Island, of approximately $100,000 in taxes. In addition to restitution and a $10,000 fine, he agreed to be barred from any future role in LIUNA or its subordinate entities.

C. Conclusions

Historically, LIUNA, at the international and local levels, especially in Chicago and New York City, has been closely tied to Cosa Nostra crime families. Tony Accardo, one of the leading organized crime figures of this half century, exercised a great deal of influence in the union for many years. Accardo, his henchmen, and their successors controlled LIUNA's general president and the officers of many locals.

In 1994 the DOJ prepared the first major attack on LIUNA labor racketeering at the national level. The looming RICO suit led to a creative settlement between the government and the union. The monitors whom LIUNA hired to enforce its new code of ethics, all former federal law enforcement figures, appear to have made headway in cleaning up the international union. Nevertheless, the extent of the international union's commitment to reform remains to be seen. Clearly, a great deal of labor racketeering remains in the locals. Indeed, a number of the most notorious locals have themselves been put under court-ordered trusteeship (United States Department of Justice 2000).

The international union suspended John Serpico, labor racketeer and political power broker, from his union positions in 1995. Serpico then became a consultant for another union, a local of the International Union of Allied Novelty and Production Workers. He also served as president emeritus of the Central States Joint Board, which provides administrative services to Chicago-area locals. In the summer of 2001, Serpico and two associates were convicted of fraud and taking kickbacks in connection with steering union business to certain companies.

V. The International Longshoremen's Association

Drawing on labor leaders' statements, FBI investigations, prosecutions, and legislative hearings, PCOC called the International Longshoremen's Association "virtually a synonym for organized crime in the labor movement" (PCOC 1986, p. 33).[22] Ships entering harbors, day or night, need to be unloaded and reloaded quickly. Delay is expensive, even ruinous. This gave the longshoremen enormous leverage over shippers who were extorted for labor peace payoffs. (Admittedly, the containerization of seaborne cargo since the late 1950s undermined this leverage.) Labor racketeers also corrupted port employees to facilitate cargo theft, solicited illegal labor payoffs, and extorted stevedores (companies that load and unload seaborne cargo) (PCOC 1986, p. 35). "Throughout its history, the international has done little, if anything, to disturb *La Cosa Nostra* influence in its locals" (PCOC 1986, p. 37).

According to the PCOC, Cosa Nostra became the primary power

---

[22] David Dubinsky, president of the International Ladies Garment Workers Union, and a well-respected labor leader and reformer, proclaimed that the ILA was "a nest for waterfront pirates—a racket, not a union" (Dubinsky and Raskin 1977, p. 164).

on the New York Harbor waterfront in 1937, when Anthony "Tough Tony" Anastasio (aka Anastasia) took control of the six New York harbor locals. (His brother Albert Anastasia was head of the infamous Murder Incorporated and boss of the crime group that later came to be known as the Gambino crime family.) "Under Anastasio, organized pilferage, strike insurance, kickbacks, and loansharking on the piers reached unprecedented levels" (PCOC 1986, p. 36). Anastasio delegated control of these locals to various organized crime members.

In 1953, the New York State Crime Commission issued a blistering report on labor racketeering in New York harbor. By the 1960s, organized crime exerted power and influence in ports all along the eastern and gulf coasts (PCOC 1986, pp. 39–40). The PCOC charged that Cosa Nostra completely controlled Thomas (Teddy) Gleason, who had succeeded the infamous Joseph Ryan as ILA international president (PCOC 1986, p. 39). The Gambino crime family controlled the ILA international union.[23] The Gambinos mostly controlled the New York side and the Genovese the New Jersey side of the New York/New Jersey harbor. After Anastasio died in 1963, control of ILA Local 1814 passed to Anthony Scotto, a son-in-law, who (from 1963 to 1979) flourished in the union, in organized crime as a capo in the Gambino crime family, and in New York City political circles.

In 1972, a Florida investigator told the Senate Permanent Subcommittee on Government Operations that "our information established that virtually every commodity affecting the transportation industry on the Dodge Island Seaport was under the control and domination of a small group of highly sophisticated and organized criminals" (United States Congress 1984*b*). In 1975, the FBI launched UNIRAC, an investigation of ILA racketeering in the ports of New York City, Miami, Wilmington, Charleston, and Mobile. Using undercover agents, electronic intercepts, and consensual recordings, UNIRAC uncovered systematic criminality and labor racketeering in every port. Ultimately, UNIRAC led to the conviction of over 100 persons, including twenty ILA leaders, among them Michael Clemente and Anthony Scotto, who held positions in both the ILA and Cosa Nostra. In 1979, Scotto was convicted of taking more than $200,000 in cash payoffs from employers (*United States v. Clemente et al.*, 494 F. Supp. 1310 [1980 U.S. Dist.]). New York's governor Hugh Carey, and two former New York

---

[23] The PCOC report found that the Genovese crime family controlled the Manhattan locals and the union's international. This is likely a typographical error. The Gambino family was known to control these locals and the international.

City mayors, John Lindsay and Robert Wagner, testified in his behalf at the sentencing hearing. (Scotto, a prominent Democratic Party fund-raiser, raised $1 million for Governor Hugh Carey's 1974 campaign and $50,000 for Mario Cuomo.)

The PCOC complained that, while UNIRAC was "a very successful operation demonstrating law enforcement skill and tenacity," there had been only sporadic subsequent investigations and prosecutions, leaving organized crime's influence intact all along the eastern seaboard (PCOC 1986, p. 43). In February 1981, the Senate Permanent Subcommittee on Investigations held hearings on waterfront corruption. The subcommittee's report summarized its findings:

> Witnesses testified that payoffs were a part of virtually every aspect of the commercial life of a port. Payoffs insured the award of work contracts and continued contracts already awarded. Payoffs were made to insure labor peace and allow management to avoid future strikes. Payoffs were made to control a racket in workmen's compensation claims. Payoffs were made to expand business activity into new ports and to enable companies to circumvent ILA work requirements.
>
> Organized crime was found to have great influence in the operation of the ILA and many shipping companies. Some shipping firms, because of fear or a willingness to participate in highly profitable schemes, have learned how to prosper in the corrupt waterfront environment. They treat payoffs as a cost of doing business.
>
> The free enterprise system has been thrown off balance. Contracts were not awarded on the basis of merit. The low bid did not beat the competition. Profitability was not based on efficiency and hard work but rather on bribery, extortion and questionable connections. The combination of these corrupt practices was a recipe for inflationary costs and economic decline.
>
> Much of the corruption on the waterfront stemmed from the control organized crime exercises over the ILA, a condition that has existed for at least 30 years. (United States Congress 1984b)

Quoting the 1984 Senate Permanent Subcommittee on Investigations' findings, PCOC concluded that, despite its successes, UNIRAC had not purged organized crime from the ports. "Corrupt practices . . . already have begun to return to the Atlantic and Gulf Coast docks. What is needed, then, is continued scrutiny of the maritime industry by government agencies" (PCOC 1986, p. 65). In 1987, Teddy Gleason retired as general president of the international union and was succeeded by his vice president, John Bowers, who has held the presidency ever since (Gleason died in 1992).

A. Civil RICO Suit against Six ILA Locals

On February 14, 1990, the U.S. Department of Justice filed a civil RICO suit (*United States v. Local 1804-1 et al., International Longshoremen's Association*, complaint, No. 90 Civ. 0963 [LBS] [S.D.N.Y. 1990]) against six New York harbor ILA locals, their executive boards and officers, the Genovese and Gambino crime families, the Westies, an Irish organized crime group allied with the Gambino family, and five waterfront employers.[24] The 125-page complaint charged that the waterfront had "been the setting for corruption, violence, and abuse of waterfront labor and business by New York La Cosa Nostra Families" for more than fifty years (*United States v. Local 1804-1 et al.*, complaint, p. 4). It further alleged that Cosa Nostra controlled the waterfront labor unions, that is, that the Genovese and Gambino crime families had exploited the locals, the shipping industry, and the longshoremen (*United States v. Local 1804-1 et al.*, complaint, p. 38). According to the government, despite the UNIRAC investigation and convictions, the Genovese and Gambino crime families, by means of their control of the ILA, continued to dominate many ports (*United States v. Local 1804-1 et al.*, complaint, p. 44). The complaint quoted the Senate Permanent Subcommittee on Investigations' 1988 report: "Organized crime continues to exercise control over the International and New York-New Jersey ILA locals" (*United States v. Local 1804-1 et al.*, complaint, p. 45). The civil RICO complaint compiled allegations of embezzlement, solicitation of bribes, benefit fund fraud, extortion of employers, and violation of the rank and file's rights through force and violence.

The U.S. Department of Justice asked the court to enjoin the organized crime defendants from participating in ILA affairs, from having any dealings with union officers and employees (*United States v. Local 1804-1 et al.*, complaint, p. 118), and from committing any acts of racketeering; DOJ sought to enjoin the defendant labor officials from associating with Cosa Nostra members or associates (pp. 118–19). The complaint sought a court-appointed liaison officer for each of the ILA

---

[24] The complaint did not include the ILA's international organization. However, International President John Bowers was named individually, as president of three of the six locals.

locals to "discharge those duties of the Executive Board[s]" and to "review the proposed actions of the Executive Board[s]" (*United States v. Local 1804-1 et al.*, complaint, p. 119), general elections to be run by a court-appointed trustee (*United States v. Local 1804-1 et al.*, complaint, p. 122), appointment of administrators to oversee the clean-up of the unions (*United States v. Local 1804-1 et al.*, complaint, p. 123), and the defendants' disgorgement of the proceeds of their labor racketeering (*United States v. Local 1804-1 et al.*, complaint, pp. 123–24). Rather than go to trial, the defendants entered into consent agreements.

B. Local 1804-1 (Bergen, N.J.)

On March 25, 1991, ILA Local 1804-1, and its executive board and officers entered into a consent judgment with the DOJ. Local 1804-1's current and future executive board and officers agreed to be enjoined from committing any acts of racketeering activity and from knowingly associating with members or associates of organized crime (*United States v. Local 1804-1 et al.*, consent judgment for Local 1804-1, p. 3). The consent judgment provided for the appointment of a monitor to oversee the local's operations until the 1997 election. The monitor would have blanket access to all union documents or information, authority to discipline union officers, agents, employees, and members, power to investigate corruption or abuse of union funds, and supervisory authority over the union's 1994 and 1997 elections (*United States v. Local 1804-1 et al.*, consent judgment for Local 1804-1, pp. 4–5). In addition, the monitor would have authority to review and veto union expenditures, union contracts, personnel decisions, and changes to the union's constitution and bylaws (*United States v. Local 1804-1 et al.*, consent judgment for Local 1804-1, pp. 5–6).

Local 1804-1 agreed to pay the monitor's salary and operating expenses, and not to oppose or interfere with the monitor's duties in any way (*United States v. Local 1804-1 et al.*, consent judgment for Local 1804-1, pp. 3–6). The consent judgment also provided for amendments of Local 1804-1's constitution, including salary limits for union officers, election of shop stewards, and discontinuation of union loans to union officers and members (*United States v. Local 1804-1 et al.*, consent judgment for Local 1804-1, pp. 7–8). The consent judgment permitted Local 1804-1's executive board to remain in office but required several board members to pay $100,000 to Local 1804-1's treasury (*United States v. Local 1804-1 et al.*, consent judgment for Local 1804-1, p. 11).

James Gill was appointed as 1804-1's monitor. The union's strategy was to strike a deal: if it expelled certain people, the union would be permitted to reform itself. This appears to have been exactly what happened; ten years after the settlement, very little appears to have changed.

C. Local 824, Local 1809, and Local 1909 (West Side Locals)

On March 26, 1991, Locals 824, 1809, and 1909 (collectively known as the West Side Locals), and their executive boards and officers entered into a consent judgment. The defendant union officials, without admitting wrongdoing or violation of law, agreed that persons holding office in the West Side Locals would be enjoined from knowingly associating with any member or associate of organized crime (*United States v. Local 1804-1 et al.*, consent judgment for the West Side Locals, p. 8). The consent judgment provided for the resignation of executive board members John Potter and Thomas Ryan, and enjoined both men from holding ILA office in the future (*United States v. Local 1804-1 et al.*, consent judgment for the West Side Locals, p. 2). ILA international president John Bowers (also president of the three West Side Locals) and executive board member Robert Gleason agreed to resign their memberships in an employer association, the NYSA (New York Shipping Association)–ILA Contract Board (*United States v. Local 1804-1 et al.*, consent judgment for the West Side Locals, p. 4). The consent judgment stipulated Department of Labor supervision over the 1991 and 1994 elections in the three locals and gave the DOL full access to union records and information necessary to carry this out (*United States v. Local 1804-1 et al.*, consent judgment for the West Side Locals, pp. 3–4).

Local 1909 agreed to a court-appointed employment practices officer to develop and implement rules and procedures to assure fair hiring, to discontinue no-show jobs, and to discipline those who violate hiring or employment procedures (*United States v. Local 1804-1 et al.*, consent judgment for the West Side Locals, pp. 4–6). The employment practices officer was granted full access to union records necessary to fulfill his duties, was to report at least every six months to the court, was to be paid by the union, and was to continue in office until the certification of the 1994 union election (*United States v. Local 1804-1 et al.*, consent judgment for the West Side Locals, pp. 6–7). The West Side Locals agreed not to obstruct, oppose, or otherwise interfere with the work of the DOL or the employment practices officer (*United States v. Local 1804-1 et al.*, consent judgment for the West Side Locals, p. 9). John Bowers and the ILA proclaimed the consent judgment a complete victory, saying it was just short of the judge throwing the case out, and claiming that nothing exceptional had been granted to the government in exchange for the settlement.

D. The Civil RICO Suit's Individual Defendants

The remaining defendants went to trial in spring 1991, but only four defendants persisted to judgment; the rest settled. On June 1, 1991, Anthony Scotto, one of the most powerful labor racketeers in U.S. history because of his high rank in both the Cosa Nostra and the union, settled with the government attorneys, agreeing to pay $50,000 and to be permanently banned from union office or any activity that would associate him with the union or any of the union's employers. On account of ERISA's antiforfeiture provision, Scotto would still receive his pension.

E. Local 1814 Consent Decree

On December 17, 1991, ILA Local 1814, its executive board and officers entered into a consent decree with the DOJ. The individual defendants and officers, without admitting wrongdoing, acknowledged past allegations, testimony, public findings, and criminal prosecutions. They agreed to be enjoined from knowingly associating with any member of organized crime (*United States v. Local 1804-1 et al.*, consent decree for Local 1814, pp. 2–3).

The consent decree provided for a court-appointed monitor with full access to the union's books, records, and other information, disciplinary authority, and supervisory authority over the 1993 and 1996 elections (*United States v. Local 1804-1 et al.*, consent decree for Local 1814, pp. 3–7). The monitor, who would be paid by the union, was authorized to review and veto union expenditures, contracts, appointments, and proposed amendments to the constitution and bylaws (*United States v. Local 1804-1 et al.*, consent decree for Local 1814, pp. 8–9). The monitor had authority to hire legal counsel, accountants, consultants, investigators, and any other personnel necessary to assist in his duties (*United States v. Local 1804-1 et al.*, consent decree for Local 1814, p. 10).

The consent decree included amendments to Local 1814's constitution providing for secret-ballot rank-and-file elections of shop stewards, and limitations on officers' compensation (*United States v. Local*

1804-1 et al., consent decree for Local 1814, p. 14). Moreover, executive board members Anthony Pimpinella and Joseph Colozza had to resign from their Local 1814 positions and agree never to hold ILA employment again (*United States v. Local 1804-1 et al.*, consent decree for Local 1814, p. 16). Anthony Ciccone had to resign but was permitted to remain a union member and continued to receive union benefits (*United States v. Local 1804-1 et al.*, consent decree for Local 1814, p. 16). The other members of the executive board were permitted to keep their positions. Local 1814 is no longer the influential local it once was because there are few functioning docks left in Brooklyn, but the Gambino crime family's influence remains strong.

F. Local 1588 (Bayonne, N.J.)

On January 3, 1992, the last of the six locals named in the 1990 civil RICO suit, Local 1588 and its executive board, entered into a consent agreement with the government.[25] The consent agreement created the office of ombudsman, which would exist until the 1993 election, and extend beyond at the option of the union's executive board or membership (*United States v. Local 1804-1 et al.*, consent order for Local 1588, p. 7). This ombudsman's office was to be staffed by two individuals, one appointed by the court and one by the union (*United States v. Local 1804-1 et al.*, consent order for Local 1588, pp. 3–4). The ombudsman was charged with enforcing the union's constitution and by-laws (*United States v. Local 1804-1 et al.*, consent order for Local 1588, p. 3). The ombudsman's office had power to file disciplinary charges, but only after consulting with the union's executive board (*United States v. Local 1804-1 et al.*, consent order for Local 1588, p. 4). Rank-and-file union members were encouraged to file confidential complaints with the ombudsman's office.

The consent agreement provided for election of stewards and constitutional changes to disciplinary procedures (*United States v. Local 1804-1 et al.*, consent order for Local 1588, pp. 10–11), Department of Labor supervision of the local's 1993 election (p. 8), and an injunction

---

[25] Local 1588's secretary-treasurer, Donald Carson, was convicted in 1988 of RICO conspiracy and extortion involving Local 1588 (United States v. DiGilio, 86 Cr. 340 [D.N.J.][DRD], aff'd mem., 870 F.2d 652 [3d Cir. 1989], vacated and remanded, 110 S. Ct. 2162 [1990]). Following his conviction and incarceration, Local 1588's president and secretary-treasurer declined to run for office in 1990. The consent order acknowledged that "the new executive board already has taken steps to return Local 1588 to fiscal soundness and to remove the taint of organized crime corruption" (United States v. Local 1804-1 et al., consent order for Local 1588, p. 2).

preventing George Weingartner and Robert Lake from serving as shop stewards or in any other ILA office or position (pp. 9–10). Robert Gaffey was appointed as Local 1588's ombudsman. (He had formerly served as an assistant U.S. attorney and as chief counsel to the investigations officer in the IBT International case.) During his time in office, Gaffey's main contribution to the cleanup of Local 1588 was to assist in the creation of a slate of reform candidates to oppose Donald Carson's Genovese-controlled slate. The leader of the "reform" slate was convicted of stealing union funds and was removed from office. Allegedly, the Genovese crime family continues to exercise substantial influence in Local 1588.

G. Conclusions

Recent legal developments demonstrate that the government's efforts to reform the ILA since the PCOC report have not fundamentally changed the structure and personnel of the ILA international union. In January 2002, the U.S. attorney's office (Brooklyn) announced an indictment against eight leaders and members of the Genovese crime family, alleging extortion from waterfront employers and businesses in the New York metropolitan area, northern New Jersey, and Miami (*United States v. Liborio "Barney" Bellomo et al.*, Cr. No. 01-416 (S-8) ILG [2002]). The indictment accuses the mob defendants of violating ILA members' Landrum-Griffin rights and of defrauding the ILA's pension and welfare fund.

In May 2002, a major investigation by the New York–New Jersey Waterfront Commission resulted in the indictment of eight persons connected to the Genovese crime family or ILA Local 1588, including the local's president, John Timpanaro. The indictment charges that through extortion and the withholding of premium job assignments, the defendants demanded kickbacks and cash payments from dozens of Local 1588 members. Some defendants were also charged with participating in a scheme to bill the marine terminal for truck chassis parts that were never delivered. On June 3, 2002, the U.S. attorney (E.D.N.Y.), the New York state attorney general, and the FBI announced the arrests and indictments of seventeen members and associates of the Gambino crime family or officials of ILA Local 1814 and Local 1 involved with waterfront racketeering. The defendants, including Local 1814 president and ILA vice president, Frank Scollo, are charged with extortion, wire fraud, loan sharking, operating illegal gambling businesses, money laundering, witness tampering, and other related crimes. Among other things, the indictment charges the defendants with placing mob members and associates in top union jobs, carrying out day-to-day extortion, loan sharking, and a scheme to defraud the ILA health fund. In late June 2002, the *New York Times* reported that the government is considering a RICO suit against the ILA international union.

VI. Perspectives on Labor Racketeering

Labor racketeering has been a major form of crime throughout the twentieth century. It has involved tens of thousands of individual crimes, some of which have been perpetrated by some of the nation's most powerful criminals and crime families. It has victimized tens of thousands of workers who have had their rights trampled on, their contracts sold out, and their pension funds looted. It has undermined the labor movement, one of the most powerful and important sociopolitical institutions in American society. While the problem has attracted enormous law enforcement, political, and media attention, especially in the last two decades, it has attracted practically no criminological attention.[26]

A. Criminology and Labor Racketeering

Labor racketeering could be studied as a form of organizational crime; from this perspective a comparative analysis of corporate crime and union crime would be especially fruitful. What kinds of criminal opportunities do both types of organizations generate? What potential and limits do corporate stakeholders and rank-and-file union members, respectively, have for preventing and remediating racketeering? Do other stakeholders in either type of organization play a role in preventing or facilitating corruption?

Labor racketeering could also be approached from the standpoint of the criminal offenses that it spawns: extortion, embezzlement, fraud, violence, hijacking, restraint of trade (enforcing cartels), and denial of intangible rights of union members to a democratically run union. Yet another option is to approach labor racketeering from the standpoint of the offender, either as a subcategory of white-collar crime or as a subcategory of organized crime. This essay approaches the topic from the latter perspective. Our thesis is that the twentieth-century history

---

[26] Likewise, it has attracted practically no interest among labor law scholars. But see Goldberg 1989; Summers 1991.

of American organized (some say "syndicate") crime could not be properly written without paying a great deal of attention to the influence, power, and wealth that the Cosa Nostra crime families derived from their association with international and local unions.

The Italian-American organized crime families obtained their foothold in the unions in the 1920s and 1930s when management and labor both called on gangsters for protection and as a counterforce to communist and socialist elements. During this period, the crime groups were able to take advantage of an immigrant culture of which they were a part. With the repeal of national alcohol prohibition in 1933, labor racketeering became an even more important source of revenue and power for organized crime. After a brief effort in the mid-1950s to oppose organized crime infiltration, the AFL-CIO apparently concluded that the labor movement would suffer more from opposing organized crime than from accommodating it (Hutchinson 1970).[27]

Unions have proved highly vulnerable to corruption and racketeering. Once the dues checkoff privilege was recognized, unions became the recipients of a steady stream of money deducted from workers' paychecks. Corrupt union officers easily diverted funds into their own pockets, sometimes by theft but sometimes via extravagant salaries and perks. The emergence of huge union pension and welfare funds in the 1950s made unions even more attractive to organized crime. As Lipset, Trow, and Coleman (1956) recognized nearly a half century ago, most union members are apathetic. They have certainly not been able to successfully oppose organized crime groups.

The sociopolitical status and economic strength of the Cosa Nostra organized crime families throughout the twentieth century have been significantly augmented by their influence in local and international

---

[27] An excellent example of the AFL-CIO attitude toward corruption and racketeering in unions is David Elbaor and Larry Gold's (1985) monograph, *The Criminalization of Labor Activity: Federal Criminal Enforcement against Unions, Union Officials and Employees.* This short monograph (by the chief counsel of the AFL-CIO) denies the existence of any significant organized crime problem in the labor movement and attributes investigations and prosecutions to a sinister plan by big business and big government to undermine the labor movement. The following excerpt provides a flavor: "The government continues to seek a substantial increase in money and personnel to carry out its prosecutorial campaign against organized labor, peddling sensational recitations of union crime and preying on public willingness to equate labor with corruption. Ironically, the motley assortment of prosecutions in recent years suggests not that the government's substantial investigatory resources have produced great results, or proven organized crime's permeation of the labor movement, but that most union crime is isolated, unconnected with larger criminal networks, involves relatively small sums of money, and is of a technical nature" (p. 66).

unions. Unions have provided organized crime with jobs, patronage, money, and power. Businesses and government agencies have to deal with organized crime figures who hold union office. Corrupt business-men have allied themselves with corrupt union bosses, bribing them for sweetheart contracts and for ignoring or circumventing terms of collective bargaining agreements. The status that the labor racketeers derived from their positions or associations with unions translated into political power, especially in the heyday of the urban political ma-chines. Unions provided endorsements, workers, and campaign contri-butions to political candidates. In return, the politicians looked the other way when the union bosses lined their own pockets.

There are many reasons why the American labor movement has de-clined over the twentieth century, but one factor worth considering is the negative impact of racketeering. To an extent, perhaps, some unions at some time, under some leaders, benefited from being allied with organized criminals; such alliances may have increased their lever-age at the bargaining table. But labor racketeers are out for themselves and their organized crime cronies, not for the rank and file. They pro-mote themselves and their cronies to leadership positions within the unions, draw excessive salaries, sell out the members' contractual rights, and loot the pension and welfare funds. They show no interest in organizing and no interest, of course, in union democracy. Labor idealists who wish to democratize and strengthen their unions cannot succeed in unions penetrated by organized crime. Indeed, the taint of organized crime may partly explain the failure of the labor movement in the second half of the twentieth century to attract the energy and idealism of the younger generations.

B. Criminal Justice and Labor Racketeering

As late as the 1980s members of Congress, labor officials, business-men, politicians, and scholars considered the Italian-American Cosa Nostra crime families invincible. The 1986 President's Commission on Organized Crime was highly pessimistic about the prospects for purg-ing the labor movement of Cosa Nostra racketeers.

Less than two decades later, the prospects for change look much brighter. The Cosa Nostra crime families, under constant legal attack for almost two decades, have been significantly weakened, in some cities practically eliminated (Jacobs and Gouldin 1999). The boss of every Cosa Nostra crime family has been imprisoned; in many cases their successors and their successors' successors have followed them to jail. Dozens of high-level Cosa Nostra members have become cooperating witnesses, assisting in the investigation and prosecution of their former colleagues, their rackets, and corrupted unions and businesses. This unprecedented attack on "traditional organized crime" has had repercussions for labor racketeering. For one thing, the organized crime families are much weaker than they were a generation ago; they have fewer and weaker resources to bring to bear in support of labor racketeering activities. For another thing, the federal government has attacked Cosa Nostra by powerfully attacking its base in labor unions.

Civil RICO has been the great engine of the government's onslaught. Beginning with the 1982 suit against IBT Local 560, government lawyers have brought one major labor racketeering case after another against local unions and international unions, including the IBT, HEREIU, ILA, and LIUNA (complaint prepared but not filed). Civil RICO allows the government to address an entire crime problem, like a mobbed-up union. There have been approximately twenty trusteeships resulting from DOJ civil RICO suits brought against unions (see app. table A1); unfortunately, there has never been a comprehensive accounting.

The civil RICO suits have been advantageous for the government because they have led to court-appointed trustees, almost always former prosecutors with major experience investigating and prosecuting organized crime cases. There is no uniform role or set of powers for these court-appointed trustees. Each judge or each consent agreement provides the trustee or trustees with case-specific authority. Moreover, each court or consent decree provides for how the trusteeship will be funded and for how long; funding has varied from generous to inadequate.

The continued interest and support of the presiding judge is critical to the court-appointed trustee's success. If the judge makes it clear that reform of the union is a nonnegotiable goal that the court will see through until victory, rank-and-file members will be more willing to step forward to work with the trustee and to challenge the racketeers for union office. But as long as a feeling persists in the union that the judge will lose interest, the trusteeship run out of funds, and the trustee become distracted with other work, the rank and file will remain intimidated, demoralized, and disorganized, anticipating the return of mob dominance.

The FBI, DOL, OCRS, and the U.S. attorney's office also play key roles in determining the success of the trusteeship. If they stay involved, they can help the trustee identify union members who continue to associate with organized crime, and they can assist in putting together disciplinary cases seeking a corrupt member's expulsion from the union. Continued investigations can also lead to a new round of criminal charges and civil RICOs. The FBI, DOL, and U.S. attorney can also keep the pressure on the trustee to be aggressive and creative in his reform efforts. The trustee's success depends upon his authority and resources, whether he can appoint paid assistants, and whether the union members are persuaded that he will be on the job until the racketeers are purged and union democracy restored. Perhaps even more important are the skills, creativity, determination, and competency of the trustee. Most of the trustees are former prosecutors. This facilitates coordination with the Department of Justice and equips the trustee to investigate racketeering and other wrongdoing. But it does not facilitate the fostering of union democracy and the energizing of a plundered and demoralized union. Those tasks can best be carried out by knowledgeable, skilled, and charismatic trade unionists. Some trusteeships have been fortunate to have had both types of trustees, but many have not.

A court-appointed trusteeship is not a panacea. Many trustees have not been successful. While there has never been a study of the successes and failures of RICO suits against mobbed-up international and local unions, our impression is that less than half could be called successful and only a few, at least to this point, could be called completely successful. If the court-appointed trusteeships are to fulfill their potential as an organized crime control strategy, much research needs to be done on how to achieve success. To date, only the IBT Local 560 trusteeship has attracted scholarly attention (Goldberg 1989; Summers 1991; Jacobs and Santore 2001).

The dozens of trustees who have been appointed to clean up corrupt unions have never been brought together for a conference.[28] Their numerous reports to their respective judges have not been assembled and therefore are not available to new trustees. After almost twenty years of such initiatives, there are neither "how to" manuals nor any materials whatsoever on how a trustee can maximize the chances of success. Here there are surely roles for the National Institute of Justice, private foundations, and university-based criminologists, among others.

It is hard for someone interested in labor racketeering to understand

---

[28] In 1989, some of the court-appointed trustees testified regarding the successes and failures of their trusteeship (see United States Congress 1989).

why the National Institute of Justice has shown no interest in sponsoring research on labor racketeering or its remediation; such research would undoubtedly be valuable to scholars and law enforcement officials in other countries that face serious organized crime problems. Perhaps the "blame" lies with the academic research community that, for one reason or another, has not focused much attention on organized crime, much less on labor racketeering. The subject, of course, is somewhat politically sensitive. But if political sensitivity has not prevented DOJ's prosecutorial wing from exposing and attacking labor racketeering, it makes no sense for DOJ's research wing to avoid studying the subject in aid of the department's future remedial efforts.

This is not the place to present a full-scale research agenda on the subject of labor racketeering. Suffice it to say that we need case studies on each of the major initiatives against labor racketeering. We need to carefully document and analyze the strategies used to purge corrupt elements from the unions and to rebuild the unions' democratic structures and processes. Such case studies, carefully coordinated and analyzed, and supplemented by joint meetings with the individuals who carried out these remedial efforts, would yield policy recommendations of great assistance to future initiatives in the United States and in other countries facing similar or analogous organized crime problems.

A final note. While organized crime controlled labor racketeering may be fading, that does not mean that labor corruption will die out as well. Dishonest officials, unconnected to organized crime, will always be in a position to embezzle money, defraud their unions, and extract excessive fees and reimbursements. The government cannot (and should not) try to monitor and regulate all the union locals and internationals in the country. In the final analysis, only an energized and watchful rank and file can assure that dishonest union officials will be swiftly exposed and deposed.

TABLE A1

Civil RICO Suits against "Mobbed-Up" Unions

Case Name	Date Filed	Published Opinions Discussing Various Aspects of the Case
1. U.S. v. IBT Local 560, No. Civ. 82-689	March 9, 1982, D.N.J.	*U.S. v. Local 560*, 581 F. Supp. 279 (D.N.J. 1984), *aff'd* 780 F.2d 267 (3d Cir. 1985)
2. U.S. v. Local 6A, Cement and Concrete Workers, LIUNA, No. 86 Civ. 4819	June 19, 1986, S.D.N.Y.	*U.S. v. Local 6A*, 663 F. Supp. 192 (S.D.N.Y. 1986)
3. U.S. v. The Bonanno Organized Crime Family of La Cosa Nostra, Philip Rastelli, et al., No. Civ. 87-2974 (IBT Local 814)	August 25, 1987, E.D.N.Y.	*U.S. v. Bonnano*, 683 F. Supp. 1411 (E.D.N.Y. 1988); 695 F. Supp. 1426 (E.D.N.Y. 1988); 879 F.2d 20 (2d Cir. 1989)
4. U.S. v. Local 30, United Slate Tile and Composition Roofers, et al., Civil Action No. 87-7718	December 2, 1987, E.D. Pa.	*U.S. v. Local 30*, 686 F. Supp. 1139 (E.D. Pa. 1988), *aff'd*, 871 F.2d 401 (3d Cir. 1989)
5. U.S. v. John F. Long, John S. Mahoney, et al., No. 88 Civ. 3289 (IBT Locals 804 and 808)	May 1988, S.D.N.Y.	*U.S. v. Long*, 697 F. Supp. 651 (S.D.N.Y. 1988); 917 F.2d 691 (2d Cir. 1990)
6. U.S. v. International Brotherhood of Teamsters, Chauffeurs, Warehousemen and Helpers of America, et al., No. 88 Civ. 4486 ("IBT International Case")	June 28, 1988, S.D.N.Y.	*U.S. v. IBT*, 708 F. Supp. 1388 (S.D.N.Y. 1989); 723 F. Supp. 203 (S.D.N.Y. 1989); 725 F. Supp. 162 (S.D.N.Y. 1989); 728 F. Supp. 1032 (S.D.N.Y. 1990); 899 F.2d 143 (2d Cir. 1990); 905 F.2d 610 (2d Cir. 1990); 907 F.2d 277 (2d Cir. 1990); 931 F.2d 117 (2d Cir. 1991); 941 F.2d 1292 (2d Cir. 1991); 964 F.2d 180 (2d Cir. 1992)
7. U.S. v. Locals 1804-1, 824, 1809, 1909, 1588, and 1814, International Longshoremen's Ass'n, et al., No. 90 Civ. 0963*	February 14, 1990, S.D.N.Y.	*U.S. v. Local 1804-1*, 745 F. Supp. 184 (S.D.N.Y. 1990); 812 F. Supp. 1303 (S.D.N.Y. 1993); 44 F.3d 1091 (2d Cir. 1995); *U.S. v. Carson*, 52 F.3d 1173 (2d Cir. 1995)
8. U.S. v. IBT Local 295, No. Civ. 90-0970	March 20, 1990, E.D.N.Y.	*U.S. v. Local 295*, 1991 WL 35497 (E.D.N.Y. 1991); 1991 WL 340575 (E.D.N.Y. 1991); 784 F. Supp. 15 (E.D.N.Y. 1992)

TABLE A1 (*Continued*)

Case Name	Date Filed	Published Opinions Discussing Various Aspects of the Case
9. U.S. v. District Council of NYC and Vicinity of the United Brotherhood of Carpenters and Joiners of America, et al., No. 90 Civ. 5722	September 6, 1990, S.D.N.Y.	*U.S. v. District Council*, 778 F. Supp. 738 (S.D.N.Y. 1991); 941 F. Supp. 349 (S.D.N.Y. 1996)
10. U.S. v. Edward T. Hanley, et al., Civil Action No. 90-5017 (HEREIU Local 54)	December 19, 1990, D.N.J.	*U.S. v. Hanley*, 1992 WL 684356 (D.N.J. 1992)
11. U.S. v. Anthony R. Amodeo, Sr., et al., No. 92 Civ. 7744 (HEREIU Local 100)	October 23, 1992, S.D.N.Y.	*U.S. v. Amodeo*, 44 F.3d 141 (2d Cir. 1995)
12. U.S. v. IBT Local 282, No. Civ. 94-2919	June 21, 1994, E.D.N.Y.	*U.S. v. Local 282*, 13 F. Supp.2d 401 (E.D.N.Y. 1998)
13. U.S. v. Mason Tenders District Council of New York and Vicinity of LIUNA, No. 94 Civ. 6487	September 7, 1994, S.D.N.Y.	*U.S. v. Mason Tenders*, 1994 WL 742637 (S.D.N.Y. 1995); 909 F. Supp. 882 and 891 (S.D.N.Y. 1995)
14. U.S. v. LIUNA (International Union "voluntarily" instituted reforms in exchange for government not filing complaint)	Never filed	*Serpico v. LIUNA*, 97 F.3d 995 (7th Cir. 1996)
15. U.S. v. Edward T. Hanley, HEREIU, and HEREIU's General Executive Board, Civ. No. 95-4596	September 5, 1995, D.N.J.	*U.S. v. HEREIU*, 974 F. Supp. 411 (D.N.J. 1997); Agathos v. Muellenberg, 932 F. Supp. 636 (D.N.J. 1996)
16. U.S. and LIUNA v. Construction and General Laborers' District Council of Chicago and Vicinity, Civil No. 99C 5229	August 8, 1999, N.D. Ill.	*LIUNA v. Caruso*, 1999 WL 14496 (N.D.Ill. 1999), *aff'd*, 197 F.3d 1195 (7th Cir. 1999)
17. U.S. v. LIUNA Local 210, Civil No. 99 CV-0915A	November 18, 1999, W.D.N.Y.	*Panczykowski v. LIUNA*, 2000 WL 387602 (W.D.N.Y. 2000); *Caci v. LIUNA*, 2000 WL 387599 (W.D.N.Y. 2000)
18. U.S. v. HEREIU Local 69	April 17, 2002	

* The civil RICO suit in this case resulted in four separate trusteeships.

REFERENCES

Abadinsky, Howard. 1990. *Organized Crime.* 3d ed. Chicago: Nelson Hall.

Bell, Daniel. 1962. *The End of Ideology: On the Exhaustion of Political Ideas in the Fifties.* New York: Free Press.

Brill, Steven. 1978. *The Teamsters.* New York: Simon & Schuster.

Coleman, Barbara J. 1989. *Primer on ERISA.* 3d ed. Washington, D.C.: Bureau of National Affairs.

Crowe, Kenneth C. 1993. *Collision: How the Rank and File Took Back the Teamsters.* New York: Scribners & Sons.

Dean, Andrew B. 2000. "An Offer the Teamsters Couldn't Refuse: The 1989 Consent Decree Establishing Federal Oversight and Ending Mechanisms." *Columbia Law Review* 100:2157–94.

Dewey, Thomas. 1974. *Twenty against the Underworld.* Edited by Rodney Campbell. Garden City, N.Y.: Doubleday.

Dubinsky, David, and A. Raskin. 1977. *David Dubinsky: A Life with Labor.* New York: Simon & Schuster.

Elbaor, David, and Larry Gold. 1985. *The Criminalization of Labor Activity: Federal Criminal Enforcement against Unions, Union Officials and Employees.* Washington, D.C.: Connerton, Bernstein, & Katz.

Foner, Philip S. 1950. *The Fur and Leather Workers Union.* Newark, N.J.: Nordon.

Fox, Stephen. 1989. *Blood and Power: Organized Crime in Twentieth-Century America.* New York: Morrow.

Goldberg, Michael J. 1989. "Cleaning Labor's House: Institutional Reform Litigation in the Labor Movement." *Duke Law Journal* 1989:903–1011.

Goldfarb, Ronald. 1995. *Perfect Villains, Imperfect Heroes: Robert F. Kennedy's War against Organized Crime.* New York: Random House.

Hughes, Rupert. 1940. *Attorney for the People: The Story of Thomas E. Dewey.* Boston: Houghton Mifflin.

Hutchinson, John. 1970. *The Imperfect Union: A History of Corruption in American Trade Unions.* New York: Dutton.

Isaac, Rael Jean. 1998. "A Corrupt Union Escapes Justice." *Wall Street Journal* (July 27), p. A14.

Jacobs, James B., Coleen Friel, and Edward O'Callaghan. 1997. "Pension Forfeiture: A Problematic Sanction for Public Corruption." *American Criminal Law Review* 35:57–92.

Jacobs, James B., and Lauryn Gouldin. 1999. "Cosa Nostra: The Final Chapter?" In *Crime and Justice: A Review of Research,* vol. 25, edited by Michael Tonry. Chicago: University of Chicago Press.

Jacobs, James B., Christopher Panarella, and Jay Worthington III. 1994. *Busting the Mob: United States v. Cosa Nostra.* New York: New York University Press.

Jacobs, James B., and David Santore. 2001. "The Liberation of IBT Local 560." *Criminal Law Bulletin* 37(2):125–58.

Jensen, Vernon H. 1974. *Strife on the Waterfront: The Port of New York since 1945.* Ithaca, N.Y.: Cornell University Press.

Johnson, Malcolm. 1950. *Crime on the Labor Front.* New York: McGraw-Hill.

Kazan, Elia. 1954. "On the Waterfront." Motion picture. United States: Columbia Pictures.

Kefauver, Estes. 1951. *Crime in America.* Garden City, N.Y.: Doubleday.

Kennedy, Robert F. 1960. *The Enemy Within.* New York: Harper & Row.

Kimeldorf, Howard. 1988. *Reds or Rackets?: The Making of Radical and Conservative Unions on the Waterfront.* Berkeley: University of California Press.

La Botz, Dan. 1990. *Rank and File Rebellion: Teamsters for a Democratic Union.* London: Verso Books.

Lacey, Frederick. 1992. "The Independent Administrator's Memorandum on the Handling and Disposition of Disciplinary Matters." Unpublished report to Judge Edelstein, October 7, 1992.

Landesco, John. 1968. *Organized Crime in Chicago.* Originally published in 1929 by the Illinois Association for Criminal Justice. Chicago: University of Chicago Press.

Lipset, Seymour M., Martin Trow, and James Coleman. 1956. *Union Democracy.* Glencoe, Ill.: Free Press.

Lynch, Gerald. 1987*a*. "RICO: The Crime of Being a Criminal, Part 1." *Columbia Law Review* 87:661–764.

———. 1987*b*. "RICO: The Crime of Being a Criminal, Part 2." *Columbia Law Review* 87:920–84.

McClellan, John. 1962. *Crime without Punishment.* New York: Duell, Sloan, & Pearce.

Mencimer, Stephanie. 1998. "Ex-FBI Official Pulls at Union's Infamous Roots." *Washington Post* (June 7), sec. A., p. 1.

Methvin, Eugene H. 1998. "A Corrupt Union and the Mob." *Weekly Standard* 3(48):25–29.

Moldea, Dan E. 1978. *The Hoffa Wars: Teamsters, Rebels, Politicians and the Mob.* New York: Paddington.

Muellenberg, Kurt W. 1998. "Final Report as Monitor of HEREIU, August 26, 1998." Available at http://www.heretics.net.

Mulligan, John E. 1999. "Coia Resigns as Head of Laborer's Union." *Providence Journal* (December 7), p. 1.

Mulligan, John E., and Dean Starkman. 1996. "An F.O.B. and the Mob (Laborer's International Union of North America President Arthur A. Coia)." *Washington Monthly* 28(5):11–13.

Navasky, Victor S. 1971. *Kennedy Justice.* New York: Atheneum.

Neff, James. 1989. *Mobbed Up: Jackie Presser's High-Wire Life in the Teamsters, the Mafia, and the FBI.* New York: Atlantic Monthly Press.

Nelson, Michael. 2000. "Slowing Union Corruption: Reforming the Landrum-Griffin Act to Better Combat Union Embezzlement." *George Mason Law Review* 8:527–86.

New York State Crime Commission. 1953. "Final Report of the New York State Crime Commission to the Governor, the Attorney General and the Legislature of the State of New York." Albany: State of New York.

New York State Organized Crime Task Force. 1990. *Corruption and Racke-*

teering in the New York City Construction Industry: Final Report to Governor Mario M. Cuomo. New York: New York University Press.

Nunn, Sam. 1986. "The Impact of the Senate Permanent Subcommittee on Investigations on Federal Policy." *Georgia Law Review* 21:17–56.

Office of the Independent Hearing Officer (LIUNA). 1999. "Executive Summary of IHO Decision re: LIUNA General President Arthur A. Coia." March 8, 1999. Available at http://www.laborers.org.

President's Commission on Organized Crime. 1986. *The Edge: Organized Crime, Business, and Labor Unions.* Washington, D.C.: President's Commission on Organized Crime.

Rauh, Joseph. 1971. "LMRDA—Enforce It or Repeal It." *Georgia Law Review* 5:643–86.

Seal, Kathy. 1997. "Union Monitor Remains; HEREIU." *Hotel and Motel Management* 212(6):3–5.

Seidman, Harold. 1938. *Labor Czars: A History of Labor Racketeering.* New York: Liveright.

Sheridan, Walter. 1972. *The Fall and Rise of Jimmy Hoffa.* New York: Saturday Review Press.

Sifakis, Carl. 1987. *The Mafia Encyclopedia.* New York: Facts on File.

Stier, Anderson, & Malone, LLC. 2002. *The Teamsters: Perception and Reality: An Investigative Study of Organized Crime Influence in the Union.* Report prepared for the International Brotherhood of Teamsters. Washington, D.C.: Stier, Anderson, & Malone, LLC.

Stolberg, Mary E. 1995. *Fighting Organized Crime: Politics, Justice, and the Legacy of Thomas E. Dewey.* Boston: Northeastern University Press.

Summers, Clyde. 1991. "Union Trusteeships and Union Democracy." *University of Michigan Journal of Law Reform* 24:689–707.

Summers, Clyde W., Joseph L. Raub, and Herman Benson. 1986. *Union Democracy and Landrum-Griffin.* Brooklyn, N.Y.: Association for Union Democracy.

Taft, Phillip. 1964. *Organized Labor in American History.* New York: Harper & Row.

———. 1970. *Corruption and Racketeering in the Labor Movement.* 2d ed. Ithaca, N.Y.: Cornell Industrial & Labor Relations Press.

United States Congress. 1933. *Investigation of So-Called "Rackets."* [Commonly known as the Copeland Committee]. Hearings before the Subcommittee of the Senate Committee on Commerce, 73d Cong., 1st sess. Washington, D.C.: U.S. Government Printing Office.

———. 1960. *Final Report of the Select Committee on Improper Activities in the Labor or Management Field.* [McClellan Commission Rpt.]. 86th Cong., 2d sess., S. Rept. 1139. Washington, D.C.: U.S. Government Printing Office.

———. 1977. *Teamsters Central States Pension Fund: Hearings before the Permanent Subcommittee on Investigations of the Committee on Governmental Affairs, United States Senate.* 95th Cong., 1st sess., July 18 and 19, 1977. Washington, D.C.: U.S. Government Printing Office.

———. 1978. *Labor Management Racketeering: Hearings before the Permanent Subcommittee on Investigations of the Committee on Governmental Affairs, United States Senate.* 95th Cong., 2d sess., April 24 and 25, 1978. Washington, D.C.: U.S. Government Printing Office.

———. 1983. *Prepared Statement of Donald Wheeler, Special Agent in Charge, Chicago Office, Organized Crime and Racketeering Section, Inspector General's Office, Department of Labor.* Prepared statement before the Permanent Subcommittee on Investigations of the Committee on Governmental Affairs, United States Senate, Chicago, Illinois, March 4, 1983. Washington, D.C.: U.S. Government Printing Office.

———. 1984a. *Hearings before the Permanent Subcommittee on Investigations of the Committee on Governmental Affairs, United States Senate.* 98th Cong., 2d sess., August 27, 1984. Washington, D.C.: U.S. Government Printing Office.

———. 1984b. *Waterfront Corruption: Report Made by the Permanent Subcommittee on Investigations of the Committee on Governmental Affairs, United States Senate.* 98th Cong., 2d sess., March 27, 1984. Washington, D.C.: U.S. Government Printing Office.

———. 1985. *Organized Crime and Labor Management Racketeering: Hearings before the President's Commission on Organized Crime.* 99th Cong., 1st sess., April 24, 1985. Washington, D.C.: U.S. Government Printing Office.

———. 1989. *Federal Government's Use of Trusteeships under the RICO Statute: Hearings before the Permanent Subcommittee on Investigations of the Committee on Governmental Affairs, United States Senate.* 101st Cong., 1st sess., April 4, 6, and 12, 1989. Washington, D.C.: U.S. Government Printing Office.

———. 1996. *Testimony of Robert Luskin before the Subcommittee on Crime of the Committee on the Judiciary, United States House of Representatives.* 104th Cong., 2d sess., July 25, 1996. Washington, D.C.: U.S. Government Printing Office.

———. 1997. "Administration's Effort against the Influence of Organized Crime in LIUNA." House Judiciary Committee, 105th Cong., 1st sess., Jan. 2, 1997. Washington, D.C.: U.S. Government Printing Office.

———. 1999. *Subcommittee on House Employer-Employee Relations, Committee on Education and the Workforce.* Hearing on the HEREIU. 106th Cong., 1st sess. Washington, D.C.: U.S. Government Printing Office.

United States Department of Justice. 2000. "Justice Department Announces New Agreement Continuing Laborers Union Reforms until 2006." Press release. January 20. Available at http://www.usdoj.gov.

Vaira, Peter, and Douglas P. Roller. 1978. *Report on Organized Crime and the Labor Unions.* Prepared for the White House. Available at http://www.americanmafia.com/crime_and_labor.html.

Witwer, David. 1994. *Corruption and Reform in the Teamsters Union, 1898 to 1991.* UMI Dissertation Services. Ph.D. thesis, History Department, Brown University.

———. 2001. "Depression-Era Racketeering in the Building Services Union." Association for Union Democracy. *$100 Club News,* no. 82 (November 2001), p. 1.

Tom R. Tyler

Procedural Justice, Legitimacy, and the Effective Rule of Law

ABSTRACT

Legal authorities gain when they receive deference and cooperation from the public. Considerable evidence suggests that the key factor shaping public behavior is the fairness of the processes legal authorities use when dealing with members of the public. This reaction occurs both during personal experiences with legal authorities and when community residents are making general evaluations of the law and of legal authorities. The strength and breadth of this influence suggests the value of an approach to regulation based upon sensitivity to public concerns about fairness in the exercise of legal authority. Such an approach leads to a number of suggestions about valuable police practices, as well as helping explain why improvements in the objective performance of the police and courts have not led to higher levels of public trust and confidence in those institutions.

This essay presents and defends a process-based model of regulation (Tyler and Huo 2002). The model addresses two key concerns underlying effective regulation. The first is with the ability of the police and the courts to gain immediate and long-term compliance with decisions made by legal authorities in situations in which members of the public deal with legal authorities about particular issues. For example, when the police are called and intervene in a domestic dispute by telling someone to stop beating his or her spouse it is important that they be able to stop the aggressive behaviors that are occurring. It is further desirable if they can intervene in a way that discourages similar behavior in the future.

Tom R. Tyler is University Professor of Psychology, New York University. He thanks Cheryl Fischman, Ayelet Kattan, Michael Tonry, and several anonymous reviewers for comments on a draft of this chapter.

The second concern is with the ability of the legal system to encourage general compliance with the law and cooperation with the police. For example, the law tells people not to speed, not to run red lights, and not to murder their neighbors. To be effective, such laws need generally to be widely obeyed by members of the public in their everyday lives (Tyler 1990). The police and courts depend upon public cooperation for their effectiveness. For example, the police need community help in identifying criminals and fighting crime.

The process-based model argues that both aspects of the public's law-related behavior outlined above are powerfully influenced by people's subjective judgments about the fairness of the procedures through which the police and the courts exercise their authority (Tyler 1990; Tyler and Huo 2002). In particular, people's reactions to legal authorities are based to a striking degree on their assessments of the fairness of the processes by which legal authorities make decisions and treat members of the public. Drawing on both psychological research on procedural justice (Lind and Tyler 1988; Tyler and Lind 1992; Tyler et al. 1997; Tyler and Smith 1997; Tyler 2000) and on studies of the police and courts (Tyler 1990; Tyler and Huo 2002), the model suggests that people's willingness to accept the constraints of the law and legal authorities is strongly linked to their evaluations of the procedural justice of the police and the courts.

The key elements of the model are shown in figure 1. The focus is on two consequences of public feelings about law and legal authorities:

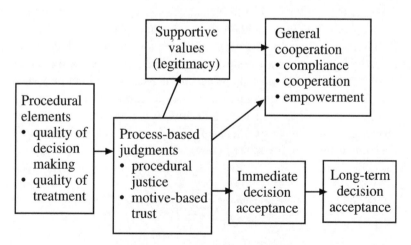

Fig. 1.—Process-based regulation (compiled by author)

variations in willingness to accept decisions and differences in the level of general cooperation. Each is linked to process-based judgments of procedural justice and motive-based trust. Those process-based judgments, in turn, flow from antecedent assessments of two procedural elements: quality of decision making and the quality of treatment.

This model is explicitly psychological, viewing subjective judgments on the part of the public about the actions of the police and the courts as central to the effectiveness of legal authorities. In particular, it is concerned with the social science question of why people do or do not comply with legal authorities. Viewed from an organizational perspective, compliance is important because it facilitates the ability of the authorities in a group, organization, or society effectively to manage those within the group (Tyler and Blader 2000). The ability to secure compliance increases the efficiency, effectiveness, and viability of the group.

As a psychological model, the model does not address normative issues concerning whether people ought to defer to legal authorities and generally obey the law. These issues are the focus of much of the philosophical literature on obedience (see, e.g., Raz 1979). The philosophical literature seeks to define conditions under which people ought to feel an obligation to obey the law.

Similarly, social theorists have argued that issues of hierarchy and structural inequality have created objective social conditions that are unfair and that the disadvantaged might reasonably respond to such conditions by ignoring or defying social authorities and rules (Tyler and McGraw 1986; Jost and Banaji 1994; Sidanius and Pratto 1999). If the social structure is viewed as fundamentally unfair by particular people or groups, then their willingness to comply might be regarded as "false consciousness"—that is, as a willingness that should be discouraged (Parkin 1971; Haney 1991). These issues are not addressed here.

This review focuses instead on empirical support concerning the importance of process-based judgments in the context of the social regulatory activities of the police and the courts. That support comes from studies in which people are interviewed about their attitudes, values, and behaviors toward law and legal authorities. These studies consider the views of people who have had personal experiences with the police and the courts and are making judgments about those experiences and the views of community residents evaluating the overall behavior of the police. In the context of personal experiences, the issue of concern is why people defer to or resist the decisions and directives of legal authorities, both in the immediate situation and over time. With people's general judgments about law and legal authorities the question is why, in their everyday lives, people obey the law, cooperate with legal authorities, and support the empowerment of those authorities.

The key argument of the process-based approach is that, while the police can and often do compel obedience through the threat or use of force, they can also gain the cooperation of the people with whom they deal. Cooperation and consent—"buy in"—are important because they facilitate immediate acceptance and long-term compliance. People are more likely to adhere to agreements and follow rules over time when they "buy into" the decisions and directives of legal authorities.

In the context of particular encounters with police officers and judges, people are more likely to consent and cooperate if they feel that they have been fairly treated. Procedural justice judgments consistently emerge as the central judgment shaping people's reactions to their experiences with legal authorities. As a consequence, the police and courts can facilitate acceptance by engaging in strategies of process-based regulation—treating community residents in ways that lead them to feel that the police and courts exercise authority in fair ways.

People also accept the directives of police officers and judges because they believe that such legal authorities are entitled to be obeyed. This feeling of obligation is rooted in a general judgment that the police are legitimate or in features of the situation or the actions of particular police officers that create feelings of legitimacy within the context of particular settings and particular legal authorities. However such feelings are formed, to the degree that people do regard the police and courts as legitimate, they are more willing to accept the directives and decisions of the police and courts, and the likelihood of defiance, hostility, and resistance is diminished.

What encourages legitimacy? Studies again suggest that the public is very sensitive to the manner in which authorities exercise their authority—that is, to issues of procedural justice. Views about legitimacy are rooted in the judgment that the police and the courts are acting fairly when they deal with community residents. Interestingly, this is true both when the public makes general evaluations of the police and the courts in their community and when particular members of the public are reacting to their personal encounters with police officers or judges. On both levels, issues of process dominate public evaluations of the police, the courts, and social regulatory activities.

Finally, preexisting legitimacy is found to shape the judgments that people make within the context of their particular experiences with police officers or judges. If people believe that legal authorities are legitimate, they are more likely to defer in encounters with particular members of those groups of authorities because they act fairly. This makes it easier for specific police officers or judges to enact process-based strategies of regulation. In other words, prior general views facilitate or hinder the social regulatory efforts of particular legal authorities. Hence, there is a favorable or unfavorable spiraling effect, with each personal contact with a legal authority being one in which it is progressively more or less likely that authorities will be able to gain deference through the use of fair procedures. When they do, they also build legitimacy, making process-based regulation more likely to be effective in the future. When they do not, and have to move to the use of a force- or sanction-based orientation, they are less able to act in ways that will be experienced by people as being fair. This undermines legitimacy and makes the likelihood of effectively using a process-based approach less likely in the future.

This essay first considers, in Section I, the types of public behavior relevant to regulation and regulatory authorities. These include immediate and long-term compliance with decisions and general compliance with law and cooperation with legal authorities in everyday life. The reasons for such public behavior are then examined in Section II, first in the context of compliance with decisions and then with general cooperation with legal authorities. Section III contrasts the influence of instrumental reasons with those of process-based judgments and assessments of legitimacy. The goal in Sections IV and V is to show that process-based models have substantial influence and can be the basis for effective strategies of regulation. Racial profiling is then used in Section VI to illustrate the policy implications of process-based regulation. Finally, the relationship of process-based regulation to other models of regulation is examined in Section VII.

I. Compliance

The ability to secure compliance is always a central issue in discussions of regulation. Legal authorities must often resolve disputes in ways that lead people to receive outcomes that are less than they want and may be less than they feel they deserve. Similarly, when enforcing the law, authorities may be called upon to tell people to cease behavior that they enjoy and may not feel is morally inappropriate. In such situations, gaining public compliance is always problematic.

A. Immediate Compliance

When judges or police officers deal with members of the public in particular situations involving regulation, their primary goal is to enforce the law. That goal leads them to want to gain immediate compliance with their decisions. Law is about the regulation of people's conduct, and its success rests on the ability of particular legal authorities effectively to shape people's behavior during personal encounters between legal authorities and members of the public. When the police, for example, tell someone to stop drinking beer in public or cease abusing his or her spouse, or if a judge directs someone to pay child support, an important measure of the success of those authorities is whether the behavior changes.[1]

Concern about compliance leads to an interest in understanding how legal authorities might act so as to encourage voluntary deference to their decisions. In other words, police officers and judges are often unsure whether they can issue directives and expect that they will be obeyed. They must focus on understanding how they might encourage consent and cooperation with their decisions through their own behavior. This raises questions about how particular legal authorities can through their actions facilitate acceptance of their decisions.

These concerns draw attention to the psychology of deference. We want to understand why people are willing to cede authority over their behavior to legal authorities, allowing those authorities to resolve disputes and regulate behavior. In particular, we want to understand how to gain public "buy in," so that people continue to follow decisions even when the authorities are no longer present and are less directly observing people's behavior.

The assumption underlying our concern over compliance is that people will naturally resist the efforts of legal authorities to restrict and regulate their behavior and to sanction them for past wrongdoing. Simple self-interest suggests that people will resist complying when the

[1] While our discussion is framed in terms of regulation, Tyler and Huo (2002) found that the primary form of contact that people had with the police came as a result of members of the public calling the police for help. In such situations the caller, at least, did not see the issue as one of restricting their own behavior to conform to the law. However, regulatory situations are central to discussions of the effectiveness of legal authorities, since resistance to law is often strong when authorities are acting as regulators.

actions involved are not in their own personal interest. Hence, the job of regulatory authorities is an inherently difficult one, and one that by its very nature generates public resistance.

These models are important for policing, since compliance by members of the public can never be taken for granted. As Mastrofski, Snipes, and Supina suggest, "Although deference to legal authorities is the norm, disobedience occurs with sufficient frequency that skill in handling the rebellious, the disgruntled, and the hard to manage—or those potentially so—has become the street officer's performance litmus test" (1996, p. 272). Similarly, Sherman (1993) highlights the problem of defiance by the public and the need to minimize resistance to the directives of the police.

The Mastrofski, Snipes, and Supina (1996) study, in which social scientists observed police encounters with the public in Richmond, Virginia, provide some evidence about the frequency of such problems. They found an overall noncompliance rate of 22 percent: 19 percent of the time when the police told a person to leave another person alone, 33 percent of the time when the police told a person to cease some form of disorder, and 18 percent of the time when the police told a person to cease illegal behavior. A replication in Indianapolis, Indiana, and St. Petersburg, Florida, found an overall noncompliance rate of 20 percent: 14 percent of the time when the police told people to leave another person alone, 25 percent of the time when the police told a person to cease some form of disorder, and 21 percent of the time when the police told a person to cease illegal behavior (McCluskey, Mastrofski, and Parks 1998).

The studies described look at immediate compliance—whether the person did as instructed—not at whether people willingly accepted the decisions made by the authorities, buying into their resolution to a problem, or understanding why the restrictions on their behavior that are occurring are appropriate and reasonable. As the researchers note, "citizens who acquiesce at the scene can renege" (Mastrofski, Snipes, and Supina 1996, p. 283). People may renege in their future behavior if they have complied in the face of coercive power. If they do so, this requires further police intervention at future times.

B. Long-Term Compliance

In the immediate presence of a police officer, or when in court in front of a judge, people are likely to comply with the decisions made by these legal authorities. When the authorities are present, and the person's behavior is observable, the possibility of bringing the power of legal authorities to bear is the greatest, and people are likely to defer in the face of such displays of potential coercion.

Such compliance might continue over time because authorities continue to be present. However, legal authorities are seldom in a position from which they are able easily to maintain such surveillance, so long-term decision acceptance is an additional concern that legal authorities must consider. If people return to their prior behavior once they are beyond the surveillance of the authorities, the police have to continually revisit issues they have dealt with when dealing with problem people, and the courts have to keep reordering people to engage in desired behavior. When this happens, the effectiveness of regulatory authorities is diminished.

Hence, a second goal of legal authorities is to obtain long-term compliance with decisions. Such long-term compliance is more strongly voluntary in character, since legal authorities are seldom able to maintain the physical presence that makes the risk of being sanctioned for wrongdoing immediate and salient. Instead, they must rely more heavily upon self-regulatory motivations among the members of the public whose continued compliance is being sought. Of course, the possibility of sanctioning is never totally absent when dealing with authorities of any type, but it is less realistic and salient when authorities are not present.

C. Everyday Law-Related Behavior

While compliance during personal encounters with members of the public is a key issue to legal authorities, it is not all that the legal system wants or values. The legal system seeks to promote three types of desirable general public behavior among the public. These are compliance with the law, cooperation with legal authorities, and support for the empowerment of the law.

One key public behavior is everyday compliance. It is important that people generally comply with the laws that apply to their everyday lives. Such general compliance is central to the effectiveness of the legal system, since the authorities are not able to control the entire population via sanctioning strategies. If they can rely on most people to comply with the law voluntarily, they can direct a more limited set of resources at a small group of problematic people (Ayres and Braithwaite 1992).

The need for legal authorities to be able to secure compliance has been widely noted by legal scholars and social scientists, who have argued that, "The lawgiver must be able to anticipate that the citizenry as a whole will . . . generally observe the body of rules he has promulgated" (Fuller 1971, p. 201). This is because the effective exercise of legal authority requires compliance from most citizens most of the time (Easton 1975). Decisions by police officers or judges mean very little if people generally ignore them, and laws lack importance if they do not affect public behavior (Tyler 1990).

The issue of gaining public compliance has gained heightened attention for several reasons. One is that confidence in the institutions of the legal system has declined, and people are less likely to express "trust and confidence" in law and legal authorities than in the past. This declining confidence in law and legal authorities may lead to declining feelings of obligation to obey the police, the courts, and the law (Tyler 1998), raising the possibility that compliance may be increasingly problematic. The popular press has noted this possibility, commenting on seeming increases in law-breaking behaviors ranging from not paying taxes to speeding and running red lights to widespread drug use.

In addition to trying to encourage public compliance, legal authorities seek the voluntary cooperation of members of the public in their efforts to combat crime and community problems. It has always been recognized that the police and courts benefit when those in the communities they regulate cooperate with them in a joint effort to enforce the law and to fight crime and criminal behavior. Recent research emphasizes this point and even raises questions about whether legal authorities can effectively manage the problems of community crime control without public cooperation (Sampson and Bartusch 1998). As Moore notes, "The loss of popular legitimacy for the criminal justice system produces disastrous consequences for the system's performance. If citizens do not trust the system, they will not use it" (Moore 1997, p. 17).

Legal authorities also seek empowerment from the public. Such empowerment involves the public's legitimization of policing activities and of the role of the police. In particular, the public must be willing to accept the use of discretion by legal authorities. In democratic societies such as the United States, the line between an abridgement of personal freedom and a legitimate policing activity is often controversial and contested. Hence, one important issue is the degree to which the public is willing to empower the police to undertake policing activities. Those activities give the police and the courts discretionary authority to decide whom to arrest and question, and how to dispose of criminal and civil cases.

When the public is unwilling to give authorities the discretion to make judgments, the actions of legal authorities are constrained. For example, concerns about bias in sentencing by judges have led to the use of sentencing guidelines that constrain judges' behavior, while concern about leniency has led to mandatory sentencing laws, such as "three strikes" laws. Concerns about bias among the police have led to recent controversy about racial profiling, which focuses on the role of race in shaping police actions. Granting discretion is linked to viewing the police and courts as legitimate authorities who are entitled to make judgments about how the law should be interpreted and enforced.

II. Reasons for Compliance

Social psychologists argue that one way authorities can gain people's acceptance for decisions that are not in their self-interest is by tapping into people's desire to see justice done. Such justice motivations include the willingness to accept outcomes if they are viewed as being fair (distributive justice) and the willingness to accept outcomes that are arrived at through procedures that are viewed as being fair (procedural justice). Either of these justice motivations could potentially serve as the basis for gaining acceptance for the decisions of legal authorities (Tyler 2000).

A. Reasons for Immediate Compliance

Studies of decision acceptance suggest that it is usually procedural justice that is especially important in shaping people's willingness to defer to the decisions made by legal authorities (Lind and Tyler 1988). In other words, while people could potentially be influenced by either the fairness of the outcomes they receive or the fairness of the procedures by which legal authorities exercise their authority, procedural fairness typically shapes both decision acceptance and evaluations of the decision maker (Tyler et al. 1997; Tyler and Smith 1997).

This does not mean that evaluations of decision fairness are irrelevant. Like assessments of the favorableness of outcomes, distributive justice judgments have a role in shaping people's reactions to their encounters with legal authorities. However, procedural justice judgments consistently are found to have the major influence. In particular, people who receive outcomes that they regard as unfavorable or unfair are more willing to accept those outcomes if they are arrived at through procedures they regard as being fair (Tyler 1990).

This procedural justice influence was first demonstrated empirically by Thibaut and Walker (1975) in a series of laboratory studies of simulated trials. Their studies place people in situations in which they are accused of wrongdoing and have the allegations adjudicated using either an adversary or an inquisitorial system of decision making. Their subjects viewed the adversary system as a fairer procedure. In these simulated trials, people are more accepting of verdicts that resulted from fair trial procedures, independent of the favorableness or fairness of those verdicts. This procedural justice effect is linked to the use of the "fairer" adversary, as opposed to the "less fair" inquisitorial, trial procedure.

Subsequent field studies find that when third parties make their decisions in ways that people view as fair, people are more willing to accept them (MacCoun et al. 1988; Kitzmann and Emery 1993; Lind et al. 1993; Poythress 1994; Wissler 1995; Lind et al. 2000). Procedural justice effects are found in real disputes, in real settings. For example, Lind and colleagues (1993) studied the willingness of disputants to defer to mediation decisions reached in federal court and found that the perceived fairness of mediation shaped deference. Similarly, Lind and colleagues (2000) studied employees fired or laid off from their jobs and showed that if the termination process was judged to be fair, employees were less likely to sue. In the context of child custody disputes, Kitzmann and Emery (1993) found that the fairness of mediation hearings shaped parent satisfaction. Hence, the early experimental work of Thibaut and Walker was strongly confirmed in nonexperimental settings (Lind and Tyler 1988).

Tyler and Huo (2002) directly study the basis of public willingness to accept the decisions of legal authorities during their personal encounters with police officers and judges. They do so in an interview-based study of 1,656 people living in Oakland and Los Angeles, California, each of whom had recently had a personal experience with legal authorities. Participants were asked a series of questions about their recent personal experience, and those questions were linked to their willingness to accept the decisions made by legal authorities about how to handle the situation.

The study finds that two types of factors shape people's deference to legal authorities during personal encounters. The first is linked to outcomes. People's willingness to accept decisions is based in part on the degree to which they regard the decisions made by legal authorities as being fair or favorable. Not surprisingly, people are more willing to accept decisions that provide them with outcomes that they view as desirable or fair or both. When people feel that they have won, they are more willing to accept the decisions made.

People can potentially have contact with legal authorities either because they seek them out for help with problems or because the authorities approach them. People can potentially deal with the police, the courts, or with both. Tyler and Huo (2002) found that the most frequent form of contact in their study involved people calling the police for help. Most personal contact was with the police (85 percent of encounters). However, irrespective of the type of contact involved or the authority involved, the process-based model best accounted for people's willingness to accept the decisions made.

In this model, people are viewed as influenced by non-outcome-based judgments about procedural justice and motive-based trust. First, they defer to the decisions of legal authorities because those authorities are viewed as exercising their authority in fair ways. Second, people are influenced by their judgments about their trust in the motives of the authorities with whom they deal. People are more willing to defer to authorities when they trust their motives. Tyler and Huo (2002) find that procedural justice judgments and judgments about motive-based trust are more important in shaping both decision acceptance and evaluations of legal authority than are evaluations of the fairness or favorableness of the decisions made by those authorities.

The results of a regression analysis illustrating this are shown in table 1. The results shown indicate that both procedural justice and motive-based trust influence decision acceptance and satisfaction with the decision maker. Interestingly, those influences occur beyond any influence of outcome issues or concerns. In fact, 44 percent of the variance in people's willingness to accept decisions is uniquely shaped by procedural justice and motive-based trust, while only 1 percent of the variance is uniquely shaped by outcome judgments.

Tyler and Huo (2002) further find that procedural justice and motive-based trust play the same central role among whites, Hispanics, and African Americans. The results suggest that members of these three ethnic groups have similar concerns when evaluating and reacting to their personal experiences with legal authorities. Tyler and Huo (2002) find, as do many prior studies, that minority group mem-

TABLE 1

Procedural Justice, Motive-Based Trust, and Reactions
to Legal Authorities

	Decision Acceptance/ Satisfaction with the Decision Maker
Beta weights:	
Social motives:	
Motive-based trust	.47***
Procedural justice	.38***
Instrumental motives:	
Distributive justice	.08***
Outcome favorability	.08***
Expected?	−.02
Predictability	.04**
Adjusted R-squared (percent):	
Unique influence of social motives	44
Unique influence of instrumental motives	1
Total	81

Source.—Tyler and Huo 2002.
* $p < .05$.
** $p < .01$.
*** $p < .001$.

bers are less willing to accept the decisions of legal authorities and less satisfied with those authorities with whom they deal (Meares 1997; Sampson and Bartusch 1998; Stuntz 1998). However, as shown in table 2, when we include ethnicity into Tyler and Huo's psychological model (2002), we find that ethnicity effects upon decision acceptance disappear. In other words, minority group members are less likely to accept decisions because they feel unfairly treated.

In addition, procedural justice and motive-based trust are the key factors shaping decision acceptance both when the police imposed themselves on members of the public as part of their social regulatory activities and when people called the police for help. This discussion has focused primarily on issues of gaining compliance. However, people are more likely to have personal contact with legal authorities because they have called them to ask for help than for any other reason. This situation, however, has similar psychological dynamics to those concerning compliance, since the police are often unable to solve people's problems and must seek their acceptance of partial solutions.

TABLE 2

Ethnicity and Decision Acceptance

	Decision Acceptance/Satisfaction with the Decision Maker			
Beta weights:				
African American/White	.13	.09	.16	−.03
Hispanic/White	.15	.09	.13	−.02
Social motives:				
Procedural justice	.75***	. . .	. . .	. . .
Motive-based trust	. . .	.76***	. . .	. . .
Quality of decision making	. . .	. . .	.69***	. . .
Quality of treatment	. . .	. . .	. . .	.68***
Instrumental motives:				
Distributive justice	.11***	.11***	.12***	.13***
Outcome favorability	.11***	.12***	.18***	.16***
Adjusted R-squared (percent)	73	75	68	67

SOURCE.—Tyler and Huo 2002.
* $p < .05$.
** $p < .01$.
*** $p < .001$.

These findings support the suggestion that legal authorities should engage in process-based regulation in which they are attentive to how they treat members of the public. If police officers and judges behave in ways that are experienced as fair, this increases their ability to gain immediate voluntary deference.

B. Reasons for Long-Term Compliance

Procedural justice judgments are especially important in shaping people's behavior over time. People are more willing to buy into a decision and adhere to it later if they feel that it was fairly made. Pruitt and his colleagues studied factors that lead those involved in disputes to adhere to mediation agreements that end those disputes. They interviewed both parties to a mediation six months later to determine which elements of the initial mediation predicted compliance six months later. They find that the procedural fairness of the initial mediation session is a central determinant (Pruitt et al. 1990; Pruitt et al. 1993) and is more important than the quality of the agreement itself.

Another example of the ability of procedural justice to encourage compliance over time is provided by Paternoster and colleagues (1997) who interviewed men who had dealt with the police because of domes-

tic violence calls. They examined which aspects of police behavior predict later compliance and found that procedural justice during the initial encounter predicts the extent of future law abiding behavior. This
suggests that, if the key issue to the police is to encourage long-term
law abidingness among those with whom they deal, they will be more
successful if they focus on treating people in ways experienced as fair.
This fairness judgment was a better predictor of long-term behavior
than were indicators of the severity of police punishment of the initial
domestic violence behavior (i.e., whether the police warned or arrested
the person, the severity of punishments administered, etc.).

The reason procedural justice is a key antecedent of long-term compliance is that it builds up support for people's "buy in" to agreements
and relationships. Procedural justice shapes people's feelings of responsibility and obligation to obey rules and accept decisions because
it enhances the legitimacy of rules and authorities. Procedural justice
also enhances the quality of the relationship among the parties to disputes as well as their mutual relationship to authorities. So, people
continue to accept decisions both because of their respect for the law
and because of their continued commitment to the relationship underlying the conflict or problem about which they dealt with a third-party
authority.

C. Implications for the Exercise of Legal Authority

When people deal with the police and courts, they often receive outcomes that they evaluate as unfavorable, and even unfair. Yet, the success of the legal system depends on the ability of legal authorities to
gain deference to those decisions. One promising approach to addressing this compliance issue is to focus on the procedures through
which legal authorities exercise their authority. Evaluations of the fairness of the procedures experienced when dealing will legal authorities
have a strong influence on people's willingness to accept their decisions and on their evaluations of those authorities.

These findings help us understand why the public often views legal
authorities negatively. Rather than viewing such negative feelings as
the inevitable results of being regulatory authorities, they suggest that
people's feelings are linked to how regulation occurs, that is, to how
legal authorities act. As Sherman et al. (1997) note, "One of the most
striking recent findings is the extent to which the police themselves
create a risk factor for crime simply by using bad manners. Modest but
consistent scientific evidence supports the hypothesis that the less re-

spectful police are towards suspects and citizens generally, the less people will comply with the law. Changing police 'style' may thus be as important as focusing police 'substance.' Making both the style and substance of police practices more 'legitimate' in the eyes of the public, particularly high-risk juveniles, may be one of the most effective long-term police strategies for crime prevention" (p. 8-1).

These findings also suggest how style might be changed to encourage deference to the legal authorities—by focusing on how people are treated and decisions are made when people deal with legal authorities. To better understand what that style should be, we need to examine what issues shape public views about the fairness of legal procedures.

D. What Leads a Procedure to Be Viewed as Fair?

A wide variety of issues influence the degree to which people evaluate a procedure's fairness (Lind and Tyler 1988; Tyler 1988). Further, the importance of procedural criteria varies depending upon the situation (Tyler 1988). For example, when the authorities are managing a dispute, the fairness of their approach is linked to whether they allow disputants to participate in finding a solution to the dispute. However, when people are seeking help with their problems, they are not influenced by participation and evaluate fairness more strongly in terms of whether they think the authority made a good faith effort to help them.

Despite these situational variations, studies consistently point to several elements as key. The literature on the antecedents of trust is less extensive but points to the importance of these same elements (Tyler and Huo 2002).

One key element is the quality of decision making. People think that decisions are being more fairly made when authorities are neutral and unbiased and make their decisions using objective indicators, not their personal views. As a result, evidence of even-handedness and objectivity in decision making enhances perceived fairness (Tyler and Lind 1992). Authorities benefit from openness and explanation, because it provides them an opportunity to communicate evidence that their decision making is neutral.

People also value the quality of their interpersonal treatment by the authorities, whether they feel they are being treated with dignity and respect by the authorities with whom they deal. The quality of interpersonal treatment is consistently found to be a distinct element of procedural fairness, separate from the quality of the decision-making process. Above and beyond the quality of the procedures used in the resolution of their problem, people value being treated with dignity and having their rights acknowledged.

Models of procedural justice focus on two key antecedents of procedural justice: the quality of decision making and the quality of interpersonal treatment. Models of motive-based trust also emphasize these factors and focus on whether people say they understand why the authorities acted as they did and whether people say they share social bonds with those authorities. People are more trusting of the motives of others whose actions they feel they can understand or with whom they feel they have shared social bonds. Trust and procedural justice are closely intertwined—people perceive procedures enacted by those they trust as being fairer, and authorities become more highly trusted when they are seen to exercise their authority in fair ways.

Figure 2 shows an expanded model examining the influence of procedural justice and motive-based trust on decision acceptance and satisfaction with the decision maker. This new model includes the antecedents of procedural justice and motive-based trust that have been

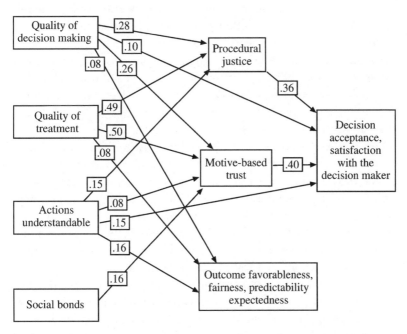

FIG. 2.—Conceptual model for the overall influence of process-based judgments (Tyler and Huo 2002).

outlined. The results suggest that both procedural justice and motive-based trust influence decision acceptance and satisfaction with the decision maker. In addition, they show that the quality of decision making, the quality of interpersonal treatment, and the understandability of actions are antecedents of procedural justice. Quality of interpersonal treatment, the strength of social bonds, and the understandability of actions are antecedents of motive-based trust. In both cases, the primary factor shaping how people reacted to their experience is the quality of their treatment by the authority.

The findings shown in figure 2 suggest that an overall outcome factor, which includes outcome favorableness and fairness, predictability, and expectedness, does not shape decision acceptance. This reinforces the argument that people react primarily to their judgments about the fairness of the procedures they experience and the related assessment of whether they trust the motives of the authority with whom they are dealing.

Early discussions of procedural justice emphasized the importance of participation in the process (Thibaut and Walker 1975). Consistent with that emphasis, people are more satisfied with a procedure that allows them to participate by explaining their situation and communicating their views to the authorities about that situation and how it should be handled. This participation effect makes clear why procedures such as mediation are more popular than the courts. Of primary importance is the ability to state one's views to an authority and to feel that those views are being considered. People are less concerned about their direct control over the decisions made.

Tyler and Huo (2002) suggest that participation does not independently influence assessments of procedural justice. This is consistent with prior analyses of the antecedents of procedural justice (Tyler and Blader 2000). However, participation does have an important indirect influence over procedural justice judgments, because people are more likely to rate the quality of decision making and the quality of interpersonal treatment to be high when the procedure includes opportunities for them to participate. As a result, allowing opportunities to participate is also important in creating fair procedures.

Taken together, these findings suggest some key elements in a procedure that will be generally viewed as being fair. Those elements are that decision making is viewed as being neutral, consistent, rule-based, and without bias; that people are treated with dignity and respect and their rights are acknowledged; and that they have an opportunity to participate in the situation by explaining their perspective and indicating their views about how problems should be resolved.

One important feature of procedures is that there is widespread agreement about the importance of these procedural elements, so that the various parties to a dispute or problem typically have general agreement about the fairness of particular ways of resolving a problem. Studies do not usually find differences in the criteria used to judge the fairness of a procedure that are linked to race, class, or ideology (Tyler 1988, 1994). However, there not is a single procedure that is universally regarded as fair. People's views of the attributes of a fair procedure vary when the procedure is being used to resolve different types of problems. For example, when the police are dealing with a dispute, people rate having opportunities to state their point of view as being key to the fairness of a procedure; but, when the police are trying to solve a problem, people are primarily focused on whether they trust the motives of the officers involved (Tyler 1988).

III. Why Do People Obey the Law and Cooperate with Legal Authorities?

A complicated and interacting set of considerations shapes people's obedience to law and cooperation with legal authorities. These include procedural fairness, legitimacy, and instrumental concerns. We've learned a great deal about these interactions.

A. Instrumental Models of Behavior

Why would people generally comply with, cooperate with, and empower the police or other legal authorities? In this subsection, I contrast three instrumental models—risk, performance, and distributive justice—to the procedural justice that is the focus of this essay.

1. *Risk.* One straightforward and widely noted perspective on social regulation builds upon the basic set of human motivations that are instrumental or "rational" in character. People, as rational self-interested actors, want to minimize their personal costs and maximize their attainment of rewards when dealing with others. This image of the person underlies deterrence, sanctioning, and social control models of social regulation (Nagin 1998).

Such models focus on the ability of legal authorities and institutions to shape people's behavior by threatening to deliver or actually delivering negative sanctions. To implement such strategies, police officers carry guns and clubs and can threaten citizens with physical injury, incapacitation, or financial penalties. Their goal is to establish their authority and "the uniform, badge, truncheon, and arms all may play a role in asserting authority" in the effort to "gain control of the situation" (Reiss 1971, p. 46). The police seek to control the individual's behavior "by manipulating an individual's calculus regarding whether 'crime pays' in the particular instance" (Meares 2000, p. 396). Judges similarly shape people's acceptance of their decisions by threatening fines or even jail time for failure to comply.

Research suggests that the ability to threaten or deliver sanctions is usually effective in shaping people's law-related behavior. In particular, a number of studies on deterrence suggest that people are less likely to engage in illegal behaviors when they think that they might be caught and punished. This core premise of deterrence models is supported by many, but not all, studies examining the factors that shape people's law-related behavior (Paternoster et al. 1983; Paternoster and Iovanni 1986; Paternoster 1987; Tyler 1990; Nagin and Paternoster 1991; Nagin 1998).

Consider a specific policing example. In a study of 346 police encounters with people in Richmond, Virginia, Mastrofski, Snipes, and Supina (1996) asked neutral observers to rate interactions between members of the public and the police. They found that the coercive balance of power between the police and members of the public shaped the degree of compliance on the part of the public. As would be expected based upon a deterrence model, people complied in the face of superior police power.

Studies of deterrence also point to factors that limit the likely effectiveness of deterrence models. Perhaps the key factor limiting the value of deterrence strategies is the consistent finding that deterrence effects, when found, are small in magnitude. For example, in a review of studies of deterrence of drug use, MacCoun (1993) found that around 5 percent of the variance in drug use behavior can be explained by variations in the expected likelihood or severity of punishment. This suggests that much variance in law-related behavior flows from factors other than risk estimates.

A further possible limitation of deterrence strategies is that, while deterrence effects can potentially be influenced by estimates either of the certainty of punishment or its severity, studies suggest that both factors are not equally effective. Unfortunately from a policy perspective, certainty more strongly influences people's behavior than severity, and certainty is the more difficult to change.

When legal authorities heighten the likelihood of being caught and punished or the severity of punishment, they are increasing the objective risks that law-breaking behavior will lead to costs for the law-breaker. The assumption is that these changes will alter people's subjective estimates of the likelihood and severity of punishment for wrongdoing, and, as a consequence, lead to lower levels of rule breaking. Research suggests that deterrence effects are more strongly associated with people's estimates of the likelihood of being caught and punished than they are by the anticipated severity of punishment (Paternoster and Iovanni 1986; Paternoster 1987; Nagin and Paternoster 1991). The implication is that efforts to increase compliance need to focus on increasing the presence of the police to encourage apprehension or on raising the likelihood of conviction in the courts. Efforts to lower the crime rate by intensifying penalties—for example, the recent proliferation of death penalty laws—are likely to be less effective.

Focusing on people's estimates of the likelihood of being caught and punished highlights another reason why deterrence approaches have difficulty shaping public compliance—the occurrence of threshold effects. To influence people's behavior, risk estimates need to be high enough to exceed some threshold of psychological meaningfulness (Teevan 1975; Ross 1982).

In most actual situations, the objective risk of being caught and punished is quite low. For example, according to an analysis of crime and arrest rates, the objective risk of being caught, convicted, and imprisoned for rape is about 12 percent; for robbery 4 percent; and for assault, burglary, larceny, and motor vehicle theft 1 percent (Robinson and Darley 1997). Of course, the psychological or subjective estimates of risk are the key to people's behavior, not the objective risk.

Ross (1982) uses drunk driving to outline the problems associated with using deterrence to shape law-related behavior. He suggests that raising risk estimates to a level that is high enough to lower the rate of law-breaking behavior, while not impossible, involves prohibitively high costs in terms of police manpower and citizen willingness to accept state intrusions into their personal lives. Interestingly, Ross finds that changes in laws can lead to short-term declines in law breaking because the high level of media exposure to police activities leads people to overestimate the risks of being caught and punished. However, as this heightened publicity fades over time, people's actual experience leads them to make more realistic risk estimates, which are lower, and those low risk estimates are not enough to deter law-breaking behavior. These findings make clear that risk estimates, if they are high enough, deter law-breaking behavior, but it is difficult to sustain such high risk estimates with the level of police activity typically associated with efforts to limit everyday crimes.

Ross argues that it is difficult to implement deterrence approaches within the political realities of democratic societies. Ross points out that even the intensive efforts of Scandinavian authorities to create high estimates of risk by using random road blocks and other similar expensive and intrusive law enforcement measures are insufficient to create and maintain subjective risk estimates that are high enough to deter drunk driving over the long term.

Of course, many of the problems associated with deterrence-based strategies are structural and involve variations in the degree to which the police are able to monitor people's law-related behavior. This suggests that there are situations in which deterrence strategies will be more or less effective. The two key variables are the ease of behavioral surveillance and the level of resources that society is willing to devote to surveillance. The influence of the conduciveness of the situation to surveillance on the rate of law-breaking behavior is illustrated by tax payments. If people are wage earners, their income is recorded, and the possibility of hiding cheating is low. In a setting of this type the opportunities for effective deterrence of law-breaking behavior are high.

The issue of societal resources is illustrated by considering the case of murder. The objective risk of being caught and punished for murder is high (around 45 percent; Robinson and Darley 1997) because society has committed considerable resources to resolving this type of crime. The likelihood of being caught is high enough for deterrence to be effective in lowering the murder rate (to be above the threshold at which risk shapes behavior; Teevan 1975).

The example of the deterrence of murder makes clear that one element in any deterrence strategy is the need and the willingness to devote resources to surveillance. Instrumental approaches are not self-sustaining and require the maintenance of institutions and authorities that can keep the probability of detection for wrongdoing at a sufficiently high level to motivate the public.

The effectiveness of "instrumental means of producing compliance always depend[s] on resource limits" (Meares 2000, p. 401). The question is how much of the resources society is willing to deploy to control crime, and how much power to intrude into people's lives legal authorities are allowed to have. Those resources need to be deployed in strategic and effective ways. Sherman (1998), for example, notes that police resources within the United States are typically deployed more in response to political pressures than to actual crime threats, with the consequence that the ability of the police to deter crime is nonoptimal.

The murder example illustrates another important limit to deterrence strategies. They are more effective in relation to crimes that are committed for instrumental reasons. For example, car theft, burglary, and crimes of this type are typically motivated by calculations about costs and benefits. However, other crimes are more expressively motivated and are, as a consequence, more strongly shaped by a person's emotional state and by events of the moment. Crimes of this type, such as rape and many murders, occur on the "spur of the moment" and in the "heat of passion." Such crimes are less strongly influenced by deterrence considerations, irrespective of the possibility of being caught and punished for wrongdoing.

The problem faced by those responsible for the everyday law enforcement is that, for most crimes, the resources devoted to law enforcement are low and the opportunities for cheating are high. As a consequence, deterrence strategies are unlikely to be a sufficient basis for effective social regulation. Deterrence can form the foundation of efforts to maintain the legal order but cannot be a complete strategy for gaining compliance (Ayres and Braithwaite 1992). To have an effective strategy for dealing with public compliance, we would benefit from being in a situation in which people have additional reasons for obeying the law beyond their fear of being caught and punished for wrongdoing (Tyler 1990; Sherman 1993, 1998, 1999).

2. *Performance.*   A second model links public behavior to evaluations of the effectiveness of the authorities. This perspective argues that people will cooperate with the police and courts when they see those authorities as being able to manage problems in their community. In the case of the police and courts, the problem being managed is social disorder.

As an example of strategies of regulation linked to performance, aggressive policing strategies, such as "zero tolerance" for minor crimes, are based on the view that the key goal of policing is to manage crime in communities effectively. The role of the police, in other words, is to assert authority over minor crimes and "lifestyle" offenses. By so doing, the police communicate to the public that they can and will manage crime and disorder effectively. The public responds by cooperating with police efforts.

3. *Distributive justice.*   A third model links public behavior and policy support to issues of police fairness in the distribution of their services and protection across the community. Here the issue is whether the police fairly distribute police services, providing "equal protection to all." Sarat (1977) argues that the demand for equal treatment is a core theme running through public evaluations of the police and the courts. He suggests that the "perception of unequal treatment is the single most important source of popular dissatisfaction with the American legal system. According to available survey evidence, Americans believe that the ideal of equal protection, which epitomizes what they find most valuable in their legal system, is betrayed by police, lawyers, judges, and other legal officials" (Sarat 1977, p. 434). This argument roots evaluations of the police and public reactions to them in views about how they distribute public resources and services.

B. Procedural Justice Models of Motivation

The procedural justice model involves two stages. The first involves the argument that public behavior is rooted in evaluations of the legitimacy of the police and courts. People's social values—in this case, their feelings of obligation and responsibility to obey legitimate authorities—are viewed as key antecedents of public behavior. In other words, people cooperate with the police and courts in their everyday lives when they view those authorities as legitimate and entitled to be obeyed.

The second involves the antecedents of legitimacy. The procedural justice argument is that process-based assessments are the key antecedent of legitimacy (Tyler 1990). In this analysis, four indicators—summary judgments of procedural justice, inferences of motive-based trust, judgments about the fairness of decision making, and judgments about the fairness of interpersonal treatment—are treated as indices of an overall assessment of procedural justice in the exercise of authority. These arguments, taken together, lead to the model shown in figure 3.

One particular advantage of procedural justice is that it leads to compliance over time. This suggests that experiencing procedural justice changes people's values concerning the law. The particular value of importance in this discussion is legitimacy—the belief that legal authorities are entitled to be obeyed. In other words, when people expe-

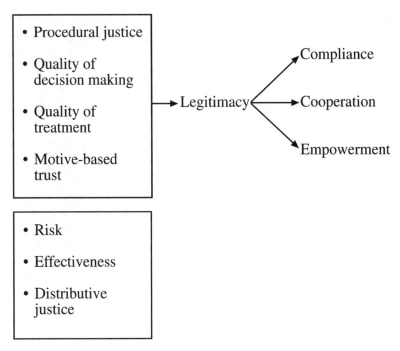

Fig. 3.—Conceptual view of the process-based model of regulation

rience procedural justice, their feelings of responsibility and obligation to obey the law increase. This leads to compliance that is sustained over time. Here that argument is expanded to address the motivations underlying people's everyday behavior. If people view law as legitimate, they generally follow it. That view, in turn, is linked to the manner in which people view the authorities as conducting themselves when they engage in regulatory activities.

C. Legitimacy

The model outlined is based on one distinct social value—legitimacy. Legitimacy is the property that a rule or an authority has when others feel obligated to defer voluntarily. In other words, a legitimate authority is an authority regarded by people as entitled to have their decisions and rules accepted and followed by others (French and Raven 1959). The roots of the modern discussion of legitimacy are usually traced to Weber's writings on authority and the social dynamics of authority (Weber 1968).

Weber argues that the ability to issue commands that will be obeyed does not rest solely upon the possession and ability to use power. In addition, there are rules that people will voluntarily obey and authorities whose directives will be voluntarily followed. Legitimacy, therefore, is a quality possessed by an authority, a law, or an institution that leads others to feel obligated to obey its decisions and directives. It is "a quality attributed to a regime by a population" (Merelman 1966, p. 548).

Similar views of responsibility and obligation are also articulated by other social scientists. As Hoffman notes: "The legacy of both Sigmund Freud and Emile Durkheim is the agreement among social scientists that most people do not go through life viewing society's moral norms as external, coercively imposed pressures to which they must submit. Though the norms are initially external to the individual and often in conflict with [a person's] desires, the norms eventually become part of [a person's] internal motive system and guide [a person's] behavior even in the absence of external authority. Control by others is thus replaced by self control [through a process labeled internalization]" (Hoffman 1977, p. 85).

The key issue Durkheim and Freud addressed is the personal taking on of obligations and responsibilities that become self-regulating, so that people acknowledge and act on internal values that lead to deference to society, social rules, and authorities. However, Hoffman, like Durkheim and Freud, focuses on the development of moral values. Those values lead to self-regulatory behavior, but behavior in which people take the responsibility to bring what they do into line with their views about what is right and wrong (Darley, Tyler, and Bilz 2002).

More recently, Beetham (1991) has also addressed issues of legitimacy. Like Weber, Beetham suggests that legitimacy is distinct from issues of rational choice or self-interest and that people relate to the powerful both as moral agents and as self-interested actors. He argues that people cooperate and comply for reasons of legitimacy, and in response to estimates of potential risk or gain from rule following or rule breaking. Beetham suggests that legitimacy is necessary in almost all situations of authority, except for rare cases such as slavery, and that it is central to the maintenance of order, to obtaining cooperation from subordinates, and to effective performance of government.

Sparks and Bottoms (1995) and Sparks, Bottoms, and Hay (1996) support the argument that legitimacy has wide importance by showing that it matters even in highly coercive environments such as prisons. They compare two prison environments, differing in their legitimacy in the eyes of prisoners. Their work suggests that when prisoners view prison as more legitimate, there is less individual and collective disorder. They argue that legitimacy develops out of the use of fair procedures and the provision of respectful treatment.

Kelman and Hamilton (1989) refer to legitimacy as "authorization" to reflect the idea that a person authorizes an authority to determine appropriate behavior within some situation and then feels obligated to follow the directives or rules that authority establishes. As they indicate, the authorization of actions by authorities "seem[s] to carry automatic justification for them. Behaviorally, authorization obviates the necessity of making judgments or choices. Not only do normal moral principles become inoperative, but—particularly when the actions are explicitly ordered—a different type of morality, linked to the duty to obey superior orders, tends to take over" (Kelman and Hamilton 1989, p. 16).

One way to think about legitimacy is as a property of an institution or group of authorities. For example, studies of confidence in government ask people to rate the overall government, and its institutions and authorities. Studies of the legitimacy of legal authorities similarly ask people to evaluate their general feelings of responsibility and obligation to obey the law and legal authorities.

This essay focus on the internalization of the obligation to obey authorities, as opposed to the internalization of the responsibility to follow principles of personal morality (for discussions of morality, see Robinson and Darley 1995; Tyler and Darley 2000; Darley, Tyler, and Bilz 2002). This feeling of responsibility reflects a willingness to suspend personal considerations of self-interest and to ignore personal moral values because a person thinks that an authority or a rule is entitled to determine appropriate behavior within a given situation or situations.

Researchers have measured legitimacy in a variety of ways. In the case of local laws and legal authorities, studies have often used an index of perceived obligation to obey. Typical items from such a scale, in this case drawn from Tyler (1990), include "People should obey the law even if it goes against what they think is right" (82 percent yes); "I always try to follow the law, even if I think it is wrong" (82 percent yes); "Disobeying the law is seldom justified" (79 percent yes); "It is difficult to break the law and keep one's self-respect" (69 percent yes); "If a person is doing something, and a police officer tells them to stop, they should stop even if they feel that what they are doing is legal" (84 percent); and "If a person goes to court because of a dispute with another person, and the judge orders them to pay money to the other person, they should pay that person money, even if they think the judge is wrong" (74 percent yes).

The perceived obligation to obey is the most direct extension of the concept of legitimacy. This sense of obligation can be directly measured ("I should obey") or it can be asked in a situation of conflict with the person's feelings about what is right or desirable ("I should obey when I disagree"; "I should obey when I think the decision is wrong").

Building on studies by political scientists, and Easton's conceptual framework (Easton and Dennis 1969), legitimacy has been measured in terms of support, allegiance, institutional trust, or confidence. Drawing on this literature, Tyler (1990) measured legitimacy by asking people's agreement with the statements "I have a great deal of respect for the Chicago police," "On the whole Chicago police officers are honest," "I feel proud of the Chicago police," and "I feel that I should support the Chicago police."

An additional measure, along these same lines, is to measure legitimacy using a thermometer to register positive or negative feeling. Tyler and Huo (2002) ask people to rate the police on a thermometer ranging from zero to ten, with five being the middle rating. People are asked to think about how warmly they feel about the police and to give a temperature rating on this scale.

More recently, legitimacy has been conceptualized as lack of cynicism about the law (Ewick and Silbey 1998). This analysis considers the degree to which people feel that the law and legal authorities represent their interests, as opposed to the interests of those in power. Based upon this model, Tyler and Huo (2002) operationalized cynicism using several items, including "The law represents the values of the people in power, rather than the values of people like me," "People in power use the law to try to control people like me," and "The law does not protect my interests." This approach is designed to establish the degree to which people feel that legal authorities are not motivated to protect their interests (i.e., as not legitimate).

D. Testing the Model

Four studies test the dynamics of the process-based model of regulation. Tyler (1990) reports the results of a panel study of residents in Chicago. Tyler, Casper, and Fisher (1989) report the findings of a panel study of a group of individuals charged with felonies. Sunshine and Tyler (2003) report the results of two studies of the residents of New York City. Tyler (2001*a*) presents the results of secondary analyses of four studies of public opinion about the police and the courts.

1. *Tyler (1990).* My early work on regulation explored the antecedents of people's everyday compliance with the law (Tyler 1990). I used the results of telephone interviews conducted with a random sample of Chicago residents to examine the basis of public compliance with the law. The study uses a panel design with 1,575 residents interviewed during wave 1 and 804 reinterviewed one year later. Each was asked about recent personal experiences with the police or courts and about their general views concerning the legitimacy of these authorities.

The results suggest that legitimacy has an important role in shaping compliance with the law. Those members of the public who feel that the law is legitimate and ought to be obeyed, and who have institutional trust in legal authorities, are more likely to follow the law. Using regression analyses, the study examines the ability of a combined measure of legitimacy to influence compliance with the law. Legitimacy is found to have an independent influence on compliance, even when controls are placed upon estimates of the risk of being caught and punished, peer disapproval, the morality of law breaking, performance evaluations of the authorities, and demographic characteristics. This was true both for an analysis of the wave 1 cross-sectional sample of 1,575 and for a panel study of 804 of these respondents reinterviewed one year later.

One particularly compelling test involved examining the relationship between legitimacy and compliance at time 2, controlling for compliance at time 1. This analysis, which makes use of the panel features of the study, is shown in table 3. Again, legitimacy has a unique significant influence on compliance.

Further, it is true of both white and minority group respondents. When separate subgroup analyses were conducted among the three major demographic groups in the sample—whites ($n = 826$), African Americans ($n = 520$), and Hispanics ($n = 154$)—influences of legitimacy on compliance were found among the members of each ethnic group (see table 4). These analyses suggest that legitimacy is an important influence on compliance with the law that is distinct from the influence of risk assessments or demographic background.

The second important finding in that study is that using fair procedures is the way for legal authorities to tap into people's feelings of

TABLE 3

Does Legitimacy Influence Compliance?

	Compliance at Time 2 (Beta Weights)
Beta weights:	
Legitimacy at time 2	.11*
Risk at time 2	.10*
Race	.00
Compliance at time 1	.65*
Adjusted R-squared (percent)	51

Source.—Tyler 1990. Wave 2 findings for panel data.
Note.—$n = 804$.
* $p < .05$.
** $p < .01$.
*** $p < .001$.

responsibility and obligation to defer to their rules and decisions. Hence, procedural justice is the key to voluntary compliance. Tyler (1990) uses the impact of personal experiences with police officers and judges upon views about the legitimacy of legal authorities to establish this procedural justice influence.

I used the results of the panel analysis to explore the impact of personal experience upon legitimacy and performance evaluations to un-

TABLE 4

Compliance with the Law

	Whites ($n = 826$)	African Americans ($n = 520$)	Hispanics ($n = 154$)
Beta weights:			
Legitimacy of legal authorities	.25*	.15*	.19*
Risk	.13*	.14*	.14
Income	.07*	.09*	.01
Education	.03	.08	.00
Gender	.31*	.25*	.25*
Age	.08*	.04	.16*
Adjusted R-squared (percent)	21	14	12

Source.—Tyler 1990. Respondents are those interviewed in wave 1 of the panel data.
Note.—$n = 1,575$.
* $p < .05$.
** $p < .01$.
*** $p < .001$.

derstand the procedural justice findings. In the study, 804 residents were interviewed at two times, one year apart. In each interview, respondents were asked to indicate how legitimate they judged legal authorities to be and to assess the quality of their job performance. During the one-year interval, 329 of the 804 respondents had a personal experience with legal authorities. This subsample was asked to evaluate two aspects of their experiences: the outcome and the procedures used to reach those outcomes. In the case of outcomes, respondents evaluated the fairness of the outcome they received (distributive justice), the favorableness of their outcome, and the degree to which that outcome equaled, exceeded, or failed to match their prior expectations. For procedures, respondents were asked to evaluate the fairness of the procedures, and the degree to which that procedure equaled, exceeded, or failed to match their prior expectations.

The results, shown in figure 4, indicate that procedural justice is the aspect of personal experience that most strongly influences legitimacy. Of the five judgments outlined, only procedural justice evaluations play a role in shaping postexperience evaluations of legitimacy. This suggests that a key antecedent of legitimacy is the procedural fairness that people have experienced during their past personal experiences with legal authorities. These procedural fairness judgments are found to affect people's general views about legitimacy. They also affect their performance evaluations.

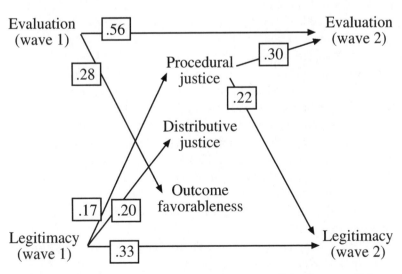

Fig. 4.—Does procedural justice influence legitimacy? (Tyler 1990; $n = 804$)

2. *Tyler, Casper, and Fisher (1989).*   Other work also supports this focus on procedural justice. Tyler, Casper, and Fisher (1989) used a panel design to interview 628 people accused of felonies. Those people were interviewed prior to and following the adjudication of their cases. The question addressed was how the experience of going through the criminal justice system influenced people's views about that system and its authorities.

The results indicate that procedural justice is the key factor shaping people's overall orientations toward legal authorities, government, and law. Neither outcome fairness nor outcome favorableness separately influenced people's views about the legal system. Hence, as in Tyler (1990), procedural justice was the key aspect of experience that shaped people's views about law and legal authorities.

3. *Sunshine and Tyler (2003).*   Sunshine and Tyler (2003) explored the role of legitimacy in shaping compliance, cooperation, and empowerment. They did so using the findings of two surveys of residents in New York City. The first, a sample of 483 residents, was asked to evaluate the New York City Police Department (NYPD) during spring–summer 2001. The sample was drawn from registered voters who responded to a mailed questionnaire and was weighted to reflect the city's ethnic, educational, and gender composition. The second sample was of 1,653 residents asked to evaluate the NYPD during the summer of 2002. This sample was drawn by random digit dialing and weighted to reflect ethnicity.

The study addresses two issues: whether the legitimacy of the police shapes compliance, cooperation, and empowerment; and whether legitimacy is linked to procedural fairness. At both levels, these influences were contrasted to the influence of the three instrumental judgments already outlined: distributive fairness, police effectiveness, and the likelihood of a serious risk of being sanctioned.

The regression analyses shown in table 5 based on data from the first sample indicate that legitimacy independently shapes cooperation, compliance, and empowerment. This is found even when controls are included for each of the three instrumental judgments. Of course, as we might expect, those instrumental judgments are also important. Risks of being caught and punished shape compliance, while judgments of the distributive fairness of the police shape empowerment.

A further analysis suggests that the key antecedent of legitimacy is procedural justice (table 6). It supports the general argument being advanced here by suggesting the key role of procedural justice assess-

TABLE 5

Influences on Compliance, Cooperation, and Empowerment, Study 1

	Compliance	Compliance (Tobit)	Cooperation	Empowerment
Legitimacy	.22**	.14***	.30***	.40***
Distributive justice	−.09	−.05	−.06	.21***
Performance	−.08	−.06	.11	.06
Risk	.18***	.07*	.04	.03
Ethnicity	−.11*	−.14*	−.19***	.05
Age	.08	.03	.07	.04
Education	.08	.04	.12*	−.02
Income	.17**	.05	.14**	−.10*
Gender	.10*	.13**	−.05	.01
Adjusted R-squared (percent)	9	. . .	14	40

Source.—Sunshine and Tyler 2003.

Note.—All entries are standardized beta weights. Sample is weighted by ethnicity, income, and education.

* $p < .05$.
** $p < .01$.
*** $p < .001$.

TABLE 6

Influences on Legitimacy, Study 1

	Legitimacy
Procedural justice	.62***
Distributive justice	.11**
Performance	.20***
Risk	−.03
Ethnicity	.01
Age	.03
Education	−.08*
Income	.05
Gender	.03
Adjusted R-squared (percent)	73

Source.—Sunshine and Tyler 2003.

Note.—All entries are standardized beta weights. They indicate the independent influence each variable has on the dependent variable. Sample is weighted by ethnicity, income, and education.

* $p < .05$.
** $p < .01$.
*** $p < .001$.

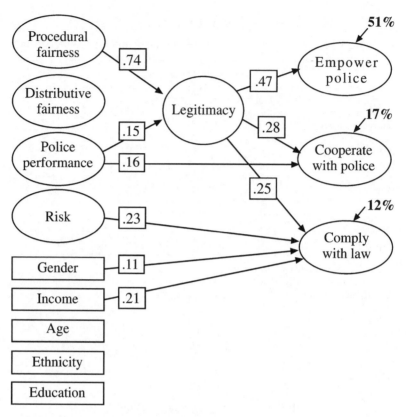

FIG. 5.—Structural equation model for study 1: testing the process-based model of regulation (Sunshine and Tyler 2003).

ments in conferring or undermining the legitimacy of the police. In addition, the police are viewed as more legitimate if they distribute services fairly and if they perform more effectively in fighting crime.

These two analyses are combined into one overall model, shown in figure 5. It supports the basic process-based regulation argument by showing that legitimacy shapes all three forms of public connection to legal authorities—compliance, cooperation, and empowerment. Further, legitimacy is shaped primarily by procedural justice. This analysis does not suggest that instrumental factors are irrelevant, because they are not. Rather it suggests that there is an independent influence of process-based judgments.

This overall analysis was replicated using data from the second sam-

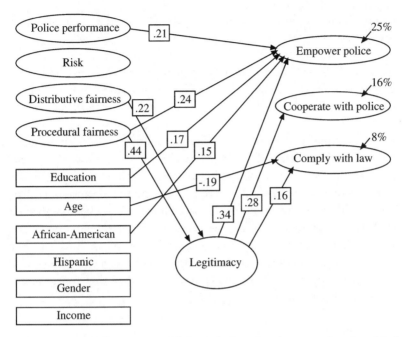

Fig. 6.—Structural equation model for study 2: testing the process-based model of regulation (Sunshine and Tyler 2003).

ple. Results are shown in figure 6. Again, the model supports the basic process-based regulation argument by showing that legitimacy shapes all three forms of public connection to legal authorities—compliance, cooperation, and empowerment. Legitimacy is again primarily linked to procedural justice.

Procedural justice matters when people are making general evaluations of the police or courts by expressing their degree of trust and confidence. Such institutional evaluations are important because they express political support for the legal system and its authorities.

4. *Tyler (2001a).* Tyler (2001a) explored the factors underlying public trust and confidence using data from several survey-based studies of the police and courts. The studies look at the general population rather than focusing on people with personal experiences. Further, people are asked about their overall evaluations of legal authorities, rather than about their willingness to accept particular decisions. The analysis contrasts the influence of performance evaluations (judgments about whether the police are effectively controlling crime) with judg-

ments about the fairness of police treatment of citizens. It compares their importance as antecedents to confidence in the police.

The findings (Tyler 2001a) suggest that people, when evaluating the police and the courts, consider both their effectiveness in controlling crime and their procedural fairness. The major factor, however, is consistently found to be the fairness of the manner in which the police and the courts are believed to treat citizens when exercising their authority.

For example, a study of 346 Oakland, California, residents living in high crime areas found that the primary factor shaping overall evaluations of the police was the quality of their treatment of community residents (which explained 26 percent of the unique variance in evaluations), with a secondary influence of performance evaluations (which explained 5 percent of the unique variance). Similarly, a national survey of 1,826 people's views about local and state courts shows that the primary source of public discontent is the judgment that people receive poor quality treatment from the courts, rather than that court performance is of poor quality.

E. Implications

These findings on the evaluation of legal institutions also support the process-based model of regulation. We already knew that people shaped their reactions to their personal experiences by focusing on the procedural fairness of their treatment. We now know that they also shape their evaluations of the police and courts as institutions of government by attention to whether they think that these authorities generally treat members of the public fairly.

Both Sunshine and Tyler (2003) and Tyler (2001a) found that these conclusions apply equally strongly to white and minority respondents. Those within both groups evaluate legal authorities in basically the same way. It might be speculated, for example, that whites would be less concerned about fair treatment, since minorities are the primary target of disrespect by the police and courts. However, no such evidence is found. Both whites and minorities are influenced by quality of treatment issues and judgments of procedural justice.

Of course, it is important to remember that these findings are linked to the subjective fairness of the procedures people experience. They are concerned about regulation as it is experienced by the people being regulated. From the perspective of the legal authorities, the thoughts and feelings of members of the public are primarily important because they shape whether those people comply with the law and cooperate with the authorities. In this sense, personal experiences can be thought of as adult socialization experiences that teach people about the nature of legal authority. These evolving views about law and legal authority, in turn, shape people's law-related behaviors.

While these findings suggest that the key to socialization during personal experience is the fairness of the procedure experienced by members of the public when they deal with legal authorities, the subjectivity of such experiences directs our attention to the psychology of procedural justice. When we look at the fairness ratings of various legal forums, it becomes clear that such subjective judgments can deviate from procedural justice as it is thought of by legal scholars. For example, Tyler, Casper, and Fisher (1989) examined criminal justice procedures and found that people rate plea bargaining to be fairer than a trial, while studies of civil justice often find that people rate mediation to be fairer than a trial (Tyler 1988). Hence, subjectively fair procedures should not be viewed as equivalent to normatively fair procedures. However, they are the procedures that shape people's behavior. For example, mediation encourages compliance (McEwen and Maiman 1984).

IV. The Impact of Legitimacy on Decision Acceptance during a Personal Experience

One argument for the importance of general legitimacy is that it influences what people do during personal interactions with police officers and judges. The question is whether people's views about the legitimacy of these legal authorities influence how people act during their personal experiences, how they evaluate those experiences and the authorities with whom they have them, and whether they cooperate and defer to the decisions made by the police officers with whom they are dealing.

We would expect, based upon theories of legitimacy, that people who view legal authorities as more legitimate, and hence more entitled to be obeyed, would be more likely to defer to legal authorities, accepting their decisions about how to resolve problems or how to restrict their own behavior. We would predict that consent and cooperation would be greater when people think authorities are legitimate. Further, we would predict that such cooperation is more likely to result in continued adherence to the decisions and agreements made during those personal encounters. Authorities want to gain cooperation and consent in the immediate situation.

TABLE 7

What Shapes the Willingness to Defer in Specific Personal
Encounters with Legal Authorities?

	Willingness to Accept the Decision/Satisfaction with the Decision Maker
Beta weights:	
How favorable/fair was the decision in the encounter?	.40***
General legitimacy of legal authorities	.36*
Adjusted R-squared (percent)	38

Source.—Tyler and Huo 2002.
Note.—$n = 1,656$.
* $p < .05$.
** $p < .01$.
*** $p < .001$.

Tyler and Huo (2002) found that, as predicted, people are more willing to accept the decisions of police officers and judges in a given situation if they regard those authorities as being generally legitimate legal authorities (see table 7). Hence, general legitimacy facilitates decision acceptance.

This study illustrates the potential benefits of legitimacy for legal authorities. If a police officer or judge comes into a personal encounter representing an institution that people regard as more legitimate, they are more likely to accept decisions. So, as predicted by theories of legitimacy, legitimacy encourages consent and cooperation.

Tyler and Huo (2002) found that the procedural justice has an important role in shaping people's willingness to consent and cooperate with the police. People who view authorities as legitimate generally decide whether to accept the decisions of police officers based upon whether they are fairly made. People who view authorities as illegitimate generally decide whether to accept the decisions of police officers based upon whether they perceive those decisions to be fair or favorable. This is shown in table 8 by the presence of an interaction between legitimacy and procedural justice, and in table 9 by differences in the weight given to procedural justice in the high and low legitimacy subgroups. Since the police are often in situations in which they cannot provide people with outcomes that they view as fair or favorable, the police benefit if people defer to their decisions because those decisions are fairly made.

TABLE 8

What Shapes Reactions to Personal Experiences
with Legal Authorities?

	Willingness to Accept the Decision/Satisfaction with the Decision Maker
Beta weights:	
Procedural fairness in the situation (A)	.77*
Favorability/fairness of the outcome in the situation (B)	.11*
Overall legitimacy of legal authorities (C)	.05*
A * C	.06*
B * C	−.01
Adjusted R-squared (percent)	80

SOURCE.—Tyler and Huo 2002.
NOTE.—$n = 1,656$.
* $p < .05$.
** $p < .01$.
*** $p < .001$.

TABLE 9

Subgroup Analysis

	Decision Acceptance/ Satisfaction with the Decision Maker
Low legitimacy:	
Beta weights:	
Process judgments	.74
Outcome judgments	.10
Adjusted R-squared (percent)	75
High legitimacy:	
Beta weights:	
Process judgments	.83
Outcome judgments	.00
Adjusted R-squared (percent)	75

SOURCE.—Tyler and Huo 2002.
NOTE.—Separate regression analyses for subgroups representing those high and low in general legitimacy.
* $p < .05$.
** $p < .01$.
*** $p < .001$.

In other words, Tyler and Huo (2002) demonstrated that legitimacy changes the basis upon which people decide whether to cooperate. They contrast two reasons for deferring to the decisions made by police officers and judges: first, because the decisions are viewed as desirable—they are seen as being a fair resolution to the issues involved in the encounter or as providing desirable outcomes such as letting the person go free without arrest, and, second, because the police officers or judges involved are seen as exercising their authority in fair ways. The findings suggest that those who view legal authorities as more legitimate rely more heavily on procedural justice judgments when deciding whether to accept decisions.

These findings show that legitimacy has two positive influences on policing. The first is that people who view the police to be legitimate are generally more willing to defer to the directives of particular police officers. The second is that people who view the police to be legitimate evaluate particular police officers in more strongly procedural terms. For both of these reasons, Tyler and Huo (2002) advocate a proactive strategy of regulation in which the police act in ways that build and maintain legitimacy.

Separate analyses among the various ethnic groups studied by Tyler and Huo (2002) suggest that these legitimacy effects are found among whites, African Americans, and Hispanics. Within each group, the willingness to accept the decisions made by particular police officers is linked to people's views about the overall legitimacy of law and legal authorities. If people view the police as legitimate, they are more willing to accept decisions. Further, within each group, legitimacy facilitates process-based deference to particular police officers.

While Tyler and Huo (2002) focused on the police, interactions with the courts were also considered. The police became the primary focus of attention because 85 percent of subjects' personal experiences were with the police. However, the psychological processes underlying acceptance or resistance to decisions were found to be similar irrespective of which type of authority was involved, suggesting that the arguments apply equally strongly to the police and the courts. Many other studies of courts also strongly support a process-based model (MacCoun et al. 1988; Tyler, Casper, and Fisher 1989; Lind et al. 1993; Wissler 1995).

V. The Idea of a Self-Regulating Society

The distinction between instrumental judgments and legitimacy as antecedents of compliance with the law highlights the possibility of two types of legal culture. The first builds public compliance on the basis of people's concerns about the possibility of being caught and punished. Such a deterrence-based society depends upon the ability of legal authorities to create and maintain a credible threat of punishment for wrongdoing. The studies outlined demonstrate that, while deterrence influences law-related behavior, the social context of democratic societies makes it difficult for authorities to engage in the levels of surveillance needed to sustain a viable legal system simply based upon deterrence.

The important role legitimacy plays in shaping people's law-related behavior indicates the possibility of a self-regulating society in which citizens internalize values that lead to voluntary deference to the law and to legal authorities. Such a society is based upon consent and cooperation. That cooperation develops from people's own feelings about appropriate social behavior and is not linked to risks of apprehension and punishment. Tyler (2001*a*) refers to such a society as a law-abiding society. The studies outlined make clear that such a society is possible. If people think authorities are legitimate, they are more likely to obey them.

A law-abiding society cannot be created overnight through changes in the allocation of resources within government agencies, changes that would alter the expected gains or risks associated with compliance. It depends upon the socialization of appropriate social and moral values among children and the maintenance of those values among adults (Tyler and Darley 2000; Tyler 2001*b*).

Evidence suggests that a core element to the creation and maintenance of such social values is the judgment that legal authorities exercise their authority following fair procedures. This is true both during personal experiences with the police and the courts and in general evaluations of these authorities.

While the process-based approach to regulation proposed here is based upon the results of studies of public reactions to the police and the courts, similar argument have been advanced by others based upon their observations of police interactions with members of the public. Wilson (1968) described a service style of policing that is similar in many ways to the process-based model. Similarly, Muir's (1977) discussion of what constitutes a good police officer notes the importance of treating people with dignity and respect.

The difference in the approach taken here lies in the effort to provide empirical support for the value of a particular style of policing as part of a broader effort to provide an empirically grounded model of effectiveness in regulation, as one element in a broader "evidence-based" approach to crime prevention (Sherman et al. 2002). This effort involves assessing the impact of policing on the members of the public who deal with the police.

This approach constitutes a useful general approach to the exercise of police authority. While not all people respond to fair processes, the work outlined suggests that such an approach is broadly effective. In particular, it is effective within the subgroup of the population that is the particular target of policing activity—the young minority male.

VI. Racial Profiling as an Example

Issues of racial profiling have recently been central to public discussions of police-community relations. President George W. Bush has condemned racial profiling. Both Congress and a number of states have considered or passed laws designed to lessen racial profiling. More than 80 percent of Americans have said that they "disapprove" of racial profiling (Gallup poll, December 1999). Racial profiling has been blamed for a variety of ills, from friction between the police and minority communities to overall decreased confidence in and cooperation with the police.

Racial profiling—situations in which legal authorities act, at least in part, based on the race of a person—can be considered from a number of perspectives. Legal scholarship focuses on whether and when profiling based on ascribed characteristics such as race, gender, or age is or ought to be illegal (Kadish 1997; Harris 1999; Thompson 1999; Meeks 2000; Knowles and Persico 2001). Criminologists try to determine how often profiling based upon ascribed characteristics occurs (Lamberth 1998; Rudovsky 2001). Police institutions have focused on profiling as a reflection of possible racism among legal authorities that leads to "bias based" policing (Fridell et al. 2001). These perspectives differ in their specific focus, but all define racial profiling in terms of the behavior of legal authorities.

This analysis approaches profiling from a psychological perspective (see Tyler and Wakslak 2002 for an extended discussion). It treats profiling as an attribution or inference made by a member of the public that the motivation for the behavior of a legal authority lies in ascribed characteristics of the people with whom that authority is dealing, rather than in their actual behavior. In other words, this analysis treats profiling as a subjective judgment made by a member of the public about the motives behind the actions of legal authorities—about why legal authorities are acting as they are.

This psychological approach is different from other treatments of racial profiling. In contrast to the usual focus on profiling behavior, we argue that the subjective experience of receiving police attention based upon one's race (profiling)—regardless of whether profiling has actually occurred—is responsible for many of the negative effects associated with profiling. It is the perception of profiling, not the objective reality, that may be the important psychological issue.

Observational studies suggest that legal authorities seldom make overt statements that link their behavior to racial profiling. They do not say, for example, "I stopped you because you are black" (Sherman 1999). When authorities do provide reasons or explanations for their actions, those reasons legitimize their actions, as when the police say that the person "fits the description of someone who is wanted for a crime." Hence, a person stopped by the police must make an inference as to why he or she was stopped, often based on unclear, ambiguous cues. From this perspective, the key issue is not the motivation or behavior of legal authorities, but how their actions are understood by the members of the public.

We can view the subjective experience of racial profiling as an aspect of people's more general desire to understand why events happen to them. Inferences about observed behavior are central to the social psychology of attribution (Heider 1958), which recognizes that a key task of social inference is to infer motivations underlying the observed behavior of others (Fiske and Taylor 1991; Nisbett and Ross 1980). People are constantly engaged in an effort to understand the social world by inferring the reasons underlying actions, and profiling is a subset of such efforts. We hypothesize that the key to people's reactions to authorities lies in their attributions of motives to those authorities.

A core distinction made by attribution theory is between causes that are "achieved," that is, that are due to the person's actions, and causes that are linked to "ascribed characteristics" of the person—their race, age, or gender. People have considerable control over their actions and therefore feel responsible and accountable for behavior they choose to engage in. Ascribed characteristics, however, are not generally the result of choice and are not within the person's control. People do not feel responsible and accountable for ascribed characteristics. Hence, people are typically more comfortable and accepting of being judged by others based upon what they choose to do rather than on aspects of who they are, such as their race, gender, or age (Fiske and Taylor 1991).

In the case of an encounter with legal authorities, people might infer that their own actions have led to or caused the behavior of the authorities ("The police stopped me because I was speeding"). This attribution for the actions of the police puts the causality for the police action in the actions of the person, in the things he or she was doing. Conversely, people might infer that the actions of authorities were motivated by their ascribed characteristics ("The police stopped me because I am black, a woman, a young person, etc."). This judgment that authorities are acting in reaction to ascribed characteristics is the core of an attribution of profiling.

In each encounter between a legal authority and a member of the public, the actions of the authority are possibly based upon ascribed characteristics and possibly based upon behavior. The person must make an inference about the cause of the police behavior. Our focus is not on the validity of that inference but, rather, on the factors that shape inferences and the consequences of inferences, when made, on attitudes toward the police. We focus not upon the actual motivations of the police, as revealed in their behavior, but on the perceived motives of the police, as revealed in inferences about their behavior drawn by members of the public.

A. Profiling as an Inference about Police Behavior

Treating profiling as an attributional inference allows us to address important questions not addressed when treating profiling as a behavioral occurrence (such as, asking "Are people being profiled?"). First, what are the consequences of a person making a profiling attribution for the behavior of the police? Does this inference, independent of its validity, have negative organizational consequences for police institutions? The studies described below test the hypothesis that attributions made about behavior shape reactions to that behavior.

Second, what are the factors that shape inferences of profiling? What variables are people relying on when they make judgments about the reasons for police behavior? The studies presented here test the process-based hypothesis that people use procedural cues to assess the motives of legal authorities. In other words, they test the value of using a process-based approach to dealing with issues of racial profiling.

These issues become vital when thinking of the consequences of defining profiling as an attribution made by the public. One might suppose, and would be supported by conventional treatments of racial profiling, that the best way to stop all problems associated with racial profiling is to stop profiling from occurring. This is obviously the tack taken by legislative bodies that have created laws making racial profiling illegal.

The psychological treatment of profiling, however, argues that if people feel that they are being profiled, it may not be sufficient "actually" to stop it. If profiling inferences are responsible for negative consequences to the police, police and other authorities must make sure that they not only deal with actual profiling, but also with the public's perception of profiling. It is easy to imagine a situation in which objective profiling is eliminated, but people still think that they are being profiled. Thus, knowledge of the factors that shape whether a person will make a profiling attribution becomes crucial.

B. Consequences of Profiling Attributions

The police rely heavily on the cooperation of the public. They depend on voluntary deference to police decisions (Tyler and Huo 2002), on general everyday compliance with the law (Tyler 1990), and on active cooperation with police officers to control crime (Sunshine and Tyler 2003). These forms of cooperation diminish when the public becomes less supportive of the police (Sunshine and Tyler 2003). It is predicted that racial profiling, with its implications that the police are biased, will lead the public to show less support for the police. A first hypothesis therefore is as follows: attributions of racial profiling undermine the legitimacy of and support for the police and, in doing so, negatively affect the public's compliance and cooperation with police authorities.

C. Antecedents of Profiling Attributions

Based on the expectation that inferences of racial profiling lead to negative consequences for police institutions, it becomes obvious that it is in the best interests of the police to reduce the occurrence of profiling attributions. But what determines whether a person stopped by the police will make a profiling attribution? Put more broadly, the issue is when people will view themselves as being the targets of discrimination (negative treatment linked to membership in a stigmatized group).

Work by many researchers has focused on factors that influence whether a person will feel that he or she has been discriminated against

(Major and Crocker 1993; Major, Quinton, and McCoy 2002). There is reason to suspect that the situation I am describing, of being stopped by a police officer, is one that may be particularly subject to an interpretation of discrimination. Work by Steele and his colleagues (Steele, Spencer, and Aronson 2002) on social identity threats suggests that members of frequently stigmatized groups are especially sensitive to cues that allow them to judge whether their identity as a member of a stigmatized group is relevant to the situation.

Cues that may not be meaningful to others can nonetheless signal to members of frequently devalued groups that a negative stereotype associated with their social identity is a possible explanation for their behavior. For example, cues signaling the subjective nature of evaluation by authorities may cause identity threat in members of traditionally stigmatized social groups who may worry that their devalued identity may influence subjective evaluations.

Based on this logic, the experience of being stopped by the police is a situation that entails a high level of potential identity threat for minority group members. It is a situation that is very subjective, with the choice of whom to stop being largely in the hands of the police, and the criteria used being unclear. It is a situation in which the person stopped has very little control over the situation, and lack of control increases social identity threat (Steele, Spencer, and Aronson 2002).

Finally, and perhaps most importantly, police-citizen interactions have been publicized in the media as ones tinged with bias, so people enter into the interaction with identity concerns highly salient. There has been much recent publicity about racial profiling in particular (Harris 1999; Meeks 2000; Knowles and Persico 2001) and tension-riddled police-minority relations in general (Fridell et al. 2001). The simple fact that a police officer has stopped a member of a minority group may in itself be a cue that a negative stereotype about the person stopped may be relevant to the situation. Given the current dynamic between the police and minorities, a profiling attribution may be one that is particularly easy for people in the minority community to make.

Can the police do anything to inhibit people from making profiling attributions? One suggestion is that people's belief in the fairness of the manner in which the police exercise their authority might prevent them from making profiling attributions, as a profiling attribution is a judgment that the police are in some way being unjust. But what determines whether people will find the police fair?

The procedural justice model argues that people judge fairness based on several process-based criteria (Tyler et al. 1997). Fair process has been argued here to consist of two primary categories: quality of decision making—perceived neutrality and consistency—and quality of treatment—being treated with dignity and respect, having one's rights acknowledged, and having one's needs acknowledged and considered (Tyler and Blader 2000).[2]

As I have already explained, the procedural justice perspective has been widely applied to the issue of regulation. The process-based model of regulation (Tyler and Huo 2002) hypothesizes that people will evaluate the actions of the police against criteria of procedural justice (Tyler et al. 1997; Tyler and Smith 1997). In particular, one hypothesis is that exercise of legal authority via fair procedures minimizes inferences of bias (Tyler and Huo 2002). The model implies that the way the police exercise their authority when they stop people—both in terms of quality of their decision making and the quality of their treatment of people—shapes the attributions those people make about whether they are being racially profiled.

The process-based hypothesis is that procedural justice information acts as a cue that bias is or is not taking place. It provides people, especially people who are potentially vulnerable to stereotyping, with cues suggesting that their identities are or are not secure and will or will not be challenged or diminished by evidence of bias or application of stereotypes (Tyler and Blader 2002). Experiencing fair procedures reassures people that they are not the target of a negative stereotype. I believe these factors will be enough largely or completely to override any cues inherent in the situation that would lead a person to conclude that profiling had taken place.

Another model of justice, the instrumental model (Thibaut and Walker 1975), makes a different argument. It argues that people's decisions are affected by their outcomes. In other words, people evaluate their experience based on the fairness or the favorableness of the outcomes they receive and the desirability of those outcomes. The model argues that people evaluate the police based on issues related to their

---

[2] In our previous discussion we treated procedural justice and motive-based trust as two parallel inferences developing from the quality of decision making and quality of interpersonal treatment that people believe characterizes the police. In this discussion of racial profiling we will focus on issues of procedural justice. Motive-based trust will be used as a check on our argument that attributions about why behavior occurs shape inferences about the character of authorities.

outcome—including both the favorableness of outcomes and distributive fairness—and this evaluation affects the likelihood that they will believe that the police are engaging in racial profiling.

Many studies have found instrumental concerns to be important predictors of people's feelings of justice (Tyler 1990; Tyler and Huo 2002), although procedural justice factors have often been found to be even more influential (Tyler et al. 1997). Thus, our second argument is the following: both instrumental factors and procedural justice will influence people's profiling attributions, but procedural justice factors will have a stronger influence.

D. Empirical Tests of the Profiling Argument

We test these two hypotheses—(1) that inferences of profiling have negative consequences for police institutions because they undermine acceptance of the actions of the police and (2) that police can lessen the occurrence of inferences that their behavior results from profiling through exercising their authority via fair procedures—through three studies. The first tests these arguments using people's inferences about the causes of their own personal experiences with the police. It is based upon a study of a sample of the residents of Oakland and Los Angeles, California. The second study, using a sample of registered voters in New York City, tests the same arguments using people's judgments about the general prevalence of profiling. Finally, the third study tests these arguments on both levels. It is based upon a study of a sample of young people living in New York City.

1. *Study 1.* Study 1 examines people's personal experiences with the police and the judgments they make about those experiences. It examines the extent to which people attribute their being stopped to behavioral or profiling factors and the effect that this attribution has on two aspects of public support for the police: willingness to accept the decision made by the police and satisfaction with the police. Additionally, it treats attributions about the experience as a dependent variable, examining possible factors that affect the attribution people make. These factors include procedural justice factors (overall procedural justice, quality of treatment, and quality of decision making), distributive justice factors (fairness of outcome, and objective and subjective favorableness of outcome), and a number of demographic variables. We expect that attributions of profiling will lead to less acceptance of police decisions and satisfaction with the police and that these attributions will be most affected by procedural justice information.

Telephone interviews with residents of the two cities in California were used to explore the inferences that people make about their personal encounters with the police in situations in which they are stopped by the police while on the street or in their cars. Residents of Oakland and Los Angeles were drawn from the population using a sampling frame that oversampled from minority areas. Subjects were screened for recent personal contacts with the police or courts to produce a sample of 1,656 respondents, each of whom had recent personal contact with one of these authorities. Each was interviewed about their most recent contact. This analysis focuses on those 521 respondents whose most recent contact was being stopped by the police: 163 were white, 186 African-American, and 172 Hispanic.

People were generally slightly more likely to make profiling attributions (28 percent) than behavioral attributions (23 percent). Minority respondents were significantly more likely to make profiling attributions (34 percent of African Americans and 33 percent of Hispanics vs. 15 percent of whites), while the frequency of behavioral attributions did not vary across ethnic groups.

To test the argument that attributions shape inferences about motives, we measured people's assessments of the trustworthiness of the motives of the police officers involved in their personal experience. As expected, we found that attributions shaped inferences of trustworthiness (adjusted R-squared = 28 percent). Those making behavioral attributions judged the police to be more trustworthy (beta = 0.37, $p <$ .001), while those making profiling attributions judged the police to be less trustworthy (beta = -0.34, $p <$ .001). Hence, attributions shaped inferences of trustworthiness.

The first argument is that when people make profiling attributions, they will view police actions less favorably and will become more resistant to accepting the decisions of the police. Regression analysis was used to test this argument. The dependent variables were the willingness to accept the decision and evaluation of the authority. The independent variables were attributions and demographic variables. Table 10 shows the results of the regression analysis. People who made a behavioral attribution were more willing to defer to authorities (beta = 0.32) and evaluated them more positively (beta = 0.35). Those who made a profiling attribution were less willing to defer (beta = -0.33) and evaluated authorities more negatively (beta = -0.35).

The second argument is that the police shape the attributions that people make by the way they treat them. In particular, the procedural

TABLE 10

Attributions for Event and Reactions to the Event, Study 1

	Willingness to Accept the Decision	Evaluation of the Authority
Beta weight:		
Behavioral attribution	.32***	.35***
Profiling attribution	−.33***	−.35***
Hispanic/white	−.10***	−.07**
African American/white	−.13***	−.12***
Age	.08***	.08***
Gender	.03	.03
Adjusted R-squared (percent)	23	26

Source.—Tyler and Wakslak 2002.

Note.—If a person thinks that the behavior of the police was caused by their behavior, they are more willing to accept police decisions, and they feel more positively about the police. If they think the behavior of the police was caused by profiling, they are less willing to accept police decisions and feel more negatively about the police.

$* p < .05$.
$** p < .01$.
$*** p < .001$.

justice model argues that the fairness of police actions shapes people's judgments about those actions. The findings, shown in table 11, strongly support this perspective. Irrespective of whether procedural justice is assessed as an overall procedural justice scale, as evaluations of the quality of decision making, or as evaluations of the quality of interpersonal treatment, people are significantly less likely to make profiling attributions when they are treated fairly (average beta = −0.39). They are also less likely to make profiling attributions when they receive fair outcomes (average beta = −0.13) or outcomes that are favorable (average beta = −0.09). Conversely, they are more likely to make behavioral attributions when procedures or outcomes are fair and when outcomes are favorable.

The findings in table 11 also show an interesting distinction between profiling attributions and behavioral attributions. If people feel that they are fairly treated, they are much less likely to say they were profiled (average beta = −0.39). However, they are not correspondingly strongly more likely to say that they caused the police actions by their own behavior (average beta = 0.22). Hence, we need to distinguish blaming the police from taking personal responsibility for one's actions, since the two are not mirror images. People are more likely not

TABLE 11
Influence of Police Behavior on Profiling Attributions, Study 1

	Profiling Attributions			Behavioral Attributions		
Beta weights:						
Procedural fairness	−.35***	⋯	⋯	.21***	⋯	⋯
Quality of decision making	⋯	−.47***	−.45***	⋯	.16***	.35***
Quality of treatment	⋯	−.13*	−.20**	⋯	⋯	.11
Distributive fairness	−.07**	⋯	⋯	.06	.01	⋯
Outcome favorability:						
Objective	−.09**	−.10***	−.14**	.03	.15***	.15***
Subjective	−.12	−.08	−.15*	.01	.08	.00
Race						
Hispanic	.05	.05	.07*	.09**	.08**	.03
African American	.02	.02	.02	.06*	.06*	.02
Age	.01	−.01	.01	.02	.02	.06
Gender	.03	.02	.06	.06*	−.06*	.10
Adjusted R-squared (percent)	13	22	22	1	9	18

Source.—Tyler and Wakslak 2002.

Note.—If people evaluate the procedures to be fair, they are less likely to make profiling attributions and more likely to make behavioral attributions. If they receive an outcome they think is fair, they are less likely to make profiling attributions and more likely to make behavioral attributions. If they receive a favorable outcome, they are generally less likely to make profiling attributions and generally more likely to make behavioral attributions. Minorities are more likely to make both profiling and behavioral attributions. Women are less likely to make behavioral attributions.

* $p < .05$.

** $p < .01$.

*** $p < .001$.

to blame the police when treated fairly than they are to take personal responsibility for their actions. Nonetheless, people are more likely to take personal responsibility for their actions when they feel fairly treated. And, from the perspective of the police, the key issue is that people do not blame them for having been profiled.

When people think the police are profiling them, it hurts the authority of the police and makes it more difficult to gain public deference to their decisions. However, there are clear policing strategies that effectively minimize the likelihood of profiling attributions. In particular, the police are less likely to be viewed as profiling if they treat people fairly.

This procedural justice finding can be divided into two distinct components corresponding to the two components of procedural justice (Tyler and Blader 2000). The first is linked to issues of decision making. People are less likely to infer that they are being profiled if the police make their decisions in neutral, objective, consistent ways. This points to the value of "transparency" in police activities—that is, of making decisions in ways that make clear that the authorities are acting neutrally. If the police make such efforts, they are less likely to be viewed as profiling. We speculated earlier that the possible subjectivity of the situation acts as a cue that increases social identity threat in minority members; perhaps transparency inhibits evaluations of discrimination by removing that subjectivity.

The second aspect of procedural justice is linked to issues of quality of treatment. It is striking that if the police treat people politely and respectfully, those people are less likely to infer that the police stopped them due to ascribed characteristics. So, by acting respectfully, the police can minimize inferences about their behavior that undermine trust and confidence. This finding is striking because whether the police are respectful has no direct connection to their motivations in stopping people on the street. Nonetheless, people connect the two issues and are less likely to say that they have been profiled when they are treated with respect.

2. *Study 2.*   Study 1 focused on people's personal experiences with the police. Study 2 examines people's general judgments about the police. Here we examine the effect of people's general judgments about the prevalence of profiling on support for the police by looking at judgments of police legitimacy and performance in fighting crime. Legitimacy has been previously conceptualized as a measure of obligation

to obey, confidence in the police, and positive affect toward the police (Tyler 1990; Tyler and Huo 2002).

We also look at possible antecedents of people's judgments about the prevalence of profiling, including procedural justice (general procedural justice, quality of treatment, and quality of decision making), instrumental judgments about the police (crime rate and fear of crime), and several demographic variables. We predict that judgments of profiling will be associated with less support for the police and that these profiling judgments will be most affected by judgments of procedural justice.

In study 2, questionnaires were mailed to a random sample of registered voters, who completed and returned them by mail. A subset of 586 (22 percent) completed and returned the questionnaires. This resulted in a diverse sample of respondents (57 percent white, 15 percent Hispanic, 22 percent African American, 75 percent female, mean age 48). Because of the low response rate, the sample collected is not representative of the population of New York City. It is more heavily white and more highly educated than the general population. For this reason, we used a weighted subsample of respondents that was weighted by ethnicity, education, and income to reflect the population of New York City. This weighted subsample included the 483 respondents who were both members of one of the three major ethnic groups (white, Hispanic, and African American) and who provided education and income information.

The mean prevalence of profiling is shown in table 12. The results shown indicate that people generally feel that profiling occurs (mean = 4.08). Further, as would be expected, minority group members are significantly more likely to say that they feel that profiling occurs (mean = 4.30 vs. 3.89; $t(441) = 4.21, p < .001$).

As in study 1, we can test the argument that profiling attributions shape inferences of trustworthiness using our index of trust in the motives of the police. That analysis found that prevalence estimates shaped motive inferences (adjusted R-squared = 28 percent, $p < .001$), with those who think the police profile more often indicating that the motives of the police are less trustworthy.

The first prediction is that support for the police is undermined if the police are viewed as profiling. A regression analysis was used to test this argument. Two dependent variables were considered: police legitimacy and police performance. The results indicate that profiling

TABLE 12

Items for the Scale Indexing the Public's Judgment of Frequency
of Police Profiling, Study 2

	All Respondents	White Respondents	Minority Respondents
Some people say that the police treat people differently based on their ethnicity. How much do you think that the police consider a person's race or ethnicity when deciding . . .			
Which cars to stop for possible traffic violations	4.28 (1.47)	4.06 (1.47)	4.55 (1.42)
Which people to stop and question in the street	4.40 (1.42)	4.17 (1.38)	4.68 (1.42)
Which people to arrest and take to jail	4.12 (1.48)	3.90 (1.47)	4.38 (1.46)
Which people in the neighborhood to help with their problems	3.78 (1.54)	3.62 (1.51)	3.97 (1.55)
Which people in the neighborhood to patrol the most frequently	4.24 (1.54)	4.15 (1.47)	4.34 (1.61)
Which calls for help to answer first	3.63 (1.58)	3.42 (1.51)	3.88 (1.62)

NOTE.—High scores indicate more profiling (6 = "a great deal"; 1 = "not much at all").

was negatively related to both. Those respondents who viewed profiling as more prevalent viewed the police as less legitimate (beta = −0.45) and gave the police lower performance ratings (beta = −0.26). These results are shown in table 13.

What can the police do to minimize public judgments that they are profiling? The procedural justice prediction is that the police can maintain their legitimacy by exercising their authority in fair ways. Study 1 found support for this argument in the context of personal experiences. This study tests it in terms of general evaluations of the police. Again, regression analyses were used to test the argument, and the results are shown in table 14. Three aspects of police procedural fairness were examined: general procedural justice judgments, judgments about the quality of police decision making, and judgments about the quality of treatment that people receive.

The results support the argument with each of the three indices of procedural justice. In each case, people were less likely to feel that profiling occurs if they say that the police exercise their authority using

TABLE 13

Impact of Profiling, Study 2

	Legitimacy of the Police	Performance Evaluations
Beta weights:		
Prevalence of profiling	−.45***	−.26***
Race	−.18***	−.24***
Age	.16***	.06
Gender	.02	.01
Adjusted R-squared (percent)	30	15

Source.—Tyler and Wakslak 2002.

Note.—High scores indicate high legitimacy, high performance evaluations, high prevalence of profiling, being minority, being old, and being male.

* $p < .05$.
** $p < .01$.
*** $p < .001$.

TABLE 14

Police Behavior and Profiling Inferences, Study 2

	Prevalence of Profiling		
Beta weights:			
Police generally act in fair ways	−.41***	. . .	. . .
Police make decisions fairly	. . .	−.53***	. . .
Police treat people fairly	. . .	. . .	−.51***
Estimated crime rate	.06	.03	.01
Fear of crime	.04	.04	.10*
Race	.05	.02	.07
Age	.00	.05	.02
Gender	.03	.02	.02
Adjusted R-squared (percent)	17	27	26

Source.—Tyler and Wakslak 2002.

Note.—High scores indicate high prevalence of profiling, that the police act fairly, that the crime rate is high, that one is afraid of crime, being minority, being old, and being male.

* $p < .05$.
** $p < .01$.
*** $p < .001$.

fair procedures (average beta $= -0.49$). In other words, by being seen as making their decisions in neutral ways and treating people with dignity and politeness, the police lead members of the public to infer that they are not profiling.

Study 1 explored people's interpretations of their personal experiences. When people had a personal experience with the police, they had to infer why that experience occurred. If they inferred that it was due to profiling, their response to the encounter was more negative than if they inferred that it was due to their behavior. Which of the two attributions they made was found to be related to procedural justice factors. Study 2 looks not at personal experiences, but at general judgments. If people judge that police profiling is widespread, they make more negative evaluations of the police. Profiling judgments are related to judgments of whether the police act in a fair manner. Hence, both on the personal and on the general levels, procedural justice is related to profiling judgments, and profiling judgments are harmful to the police.

3. *Study 3.* Study 3 examines both general views of the police and personal experiences. It looks at the effects of feeling that profiling is prevalent and feeling personally profiled on support for the police; it examines the effects of two types of support: judgments regarding the quality of the police's performance and those regarding police-minority relations. It also looks at factors influencing profiling judgments, including procedural justice (respect) and instrumental judgments about the police, and a number of demographic variables. We predict that profiling judgments will influence support for the police and will themselves be influenced most strongly by procedural justice factors.

In January of 2001, a *New York Times* poll of New Yorkers focused on the NYPD. The poll completed 721 interviews with a sample of residents between the ages of eighteen and twenty-six. This age group was targeted because young people are the frequent focus of policing activities. The sample was interviewed over the telephone. Of those interviewed, 37 percent were white, 25 percent African American, 27 percent Hispanic, and 11 percent other races or ethnicities.

Profiling was indexed in two ways: first, the judgment that profiling occurs and, second, the personal experience of feeling that one has been profiled. The results shown in table 15 suggest that both profiling inferences undermine performance evaluations and judgments of the quality of the relationship between the police and the minority community.

TABLE 15

Influence of Profiling Attributions on Performance
Evaluations, Study 3

	Performance		Relations with Minorities	
Beta weights:				
Prevalence of profiling	−.27***	. . .	−.40***	. . .
I was profiled	. . .	−.23***	. . .	−.29***
Race	−.15***	−.12***	−.21***	−.20***
Gender	−.13***	−.20***	−.04	−.13***
Adjusted R-squared (percent)	13	11	25	16

NOTE.—High scores indicate high performance, positive relations with minorities, high prevalence of profiling, having been profiled, minority status, and being male.
* $p < .05$.
** $p < .01$.
*** $p < .001$.

If the police are procedurally fair, are they less likely to be viewed as profiling minorities? This issue is addressed using regression analysis. The results are shown in table 16. They suggest that when people experience unfair treatment, they are both more likely to say that they were profiled and to indicate that profiling is prevalent. Hence, as in

TABLE 16

Behavior of the Police and Inferences of Profiling, Study 3

	Prevalence of Profiling	I Was Profiled
Beta weights:		
I was treated procedurally fairly (respectfully) by the police	−.28***	−.53***
Instrumental judgments about the police (feel safe, not fearful around the police)	−.14**	−.21***
Race	.16***	.25***
Gender	.12**	.15***
Adjusted R-squared (percent)	8	30

SOURCE.—Tyler and Wakslak 2002.
NOTE.—High scores indicate feeling that profiling is prevalent, that one has been profiled, that treatment was fair, that the police are safe, not dangerous; being minority; being male.
* $p < .05$.
** $p < .01$.
*** $p < .001$.

studies 1 and 2, the experience of profiling was damaging to the police because it led the people personally involved to have more negative views about the police, as well as leading the public generally to have more negative views about the police. This study replicates both prior effects in the context of one study.

E. Discussion

The results presented suggest that people react negatively to attributions of profiling, irrespective of whether they think that profiling occurs in their own personal experience or generally during policing activities in their neighborhood and city. This supports the hypothesis that there are widespread negative consequences when people think that they have been profiled or that profiling occurs. The inference of profiling hurts the police. These findings support the first prediction, the attributional hypothesis, by showing that people's inferences about the motives underlying police behavior shape their reactions to the police.

To test the argument, and demonstrate that the attributions measured are related to judgments about the motives of the police, both studies 1 and 2 tested the impact of attributions on motive inferences. In both studies, attributions significantly shaped people's views about the trustworthiness of the motives of the police. In study 1, this reflected judgments about particular police officers, while in study 2 it reflected judgments about the police in general. When profiling is inferred to be occurring, people evaluated the motivations of the actors involved as being less trustworthy. This supports that key attributional argument that it is motive inferences that are the key antecedent to people's reactions to authorities.

Since profiling has received wide public exposure, has attracted considerable political attention, and is rated by police chiefs as one of the central issues in policing today (Fridell et al. 2001), these findings suggest the value of psychology as a framework within which to approach issues of policing and regulation. In many ways it is the subjective experience of profiling—the first-person accounts of people's experiences of being stopped by the police—that has drawn so much attention. These experiences are not necessarily linked to actual profiling, so efforts to eliminate actual profiling may or may not resolve public beliefs that the police profile members of the minority community. It is difficult to know exactly what is going on inside a police officer's head at the moment of a stop. A psychological perspective, like the one discussed here, argues that regardless of the objective truth, racial profiling is a serious issue. People certainly feel that profiling exists, and that feeling has been linked to a marked decrease in support for the police.

In addition, the results support the hypothesis that the procedural justice framework is valuable in understanding how to manage issues of profiling. The core conclusion of the studies reported is that when people indicate that they have experienced fair procedures when dealing with the police, or when they indicate that the police generally use fair procedures when dealing with members of their community, they are less likely to infer that profiling occurs. Hence, the police can manage their relationships with members of the communities they serve through their behavior when dealing with members of the public. These findings, therefore, support the general argument about policing made by Tyler and Huo (2002)—that process-based regulation has important advantages for the police and for policing.

Two aspects of procedural fairness—quality of decision making and quality of treatment—were found to affect significantly the inferences people make about their interactions with the police. Quality of decision making refers to the degree to which the police make their decisions in neutral, objective, and consistent ways. Profiling, by definition, is a nonneutral way of making a decision. It is thus intuitively logical that quality of decision making is related to inferences of profiling. The finding does, however, highlight the value of transparency, of making decisions in ways that make clear that authorities are acting neutrally.

The finding that people are less likely to infer that they have been profiled when they are treated with politeness and respect by the police is especially striking. The quality of interpersonal treatment is not necessarily an indicator of the manner in which police make decisions. We can imagine an officer who is not a neutral decision maker but still treats people with dignity and respect. At the same time we can imagine an officer who is a neutral decision maker but treats people without dignity and respect.

Yet, people do not treat these two issues as distinct and draw inferences about profiling from indicators of respect. It is therefore critical that police officers realize the messages that their method of interaction sends. For a police force to be considered fair by the public, it must make decisions in an objective, consistent manner, while also being careful to treat citizens with dignity and respect. The process-based model of regulation (Tyler and Huo 2002) advocates an environment of fairness that incorporates both of these objectives.

Stuntz (2002) argues that in order to deal effectively with racial distrust of the police in the minority community, it is important to regulate not only whom the police stop, but how they conduct stops. According to his argument, this perspective may also offer one way of dealing with the complex issue of profiling in a post-9/11 world. Many maintain that suddenly the normative question of profiling is a lot less clear (Gross and Livingston 2002). Should all profiling, including that of potential terrorists, be disallowed?

Stuntz (2002) argues that in the type of situation faced post 9/11, in which it is unclear whether prohibiting profiling is an appropriate thing to do, we should focus on the manner in which people are stopped. Regulating the manner of stops made by the police is a way to limit the harm associated with profiling independent of whether one believes actual profiling should be prohibited under all circumstances. Of course, I am not advocating that the police simply treat people fairly and not act to reduce profiling itself. Instead, my point is that since there are some situations, like combating terrorism, in which profiling may be important and, hence, may be allowable under law, approaching the situation from a psychological perspective is especially advantageous in reducing public dissatisfaction about profiling.

Throughout this essay my main focus has been the benefits to the police of treating the people they deal with fairly. However, I wish to emphasize that a policing model focused on fairness is first and foremost beneficial to the community the police serve. The public gains from an increasingly neutral and respectful police force. In addition, process-based regulation creates an environment of fairness that fosters cooperation and a sense that the police are acting on behalf of the community. Increasing support for the police allows the police to function more effectively, better focusing their efforts on serving the community, a result that benefits both the police and the public.

The importance of fair procedures is particularly central in interactions between authorities and minority group members. People who belong to groups that are potentially stigmatizable are especially sensitive to social cues concerning the motivations underlying the behavior of others. If people feel that the authorities are exercising their authority fairly, they are less likely to believe that prejudices, stereotypes, or personal biases are guiding their actions. While members of minority groups vary in their sensitivity to race-based rejection, people in groups vulnerable to the application of stereotypes are generally more sensitive to such social cues and therefore especially likely to react to evidence of race-based practices such as profiling (Mendoza-Denton et al. 2002).

Of course, these findings do not apply only to the minority community. Everyone views being stopped by the police as an ambiguous situation that has the potential for negative social implications. So all members of the community are sensitive to how they are treated by police officers, judges, and other public officials. As representatives of the group, the actions of authorities such as the police carry an important message about one's position and status in the group, and thereby communicate to that person whether their identity is secure (Tyler and Blader 2002). The findings reported in this essay support the hypothesis that procedural justice is the cue that people use most heavily when evaluating their reactions to social authorities.

Since there is a major ethnic group gap in trust and confidence in the law and the police, these findings have particular relevance to the task of managing the relationship between the police and the minority community. The procedural justice findings point to a clear strategy that the police can use to create and sustain the trust and confidence of minority group members. Members of minority groups have been of greatest concern to legal authorities since they have consistently been found to be the most disaffected and defiant members of our society. It is especially striking, therefore, that the three studies, like the findings of Tyler and Huo (2002), equally characterized the majority and minority populations.

Because the focus of this section is on racial profiling, an issue that is important in the context of regulation (Tyler and Huo 2002), the focus has been on the willingness of people to defer to legal authorities. This focus can be expanded to general rule following and cooperation with authorities. Results of studies of general rule following suggest that general rule following is also linked to the overall fairness of group procedures (Tyler 1990; Tyler and Blader 2002). Similarly, studies of cooperation find that this, too, is linked to perceptions of procedural fairness (Sunshine and Tyler 2003).

A broadened focus is important because authorities want more from the public than deference to laws and the decisions of legal authorities. They also want proactive involvement. Studies of crime and urban disorder emphasize that the community must play an active role for the police to control crime effectively in their communities (Sampson,

Raudenbush, and Earls 1997; Sampson and Bartusch 1998). Hence, the authorities also want to motivate proactive behavior on the part of those within their groups. A broader implication of these findings is that procedural fairness motivates proactive behavior on the part of group members. In this case, broader behavior involves cooperation with the police.

The issue of antiterror profiling illustrates how the police and community can gain from treating people fairly and building their legitimacy within minority communities. People of Middle Eastern appearance are often the targets of profiling antiterror efforts. At the same time, authorities depend upon the cooperation of the members of the Arab community to warn the authorities about terrorist activities. The key to successful terrorism is the ability to blend into the minority community without detection. As with community cooperation in fighting everyday crime, community cooperation is important in fighting terrorism. And, in both cases, cooperation flows from the belief that the police are legitimate social authorities.

This point can be extended beyond the police to represent a general management strategy. People's willingness to cooperate with groups is generally facilitated by their judgments that the group functions using fair procedures (Tyler and Blader 2000). As a consequence, authorities in groups should generally recognize the importance of creating and maintaining organizational integrity in the eyes of citizens, employees, or other group members. This should be equally true of community residents dealing with the police and courts, of employees dealing with managers, of students dealing with teachers, and of citizens dealing with political leaders.

The importance of cooperation from the public makes clear that the concern when dealing with minority group members is not just with encouraging their deference to authorities and institutions. We are more broadly interested in understanding how authorities and institutions can encourage the members of vulnerable minority groups to engage in society behaviorally and psychologically. The willingness to work with others in one's community is one example of such engagement, as are achievement in school and integration into the workforce. Research on this broader engagement suggests that people in minority groups are more willing to engage in groups when they experience those groups and their authorities as acting using fair procedures (Davis and Tyler 2002). Hence, more broadly, organizations that are characterized by procedural fairness are better able to encourage the engagement of minority group members in themselves.

Some researchers have suggested that attributing a negative event to discrimination may, in fact, benefit members of stigmatized groups by protecting their self-esteem (Major and Crocker 1993), an argument that is at odds with the claim that attributions to profiling are harmful for minority group members. We examined this possibility using the data in study 1 by looking at the relationship between attributions concerning the cause of being stopped and general measures of self-esteem and respect by others. This allows us to determine whether one attribution has more positive implications for well-being. In the case of being stopped by the police, it is not clear that feeling one has been stopped because of one's behavior ("I was breaking the law") has more positive implications than being stopped due to one's race. Consistent with this, we found no differential effects of attribution in study 1. In other words, being stopped by the police has small, but identifiable, negative effects on measures of self-worth. But the magnitude of these effects was similar irrespective of which attribution was made about the cause of the event.

F. Profiling as an Example of the Value of a Procedural Justice Perspective

The results of the profiling studies suggest that people react negatively to the inference of profiling, irrespective of whether it occurs in their own personal experience or is generally viewed as occurring during policing activities in their neighborhood and city. The results also support the argument that the psychology of procedural justice is a valuable framework within which to understand how to manage issues of profiling. When people indicate that they have experienced fair procedures when dealing with the police, or when they indicate that the police generally use fair procedures when dealing with members of their community, they are less likely to infer that profiling occurs. Hence, the police can manage their relationships with members of the communities they serve through their behavior when dealing with members of the public.

It is especially striking that people are less likely to infer that they have been profiled when they are treated with politeness and respect. The quality of interpersonal treatment is distinct from the manner in which the police make decisions, and we can imagine that police officers could be nonneutral and biased, and could make decisions based upon personal prejudices, while still treating people with dignity and respect. However, people do not treat these two issues as distinct. Instead, they infer that they have not been profiled if they are treated more politely.

VII. The Relationship of the Procedural Justice Approach to Other Models

Legitimacy and procedural justice together make up one of three major conceptual initiatives of the 1980s and 1990s that have influenced thinking about the criminal justice system. Restorative justice and community policing are the others.

A. Restorative Justice

The suggestion that the maintenance of internal values in community residents is important to effective policing is also made by the literature on restorative justice (see Braithwaite 1989, 1999, 2002; Strang and Braithwaite 2000, 2001). The core argument is that the police and courts should behave in ways that "restore" people to law-following behavior. The goal is to reconnect offenders to an awareness of their own social values and to their stake in maintaining social relationships. This awareness will discourage them from law-breaking behavior in the future because they will recognize that their behavior violates personal values that define appropriate conduct. They will see that rule breaking damages social relationships with friends, family, and the community.

The effectiveness of this model is being tested in a set of restorative justice field experiments being conducted in Canberra, Australia. Those studies explore the long-term impact of restorative justice experiments on law-abiding behavior. While data on long-term behavior are still being collected, data already available suggest that people who experience restorative justice conferences express greater respect for the law and view the police as more legitimate than do those whose cases are processed via traditional court procedures (Sherman 1999).

Like procedural justice, restorative justice is oriented toward future conduct. Both models suggest that one important goal for legal authorities is to encourage activation of people's internal values so that they will feel personally responsible for rule-abiding conduct in the future. Restorative justice focuses on people's feelings of shame, which are linked to their relationships to others in the community. Most people

TABLE 17

Self-Regulatory Motivations

Model	Focus	Motivation That Is Activated
Procedural justice models	Legitimacy of authority	Obligation
Restorative justice models	Relationships to others	Shame
Moral development models	Principles of right and wrong	Guilt

feel a responsibility to act in ways that will be respected by others and are ashamed when they have let others down. Restorative justice seeks to communicate to offenders that they are valued and respected people who have positive relationships with others. While condemning the law-breaking actions that occurred and trying to find appropriate ways to make up for the harms done, restorative justice also tries to increase the offender's motivation to act in appropriate ways in the future.

Procedural justice does not focus on shame. It focuses on obligation and responsibility. However, both shame and obligation are internal motivations for self-regulatory behavior. We can combine these with a third motivation mentioned earlier—morality—to identify three self-regulatory motivations. These are shown in table 17. While all three are united in their goal of activating people's internal values, they focus on different issues. Procedural justice focuses on feelings of obligation and responsibility to authorities. Restorative justice is concerned with people's relationships to others and the shame that occurs when people disappoint others. Moral values lead to guilt when a person violates his own personal standards of right and wrong.

B. Community and Problem-Oriented Policing

Many of the ideas outlined here are also part of the community and problem-oriented approaches to policing. Those approaches emphasize police efforts to move beyond reacting to committed crimes to making efforts to work proactively with communities to solve community problems.

Studies suggest that people value having the police talk to citizens and cooperate with citizens to solve community problems. They support more bike and pedestrian patrols because they "like to perceive the police as friends and helpers and they would support endeavours to improve the work of the police force much in the sense of what community and problem oriented policing propose" (Weitekamp, Kerner, and Meier 1996, p. 16). Similarly, a study of public complaints about the police showed that the two primary reasons for complaining were "rude, arrogant, unfriendly, over-casual treatment" (38 percent) and "unreasonable, unfair behavior" (46 percent) (see Skogan 1994).

These findings suggest that people would like to improve the relationships between citizens and the police, a core concern of problem-oriented and community policing. Weitekamp, Kerner, and Meier (1996) proposed a restorative problem-solving police prevention program that views reconciliation between victims, the community as a whole, and perpetrators as a key goal. They argue that four groups—the police, the community, the offender, and the victim—should be involved in efforts to reconcile following wrongdoing. All of these groups should be jointly concerned to make their community safer, reduce fear, prevent future crime, improve the quality of life, and increase interpersonal harmony among the people in communities.

Several conceptual issues underlay the distinctions among restorative, problem-oriented, and community policing. One is what the appropriate responsibilities of the police should be. Traditionally the police are responsible for enforcing the law by regulating public behavior and apprehending lawbreakers. Those people are evaluated and potentially punished by the courts. Recently there have been arguments for an expanded police role in helping to solve community problems and helping communities to solidify themselves as communities. These arguments stem in part from the recognition that the police cannot effectively control crime without community assistance (Sampson, Raudenbush, and Earls 1997; Sampson and Bartusch 1998), and in part from the suggestion that at least some members of the public would prefer the police play a broader role in the community than just rule enforcement and crime control.

A second issue is who should deal with rule breaking. Within modern societies, the state has the central authority for deciding how to react to rule breaking, with the police and courts deciding whom to arrest, how to determine wrongdoing, and how much to punish. This has led to a variety of types of discontent. Victims of crime feel excluded from the determination of punishment and would like to have a greater role in deciding how to deal with criminals. Communities would also like a greater role, in part because they feel that the punishments of the formal legal system depart from the communities' feelings about what is right and wrong (Robinson and Darley 1995). These groups have argued for greater opportunities to participate in determinations of how to deal with crime and criminals.

Finally, there is the question of how crime should be dealt with. The current legal system emphasizes determinations of guilt and the application of punishment. However, approaches such as restorative justice argue for the value of seeking to rehabilitate offenders—emphasizing the encouragement of future law-abiding behavior as the goal over punishment for past wrongs. This leads to efforts to work with the families and communities affected by the crime to encourage the criminal to come into compliance with community norms and values. Restorative justice itself is a model for the goal that should shape reactions to wrongdoing. It does not speak to the issue of who—the community, the police, the courts—should have the authority to manage responses to deviant behavior. In the RISE experiments conducted in Australia, for example, the police managed restorative justice sessions (Braithwaite 1999, 2002). However, in many of the traditional dispute resolution approaches from which restorative justice draws its inspiration, the community and community leaders were the key authorities. The restorative justice approach is a model for how to react to wrongdoing, rather than a model of policing, but it can be applied to policing if the police adopt a restorative justice approach to their dealings with wrongdoers.

The goal of law, legal institutions, and legal authorities is to regulate effectively the behavior of those within society. If the law is to be effective, most people must accept the directives of the law most of the time, they must generally cooperate with legal authorities, and they must support the empowerment of those authorities. Gaining such cooperation is always difficult, since legal authorities are often in the position of restricting people's behavior or asking people to take actions that benefit the community rather than themselves.

This essay presents a perspective on how public cooperation can be secured. It argues that people evaluate and react to the law and to legal authorities in large part by evaluating the processes through which legal institutions and authorities exercise their authority. In particular, people evaluate the actions of authorities and institutions by applying an ethical framework and assessing the justice of the manner in which these institutions and authorities make decisions and treat people.

This process-based perspective suggests that the authorities need to be concerned with understanding the ethical frameworks through which their actions are viewed by the public. In particular, they need to be sensitive to people's judgments about what makes legal procedures fair. Assessments of procedural justice, more than any other aspect of public judgments, shape reactions to the police, the courts, and the law. This is true both when people are reacting to their personal experiences and when they are making general evaluations of the police and the courts. Together with judgments about the trustworthiness of the motivations of legal authorities, the other important process-based judgment about legal authorities, procedural justice judgments are the key antecedent of deference to decisions and cooperation with legal authorities.

One procedural element consistently found to shape evaluations of procedural justice and inferences of motive-based trust is the quality of decision making. When people judge that legal authorities and institutions are making their decisions fairly, they view those authorities as more legitimate and more willingly defer to and cooperate with them in personal encounters and in their everyday law-related behaviors. Quality of decision making involves making decisions in neutral and unbiased ways using objective information, and not personal biases and prejudices. In neutral decision making, authorities make decisions based upon rules consistently applied across people and situations. Because neutrality involves the use of objective information about the situation, people are more likely to view procedures as neutral when they are given an opportunity to present evidence and explain their situation.

A second procedural element that shapes evaluations of procedural justice and inferences of motive-based trust is the quality of the interpersonal treatment that people experience when dealing with authorities. This includes treatment with dignity and respect, acknowledgment of one's rights and concerns, and a general awareness of the importance of recognizing people's personal status and identity and treating those with respect, even while raising questions about particular conduct. As with neutrality, one factor that accords respect is allowing people to voice their concerns. In addition, people value having the reasons for the actions of authorities justified and explained, and having their right to appeal unfair decisions affirmed.

While both process-based elements play an important role in shaping people's reactions to the police, the courts, and the law, it is particularly striking that many studies find that a key issue to people when dealing with legal authorities is the respect and dignity with which they are treated. This aspect of quality of treatment is found by Tyler and Huo (2002) to be the most important antecedent of both procedural justice assessments and judgments about the trustworthiness of the motives of legal authorities. The studies of public evaluations of the police and courts outlined always find that assessments of how these authorities treat community members are important elements in overall evaluations of performance and legitimacy, and a major antecedent of compliance, cooperation, and empowerment.

These findings have clear implications for the exercise of legal authority. They suggest that in addition to their concerns about performance and effectiveness in fighting crime and urban disorder, legal authorities need to be sensitive to the need to manage the public in ways that accord respect to and acknowledge the rights and concerns of community residents.

It is ironic that, while appearing to be increasingly successful in dealing with crime, legal authorities have not achieved greater legitimacy in the eyes of the public. Legitimacy and cooperation, however, are not solely, or even primarily, shaped by performance. Rather, the views of the public are shaped to an important degree by the manner in which the police exercise their authority.

Consider a concrete example. The New York City Police Department feels considerable pride in their adoption of innovative policing techniques, such as COMPSTAT, which have enabled them to fight crime more effectively. However, views about the NYPD continue to be widely negative, especially among members of the minority community. This frustrates police officials, whose underlying assumption is that the public links their views to estimates of the crime rate, fear of crime, or judgments about police performance in fighting crime. If the public focuses instead on issues of process, then policies such as aggressive policing or racial profiling may have the consequence of undermining public support, even if they effectively lower crime. Increased attention to quality of treatment, if accepted as a goal in and of itself, would enhance public views.

The argument for increased attention to process-based issues is not intended to replace efforts to manage crime and urban disorder effectively. Rather, the goal is to create a second criterion against which the police and courts might evaluate themselves—a "fairness" criterion re-

flecting public views about how those authorities exercise their authority. Inevitably an effort to implement such a strategy involves focusing
on what fairness means to people in the community.

REFERENCES

Ayres, Ian, and John Braithwaite. 1992. *Responsive Regulation: Transcending the Deregulation Debate.* Oxford: Oxford University Press.

Beetham, David. 1991. *The Legitimation of Power.* Atlantic Highlands, N.J.: Humanities International Press.

Braithwaite, John. 1989. *Crime, Shame, and Reintegration.* Cambridge: Cambridge University Press.

———. 1999. "Restorative Justice: Assessing Optimistic and Pessimistic Accounts." In *Crime and Justice: A Review of Research,* vol. 25, edited by Michael Tonry. Chicago: University of Chicago Press.

———. 2002. *Restorative Justice and Responsive Regulation.* Oxford: Oxford University Press.

Darley, John, Tom R. Tyler, and Kenworthey Bilz. 2002. "Enacting Justice: The Interplay of Individual and Institutional Perspectives." In *Handbook of Social Psychology,* edited by Michael A. Hogg and Joel Cooper. London: Sage.

Davis, Angelina E., and Tom R. Tyler. 2002. "The Influence of Biculturalism and Fair Treatment on Successful Ethnic Minority Engagement." Unpublished manuscript. New York: New York University, Psychology Department.

Easton, David. 1975. "A Reassessment of the Concept of Political Support." *British Journal of Political Science* 5:435–57.

Easton, David, and Jack Dennis. 1969. *Children in the Political System: Origins of Political Legitimacy.* Chicago: University of Chicago Press.

Ewick, Patrick, and Susan S. Silbey. 1998. *The Common Place of Law: Stories from Everyday Life.* Chicago: University of Chicago Press.

Fiske, Susan T., and Shelley E. Taylor. 1991. *Social Cognition.* 2d ed. New York: McGraw-Hill.

French, J. R. P., and B. Raven. 1959. "The Bases of Social Power." In *Studies in Social Power,* edited by Dorwin Cartwright. Ann Arbor: Research Center for Group Dynamics, Institute for Social Research, University of Michigan.

Fridell, Lorie, Robert Lunney, Drew Diamond, and Bruce Kubu. 2001. *Racially Biased Policing: A Principled Response.* Washington, D.C.: Police Executive Research Forum.

Fuller, L. 1971. "Human Interaction and the Law." In *The Rule of Law,* edited by R. P. Wolff. New York: Simon & Schuster.

Gross, Sam R., and Debra Livingston. 2002. "Racial Profiling under Attack." *Columbia Law Review* 102:1413–38.

Haney, Craig. 1991. "The Fourteenth Amendment and Symbolic Legality." *Law and Human Behavior* 15:183–204.

Harris, David A. 1999. "The Stories, the Statistics, and the Law: Why 'Driving While Black' Matters." *Minnesota Law Review* 84:265–326.

Heider, Fritz. 1958. *The Psychology of Interpersonal Relations.* New York: Wiley.

Hoffman, Martin 1977. "Moral Internalization." *Advances in Experimental Social Psychology* 10:85–133.

Jost, John T., and Mahzarin R. Banaji. 1994. "The Role of Stereotyping in System-Justification and the Production of False Consciousness." *British Journal of Social Psychology* 33:1–27.

Kadish, Mark J. 1997. "The Drug Courier Profile: In Planes, Trains, and Automobiles; and Now in the Jury Box." *American University Law Review* 46: 747–91.

Kelman, Herbert C., and V. Lee Hamilton. 1989. *Crimes of Obedience: Toward a Social Psychology of Authority and Responsibility.* New Haven, Conn.: Yale University Press.

Kitzmann, Katherine M., and Robert E. Emery. 1993. "Procedural Justice and Parents' Satisfaction in a Field Study of Child Custody Dispute Resolution." *Law and Human Behavior* 17:553–67.

Knowles, John, and Nicola Persico. 2001. "Racial Bias in Motor Vehicles: Theory and Evidence." *Journal of Political Economy* 109:203–29.

Lamberth, John 1998. "Driving While Black: A Statistician Proves That Prejudice Still Rules the Road." *Washington Post* (August 16), p. C1.

Lind, E. Allan, Jerald Greenberg, Kimberly S. Scott, and Thomas D. Welchans. 2000. "The Winding Road from Employee to Complainant." *Administrative Science Quarterly* 45:557–90.

Lind, E. Allan, Carol T. Kulik, Maureen Ambrose, and Maria de Vera Park. 1993. "Individual and Corporate Dispute Resolution." *Administrative Science Quarterly* 38:224–51.

Lind, E. Allan, and Tom R. Tyler. 1988. *The Social Psychology of Procedural Justice.* New York: Plenum Press.

MacCoun, Robert J. 1993. "Drugs and the Law: A Psychological Analysis of Drug Prohibition." *Psychological Bulletin* 113:497–512.

MacCoun, Robert J., E. Allan Lind, Deborah R. Hensler, D. L. Bryant, and Patricia A. Ebener. 1988. *Alternative Adjudication: An Evaluation of the New Jersey Automobile Arbitration Program.* Santa Monica, Calif.: RAND.

Major, Brenda, and Jennifer Crocker. 1993. "Social Stigma: The Affective Consequences of Attributional Ambiguity." In *Affect, Cognition, and Stereotyping: Interactive Processes in Intergroup Perception,* edited by Diane M. Mackie and David L. Hamilton. New York: Academic.

Major, Brenda, Wendy J. Quinton, and Shannon K. McCoy. 2002. "Antecedents and Consequences of Attributions to Discrimination: Theoretical and Empirical Advances." In *Advances in Experimental Social Psychology,* vol. 34, edited by M. Zanna. New York: Academic.

Mastrofski, Stephen D., Jeffrey B. Snipes, and Anne E. Supina. 1996. "Com-

pliance on Demand: The Public's Responses to Specific Police Requests."
Journal of Crime and Delinquency 33:269–305.

McCluskey, John D., Stephen D. Mastrofski, and Roger B. Parks. 1998. "To
Acquiesce and Rebel: Predicting Citizen Compliance with Police Requests."
Unpublished manuscript. Arlington, Va.: George Mason University, De-
partment of Political Science.

McEwen, Craig, and Richard J. Maiman. 1984. "Mediation in Small Claims
Court." *Law and Society Review* 18:11–49.

Meares, Tracey L. 1997. "Charting Race and Class Differences in Attitudes
toward Drug Legalization and Law Enforcement." *Buffalo Criminal Law Review* 1:137–74.

———. 2000. "Norms, Legitimacy, and Law Enforcement." *Oregon Law Review* 79:391–415.

Meeks, Kenneth. 2000. *Driving While Black: Highways, Shopping Malls, Taxi-
cabs, Sidewalks: How to Fight Back if You Are a Victim of Racial Profiling.* New
York: Broadway Books.

Mendoza-Denton, Rudolfo, Geraldine Downey, Valeria J. Purdie, Angelina
Davis, and Janina Pietrzak. 2002. "Sensitivity to Status-Based Rejection:
Implications for African-American Students' College Experience." *Journal
of Personality and Social Psychology* 83:896–918.

Merelman, Richard J. 1966. "Learning and Legitimacy." *American Political Science Review* 60:548–61.

Moore, Mark 1997. "Legitimizing Criminal Justice Policies and Practices."
FBI Law Enforcement Bulletin (October):14–21.

Muir, William Ker, Jr. 1977. *Police: Streetcorner Politicians.* Chicago: University
of Chicago Press.

Nagin, Daniel S. 1998. "Criminal Deterrence Research at the Outset of the
Twenty-First Century." In *Crime and Justice: A Review of Research,* vol. 23,
edited by Michael Tonry. Chicago: University of Chicago Press.

Nagin, Daniel S., and Raymond Paternoster. 1991. "The Preventive Effects of
the Perceived Risk of Arrest: Testing an Expanded Conception of Deterrence." *Criminology* 29:561–87.

Nisbett, Richard, and Lee Ross. 1980. *Human Inference: Strategies and Short-
comings of Social Judgment.* Englewood Cliffs, N.J.: Prentice-Hall.

Parkin, Frank. 1971. *Class Inequality and Political Order: Social Stratification in
Capitalist and Communist Societies.* New York: Praeger.

Paternoster, Raymond. 1987. "The Deterrent Effect of the Perceived Certainty and Severity of Punishment." *Justice Quarterly* 4:173–217.

Paternoster, Raymond, Robert Brame, Ronet Bachman, and Lawrence Sherman. 1997. "Do Fair Procedures Matter?" *Law and Society Review* 31:163–
204.

Paternoster, Raymond, and Leeann Iovanni. 1986. "The Deterrent Effect of
Perceived Severity." *Social Forces* 64:751–77.

Paternoster, Raymond, Linda E. Saltzman, Gordon P. Waldo, and Theodore
G. Chiricos. 1983. "Perceived Risk and Social Control: Do Sanctions Really
Deter?" *Law and Society Review* 17:457–79.

Poythress, Norman G. 1994. "Procedural Preferences, Perceptions of Fairness, and Compliance with Outcomes." *Law and Human Behavior* 18:361–76.

Pruitt, Dean, Robert S. Peirce, Neil B. McGillicuddy, Gary L. Welton, and Lynn M. Castrianno. 1993. "Long-Term Success in Mediation." *Law and Human Behavior* 17:313–30.

Pruitt, Dean, Robert S. Peirce, Jo M. Zubek, Gary L. Welton, and Thomas H. Nochajski. 1990. "Goal Achievement, Procedural Justice, and the Success of Mediation." *International Journal of Conflict Management* 1:33–45.

Raz, Joseph. 1979. *The Authority of Law: Essays on Law and Morality.* Oxford: Oxford University Press.

Reiss, Albert J., Jr. 1971. *The Police and the Public.* New Haven, Conn.: Yale University Press.

Robinson, Paul H., and John M. Darley. 1995. *Justice, Liability, and Blame: Community Views and the Criminal Law.* Boulder, Colo.: Westview.

———. 1997. "The Utility of Desert." *Northwestern University Law Review* 91: 453–99.

Ross, H. Laurence. 1982. *Deterring the Drinking Driver: Legal Policy and Social Control.* Lexington, Mass.: Lexington Books.

Rudovsky, David. 2001. "Law Enforcement by Stereotypes and Serendipity: Racial Profiling and Stops and Searches without Cause." *University of Pennsylvania Journal of Constitutional Law* 3:296–349.

Sampson, Robert J., and Dawn J. Bartusch. 1998. "Legal Cynicism and (Subcultural?) Tolerance of Deviance." *Law and Society Review* 32:777–804.

Sampson, Robert J., Stephen W. Raudenbush, and Felton Earls. 1997. "Neighborhoods and Violent Crime." *Science* 277:918–24.

Sarat, Austin 1977. "Studying American Legal Culture." *Law and Society Review* 11:427–88.

Sherman, Lawrence W. 1993. "Defiance, Deterrence, Irrelevance: A Theory of the Criminal Sanction." *Journal of Research on Crime and Delinquency* 30: 445–73.

———. 1998. "Alternative Prevention Strategies and the Role of Policing." Presentation at a conference on "beyond incarceration," Harvard University, Cambridge, Mass., November.

———. 1999. "Consent of the Governed: Police, Democracy, and Diversity." Paper presented at a conference in honor of Professor Menachem Amir, Institute of Criminology, Hebrew University of Jerusalem, Jerusalem, January 7.

Sherman, Lawrence W., David P. Farrington, Brandon C. Welsh, and Doris Layton MacKenzie, eds. 2002. *Evidence-Based Crime Prevention.* London: Routledge.

Sherman, Lawrence W., Denise Gottfredson, Doris MacKenzie, John Eck, Peter Reuter, and Shawn Bushway. 1997. *Preventing Crime: What Works, What Doesn't, What's Promising: A Report to the United States Congress.* Prepared for the National Institute of Justice. Washington, D.C.: Office of Justice Programs, U.S. Department of Justice.

Sidanius, Jim, and Felicia Pratto. 1999. *Social Dominance: An Intergroup Theory of Social Hierarchy and Oppression.* New York: Cambridge University Press.

Skogan, Wesley G. 1994. *Contacts between Police and Public: Findings from the 1992 British Crime Survey*. London: H. M. Stationery Office.

Sparks, J. Richard, and Anthony Bottoms. 1995. "Legitimacy and Order in Prisons." *British Journal of Sociology* 46(1):45–62.

Sparks, J. Richard, Anthony Bottoms, and Will Hay. 1996. *Prisons and the Problem of Order*. Oxford: Clarendon Press.

Steele, Claude, Steven Spencer, and Joshua Aronson. 2002. "Contending with Group Image." In *Advances in Experimental Social Psychology*, vol. 34, edited by M. Zanna. New York: Academic.

Strang, Heather, and John Braithwaite, eds. 2000. *Restorative Justice: Philosophy to Pratice*. Burlington, Vt.: Ashgate.

———. 2001. *Restorative Justice and Civil Society*. New York: Cambridge University Press.

Stuntz, William. 1998. "Race, Class and Drugs." *Columbia Law Review* 98: 1795–1842.

———. 2002. "Local Policing after the Terror." *Yale Law Journal* 111:2137–94.

Sunshine, Jason, and Tom R. Tyler. 2003. "The Role of Procedural Justice and Legitimacy in Shaping Public Support for Policing." *Law and Society Review* 37(3), forthcoming.

Teevan, James J. 1975. "Perceptions of Punishment." In *Perception in Criminology*, edited by Richard L. Henshel and Robert A. Silverman. New York: Columbia University Press.

Thibaut, John W., and Laurens Walker. 1975. *Procedural Justice: A Psychological Analysis*. Hillsdale, N.J.: Erlbaum.

Thompson, Anthony C. 1999. "Stopping the Usual Suspects: Race and the Fourth Amendment." *New York University Law Review* 74:956–1013.

Tyler, Tom R. 1988. "What Is Procedural Justice? Criteria Used by Citizens to Assess the Fairness of Legal Procedures." *Law and Society Review* 22:103–35.

———. 1990. *Why People Obey the Law*. New Haven, Conn.: Yale University Press.

———. 1994. "Governing amid Diversity: Can Fair Decision-Making Procedures Bridge Competing Public Interests and Values?" *Law and Society Review* 28:701–22.

———. 1998. "Public Mistrust of the Law: A Political Perspective." *University of Cincinnati Law Review* 66:847–76.

———. 2000. "Social Justice." *International Journal of Psychology* 35:117–25.

———. 2001a. "Public Trust and Confidence in Legal Authorities: What Do Majority and Minority Group Members Want from Legal Authorities?" *Behavioral Sciences and the Law* 19:215–35.

———. 2001b. "Trust and Law Abidingness: A Proactive Model of Social Regulation." *Boston University Law Review* 81:361–406.

Tyler, Tom R., and Steven L. Blader. 2000. *Cooperation in Groups: Procedural Justice, Social Identity, and Behavioral Engagement*. Philadelphia: Psychology Press.

———. 2002. "Procedural Justice, Identity, and Cooperative Behavior." *Personality and Social Psychology Review*. Forthcoming.

Tyler, Tom R., Robert Boeckmann, Heather J. Smith, and Yuen J. Huo. 1997. *Social Justice in a Diverse Society.* Boulder, Colo.: Westview.

Tyler, Tom R., Jonathan D. Casper, and Bonnie Fisher. 1989. "Maintaining Allegiance toward Political Authorities." *American Journal of Political Science* 33:629–52.

Tyler, Tom R., and John Darley. 2000. "Building a Law-Abiding Society: Taking Public Views about Morality and the Legitimacy of Legal Authorities into Account When Formulating Substantive Law." *Hofstra Law Review* 28:707–39.

Tyler, Tom R., and Yuen J. Huo. 2002. *Trust in the Law: Encouraging Public Cooperation with the Police and Courts.* New York: Russell-Sage Foundation.

Tyler, Tom R., and E. Allan Lind. 1992. "A Relational Model of Authority in Groups." In *Advances in Experimental Social Psychology*, vol. 25, edited by M. Zanna. New York: Academic.

Tyler, Tom R., and Kathleen M. McGraw. 1986. "Ideology and the Interpretation of Personal Experience." *Journal of Social Issues* 42:115–28.

Tyler, Tom R., and Heather J. Smith. 1997. "Social Justice and Social Movements." In *Handbook of Social Psychology*, vol. 2., 4th ed., edited by Daniel Gilbert, Susan Fiske, and Gardner Lindzey. New York: McGraw-Hill.

Tyler, Tom R., and Cheryl Wakslak. 2002. "Profiling and the Legitimacy of the Police." Unpublished manuscript. New York: New York University, Department of Psychology.

Weber, Max. 1968. *Economy and Society: An Outline of Interpretive Sociology.* Edited by Guenther Roth and Claus Wittich. New York: Bedminster.

Weitekamp, Elmer G. M., Hans-Jurgen Kerner, and Ulrike Meier. 1996. "Problem-Solving Policing: Views of Citizens and Citizen's Expectations." Paper presented at the international conference on problem-solving policing as crime prevention. Stockholm, September.

Wilson, James Q. 1968. *Varieties of Police Behavior: The Management of Law and Order in Eight Communities.* Cambridge, Mass.: Harvard University Press.

Wissler, Roselle L. 1995. "Mediation and Adjudication in Small Claims Court." *Law and Society Review* 29:323–58.

Alex R. Piquero, David P. Farrington,
and Alfred Blumstein

The Criminal Career
Paradigm

ABSTRACT

Criminal careers have long occupied the imaginations of criminologists.
Since the 1986 publication of the National Academy of Sciences report on
criminal careers and career criminals, a variety of theoretical, empirical,
and policy issues have surfaced. Data on key criminal career dimensions of
prevalence, frequency, specialization, and desistance have raised theoretical
questions regarding the patterning of criminal activity over the life course.
Recent research has identified important methodological issues, including
the relationship between past and future criminal activity, and potential
explanations for this relationship: state dependence and persistent
heterogeneity. Advanced statistical techniques have been developed to
address these challenges. Criminal career research has identified important
policy issues such as individual prediction of offending frequency and
career duration, and has shifted the focus toward the interplay between
risk and protective factors.

Researchers have long been interested in the patterning of criminal activity throughout the course of criminal careers. Von Scheel (1890,
p. 191) pointed out that "Ideal criminal statistics . . . would follow
carefully the evolution of criminal tendencies in a given population."
Kobner (1893, p. 670) noted that "correct statistics of offenders can be
developed only by a study of the total life history of individuals." Von
Mayr (1917, pp. 425–26) argued that a "deeper insight into the statistics of criminality is made possible by the disclosure of developmental

Alex R. Piquero is associate professor of criminology and law, Center for Studies in
Criminology and Law, University of Florida. David P. Farrington is professor of psychological criminology at Cambridge University. Alfred Blumstein is J. Erik Jonsson Professor of Urban Systems and Operations Research, H. John Heinz III School of Public
Policy and Management, Carnegie Mellon University.

regularities in which criminality develops in the course of a human life-time. To do this it is necessary to identify the offender and his offense in the population and to keep him under constant statistical control so that it is possible for each birth cohort entering punishable age and until all its members are dead, to study statistically its participation or nonparticipation in criminality and the intensity of such participation in its various forms." Soon after these statements appeared, original studies of career criminals emerged including notably Shaw's *The Jack-Roller* (1930) and Sutherland's *The Professional Thief* (1937). Although these and related works offered insightful observations about the most serious or most interesting criminals, they were largely uninformative about typical criminal careers.

Another line of research focused on the relationship between age and crime. In 1831, Quetelet recognized that age was closely related to the propensity for crime. Using data on crimes committed against persons and property in France from 1826 to 1829, Quetelet found that crimes peaked in the late teens through the mid-twenties (Quetelet [1831] 1984, pp. 54–57). Since Quetelet's findings, a number of researchers have pursued the relationship between age and crime, across cultures and historical periods, and for a number of different crime types (see Hirschi and Gottfredson 1983). Research on the relationship between age and crime has been one of the most studied issues within criminology (Greenberg 1977; Rowe and Tittle 1977; Tittle 1988; Steffensmeier et al. 1989; Britt 1992; Tittle and Grasmick 1997).

The relationship between age and crime raises the question of the degree to which the aggregate pattern displayed in the age/crime curve is similar to—or different from—the pattern of individual careers and whether conclusions about individuals can be validly drawn from aggregate data. For example, how far does the observed peak of the aggregate age/crime curve reflect changes within individuals as opposed to changes in the composition of offenders? In other words, is the peak in the age/crime curve a function of active offenders committing more crime or of more individuals actively offending during those peak years? Some evidence suggests that the aggregate peak age of offending primarily reflects variations in prevalence (Farrington 1986; but see Loeber and Snyder 1990).

Within individuals, to what extent is the slowing past the peak age a function of deceleration in continued criminal activity or stopping by some of the individuals? Across individuals, how much of the age/crime curve can be attributed to the arrival/initiation and departure/

termination of different individuals? What about the role of co-offending? How much of the continuation of offending by lone/solo offenders is attributable to identifying theirs as the key criminal careers of long duration, with their co-offenders serving merely as transients with shorter careers? How much of the age/crime curve for any particular crime type is a consequence of individuals persisting in offending, but switching from less serious crimes early in the career to more serious crimes as they get older?

These questions are central to theory, as well as policy, especially those policies that are geared toward incapacitative effects of criminal sanctions, as well as to changes in the criminal career (e.g., rehabilitation or criminalization patterns as a result of actions by the criminal justice system). For example, if crime commission and arrest rates differ significantly among offenders and over the career, the effect of sentence length on overall crime will depend on who is incarcerated and for how long (Petersilia 1980, p. 325). Addressing these and related issues requires knowledge about individual criminal careers, their initiation, their termination, and the dynamic changes between these end points.

A criminal career is the longitudinal sequence of crimes committed by an individual offender (Blumstein et al. 1986, p. 12). The criminal career approach partitions the aggregate rate of offending into two primary components: participation, or the distinction between those who commit crime and those who do not, and frequency, or the rate of activity of active offenders, commonly referred to by the Greek letter lambda (λ) (Blumstein et al. 1986, p. 12). Two other dimensions affecting aggregate crime rates are duration, or the length of an individual career, and seriousness, which includes both the offenses committed and patterns of switching among offenses (Blumstein et al. 1986, p. 13). To study these issues, a Panel on Research on Criminal Careers was convened by the National Academy of Sciences (NAS) at the request of the U.S. National Institute of Justice in 1983 and charged with evaluating the feasibility of predicting the future course of criminal careers, assessing the effects of prediction instruments in reducing crime through incapacitation, and reviewing the contribution of research on criminal careers to the development of fundamental knowledge about crime and criminals (Blumstein et al. 1986, p. x).

Since publication of the report, numerous theoretical, empirical, and policy issues have surfaced regarding the longitudinal patterning of criminal careers. One concerned the relevance (or lack thereof) of criminal career research for criminology generally and public policy in particular. Michael Gottfredson and Travis Hirschi (1986, 1987, 1988) levied a series of critiques against the criminal career approach in which they claimed that attempts to identify career criminals and other types of offenders were doomed to failure. Perhaps the most important issue they raised concerns causality. Although the criminal career paradigm necessitates a longitudinal focus in order to study both the between- and within-individual patterning of criminal activity, Gottfredson and Hirschi questioned whether longitudinal research designs could actually resolve questions of causal order. They also argued that, since correlations with offending were relatively stable over the life course, cross-sectional designs were suitable for studying the causes of crime.

Gottfredson and Hirschi's challenge precipitated theoretical and methodological advances in the study of the longitudinal sequence of criminal careers. Ensuing research showed that, while the between-individual patterning of criminal careers was important, the within-individual differences in criminal activity over time that were not reflected in the aggregate age/crime curve were more important. Theoretical developments emerged claiming that the aggregate age/crime curve masked the offending trajectories of distinct groups of offenders who offend at different rates over the life course, and whose criminal activity is caused by unique factors. Empirical research has tended to confirm these and related theoretical expectations.

Research on criminal careers has generated a wealth of information regarding the longitudinal patterning of criminal activity. For example, researchers have been able to document and account for important empirical regularities such as the relationship between past and future criminal activity, isolate important life circumstances and events that lead to within-individual changes in criminal activity over time, and develop improved statistical techniques to study criminal careers in more detail. Still, much more research is needed. Little is known about how the development and progression of criminal careers varies across race and gender or about how individual criminal careers vary across neighborhood contexts. Similarly, researchers have identified only a small number of life circumstances that relate both positively and negatively to criminal activity, and they are only beginning to understand some of the methodological difficulties encountered in longitudinal research on criminal careers. Also, the relevance and use of criminal career research for incapacitation decisions remains unknown. As prison populations have soared, few incarceration decisions are likely to have been based on sound empirical knowledge of the longitudinal patterning of criminal careers or of career duration estimates in particular.

This essay surveys background and recent developments associated with the criminal career paradigm. Section I introduces studies that have served as platforms for criminal career research and reviews the findings of some of the major cohort and longitudinal studies. Section II provides a brief review of the criminal career report published by the NAS in 1986. Section III identifies theoretical challenges and developments since the NAS report and discusses newly articulated criminal career features. Section IV outlines methodological issues that arise in criminal career research including issues relating to data, research designs, analytic techniques, and general analytic issues. Section V provides an overview of the empirical findings generated by criminal careers research, with an explicit concentration on the dimensions of criminal careers. Section VI presents a discussion of selected policy implications including the identification of career criminals and policies associated with sentence duration. Section VII offers a modest agenda for future theoretical, empirical, and methodological research.

I. Sources of Knowledge

Many longitudinal studies throw light on criminal career issues, but a relatively small number of classic and contemporary studies are especially important. Table 1 presents a summary of the main features of each.

Several early longitudinal studies shaped the landscape of criminal career research: the Gluecks' Unraveling Juvenile Delinquency study, McCord's Cambridge/Somerville study, Wolfgang's Philadelphia Birth Cohort Studies, Farrington's Cambridge Study in Delinquent Development, Elliott's National Youth Survey, Le Blanc's Montreal adjudicated and adolescent samples of youth, and two Swedish studies, Project Metropolitan and the "Individual Development and Environment" research program. These projects differ in the samples used, the issues addressed, the data used, and the methodological approaches taken.

A. The Gluecks' Unraveling Juvenile Delinquency (UJD) Study

The Gluecks compared the criminal activity of 500 nondelinquents with that of 500 boys officially designated as delinquent and selected from the Massachusetts correctional system. The delinquent boys were

TABLE 1
Sources of Knowledge

Study	Sample	Measure of Crime
Early studies:		
Gluecks	500 delinquent and 500 nondelinquent males from Massachusetts	Official and self-, teacher-, and parent-report records
McCord	506 boys from Cambridge and Somerville, Massachusetts	Official records
Philadelphia Birth Cohort Studies:		
1. 1945 cohort	9,945 boys born in Philadelphia in 1945 and who lived in Philadelphia through age 17	Official records
2. 1958 cohort	27,160 boys and girls born in Philadelphia in 1958 and who lived in Philadelphia through age 17	Official records
Cambridge Study in Delinquent Development	411 London males selected at ages 8–9 from registers of six state primary schools	Official and self-report records
National Youth Survey	1,725 male and female adolescents aged 11–17	Self-report records (official records are not publicly available)
Montreal Adjudicated Youths	505 male and 150 female delinquents recruited in 1992 at an average age of 15 in 1974 and followed to age 23	Official and self-report records

Study	Description	Records
Montreal Adolescent Sample	3,070 Montreal adolescents age 14 in 1974 followed to age 40. A subsample of 458 boys was reinterviewed at 16, 30, and 40 years old	Self-report records
Project Metropolitan	15,117 males and females born in the Stockholm metropolitan area in 1953 and still residing there in 1963	Official records
Individual Development and Environment	1,027 third-grade school children in Orebro, Sweden, in 1965 followed from the age of 10 to 30	Official records
Contemporary studies: Causes and correlates studies:		
1. Pittsburgh	1,517 boys in Pittsburgh public schools, ages 7, 10, 13	Official and self-report records
2. Denver	1,527 youths from high-risk Denver neighborhoods, ages 7–15	Official and self-report records
3. Rochester	1,000 youths from Rochester public schools, age 12	Official and self-report records
Dunedin Multidisciplinary Study	1,037 youths of an unselected birth cohort from Dunedin, New Zealand, born in 1972–73	Official and self-report records
Project on Human Development in Chicago Neighborhoods	6,500 individuals in 80 communities in Chicago	Official and self-report records

white males, aged ten to seventeen, who had recently been committed to either the Lyman School for Boys in Westboro, Massachusetts, or the Industrial School for Boys in Shirley, Massachusetts (Glueck and Glueck 1950, p. 27). The nondelinquents, also white males aged ten to seventeen, were chosen from Boston public schools. Their nondelinquent status was determined on the basis of official record checks and interviews with parents, teachers, local police, social workers, recreational leaders, and the boys themselves (Sampson and Laub 1993, p. 26). In general, the nondelinquents were well behaved.

One particularly interesting feature of the UJD study was its matching design. The two groups were matched, case by case, on age, nationality, neighborhood, and measured intelligence. Data on a number of characteristics were collected on both sets of boys including social, psychological, and biological characteristics, aspects of family life, school performance, work experience, and other life events, as well as delinquent and criminal behavior from self-, teacher-, and parent-reports and official records. The Gluecks and their research team followed up the UJD subjects from an average age of fourteen to ages twenty-five and thirty-two. Follow-up information included extensive criminal history record checks in a number of different states, items related to the subjects' living arrangements (including marriage, divorce, children, etc.), military experience, employment, and schooling history.

The Gluecks studied the correlates of onset, persistence, and desistance. A number of key findings emerged. First, they found a strong relationship between age and crime. In particular, they found that, as the sample of offenders aged, their individual crime rates declined. Second, they observed that an early age of onset was related to a lengthy and persistent criminal career. Third, the Gluecks found strong evidence in favor of the stability postulate; that is, that the best predictor of future antisocial behavior was past antisocial behavior. They observed that many of the juvenile delinquents went on to engage in criminal activity as adults. Finally, their analysis uncovered strong family influences. Those families with lax discipline combined with erratic/threatening punishment, poor supervision, and weak emotional ties between parent and child generated the highest probability of persistent delinquency.

Recently, Sampson and Laub (1993) recoded and reanalyzed the Glueck data using contemporary statistical and methodological techniques. They found patterns of both stability and change in criminal behavior over the life course. For example, they found that, even after controlling for stable individual differences in offending propensity, life events (e.g., marriage) and, in particular, attachment to informal social control agents fostered cessation from criminal activity (Laub, Nagin, and Sampson 1998). Laub and Sampson (2001) are continuing to follow the Glueck men through late adulthood.

B. McCord's Cambridge-Somerville Project

The Cambridge-Somerville Youth Study was designed to learn about the development of delinquency and to test the notion that children could be steered away from delinquency through guidance and prevention (McCord 1992, 2000, p. 240). The study's original investigator, Richard Cabot, selected high-poverty/high-crime sites in eastern Massachusetts for study. Police, scout leaders, shopkeepers, and social workers identified eligible candidates for inclusion in the project. Between 1935 and 1939, staff obtained relevant information from families, schools, and neighborhoods. From this information they were able to match pairs of boys similar in age, intelligence, family structure, religion, social environment, and delinquency-prone history. The selection committee flipped a coin to decide which member of the pair would receive treatment and which would be placed in the control group (McCord 2000, p. 240). The "treatment" administered by adult counselors included intensive individual help and guidance for continuing social, physical, intellectual, and spiritual growth. All subjects were male, their average age was approximately eleven at the outset, nearly all were white, and nearly all were from working-class backgrounds. By May 1939, 650 subjects were involved in the study, equally split between the experimental and control groups.

Initial data were collected in 1942, with follow-ups in 1955 and 1976. Early results indicated that the special work of the guidance counselor did no better than the usual forces in the community in preventing involvement in delinquency. In several respects, boys in the experimental group actually did worse (e.g., went to court more, committed more offenses). The first follow-up, undertaken in 1955, showed that nearly equal numbers of experimental- and control-group members had been convicted as adults. In the second follow-up (1976), McCord found that "none of the . . . measures confirmed hopes that treatment had improved the lives of those in the treatment group" (McCord 1978, p. 288). Recent analysis of the experimental group members showed that they tended to die earlier and had more mental illness (Dishion, McCord, and Poulin 1999).

Still, the study produced four key findings, which have been observed in other criminal career studies. First, the earlier the age of onset, the greater the likelihood of continued offending in adulthood. Second, although most juvenile delinquents committed a crime as an adult, the majority of adult offenders had no history of offending as juveniles. Third, family factors were important predictors of offending (McCord 1978). In particular, McCord (1991) found that maternal behavior influenced juvenile delinquency and through those effects, adult criminality, and that paternal interaction with the family appeared to have a more direct influence on adult criminal behavior. Finally, McCord's research has also uncovered strong evidence that both alcoholism and criminality tend to run in families and that, in part, alcoholic and criminal parents tend to provide poor socializing environments. In particular, McCord (1999, p. 114) observed "that alcoholic and criminal men were disproportionately likely to be aggressive in their families and to have fathered sons whose mothers were disproportionately incompetent in their maternal roles."

C. Wolfgang's Philadelphia Birth Cohort Studies

Marvin Wolfgang and colleagues (1972) traced the delinquent careers of 9,945 males who were born in Philadelphia in 1945 and who lived in Philadelphia between ages ten and seventeen. Because of the structure of the data set, Wolfgang, Figlio, and Sellin "were able to use sophisticated stochastic models to examine some long-standing but untested assumptions concerning the dynamics of specialization in illegal behavior and developmental trends in the seriousness of that behavior" (Bursik 1989, p. 390). This study has been described as one of the seminal pieces of criminal career scholarship produced in the twentieth century (Morris 1972; Bursik 1989).

Several important findings emerged. First, 35 percent of the boys were involved with the police at least once. Second, a very small percentage of offenders (6 percent of the cohort, 18 percent of the delinquent subset) was responsible for 52 percent of all delinquency in the cohort through age seventeen. Third, the tendency to specialize in particular offenses was small. Finally, (early) age-at-onset was consistently related to persistent and serious criminality.

A second Philadelphia birth cohort study, conducted by Tracy, Wolfgang, and Figlio (1990), traced the criminal records of 27,160 boys and girls born in Philadelphia in 1958 and followed through age seventeen. Although the main results of the 1945 cohort were replicated, including that the prevalence of arrest up to age eighteen was about the same (35 percent) as in the 1945 cohort, and the substantive male findings (e.g., chronicity) from the 1945 cohort were replicated among females in the 1958 cohort, there were a few important exceptions. For example, the prevalence of police contacts of both whites and blacks was lower in the 1958 cohort than for the whites and blacks in the 1945 cohort. The aggregate prevalence was the same because there were more blacks in the 1958 cohort, and blacks had a higher prevalence of offending than whites. One reason why both groups had a lower total prevalence of offending was that there were many fewer minor arrests. A second difference was that the offense rate for the 1958 cohort (1,159 offenses per 1,000 subjects) was higher than the rate for the 1945 cohort (1,027 offenses per 1,000 subjects) (Tracy, Wolfgang, and Figlio 1990, p. 276). A third difference across the two cohorts was that the 1958 cohort evidenced more severe (violent) criminality. For example, the 1958 cohort rate exceeded the 1945 cohort by factors of 3:1 for homicide, 1.7:1 for rape, 5:1 for robbery, and almost 2:1 for aggravated assault and burglary (Tracy, Wolfgang, and Figlio 1990, p. 276).

Tracy and Kempf-Leonard (1996) collected criminal records up to age twenty-six for the 1958 cohort. Their analysis indicated that career continuity was more common than discontinuity. In other words, adult crime was more likely among former delinquents, while nondelinquents more often remained noncriminal as adults. Also, the key predictors of adult criminality included an early onset as well as being active in the juvenile period (prior to age seventeen). They also found that early imposition of probation was associated with a lower probability of continuation into adult offending for males, but this effect was insignificant for females. No form of juvenile incarceration seemed to inhibit adult offending. These results could be due to a selection effect in that judges were more likely to sentence "less serious" offenders to probation.

D. Farrington's Cambridge Study in Delinquent Development

The Cambridge Study in Delinquent Development is a prospective longitudinal survey of the development of offending and antisocial behavior in 411 South London males born mainly between September 1952 and August 1954. The study was initiated in 1961 and for the first twenty years was directed by Donald West. Since 1982, it has been directed by David Farrington. The males have been personally interviewed nine times (at ages eight, ten, fourteen, sixteen, eighteen, twenty-one, twenty-five, thirty-two, and forty-six), and their parents were interviewed annually between their ages of eight and fifteen. Peer ratings were obtained at ages eight and ten, and criminal records (and the criminal records of all their immediate relatives—brothers, fathers, mothers, sisters, and wives) have been searched up to age forty.

The conviction data from the Cambridge study have generated an impressive array of research reports and a number of key findings regarding the development of crime over the life course (Farrington 2002). First, excluding minor crimes such as common assault, traffic infractions, and drunkenness, the most common offenses were theft, burglary, and unauthorized taking of vehicles. Second, the annual prevalence of offending increased up to age seventeen and then decreased. Also, while the modal age for offending was seventeen, the mean age was twenty-one, reflecting the inherent individual skewness of the age-crime curve. Third, 40 percent of the males in the Cambridge study were convicted of criminal offenses up to age forty. Fourth, up to age forty, the mean age of onset (measured as the age at first conviction) was 18.6, while the mean age of desistance (measured as the age at last conviction) was 25.7. Fifth, the average number of offenses per active offender was 4.6 crimes. Sixth, for offenders with two or more offenses, the average duration of criminal careers from first to last recorded conviction was 10.4 years.

Other developmental aspects of criminal careers have also been examined with the Cambridge data. For example, Farrington, Lambert, and West (1998) studied the criminal careers of brothers and sisters of the study's subjects and reported prevalence estimates of 43.4 percent and 12.1 percent for brothers and sisters, respectively. Regarding specialization, Farrington found that most males convicted for a violent offense tended to be convicted for a nonviolent offense as well and that violent crimes occurred almost at random in criminal careers (Farrington 1991). The chronic offender effect also showed up in the Cambridge data. A small number of chronic offenders, usually coming from multiproblem families, accounted for substantial proportions of all official and self-reported offenses, and they were, to a considerable extent, predictable in advance (Farrington 2002). Finally, several childhood factors predicted criminality throughout the life course, including impulsivity, low intelligence, family criminality, broken families, and poor parental supervision.

E. Elliott's National Youth Survey

The National Youth Survey (NYS) is a prospective longitudinal study of a U.S. national probability sample concerning delinquency and drug use. The NYS sample was obtained through a multistage probability sampling of households in the United States. Originally, 7,998 households were randomly selected, and all 2,360 eligible youths aged eleven to seventeen living in the households were included. Seventy-three percent of those youths (1,725) agreed to participate, signed consent forms, and, along with one of their parents, completed first-wave interviews in 1977. The demographic characteristics of the sample are generally representative of eleven- to seventeen-year-olds in the United States (see Elliott, Huizinga, and Ageton 1985; Elliott, Huizinga, and Menard 1989). Nine waves of data are available on the panel, which was age twenty-seven to thirty-three when last interviewed in 1993. Both official and self-reported records of crime and delinquency are available for all respondents. In each wave of the NYS, respondents were asked a large number of questions about events and behavior that occurred during the preceding calendar year, including involvement in a variety of illegal acts. In addition, a number of questions were asked regarding key theoretical constructs from control, strain, and differential association theories.

Elliott (1994) has conducted the most elaborate analysis of the onset, developmental course, and termination of serious violent offenders in the NYS, where serious violent offending included aggravated assaults, robberies, and rapes that involved some injury or a weapon (Elliott 1994, p. 4). Regarding involvement in serious violent offending, Elliott found that at the peak age (seventeen), 36 percent of African-American males and 25 percent of the white males reported committing one or more serious violent offenses. Among females, nearly one African-American female in five and one white female in ten reported involvement in serious violent offending. The decline with age in serious violent offending is steeper for females, and the gender differential becomes greater over time. Regarding the onset of a serious, violent career, Elliott found that serious violent offending begins between ages twelve and twenty, with negligible risk of initiation after age twenty. African-American males exhibit an earlier age of onset for serious violent offending, and more African-American males become involved than white males.

Elliott studied the progression of offenses in the behavioral repertoire. In general, he found that minor forms of delinquency and alcohol use were added to the behavioral repertoire before serious forms of criminal theft and violence. Elliott suggested that the self-report data indicated that criminal behavior escalated over time in a criminal career and that serious violent offenders exhibited versatile offending patterns. Finally, Elliott examined continuity rates for serious violent offending after age twenty-one. Nearly twice as many African Americans compared to whites continued their violent careers into their twenties and thus were likely to have longer criminal careers.

F. Le Blanc's Montreal Sample of Adjudicated Youths

Le Blanc and associates recruited a sample of 470 males adjudicated at the Montreal Juvenile Court over a two-year period (see Le Blanc and Fréchette 1989 for a detailed summary of the self-reported and official careers of these youths). They were interviewed at the average ages of fifteen, seventeen, twenty-two, thirty, and forty. Le Blanc and associates also recruited a representative sample of Montreal adolescents comprised of 3,100 boys and girls, of which a random subset of 458 boys was reinterviewed at ages sixteen, thirty, and forty. In 1992, they recruited a replication sample of 505 male and 150 female adjudicated youth from the Montreal Juvenile Court who were between thirteen and seventeen years of age and adjudicated for a criminal offense under the Young Offender Act or for problem behavior under the Youth Protection Act. All of the youths were sentenced to probation or placed in a correctional institution with a treatment philosophy. The sample includes almost all of the adolescents who were adjudicated in that court over two years. These individuals have been interviewed twice since (Le Blanc and Kaspy 1998).

Also, for these three samples, in addition to official records, a self-report card-sorting interview was administered to the youths in private settings. For a number of criminal and deviant behaviors, researchers collected information on the variety or number of different acts ever committed, the age at which various acts were first committed (including the onset age), the frequency with which the act was committed, and the last age at which the act was committed. A detailed summary of the offense histories of these adjudicated youths appears in Le Blanc and Fréchette (1989). The males, and a sample of male adolescents, were later interviewed at age thirty-two. For all these samples, personality and social (family, school, work, leisure, attitudes, etc.) data were collected at each age.

G. Swedish Studies

Project Metropolitan is a large-scale, longitudinal study that provides offending information for all individuals born in the Stockholm metropolitan area in 1953 and still residing there in 1963. It comprises 15,117 males and females. Data come from police-recorded criminality (i.e., those crimes reported to the police that have been cleared by connecting a suspect to the crime). A number of criminal career studies have been carried out with these data, including a study on the relationship between age and crime (Wikström 1990) and a study on gender and age differences in crime continuity (Andersson 1990).

The Project on Individual Development and Environment was initiated in 1965 by David Magnusson, with one of its primary purposes being an investigation of criminal activity over the life span. Subjects were 1,027 third-grade children (age ten) in Orebro, Sweden, in 1965, who have been followed with criminal records from the age of ten to thirty. The data cover a broad range of individual physiological and behavioral factors as well as structural and social factors. Outcome data were collected from official registers (including information on criminal offenses, mental health, employment, education, alcohol abuse, etc.). Several studies have used these data to analyze the relationship between age and crime (Stattin, Magnusson, and Reichel 1989) and patterns of stability and change in criminal activity (Stattin and Magnusson 1991).

H. Causes and Correlates Studies

In 1986, the Office of Juvenile Justice and Delinquency Prevention (OJJDP) of the U.S. Department of Justice created the Program of Research on the Causes and Correlates of Delinquency by supporting three coordinated, prospective longitudinal research projects in Pittsburgh, Pennsylvania, Rochester, New York, and Denver, Colorado. The Pittsburgh study, which oversampled high-risk boys, consists of 1,517 boys (cohorts of first-, fourth-, and seventh-grade boys) in the public school system in Pittsburgh. The Rochester sample consists of 1,000 youth (73 percent boys) and represents the entire range of seventh- and eighth-grade students attending Rochester's public schools. The Denver sample consists of 1,527 youth (slightly more than 50 percent boys) who represent the general population of youth residing in households in high-risk neighborhoods in Denver.

These studies represent a milestone in criminological research because they constitute the largest shared-measurement approach ever achieved in delinquency studies. As of 1997, the research teams had interviewed nearly 4,000 participants at regular intervals for nearly a decade, recording their lives in great detail (Kelley et al. 1997). The research teams continue to follow up participants across sites as the study subjects enter adulthood.

In general, the causes and correlates studies are designed to improve understanding of serious delinquency, violence, and drug use through the examination of how individual youth develop within the context of family, school, peers, and community (Kelley et al. 1997). The numbers are sufficient to study race, gender, and community-level differences in the determinants of criminal and antisocial behavior. Although each site has unique features, they share several common elements.

All three sites are longitudinal investigations that involve repeated contacts (at six- or twelve-month intervals) with and about the same individual in an effort to assess both the subject's involvement in antisocial and criminal activity and the correlates of such involvement. The causes and correlates studies entail a shared-measurement approach in that each of the three sites uses common core measures to collect data on a wide range of key variables including delinquent and criminal involvement, drug and alcohol use, family, peer, and community-level characteristics, educational experiences and, as the samples move into adulthood, marriage and employment. Importantly, besides detailed assessments of self-reported offending, researchers at each site are collecting juvenile justice and adult criminal records.

Thus far, a number of reports and publications have been produced that have examined key features of criminal career dimensions (see Huizinga, Loeber, and Thornberry 1993; Kelley et al. 1997; Loeber et al. 1998, 1999). Researchers have documented important information related to involvement in serious violence and the progression of criminal activity over the life course.

I. The Dunedin Multidisciplinary Health and Human Development Study
The Dunedin Study is a longitudinal investigation of the health, development, and behavior of a complete cohort of births between April 1, 1972, and March 31, 1973, in Dunedin, a provincial capital city of 120,000 on New Zealand's South Island (Silva and Stanton 1996).

Perinatal data were obtained at delivery, and when the children were later traced for follow-up at age three, 91 percent ($N = 1,037$) of the eligible births, 52 percent of whom were boys, participated in the assessment, forming the base sample for the longitudinal study (Moffitt et al. 2001). The sample turns thirty in 2002–3 and researchers continue to follow up sample members and most recently have included assessments of the subjects' partners, peers, and children.

The Dunedin data are designed for three specific types of studies (Moffitt et al. 2001, p. 10): childhood predictors of later health and behavior outcomes, developmental studies of continuity and change in health and behavior, and epidemiological studies of the prevalence and incidence of health problems, behavior problems, and associations among problem types. Although it was not originally initiated to examine antisocial and criminal activity, it has considerably advanced knowledge about offending.

Within the realm of criminal and antisocial behavior, researchers have collected a wealth of information including early forms of antisocial behavior, juvenile delinquency, and official records from the police and court systems. In addition, researchers have collected information on the correlates of antisocial and criminal activity including neuropsychological tests, peer associations, family and school experiences, and, most recently as the subjects entered adulthood, information related to partner violence.

Since 1975, over 600 publications have appeared. With regard to key dimensions of criminal careers, a number of studies have examined general issues related to the patterning of criminal activity, gender differences, and characteristics associated with—and determinants of—criminal and antisocial activity over the life course (see review in Moffitt et al. 2001).

J. Project on Human Development in Chicago Neighborhoods
The Project on Human Development in Chicago Neighborhoods (PHDCN) is a major, interdisciplinary study aimed at understanding the causes and pathways of juvenile delinquency, adult crime, substance abuse, and violence in Chicago neighborhoods (Earls 2001). Throughout its course, the project has followed approximately 6,500 individuals and eighty communities in the city of Chicago and includes equal numbers of males and females drawn from African-American, Latino, white, and mixed ethnic communities and from all social classes within each of these groups.

The project is unique in that it combines two studies into a single study. The first is an intensive investigation of Chicago's neighborhoods, including their social, economic, organizational, political, and cultural structures, and the dynamic changes that take place in these structures within and across neighborhoods. The second is a series of coordinated longitudinal studies including about 6,500 randomly selected children, adolescents, and young adults, in an effort to examine the changing circumstances of their lives, as well as the personal characteristics, that may lead them toward or away from a variety of antisocial behaviors. The project employs an accelerated longitudinal design that, unlike traditional longitudinal studies that follow a single group of people for a long period of time, begins with nine different age groups, from prenatal to age eighteen, and follows them for several years (Tonry, Ohlin, and Farrington 1991). The age groups are separated by three-year intervals, so three years after the data collection started, the overall age range was continuous. Information concerning human development will be available covering all ages, but with the additional complexity of linking across the groups.

In addition to a wealth of information related to neighborhoods, families, and individuals growing up in these contexts, researchers are collecting information on systematic social observations of face blocks across the neighborhoods as well as various sorts of antisocial and criminal activity from early childhood through adulthood for subjects. Most recently, the project has expanded to include two other studies, one on children's exposure to violence and its consequences, and a second on child care and its impact on early child development. A number of publications have appeared, and a considerable number are in process (Earls and Visher 1997; Sampson, Raudenbush, and Earls 1997).

These contemporary studies have paid significant attention to key criminal career dimensions, particularly in describing involvement in criminal activity. For example, data from the three causes and correlates studies have generated important new information on the prevalence and frequency of criminal activity among samples of inner-city boys and girls, and as these samples enter adulthood, researchers will be better able to describe and empirically assess the patterning and causes of specialization and desistance. Data from the Dunedin study have been used to describe the sample's involvement in delinquency, arrest, and conviction, as well as the causes of participation and frequency of offending through age twenty-six. The Dunedin data are especially useful because they also contain a rich array of data on other noncriminal antisocial behaviors including data from the *Diagnostic and Statistical Manual of Mental Disorders* (DSM-IV). Finally, the PHDCN may prove to be the largest data collection effort designed to understand criminal activity using several levels of analysis. This study will allow for unique insight into the embeddedness of individuals within family and neighborhood contexts in an effort to document involvement in criminal activity from birth through the twenties.

II. Models of Criminal Careers

Several of the early criminal career studies stimulated a major initiative by the NAS. In 1986, the NAS published the two-volume report *Criminal Careers and "Career Criminals"* that presented a systematic overview (Blumstein et al. 1986). The aim was to synthesize the research on criminal careers, evaluate the feasibility of predicting the future course of criminal careers, assess the potential of prediction instruments in reducing crime through incapacitation, and review the contribution of research on criminal careers to the development of basic knowledge about crime and criminals.

A. Dimensions of a Criminal Career

The criminal career paradigm recognizes that individuals start their criminal activity at some age, engage in crime at some individual crime rate, commit a mixture of crimes, and eventually stop. Hence, the criminal career approach emphasizes the need to investigate issues related to why and when people start offending (onset), why—and how—they continue offending (persistence), why and if offending becomes more frequent or serious (escalation) or specialized, and why and when people stop offending (desistance). In sum, the criminal career approach provides a focus on both between- and within-individual changes in criminal activity over time.

1. *Definition of a Criminal Career.*   At its most basic level, a criminal career is the "characterization of the longitudinal sequence of crimes committed by an individual offender" (Blumstein et al. 1986, p. 12). This definition helps to focus researchers' attention on entry into a career when or before the first crime is committed and dropout from the career when or after the last crime is committed. Importantly, the concept recognizes that, during a criminal career, offenders have a continuing propensity to commit crimes, they accumulate some number of arrests, and are sometimes convicted and less frequently incarcerated

(Blumstein, Cohen, and Hsieh 1982, p. 2). The study of criminal careers does not imply that offenders necessarily derive their livelihood exclusively or even predominantly from crime; instead, the concept is intended only as a means of structuring the longitudinal sequence of criminal events associated with an individual in a systematic way (Blumstein, Cohen, and Hsieh 1982, p. 5).

2. *Participation.* The criminal career approach partitions the aggregate crime rate into two primary components: "participation," the distinction between those who commit crime and those who do not; and "frequency," the rate of offending among active offenders (Blumstein et al. 1986, p. 12). Participation is measured by the fraction of a population ever committing at least one crime before some age or currently active during some particular observation period. In any period, active offenders include both new offenders whose first offense occurs during the observation period and persisting offenders who began criminal activity in an earlier period and continue to be active during the observation period. Importantly, the longer the average duration of offending, the greater the contribution of persisters to measured participation in successive observation periods.

Blumstein and colleagues noted that demographic differences in participation, as measured by arrest, were large, the most striking of which involved gender discrepancies. The authors concluded that about 15 percent of males were arrested for an index offense by age eighteen and about 25–35 percent were arrested for such an offense sometime in their lifetime. The cumulative prevalence of self-reported offenses is even more striking. For example, in the Cambridge study, Farrington (1989) found that 96 percent of the males had reported committing at least one of ten specified offenses (including burglary, theft, assault, vandalism, and drug abuse) up to age thirty-two. When participation is restricted to serious offenses, the demographic differences are much larger, and race takes on more importance. Regarding age, the panel concluded, about half of those ever arrested during their lifetimes were first arrested before age eighteen, which was true among both African Americans and whites. Blumstein and colleagues also reported that ineffective parenting, poor school performance, low measured IQ, drug use, and parental criminality were related to participation.

3. *Key Dimensions of Active Criminal Careers.* The criminal career paradigm encompasses several dimensions of active criminal careers including offending frequency, duration, crime-type mix and seriousness, and co-offending patterns. Although desistance is also a key dimension

of the criminal career, a recent review of this literature was published in *Crime and Justice* (Laub and Sampson 2001).

a. Offending Frequency. The offending rate for individual offenders, λ, reflects the frequency of offending by individuals who are actively engaged in crime (Blumstein et al. 1986, p. 55). Much criminal career research has been concerned with estimating the individual offending frequency of active offenders during their criminal careers (see Blumstein and Cohen 1979; Cohen 1986). According to Blumstein et al. (1986, p. 76), individual frequency rates for active offenders do not vary substantially with demographics (age, gender, and race). However, active offenders who begin criminal activity at young ages, use drugs heavily, and are unemployed for long periods of time generally commit crimes at higher rates than most other offenders. The distribution of individual offending frequencies is highly skewed, which ultimately leads to a focus on the "chronic" (i.e., high frequency [λ]) offender. The identification of chronic offenders, however, has been difficult (see Chaiken and Chaiken 1982; Blumstein, Farrington, and Moitra 1985; Greenwood and Turner 1987).

b. Duration—the Interval between Initiation and Termination. One aspect of the criminal career paradigm that has received a great deal of research attention is initiation, or the onset of antisocial and criminal activity (Farrington et al. 1990; Tremblay et al. 1994). A number of studies have reported higher recidivism rates among offenders who have records of early criminal activity as juveniles (Blumstein et al. 1986; Farrington et al. 1990). Although many researchers argue that individuals who begin offending early will desist later and thus have lengthy careers (Hamparian et al. 1978; Krohn et al. 2001), there has been much less research on the duration of criminal careers, primarily because of the difficulty involved in determining the true end of an individual's criminal career. It is more tenable, however, to measure a rate of desistance for an identified group of offenders. Based on their research, Blumstein, Cohen, and Hsieh (1982) concluded that most criminal careers are relatively short, averaging about five years for offenders who are active in Index offenses as young adults. Residual careers, or the length of time still remaining in careers, increase to an expected ten years for Index offenders still active in their thirties. Research on desistance, or the termination of a criminal career, has received even less attention because of measurement and operationalization difficulties (Laub and Sampson 2001).

c. Crime-Type Mix and Seriousness. The mix of different offense types among active offenders is another important criminal career dimension. Issues underlying the offense mix include specialization, or the tendency to repeat similar offense types over a criminal career; seriousness; and escalation, or the tendency for offenders to move to more serious offense types as offending continues. Blumstein and colleagues reported that offenders tend to engage in a diversity of crime types, with a somewhat greater tendency to repeat the same crime or to repeat within the group of property crimes or the group of violent crimes. In addition, there appeared to be some evidence of increasing seriousness, specialization, and escalation during criminal careers.

d. Co-offending Patterns. Another important criminal career feature is whether a person commits an offense alone or with others (see Reiss 1986a). Research tends to suggest that the incidence of co-offending is greatest for burglary and robbery and that juvenile offenders primarily commit their crimes with others, whereas adult offenders primarily commit their crimes alone (Reiss and Farrington 1991). Although the decline in co-offending may, at first glance, be attributed to co-offenders dropping out, it seems to occur because males change from co-offending in their teenage years to lone offending in their twenties. Recent efforts continue to assess the extent of co-offending (Sarnecki 2001; Warr 2002).

B. Policy Issues

The criminal career paradigm suggests three general orientations for crime control strategies: prevention, career modification, and incapacitation. Knowledge concerning the patterning of criminal careers is intimately related to these policy issues. Prevention strategies, including general deterrence, are intended to reduce the number of nonoffenders who become offenders. Career modification strategies, including individual deterrence and rehabilitation, are focused on persons already known to be criminals and seek to reduce the frequency or seriousness of their crimes. In addition, these strategies encourage the termination of ongoing criminal careers through mechanisms such as job training and drug treatment. Incapacitative strategies focus on the crimes reduced as a result of removing offenders from society during their criminal careers. Two types of incapacitation are general, or collective, and selective, which focuses on the highest frequency offenders. These three crime control strategies are intimately related to specific laws, including habitual offender statutes, truth-in-sentencing laws, three-strikes laws, and mandatory minimum sentence laws.

1. *Crime Control Strategies.* The criminal career paradigm has focused extensive attention on incapacitation. General or collective incapacitation strategies aim to reduce criminal activity as a consequence of increasing the total level of incarceration while selective incapacitation policies focus primarily on offenders who represent the greatest risk of future offending. The former approach is consistent with the equal treatment concerns of a just-deserts sentencing policy while the latter focuses as much on the offender as the offense. Importantly, the degree to which selective incapacitation policies are effective depends on the ability to distinguish high- and low-risk offenders and to identify them early enough before they are about to terminate criminal activity. Three related issues arise: the ability to classify individual offenders in terms of their projected criminal activity, the quality of the classification rules, and the legitimacy of basing punishment of an individual on the possibility of future crimes rather than only on the crimes already committed (and the consequent level of disparity that is considered acceptable).

Regarding collective incapacitation, Blumstein et al. (1986) suggest that achieving a 10 percent reduction in crime may require more than doubling the existing inmate population. However, under selective incapacitation policies, long prison terms would be reserved primarily for offenders identified as most likely to continue committing serious crimes at high rates. Blumstein et al. conclude that selective incapacitation policies could achieve 5–10 percent reductions in robbery with 10–20 percent increases in the population of robbers in prison, while much larger increases in prison populations are required for collective incapacitation policies.

2. *Relationship to Laws.* Though not directly addressed in the report, both collective and selective incapacitation policies are directly influenced by laws and policies that govern criminal justice decisions regarding the punishment of offenders. For example, habitual offender statutes give special options to prosecutors for dealing with repeat offenders. Truth-in-sentencing laws are intended to increase incapacitation by requiring offenders, particularly violent offenders, to serve a substantial portion of their prison sentence, and parole eligibility and good-time credits are restricted or eliminated. Three-strikes laws pro-

vide that any person convicted of three, typically violent, felony offenses must serve a lengthy prison term, usually a minimum term of twenty-five-years to life. Mandatory-minimum sentence laws require a specified sentence and prohibit offenders convicted of certain crimes from being placed on probation, while other statutes prohibit certain offenders from being considered for parole. Mandatory-minimum sentence laws can also serve as sentencing enhancement measures, requiring that offenders spend additional time in prison if they commit particular crimes in a particular manner (e.g., committing a felony with a gun). The net effect of these laws is to increase prison populations by incarcerating certain kinds of offenders or increasing the sentence length of those offenders convicted for certain types of crimes.

C. *The Report's Suggestions and Needs for Future Research*

The criminal careers report was expansive in its review of the evidence and in the identification of unanswered theoretical and policy questions. The report outlined an agenda for future research that called for improved measurement of the dimensions of criminal careers, measurement of their distributions over offenders, measurement of the variation of the dimensions over the course of a criminal career, and better identification of the factors that influence the criminal career parameters. Many of these issues are best addressed, the report claimed, through a longitudinal research design.

Blumstein et al. (1986) argued that the most important criminal career dimension is individual frequency and, in particular, noted that research should focus especially on the rate of λ over time as offenders age, variation in λ with age for active offenders, the factors associated with intermittent spurts of high-rate and low-rate offending, and differences in λ by crime type. In addition, the report concluded that further research should assess the influence of various life events on an individual's criminal career and the effects of interventions on career development and should distinguish between developmental sequences and heterogeneity across individuals in explaining apparent career evolution (Blumstein et al. 1986, p. 199). These issues are best addressed through a prospective, longitudinal research design, especially in light of the inherently longitudinal and dynamic character of criminal careers. Individuals of different ages (i.e., several cohorts) should be studied. Such a project, the report noted, would provide for more detailed measurement of the initiation and termination of individual criminal careers, including a focus on the distinction among different kinds of crimes and a better sequential ordering of life events and criminal behavior that would begin to suggest directions of causal influence (Blumstein et al. 1986, p. 200).

III. Theoretical Developments since the Criminal Career Report

In their recent review of the desistance literature, Laub and Sampson (2001, p. 17) asserted that, while the criminal career approach represented a significant movement in criminology, "it appear[ed] to have reached a point of stagnation . . . because of its narrow focus on measurement and policy." In this section, we outline the various theoretical challenges and developments that were spurred as a result of the criminal careers report. We believe that the research following the publication of the criminal careers report led to important challenges to the criminal career paradigm, identification and development of other criminal career features, attention to the relationship between past and future criminal activity (and the subsequent identification of state dependence and persistent heterogeneity as two potential explanations of this relationship), and development of theories that follow from the criminal career paradigm.

A. Challenge and Response to the Criminal Career Paradigm and Report

The criminal career paradigm—and its emerging policy implications—was not embraced by the entire academic community. Michael Gottfredson and Travis Hirschi, in particular, launched a series of critiques.

1. *The Gottfredson and Hirschi Critique.* The basis of their critique lies in their explication and interpretation of the aggregate age/crime curve. Hirschi and Gottfredson (1983) contend that the shape of the aggregate age/crime relationship is pretty much the same for all offenders, in all times and places, and is largely unaffected by life events that occur after childhood. They assert, then, that involvement in crime (and other analogous behaviors) is sufficiently stable over the life course to obviate the need to collect longitudinal data, which is a prerequisite for pursuing the criminal career paradigm. This is especially the case in their denial of the need to distinguish prevalence and frequency (because both reflect underlying propensity). They claim that prevalence and frequency vary similarly with age. For the most part, however, research fails to support their claim.

Gottfredson and Hirschi do not deny that some offenders offend at a much higher rate than other offenders, but they argue that offenders differ in degree and not kind; that is, offenders can be arrayed on a continuum of criminal propensity (which they term low self-control) with individuals at the higher end of the continuum evidencing higher criminal activity and vice versa. This is a key point because Gottfredson and Hirschi do not allow for the existence of qualitatively distinct groups of offenders.

Gottfredson and Hirschi are concerned with the proposed identification of the "career criminal" and the implied policy response of selective incapacitation. Their concern derives from the small number of chronic offenders and the limited ability of the criminal justice system to identify chronic offenders prospectively, before they reach their offending peak. In particular, Gottfredson and Hirschi argue that, by the time the criminal justice system is able to identify a career criminal, he tends no longer to be as active as he once was. That is, career criminals cannot be identified early enough in their careers to be useful for policy purposes. Thus, since Hirschi and Gottfredson believe that crime declines with age for everyone, they argue that the policy of selective incapacitation makes little sense because career criminals would likely not be committing crimes at high rates if they were free.

Gottfredson and Hirschi (1987) are also unfriendly to the prospect of longitudinal cohort data. Their critique is forceful and centers around five issues: the longitudinal cohort study is not justified on methodological grounds, such a design has taken criminological theory in unproductive directions, it has produced illusory substantive findings, it has promoted policy directions of "doubtful utility," and such research designs are very expensive and entail high opportunity costs (Gottfredson and Hirschi 1987, p. 581). They argue instead for more emphasis on cross-sectional studies, which they claim tend to provide similar substantive conclusions to those reached by longitudinal studies but at a much smaller cost. They conclude that neither the criminal career paradigm, its constructs (prevalence, λ, etc.), nor longitudinal research has much to offer criminology.

Gottfredson and Hirschi (1988) question whether the concept of a "career" is valuable to the study of crime. They claim that there is no empirical support for the use of the career concept and its related terminology (p. 39). Gottfredson and Hirschi go on to critique the participation/frequency distinction and, in so doing, employ data from the Richmond Youth Project, which collected, cross-sectionally, police records and self-report data on over 2,500 males and females. They conclude that the substantive conclusions about the causes and correlates of crime do not depend on career distinctions. They show that as one moves from λ for any kind of offending to the smaller λ for serious offending, the correlations between demographic characteristics and criminal career offending dimensions become even smaller, largely as a result of decreasing sample size. In sum, Gottfredson and Hirschi claimed that the factors associated with different criminal career parameters are more similar than different.

2. *Blumstein and Colleagues' Response.*   Blumstein, Cohen, and Farrington (1988a) provided a response to the main critiques. They noted (1988a, p. 4) that the construct of a criminal career is not a theory of crime—instead it is a way of structuring and organizing knowledge about certain key features of individual offending for observation and measurement—and that the distinction between participation and frequency is important because it permits isolation of different causal relationships. However, they also suggest that the criminal career concept is useful for the development and assessment of theory as it may help researchers understand differences among offenders, especially with regard to their various criminal career parameters. Thus, unlike Gottfredson and Hirschi, who assume that as criminal propensity increases so too do participation, frequency, and career length, the criminal career paradigm suggests that the predictors and correlates of one criminal career parameter may differ from the predictors and correlates of another.

The key point of contention between Gottfredson and Hirschi and Blumstein et al. lies in their respective interpretations of the age/crime curve. For Gottfredson and Hirschi, the decline in the age/crime curve in early adulthood reflects decreasing offending frequency (λ) after the peak age. Blumstein, Cohen, and Farrington claim that the decline in the aggregate arrest rate after a teenage peak does not require that offending frequency (λ) follow a similar pattern. According to Blumstein, Cohen, and Farrington (1988a, p. 27), this is precisely where the distinction between participation and frequency becomes critical. The decline in the aggregate age/crime curve may be entirely attributable to the termination of criminal careers, and the average value of λ could stay constant (or increase or decrease with age) for those offenders who remain active after that peak. This ultimately is an empirical question, yet Blumstein, Cohen, and Farrington (1988a, p. 32) suggest that participation in offending, and not frequency as Gottfredson and Hirschi suggest, is the key dimension that varies with age.

Blumstein, Cohen, and Farrington (1988b, p. 57) suggest that Gottfredson and Hirschi misunderstand key criminal career evidence, "especially the evidence of a decline in offending with age, regarding which the distinction between participation and frequency is crucial." They claim that Gottfredson and Hirschi misinterpreted the concepts of individual crime rates, lambda (λ), and career duration and, as a result, miscalculated such estimates because of their failure to take into account the length of active criminal careers for individual offenders (Blumstein, Cohen, and Farrington 1988*b*, pp. 58–59, 62). In addition, they challenge Gottfredson and Hirschi's interpretation of declines in offending with age: "just *what* is declining . . . Are still-active offenders committing crimes at lower frequencies or are increasing numbers of offenders ending their careers and ceasing to commit crimes altogether? The former is a change in λ, and the latter is a change in *participation*, and measuring these changes with age is an empirical issue" (Blumstein, Cohen, and Farrington 1988*b*, p. 66; emphasis in original). In sum, they conclude that cross-sectional studies can study only between-subject differences, while longitudinal surveys allow for the analysis of both between- and within-subject changes, and it is this latter type of analysis that frames the criminal career focus on participation, frequency, and termination. Within-subject changes are also more relevant to issues of prevention and treatment of offending.

3. *What Is the Relevance of This Debate?* The debate has relevance for policy issues. In Gottfredson and Hirschi's view, the most important distinction should be between offenders and nonoffenders (i.e., participation). The criminal career paradigm, by contrast, does not dispute a focus on participation, but also places emphasis on the frequency of active offenders. This focus on frequency reflects, not only an interest in systematic differences in offending frequencies among active offenders but also an interest in changes in offending frequency during active criminal careers. Both participation and frequency, according to the criminal career paradigm, are relevant for policy purposes since affecting both can generate payoffs in crime reduction. Blumstein, Cohen, and Farrington argue that longitudinal data are superior to cross-sectional data in testing causal hypotheses, because longitudinal data permit observation of the time ordering of events observed and provide better control of extraneous variables because each person acts as his/her own control.

B. Other Criminal Career Features

The criminal career paradigm, and the ensuing sets of exchanges, resulted in the continued study of the different trajectories and dimensions associated with criminal careers (Le Blanc and Fréchette 1989; Loeber and Le Blanc 1990; Le Blanc and Loeber 1998). Researchers continued in the criminal career tradition by identifying other criminal career dimensions, including activation, aggravation, and desistance.

1. *Activation.* According to Le Blanc and Loeber, activation refers to "the way the development of criminal activities, once begun, is stimulated and the way its continuity, frequency, and diversity are assured" (1998, p. 123). There are three subprocesses of activation. The first is acceleration, which refers to an increase in the frequency of offending over time. The second is stabilization, which refers to a tendency toward continuity over time. The third is diversification, which refers to the propensity for individuals to become involved in a more diverse set of criminal activities over time. The timing of onset (i.e., onset age) is a central feature of activation, and research shows that an early age of onset predicts each of the three subprocesses of activation, regardless of whether onset is measured by self-reports or official records. While an early onset of offending is typically associated with a higher rate of offending, a diverse pattern of offending, and a longer criminal career (see Blumstein et al. 1986; Farrington et al. 1990), the conceptual interpretation linking early onset to other dimensions of criminal careers has not been fully resolved (Nagin and Farrington 1992*a*, 1992*b*).

Regarding acceleration, several studies have shown that individuals who exhibit an early onset age tend to commit crimes at a much higher rate than those with a later age of onset (see Cohen 1986; Loeber and Snyder 1990). Regarding stabilization, research tends to find that an early onset age is predictive of both chronic offending and a longer duration of offending (Le Blanc and Fréchette 1989). An early onset age is also predictive of diversification. For example, using self-report data Tolan (1987) found that early onset offenders averaged 3.2 types of offenses in a one-year recall period, compared with 2.3 offenses for late-onset offenders. However, using official records from the 1958 Philadelphia birth cohort through age twenty-six, Piquero et al. (1999) found that onset age was related to offending versatility, but the association vanished after controlling for age. These authors showed that there was a tendency for offenders to become more specialized in their offending over time, regardless of the age at which they initiated offending (see also Peterson and Braiker 1980; Cohen 1986).

2. *Aggravation.* The second dynamic process added by Le Blanc and Loeber is aggravation. This process refers to the "existence of a *developmental sequence* of diverse forms of delinquent activities that *escalate* or increase in seriousness over time" (1998, p. 123; emphasis in

original). Some evidence indicates that offenders tend to progress to more serious offense types as offending continues over time (see Glueck and Glueck 1940; Wolfgang, Figlio, and Sellin 1972; Smith, Smith, and Noma 1984; Le Blanc and Fréchette 1989; Tracy, Wolfgang, and Figlio 1990), while others report mixed evidence in this regard (Blumstein et al. 1988), and still others fail to uncover escalation patterns (Datesman and Aickin 1984; Shelden, Horvath, and Tracy 1987).

Perhaps the most detailed investigation to date on escalation was conducted by Le Blanc and Fréchette (1989) using data from Montreal adjudicated youths. These authors summarized the escalation process into five developmental stages: emergence, exploration, explosion, conflagration, and outburst. In the emergence stage, between ages eight and ten, petty larceny takes shape as the key offense type. During the exploration stage (ages ten to twelve), offenses tend to become diversified and more aggravated and include shoplifting and vandalism. In the third stage, around age thirteen, there is a substantial increase in the variety and seriousness of offending, and new crimes are committed, including common theft, burglary, and personal larceny. Around age fifteen, during the conflagration stage, the variety and seriousness of offending increases and is complemented by drug trafficking, motor vehicle theft, and armed robbery. Finally, during adulthood, outburst occurs, and crimes become more serious and tend to include fraud and homicide. Le Blanc and Fréchette (1989) showed that, up to age twenty-five, 92 percent of their convicted delinquent sample moved through this particular developmental escalation sequence. Loeber et al. (1999) reached similar substantive conclusions regarding the escalation progression using data from three large-scale self-report studies from Pittsburgh, Denver, and Rochester.

3. *Desistance.* The third process identified by Le Blanc and Loeber (1998) is desistance, but their view of desistance is much broader than the usual exposition in the criminal careers report. According to Le Blanc and Loeber, desistance is a slowing down in the frequency of offending (deceleration), a reduction in the variety of offending (specialization), a reduction in the seriousness of offending (de-escalation), or reaching a plateau or ceiling in offense seriousness. The study of desistance has been hampered by both theoretical and measurement problems (see Laub and Sampson 2001). For example, questions have been raised regarding whether desistance is an event or a process (see Fagan 1989; Maruna 2001), can be studied while individuals are still

alive (i.e., the cutoff age problem; see Farrington 1979), and can be identified from short periods of nonoffending (Blumstein et al. 1986; Barnett, Blumstein, and Farrington 1987, 1989; Bushway et al. 2001). Still, these concerns have not deterred researchers from studying desistance (see Mulvey and Larosa 1986; Farrington and Hawkins 1991; Loeber et al. 1991; Laub, Nagin, and Sampson 1998; Warr 1998).

Le Blanc and Loeber (1998, p. 162) suggest that deceleration may occur in three ways: aging out of the criminal career in midlife, early desistance from offending in adolescence, and desistance from specific offense types in the middle of a delinquent career. Researchers have found that the rate of offending, λ, tends to decrease with age, and this especially takes place in the thirties and forties (see Blumstein et al. 1986; Piquero et al. 2001). In addition, researchers have identified some desistance from offending during adolescence (Le Blanc and Fréchette 1989). Finally, some research indicates that some offenders tend to drop minor offenses over their careers (Le Blanc and Fréchette 1989).

Regarding de-escalation, some limited evidence indicates that this occurs during adulthood (Robins 1966; Le Blanc, Côté, and Loeber 1991). For example, Blumstein and his colleagues (1988) found some de-escalation among Michigan offenders during adulthood. Le Blanc and Fréchette (1989) reported that 61 percent of the subjects in their delinquent sample reached their maximum level of seriousness in offending during adolescence; however, little research has examined desistance as reaching a ceiling, primarily because the ceiling is difficult to detect reliably. Finally, Le Blanc and Loeber's (1998) definition of specialization refers to desistance from a versatile pattern of criminal activity into a more homogenous pattern. Thus, specialization involves desistance from some kinds of offenses. Research has analyzed offending careers spanning the juvenile and adult years and suggests that specialization tends to increase with age (see Blumstein et al. 1986; Le Blanc and Fréchette 1989; Stattin, Magnusson, and Reichel 1989; Piquero et al. 1999).

C. Issues of State Dependence and Persistent Heterogeneity

One of the key criminal career findings was the consistent relationship between past and future criminal activity. Although research consistently documented such a positive relationship, current theory has not agreed about the cause of the relationship. Aided by theoretical and empirical research from other disciplines, two principal explanations have emerged: state dependence and persistent heterogeneity.

1. *Does Prior Behavior Reflect Differential Propensity, a True Causal Effect, or Both?* There has been intense debate about the interpretation and meaning of the correlated relationship between past and future offending. In criminology, the first acknowledgment of this issue and subsequent empirical application was achieved by Nagin and Paternoster (1991). These authors suggested that the positive relationship could reflect some combination of two processes: state dependence and persistent heterogeneity.

The state dependence argument suggests that the positive correlation between past and future criminal activity exists because the act of committing a crime transforms the offender's life circumstances in some way that increases the probability that future crimes will occur. For example, committing crimes can weaken one's involvement in a network of conventional relationships that could have provided some restraint on criminal activity. After the commission of a criminal act, future criminal acts may become more likely as a result of a closer affiliation with other offenders. In sum, the state dependence argument posits that criminal activity materially transforms conditions in the offender's life, thus increasing the probability of future offending. Theories such as Agnew's general strain theory (1992), Sutherland's differential association theory (1947), and Lemert's labeling theory (1951) attribute importance to the state dependence interpretation.

Persistent heterogeneity is the second interpretation. This explanation attributes the positive correlation to differences across persons in their propensity to commit crime. In this explanation, there is heterogeneity in the population that takes the form of a time-stable characteristic that affects the probability of criminal activity over the life course. Thus, individuals with the "highest" criminal propensity are likely to be involved in all sorts of antisocial, criminal, and deviant acts throughout the life course, and the rank-order differences between those with high criminal propensity and those with low criminal propensity tend to remain relatively stable. In sum, the persistent heterogeneity explanation attributes continuity in criminal activity over time to stable differences between individuals in factors that influence crime. Theories developed by Gottfredson and Hirschi (1990) and Wilson and Herrnstein (1985) subscribe to the persistent heterogeneity point of view.

These two explanations are not necessarily incompatible. For example, there can be mixed explanations for the relationship between past and future criminal activity that allow for both stable individual differences in criminal propensity and for criminal activity to alter the risk of future crime (Nagin and Paternoster 2000). Thus, a mixed persistent-heterogeneity/state-dependence explanation would allow for both individual differences and life events to influence and alter patterns of criminal activity. Such a mixture would accommodate both continuity and change. Sampson and Laub's (1993, 1997) age-graded informal social control theory is an example of a theory that accommodates both persistent heterogeneity and state dependence.

A number of studies have examined the extent to which persistent heterogeneity and state dependence account for the relationship between past and future criminal activity. Nagin and Paternoster (1991) used data from high school students and found that prior criminal offending had an effect on subsequent offending after controlling for both observed and unobserved heterogeneity. Using the Cambridge study, Nagin and Farrington (1992a, 1992b) found substantially stronger effects for persistent heterogeneity than for state dependence, though the latter were still significant. In further analyses of the same data, Paternoster, Brame, and Farrington (2001) also concluded that persistent heterogeneity was more important. However, Paternoster and Brame (1997) found more evidence in favor of state dependence than persistent heterogeneity in data from the NYS. Nagin and Land (1993) and Land, McCall, and Nagin (1996) found both persistent-heterogeneity and state-dependence effects using official records from the Cambridge study and the Second Philadelphia birth cohort.

Nagin and Paternoster's (2000) recent review of the persistent-heterogeneity/state dependence literature yields the important conclusion that both persistent-heterogeneity and time-varying characteristics are important. Thus, despite important differences in criminal propensity, life events still play a causal role in shaping criminal activity over the life course. Importantly, these conclusions are derived from over a decade of research employing different samples (high school students, representative population samples, offender-based samples, etc.), different types of time-varying characteristics (marriage, employment, alcohol, drug use, etc.), and different measures of criminal activity (official records, self-reports).

A number of unresolved questions remain (see Nagin and Paternoster 2000, pp. 138–40). First, little is known about the distribution of and response to opportunities to desist. Second, there is little understanding of the causal processes that underlie desistance from crime. Third, more needs to be done to identify the effect of various events and experiences that lead persons into and out of crime. Fourth, little is known about the sources of the differential propensity to commit crime. Fifth, current research does not show conclusively whether criminal justice interventions have positive or negative effects.

2. *Do Interventions Have Positive Effects?* Under the state-dependence argument, events external to the individual (i.e., association with delinquent peers, imposition of formal sanctions, etc.) are believed to exert a meaningful, causal effect on an individual's behavior. To the extent that the state-dependence argument is correct, then, interventions aimed at reducing the frequency, seriousness, or duration of offending could have a desirable effect; that is, interventions should work toward inhibiting continued criminal careers. However, as argued in labeling theory, interventions could also have undesirable effects.

Can good things happen to offenders that will cause them to settle down and turn away from their criminal patterns? This question has been taken up in several recent studies aimed at understanding how local life circumstances or life events, including crime, influence the subsequent patterning of criminal and noncriminal activity (e.g., Hagan and Palloni 1988; Ouimet and Le Blanc 1995). For example, using self-reported data from a sample of Nebraska prisoners, Horney, Osgood, and Marshall (1995) examined the extent to which changes in local life circumstances were related to changes in short-term criminal activity. They found that during months of drug use, offenders were more likely to be involved in property, assaultive, and drug-related crimes, whereas, during months of living with a wife, offenders were less likely to be involved in all sorts of crimes, particularly assaultive crimes.

Laub, Nagin, and Sampson (1998) used the Glueck data on 500 delinquent boys to study how "good marriages" were related to desistance from crime through age thirty-two. After controlling for persistent individual differences, Laub and his colleagues found that a "good marriage" rather than simply "being married" was associated with desistance.

Cernkovich and Giordano (2001) used longitudinal data from a household sample and an institutionalized sample to study stability and change in antisocial behavior. Their results indicated that prior delinquency was a stable predictor among individuals in both samples, but social bonding effects were important only for the household sample and not for the institutionalized sample. Regarding the latter result, they argued that the institutionalized sample may simply have been unable to acquire or maintain social bonding mechanisms.

Using data on 524 California Youth Authority (CYA) parolees followed for seven consecutive years, Piquero et al. (2002) examined how changes in several life circumstances, including alcohol and drug use and stakes in conformity, were related to changes in both violent and nonviolent criminal activity. Piquero and his colleagues found that changes in these life circumstances were related to changes in criminal activity, even after controlling for persistent individual differences, and that some of the life circumstances were related to one type of crime more than another. For example, stakes in conformity and heroin dependency were related to nonviolent but not violent arrests. Piquero, MacDonald, and Parker (2002) further explored the interaction between race and local life circumstances among these CYA parolees and found that, although the effects of marriage and employment operated in similar ways for white and nonwhite parolees, nonwhite parolees who were involved in common-law relationships were more likely to continue their involvement in criminal activity, while similarly situated white parolees were not. These authors speculated that the common-law relationships were crime increasing because of the additional level of commitment and accountability necessary for a marriage.

Simons and his colleagues (2002) employed data from a longitudinal sample of Iowa adolescents to explore stability and change in criminal activity into early adulthood. They tested the idea of assortative mating as a potential explanatory factor and also explored gender differences in assortative mating. Their results indicated that, among males and females, adolescent delinquency and affiliation with delinquent peers predicted having an antisocial romantic partner as a young adult; in turn, involvement with an antisocial romantic partner was related to further adult criminal activity. Among females, the quality of romantic relationships also predicted crime, an effect that was not observed among males.

The overriding conclusion from these studies is that life events (interventions) can have a positive effect on offenders' lives, over and above persistent individual differences (i.e., criminal propensity). Other interventions, external to the individual, have also been examined for their ability to reduce criminal activity. Because a review of this literature is beyond the scope of this essay, readers are referred to

Sherman et al. (2002), Wilson and Petersilia (2001), and Tonry and Farrington (1995) for extensive reviews of crime prevention and intervention efforts generally and to Tremblay and Craig's (1995) review of developmental crime prevention in particular.

3. *Does Criminal Justice Intervention (i.e., Labeling) Do Harm?* Labeling theory draws attention to the potentially negative consequences of being labeled a criminal. Labeling theory would view criminal justice intervention, especially serious criminal justice intervention, as doing more harm than good. For example, Lemert (1951) argues that societal reactions to primary deviance cause problems of adjustment that lead to additional, or secondary, deviance. Thus, as offenders move through the criminal justice process, or what Garfinkel (1965) refers to as the "status degradation ceremony," individuals are likely to incur negative prospects for employment and other prosocial outcomes later in life. Individual deterrence theory as well as rehabilitation efforts, by contrast, make the exact opposite prediction; namely, that criminal justice interventions do more good than harm. Under the deterrence argument, individuals are believed to be rational beings who avoid future criminal activity as a result of the swift, certain, and severe imposition of formal and informal sanctions. In sum, labeling theory posits that criminal justice intervention exacerbates future criminal activity, while deterrence or rehabilitation theory predicts that criminal justice interventions inhibit future criminality.

Unfortunately, very few studies have related criminal justice sentences to recidivism probabilities (though see Walker, Farrington, and Tucker 1981 for an exception). One key question is the impact of official processing as opposed to no official action. Farrington (1977) attempted to address this question with data from the Cambridge study. Youths who were first convicted between ages fourteen and eighteen were matched on self-reported delinquency at age fourteen with youths not convicted up to age eighteen, and a similar analysis was carried out between ages eighteen and twenty-one. Farrington found an increase in self-reported offending frequency after first convictions, thereby providing some support for the labeling theory argument.

Smith and Gartin (1989) used data from the 1949 Racine cohort, a longitudinal study of 2,099 residents of Racine, Wisconsin, born in 1949 and followed up to 1974, to examine two specific questions regarding the influence of arrest on future criminal activity. First, does arrest amplify or deter the future criminal activity of those arrested?

Second, does the influence of being arrested on future offending vary according to where arrest occurs in the sequence of police contacts? These scholars partitioned future offending into distinct components, including the rate of future offending, the duration of a criminally active period, and desistance from future offending. They found that, while being arrested affected specific parameters of criminal careers differently, the reduction in the future criminal activity of those offenders whom police arrested was lower than those who were contacted but not arrested (Smith and Gartin 1989, p. 102). In addition, among novice offenders, arrest was more likely to terminate their criminal careers while among more experienced offenders, arrest significantly reduced future rates of offending. Using the same data, Shannon (1980) found that severe sanctions, such as incarceration, led to increased future criminality. Thus, within the same data, Smith and Gartin find that arrest had some specific deterrent value but Shannon concluded that more severe sanctions backfired.

Smith and Paternoster (1990) used juvenile justice intake data from the Florida Department of Health and Rehabilitative Services to examine whether referring a case to juvenile court or diverting it affected a person's future delinquent or criminal behavior. To the extent that labeling theory is correct, referring the case would trigger a deviance-amplification process that ultimately results in increased criminal or delinquent activity. Smith and Paternoster raise the methodological point that a higher rate of offending among those referred to court could actually be a selection artifact. That is, since the diversion decision is discretionary, those juveniles referred to court may have more attributes that are related to future offending than those juveniles who are diverted from the system. Their initial analysis indicated that while referral to court had a significant, positive effect on recidivism, further analysis that recognized the potential heterogeneity in risk factors between referred and diverted cases revealed that the apparent labeling effect of court referral could be attributed instead to a selection artifact. In finding no support for the deviance amplification process, Smith and Paternoster (1990, p. 1128) cautioned researchers about potential selection artifact effects in nonexperimental data.

Although most studies have examined how criminal justice interventions lead to future criminal activity, Sampson and Laub have posited that criminal justice experiences could also lead to negative consequences in other aspects of offenders' lives, including employment, particularly job stability. Using the Glueck data, Sampson and Laub

(1993) found that length of juvenile incarceration had the largest over-all effect on later job stability, even after controlling for observed and unobserved persistent heterogeneity. In particular, compared to delin-quents with short incarceration histories, delinquent boys incarcerated for a longer period of time had trouble securing stable jobs as they entered young adulthood (Sampson and Laub 1997). Moreover, length of incarceration in both adolescence and young adulthood had a sig-nificant negative effect on job stability at ages twenty-five and thirty-two (Sampson and Laub 1993). Similar results regarding the destabiliz-ing effects of criminal justice intervention have been observed by other scholars (Nagin and Waldfogel 1995).

D. Theories Influenced by the Criminal Career Paradigm

The criminal career paradigm forced theorists to examine the extent to which they were able to account for the different criminal career dimensions (i.e., onset, persistence, frequency, desistance, etc.). As a result of the recognition of other criminal career features, and the im-portance of the relationship between past and future criminal activity, several life-course and developmental theories were developed that at-tempted to account for the patterning of criminal activity over time.

The life course has been defined as "pathways through the age-differentiated life span," where age differentiation "is manifested in ex-pectations and options that impinge on decision processes and the course of events that give shape to life stages, transitions, and turning points" (Sampson and Laub 1993, p. 8; see also Elder 1985). Within criminology, the life-course perspective can offer a comprehensive ap-proach to the study of criminal activity because it considers the multi-tude of influences that shape offending across different time periods and contexts (Thornberry 1997; Piquero and Mazerolle 2001). In par-ticular, two central concepts underlie the analysis of life-course dynam-ics, and of criminal activity more specifically.

The first is a trajectory, or a pathway of development over the life span such as in work life or criminal activity. Trajectories refer to long-term patterns of specific types of behavior. Second, and embedded within trajectories, are transitions, or specific life events (e.g., a first arrest) that evolve over shorter time spans. According to Elder (1985, p. 32), the interlocking nature of trajectories and transitions may gen-erate turning points or changes in the life course. According to Samp-son and Laub, "The long-term view embodied by the life-course focus on trajectories implies a strong connection between childhood events and experiences in adulthood. However, the simultaneous shorter-term view also implies that transitions or turning points can modify life trajectories—they can 'redirect paths' " (1992, p. 66). As such, the life-course perspective recognizes the importance of both stability and change in human behavior.

Developmental criminology adopts this life-course view by acknowledging that changes in social behavior, such as delinquency and crime, are related to age in an orderly way (Patterson 1993; Thornberry 1997). Developmental criminology, which focuses on all sorts of anti-social and criminal activity over the life course, studies the temporal, within-individual changes in offending over time (Le Blanc and Loeber 1998, p. 117) and focuses on two primary areas of study. The first concerns the development and dynamics of offending over age, while the second concerns the identification of explanatory or causal factors that predate or co-occur with the behavioral development and have an effect on its course (Le Blanc and Loeber 1998, p. 117).

Developmental criminology departs from traditional criminological theory that, with one principal exception (labeling theory; see Sampson and Laub 1997), adopts a relatively nondevelopmental, or static, orientation. Thornberry (1997, pp. 2–5), for example, offers four reasons why static theories have led to a stagnation of knowledge. First, static perspectives neither identify nor offer explanations for all of the key criminal career dimensions. Most static theories, with the exception of Gottfredson and Hirschi and Wilson and Herrnstein, are basically state-dependence theories. Second, static theories fail to identify types of offenders based on developmental considerations. For example, some offenders may start early and continue offending for long periods while others start later and desist earlier. Third, static explanations do not focus attention on either precursors or consequences of criminal activity. For example, what factors lead to the initiation of criminal activity, and does continued criminal activity materially affect life outcomes in other noncrime domains such as school and work? Fourth, static perspectives do not integrate the noncrime developmental changes that occur over the life course as a way to understand changes in criminal activity during the same period. For example, how do transitions in work, school, family, and interpersonal relationships relate to changes in criminal activity? Developmental criminology attempts to overcome these limitations in an effort to provide a more complete understanding of criminal activity over the life course and recognizes that there may be multiple paths to antisocial and criminal behavior (Huizinga, Esbensen, and Weiher 1991).

Within criminology, the last decade has witnessed the application of scholarly work from other disciplines that have adopted a life-course perspective to the study of criminal activity. These theories, and the ones also constructed by criminologists, take as their starting point two key facts: the relationship between age and crime and the relationship between prior and future criminal activity. These theories have also attempted to address the following observation: although antisocial behavior in children is one of the best predictors of antisocial behavior in adults, not all antisocial children become antisocial adults.

Moffitt's (1993) developmental taxonomy decomposes the aggregate age/crime curve into two distinct classes of offenders. The first group, designated "adolescence-limited," is hypothesized to engage in crimes solely during the adolescent period. The primary causal factors for this group include the maturity gap (i.e., adolescents are physically old enough to look like adults, but socially not allowed to act like adults) combined with the encouragement of peers. Moffitt anticipates that the crime repertoire of adolescence-limiteds would be restricted to mainly status- and property-oriented offenses that symbolize adult social status such as theft, smoking, vandalism, and drug use, but not violent acts. For the majority of adolescence-limiteds, their prosocial skills and attitudes allow them to recover from their delinquent experimentation and move away from their delinquent activities as they reach adulthood.

The second group of offenders in Moffitt's taxonomy, "life-course-persistent," is hypothesized to engage in antisocial activities and criminal acts throughout the life span. Composed of less than 10 percent of the population, the primary determinants of criminal activity for life-course-persistent offenders lie in the interaction between poor neuropsychological functioning and deficient home and socioeconomic environments. Unlike their adolescence-limited counterparts, life-course-persistent offenders continue their criminal involvement throughout most of their lives (i.e., they are unlikely to desist). In addition, the crime repertoire of life-course-persistent offenders is varied and includes interpersonal violence.

Thus, Moffitt's adolescence-limited offenders are likely to be influenced much more by state-dependence effects, since offending among adolescence-limited offenders depends largely on life circumstances and environmental influences such as peers. Prior criminal acts are likely to affect causally current and future offending among adolescence-limited offenders because offending is likely to alienate further parents and conventional peers. Life-course-persistent offenders, after child socialization efforts have taken place, are likely to be a consequence of persistent heterogeneity. That is, life-course-persistent offenders are "bad apples" who exhibit significant deficits in early childhood socialization and are rarely likely to get back on track.

A good deal of empirical research has tended to support some of the key hypotheses arising from Moffitt's typology (Nagin and Land 1993; Moffitt, Lynam, and Silva 1994; Dean, Brame, and Piquero 1996; Moffitt et al. 1996; Bartusch et al. 1997; Kratzer and Hodgins 1999; Tibbetts and Piquero 1999; Moffitt and Caspi 2001; Piquero 2001; Piquero and Brezina 2001), while some studies have generated useful alterations to the theory (see Nagin, Farrington, and Moffitt 1995; D'Unger et al. 1998; Aguilar et al. 2000; Fergusson, Horwood, and Nagin 2000).

Much like Moffitt's typology, Patterson and Yoerger's (1999) theory is based on a two-group model of offending that is comprised of early- and late-onset offenders. According to their perspective, early-starting offenders become involved in criminal and antisocial behaviors as a function of failed early childhood socialization due to inept parenting practices that foster oppositional/defiant behavior. The failure of children to learn effective self- and social controls leads them to be involved in deviant peer groups, which, in turn, magnifies their offending intensity. Early-starting offenders tend to be aggressive and defiant in their interactions with others and come to be rejected by conventional peers. As a result of their social rejection, early-starting offenders tend to establish friendships with each other thereby forming deviant peer groups that engage in criminal activities. Early starters, then, are at high risk for chronic offending and continued criminal careers as adults.

Late-starting offenders, however, do not suffer from failed socialization efforts. Instead, the principal cause of offending for them is their close association and interaction with deviant peer models. As a result of the aid, encouragement, and support of the peer social context, late-starting youths experiment with delinquency during mid to late adolescence. However, since late-starting offenders do not suffer from inept parenting, nor are they failed socialization products, their social skills remain relatively intact, and they are likely to turn away from criminal acts as adulthood approaches. Several empirical studies have tested Patterson's theory. For the most part, they confirm the key predictions regarding the effects of inept parenting, oppositional/defiant behavior, and deviant peers (see Simons et al. 1994, 1998; Patterson and Yoerger 1999).

Loeber and his colleagues (1998, 1999) have proposed a three-pathway model that integrates both predelinquent behavior problems and delinquent acts in attempting to describe which youths are at highest risk of becoming chronic offenders. The first pathway, the "overt pathway," begins with minor aggression, followed by physical fighting and then violence. The second pathway, the "covert pathway," consists of a sequence of minor, covert behaviors followed by property damage (such as vandalism) and then proceeds on to serious forms of delinquency. The third pathway, the "authority-conflict pathway," prior to age twelve consists of a sequence of stubborn behaviors, including defiance and authority avoidance (such as running away). According to Loeber, individuals' development can take place on more than one pathway, with some youths progressing on all three pathways. However, the most frequent offenders are overrepresented among those boys in multiple pathways, especially those displaying overt and covert behavior problems. In addition, Loeber's model also allows for specialization, for example, in covert acts only, as well as escalation along pathways.

A key assumption of Loeber's model is that behavior takes place in an orderly, not random, fashion. In other words, individuals progress through lower-order steps up through higher-order steps. The pathway model has been replicated in the youngest sample of the Pittsburgh study and applied better to boys who persisted compared to those who experimented in delinquency (Loeber et al. 1998). In addition, replications have been reported by Tolan and Gorman-Smith (1998) in samples from the NYS and the Chicago Youth Development Study (see also Elliott 1994). Finally, recent research on the pathway model in the three causes and correlates study sites (Denver, Pittsburgh, and Rochester) replicated it for steps 2 and higher in the overt and covert pathways only (Loeber et al. 1999; though see Nagin and Tremblay 1999).

Thus far, we have presented three specific developmental theories that allow for both static and dynamic effects. Another theory that was developed after the criminal careers report is Sampson and Laub's age-graded informal social control theory. Though technically a general, nondevelopmental theory, the Sampson and Laub model allows for both static and dynamic effects on criminal activity over the life course.

For Sampson and Laub (1993), crime can be understood as a product of both persistent individual differences and local life events. Their thesis entails three key ideas. First, delinquency in childhood and adolescence can be explained by the structural context, which is mediated by informal family and school social controls. Second, they recognize that there is a substantial amount of continuity in antisocial behavior from childhood through adulthood in a variety of life domains. Third, they argue that variation in the quality of informal social bonds in adulthood to family and employment explains changes in criminality over the life course, despite early childhood persistent individual differences. Sampson and Laub's theory claims that, independent of persistent individual differences, informal social control mechanisms exert a causal effect on criminal activity and that the type of social control varies at different ages. Their theory incorporates both stability and change over the life course, and "change is a central part of [their] explanatory framework" (Sampson and Laub 1993, p. 17).

Several studies have examined Sampson and Laub's conception of stability and change and have found that both persistent individual differences (stability) and local life circumstances (change) are important for understanding criminal activity over the life course. These efforts have made use of different samples, different indicators of local life circumstances, different methodologies, and different periods of the life course (see Sampson and Laub 1993; Horney, Osgood, and Marshall 1995; Laub, Nagin, and Sampson 1998; Piquero et al. 2002). Moreover, these efforts have shown that the type and quality of local life circumstances may be more important than just the presence of a particular life circumstance. For example, Laub, Nagin, and Sampson (1998) found that the quality of marriage, as opposed to marriage per se, was associated with desistance from offending in early adulthood.

Recently, Sampson and Laub (1997) have extended their age-graded theory of informal social control to incorporate a developmental conceptualization of labeling theory. In particular, this account invokes a state-dependence argument in that it incorporates the causal role of prior delinquency in facilitating adult crime through a process of "cumulative disadvantage." According to Sampson and Laub, involvement in delinquent behavior has a "systematic attenuating effect on the social and institutional bonds linking adults to society (e.g., labor force attachment, marital cohesion)" (1997, p. 144). Thus, delinquency is indirectly related to future criminal activity in that it can spark failure in school, incarceration, and weak bonds to the labor market, all of which are likely to lead to further adult crime. This cycle occurs because severe sanctions, which ultimately end up labeling offenders, limit the opportunities available to individuals to follow a conventional lifestyle. The cumulative continuity of disadvantage is the result of both persistent individual differences and the dynamic process where childhood antisocial behavior and adolescent delinquency foster adult crime through the weakening of adult social bonds (Sampson and Laub 1997, p. 145).

Cumulative disadvantage is believed to be linked to the four social control institutions of the family, school, peers, and state sanctions. For Sampson and Laub (1997), interactional continuity begins with the family. Child behaviors tend to influence parents just as much as parent behaviors influence children, and it is likely that a child's negative behavior will not only be punished by parents, but further actions may be influenced by parental labels placed on their children and their child's subsequent adoption of the label. The school also occupies a key place in Sampson and Laub's cumulative disadvantage theory. For example, teachers may react to a child's unruly behavior by retreating from a teacher-student relationship that is designed to foster intellectual and personal growth. To the extent that this rejection "undermines the attachment of the child to the school, and ultimately, the child's performance in the school," it may lead to further disruptive and delinquent behavior (Sampson and Laub 1997, p. 147). Another key aspect of their theory revolves around peers. Children who are rejected by their peers tend to be more aggressive and, for some children, peer rejection fosters association with deviant peers, many of whom share the same aggressive characteristics.

The final aspect of cumulative disadvantage for Sampson and Laub is the criminal justice and institutional reaction. Their argument here involves the negative structural consequences of criminal offending and the resulting official sanctions that limit noncriminal opportunities. According to Sampson and Laub, adolescent delinquency and its negative consequences (i.e., arrest, trial, incarceration, etc.) "increasingly 'mortgage' one's future, especially later life chances molded by schooling and employment" (1997, p. 147). Thus, the stigma associated with arrest and, especially, incarceration, tends to limit good job prospects and, as a result, job stability. Given that job stability is virtually a prerequisite for lasting interpersonal relationships, arrest and incarceration are likely to reduce an offender's marriage premium (see

Cohen 1999). In sum, Sampson and Laub claim that official (and severe) reactions to primary deviance tend to create problems of adjustment that are likely to foster additional crime in the form of secondary deviance.

In a preliminary test of this thesis, Sampson and Laub (1997) examined the role of job stability at ages seventeen to twenty-five and twenty-five to thirty-two as an intervening link between incarceration and adult crime. After controlling for a number of theoretically relevant variables, including arrest frequency, alcohol use, and persistent unobserved heterogeneity, Sampson and Laub found that, compared to delinquents with a shorter incarceration history, boys who were incarcerated for a longer period of time had greater difficulty securing stable jobs as they entered young adulthood.

The theories outlined in this section share a common theme in that they are designed to assess within-individual change in both criminal activity and the factors associated with criminal activity over the life course. Yet, they differ in important respects. Compared to the static general theories of crime that assume that there is a general cause and one pathway to crime for all offenders and that once this causal process has occurred change is highly unlikely (see Wilson and Herrnstein 1985; Gottfredson and Hirschi 1990), a dynamic general theory, such as the one postulated by Sampson and Laub, maintains the assumption of general causality but allows for the possibility that life circumstances can materially alter an individual's criminal trajectory above and beyond persistent individual differences; that is, Sampson and Laub's model allows for both persistent heterogeneity and state-dependence effects. Developmental theories, such as those advanced by Moffitt, Patterson, and Loeber, are quite complex in that they assume that causality is not general and that different causal processes explain different offender types. Moreover, this causal process may emphasize persistent heterogeneity as in Moffitt's life-course persisters and Patterson's early-starting offenders or a state-dependence effect as in the dynamic accounts found among Moffitt's adolescence-limited offenders and Patterson's late-start offenders. Empirical research has attempted to adjudicate between these theoretical models, and thus far the evidence tends to favor a middle-ground position, such as the one advanced by Sampson and Laub (see Paternoster et al. 1997). However, recent evidence tends to suggest that local life circumstances operate in somewhat different ways across distinct offender groups (see Chung et al. 2002; Piquero, MacDonald, and Parker 2002).

TABLE 2

Classification Scheme

	General	Developmental
Static	Gottfredson and Hirschi	Moffitt's life-course-persistent offender
	Wilson and Herrnstein	Patterson's early-starting offender
Dynamic	Sampson and Laub	Moffitt's adolescence-limited offender
		Patterson's late-starting offender

An important point concerns the relationship between static (persistent-heterogeneity)/dynamic (state-dependence) and general/developmental theories. Paternoster et al. (1997) presented a useful classification, reproduced here as table 2. As can be seen, developmental theories can be compared against purely static/general theories and can be viewed along a continuum of parsimony. For example, static/general theories are the most parsimonious in emphasizing a purely persistent heterogeneity explanation, followed by dynamic/general theories, which emphasize a combined persistent-heterogeneity/state-dependence explanation. These are followed by developmental/static theories and then the least parsimonious, dynamic/developmental theories, which emphasize a mixture of persistent-heterogeneity/state-dependent explanations across offender types. In sum, the sometimes competing explanations of persistent heterogeneity and state dependence are not necessarily incompatible; sometimes one is stronger, sometimes another, but they are not necessarily mutually inconsistent.

IV. Methodological Issues

Both criminal career research and developmental theory focus on longitudinal data on criminal activity over the life course. Several key methodological issues relating to types of data, research designs, and analytic techniques must be confronted.

A. Data

Because of the need to obtain a complete portrayal of criminal activity, especially activity that goes undetected by the criminal justice system, both self-report and official records are needed to study the longitudinal patterning of criminal activity. In this section, we discuss three issues related to the reliability of self-report and official data. Although both self-reports and official records are useful, each is vulnerable to sources of error that may limit the accuracy of estimates of criminal career dimensions.

1. *Reliability.* Self-report and official record data provide complementary information on the behavior of offenders. Use of both methodologies can serve as a check on one another as, oftentimes, self-report records document information not found in official records.

Self-report data can be distorted as a result of problems in the design of survey instruments, response errors, and analytical problems in inferring career dimensions from questionnaire responses (Hindelang, Hirschi, and Weis 1981; Blumstein et al. 1986; Weis 1986). First, response errors typically result from the saliency, frequency, and timing of criminal activity. For example, in many surveys, individuals are asked to provide a frequency count of the number of times they engaged in a particular act. For many individuals, especially high-rate offenders and those with a history of heavy drug and alcohol use, memory problems are likely to increase with longer recall periods and with greater intervals between the recall period and the survey date. Henry and colleagues (1994) investigated the use of recall questions, including those associated with delinquency/arrest. Their analysis concluded that recalling the precise number of events is difficult, especially when many events occur.

A second problem lies in respondent uncertainty about which events are to be counted as police contacts, arrests, or convictions, and to which crimes those events refer. This is likely magnified among high-rate offenders.

Third, respondents may misrepresent their involvement in criminal activity. They may lie about their involvement or noninvolvement in crime. Similarly, they may refuse to participate in a study or, once involved, may refuse to continue. The NYS, for example, had an original refusal rate of over 25 percent, and attrition increased over subsequent surveys. Misrepresentation of information, refusal of participation, and attrition or noncooperation are likely to be pronounced among the most serious offenders.

A fourth set of problems includes testing, period, and panel effects (Thornberry 1989). Testing effects refer to alterations in individuals' responses to a particular item or set of items caused by previously answering the same item or set of items. Panel effects refer to the observation that age-specific rates for crimes tend to change with age. Period effects can produce downward trends in age-specific rates for the majority of crimes that may or may not be indicative of a real decline.

Another potential threat to the reliability of self-reports is the changing content validity of items related to the age of the respondent. For example, people's interpretations of self-report items may change as they age, and thus changes in crime and delinquency over time may have more to do with the meaning of the questions to the respondents than with actual changes in behavior (Lauritsen 1998). Or within a cross-section of different-aged individuals, there may be changing content validity across different-aged survey respondents (Piquero, MacIntosh, and Hickman 2002). Despite these problems, self-report surveys have become one of the key pieces of data collected by researchers studying criminal careers (see Junger-Tas and Marshall 1999; Thornberry and Krohn 2000).

Official records are vulnerable to important but different errors. They are a reflection only of the "tip of the iceberg" with regard to criminal activity. Official records contain information only on offenses that come to the attention of officials. Many crimes are not reported to the police, much less solved. Two other associated problems are misclassification and nonrecording of events. Misclassification of events can occur as a result of differences among local agencies in classifying offenses (e.g., is a purse snatch a larceny or a robbery?). Relatedly, the criminal event that led to an initial arrest may end up being "redefined" on conviction. An individual arrested for rape may be convicted for a less serious offense such as a sexual assault. Nonrecording errors may also occur because the criminal event leading to formal detection may not meet reporting standards, such as the requirement for disposition data that may not be available (Blumstein et al. 1986, p. 99). Nonrecording can also vary across jurisdictions, for example, from large cities with ample resources compared to small, rural communities with few resources.

Self-reports and official records should not necessarily be viewed as in competition. Farrington (1989, p. 418) suggests that official and self-report records tend to produce "comparable and complementary results on such important topics as prevalence, continuity, versatility, and specialization in different types of offenses."

2. *Sampling.* Researchers want representative samples. However, due to resource constraints, complete populations and large representative samples are seldom possible. Two significant sampling issues involve selection bias that occurs through the arrest process and researchers' ability to obtain a sufficient number of cases of serious offending. Both issues involve trade-offs.

Selection bias occurs with the use of offender-based samples (i.e., those offenders who were arrested). Such offenders are not likely to be representative of all offenders; they are presumably the most serious, older, and possibly the most inept at avoiding detection (Blumstein et al. 1986, p. 102). Moreover, sampling arrestees involves potential errors of commission because some falsely arrested persons are wrongly included among active offenders. Similarly, selecting convicted offenders is more likely to involve errors of omission because sampling convicted offenders misses the active offenders who were not convicted. Thus, selection bias may occur at the arrest, conviction, and incarceration stages. This problem is particularly important for issues related to incapacitation. As Canela-Cacho, Blumstein, and Cohen suggest, "differential selection of offenders arising stochastically from variation in individual offending frequencies will result in measurement bias if one applies this biased estimate of offending frequency to *all offenders* and not just to those offenders processed through the same stage of the criminal justice system" (1997, p. 135; emphasis in original). Selection bias is a concern because of the heterogeneous distribution of offending frequencies observed in self-report surveys of inmates (Chaiken and Chaiken 1982; Spelman 1994; Canela-Cacho, Blumstein, and Cohen 1997).

Problems associated with researchers' ability to obtain a sufficient number of cases of serious offending are particularly relevant in self-report studies. In general population samples, arrests and crimes are relatively infrequent, and this is especially true for the more serious offense types. Cernkovich, Giordano, and Pugh (1985) concluded that high-rate offenders were often missing from general population (i.e., household) surveys. Those high-rate offenders who do show up in self-report studies may be more likely to drop out over time (Brame and Piquero, forthcoming). This nonrandom sample attrition may pose a problem for correctly estimating criminal career dimensions. Thus, the limited number of more serious offenders in self-report data will likely underestimate true offending offense rates. One potential correction is to oversample high-yield subpopulations (low-income neighborhoods) as in some of the causes and correlates studies.

It is possible to correct for biases arising from sampling processes. Such a correction involves reweighting the sample to reflect the differences in the probabilities of sample members. Thus, certain offender types who are underrepresented can be given greater weight while those who are overrepresented are given less weight. The best sample choice in any study varies with the career dimension being measured. General population samples, which include both offenders and nonoffenders, are more appropriate for estimating participation rates. However, such samples are inefficient for estimating individual offending frequencies because of the small number of high-rate offenders found within them. Samples of arrestees or inmates are better suited for estimating frequency, but corrections are required to adjust for the overrepresentation of high-rate and more serious offenders (Blumstein et al. 1986, p. 104). One compromise is to study similar questions with both sets of samples (see Le Blanc and Fréchette 1989). Cernkovich and Giordano (2001) recently used both household and institutionalized samples to study patterns of stability and change in criminal offending over time.

3. *Street Time.* Researchers develop estimates of individuals' offending over some period of time, typically over a six- or twelve-month period. However, during these periods, individuals may not be "free" to commit criminal acts. The calculation of "time at risk," "street time," or "free time," then, is crucial to estimating individual offending rates since offenders cannot commit crimes on the street while incarcerated (Weis 1986, p. 34), though they can clearly engage in crime while serving their jail or prison terms.

Estimating an individual's offending frequency without taking exposure time into consideration assumes that he is completely free to commit crimes. Under this assumption, an individual's true rate of offending is likely to be miscalculated because some offenders are not completely free. Researchers have recognized the importance of this problem and have implemented controls for street time (see Visher 1986; Barnett, Blumstein, and Farrington 1987, 1989; Hurrell 1993; Horney, Osgood, and Marshall 1995), but many self-report studies do not. The importance of this issue was recently demonstrated by Piquero et al. (2001) in their study of the recidivism patterns of serious offenders paroled from the CYA. They found that conclusions regarding persistence and desistance were contingent on knowledge of exposure time. Without controlling for street time, they found that 92 percent of their sample desisted. With controls for exposure time, only 72 percent desisted. In sum, variations in exposure time can affect measurements of criminal career dimensions and need to be considered in criminal career research (Blumstein et al. 1986, p. 106).

B. Research Design

Research on criminal careers examines individuals' variations in criminal activity over the life course. Because the paradigm devotes attention to ages at initiation and termination, and all points between, criminal career research is best carried out through longitudinal studies. Still, all criminal career research has not been carried out using longitudinal data. In this section, we discuss three different types of research designs that have been employed to study criminal activity, including longitudinal designs, accelerated longitudinal designs, and cross-sectional designs.

1. *Longitudinal Studies.* Longitudinal studies permit observations of criminal activity over an extended period. There are two principal types: cohort and panel studies. Cohort studies examine more specific samples (e.g., birth cohorts) as they change over time. Panel studies are similar except that the same set of people are interviewed at two or more time periods.

Longitudinal research can be carried out in several ways. One of the most obvious is to identify a cohort at birth and follow it prospectively for a long period. Two key problems are the costs associated with following people over long periods and the time required to study certain questions (e.g., desistance). Unfortunately, researchers age at the same rate of participants.

Another type of longitudinal design is retrospective. This approach avoids the long delay associated with the prospective design. In a retrospective design, the researcher defines a cohort, such as all persons born in 1970, and then retrospectively collects various pieces of information, such as offending histories. This approach, however, introduces potentially serious problems with recall errors.

Though useful for the study of within- and between-individual changes in criminal activity over time, prospective longitudinal designs suffer from limitations including costs; history, period, panel, and testing effects; and sample attrition. One problem is that age effects are confounded with historical effects. For example, significant social and historical events could influence the criminal activity of members of one cohort at a particular time as opposed to another cohort during another particular time (i.e., growing up during the depression, compared with during the Second World War or the Vietnam War). Sample attrition from a variety of causes including death, refusal to participate, and moving to unknown addresses, can seriously under- or overestimate criminal career dimensions. The extent to which sample attrition occurs nonrandomly is a concern. If high-rate offenders are more likely to drop out, then estimates concerning the relationship between age and crime in longitudinal designs may be biased (Brame and Piquero, forthcoming). Finally, on a practical level, human life expectancies and stakes make multidecade, longitudinal projects difficult to sustain and complete.

2. *Accelerated Longitudinal Design.*   One way to overcome problems associated with typical longitudinal designs is by drawing multiple cohorts and obtaining longitudinal data on them. The researcher identifies a cross-sectional sample of the population (thus representing multiple cohorts) and then collects longitudinal data, either prospectively or retrospectively. In such a design, several cohorts born in different years could be selected and each followed for about six years. For example, four cohorts could be followed from birth to age six, six to twelve, twelve to eighteen, and eighteen to twenty-four (see Farrington, Ohlin, and Wilson 1986, p. 18). The emphasis is on linking results from different cohorts to build up a more complete picture of the development of criminal careers from birth to young adulthood. This approach shortens the time until research results are obtained and enables investigators to distinguish between the effects of aging and the effects of a historical period. In addition, accelerated longitudinal designs also present an unusual opportunity to examine period effects since successive cohorts will reach specific ages (e.g., age twelve) in different years and their life experiences can be compared. Still, accelerated longitudinal designs present some difficulties. For example, researchers may encounter difficulty in achieving sampling-criteria consistency across cohorts, and statistical problems may arise in amalgamating data from successive cohorts.

The PHDCN uses an accelerated longitudinal design. This study started with nine different age groups, from prenatal to age eighteen, and is following each group for several years. The age groups are separated by three-year intervals; three years after the data collection started, the overall age range would be continuous. Researchers hoped to examine several aspects of development, including criminal activity, from birth to age twenty-six. Approximately 6,500 individuals are being studied.

3. *Cross-Sectional Designs.*   Cross-sectional designs are based on observations at a single time and are best suited to examine between-individual differences. In the criminal career domain, cross-sectional studies are designed to provide a glimpse of the criminal activity of sample members at one time. Although the aim is to understand causal processes that occur over time, ability to do so is compromised because the observations are made at only one time. Thus, cross-sectional designs cannot study within-individual variation over time, but research-

ers can link cohorts by age, thereby constituting an extreme example of the accelerated longitudinal design.

C. Analytic Techniques

The use of longitudinal data raises a number of analytical questions. Because data are collected on the same persons repeatedly, assessing stability and change in criminal activity becomes somewhat complicated. For example, what is the best way to study change over time? What is the best way to model the unobserved heterogeneity in the offending population? What is the best approach for handling multiple observations of the same person over time? In this section, we describe the three main techniques that have been applied to the within- and between-individual analysis of criminal activity over the life course.

1. *Random- and Fixed-Effects Models.* One way to control for persistent unobserved individual differences is with random-effects models. These models decompose the error term into two components, a random error component and an individual-specific, time-constant component that reflects time-stable differences across individuals (i.e., unobserved persistent heterogeneity). This model recognizes that some unmeasured elements will not be truly random but will instead be fixed for a given individual over time. Thus, random-effects models take care of persistent individual differences by decomposing the error term; however, these models presume that this unobserved heterogeneity is normally distributed in the population.

Fixed-effects models model unobserved heterogeneity as a time-constant intercept term that captures all individual effects that are constant over time. Unlike the random-effects model, the fixed-effects model does not conceptualize unobserved heterogeneity as part of the error term. The fixed-effects model incorporates unobserved heterogeneity by using a constant term for each individual to absorb all individual-specific effects. Because the fixed-effects model "sweeps up" all potential sources of heterogeneity by introducing dummy variables to account for the effects of all omitted variables that are specific to each individual but are constant over time, omitted variable bias is not a problem (Hsiao 1986). In addition, because a separate intercept is estimated for each individual, unlike in the random-effects model, no assumption about the distributional form of individual heterogeneity is needed in the fixed-effects model. Still, the fixed-effects model is limited because the estimation of a separate intercept for each individual uses many degrees of freedom.

2. *Clusters of Individual Trajectories.* In view of the distributional assumptions made by random-effects models, Nagin and Land (1993) developed an alternative modeling strategy, the semiparametric mixed Poisson model (SPM), which makes no parametric assumptions about the distribution of persistent unobserved heterogeneity (see also Land, McCall, and Nagin 1996; Land and Nagin 1996). Although the SPM is still a random-effects model, it no longer restricts the mixing distribution (i.e., the distribution of individual heterogeneity in the population) to be normal, as is the case with random-effects models. Instead, the SPM assumes that the distribution of unobserved persistent heterogeneity is discrete rather than continuous, and thus the mixing distribution is viewed as multinomial (i.e., a categorical variable). Each category within the multinomial mixture can be viewed as a point of support (i.e., grouping) for the distribution of individual heterogeneity. Essentially, the SPM estimates a separate intercept, or point of support, for as many distinct groups as can be identified in the data. Thus, each individual has some nonzero probability of being assigned to each discrete group and is assigned to the group to which he has the highest probability of belonging. This is an important feature of the SPM because the SPM helps isolate the sorts of offender typologies or groups that current developmental theories of crime argue exist in the offending population. This cannot be accomplished with modeling approaches that treat unobserved heterogeneity in a continuous fashion.

The SPM has two additional features that make it appealing. First, it takes into consideration periods of nonoffending, or intermittency. Researchers have made note of the importance of controlling for periods of nonoffending throughout the criminal career, and empirical research has shown that models that control for periods of intermittency tend to provide a better fit to the data than models that do not control for such periods. Second, the SPM makes use of several different types of estimators, including the Poisson, the zero-inflated Poisson, the Bernoulli, and the censored normal. The censored normal model is useful for psychometric scale data, the Poisson and the zero-inflated Poisson model for count data, and the Bernoulli model for dichotomous data. By allowing for the use of different types of estimators, the outcome data under investigation can be more appropriately modeled.

Still, the SPM has some weaknesses. For example, since the SPM assumes that unobserved individual heterogeneity (i.e., the mixing distribution) is drawn from a discrete (multinomial) probability distribution, there will likely be model misspecification bias if unobserved individual differences are actually drawn from a continuous distribution. Latent curve modeling recently adopted the conventional assumption of a continuous distribution of growth curves to accommodate the group-based approach (Muthen and Muthen 2000). Second, the identification of parameter estimates under the SPM is difficult with small periods of observations and where the prevalence of observations is small. Third, classification of individuals to distinct trajectories will never be perfect (see Roeder, Lynch, and Nagin 1999).

3. *Hierarchical Linear Models.* Hierarchical linear models (HLM) are a generalization of multiple regression models for nested or repeated-measures data and in many ways allow for more complex random effects such as growth curve approaches, which provide for individual differences in levels of propensity to offend and in trajectories of change over time (Osgood and Rowe 1994, p. 541). Hierarchical linear models separate between-person and within-person models, and the latter are determined first. In HLM, the individual-level parameters from the within-person model serve as dependent variables for the between-person model, leading to a separate equation for each parameter (Horney, Osgood, and Marshall 1995, p. 661). Estimates of within-person change are derived by transforming key independent variables to deviations from each individual's mean calculated across the entire period of observations. Then, by including the individual means for the key independent variables as explanatory variables in the equation for overall individual differences, HLM models reflect the effects of between-person differences in average independent variables as well as providing estimates that reflect the effects of within-person change. As can be seen, HLM models differ from SPM models in that they apply continuous distributions to unobserved individual heterogeneity and therefore neither assume nor estimate discrete groups of offenders. To the extent that individual heterogeneity is continuous, HLM models will likely not suffer from model misspecification bias; however, if individual heterogeneity is discrete, then HLM models will suffer this sort of bias. In addition, current HLM models assume that errors for particular observations are normally distributed, which may or may not be true.

There are thus several different analytic techniques that researchers can employ when studying the longitudinal sequence of criminal activity. For example, growth curve modeling, whether hierarchical or latent variable, is designed to identify average developmental tendencies, to calibrate variability about the average, and to explain that variability in terms of the covariates of interest. The SPM is designed to identify distinctive developmental trajectories within the population, to calibrate the probability of population members following each trajectory, and to relate those probabilities to covariates of interest (Nagin 1999, p. 153). The former set of approaches implies that people come in all shades of criminality while the latter implies qualitative differences between offenders and nonoffenders (Osgood and Rowe 1994, p. 531). Raudenbush (2001) suggests that the type of question being studied should guide the type of model used. For example, if the question is centered on what is the typical pattern of growth within the population and how this growth varies across members, then hierarchical and latent curve modeling may be more useful. However, if the concern is with phenomena that do not generally grow or change monotonically over time and do not vary regularly over the population, then techniques such as the SPM are likely to be more useful because they are designed to identify clusters of trajectories and to calibrate how individual characteristics affect cluster membership. Other techniques for the identification of trajectories such as ad hoc classifications, cluster analysis, growth curves, and so forth, have recently been reviewed elsewhere (Le Blanc, forthcoming).

D. Analytic Issues

The study of criminal careers has also led to the recognition of difficult questions that have been the source of operationalization, measurement, and empirical application concerns: first, sorting out the state dependence/persistent heterogeneity effect and, second, defining, operationalizing, and measuring desistance.

1. *Sorting Out the State-Dependence/Persistent-Heterogeneity Effect.* The positive correlation between past and future criminal activity is a key finding. Although all researchers recognize the importance of this relationship, determining the process responsible for it, some combination of state dependence and persistent heterogeneity, has been difficult. Evidence for persistent heterogeneity would consist of an observed relationship between a time-stable individual characteristic measured early in life and subsequent criminal activity, while evidence for state dependence would consist of a relationship between a time-varying individual characteristic and criminal activity net of time-stable differences in criminal propensity (Nagin and Paternoster 2000, p. 129). Because of data and measurement limitations, the disentan-

gling of persistent heterogeneity and state dependence requires that researchers control for unmeasured persistent heterogeneity (Bushway, Brame, and Paternoster 1999).

One problem with isolating a persistent-heterogeneity effect is that researchers are unlikely to agree on its distribution. Even after controlling for many different indicators of observed persistent heterogeneity, there is likely to be a sizeable amount of unmeasured, unobserved persistent heterogeneity that needs to be taken into consideration. To accomplish this, researchers have employed statistical techniques that incorporate unobserved sources of persistent heterogeneity. It is important to control for such unobserved sources since omitting them is likely to lead to biased estimates of observed time-varying factors. The effect of not controlling is an overinflated effect of time-varying variables that may overstate the state-dependence effect.

Although analytic techniques exist for estimating unobserved persistent heterogeneity, researchers have not come to agreement as to which best performs this task. Bushway, Brame, and Paternoster (1999) assessed issues related to stability (persistent individual heterogeneity) and change (state dependence) by applying three different analytic techniques (random-effects probit model, the SPM, and the fixed-effects logit model) to criminal history data from the 1958 Philadelphia birth cohort. Four key findings emerged. First, all three methods converged on the finding that there was a strong positive relationship between prior and future criminal activity even after stable unobserved individual differences were controlled. Second, the state-dependence effect, though still important, was lessened with controls for persistent unobserved heterogeneity. Third, controlling for time trends was found to be important. In particular, analysis with the random-effects model showed that time trend controls allowed for the identification of greater levels of heterogeneity in crime proneness and yielded attenuated estimates of the effect of prior criminal activity on future criminal activity. Fourth, increasing levels of positive skew (i.e., nonnormality) in the distribution of crime proneness was associated with an overestimation of the effect of prior criminal activity on future criminal activity (Bushway, Brame, and Paternoster 1999, p. 53).

2. *Defining, Operationalizing, and Measuring Desistance.*   Desistance is the least studied criminal career dimension (Loeber and Le Blanc 1990, p. 407). Laub and Sampson (2001) noted three particular reasons: conceptual, definitional, and measurement. Regarding conceptualization, Laub and Sampson (2001, p. 5) argue that there is little theo-

retical conceptualization about crime cessation, the various reasons for desistance, and the mechanisms underlying the desistance process. They note that the underlying conceptual difficulty stems from the issue of stability and change over the life course. There is no agreed on definition of desistance (Bushway et al. 2001), and this leads Laub and Sampson to raise their second concern, that desistance definitions are vague. For example, Warr (1998) employed a one-year crime-free period as desistance, while Farrington and Hawkins (1991) defined desistance as having no convictions between ages twenty-one and thirty-two following a conviction before age twenty-one. Loeber and his colleagues (1991) defined desistance as refraining from offending for a period of less than a year. Laub and Sampson point out, however, that simply because an offender desists from criminal activity, it does not necessarily follow that he has stopped engaging in other sorts of deviant acts. For example, Nagin, Farrington, and Moffitt (1995) found that although some offenders desisted from crime according to official conviction records, self-reported data indicated continued deviance and involvement in drugs and alcohol. Similar discrepant effects were reported by Le Blanc and Fréchette (1989) in their Canadian study comparing official and self-report records.

The larger measurement issue deals with the length of follow-up and censoring. For example, findings regarding desistance may reflect the cutoff of observations at a specific age (Laub and Sampson 2001, p. 9), and some researchers have even suggested that desistance is only definite when study subjects have died (Blumstein, Cohen, and Hsieh 1982; Farrington 1994). Thus, if researchers studying desistence ceased observation of study subjects at age thirty, there is no guarantee that the subjects have truly desisted; there may even be a temporary lull followed by continued criminal activity in later years, that is, intermittency (see Frazier 1976; Barnett, Blumstein, and Farrington 1989; Nagin and Land 1993; Piquero, forthcoming). Laub and Sampson (2001, p. 11) suggest that researchers distinguish termination of offending (the time at which criminal activity stops) from desistance (the causal process that supports the termination of offending and maintains the continued state of nonoffending). The former is the outcome to be explained by the latter processual cause. This is consistent with the view that desistance is both an event and a process (see Fagan 1989; Maruna 2001). In sum, it is an important process that needs to be measured and understood.

Bushway and his colleagues (2001) proposed an empirical framework for studying desistance as a developmental process. Instead of focusing on offending itself, these authors focus on changes in the offending rate. In particular, the Bushway et al. approach, which makes use of Nagin and Land's (1993) SPM, models the process by which criminality, defined as the propensity to offend, changes with age. Their approach allows researchers to trace patterns of individual offending behavior across age and to explore the developmental dynamics that generate stability or change. Thus, since age is incorporated into the dependent variable (i.e., measured as changes in offending behavior over time/age), any causal factor by definition is studied in the context of age.

V. Empirical Findings of Criminal Career Dimensions

Several new research efforts, longitudinal studies, and explanatory paradigms have been initiated since the mid-1980s to focus on the key dimensions of criminal careers. In this section, we survey findings from empirical research on the key dimensions of criminal careers, the latest round of longitudinal studies that were initiated after publication of the criminal careers report, and new questions and criminal career issues raised by the risk/protective factor paradigm.

A. Overview of Findings

We concentrate on five key subjects: participation in criminal careers; the dimensions of criminal careers and their covariates, including frequency, duration, and termination, crime-type mix and seriousness, co-offending, and specialization/crime-type switching; the extent to which the causes of one dimension are similar to—or different from— the causes of another dimension; chronic offenders; and the relevance of criminal career research to understanding incapacitation.

1. *Participation in Criminal Careers: Ever-Prevalence Estimates.* Estimates of ever-participation in criminal activity vary across reporting method (they tend to be much higher with self-report than with official records that are a filtered subset of self-reports), the crimes in which participation is being measured (there is more participation in less serious criminal activity), the level of threshold of involvement (police contact, arrest, conviction), and the characteristics and representativeness of the sample (high school students, college students, general population, offender-based, etc.). In general, ever-participation estimates are fairly common across data sets and consistent with most criminological findings.

There is a relatively high rate of participation among males in criminal activity (Elliott, Huizinga, and Morse 1987, p. 502). Blumstein et al. (1986) reported that about 15 percent of urban males are arrested for an Index offense by age eighteen, and 25–45 percent of urban males are arrested for a nontraffic offense by age eighteen. Visher and Roth's (1986) overview of several longitudinal studies employing police and court records indicates a lifetime prevalence estimate of 40–50 percent, with slightly higher rates for blacks and much lower rates among females (see, e.g., Robins 1966; Christensen 1967; Blumstein and Graddy 1982; Shannon 1982). Visher and Roth's (1986) overview of cumulative criminal participation rates in cross-sectional samples of high-school-age youths indicates differences in participation across crime types. For example, although many studies report consistent estimates of burglary participation of between 15 and 20 percent for males, and much lower estimates for females (around 3–4 percent), estimates for theft vary much more widely.

Several studies provide in-depth information on participation based on official record-based police contact/arrest data. Using the 1945 Philadelphia birth cohort, Wolfgang, Figlio, and Sellin (1972) observed a "by-age-eighteen-prevalence" of police contacts of 34.9 percent for the entire sample, with rates of 28.6 percent for whites and 50.2 percent for blacks. Using police contact data for the 1958 Philadelphia birth cohort, Tracy, Wolfgang, and Figlio (1990) reported a "by-age-eighteen-prevalence" of 32.8 percent for the entire sample, with rates of 22.7 percent for whites and 41.8 percent for blacks. In a 1970 Puerto Rico birth cohort study, Nevares, Wolfgang, and Tracy (1990) found that the arrest prevalence of delinquency by age seventeen was 6.8 percent for the full sample, with rates of 11.3 percent for males and 2.3 percent for females. Wikström (1990) reports that nearly one-fifth (19 percent) of subjects in Project Metropolitan in Sweden had a police record for a crime by age twenty-five. Polk et al. (1981) used data from police and juvenile court records for over 1,000 Oregon male high school sophomores in 1964 and observed a prevalence estimate of 25 percent, with comparable estimates reported among other high-school-aged youths (see Hirschi 1969; Hindelang, Hirschi, and Weis 1981; Elliott and Huizinga 1984). Some Scandinavian studies, however, report smaller prevalence estimates (see Guttridge et al. 1983; Mednick, Gabrielli, and Hutchings 1984).

Studies based on conviction records provide similar estimates. For example, McCord (1978) obtained a conviction prevalence estimate of

27.5 percent for over 500 males born in 1925–34 in Massachusetts and followed until 1978. Results from the Cambridge study indicated that by age forty, 40 percent of the London males were convicted of a criminal offense (Farrington 2002).

Several studies have used self-report data to obtain prevalence estimates. For example, using self-report data from the NYS, Elliott (1994) reported that the ever-prevalence (to age twenty-seven) of serious, violent offending was 30 percent. Self-report data from the three causes and correlates studies indicate that, by age sixteen at all three sites, approximately 40 percent of males reported committing one or more serious violent acts, while for females, the corresponding rates were 32 and 16 percent, respectively, in Rochester and Denver (Kelley et al. 1997). Using self-report data from the Cambridge study, Farrington (2002) found that up to age thirty-two, 96 percent of males admitted committing at least one crime that could have led to a conviction. For Canadian males, Le Blanc and Fréchette (1989, p. 60) found that 97 percent of adolescents self-reported at least one criminal infraction during their adolescence.

2. *Gender and Participation.* Regardless of the source of data, crime type, level of involvement, or measure of participation, male criminal participation in serious crime at any age is always greater than female participation (Blumstein et al. 1986, p. 40; see also Lanctôt and Le Blanc [2002] for a detailed review of gender differences), and this is especially so for serious violence (Weiner 1989, p. 67). In both the 1958 Philadelphia birth cohort and the three Racine, Wisconsin, cohorts, ratios of male to female participation were small for broad (and less serious) categories but larger for Index offenses and specific crime types. Although males in the 1958 Philadelphia birth cohort had a 32.8 percent prevalence estimate, the comparable estimate among females was 14.1 percent, and it was twice as high among black (18.5 percent) as among white (9.2 percent) females. In the three Racine cohorts, Shannon (1982) reported prevalence estimates, derived from police contacts for nontraffic and status offenses, of 41 percent, 47.3 percent, and 44.1 percent among males in the 1942, 1949, and 1955 cohorts. Female prevalence estimates were 8.7 percent, 15.1 percent, and 22.2 percent, respectively. Hamparian et al. (1978) found gender ratios in arrest prevalence as high as 6:1. Male prevalence estimates of 29 percent and 28 percent were obtained by Ouston (1984) and Miller et al. (1974) in two separate British birth cohort studies using police and juvenile court records, respectively, with female prevalence estimates of

6 percent and 5.6 percent, respectively. Also using police records, Wikström (1990) reported ever-prevalence rates in Project Metropolitan of 31 percent for males and 6 percent for females by age twenty-five. Using official record data for the Dunedin cohort through age twenty-one, Moffitt et al. (2001) found that males (20 percent) were twice as likely as females (10 percent) to have had a contact with police as juveniles, and males were significantly more likely than females to have been convicted of a crime (20 percent to 8 percent). Further, 8 percent of males were convicted for a violent offense whereas only 2 percent of females were. The sexes were more similar—yet still significantly different—to one another on convictions for drug/alcohol offenses with 5 percent of males and 2 percent of females being convicted for such an offense. Piquero's (2000) analysis of the Philadelphia National Collaborative Perinatal Project data indicated that 31 percent of males incurred a police contact by age eighteen while the comparable figure for females was 14 percent. Piquero and Buka (2002), using the Providence National Collaborative Perinatal Project data, found that 19 percent of males had a court contact by age eighteen while the comparable estimate among females was 5 percent.

The relationship between gender and participation has also been assessed via self-report records. For example, Elliott (1994) examined self-reported participation estimates for serious, violent offending using the first eight waves of the NYS. Focusing on gender differences, Elliott reported that the peak age in prevalence for serious, violent offending was earlier for females, the decline was steeper among females, and the gender differential became greater at older ages. At age twelve, the male to female differential was 2:1; by age eighteen it had increased to 3:1; and by age twenty-one it had increased to 4:1. Thus, at each age, males were more likely than females to be involved in serious, violent offending. The ever-prevalence (to age twenty-seven) of serious, violent offending was 42 percent for males and 16 percent for females.

Puzzanchera (2000) analyzed self-reported delinquency data from several thousand twelve-year-old youths participating in the National Longitudinal Survey of Youth (NLSY) 1997 and found that only 2 percent had ever been arrested; however, 22 percent of the sample reported smoking cigarettes, 21 percent reported drinking alcohol, 24 percent reported destroying property, and 14 percent reported engaging in assaultive behaviors. Males (24 percent) were somewhat more likely to drink alcohol than females (19 percent), and much more likely to carry a handgun (13 percent compared to 2 percent) and destroy property (31 percent compared to 16 percent).

Kelley et al. (1997) used self-reported data on serious violence from the causes and correlates studies to examine gender differences in cumulative prevalence. They found that 39 percent of Denver males, 41 percent of Pittsburgh males, 40 percent of Rochester males, 16 percent of Denver females, and 32 percent of Rochester females reported committing at least one serious violent act by age sixteen.

This pattern of findings regarding gender differences in participation is not observed when examining a selected population of female prisoners. In a study of self-reported crime rates of prisoners in Colorado, English (1993) found that women and men had similar participation rates in the crimes of drug dealing, assault, robbery, motor vehicle theft, and fraud, though they differed in participation in forgery, theft, and burglary. Women were significantly more likely than men to report involvement in forgery and theft.

3. *Race and Participation.*   Researchers have tended to rely on official-record estimates, and most of the studies report relatively large black/white ratios and strong associations between race and participation, particularly as the seriousness of criminal activity increases. In their synthesis of the literature using official records, Visher and Roth (1986) reported that the average black/white participation ratio was 1.8:1 for all nontraffic offenses, but 3.2:1 for Index offenses. These estimates were similar whether using a "by-age-eighteen" or "lifetime" measure. In the Philadelphia birth cohort studies, the prevalence of delinquency was 50.2 percent for nonwhites and 28.6 percent for whites in the 1945 cohort, and 41.8 percent for nonwhites and 22.7 percent for whites in the 1958 cohort (Tracy, Wolfgang, and Figlio 1990, p. 39). Moreover, black/white ratios tended to increase as the level of seriousness increased: in the 1958 cohort, the black/white ratio was 3.2:1 for offenses with injury, but only 1.8:1 for nontraffic offenses. When the 1958 Philadelphia birth cohort was followed up to age twenty-six, Kempf-Leonard, Tracy, and Howell (2001) found that more black (17.4 percent) than white (9.1 percent) subjects participated in crime as adults, as measured by municipal court data, and this was the case for subjects who were delinquent prior to age eighteen as well as for those without a juvenile record. In sum, official record studies report male race differentials (nonwhite:white) of 4:1 during the adolescent years (Wolfgang, Figlio, and Sellin 1972; Hamparian et al. 1978), and those differentials tend to continue into the adult years (Kempf-Leonard, Tracy, and Howell 2001).

Although self-report comparisons of race prevalence tended to indicate that the estimated ratio of black/white participation is only slightly above 1:1 for minor delinquent acts and self-reported serious property offenses, analysis confined to more serious offenses suggests that the black/white ratio is larger, especially at younger ages (Blumstein et al. 1986, p. 41). Elliott (1994) recently performed the most systematic race comparison of self-report prevalence in the NYS and uncovered a number of important race findings. First, by age eighteen, nearly 40 percent of black males compared to 30 percent of white males became involved in serious violence. By age twenty-seven, the ratio is quite similar—48 percent for black males and 38 percent for white males. Second, the male black-to-white ratio in ever-prevalence was about 5:4, a small but statistically significant difference. Third, blacks (male and female) exhibited a higher prevalence of serious violent offending than whites throughout adolescence and early adulthood, and the discrepancy was most pronounced in the late teenage years. The maximum black-to-white differential was 3:2 for males, and 2:1 for females. During the early to mid-twenties, the prevalence of serious violence among white and black males in the NYS was similar; however, by age twenty-seven, the male black-to-white differential was 3:2. Among black females, however, their age-specific prevalence in serious violence was higher at every age from thirteen to twenty-seven compared to white females. Moreover, between ages twenty-four and twenty-seven, the annual prevalence of serious violence among white males declined, while it increased for black males from ages twenty-five to twenty-seven by nearly 50 percent (Elliott 1994, p. 7).

Kelley et al. (1997) also presented self-reported prevalence data by race/ethnicity across the three causes and correlates study sites. They found differences in serious violence prevalence rates across ethnic groups. In particular, a greater proportion of minority groups were involved in serious violence. With the exception of eighteen-year-olds in Rochester, prevalence rates were higher among minority groups than among whites at each age and site, and this difference was substantial during adolescence.

4. *Age and Participation.* The relationship between age and participation covers two issues. The first concerns the probability of committing an offense at a given age, while the second concerns the probability of initiating a criminal career at a given age. In general, both self-report and official records indicate that, although a small fraction of youth begins criminal careers at any given age, a concentration of

initiations among youth under age eighteen is evident. In their synthesis of the literature, Blumstein et al. (1986, p. 42) report that, for both blacks and whites, about half of those ever arrested during their lifetimes were first arrested before age eighteen. According to self-report records, few males commit their first criminal offense after age seventeen (Elliott, Huizinga, and Menard 1989). With official records, initiation rates tend to increase around the beginning of adolescence and peak around ages fourteen to eighteen and fall thereafter; however, self-reported participation rates peak somewhat earlier, around ages thirteen to sixteen (see Elliott et al. 1983). The age differences occur because teenagers are active in crime for some time before they experience their first police contact, arrest, or conviction. With self-report data, age-specific participation in "serious violence" (measured as involvement in three or more aggravated assaults, sexual assaults, gang fights, and strong-arm robberies of students or others) ranged between 7 percent and 8 percent from ages twelve to seventeen, with male rates higher by a factor of about two. Further, data from seven different longitudinal studies show that nearly one-fifth of children aged seven to twelve reported that they had committed at least one or more "street offenses" (i.e., bicycle theft, purse-snatching, physical fights, etc.) (Espiritu et al. 2001). Data from the three causes and correlates studies indicate that the self-reported prevalence of serious violence peaks in the mid to late teens for males, but somewhat earlier for females, with initiation in serious violence occurring relatively early (around age thirteen) (Kelley et al. 1997). In the 1970 Puerto Rico birth cohort study, age at onset measured from arrest records was observed to be highest at age sixteen for both males and females (Nevares, Wolfgang, and Tracy 1990). In the 1945 and 1958 Philadelphia cohort studies, age of onset peaked at sixteen and fifteen, respectively. Weiner (1989) concluded that most initiation of serious violence in official records occurred between ages eighteen and twenty-four but that participation in violence declines in early adulthood after reaching its peak in the late teens or early twenties.

In one of the most comprehensive analyses of the prevalence of criminal activity at different ages, Stattin, Magnusson, and Reichel (1989) followed a representative sample of Swedish males and females from ages ten to thirty and uncovered several key findings. First, the peak age at first conviction among males was age sixteen to seventeen (31.1 percent of registered males were convicted at this age), with age of first conviction peaking at age fifteen. Very few males were convicted for their first offense after age twenty-six. Moreover, the peak participation ages for the Swedish males were fifteen to seventeen. Second, the peak age at first conviction among females was twenty-one to twenty-three (32.8 percent of registered females were convicted at this age). Unlike their male counterparts, the Swedish females were more likely to accumulate convictions in early adulthood. By age thirty, 37.7 percent of the Swedish males and 9 percent of the Swedish females were registered for a criminal offense, and these estimates would be higher if common drunkenness and disorderly conduct were included. Using data from Project Metropolitan through age twenty-five, Wikström (1985) found that peak violence initiation ages, measured in police records, occurred during late adolescence and young adulthood (ages sixteen to twenty), with the two highest initiation ages of seventeen and nineteen. In particular, the peak age for both crimes and offenders was seventeen and nineteen, respectively, with slightly different peaks across offense types.

Farrington's (2002) analysis of the criminal histories of the Cambridge study males through age forty revealed three key findings regarding age and participation. First, up to age forty, 40 percent of the study males were convicted of a criminal offense. Second, up to age forty, the mean age of onset (first conviction) was 18.6. Third, with self-report records, the cumulative prevalence of offending up to age thirty-two was 96 percent. In an interesting comparison of the Cambridge study boys with 310 boys born seven years later and living in the same small area of South London at age fourteen, Farrington and Maughan (1999) found that the average age of onset and the cumulative prevalence of convictions were almost identical in the two samples up to age thirty-three. Finally, in a comparison of the Cambridge study males to lower class males in Project Metropolitan in Sweden, Farrington and Wikström (1994) found that the cumulative prevalence curves were remarkably similar, as were the age of onset curves.

Until recently, very few researchers have presented general hazard rates for age of initiation (Elliott, Huizinga, and Morse 1987; Weiner 1989; Farrington et al. 1990). Using the first eight waves of the NYS, Elliott (1994) examined age of onset by calculating the hazard rate for self-reported serious violence through age twenty-seven. Elliott found that although the hazard rate was very low through age eleven (<0.5 percent), it increased sharply to 5.1 percent at age sixteen and then declined sharply to 1.0 percent or less for ages twenty-one to twenty-seven. Over half of all violent offenders in the NYS initiated their violence between ages fourteen and seventeen, with the risk of initiation being close to zero after age twenty. Compared to white males, black males in the NYS had a substantially higher hazard rate for serious violence between ages thirteen and sixteen, and had an earlier age of onset (age fifteen compared to age sixteen for whites). In addition, the age-specific cumulative prevalence for black males was higher than for white males at every age from twelve to twenty-seven; by age twenty-seven, the cumulative prevalence of serious violence for black males in the NYS was almost 50 percent. Finally, male hazard rates tracked the hazard rates for the full sample indicating that the male rates were driving much of the sample's overall rates (Elliott, Huizinga, and Morse 1987).

Farrington et al. (1990) calculated hazard rates for the onset of criminal conviction in the Cambridge study through age thirty-two and found age fourteen to be the peak age of conviction onset, whereas data from the Philadelphia birth cohort study indicate that arrest onset peaked at age sixteen and was earlier for nonwhites compared to whites. Other researchers using police records have found age fourteen to be the peak for onset of criminal activity (see Patterson, Crosby, and Vuchinich 1992; Tibbetts and Piquero 1999). Onset rates may also vary by crime type. For example, in the Cambridge study, the onset rate for shoplifting peaked at ages thirteen to fourteen while the onset rate for assault peaked at ages seventeen to nineteen. Le Blanc and Fréchette (1989) also found that onset rates varied by crime type, with less serious offenses having an earlier peak compared to more serious offenses.

5. *Gender and Age Participation.* Few studies have provided data on gender comparisons regarding age and crime generally and age of onset in particular. Piper (1983) found that males and females in the 1958 Philadelphia birth cohort initiated their overall delinquent careers at approximately the same ages (seven in ten of those who initiated careers in each gender group initiated before age fifteen). Elliott, Huizinga, and Morse (1987) found that male hazard rates peaked at ages sixteen through eighteen and then declined, while female hazard rates peaked earlier (thirteen to fifteen) and decreased considerably from ages sixteen to twenty-one. Moreover, the ratio of the male-to-female peak hazard rates was 4.5:1 (for males, 6.8 percent at age seventeen, and for females, 1.5 percent at age fourteen). Piquero and Chung (2001) found no gender differences in onset age with police contact data through age seventeen from the Philadelphia Perinatal Project.

Police arrest data from Project Metropolitan have also been used to study the relationship between gender and age participation in criminal activity. Wikström (1990) found that the participation rate for males (31 percent) was higher than for females (6 percent) by age twenty-five. Interestingly, while the male crime rate was highest at ages fifteen to seventeen years, the female crime rate was highest at ages twenty-two to twenty-four. The main difference in the patterning of male and female offending rates seemed to be that there was no difference in the offending rate at the oldest ages for females as there was for males (Wikström 1990, p. 72). The increase in recidivist offenders was faster for females than males. There were five times more female recidivist offenders at age twenty-five compared to age fourteen. The corresponding male figure was only 2.5 times more (Wikström 1990, p. 74). Andersson (1990) also used these data to study continuity in criminal activity from age fifteen to thirty and reported that the age-based transition probabilities for females conformed to a first-order Markov chain (i.e., the original matrices could be viewed as estimates from a single "parent" matrix); however, this was not the case for males.

Moffitt et al. (2001) examined Dunedin males' and females' age at first arrest, first conviction, first DSM-IV conduct disorder diagnosis, and first self-reported delinquency. Across all four measures, these authors found that at every age, more males than females had begun antisocial behavior; however, estimates of the age at which antisocial behavior began was dependent on the source of the data. For example, by age fifteen, only 1 percent of girls had an onset as measured by conviction, but 8 percent had an onset as measured by arrest, 12 percent had an onset as measured by diagnosis, and 72 percent had an onset as measured by self-reports; among males, the comparable estimates were 4, 15, 23, and 80 percent (Moffitt et al. 2001, p. 82). These results corroborate earlier suggestions that official data records an "onset" at a later period than other measures, primarily self-reports (see Loeber and Le Blanc 1990; OJJDP 1998). By age eighteen, almost all of the Dunedin subjects had engaged in some form of illegal behavior. In fact, only 9 percent of males and 14 percent of females remained abstinent by age eighteen, with very few new "onset" cases between ages eighteen and twenty-one (Moffitt et al. 2001, p. 85).

The Dunedin data also provide some information on age of onset across gender. For example, among those convicted by age twenty-one, the 103 boys were first convicted at a mean age of 17.7 years, and the thirty-eight girls were first convicted at a mean age of 17.9 years. And among the 101 boys who were first arrested prior to age seventeen, they were arrested at a mean of 13.5 years while the forty-nine girls who were first arrested prior to age seventeen were arrested at a mean of 13.7 years. Comparable age similarities were observed for conduct disorder and self-reported delinquency.

Espiritu et al. (2001) provided estimates on the epidemiology of self-reported delinquency for male and female child delinquents (under age twelve) in the Pittsburgh and Denver sites of the causes and correlates studies. A number of important findings emerged. First, ever-prevalence estimates for "any aggression/minor violence" were upward of 75 percent by age twelve for males and females in both studies, and many of these children reported an "onset" of such behavior prior to age nine. Second, although a higher percentage of Denver males (32 percent) relative to Denver females (23 percent) reported initiating "any aggression/minor violence" prior to age seven, the percentage initiating in several types of delinquency including "any aggression/minor violence" at ages seven to eight, nine to ten, and eleven to twelve was virtually identical across gender; however, at ages eleven to twelve, 7 percent of Denver males compared to 1 percent of Denver females reported "serious violence" initiation. Third, when examining the prevalence of combinations of delinquency and drug use at ages seven to twelve years, they found that although one-third of both the Denver and Pittsburgh children reported no involvement in minor violence, property offenses, or drug use, 13 percent in Denver and 6 percent in Pittsburgh reported involvement in all three delinquency combinations. Fourth, estimates from the Denver study indicated that males reported a higher ever-prevalence for injury-related violence, but females reported a higher ever-prevalence for "aggression/without hurt." Fifth, although males tended to report a higher ever-prevalence associated with most property-oriented offenses, males and females in the Denver study tended to report very similar ever-prevalence estimates for status/drug use offenses. Finally, the prevalence of police contacts for delinquent behaviors increased between ages seven to twelve years, regardless of the type of delinquency, in a similar fashion for males and females. For example, at ages eleven and twelve, the prevalence of a police contact for any delinquency was 10.9 percent for Denver males, 8.5 percent for Denver females, and 6.9 percent for Pittsburgh males.

When ever-participation is measured without regard for offense seriousness, participation estimates across demographic subgroups are similar; however, as more serious offenses are considered, the demographic differences get considerably larger and are likely influenced by the low base rate of participation in serious offenses. This is especially the case when comparisons are made between official and self-report records. For the most part, gender and race differentials (higher for males and nonwhites) are substantially higher in official record studies (Elliott 1994, p. 7). With official records, it seems reasonable to conclude that "by-age-eighteen-prevalence" for nontraffic offenses approaches 33 percent, while for Index offenses the comparable estimate is about 20 percent. When studying lifetime prevalence, the comparable estimates approach 60 percent and 25 percent, respectively (Visher and Roth 1986, p. 248). With self-report records, participation rates vary by crime type but across all domains tend to favor more male than female participation.

Regardless of whether official or self-report records are used to study prevalence, three main conclusions emerge. First, male participation rates are typically higher than those for females, and especially so for the more serious offenses. Second, black participation rates are typically higher than those for whites, especially when participation is examined via official records as opposed to self-reports (Hindelang, Hirschi, and Weis 1981). In self-reports, blacks have also been found to report continuing their violent offending at higher rates than whites (Elliott 1994). Third, there is a strong relationship between age and participation. In particular, the probability of initiating a criminal career at a given age is highest in the range thirteen to eighteen, on the lower end for self-report estimates and on the higher end for arrest and conviction records. Also, evidence on the probability of committing an offense at a given age is mixed, with some research indicating a consistent increase through the mid-teens to a peak at age nineteen and then subsequent decline (see Bachman, O'Malley, and Johnston 1978), while other research indicates a decline in self-reported participation through the teens (Elliott et al. 1983; Thornberry 1989; Lauritsen 1998). Studying demographic differences in prevalence remains controversial. For example, Hindelang, Hirschi, and Weis (1981) argued that there is a race difference in the validity of self-reported delinquency measures, which leads to a serious underestimation of black males' prevalence and frequency rates (but see Huizinga and Elliott 1986). A detailed summary of the ever-prevalence results may be found in table 3.

TABLE 3
Estimates of "Ever" Prevalence

Study	Overall Prevalence (percent)	Sex (percent) Male	Female	Race (percent) White	African-American	Measure of Crime
Wolfgang et al. (1972)	34.9			28.7	50.2	Recorded police contacts
Miller et al. (1974)		28	5.6			Juvenile court records
McCord (1978)	27.5					Convictions
Polk et al. (1981)	25					Police and juvenile court records
Shannon (1982):						Police records
1942 cohort		41	8.7			
1949 cohort		47.3	15.1			
1955 cohort		44	22.2			
Ouston (1984)		29	6			Police and juvenile court records
Stattin et al. (1989)		37.7	9			Convictions
Tracy et al. (1990)	32.8	32.8	14.1	22.7	41.8	Recorded police contacts
Nevares et al. (1990)	6.8	11.3	2.3			Arrests
Wikström (1990)	19					Recorded police records
Elliott (1994)	30	42	16			Self-reports
Kelley et al. (1997):	40					Self-reports
Denver		39	16			
Pittsburgh		41				
Rochester		40	32			
Piquero (2000)	22.29	31	14			Recorded police contacts
Puzzanchera (2000)	21					Self-reports
Moffitt et al. (2001)		20	10			Recorded police contacts
Moffitt et al. (2001)		20	8			Convictions
Farrington (2002)	40					Convictions
Farrington (2002)	96					Self-reports
Piquero and Buka (2002)	11.99	19.2	4.8	10.8	15.7	Juvenile court referrals and police records

6. *"Current" Annual Prevalence.* Estimates of "current" annual prevalence rates are usually based on self-reports of criminal activity within the past year. For example, in the NYS, Elliott et al. (1983) report current theft participation rates of 2.2 percent for eleven- to seventeen-year-olds, and 3.1 percent for fifteen- to twenty-one-year-olds, with slightly higher estimates among blacks than whites, and much higher for males compared to females. For breaking and entering, participation rates were 4.1 percent for the eleven to seventeen age group, and 2.4 percent for the fifteen to twenty-one age group. Finally, for assault, participation rates were 6.1 percent for the eleven to seventeen age group, and 4.6 percent for the fifteen to twenty-one age group. Once again, male rates exceed those of females, and for the most part, black rates are higher than white rates. Using self-reported data from the first five waves of the NYS, Elliott, Huizinga, and Morse (1987, p. 484) found that the annual prevalence of serious violent offending increased from age twelve to a peak at age sixteen and then declined through age twenty-one; the hazard, however, peaked at age seventeen, and by age twenty-one, the risk of onset was very low (0.4 percent). Across gender, the annual male prevalence increased to a peak of 7.8 percent at age sixteen and then began a slow decline to 3.1 percent at age twenty-one while the annual female prevalence increased to a peak of 2.8 percent at age fourteen and then began a sharp decline to 0.3 percent at age twenty-one.

The Monitoring the Future Study (MTF) (Johnston, Bachman, and O'Malley 1994) database is valuable for tracking current participation rates, especially for drug use. The MTF is a self-reported, cross-sectional survey of over 2,000 United States high school seniors performed each year. Osgood and his colleagues (1989) analyzed time trends covering the period 1975–85 with a sample of over 3,000 high school seniors and age trends covering ages seventeen to twenty-three for samples of 300–1,200 per year. These authors found that self-report (and comparison arrest) measures revealed substantial declines in illegal behavior throughout the age period covered. With the exception of arrest indices of assault, both methods showed declines from ages seventeen through twenty-three for almost all offenses examined (Osgood et al. 1989, p. 410). Although age trends in illegal behavior were consistent across offenses, time trend results indicated otherwise. For example, time trends in assault rates exhibited an increase from 1975 to 1985, while time trends in theft decreased from 1975 to 1985. Time trend analyses for other offenses, such as robbery, joyriding/car theft, and arson, were more erratic with no single peak or monotonic trend (Osgood et al. 1989, p. 405).

More recent MTF data, which includes past-year prevalence for a number of delinquent acts, spans the years 1988–2000. Between 1988 and 2000, the self-reported prevalence of theft under fifty dollars ranged between 31 and 34 percent. For serious assault, prevalence rates ranged between 11.4 percent and 14.6 percent. Between 1993 and 2000, the prevalence rate for arrest ranged around 10 percent. Male prevalence was higher than female prevalence for most delinquent/criminal acts. In 2000, the male assault prevalence rate was 21.1 percent (compared to 4.4 percent for females), 38.7 percent for theft (23.8 percent for females), and 13.1 percent for arrest (5.2 percent for females), a trend that was evident across all the years of observation.

Across race, prevalence rates were more similar than different among whites and blacks for most crime types, with only a few minor exceptions. For example, in 2000, the assault prevalence rate for whites was 3 percent higher than for blacks. For theft, the prevalence rate was about 5 percent higher for blacks compared to whites. Finally, in 2000, the white arrest prevalence was slightly over 2 percent higher than for blacks, though the two groups experienced very similar arrest prevalence rates across the years of observation.

Several other databases on elementary and high school students have also captured prevalence estimates. The PRIDE Surveys (2000) indicate that the prevalence of students reporting "trouble with the police" varied from 19 percent for students in grades six to eight to 26 percent for students in grades nine to twelve. The 1999 Youth Risk Behavior Surveillance system indicated high prevalence in a number of delinquent activities engaged in by high school students (Kann et al. 2000). For example, 17.3 percent of high school students reported carrying a weapon to school during the past thirty days, while 4.9 percent reported carrying a gun to school. Males overwhelmingly had a higher prevalence for both of these acts. Along race/ethnic lines, however, prevalence rates were highest for blacks, followed by Hispanics and whites. Over one-third of high school students (35.7 percent) reported being in a physical fight during the past twelve months, with males and blacks exhibiting the highest prevalence among the subgroups. Finally, in the thirty days preceding the survey, 33.1 percent of the high school students reported riding with a driver who had been drinking alcohol, and although males and Hispanics exhibited the highest prevalence, these rates were quite comparable across subgroups.

A similar Centers for Disease Control survey (U.S. Department of Health and Human Services, Centers for Disease Control and Prevention 2000) also asked high school students about their current and lifetime use of drugs and alcohol. Self-reported prevalence estimates from 1999 indicate that lifetime marijuana use was 47.2 percent while current (i.e., past thirty days) marijuana use was 26.7 percent. Lifetime (50 percent) and current (31.5 percent) alcohol prevalence were only slightly higher. Much smaller prevalence estimates were reported for cocaine and steroid use. A complete description of the prevalence of drug and alcohol use is beyond the scope of this essay. Interested readers should consult Johnston, O'Malley, and Bachman (2000), as well as the annual National Household Survey on Drug Abuse, which tracks prevalence of drug and alcohol use.

Using data from a male adolescent and a male delinquent sample from Canada, Le Blanc and Fréchette (1989) calculated annual participation by age in any self-reported offense and found that, among adolescents, annual participation ranged from 80 percent at age eleven to 90 percent at age nineteen, while, among delinquents, annual participation was constant (100 percent) between the ages of thirteen and nineteen. Loeber and his colleagues (1998) calculated self-reported prevalence rates of serious delinquency (including car theft, breaking and entering, strong-arming, attacking to seriously hurt or kill, forced sex, or selling drugs) for white and black boys between ages six and sixteen in the Pittsburgh site of the causes and correlates study. At age six, whites and blacks did not differ; however, while both groups evidenced an increase in prevalence between ages seven and sixteen, the prevalence rate among blacks was higher than among whites such that at age sixteen, over 25 percent of blacks reported participating in serious delinquency, while the comparable estimate among whites was almost 20 percent. Estimates of age of onset of serious delinquency show that between ages six and eight, blacks and whites report similar cumulative percentages of committing serious delinquency; however, between ages nine and fifteen, the two groups begin to differ. Compared to whites, blacks had a steeper age of onset curve. By age fifteen, 51.4 percent of blacks had engaged in serious delinquency compared to 28.1 percent of whites.

Kelley et al. (1997) compared the self-reported prevalence of serious violence (aggravated assault, rape, robbery, and gang fights) across the three sites (Pittsburgh, Denver, and Rochester) of the causes and correlates study. Several important findings emerge (see table 4). First, in

TABLE 4

Current, Annual Prevalence (Percentage) for Serious Violence from Causes and Correlates Studies

	Denver		Rochester		Pittsburgh
Age	Males	Females	Males	Females	Males
10	2	1			7
11	5	2			11
12	8	3	19	15	8
13	10	6	16	18	17
14	12	7	22	18	17
15	15	7	19	13	15
16	18	5	17	6	13
17	18	4	17	4	17
18	19	3	20	7	
19	21	1			

Source.—Kelley et al. (1997), table 1, p. 7.

Denver, between the ages of ten and nineteen, the prevalence of serious violence increased for males (reaching 21 percent at age nineteen) but declined for females after an age-fifteen peak of over 5 percent. Between ages twelve and eighteen in Rochester, the prevalence of serious violence peaked at age fourteen for both males (22 percent) and females (18 percent). After age fifteen, however, female participation declined while male participation remained fairly constant through age eighteen. In Pittsburgh, participation in serious violence was fairly constant from ages thirteen to seventeen (around 16–17 percent). When Kelly et al. (1997) examined the prevalence of serious violence across race/ethnicity, they found that a greater proportion of minority group members was involved in serious violence. With one exception (eighteen-year-olds in Rochester), prevalence rates were higher among minority groups at each age and site. In sum, unlike the decline evidenced by females in serious violence participation, males' participation remained constant in the late teens across all three sites.

Puzzanchera (2000) used the age-twelve sample of the NLSY 1997 and distinguished between lifetime and recent involvement in various behaviors. In general, more than half of the twelve-year-olds who reported ever committing a specific delinquent act said they had committed the act within the past year. Nine percent of all twelve-year-olds reported that they had engaged in assaultive behaviors in the past year, while 5 percent reported that they had carried a handgun in the past year. Interestingly, although there were similar proportions of males and females reporting recent participation in several delinquent behaviors, a pattern that was also the case among white and nonwhite youth, there were some interesting subgroup differences. For example, in the past year, males were significantly more likely than females to report that they had carried a handgun (9 percent vs. 1 percent) and engaged in assaultive behaviors (12 percent vs. 6 percent). In the past year, nonwhite youth were more likely than white youth to report having stolen something worth more than fifty dollars (4 percent vs. 2 percent), while white youth were significantly more likely than nonwhite youth to report that they had carried a handgun (6 percent vs. 2 percent).

Until recently, there has been very little self-report research describing current participation rates. In general, annual prevalence is rather low, especially for robbery (1–8 percent), assault (1–9 percent), and burglary (3–7 percent) (see review in Visher and Roth 1986, table A-4). Male prevalence is higher than female prevalence, though females do engage in delinquent acts, especially serious violence, at rates that are likely to surprise some observers. Race differences in prevalence also exist across some crime types, with minorities' participation in serious violence higher than whites (Elliott 1994; Kelley et al. 1997). Finally, age and current participation are related, with peaking and stabilization of participation in the late teens observed for males and early peaking and declining participation levels observed for most females.

B. Dimensions of Active Criminal Careers and Their Covariates

Several researchers have presented estimates across key criminal career dimensions, as well as the covariates of such dimensions. In this section, we focus on five dimensions: offending frequency (λ), duration/termination rates, crime-type mix and seriousness, co-offending patterns, and specialization/crime-type switching.

1. *Estimates of λ.* The offense rate for individuals reflects the frequency of offending by individuals who actively engage in crime (i.e., active offenders) (Blumstein et al. 1986, p. 55). Complications in estimating individual frequencies include undercounting total arrests and undercounting low-rate active offenders. Individual frequency estimates can be obtained in two ways: by adjusting estimates of mean individual arrest frequencies for active adult offenders (μ) and then dividing by arrest probability following a crime to infer λ, or by surveying samples of offenders to obtain self-reports of their offending frequen-

cies (Blumstein et al. 1986, p. 59). Weiner (1989, p. 67) points out that annual violent arrest rates tend to be modest but annual violent offense rates are higher. Most individuals tend to engage in violence at low annual rates.

Blumstein and Cohen (1979) estimated individual frequencies (λ) from Washington, D.C., arrest records. Although they were able to follow cohorts of offenders for only four to seven years, they found that λ increased with age for burglary, narcotics, and a residual category that included "all other" offenses; rates were trendless for robbery, aggravated assault, larceny, auto theft, and weapons offenses; and, for most crime types, the rates were independent of the number of prior arrests in an individual's record. They also reported that individual offending frequencies (estimated from arrest histories for adult arrestees) varied from 1.72 assaults per year free for offenders who committed aggravated assault to 10.88 larcenies per year free for those who committed any larceny. Finally, they estimated that offenders committed between nine and seventeen Index offenses per year while free.

Two surveys of sentenced prisoners, known as the Rand Inmate Surveys, provide estimates of individual crime rates for active adult male offenders (Peterson and Braiker 1980; Chaiken and Chaiken 1982). Researchers collected self-reports of offenses committed during an observation period prior to the start of the current incarceration for about 2,500 prisoners. Mean individual frequencies from the first survey (resident prisoners in 1976) indicated that offenders committed an average of 115 drug deals and 14.2 burglaries per person per year free. The second inmate survey (incoming prisoners in California, Michigan, and Texas in 1978) indicated that offenders committed between 14.9 (Texas) and 50.3 (Michigan) burglaries per year and between 4.8 (Texas) and 21.8 (California) robberies per year. Another smaller group of offenders reported committing crimes much more frequently. The most active 10 percent of the inmates reported committing about 600 of the seven survey crimes in the two-year period prior to their incarceration, more than ten crimes per week (Visher 2000, p. 603). Chaiken and Chaiken (1982) classified some inmates into a "violent predator" group who committed an average of 70 robberies, 144 burglaries, and 229 thefts in one year.

Elliott and colleagues' (1983) analysis of self-report data of active offenders in the NYS revealed somewhat similar numbers, an average of 8.4 robberies and 7.1 larcenies per year (see Blumstein et al. 1986, p. 66; Visher 1986). Le Blanc and Fréchette's (1989) analysis of two

Canadian samples yielded important differences across official and self-reported estimates of frequency. First, offense frequencies were much higher in self-reports than in official records. Second, the delinquent sample experienced three times the number of convictions as the adolescent sample, a ratio that did not differ much from age twelve through the twenties. Third, when the annual crime frequencies are calculated by age, the number of crimes of the adolescent and delinquent samples were similar, with the adolescents showing a general annual average of 2.55 while the delinquents showed a general annual average of 3.24.

Blumstein et al. summarized variation in λ by gender, age, and race. Regarding gender, they found little variation in frequency across males and females (i.e., the ratios are generally 2:1 or less) for most crimes (Blumstein et al. 1986, pp. 67–68). Thus, if active in a crime type, females commit crimes at rates similar to those of males (for an exception see Wikström 1990). Regarding age, Blumstein et al. (1986) reported little change with age in offense-specific frequency rates for active offenders, but when all offense types are combined, there tended to be an increase during the juvenile years and a decrease during the adult years. In comparing age-specific violent rates, Weiner (1989) noted that although age-specific violent juvenile arrest rates tend to rise and fall as adolescence runs its course, age-specific violent offense rates exhibited greater stability. In the Rand surveys, there appeared to be some evidence of general stability of λ over age (Peterson and Braiker 1980; Chaiken and Chaiken 1982). The number of active crime types declined with age in the Rand survey, but crime-specific frequencies tended to be stable (Peterson and Braiker 1980). Unfortunately, much prior research did not examine age-specific rates past the early twenties. Recent research, however, has indicated that among active offenders, offense-specific frequency rates vary with age (see Nagin and Land 1993; Piquero et al. 2001).

Regarding race, Blumstein et al. (1986) report that, across a number of different data sets, the ratio of black/white arrest frequencies for adult offenders who are active in a crime type are very close to 1:1 for most offenses. This conclusion has been drawn in a number of different samples (i.e., offenders, general population) and with both self-report and official records. Blumstein et al. (1986) suggest, then, that the substantial race differences in criminal activity stem from differences across the races in participation, not frequency. At any given time, there are comparatively more active black participants in crime than there are white participants, but blacks and whites who are active are similar in offending frequency.

Cohen (1986) concluded that mean λ's for violent crime are lower than for property crime. She observed that active violent offenders in the community committed an average of two to four serious assaults per year while active property offenders committed five to ten crimes per year. Prisoners, a more select population, report higher annual averages. For example, on average, they report fifteen to twenty robberies per year and forty-five to fifty burglaries. In part, this high average results from the skewed distribution of λ within the offending population, with the highest decile committing over 100 crimes per year. Although Wolfgang and colleagues (1972) did not report estimates of frequencies for active offenders in the 1945 Philadelphia birth cohort, Cohen (1986) used their data to examine this issue and found that active (i.e., ever-arrested) offenders among Philadelphia juveniles experienced an average of .84 total arrests per year.

Visher (1986) reanalyzed the Rand Inmate Surveys data to re-estimate annual individual offending frequencies (λ). Her reanalysis brought forth several insights. First, she noted that half of the offenders reported committing no more than five crimes a year, but a small group reported committing several hundred crimes per year. Similar results were obtained with a sample of New Orleans inmates (Miranne and Geerken 1991). Second, the estimates of λ for robbery and burglary were sensitive to choices in computation and in particular, the interpretation of ambiguous survey responses, the treatment of missing data, and the computation of respondents' street time. Third, because some offenders reported almost no offending prior to incarceration and others reported a significant amount, the high estimates have a particularly strong influence on the mean value of λ. Fourth, many offenders have intensive short-term criminal offending patterns while others offend more or less intermittently. Fifth, λ varied across the three states in the study (California, Texas, and Michigan), thus raising questions about whether λ varies meaningfully across jurisdictions or whether the difference results from differences in case processing and sanctioning across states. Finally, Visher questioned the validity of estimating λ for offenders who had been incarcerated for several months prior to their current arrest. Since these individuals may have been especially active in the short period during which they were on the street, generalizing that rate of offending to an entire year may overestimate the annual rate. Rolph and Chaiken (1987) proposed a model that allowed for offender switching between a "quiescent" state and an "active" state from time to time. After taking into account the length of the measurement period, they found lower λ's than the original estimates produced in the second Rand survey. In any event, Visher confirmed the main conclusion from the Rand survey, that there was an extreme skew in the distribution of λ even in a sample of serious criminals in prison.

Loeber and Snyder (1990) used juvenile court data from a large sample of juvenile offenders in Maricopa County (Phoenix), Arizona, to study how the rate of offending varied between ages eight and seventeen. Although λ varied substantially as a function of age, increasing monotonically, λ was not related to the age at first offense. That is, λ was observed to be constant at each individual age level regardless of the age at which offending began or desisted (Loeber and Snyder 1990). Since the absolute magnitude of λ among active juvenile offenders at any age was independent of how long offenders were involved in criminal activity, Loeber and Snyder (1990, p. 105) concluded that, "the only information needed to predict the average λ for active juvenile offenders at any age is age."

Using police records from Project Metropolitan, Wikström (1990) calculated age-specific values of λ for several crime types through age twenty-five. Four key findings emerged. First, λ peaked at age fifteen (5.6 crimes per offender) for total crimes, but there was variation across crime types with λ peaking at fifteen for stealing (5.3 crimes per offender), twenty-one for fraud (3.3 crimes per offender), and twenty-three for violent crime (1.6 crimes per offender). Second, recidivist offenders had a higher λ than first-time offenders. Third, males had λ's twice as high as females (9.1 compared to 4.5 crimes per offender). Finally, male λ's peaked at ages fifteen to seventeen, while female λ's peaked at ages twenty-two to twenty-four, implying that there is little decrease in the offender rate at the oldest ages for females as compared to males. In sum, Project Metropolitan data indicate that λ varies with age and is not invariant across gender.

English and Mande (1992) examined the extent to which self-reported crime frequencies among prisoners were a function of how such information was collected. These researchers examined five different methods for eliciting λ from prisoners: a confidential, written questionnaire; an anonymous—but not confidential—questionnaire; a shortened version of the self-administered questionnaire; an automated version of the questionnaire in which the inmates enter their answers directly into laptop computers; and administering the questionnaire in two different locations in the prison setting, one more and one less "neutral." In addition, these authors administered surveys to female prisoners.

A number of key findings emerged. First, there were few differences in self-reported crime participation rates across the methods explored, though blacks tended to report higher participation rates using the anonymous version of the survey than when using the other modes. Second, crime frequency estimates remained fairly stable across the different methods of survey administration with no differences found across race or age; however, the anonymous version led to much higher crime frequencies than the other methods. Third, the familiar skewed offending rates that others have found for male prisoners also characterized female prisoners. This skewed, female offending pattern has also been observed with official records in two longitudinal data sets in Philadelphia (Piquero 2000) and Providence (Piquero and Buka 2002). More women reported committing only one type of crime, while men reported more involvement in several different crimes. Fourth, participation rates changed when the definition of the crime was changed. When criminal activity was related to smaller compared to larger increments of time (i.e., weekly vs. monthly), higher frequencies were observed. Fifth, demographic comparisons of self-reported and official record data yielded complementary information; the demographic factors found to be associated with official records were the same as those found for self-report records. English (1993) reported that once active in crime, women and men committed burglary, robbery, motor vehicle theft, fraud, and drug dealing at similar rates. Moreover, with regard to drug dealing, more than 15 percent of the women, compared with only 4 percent of the men, reported more than twenty-five drug deals per day (English 1993, p. 374). Sixth, women reported higher frequencies for theft and forgery while men reported higher frequencies with assault. Finally, the lack of data on female self-reports of λ makes English and Mande's results particularly important and highlights some similarities to the pattern for males. They found that female participation rates varied by race, with blacks participating more in burglary, robbery/assault, and drug dealing than whites, and whites participating more in forgery/fraud. The frequency pattern was similar to that for male prisoners: a large percentage (almost 40 percent) of the sample reported fewer than five offenses during the observation period, while almost 20 percent reported 200-plus offenses during the observation period.

Barnett, Blumstein, and Farrington (1987, 1989) designed and tested a probabilistic model of criminal careers. Their initial analysis suggested that criminal careers in the Cambridge study (through age twenty-five) could be modeled with parameters reflecting constant individual rates of offending and constant rates of career termination. They found, however, that the offending population had to be divided into two groups: "frequents" and "occasionals" (Barnett, Blumstein, and Farrington 1987). They found that "frequents," comprising 43 percent of the sample, had an annual conviction rate of 1.14 convictions per year (constant with age) while the "occasionals," comprising 57 percent of the sample, had an annual conviction rate of .41. In a follow-up prospective test, Barnett, Blumstein, and Farrington (1989) applied their 1987 model to the Cambridge study males with five additional years of data (through age thirty). Although their original model accurately predicted the number of recidivist convictions and the time intervals between recidivist convictions, the predictions for the frequents were hampered by a few intermittent offenders who, although temporarily stopping their careers, later reinitiated offending after a long gap.

Horney and Marshall (1991) refined the Rand methodology to achieve more precise estimates of λ with a sample of Nebraska prisoners. They used individual interviews that included a detailed calendar system with month-by-month reporting of criminal activity. This allowed them to look at variability of offending within individuals over relatively short periods of time. Focusing on those offenders who reported committing more than ten of any particular target crimes during the three-year reference period, Horney and Marshall (1991) found considerable variability; that is, offenders reported periods of inactivity and low, medium, and high rates of activity. There was considerable variability in individual offenders' values of λ over the observation period. Patterns of activity varied considerably by crime type. While burglars were unlikely to be active during all months, drug dealers had the highest proportion of active months as well as the highest proportion of months offending at high rates (Horney and Marshall 1991, p. 491). Horney and Marshall suggest that λ estimates in the original Rand Inmate Surveys were overinflated, and especially for crimes with the greatest time variability in offending frequencies.

TABLE 5

Mean Offending Rate for Serious Violence from Causes and
Correlates Studies

	Denver		Rochester		Pittsburgh
Age	Males	Females	Males	Females	Males
10	1.6	. . .			2.6
11	3.5	. . .			3.3
12	3.3	3.3	4.0	. . .	2.8
13	10.1	1.5	6.9	2.7	3.3
14	10.4	2.4	7.2	5.5	4.1
15	7.7	2.3	5.7	5.4	4.9
16	11.8	2.1	5.3	4.5	6.7
17	10.9	1.4	3.7	. . .	8.6
18	12.0	1.0	5.8	. . .	
19	8.7	. . .			

SOURCE.—Kelley et al. (1997), table 1, p. 7.

Kelley et al. (1997) examined serious violence offending rates in the three causes and correlates studies (Pittsburgh, Denver, and Rochester) by calculating the number of self-reported serious violent acts committed within the annual reporting period (see table 5). Generally, active male offenders committed more serious violence than active female offenders. Between ages ten and nineteen, annual offense rates tended to increase steadily and continue throughout much of the adolescent period, but for Denver and Rochester females, the number of offenses peaked around ages fourteen to fifteen. For example, eighteen per 100 Rochester females committed ninety-nine serious, violent offenses at age fourteen, while seven per 100 Denver females committed seventeen serious violent offenses at age fourteen. There were also important differences across sites. For example, in Denver, active male offenders engaged in many more criminal acts than their female counterparts such that, by age eighteen, active males averaged twelve serious violent crimes while active females averaged one serious violent act. Moreover, Denver males exhibited the largest annual offense rate of all active offenders across all three sites: at age eighteen, nineteen per 100 Denver boys committed an estimated total of 228 offenses. In Rochester, however, the differences between boys and girls were much smaller, especially in the mid-teens. Among Pittsburgh males, increases in violent offending were observed throughout the teenage years. For example, at age seventeen, seventeen per 100 Pittsburgh boys committed an estimated total of 146 offenses.

Canela-Cacho, Blumstein, and Cohen (1997) used data from the Rand Second Inmate Surveys to develop an approach for estimating the values of mean λ for diverse offender populations. Treating the self-reported estimates of λ for prisoners as a filtered sample (i.e., all inmates have gone through the criminal justice system) and a three-component mixed exponential for all sorts of offenders (i.e., free, in prison, etc.), they found important differences in offending rates between inmates and free offenders, between robbery and burglary, and across the three states in the analysis. Free active offenders averaged one to three robberies and two to four burglaries per year, while inmates had λ values ten to fifty times higher. Moreover, different levels of offending were observed across states, with the lowest mean λ of just two to three robberies or burglaries annually by individual offenders in Texas, six to seven robberies or burglaries in California, and fifteen robberies and ten burglaries in Michigan. These differences resulted from differences in imprisonment levels and differences in the overall levels of criminality within the total offender population. These results are important because they suggest that a highly heterogeneous offending frequency in the total population of offenders can combine with relatively low imprisonment levels to lead to substantial selectivity of high-λ offenders among inmates and correspondingly low mean value of λ among those offenders who remain free (Canela-Cacho, Blumstein, and Cohen 1997, p. 133). We return to the relevance of this issue for incapacitation decisions in greater detail when we discuss the need for prediction alleviated by "stochastic selectivity."

Lattimore and her colleagues (forthcoming) studied the characteristics of arrest frequency among paroled youthful offenders from the CYA. Using negative binomials to examine the relationship between several characteristics and the frequency of offending, they found that individual and geographic characteristics were important predictors of both the average arrest frequency and its variation among the offenders in a three-year follow-up.

Contrary to the observed relationships between participation and demographic characteristics, research based on official records tends to indicate that there is not a strong relationship between offending frequency and demographic characteristics, though some recent self-report data on serious violence tends to indicate otherwise (Elliott 1994; Kelley et al. 1997). In general, active offenders who begin criminal activity at an early age, use alcohol and drugs heavily, and have extensive prior records commit crime at higher rates than other offenders.

Spelman (1994) summarized current knowledge on offending frequencies. First, there are different values for the average offense frequencies across studies because researchers provide different definitions and operationalizations of the offense rate. Second, most of the variation in offense rates can be attributed to differences in the populations sampled and especially where in the criminal justice system they are sampled. Third, the average offender commits around eight crimes per year, while offenders who are incarcerated at some point in their lives commit thirty to fifty crimes per year, and the average member of an incoming prison cohort commits between sixty and 100 crimes per year. Fourth, criminals do not commit crimes all the time; in other words, there is evidence that many offenders spend long periods of time in which they commit no crimes. Fifth, the distribution of offending frequencies is highly skewed, with a few offenders committing crimes at much higher than average rates.

2. *Estimates of Duration/Termination.*   The two most common approaches for studying career termination have been through providing estimates of termination probabilities after each arrest and estimating the time between the first and last crimes committed. Regarding termination probabilities, Blumstein et al. (1986, p. 89) calculated persistence probabilities for six different data sets and found that after each subsequent event (i.e., police contact, arrest, conviction, etc.), the persistence probability increases, reaching a plateau of .7 to .9 by the fourth event across all data sets. Farrington, Lambert, and West (1998) used conviction data to calculate recidivism probabilities for Cambridge study males through age thirty-two and found that after the third offense the recidivism probability ranged from .79 to .91 through the tenth offense. The same substantive conclusion was reached when they examined the recidivism probabilities of the subjects' brothers.

Blumstein, Farrington, and Moitra (1985) pose a model of population heterogeneity in which some members are "innocents" (i.e., refrain from offending), some are "desisters" (i.e., with relatively low persistence probabilities), and others are "persisters" (i.e., with relatively high persistence probabilities). By partitioning the sample into these three groups, Blumstein and colleagues are able to account for the rise in the observed aggregate recidivism probabilities by studying the changing composition of offenders at each stage of involvement;

with most desisters stopping early, only smaller numbers of high-recidivism persisters are left. The key assumption is that each offender has a constant desistance probability after the commission of each offense. Their analysis, applied to several different longitudinal studies, indicated a very high prevalence of official involvement in criminal activity, a high, stable recidivism rate through about the sixth involvement, and a higher but stable recidivism rate for subsequent involvements. After the first few involvements, recidivism probabilities stabilized at a high level (about 80–90 percent). By characterizing offenders' careers as a series of recidivism events, their model permits some few persisters to drop out early and some few desisters to accumulate a large number of offenses. Blumstein, Farrington, and Moitra (1985, p. 216) suggest, then, that the persister/desister characterization "encourages thinking about populations of offenders in terms of probabilistic expectations rather than in terms of retrospective characterizations" as is the case with arbitrary retrospective designations of some as "chronic" offenders. When these authors applied their model to the Cambridge study data, they found that persisters were distinguished from desisters by several "risk factors" observed at ages eight to ten including troublesomeness as assessed by peers and teachers, criminal parents, low nonverbal IQ, poor parental child-rearing practices, and so on.

Barnett and Lofaso (1985) attempted to predict future arrest rates in the Philadelphia birth cohort at a specified arrest number. Two important findings emerge. First, only past arrest rates were systematically related to future rates. Second, problems arose as a result of truncation of the arrest record at the eighteenth birthday. After assuming that arrests occurred probabilistically according to a Poisson process, Barnett and Lofaso calculated the probability of no arrest occurring between the last juvenile arrest and the eighteenth birthday, given that the offender was continuing his criminal career. They could not reject the hypothesis that all apparent desistance was false. In other words, almost all offenders were likely also to have had a subsequent adult arrest after their eighteenth birthday.

Barnett, Blumstein, and Farrington (1987) built on the work of Blumstein, Farrington, and Moitra (1985) and Barnett and Lofaso (1985) by avoiding the implication that all desistance is true (as in Blumstein, Farrington, and Moitra) or that all desistance is false (as in the case in Barnett and Lofaso). Barnett et al. developed a model that includes a conviction rate and a desistance probability. In addition, they found it necessary to postulate two populations of offenders, one with a high conviction rate and another with a low conviction rate. Using data from the Cambridge study through age twenty-five, they found that a model explicitly incorporating individual rates of conviction and a parameter characterizing the termination process, along with two separate parameters to reflect offender heterogeneity (i.e., "occasional" and "frequent" offenders), fit the data well. Barnett, Blumstein, and Farrington (1989) then engaged in a prospective test of their model using an additional five years of conviction data collected on the Cambridge subjects (through age thirty). Their results indicated that the original model accurately predicted the number of recidivist convictions, as well as the time interval between recidivistic convictions. However, the predictions for the "frequents" were hampered by a few "intermittent" offenders who reinitiated offending after a long, crime-free period.

A number of studies have attempted to derive estimates of career duration, typically measured as career length in years (see table 6). Three major studies conducted in the 1970s estimated career lengths to be between five and fifteen years (Greenberg 1975; Shinnar and Shinnar 1975; Greene 1977). Shinnar and Shinnar (1975) estimated career length with partial career information based on aggregate data on the time between first and current adult arrests of five years for all offenders and ten years for recidivists reported for a sample of offenders from FBI files. Shinnar and Shinnar had no information on juvenile offending periods, nor the age of first offending. Under several assumptions regarding estimates of the average number of Index arrests per year per offender, Greenberg (1975) approximated active Index career lengths to be about five years. His estimates, however, rest on the steady-state assumption of stationarity in the processes generating an active criminal population. Greene (1977) applied a life-table approach to the age distribution of arrestees in a single year in Washington, D.C., and assumed that all arrestees were criminally active at age eighteen. He estimated the mean adult career length for Index offenses to be twelve years. Greene's estimates, however, assumed that all active offenders were equally likely to have at least one arrest in a year, that all offenders began their adult criminal careers at age eighteen, and that the size of the offender population at each age is constant over time.

Building on Greene's work, Blumstein, Cohen, and Hsieh (1982) conducted the most detailed study of criminal career duration and used

TABLE 6
Career Length Estimates

Study	Career Length Estimate (Years)	Sex		Race		Measure of Crime
		Male	Female	White	Nonwhite	
Shinnar and Shinnar (1975)	5–10					Arrests
Greenberg (1975)	5					Arrests
Greene (1977)	12					Arrests
Blumstein et al. (1982)	5					Arrests
	4.2 (property)					
	7.0 (personal)					
Elliott et al. (1987)*	1.58					Self-reports
Le Blanc and Fréchette (1989)	1.46 (personal)					
	3.47 (burglary)					
	3.56 (petty larceny)					
Spelman (1994)	6–7					Self-reports
	7–10 (property)					Self-reports
	7–9 (personal)					
Tarling (1993)		7.4	4.9			Official records
British Home Office (1995)		9.7	5.6			Official records
Farrington et al. (1998)	10					Convictions
Piquero et al. (2002)	17.27			16.7	17.7	Police contacts and arrests

* The Elliott et al. study measured career length as the maximum number of consecutive years an individual was classified as a serious, violent offender.

data on arrests rather than on arrestees to estimate career lengths. Although the Blumstein, Cohen, and Hsieh (1982) approach has been credited with requiring fewer assumptions about the distribution of career lengths and the underlying system producing this distribution (Spelman 1994, p. 132), like all career-length studies, the Blumstein, Cohen, and Hseih (1982) approach makes several assumptions (e.g., age eighteen as the beginning of the adult criminal career, the probability of at least one arrest in a year does not vary with age, etc.). Their analysis yielded five key insights. First, the average criminal commits crimes over about a five-year career, with mean career lengths of 4.2 and 7.0 for property and personal offenders, respectively. Second, in comparing career lengths for a seven-year period (1970–76), they found that the mean career lengths were fairly stable over time.

Third, they found that the dropout rate appeared to vary over the course of a career, first falling ("break-in" failures), then leveling off, and then rising with "burn-out" in the later years. The criminal career can be construed as three distinct phases (Blumstein, Cohen, and Hsieh 1982, p. 38). In the first phase, the "break-in" period in the early years of the career, dropout rates decrease, and the mean residual career length (i.e., the expected time still remaining in a career) increases. This surprising result—residual career length increasing as the offender stays active—is a consequence of the changing composition of the offender population; through their twenties, the more committed offenders persist, the less committed drop out, and so the residual average career length of the remaining group increases as a result. This initial phase lasts for the first ten to twelve years of the career. In the second "stable" period, beginning around age thirty for eighteen-year-old starters, there are likely to be stable residual career lengths. During this second phase, the dropout rate is at its minimum, and the expected time remaining in the career is longest (i.e., about ten additional years regardless of the prior duration of careers). Thus, regardless of the number of years a person has been active in a career, the expected time remaining is similar. Then, in the final "burn-out" period, around age forty-one, which is characterized by increasing dropout rates, the expected time remaining in a career gets shorter.

Fourth, career length was associated with onset age such that younger starters tended to have longer careers. The only exception to this was the finding that for offenders with more than seven years already in a career, older starters exhibited longer remaining careers.

Finally, careers tended to vary somewhat across crime types, with property offenders exhibiting the shortest careers (about four to five years) among eighteen-year-old starters, though the careers for those who do remain active as adult property offenders in their thirties can be expected to last for another ten years (Blumstein et al. 1986, p. 94). The longest careers are found for murder and aggravated assault, which averaged about ten years among eighteen-year-old starters (Blumstein, Cohen, and Hsieh 1982, p. 66). In sum, persistent offenders who begin their adult careers at age eighteen or earlier and who are still active in their thirties are most likely to be persistent offenders and are likely to continue to commit crimes for about another ten years (Visher 2000, p. 608).

Elliott, Huizinga, and Morse (1987) studied career lengths with the first five waves of the NYS. Unlike other researchers who define career length as the period of time from the first through the last year of offending, these authors defined career length as the maximum number of consecutive years the individual was classified as a serious violent offender measured via self-reports. Elliott, Huizinga, and Morse found that the mean length of violent careers over the five-year period was rather short (1.58 years), with most serious violent offenders having a career length of one year. Still, about 4 percent have a career length of five years. Using a Canadian sample, Le Blanc and Fréchette (1989) found that career length was longer when assessed via self-reports than via official records. Career duration varied by crime type with crimes of personal attack having the shortest mean duration (1.46 years) and crimes of burglary (3.47 years) and petty larceny (3.56) having the longest mean durations.

Spelman (1994) studied career lengths with data from the three-state Rand Inmate Surveys. He made several assumptions about criminal careers and developed estimates of total career lengths from seven to ten years for property offenders and seven to nine years for personal offenders, with some slight variations across states. Spelman identified the average career length in the Rand data to be about 8.5 years. However, when he took the dropout process among adult offenders into consideration, he revised his estimates of the average career length to be about six or seven years (Spelman 1994, p. 140). Spelman (1994, p. 156) shows that young and inexperienced offenders, those in the first five years of their career, are more likely than older offenders to drop out each year, but after five years the rate of dropout levels off, rising only after the twentieth year as an active offender.

Tarling (1993) examined career durations with official records from males and females born in 1953 and followed until age thirty-one, and found that, excluding one-time offenders, the average duration was 7.4 years for males and 4.9 years for females. Later analysis of the same data through age forty found that the average duration increased for males and females to 9.7 and 5.6 years, respectively (Home Office Statistical Bulletin 1995). Similar estimates of career duration have been made in London and Stockholm (Farrington and Wikström 1994).

Farrington, Lambert, and West (1998) examined the duration of criminal careers in the Cambridge study using conviction data to age forty. Defining the duration of a criminal career as the time interval between the first and last conviction, and excluding one-time offenders, the average duration of criminal careers was ten years. Fifteen males (9.1 percent) had career durations exceeding twenty years. Farrington, Lambert, and West also collected data on the siblings and wives of the study subjects and found that brothers of study subjects had similar career durations, but the criminal careers of sisters and wives were shorter, averaging about eight years. The career duration for study subjects' fathers and mothers averaged sixteen and fifteen years, respectively, at least in part because they had more time to accumulate convictions. Finally, Farrington, Lambert, and West compared career duration to the age of onset for study subjects. Average career duration decreased significantly with increasing age of onset for study subjects and for their mothers and fathers. Those study subjects who experienced onset between ages ten and thirteen incurred 8.77 offenses and had a career duration of 11.58 years. Those individuals experiencing onset between ages twenty-one to thirty incurred 1.79 offenses and had a career duration of 2.33 years. Similar conclusions were reached regarding the relationship between onset age and career duration when brothers, fathers, mothers, sisters, and wives' criminal careers were examined (Farrington, Lambert, and West 1998, p. 102). When Farrington (2001) extended the analysis to include conviction records of one-time offenders, he found that the average duration of criminal careers, defined as the time between the first conviction and the last, was 7.1 years. Excluding one-time offenders whose duration was zero, the average duration of criminal careers in the Cambridge study was 10.4 years.

Piquero, Brame, and Lynam (2002) studied the length of criminal careers using data from a sample of serious offenders paroled from

CYA institutions in the 1970s. Defining career length as the time between the age of last arrest less the age at first police contact, average
career length was 17.27 years, with little difference between white
(16.7 years) and nonwhite parolees (17.7 years).

Because much research on career length has been descriptive, there
is almost no research predicting career duration. Smith and Gartin
(1989) used data from the Racine cohorts to study the effect of arrest
on the duration of a criminal career. Defining career duration as the
time between an individual's first and last police contact, they found
that for the sample of offenders who remained criminally active after
a kth contact, an arrest appeared to extend the duration of their criminal career. In addition, age was negatively associated with career duration. Elliott, Huizinga, and Morse (1987) used the first five waves of
the NYS to examine the extent to which career length varied by gender, race, class, residence, and age, and found that career length did
not vary much across these factors, with the exception that career
lengths varied by place of residence, with urban youths reporting
somewhat longer careers.

Piquero, Brame, and Lynam (2002) used data from a sample of parolees from the CYA to examine the correlates of career length. Several key findings emerged. First, individuals with low cognitive abilities
and reared in disadvantaged environments during childhood tended to
have the longest careers. Second, when this risk contrast was compared
for white and nonwhite parolees, it was more important for nonwhites.
The data showed three sets of findings across race. First, among parolees experiencing little risk in the risk contrast (i.e., no cognitive deficits
and no disadvantaged environments), career duration was identical
among white and nonwhite parolees (almost seventeen years). Second,
among nonwhites only, the risk contrast was related to career length
with nonwhite parolees experiencing cognitive deficits and disadvantaged environments exhibiting the longest career lengths (almost nineteen years). Third, among white parolees, the risk contrast was not related to career length; career lengths varied between sixteen and
seventeen years regardless of the level of the risk contrast.

Since many data sets used to study termination/persistence probabilities and career length duration are right-hand censored (i.e., the
observations are cut off at a particular age), estimates regarding the duration of careers are biased downward (Blumstein, Cohen, and Hsieh
1982; Greenberg 1991). In other words, attributing the absence of further events near the end of the observation period to desistance rather

than to the time between events in a still-active career will lead to overestimates of desistance, or "false desistance" (Blumstein et al. 1986, p. 91). This raises the question of how many years of non-offending have to be observed to conclude that someone has desisted (Laub and Sampson 2001; Maruna 2001).

Bushway et al. (2001) recognized the difficulties in studying termination generally and desistance in particular and outlined an empirical framework for studying desistance as a process. Instead of focusing on offending itself, these authors argued for a focus on changes in the offending rate over time. In particular, Bushway et al. (2001, p. 496) argued that it made more sense to describe, operationalize, and study desistance as a process in which criminality (i.e., the propensity to offend) changes over time. They define desistance as "the process of reduction in the rate of offending (understood conceptually as an estimate of criminality) from a nonzero level to a stable rate empirically indistinguishable from zero" (Bushway et al. 2001, p. 500). Recently, Bushway, Thornberry, and Krohn (forthcoming) compared the Bushway et al. (2001) approach with a more traditional approach of defining a desister as someone who has been observed to refrain from offending for a certain period of time. Using self-report data from the Rochester site of the causes and correlates study, these authors found that the two approaches identified different people as desisters.

The idea of desistance is a key feature of the criminal career paradigm. Since the publication of the NAS report in 1986, several desistance studies, both theoretical and empirical, have appeared (e.g., Uggen and Piliavin 1998; Kruttschnitt, Uggen, and Shelton 2000). To avoid duplication, we refer readers to a detailed review of this literature in *Crime and Justice* (Laub and Sampson 2001).

3. *Crime-Type Mix.* The study of crime-type mix involves studying seriousness (the tendency to commit serious crimes throughout one's criminal career), escalation (the tendency to move toward more serious crimes as one's career progresses), specialization (the tendency to repeat the same offense type on successive crimes), and crime-type switching (the tendency to switch types of crimes and/or crime categories on successive crimes).

Most research on offense seriousness and escalation has been carried out with official records. With data from the 1945 Philadelphia birth cohort through age seventeen, Wolfgang, Figlio, and Sellin (1972) found that although each subsequent offense tended to be somewhat more serious than the preceding offense, observed increases in seriousness scores were small. They interpreted these results as indicative of relatively stable delinquency careers. Analysis of successive transitions by Cohen (1986), however, found increases in switches to more serious offense types and decreases in switches to less serious offense types on later transitions with the Philadelphia cohort. In addition, Cohen (1986, p. 402) reported some escalation in seriousness for Philadelphia juveniles, especially for nonwhite offenders. Smith and Smith (1984) also reported evidence consistent with escalation in seriousness on successive arrests for juveniles. Data from Rojek and Erickson for juveniles in Pima County, Arizona, indicated that "there is no evidence that the probability distributions of the five types of offenses shift in any way toward more serious offenses" (1982, p. 17; see also Bursik 1980). However, reanalysis by Cohen (1986, pp. 397–98) indicated that switches from juvenile status offenses to more serious crimes on later transitions were common, a finding not corroborated in another study of status offenders (Shelden, Horvath, and Tracy 1987).

Data examining adult-only periods or combining juvenile and adult periods tend to show that average seriousness declines on successive arrests, indicating patterns of de-escalation (see Hamparian et al. 1978; Shannon 1982; Cohen 1986, p. 403). Thus, during the juvenile years, the seriousness of arrests increases somewhat throughout adolescence, while during the adult years, seriousness tends to be stable early on followed by de-escalation. Although involvement in serious offending as a juvenile is predictive of continued offending into adulthood, more so for males than females (Stattin and Magnusson 1991; Tracy and Kemp-Leonard 1996), among juveniles who remain active into adulthood, their seriousness scores tend to increase and then stabilize (Rand 1987; Visher 2000).

There have been several comprehensive examinations of escalation. Datesman and Aickin (1984) used self-report data from a sample of deinstitutionalized juvenile offenders from Delaware and found less specialization than appears from official records and that females tended to be more specialized than males. White females tended to be more specialized in status offenses than any other race/gender combination group. Little evidence was found for escalation as most of the youths did not return to court after their first referral for status offenses. Shelden, Horvath, and Tracy (1987) found that the majority of juvenile court referrals (whose first referral was a status offense) did not become serious delinquents, although male status offenders were more likely than females to escalate.

Blumstein et al. (1988) studied criminal records of Michigan offenders and found that average seriousness was stable over the careers of African-American offenders with ten arrests for serious crimes, whereas similar white offenders exhibited an increase in seriousness over successive arrests. Only a small group of offenders, however, were likely to engage in increasingly serious behavior over their careers.

Tracy, Wolfgang, and Figlio (1990, p. 173) studied escalation with both Philadelphia birth cohorts and found, generally, that when an offense was repeated, the severity was greater than that of the former offense. In addition, they found that escalation patterns did not vary across race, although injury offenses were repeated in both cohorts with substantial increases in severity.

In a test of Loeber and Hay's pathways model, Loeber et al. (1999) employed self-report data from the three causes and correlates studies (Pittsburgh, Denver, and Rochester) to examine how seriousness increases over time within a career. Their analysis at each site indicated that cumulative age of onset curves for steps in the pathways followed the expected pattern with the less serious forms of problem behavior and delinquency occurring first and the more serious forms occurring later. In addition, Loeber et al. (1999, p. 260) found that the proportion of participants who advanced to a next step in a pathway was consistent with expectations and that across the sites the fit of participants in the pathways for steps two and higher in the overt and covert pathways was consistent with the model.

Diverse methodological techniques (Wolfgang et al. 1972; Farrington, Snyder, and Finnegan 1988; Britt 1996; Paternoster et al. 1998; Piquero et al. 1999) have been employed to investigate specialization, or the tendency to repeat the same offense type on successive crimes (see review in Cohen 1986; Tracy and Kempf-Leonard 1996). In the 1945 Philadelphia birth cohort, Wolfgang, Figlio, and Sellin (1972) found that there appeared to be no evidence of specialization although offenders were most likely to have a subsequent involvement for a non-Index crime, especially theft. Similar results were obtained in the Puerto Rico birth cohort study (Nevares, Wolfgang, and Tracy 1990) and in the 1958 Philadelphia birth cohort study. In the 1958 cohort, however, specialization was slightly more evident among recidivists and became more pronounced as the number of offenses increased (Tracy, Wolfgang, and Figlio 1990, p. 173). Self-report data from the Rand studies suggest that, although there is some evidence of property specialization (Spelman 1994), incarcerated offenders tend to report much more generality than specialty (Petersilia, Greenwood, and Lavin 1978; Peterson and Braiker 1980; Chaiken and Chaiken 1982).

Bursik's (1980) study of serious juvenile offenders in Cook County, Illinois, provided evidence of specialization. Rojek and Erickson (1982) examined specialization among juvenile offenders in Pima County, Arizona, and found evidence of specialization for property offenses and a status offense (running away), but not for other offense types. Smith and Smith (1984) studied specialization with a sample of male juveniles and found some evidence of specialization, especially among those delinquents who began their careers with a robbery offense. Farrington, Snyder, and Finnegan (1988) developed the "forward specialization coefficient" (FSC) to quantify specialization among juvenile delinquents. This ranged from zero for no specialization to one for perfect specialization. Their analysis indicated that there was a small but significant degree of specialization in the midst of a great deal of versatility. Stander et al. (1989) used conviction data from a 10 percent sample survey of 698 adult males (aged twenty-one or above) under sentence in the twenty-one prisons in the southeast region of England in 1972 to study offense specialization. Three findings emerged. First, consistent with a Markov chain hypothesis (i.e., knowledge of an offender's past history of offense types adds nothing to the prediction that could be made on the basis of the present offense type), the probability of switching from one offense to another remained constant over successive convictions. At the same time, and contrary to the Markov hypothesis, the past history of offense types helped in predicting future offense types, offering some support for specialization. Second, sex offenders were the most specialized. Third, the most persistent offenders became increasingly specialized in fraud.

Some scholars have investigated specialization in violence. Using a binomial model applied to official record data, Farrington (1989), Piquero (2000), and Piquero and Buka (2002) reported little evidence of specialization in violence in the Cambridge study, or the Philadelphia and Providence perinatal cohorts, respectively, and that the commission of a violent offense in a criminal career is a function of offending frequency: frequent offenders are more likely to accumulate a violent offense in their career. Farrington (1991) tested the hypothesis that violent offenses occur at random in criminal careers and failed to reject the hypothesis. Similar results have been obtained by Capaldi and Patterson (1996) with self-report data from the Oregon Youth Study.

Two main conclusions can be drawn from the specialization literature. First, in general, the next offense type is proportional to its prevalence with some bias toward repeating. Second, although there is some evidence of specialization (Stander et al. 1989), most criminal careers are marked by versatile offending patterns (Chaiken and Chaiken 1982; Klein 1984; Cohen 1986; Stattin, Magnusson, and Reichel 1989; Lattimore, Visher, and Linster 1994).

At the same time, there is some evidence that specialization patterns may vary across demographic subgroups. Regarding age, important differences in specialization are observed between adults and juveniles. Across several studies, specialization appears to be stronger in magnitude and to be found in all offense types for adult than for juvenile offenders (Cohen 1986; though see Bursik 1980).

Two studies have examined how age at onset relates to specialization. Rojek and Erickson (1982) computed matrices of transition probabilities by onset age and concluded that none of the age-specific matrices differed from each other (though see Cohen 1986). Piquero et al. (1999) applied two different analytic techniques (the FSC and the diversity index) to data from the 1958 Philadelphia birth cohort for arrests through age twenty-six and found that, although there was an inverse relationship between onset age and offense specialization, when age was controlled by examining common offending periods for different onset age groups, the relationship vanished. It appears, then, that versatility differences between onset age groups have more to do with the effects of age itself than with onset age. In sum, although there is some limited evidence of specialization in the juvenile years for status-oriented offenses, specialization is more sporadic among juvenile offenders (Cohen 1986) but tends to increase as a career progresses (Blumstein et al. 1986). Specialization among adult offenders tends to be stronger for drugs, fraud, and auto theft (Blumstein et al. 1988).

Only a handful of studies have examined gender differences in specialization. Rojek and Erickson (1982) found that, although specialization was less frequent for female juvenile offenders, gender differences in offense switching were observed with female offenders being more likely than males to desist or to move to a runaway offense. Using official records from Maricopa County, Arizona, Farrington, Snyder, and Finnegan (1988) found that males tended to specialize in the more serious offenses, and females tended to be runaway specialists. Mazerolle et al. (2000) used official record data from the 1958 Philadelphia birth cohort and failed to find substantive differences in offending diversity between males and females across five offense transitions. In addition, when interrelationships between gender, onset age, and specialization were examined, differences in levels of offending diversity were found between males and females, differentiated by onset age criteria, a result that was corroborated when the authors substituted "persistence" for onset age. Piquero and Buka (2002) used court referral data from the Providence perinatal cohort to study specialization in violence and failed to find evidence of any gender differences. Soothill, Francis, and Fligelstone (2002) applied latent class analysis to conviction data from the 1953 and 1958 British birth cohorts to study offense specialization generally and across gender in particular. They found a different cluster solution (i.e., a different number of offense groups) across gender, with females' offending being less diverse than males' offending. As in previous research, there was an increasing tendency toward specialization with age, especially for males. While a shoplifting cluster emerged for both sexes, a cluster titled "marginal lifestyle with versatile offending" was the most common cluster across gender. Most crime switching was toward noncrime; that is, there was little tendency to switch to the same crime.

With regard to race, Wolfgang, Figlio, and Sellin (1972) found that although white offenders tend to be more specialized than nonwhite offenders, nonwhites exhibited a greater tendency to switch to violent offense types. Bursik (1980) found that both whites and nonwhites engaged in specialized offending, with nonwhite juveniles more likely than white juveniles to move to violent offenses. Rojek and Erickson (1982), however, failed to find evidence of race differences in offense switching. Using arrest records, Blumstein et al. (1988) found some evidence of specialization in each crime type among Michigan offenders; however, specialization was not uniformly strong across all crime types. For example, drugs were a highly specialized crime type among whites and blacks, but fraud was more specialized among white offenders while auto theft was more specialized among black offenders. Blumstein et al. (1988) concluded that levels of specialization were generally similar for active white and black offenders for most crime types. Tracy, Wolfgang, and Figlio (1990) examined specialization across race in both the 1945 and 1958 Philadelphia birth cohorts and found, in general, that there were no race effects with regard to specialization. However, when Tracy, Wolfgang, and Figlio removed desisters and concentrated on recidivists, they found race effects. In particular, the white "chronics" (i.e., those with more than four arrests) in the 1945 cohort repeated theft offenses, while white chronics in the 1958 cohort appeared to specialize in theft and combination offenses. Nonwhite chronics in the 1945 cohort showed evidence of repeating more offense types than their white counterparts in either cohort, and strong evidence of specialization was observed for injury offenses among nonwhite offenders in the 1958 cohort (Tracy, Wolfgang, and Figlio 1990, p. 173). The evidence for specialization was stronger in both cohorts as the number of recidivist offenses increased. Piquero and Buka (2002), however, failed to find evidence of specialization in violence with court referral data through age seventeen among white and nonwhite members of the Providence perinatal cohort.

Directly related to the specialization issue is the switching that occurs across clusters of crime types. Clusters represent natural groupings of offense types (violence, property, other), and research tends to indicate that adult offenders display a stronger tendency to switch among offense types within a cluster and a weaker tendency to switch to offense types outside a cluster, but the strong partitioning is not as sharp among juveniles (Blumstein et al. 1986; Cohen 1986). Among juveniles, there appears to be a tendency to switch between violent and property offenses. Rojek and Erickson (1982) found a sharp partition between traditional crime categories and juvenile status offenses. Interestingly, the tendency for offense types to cluster varies somewhat by race, with a stronger partition between violent and property offenses evident among black than among white offenders.

Blumstein et al. (1988) engaged in the most comprehensive analysis of crime-type switching with arrest data from Michigan offenders. Using four categories (violent, robbery, property, and drugs), they found that black offenders were more likely than white offenders to switch to violence or robbery and less likely to switch to offenses involving drugs. Rates of switching to property offenses were similar for whites and blacks (Blumstein et al. 1988, p. 331).

Le Blanc and Fréchette (1989) used data from two Canadian samples to study issues related to offense variety and changes in the crime mix. Regarding variety, they found that in both adolescent and delinquent samples, their offending behavior was more heterogeneous than homogeneous. Several important findings emerged concerning changes in the crime mix. First, burglary was a common criminal act engaged in by most delinquents. Second, when the degree of diversity increased, automobile theft increased. Third, crime severity increased throughout the juvenile period with a more serious crime mix in late adolescence as offenders moved away from crimes of theft and on to more personal crimes such as armed robbery. Fourth, as age increased, there was a tendency for more specialized offending patterns.

The empirical literature on crime-type switching and offense clusters suggests that violent and property offenses form distinct clusters and that adult offenders and incarcerated juveniles are more likely to commit offenses within a cluster than to switch to offenses outside a cluster (Cohen 1986; Visher 2000). Drug offenders, however, do not tend to switch to either violent or property offenses (Cohen 1986; Blumstein et al. 1988). There is also some evidence of increasing specialization with age.

4. *Co-offending Patterns.* Criminal activity, especially adolescent delinquency, is a group phenomenon (Cohen 1955; Zimring 1981; Tremblay 1993). Unfortunately, little empirical work has been completed on this, and little information exists regarding the group criminal behavior of youths in transition to adult status or of adult offenders at different ages (Reiss 1986*a*).

Reiss and Farrington (1991) used the Cambridge data to examine patterns of co-offending, and their results yielded five key findings. First, while most juvenile and young adult offenses were committed with others, the incidence of co-offending declined steadily with age. Males changed from co-offending to lone offending in their twenties, a finding that provides indirect support for Moffitt's contention that peers are important during adolescence but become less of a factor in adulthood. Second, burglary, robbery, and theft from vehicles were particularly likely to involve co-offenders, which raises the possibility that co-offending matters more for some crimes than others. Third, there was some consistency in co-offending from one offense to the next. Fourth, co-offenders tended to be similar in age, gender, and race, and typically lived close to the locations of the offenses. Fifth, about one-third of the most persistent offenders continually offended with less criminally experienced co-offenders, perhaps indicating that these persistent offenders repeatedly recruited others, a finding also consistent with Moffitt's prediction that persistent offenders recruit others into criminal activities.

Warr (1996) used self-report data from the National Survey of Youth to study organization and instigation in delinquent groups and offered four key findings. First, although delinquent groups were small and transitory, offenders belonged to multiple groups. Second, groups appeared to be more specialized in offending than did individuals.

Third, most delinquent groups had an older, more experienced leader. Fourth, roles within delinquent groups changed over time contingent on the situational interaction of both group and individual characteristics.

In the Swedish Borlänge study, a project that studied all juveniles suspected of offenses in the Borlänge police district between 1975 and 1977, Sarnecki (1990) found that 45 percent of all youths suspected of offenses at some stage during the six-year study period could be linked together in a single large network that accounted for the majority of all offenses. Network membership was important for youths' introduction to—and continued involvement in—delinquency. Further, Sarnecki found a large overlap between the juveniles' circle of friends and their circle of co-offenders.

Recently, Sarnecki (2001) completed the most comprehensive study of delinquent networks. Using data from all individuals aged twenty or less who were suspected of one or more offenses in Stockholm during 1991–95, Sarnecki examined official records to assess the extent and role of co-offending. A number of important findings emerged. First, 60 percent of the individuals had a co-offender at some point. Second, the more active delinquents tended to have the most co-offenders. Third, like Warr, Sarnecki observed that much co-offending was transient and short-lived. Fourth, burglary and shoplifting were the most common co-offending crimes. Fifth, most co-offending and co-offenders tended to be of the same age. However, there were some important gender differences in co-offending. Males tended to co-offend primarily with other males; this was the case for over 94 percent of the offenses among males between ages ten and twenty-one. Among females, however, the proportion of girls choosing other females was lower than the proportion of boys choosing other males as co-offenders (Sarnecki 2001, p. 65). Interestingly, and consistently with Warr's (1996) observations, the older girls chose males as co-offenders much more often than did younger girls. Moreover, the male co-offenders chosen by girls were on average considerably older than the girls were themselves (p. 65). When a girl was suspected of co-offending with a male, the age difference was almost four years, while the age difference between female co-offenders and male co-offenders was one and 1.2 years, respectively. Sixth, co-offenders tended to live close to offenders, though the distance between co-offenders' places of residence increased with age (p. 65).

Conway and McCord (2002) conducted the first co-offending study

designed to track patterns of violent criminal behavior over an eigh-
teen-year period (1976–94) among a random sample of 400 urban
offenders and their accomplices in Philadelphia. The distinctive aspect
of this research was its use of court records. Conway and McCord argued that self-report records may overestimate the role that peers play
in criminal activity. Using crime data collected from Philadelphia court
records and "rap sheets," they found that nonviolent offenders who
committed their first co-offense with a violent accomplice were at increased risk for subsequent serious violent crime, independent of the
effects of age and gender (Conway and McCord 2002, p. 104). This
suggests that violence may "spread" from violent offenders to those
inexperienced in violence.

Though not directly related to co-offending patterns, Haynie (2001)
used data from the National Longitudinal Study of Adolescent Health
to examine how network structures are incorporated into the roles of
delinquent peers more generally. Two main findings emerged. First,
friends' delinquency, as measured by responses from friends who composed the adolescent's friendship network, was associated with an adolescent's own self-reported delinquency. Second, network properties summarizing the structure of friendship networks moderated the
delinquency/peer association. In particular, delinquent friends had a
weaker association with delinquency when adolescents were located in
a peripheral position within their peer network, when their peer network was not very cohesive, and when they had less prestige. Delinquent friends had a stronger association when adolescents were located
in a central position within their friendship networks, when their
friendship network was very dense, and when they were nominated as
friends by others.

C. Comparing Causes of Criminal Career Dimensions

One of the key questions raised by the criminal career paradigm is
the extent to which the causes of one dimension, for example, onset,
are the same as the causes of another dimension, for example, frequency. Evidence on this question is important because it is relevant to
matters related to both theory and policy. For example, if the different
criminal career dimensions result from the same causal process, then
specific theories of onset, persistence, specialization, and desistance are
unnecessary and more general theories of crime should suffice. If different causal processes are associated with different criminal career dimensions, then more dimension-specific or typological theories would

be needed. Relatedly, if the causes of criminal career dimensions are more similar than different, then policy proscriptions do not need to be as specific as they would need to be if the causes of various criminal career dimensions were different.

Several studies are germane. Paternoster and Triplett (1988) examined self-report data from South Carolina high school students and found that causal processes relating to prevalence and incidence were different. Paternoster (1989) examined the relations of several different criminological variables (i.e., peers, sanction risk, etc.) to onset, persistence/desistance, and frequency of delinquency, using the same data, and found many similarities across the offending dimensions, with the exception that peer involvement in delinquency had no impact on initiation but was related to continuation. Nagin and Smith (1990) used self-report data from the NYS to study the determinants of participation and frequency and found that, while some variables were associated with one but not the other dimension, the majority of variables were related to both dimensions. Loeber et al. (1991) used self-report data from the Pittsburgh site of the causes and correlates study to investigate the correlates of initiation, escalation, and desistance in juvenile offending. Although they had data for only two years, they, somewhat surprisingly, found that the correlates of initiation were distinct from the processes explaining escalation but were similar to the correlates of desistance. Using data from the Cambridge study, Farrington and Hawkins (1991) investigated whether several variables were similarly related to participation, early onset, and persistence. They found that, in general, the three crime outcomes were predicted by different variables measured in childhood.

Smith, Visher, and Jarjoura (1991) studied the correlates of participation, frequency, and persistence in delinquency with self-report data from the NYS and found that while some variables were related to specific dimensions of delinquency, a core of variables were related to multiple dimensions of delinquency. Nagin and Farrington (1992b) used the Cambridge data to examine the correlates of initiation and persistence and found that low IQ, having criminal parents, a "daring" or risk-taking disposition, and poor child rearing were associated with an initial conviction as well as subsequent convictions. Smith and Brame (1994) used self-report data from the NYS and found that, while many variables similarly predicted initial and continued involvement in delinquency, other variables predicted only one of these dimensions. For example, moral beliefs were related only to initiation and not continuation. Triplett and Jarjoura (1994) also used the NYS to study the disaggregation issue and found that, consistent with labeling theory, informal labels were predictive of the decision to continue rather than to initiate delinquent behavior.

Mazerolle (1997) used the first five waves of the NYS to examine whether, on the basis of prevailing developmental theories, different factors such as exposure to delinquent peers, social class, and so on, predicted early and late onset of self-reported delinquency. He also examined whether the relationships differed for serious as opposed to more general or trivial acts of delinquency. In a series of logistic regression models, Mazerolle found support for different predictors of delinquency, dependent on participation age; however, the relationships were not observed for trivial acts of delinquency. In sum, he found support for developmental theories that assert that different factors differentiate early and late onset to delinquency, but only when serious acts of delinquency are considered.

Using data from the Seattle Social Development Project, Ayers et al. (1999) examined the correlates of onset, escalation, de-escalation, and desistance from age twelve to fifteen and found that many of the correlates distinguished those juveniles who remained involved in delinquency from those who de-escalated or desisted from delinquency. Ayers and his colleagues also found some similarities and differences across gender in how the different correlates were associated across the offending dimensions. Piquero (2001) used police contact data from the Philadelphia Perinatal Project and found that neuropsychological risk was related to early onset, chronic offending, as well as crime seriousness through age seventeen.

The evidence thus far on the correlates of different criminal career dimensions suggests that in most studies, some variables are associated with two or more dimensions and some are uniquely associated with just one dimension. Thus, no clear pattern has yet emerged. Even less is known about the relative magnitude of these effects. However, it does not appear that correlations are similar for all dimensions, as Gottfredson and Hirschi argued.

D. "Chronic" Offenders

Criminologists have long recognized that a small group of individuals is responsible for a majority of criminal activity. This finding is one of the key foundations of the criminal career paradigm and its resultant policies.

1. *Recognition of Chronic Offenders.* Wolfgang, Figlio, and Sellin (1972) focused attention on the chronic offender. They applied that label to the small group of 627 delinquents in the 1945 Philadelphia birth cohort who were found to have committed five or more offenses. This group constituted just 6 percent of the full cohort of 9,945 males and 18 percent of the delinquent subset of 3,475, but was responsible for 5,305 offenses, or 52 percent of all delinquency in the cohort through age seventeen. The chronic offenders were responsible for an even larger percentage of the more serious, violent offenses. The finding that a small subset of sample members is responsible for a majority of criminal activity is supported by data from other longitudinal data sets, including the second 1958 Philadelphia birth cohort (Tracy, Wolfgang, and Figlio 1990), the Puerto Rico Birth Cohort Study (Nevares, Wolfgang, and Tracy 1990), the Dunedin Multidisciplinary Health Study (Moffitt et al. 2001), the Philadelphia (Piquero 2001) and Providence (Piquero and Buka 2002) perinatal projects, the Racine birth cohorts (Shannon 1982), the Cambridge study (Farrington 2002), and also by cohort studies in Sweden (Wikström 1985), Finland (Pulkkinen 1988), and Denmark (Guttridge et al. 1983). The finding is also replicated across gender and race (see Moffitt et al. 2001; Piquero and Buka 2002) and emerges from both official and self-report data (Dunford and Elliott 1984). Research indicates that chronic offenders tend to exhibit an early onset, a longer career duration, and involvement in serious offenses—including person/violent-oriented offenses—than other offenders (Farrington et al. 1990; Piquero 2000; Farrington 2002). Thus, in any group or cohort of subjects, there is likely to be an uneven distribution of offenses with most individuals committing zero offenses, some individuals committing one or two offenses, and a very small number of individuals accumulating many offenses (Fox and Tracy 1988; Tracy and Kempf-Leonard 1996). It is no surprise then, that theorists have directly incorporated the chronic offender into their explanatory frameworks (see in particular Moffitt 1993).

2. *Defining Chronicity and Related Problems.* Wolfgang, Figlio, and Sellin (1972) defined as chronic offenders those individuals with five or more police contacts by age seventeen. This five-plus cutoff has been employed in several studies (Hamparian et al. 1978; Shannon 1978; Kempf-Leonard, Tracy, and Howell 2001). However, since theoretical or empirical definitions of chronicity have yet to be established (Dunford and Elliott 1984; Le Blanc 1998, p. 169; Loeber et al. 1998, p. 15), questions have been raised about the extent to which similar definitions

of chronicity should be used across gender (Farrington and Loeber 1998; Piquero 2000), and researchers have also called into question the relatively arbitrary designation of five-plus offenses as characteristic of chronicity (Blumstein, Farrington, and Moitra 1985). For example, regarding gender, Piquero (2000) found only seven women who had five-plus offenses through age seventeen in the Philadelphia Perinatal Project and thus had to employ four-plus as the chronic offenders criterion for females. Piquero and Buka (2002), using data from the Providence Perinatal Project, were forced to use the criteria of two-plus for chronicity among females, because of the very small number of female delinquents who incurred more than three offenses.

Blumstein, Farrington, and Moitra (1985) raised other concerns with the use of five-plus as the chronicity cut point. They argued that the chronic offender calculation, which was based on the full cohort, overestimates the chronic offender effect because many cohort members will never be arrested. Instead, they urge that the ever-arrested subjects should be the base used to calculate the chronic offender effect. With this base, the 627 chronics with five-plus arrests represented 18 percent of those arrested, as opposed to 6 percent of the cohort. Blumstein, Farrington, and Moitra (1985) also argued, based on evidence presented by Blumstein and Moitra (1980), that the proportion of chronic offenders observed by Wolfgang, Figlio, and Sellin (1972) could have resulted from a homogenous population of persisters. Blumstein and Moitra tested the hypothesis that all persisters (those with more than three arrests) could be viewed as having the same re-arrest probability. Such an assumption could not be rejected. Although those with five or more arrests accounted for the majority of arrests among the persisters, such a result could have occurred even if all subjects with three or more arrests had identical recidivism probabilities (Blumstein, Farrington, and Moitra 1985, p. 189). Thus, the chronic offenders who were identified retrospectively as those with five or more arrests could not have been distinguished prospectively from nonchronics with three or four arrests.

3. *Difficulty of Prospective Predictability.* Blumstein, Farrington, and Moitra (1985) also raised the concern that not all persisters are homogenous. As a result, they argued that researchers and policy makers should want to be able to distinguish prospectively the offenders who are likely to accumulate the largest number of arrests. Since Wolfang, Figlio, and Sellin (1972) identified the chronic offenders retrospectively, they offered no discriminators that could distinguish, in

advance, those individuals who were likely to emerge as chronic offenders.

Blumstein, Farrington, and Moitra (1985) developed a model that divided the Cambridge study into three groups: innocents (those with no offenses), persisters (those with relatively high recidivism probabilities), and desisters (those with relatively low recidivism probabilities). Several important findings emerged. First, identification of chronic offenders in the 1945 Philadelphia birth cohort as those with five or more arrests was inappropriate; instead, on the basis of transition probabilities, it was more reasonable to identify those with six or more arrests as a relatively more homogenous group of chronic offenders (Blumstein, Farrington, and Moitra 1985, p. 195). Second, they calculated recidivism probabilities for innocents, desisters, and persisters in the Cambridge study. Third, using observations made at age ten of boys in the Cambridge study to identify persisters prospectively, they formulated two models: an aggregate model in which the entire cohort of active offenders was characterized by three parameters and an individual model in which each boy was characterized as a persister or desister at his first conviction based on individual characteristics measured at ages eight to ten. Blumstein, Farrington, and Moitra (1985) found that the strongest discriminator of chronics versus nonchronics was "convicted by age thirteen," followed by "convicted sibling," and "troublesomeness." The fifty-five youths scoring four or more points out of seven on a risk variable included the majority of the chronics (fifteen out of twenty-three), twenty-two of the nonchronic offenders, and eighteen of those never convicted. Further analysis indicated that it is appropriate to distinguish individuals based on differential recidivism probabilities rather than some arbitrary number of arrests, and this is especially important since their probabilistic model also permits some persisters to drop out early and some few desisters to accumulate a large number of arrests. Their analysis indicated that "to a reasonable degree, many of the chronics can be identified at their first conviction on the basis of information available at age ten" (Blumstein, Farrington, and Moitra 1985, p. 201).

E. Relevance to Incapacitation

Incapacitation effects are maximized when highest λ, longest duration, most serious offenders are incarcerated. Knowledge of offenders' involvement in the various criminal career dimensions, especially the frequency of offending, has direct import for incapacitation decisions and outcomes. Identification of those offenders with the highest λ, exhibiting the longest career duration, and engaging in the most serious offenses would be an achievement of incapacitation goals. To the extent that incapacitation decisions are targeted on individuals exhibiting these offending characteristics, then incapacitation effects (realized by lower crime rates, shorter careers, and lower overall levels of criminal activity) would be maximized.

Crime control effects through incapacitation increase with the magnitude of individual offending frequency (λ), with the length of incarceration, and with the expected duration of the criminal career (Blumstein et al. 1986). To the extent that high λ offenders are incapacitated during the period in which they are at high risk of offending and not during the period when they are at low or no risk of offending, then more crimes will be averted by their incarceration. Incapacitation policies are more likely to be effective if they are applied during active careers and not after criminal careers have ceased or when careers are in a downswing, when offenders tend to commit crimes at rates "indistinguishable from zero" (see Cohen and Canela-Cacho 1994; Bushway et al. 2001). Incapacitative effects will depend on the effectiveness of the criminal justice system in identifying and incarcerating high-rate offenders during the peaks of their careers.

F. New Questions/Criminal Career Issues Recently Raised

A number of research efforts have been designed to understand better the patterning and determinants of criminal activity over the life course. There appears to be a paradigm shift away from measurement of criminal career parameters and toward a search for risk and protective factors, a perspective very common to the public health field. In this section, we examine four key themes that emanate from longitudinal studies and current research, including how these studies have led to a new focus on risk and protective factors, why risk and protective factors are easy for practitioners to understand, why risk and protective factors provide policy guidance, and how risk and protective factors link research and intervention.

1. *Focus on Risk/Protective Factors.* Blumstein et al. (1986) sought to describe the longitudinal patterning of crime over the life course, especially the manner in which the key demographic correlates of age, gender, and race were associated with criminal career dimensions. The report did not devote great attention to identification and explanation of factors associated with continued or curtailed involvement in criminal

activity over time. Much of the data and analysis reviewed in the report were from prior to 1985 when data collections were difficult and costly, especially those following individuals over long periods.

Since then, researchers have paid explicit attention to risk and protective factors associated with criminal activity over the life course. The risk factor prevention paradigm, imported from medicine and public health (Hawkins and Catalano 1992), focuses on factors that predict an increase in the probability of later offending (i.e., a risk factor) or a decrease (i.e., a protective factor) (Kazdin et al. 1997). Defining risk and protective factors has been controversial, and researchers continue to suggest that a uniform definition be developed (Farrington 2000). Risk and protective factors may also interact with one another; a protective factor (such as high IQ) may interact with a risk factor (such as poor socioeconomic status) to minimize the risk factor's effect (see Rutter 1985). It is also important to distinguish between risk factors that are predictive but not changeable (e.g., race) from those that are changeable (e.g., poor parenting). With knowledge of the effects of risk and protective factors, prevention and intervention efforts can be developed and targeted at the most appropriate individuals, families, and communities (see Tremblay and Craig 1995). In short, the risk factor paradigm aims to identify the key risk factors for offending, implement prevention methods to counteract them, and identify and enhance protective factors (Farrington 2000).

2. *Risk/Protective Factors in Practice.* A principal advantage of the risk factor paradigm is that it links explanation and prevention, fundamental and applied research, and scholars and practitioners (Farrington 2000, p. 7). It provides for the easy identification of factors that are associated with increased and decreased probabilities of criminal activity and allows for the implementation of prevention and intervention efforts aimed at reducing risk factors and enhancing protective factors. When a fatty diet and a lack of exercise are used as examples of risk factors for heart disease, it is easy to conceive of prevention and intervention efforts as encouraging people to eat healthier and exercise. A risk factor like family history of heart disease, by contrast, cannot be prevented but serves as a stimulus to other preventive actions. In the context of crime then, practitioners can be shown risk factors (i.e., poor parenting) and then asked to identify appropriate prevention and intervention efforts (e.g., parent training).

3. *Policy Guidance.* The risk factor paradigm is based largely on medical terminology and is easy to understand and to communicate. It

is no surprise that it is readily accepted by policy makers, practitioners, and the general public (Farrington 2000). Furthermore, because it involves establishing the key risk factors for delinquency, the risk factor paradigm provides useful information for implementing prevention programs designed to target those risk factors. Similarly, research on establishing the protective factors against delinquency provides important information for enhancing such factors. Hawkins and Catalano's (1992) Communities That Care (CTC) is a risk-focused prevention program that is based on the social development model that organizes risk and protective factors, and each community tailors the interventions according to its particular risk and protection profile. In general, CTC aims to reduce delinquency and drug use by implementing particular prevention efforts that have demonstrated effectiveness in reducing risk factors or enhancing protective factors (Farrington 2000, p. 11). In sum, the risk factor paradigm represents a clear advance over vague theories of criminal activity that were often difficult to assess empirically and provides clearer direction for prevention and intervention (Guerra 1998, p. 398).

4. *Link between Research and Intervention.* The risk factor paradigm is well suited for the interplay between research and intervention. For example, the CTC program begins with community mobilization. Key community leaders (e.g., mayor, police chief, etc.) are brought together with the idea of getting them to agree on the goals of the prevention program and to support the implementation of CTC. Then the leaders set up a community board (e.g., including representatives of schools, parents, church groups, social services, police, etc.) that articulates the prevention effort. The board then carries out a risk and protective factor assessment in its particular community. After the assessment, the board develops a plan for intervention. Research is conducted on the implementation of the intervention and the intervention outcome. That information is then used either to strengthen the intervention effort or to modify it. The process is repeated over time as risk and protective factors may change within individuals, as well as within families, schools, and communities.

A number of efforts have generated important insight into the risk and protective factors associated with antisocial and criminal activity (Werner and Smith 1982; Stouthamer-Loeber et al. 1993). A recent comprehensive review of the various risk and protective factors associated with criminal activity, especially among serious offenders, has been influential in furthering research and intervention efforts following the risk factor paradigm (Loeber and Farrington 1998). This paradigm shift into searching for risk and protective factors represents a significant advance in criminology and has fostered links between explanation and prevention, fundamental and applied research, and scholars, policy makers, and practitioners (Farrington 2000, p. 16).

VI. Policy Implications

Research on criminal careers has direct import for decision making in the criminal justice system. Policy officials are interested in preventing criminal activity from starting and in modifying and terminating current criminal activity. In this section, we address four implications of criminal career research: the role of criminal career research in policy and individual decision making, individual prediction of offending frequencies (λ), sentence duration, and research on career length and desistance and its relation to intelligent sentencing policy.

A. Role of Criminal Career Research in Policy and Individual Decision Making

Criminal career research relates to decisions made throughout the criminal justice process and system (i.e., arrest, pretrial release, prosecution, sentencing, and parole). A principal example of the importance of criminal career research for criminal justice policy is the length of criminal careers. Three-strikes and selective incapacitation philosophies assume that high-rate offenders will continue to offend at high rates and for long periods of time if they are not incarcerated. However, from an incapacitative perspective, incarceration is only effective in averting crimes when it is applied during an active criminal career. Thus, incarceration after the career ends, or when a career is abating, is wasted for incapacitation purposes (Blumstein, Cohen, and Hsieh 1982, p. 70).

1. *General Policy Guidance.* By identifying career lengths, especially residual career lengths, policy makers can better target incarceration on offenders whose expected remaining careers are longest. Incarceration policies should be based on career duration distribution information. The more hard-core committed offenders with the longest remaining careers are identifiable only after an offender has remained active for several years (Blumstein, Cohen, and Hsieh 1982). Earlier and later in criminal careers, sanctions will be applied to many offenders who are likely to drop out shortly anyway (Blumstein, Cohen, and Hsieh 1982, p. 71). In sum, the benefits derived from incapacitation

will vary depending on an individual's crime rate and the length of his or her remaining criminal career. Continuing to incarcerate an offender after his or her career ends limits the usefulness of incarceration.

2. *Identification of Serious "Career Criminals."* Since Wolfgang, Figlio, and Sellin's (1972) recognition of the "chronic offender," a search has been underway for "career criminals." Here, we describe three aspects of identifying career criminals, including recognition that skewness in the λ distribution suggests seeking those in the high tail, the problem of identifying career offenders (i.e., false positives), and the limited usefulness of the concept in individual cases because of the need for prediction, including limited prediction validity and concern over false positives.

a. Skewness. Three main findings emerge from a number of different longitudinal crime studies, in different countries, in different time periods, and with different measurements of criminal activity. First, many individuals never commit, or are arrested for, a criminal act. Second, some individuals commit one or two crimes and desist. Third, a small number of individuals offend frequently over time. In any cohort of subjects, there will be an uneven distribution of offenses (Fox and Tracy 1988). It is this third finding, the recognition of skewness, that has led researchers and policy makers to study chronic or career criminals.

b. Problems with Identification. To the extent that criminal justice personnel can correctly identify and selectively target the small group of chronic/career criminals, criminal activity could be substantially reduced. Predictive classifications, however, have been fraught with problems including a high false positive rate (i.e., an offender is predicted to be a chronic offender but turns out not to be). Moreover, prospectively identifying career criminals early in their careers, when such information would be most useful, has been particularly difficult.

c. Limited Usefulness in Individual Cases. Since most of the criminal career research aimed at identifying serious career criminals has tended to examine aggregate distributions of offense rates in large samples, such information has limited usefulness in predicting chronicity in individual cases. This is largely because of the need for prediction on a more aggregate level. Current prediction tools have limited validity because of the inherent errors in predictions (Visher

2000). As many as one-half to two-thirds of such predictions have been shown to be incorrect (Blumstein et al. 1986; Decker and Salert 1986; Farrington 1987; Chaiken, Chaiken, and Rhodes 1993; Gottfredson and Gottfredson 1994; Spelman 1994). Visher (1986), for example, found that Greenwood's scale for predicting future criminal activity was unable to predict very accurately which inmates would commit new crimes, much less which inmates would go on to become career offenders. Still, researchers continue to develop tools for predicting high-rate offenders (Gottfredson 1999).

B. Individual Prediction of λ

Rand's second inmate survey (Chaiken and Chaiken 1982) highlighted the extreme skewness of the distribution of λ for a sample of serious criminals (Visher 1986). Naturally, the identification of a small number of inmates who reported committing several hundred crimes per year led to the search for a method to identify these offenders in advance. If high-rate offenders cannot be identified prospectively, then crime control efforts will be hampered (Visher 1987). In this section, we highlight two related issues: the difficulty in identifying high λ individuals and the alleviation of the concern over prediction by "stochastic selectivity."

1. *Difficulty in Identifying High λ Individuals.* Although high λ individuals emerge in the aggregate, it has been difficult to identify specific individuals. Greenwood and Turner (1987) used data consisting of follow-up criminal history information on the California inmates who were included in the original Rand survey and who had been out of prison for two years to examine the extent to which Greenwood's seven-item prediction scale succeeded in predicting recidivism. The scale was not very effective in predicting postrelease criminal activity when the recidivism measure is arrest. The majority of released inmates, regardless of whether they were predicted to be low- or high-rate offenders, were rearrested within two years. Moreover, the seven-item scale was also a poor predictor of "safety" arrests (i.e., murder, aggravated assault, rape, robbery, or burglary) as 46.9 percent of low-rate offenders and 54.7 percent of high-rate offenders were arrested for a safety offense. Greenwood and Turner (1987, tables 3.11, 3.12) also created a measure of the offender's annual arrest rate (i.e., the number of arrests per year of street time) for the follow-up sample and defined high-rate offenders as those inmates who had an actual arrest rate greater than 0.78. They found that the seven-item scale

was less accurate in predicting annual arrest rates than it was in predicting reincarceration. For example, among those predicted to be low-moderate-rate offenders, 39.1 percent had a high annual arrest rate, while the comparable estimate among high-rate offenders was 57.4 percent. In part, this was a weak test because it used the arrest rate (μ) rather than λ as the outcome measure. To the extent that there is a negative association between λ and the arrest probability, then that would diminish any power to the prediction based on factors associated with high λ.

There are also concerns related to the false positive prediction problem in identifying high λ individuals. For example, Visher (1986, pp. 204–5) reanalyzed the Rand second inmate survey and generated a number of important conclusions. First, the estimates of λ for robbery and burglary were sensitive to choices in computation (i.e., handling missing data, street time, etc.). Second, some inmates convicted of robbery and burglary denied committing any robberies and burglaries. Third, some inmates reported annual rates of 1,000 or more robberies or burglaries, thus strongly affecting the distribution of λ, and especially its mean. Fourth, λ varied considerably across the three state samples. Fifth, Visher's analysis of the Greenwood scale for identifying high-rate offenders indicated that 55 percent of the classified high-rate group (27 percent of the total sample) were false positives who did not commit crimes at high rates. In fact, the prediction scale worked better in identifying low-rate offenders. Sixth, the anticipated reduction in the California robbery rate identified by Greenwood and Abrahamse (1982) was overestimated. Finally, because the scale captured only frequency and not termination of careers, its prospective accuracy is likely to deteriorate further as careers end.

Using longitudinal data on a sample of serious California offenders released on parole, Haapanen (1990) tested the assumption underlying the selective incapacitation model that criminal careers are characterized by a reasonably constant rate of criminal behavior, especially among high-rate offenders. Haapanen found that arrest rates were not stable and declined with age. He found that few offenders maintained a consistent pattern of being in the lowest, middle, or highest third of the sample in terms of their rates of arrest over a four-year period (Haapanen 1990, p. 140). A small minority (28 percent over three periods and 12 percent over four periods) were in the highest third over most of the periods. Thus, the assumption that rates are stable will likely overestimate the amount of crime that could be prevented by selectively incapacitating those identified as high-rate offenders because high-rate offenders are not always high rate. Another important finding emerging from Haapanen's analysis is that in the four years prior to incarceration, offenders were accelerating in criminal activity (as measured by their arrests), suggesting that the preincarceration period may not be appropriate for establishing typical levels of distributions of offense rates. Arrest rates tended to be much lower after release from incarceration. Finally, of those offenders who had the highest rates of arrest prior to prison, only 40 percent were among the highest third after release, as compared to almost 30 percent of those who were not high rate prior to prison (Haapanen 1990, p. 141). Haapanen (1990, pp. 142–43) concluded that the identification of high-rate offenders is "problematic" and likely to produce a large proportion of false positives.

Recently, Auerhahn (1999) replicated Greenwood and Abrahamse's (1982) selective incapacitation study with a representative sample of California state prison inmates. She found that the selective incapacitation scheme advocated by Greenwood and Abrahamse performed poorly with a scale that closely mimicked the one developed and employed by Greenwood and Abrahamse. Auerhahn found that the overall predictive accuracy of her scale was 60 percent, indicating a great deal of error in identifying serious, high-rate offenders. In sum, the problem of identifying high-rate offenders appears to limit the utility of sentencing strategies based on selective incapacitation (Visher 1987, p. 538).

2. *Concern and Need for Prediction Alleviated by "Stochastic Selectivity."* Many analyses of the crime control potential of increasing incarceration rely on a single estimate of mean λ derived from prison inmates and applying it indiscriminately to all related populations of offenders (Canela-Cacho, Blumstein, and Cohen 1997). This assumes that all offenders engage in the same amount (λ) of criminal behavior—regardless of whether they are in prison or jail, or free in the community—and that the probability of their detection and incarceration is equal. Unfortunately, measures of λ derived from arrestee/convictee populations display a strong selection bias because individuals who have gone through the criminal justice process are unlikely to be representative of the total offender population. This selection bias could be because samples of arrestees have a higher propensity for arrest or different offending frequencies. Regardless of the source of bias, there is considerable diversity among offender populations. A highly heterogeneous

distribution of offending frequency in the total population of offenders combines with relatively low imprisonment levels to lead to substantial selectivity of high λ offenders among resident inmates and a correspondingly low mean value of λ among those offenders who remain free (Canela-Cacho, Blumstein, and Cohen 1997). "Stochastic selectivity," then, draws new inmates disproportionately from the high end of the distribution of free offenders. These new inmates will selectively display high average λ's, but their average λ will be lower than that of the current inmates. Furthermore, the higher the incarceration probability following a crime, the deeper into the offender pool incarceration will reach, and the lower will be the incapacitation effect associated with the incoming cohorts (Canela-Cacho, Blumstein, and Cohen 1997).

Using data from the second Rand Inmate Surveys, Canela-Cacho, Blumstein, and Cohen (1997) studied the issue of stochastic selectivity by applying a mixture model that measures the overrepresentation of high λ offenders among prison inmates as a function of variability in individual offending frequencies and severity of criminal justice sanction policies. Focusing on the crimes of robbery and burglary among inmates in California, Texas, and Michigan, they derived estimates of λ for offenders in prison, entering prison, free in the community, and the entire population of similar offenders.

A number of important findings emerged. First, if all offenders within a state and crime type were assumed to face an identical imprisonment risk and time-served distribution, the share of similar offenders who were in prison increased substantially with increasing λ. Second, the proportion of low λ burglars and robbers among free offenders was much larger than among resident inmates, while at the high end of the offending frequency distribution, there was a larger proportion of high λ burglars and robbers among resident inmates than among free offenders. Thus, the concentration of high λ offenders found among inmates results from stochastic selectivity operating on heterogeneous distributions of λ. In other words, selectivity occurred naturally as high λ offenders experienced greater opportunities for incarceration through the greater number of crimes they committed (Canela-Cacho, Blumstein, and Cohen 1997, p. 142), thereby obviating the need for efforts to identify explicitly individual high λ offenders. Since high λ offenders represent a small fraction of the total population of offenders, it seems unwise to use the mean λ of prisoners to represent the mean for the total population of offenders. In sum, analyses of the impact of incarceration policies that rely on mean values of λ will substantially overstate the likely crime reduction to be derived from expanding imprisonment because the population of free offenders is dominated by lower λ offenders.

C. Sentence Duration

Information about crime rates and career lengths is particularly useful for incapacitation and incarceration decisions and policies. Principal among these is the decision regarding sentence length.

1. *Estimates of Criminal Career Duration.*   Many current sentencing policies are based on the assumption that high-rate offenders will continue committing crimes at high rates and for lengthy periods. Thus, many policies prescribe either an additional period of years to a particular sentence or a lengthy incarceration stint (i.e., a twenty-five-year sentence for a third strike). The extent to which this policy is effective, however, is contingent on the duration of a criminal career.

Much debate regarding sentence length has centered on three-strikes policies. These policies severely limit judges' discretion because they prescribe a mandatory prison sentence of (typically) twenty-five years to life. The incapacitation effectiveness of three-strikes laws, however, depends on the duration of criminal careers. To the extent that sentencing decisions incarcerate individuals with short residual career lengths, a three-strikes law will waste incarceration resources (Stolzenberg and D'Alessio 1997, p. 466).

California's three-strikes statute requires enhanced penalties for any felony conviction if one prior conviction was for a listed strike offense and for those convicted two or more times of a strike offense. For the former group, imprisonment is mandatory, and prison sentences are three times longer than the usual time served for the particular felony. For the latter group, any felony conviction can result in a minimum of twenty years served in prison (Zimring, Kamin, and Hawkins 1999, p. 1).

Early research by Greenwood and his colleagues (1994) estimated that a fully implemented three-strikes law would reduce serious felonies by 22–34 percent. Stolzenberg and D'Alessio (1997) used aggregate data drawn from the ten largest cities in California to examine the impact of California's three-strikes law on serious crime rates. Using an interrupted time-series design, they found that the three-strikes law did not decrease serious crime or petty theft rates below the level expected on the basis of preexisting trends. Zimring, Kamin, and

Hawkins (1999) obtained a sample of felony arrests (and relevant criminal records) in Los Angeles, San Francisco, and San Diego, both before and after the California law went into effect. First, 10 percent of all felonies were committed by the two groups that were targets of the law, and two-thirds of those were committed by persons with only one prior strike (p. 2). Second, the profile of crimes committed by the two targeted groups was similar to the profile of crimes committed by other people. Third, while both second-strike- and third-strike-eligible defendants had more extensive criminal histories than ordinary felony defendants, they were not more active than defendants with two or more prior felony convictions who did not have strikes on their records. Fourth, while the three-strikes law was applied to between 30 and 60 percent of the second-strike-eligible cases, only 10–20 percent of the third-strike-eligible cases received the full third-strike treatment (p. 3). However, among those receiving the third-strike treatment, their imprisonment length was considerably increased (p. 51). Fifth, the mean age at arrest for two strikes and above was 34.6 years. That is not surprising because offenders with strikes tend to be older since they have had time to accumulate adult felony records (Zimring, Kamin, and Hawkins 1999, p. 34). This is particularly important because "on average the two or more strikes defendant has an almost 40 percent longer criminal adult career behind him (estimated at 16.6 years) than does the no-strikes felony defendant. All other things being equal, this means that the twenty-five-years-to-life mandatory prison sentence will prevent fewer crimes among the third-strike group than it would in the general population of felons because the group eligible for it is somewhat older" (Zimring, Kamin, and Hawkins 1999, p. 34). Older felons, then, are likely to be further along—and closer to the end of—their criminal careers. Finally, when comparing crime trends in the three cities before and after the law, Zimring, Kamin, and Hawkins found that there was no decline in the crimes committed by those targeted by the new law. In particular, the lower crime rates in 1994 and 1995 (just immediately after the three-strikes law went into effect) were evenly spread among targeted and nontargeted populations, suggesting that the decline in crime observed after the law went into effect was not the direct result of the law (p. 83).

Caulkins (2001) investigated whether the use of different definitions for the first, second, and third strikes, or different sentence lengths, could make incarceration more efficient (i.e., reduce more crimes). He used data from California (see Greenwood et al. 1994). Assuming that the lengths of criminal careers were exponentially distributed, he found that the broader the definition of what constituted a strike, the greater the reduction in crime but the greater the cost per crime averted (p. 240). The problem with a very broad definition is that it fails to take advantage of stochastic selectivity, or the notion that high-rate offenders make up a larger proportion of third- rather than first-strike offenders (Caulkins 2001, p. 242). Caulkins concludes that the three-strikes law would be more effective if second- and third-strike offenders served six- and ten-year terms instead of the ten- and twenty-year terms required by the current law, and if sentences were lengthened for first-strike offenders.

Using data from Florida, Schmertmann, Amankwaa, and Long (1998) concluded that the aging of prison populations under three-strikes policies in that state will undermine their long-run effectiveness. In particular, they noted that the policies will cause increases in prison populations due to the addition of large numbers of older inmates who are unlikely to commit future offenses (p. 445).

The key to the sentence duration issue, and why estimates of criminal career duration are so important, rests on the characteristics of the person-years—not the people—that are removed from free society as a result of such policies (Schmertmann, Amankwaa, and Long 1998, p. 458). Such policies will be effective only to the extent that they incarcerate offenders during the early stages of their criminal careers when they are committing crimes at a high rate and not when they are older and winding down their criminal careers. Research on the rehabilitative and deterrence effects of incarceration on criminal career parameters is sorely needed.

D. Research on Career Length and Desistance

Sentencing practices involving lengthy sentence durations assume that affected offenders will continue to commit crime at a high rate and for a long period. To the extent that this is the case, incapacitation policies will avert crimes and thwart continued careers. However, to the extent that offenders retire before the expiration of a lengthy sentence, shorter career durations will reduce the effects of lengthy sentences (see Blumstein, Cohen, and Hsieh 1982; Spelman 1994; Caulkins 2001).

Unfortunately, research on career duration and desistance is in its infancy. Empirical research on these issues is difficult, but not impossible. Knowledge on this subject will be important for furthering criminal justice policy and the cost-effective use of criminal justice resources.

VII. Directions for Future Criminal Career Research

The criminal career paradigm was developed to structure and organize knowledge about features and dimensions of individual offending and the patterning of criminal activity over the life course. Researchers have provided important evidence on criminal career dimensions, have developed between- and within-individual hypotheses regarding the causes and patterning of criminal activity, and have developed methodological and statistical techniques that furthered the study of criminal careers. Researchers have also provided evidence regarding the within-individual patterns of criminal activity that underlie the aggregate age/crime curve that challenges Gottfredson and Hirschi's claims that the shape of the aggregate age/crime curve is the same for all offenders and is unaffected by life events after childhood.

Much work remains to be done. We discuss the sorts of research needed to inform theory and policy, the types of data collection and modeling required for each criminal career dimension, and the methodological issues that need to be addressed.

A. Research Needed for Informed Theory and Policy

Evidence on criminal career issues cuts to the heart of theory and policy. On the theoretical side, knowledge on the correlates of criminal career dimensions is relevant to the necessity for general versus typological models. If research indicates that the correlates of one offending dimension are similar to another offending dimension, then more general and non-dimension-specific theories are warranted. If the correlates of one offending dimension are different from another offending dimension, then the causal processes underlying these two particular dimensions are probably different, and different explanations and theories are required.

Better knowledge on various criminal career dimensions would aid policy initiatives designed to prevent initial involvement, curtail current offending, and accelerate the desistance process. If research suggests that poor parental socialization is related to early initiation, then prevention efforts should include parent-training efforts. Similarly, if drug use is associated with continued involvement in delinquent and criminal behavior, then intervention efforts should include drug treatment. Finally, if some set of correlates is associated with desistance, then policy efforts may wish to provide for specific prevention and intervention efforts.

Knowledge on career length and residual career length could best inform criminal justice policies because it deals directly with sentencing and incapacitation policies that are now driven more by ideology than by empirical knowledge. For example, if residual criminal career lengths average around five years, criminal justice policies advocating multidecade sentences waste scarce resources. Similarly, if offenders are incarcerated in late adulthood when their residual career lengths have diminished, incarceration space will be wasted, and health care costs will increase, thereby further straining scarce resources.

B. Data Collection and Modeling for Each Dimension

Empirical study of criminal careers requires data collection for large samples of individuals beginning early in life and continuing for a lengthy period into adulthood. Such data are needed if questions surrounding initiation, continuation, and desistance are to be adequately addressed. Continued data collection and research are important to identify and study unaddressed and unresolved criminal career issues and to update thirty-year-old estimates.

1. *What Is Known, Not Known, and Needs to Be Known.* A number of empirical efforts have generated important information on key criminal career dimensions that has been both descriptive and etiological. For example, researchers have identified important determinants of initiation, persistence, and desistance, have discovered that specialization is more the exception than the rule, and have shown that career lengths are not as long as current criminal justice policies presume them to be. Still, a number of important questions remain unanswered.

First, evidence on the correlates of particular criminal career dimensions has tended to indicate that there are some important differences, although there are also some common correlates. Much of this work has employed samples of adolescents and typically only males. Future studies should use data from the adult period and with disaggregation across race and gender and explore how risk and protective factors relate to various criminal career dimensions.

Second, only a handful of studies have studied how sanction effects influence criminal careers (Farrington 1977; Smith and Gartin 1989; Manski and Nagin 1998). Work is needed on the effects of different penal treatments on various criminal career dimensions and whether these relationships vary across age, race, and gender.

Third, evidence is beginning to mount concerning heterogeneity within offending populations, suggesting that theories cannot treat all serious offenders in the same way (see Canela-Cacho, Blumstein, and Cohen 1997). Research is needed on why some serious offenders continue their antisocial behavior while others stop, whether and why persistent heterogeneity or state dependence matters for some but not all offenders, and why some correlates are related to continuation but not desistance, and vice versa.

Fourth, researchers have provided some information on recidivism probabilities, but much more work remains to be done. We know perilously little, from self-reports, about how recidivism probabilities fluctuate in the period from adolescence into adulthood, and how such probabilities are conditioned by neighborhood characteristics. Little information exists on how recidivism probabilities vary across crime types over time.

Fifth, researchers have tended to report data from either self-reports or official records, with few reporting information from both self-reports and official records linking the juvenile and adult periods. Important questions remain as to whether these different measurement approaches provide similar or different information with regard to key criminal career dimensions (see Dunford and Elliott 1984; Weiner 1989, p. 67). In addition, future efforts should attempt to determine if expectations derived from several of the recently articulated developmental theories apply equally well to self-reported and official records. Lynam, Piquero, and Moffitt (2002) found that specialization in violence varied by the type of measurement approach, with violence specialists in the Dunedin study identified in self-reports but not in official records through age twenty-six.

Sixth, co-offending has gone relatively underinvestigated. Although some research has examined the extent to which co-offending patterns vary in the juvenile years, almost no research has explored co-offending in adulthood and across subgroups defined by race and gender. This may have much to do with measures of criminal activity. Official records seldom contain data on co-offending, and researchers seldom ask explicit co-offending questions in their self-report surveys. Future work should investigate this subject, especially regarding recruitment.

Seventh, much criminal career research has concentrated on male subjects. Less information is available comparing male and female offending patterns (though see Piper 1985; English 1993; Baskin and Sommers 1998; Moffitt et al. 2001; Broidy et al. 2002; D'Unger, Land,

and McCall 2002; Giordano, Cernkovich, and Rudolph 2002). Research may help explain the longitudinal patterning of female criminality generally and the relevance of gender-specific theories (Lanctôt and Le Blanc 2002).

In a recent study comparing male and female offending trajectories using data from the Christchurch Health and Development Study, Fergusson and Horwood (2002) found that the same five trajectory groups applied to both males and females and that the risk factors associated with trajectory-group membership operated similarly for males and females. The only gender differences were that females were more likely to exhibit low-risk or early onset adolescent-limited offending while males were more likely to exhibit chronic offending or later adolescent-limited onset. Future work should explore criminal career dimensions of female offenders, gender-specific theoretical models, and whether policy implications vary across gender (see Warren and Rosenbaum 1987). For example, do males' and females' deviant behavior develop and escalate through similar processes (Lanctôt and Le Blanc 2002)? Are state-dependent effects more important for females than males? Such research is particularly important in the wake of recent challenges regarding the generality (across gender) of Moffitt's typology (see Silverthorn and Frick 1999).

Eighth, much research on criminal careers has been quantitative. While it has generated important insights, more qualitative work is needed into subjects' lives. Several qualitative studies have provided unique insights into desistance (see Shover 1996; Baskin and Sommers 1998; Maruna 2001; Giordano, Cernkovich, and Rudolph 2002).

Ninth, career length has received little empirical attention. This is unfortunate because career length has relevance to sentencing and incapacitation decisions. One problem with studying career length is the right-hand censoring that occurs because offenders are not studied until their deaths. Future research should provide both descriptive and etiological information on career lengths, especially how career lengths vary for different types of offenders, for different types of crime, and for age, race, and gender subgroups.

Tenth, much research has concentrated on "classic" depictions of street offenders. Recent work has examined the criminal career pattern of white-collar offenders (Weisburd and Waring 2001). Efforts should be made better to understand the differences between street and suite offenders.

Eleventh, continued work unpacking the relationship between past and future criminal activity is warranted. Paternoster, Brame, and Farrington (2001) used conviction records from the Cambridge study to examine whether variation in adult offending was consistent with a conditional random process. Through age forty, adult offending was consistent with a random process, after conditioning on adolescent differences in the propensity to offend. Further research with different samples and offending measures is necessary.

Twelfth, the ecological context within which offenders reside and operate is an underdeveloped research area (Lynam et al. 2000; Wikström and Loeber 2000; Wikström and Sampson, forthcoming). Since certain ecological contexts contain high rates of criminal activity, a basic question arises: are high crime areas simply those populated with the highest rate offenders? Little criminological research has examined the criminal careers of places (see Reiss 1986*b*; Spelman 1995), and even less research has tracked the criminal careers of high-rate offenders in high crime ecological contexts over time.

Thirteenth, few efforts have been made to link self-reports and official records to estimate q, or the probability of arrest per crime, and its relationship to λ (see Blumstein and Cohen 1979; Dunford and Elliott 1984; Cohen 1986; Farrington et al., forthcoming). Such analyses will help develop offense-specific estimates of the probability of arrest for a particular crime and indicate whether offenders differ from one another in their arrest risk per crime. Variations in q for any offense type may result from differential enforcement practices that increase arrest vulnerability for some offenders compared to others (Cohen 1986, p. 335). Thus, a lower q for certain subgroups will lead to their underrepresentation among arrestees and to a corresponding overestimate of their λ if the same q was applied uniformly to all subgroups in offense-specific analyses (Cohen 1986, p. 335). It would also be interesting to know if the probability of arrest per crime increases or decreases with increasing frequency. If it decreases with offending frequency, then this may suggest some sort of "learning" effect by which high λ offenders become apt at avoiding detection (see Spelman 1994).

Fourteenth, although traditionally believed rare, adult onset of offending has been a neglected criminal career dimension. Recent work by Eggleston and Laub (2002) shows the importance not only of describing adult onset but of understanding its correlates.

Finally, although researchers have documented patterns of non-offending, or intermittency, throughout offenders' careers (Frazier 1976; Barnett, Blumstein, and Farrington 1989; Nagin and Land

1993), little research has been done on this issue (Piquero, forthcoming). Future research should attempt to determine whether intermittency periods become longer over time (with age) and whether some crimes evidence different intermittent patterns than other crimes.

2. *Update Thirty-Year-Old Estimates.* Much of the knowledge base surrounding criminal careers emerged from classic data sets and from inmate surveys completed almost thirty years ago. Much more recent information is needed across different types of samples and with different measurement protocols. For example, an updating of participation, frequency, and career duration estimates is needed as they are likely to provide important information that could be used in designing and implementing more effective criminal justice policies. Such information is particularly important because of the increases in prison populations over the last thirty years. Such updates should also examine the changes that have occurred in sanction rates and the degree to which the various λ distributions have changed, particularly the extent to which the λ distribution of inmates may have declined as a result of the much higher incarceration rates (see Canela-Cacho, Blumstein, and Cohen 1997, p. 167).

C. Methodological Issues

Empirical study of criminal careers must overcome several methodological issues including accounting for street time and death, the strengths and weaknesses of modeling approaches, and sample attrition. These issues are relevant for both official and self-report records.

1. *Accounting for Street Time and Death.* Much analysis of criminal careers centers on the importance of controlling for street, or exposure, time. Unfortunately, because of the difficulty of collecting such data, researchers have been frequently unable to implement controls for street time. The importance of this issue was recently demonstrated by Piquero et al. (2001) who found that the conclusions regarding the size and shape of criminal trajectories varies considerably depending whether street time is controlled. Future research should control for street time as desistance patterns may reflect street time more than desistance.

Similarly, mortality should continue to be examined. Before age forty, delinquent individuals are more likely than nondelinquent individuals to die from unnatural causes such as accidents and homicide (Laub and Vaillant 2000). If such individuals are assumed to have desisted from crime in longitudinal studies, researchers will incorrectly identify these deceased delinquents as desisting delinquents. Mortality information should be a key priority in longitudinal studies, especially those that focus on high-risk populations as they enter into adulthood (Lattimore, Linster, and MacDonald 1997).

Laub, Sampson, and Eggleston (2001) reinforced these points. They showed that the shape and size of offending trajectories in the Glueck data were highly influenced by controls for street time, length of observation windows, and mortality, thereby underscoring the importance of considering such methodological issues.

2. *Various Modeling Approaches.*   A number of modeling approaches are used to describe criminal career patterns. Each attempts to ask and answer similar questions regarding the nature of offending over the life course. Most studies, however, have tended to rely on solely one approach. In an important study that applies several different modeling approaches to the same research question and data set, Bushway, Brame, and Paternoster (1999) found that modeling strategies generally converged on the same substantive result, though some important differences emerged. They suggested that researchers continue to apply multiple models in order to learn more about the strengths and weaknesses of each.

Researchers should continue to extend current modeling approaches and to develop new ones. Recent efforts have extended modeling approaches to account for the joint distribution of two outcomes. Brame, Mulvey, and Piquero (2001) extended the semiparametric model to study violent and nonviolent offending simultaneously. Their results, using the 1958 Philadelphia birth cohort study, indicated that individuals scoring high on the violent measure were the same as those scoring high on the nonviolent measure.

Finally, researchers should develop and apply unique methodologies for understanding and visualizing lives. Maltz and Mullany (2000) outlined an analytic framework designed to explore issues related to criminal careers generally and life-course issues specifically. Their approach is chronological, recognizes that different people may have experienced different events and thus may need different variables to understand their behavior, recognizes that people may have different reactions to similarly experienced events, and can be studied using an exploratory graphical analysis that is more free form than algorithmic. Their analytic technique can be viewed as a complement to the more advanced quantitative methods described earlier.

3. *Sample Attrition.*   Longitudinal studies inevitably incur sample attrition. This is especially relevant for serious offenders, who are notoriously absent from longitudinal studies and who tend to drop out much more frequently than non- or less-serious offenders (Cernkovich, Giordano, and Pugh 1985). Sample attrition would not be much of a concern if the attrition was random; however, to the extent that the sample attrition is nonrandom, estimates of delinquent/criminal behavior will be biased.

Brame and Piquero (forthcoming) used the first and fifth wave of the NYS to examine sample attrition and found that some of the attrition was nonrandom. This is important because it indicates that attrition is related to involvement in criminal activity, and thus time-trend estimates of delinquent/criminal activity may be biased. Future research should attempt to sort out random and nonrandom components of sample attrition. In general, greater efforts should be made to minimize attrition (Farrington et al. 1990).

Criminal career research focuses on between- and within-individual differences in offending over time. Researchers should continue their efforts to address the important methodological issues that confront this line of research. Information derived from criminal career research is important to advance fundamental knowledge about offending and to assist criminal justice decision makers in dealing with offenders.

REFERENCES

Agnew, Robert. 1992. "Foundation for a General Strain Theory of Crime and Delinquency." *Criminology* 30:47–87.
Aguilar, Benjamin, L. Alan Sroufe, Byron Egeland, and Elizabeth Carlson. 2000. "Distinguishing the Early-Onset/Persistent and Adolescence-Onset Antisocial Behavior Types: From Birth to 16 Years." *Development and Psychopathology* 12:109–32.
Andersson, Jan. 1990. "Continuity in Crime: Sex and Age Differences." *Journal of Quantitative Criminology* 6:85–100.
Auerhahn, Kathleen. 1999. "Selective Incapacitation and the Problem of Prediction." *Criminology* 37:703–34.
Ayers, Charles D., James Herbert Williams, J. David Hawkins, Peggy L. Peterson, Richard F. Catalano, and Robert D. Abbott. 1999. "Assessing Cor-

relates of Onset, Escalation, Deescalation, and Desistance of Delinquent Behavior." *Journal of Quantitative Criminology* 15:277–306.

Bachman, Jerald G., Patrick M. O'Malley, and Jerome Johnston. 1978. *Adolescence to Adulthood: Change and Stability in the Lives of Young Men*. Vol. 7 of *Youth in Transition*. Ann Arbor: Institute for Social Research, University of Michigan.

Barnett, Arnold, Alfred Blumstein, and David P. Farrington. 1987. "Probabilistic Models of Youthful Criminal Careers." *Criminology* 25:83–107.

———. 1989. "A Prospective Test of a Criminal Career Model." *Criminology* 27:373–88.

Barnett, Arnold, and Anthony J. Lofaso. 1985. "Selective Incapacitation and the Philadelphia Cohort Data." *Journal of Quantitative Criminology* 1:3–36.

Bartusch, Dawn R. Jeglum, Donald R. Lynam, Terrie E. Moffitt, and Phil A. Silva. 1997. "Is Age Important? Testing a General versus a Developmental Theory of Antisocial Behavior." *Criminology* 35:13–48.

Baskin, Deborah R., and Ira B. Sommers. 1998. *Casualties of Community Disorder: Women's Careers in Violent Crime*. Boulder, Colo.: Westview.

Blumstein, Alfred, and Jacqueline Cohen. 1979. "Estimation of Individual Crime Rates from Arrest Records." *Journal of Criminal Law and Criminology* 70:561–85.

Blumstein, Alfred, Jacqueline Cohen, Somnath Das, and Soumyo D. Moitra. 1988. "Specialization and Seriousness during Adult Criminal Careers." *Journal of Quantitative Criminology* 4:303–45.

Blumstein, Alfred, Jacqueline Cohen, and David P. Farrington. 1988a. "Criminal Career Research: Its Value for Criminology." *Criminology* 26:1–35.

———. 1988b. "Longitudinal and Criminal Career Research: Further Clarifications." *Criminology* 26:57–74.

Blumstein, Alfred, Jacqueline Cohen, and Paul Hsieh. 1982. *The Duration of Adult Criminal Careers*. Final report submitted to U.S. Department of Justice, National Institute of Justice, August 1982. Pittsburgh: School of Urban and Public Affairs, Carnegie-Mellon University.

Blumstein, Alfred, Jacqueline Cohen, Jeffrey A. Roth, and Christy A. Visher, eds. 1986. *Criminal Careers and "Career Criminals."* 2 vols. Panel on Research on Career Criminals, Committee on Research on Law Enforcement and the Administration of Justice, Commission on Behaviorial and Social Sciences and Education, National Research Council. Washington, D.C.: National Academy Press.

Blumstein, Alfred, David P. Farrington, and Soumyo Moitra. 1985. "Delinquency Careers: Innocents, Desisters, and Persisters." In *Crime and Justice: An Annual Review of Research*, vol. 6, edited by Michael Tonry and Norval Morris. Chicago: University of Chicago Press.

Blumstein, Alfred, and Elizabeth Graddy. 1982. "Prevalence and Recidivism in Index Arrests: A Feedback Model." *Law and Society Review* 16:265–90.

Blumstein, Alfred, and Soumyo Moitra. 1980. "The Identification of 'Career Criminals' from 'Chronic Offenders' in a Cohort." *Law and Policy Quarterly* 2:321–34.

Brame, Robert, Edward Mulvey, and Alex R. Piquero. 2001. "On the Development of Different Kinds of Criminal Activity." *Sociological Methods and Research* 29:319–41.

Brame, Robert, and Alex R. Piquero. Forthcoming. "The Role of Sample Attrition in Studying the Longitudinal Relationship between Age and Crime." *Journal of Quantitative Criminology*, vol. 19.

Britt, Chester L. 1992. "Constancy and Change in the U.S. Age Distribution of Crime: A Test of the 'Invariance Hypothesis.'" *Journal of Quantitative Criminology* 8:175–87.

———. 1996. "The Measurement of Specialization and Escalation in the Criminal Career: An Alternative Modeling Strategy." *Journal of Quantitative Criminology* 12:193–222.

Broidy, Lisa M., Daniel S. Nagin, Richard E. Tremblay, John E. Bates, Bobby Brame, Kenneth Dodge, David Fergusson, John Horwood, Rolf Loeber, Robert Laird, Donald Lynam, Terrie E. Moffitt, Gregory S. Petit, and Frank Vitaro. 2002. "Developmental Trajectories of Childhood Disruptive Behaviors and Adolescent Delinquency: A Six Site, Cross-National Study." *Developmental Psychology*. Forthcoming.

Bursik, Robert J., Jr. 1980. "The Dynamics of Specialization in Juvenile Offenses." *Social Forces* 58:851–64.

———. 1989. "Erickson Could Never Have Imagined: Recent Extensions of Birth Cohort Studies." *Journal of Quantitative Criminology* 5:389–96.

Bushway, Shawn, Robert Brame, and Raymond Paternoster. 1999. "Assessing Stability and Change in Criminal Offending: A Comparison of Random Effects, Semiparametric, and Fixed Effects Modeling Strategies." *Journal of Quantitative Criminology* 15:23–64.

Bushway, Shawn D., Alex R. Piquero, Lisa M. Broidy, Elizabeth Cauffman, and Paul Mazerolle. 2001. "An Empirical Framework for Studying Desistance as a Process." *Criminology* 39:491–515.

Bushway, Shawn D., Terence P. Thornberry, and Marvin D. Krohn. Forthcoming. "Desistance as a Developmental Process: A Comparison of Static and Dynamic Approaches." *Journal of Quantitative Criminology*, vol. 19.

Canela-Cacho, José E., Alfred Blumstein, and Jacqueline Cohen. 1997. "Relationship between the Offending Frequency λ of Imprisoned and Free Offenders." *Criminology* 35:133–76.

Capaldi, Deborah N., and Gerald R. Patterson. 1996. "Can Violent Offenders Be Distinguished from Frequent Offenders: Prediction from Childhood to Adolescence." *Journal of Research in Crime and Delinquency* 33:206–31.

Caulkins, Jonathan P. 2001. "How Large Should the Strike Zone Be in 'Three Strikes and You're Out' Sentencing Laws?" *Journal of Quantitative Criminology* 17:227–46.

Cernkovich, Stephen A., and Peggy C. Giordano. 2001. "Stability and Change in Antisocial Behavior: The Transition from Adolescence to Early Adulthood." *Criminology* 39:371–410.

Cernkovich, Stephen A., Peggy C. Giordano, and M. D. Pugh. 1985. "Chronic Offenders: The Missing Cases in Self-Report Delinquency Research." *Journal of Criminal Law and Criminology* 76:705–32.

Chaiken, Jan M., and Marcia R. Chaiken. 1982. *Varieties of Criminal Behavior.* Rand Report no. R-2814-NIJ. Santa Monica, Calif.: Rand.

Chaiken, Jan, Marcia Chaiken, and William Rhodes. 1993. "Predicting Violent Behavior and Classifying Violent Offenders." In *Understanding and Preventing Violence*, vol. 4, edited by Albert J. Reiss, Jr., and Jeffrey A. Roth. Washington, D.C.: National Academy Press.

Christensen, Ronald. 1967. "Projected Percentage of U.S. Population with Criminal Arrest and Conviction Records." In *Task Force Report: Science and Technology.* Report to the President's Commission on Law Enforcement and the Administration of Justice, prepared by the Institute for Defense Analysis. Washington, D.C.: U.S. Government Printing Office.

Chung, Ick-Joong, Karl G. Hill, J. David Hawkins, Lewayne D. Gilchrist, and Daniel S. Nagin. 2002. "Childhood Predictors of Offense Trajectories." *Journal of Research in Crime and Delinquency* 39:60–92.

Cohen, Albert K. 1955. *Delinquent Boys: The Culture of the Gang.* Glencoe, Ill.: Free Press.

Cohen, Jacqueline. 1986. "Research on Criminal Careers: Individual Frequency Rates and Offense Seriousness." In *Criminal Careers and "Career Criminals,"* vol. 1, edited by Alfred Blumstein, Jacqueline Cohen, Jeffrey A. Roth, and Christy A. Visher. Washington, D.C.: National Academy Press.

Cohen, Jacqueline, and José A. Canela-Cacho. 1994. "Incarceration and Violent Crime: 1965–1988." In *Consequences and Control*, vol. 4 of *Understanding and Preventing Violence*, edited by Albert J. Reiss, Jr., and Jeffrey A. Roth. Panel on the Understanding and Control of Violent Behavior, Committee on Law and Justice, Commission on Behavioral and Social Sciences and Education, National Research Council. Washington, D.C.: National Academy Press.

Cohen, P. N. 1999. "Racial-Ethnic and Gender Differences in Returns to Cohabitation and Marriage: Evidence from the Current Population Survey." U.S. Census Bureau, Population Division Working Paper no. 35. Washington, D.C.: U.S. Census Bureau.

Conway, Kevin P., and Joan McCord. 2002. "A Longitudinal Examination of the Relation between Co-offending with Violent Accomplices and Violent Crime." *Aggressive Behavior* 28:97–108.

Datesman, Susan K., and Mikel Aickin. 1984. "Offending Specialization and Escalation among Status Offenders." *Journal of Criminal Law and Criminology* 75:1246–75.

Dean, Charles W., Robert Brame, and Alex R. Piquero. 1996. "Criminal Propensities, Discrete Groups of Offenders, and Persistence in Crime." *Criminology* 34:547–74.

Decker, Scott H., and Barbara Salert. 1986. "Predicting the Career Criminal: An Empirical Test of the Greenwood Scale." *Journal of Criminal Law and Criminology* 77:215–36.

Dishion, Thomas J., Joan McCord, and Francois Poulin. 1999. "When Interventions Harm: Peer Groups and Problem Behavior." *American Psychologist* 54:755–64.

Dunford, Franklyn W., and Delbert S. Elliott. 1984. "Identifying Career Offenders Using Self-Reported Data." *Journal of Research in Crime and Delinquency* 21:57–87.

D'Unger, Amy V., Kenneth C. Land, and Patricia L. McCall. 2002. "Sex Differences in Age Patterns of Delinquent/Criminal Careers: Results from Poisson Latent Class Analyses of the Philadelphia Cohort Study." *Journal of Quantitative Criminology* 18:349–75.

D'Unger, Amy V., Kenneth C. Land, Patricia L. McCall, and Daniel S. Nagin. 1998. "How Many Latent Classes of Delinquent/Criminal Careers? Results from Mixed Poisson Regression Analyses." *American Journal of Sociology* 103:1593–1630.

Earls, Felton J. 2001. "Connecting Social Science to the World." Available on-line at http://www.phdcn.harvard.edu (visited February 2002).

Earls, Felton J., and Christy A. Visher. 1997. *Project on Human Development in Chicago Neighborhoods: A Research Update*. Washington, D.C.: National Institute of Justice, Office of Justice Programs, U.S. Department of Justice.

Eggleston, Elaine P., and John H. Laub. 2002. "The Onset of Adult Offending: A Neglected Dimension of the Criminal Career." *Journal of Criminal Justice* 30:603–22.

Elder, Glen H., Jr. 1985. "Perspectives on the Life Course." In *Life Course Dynamics: Trajectories and Transitions, 1968–1980*, edited by Glen H. Elder, Jr. Ithaca, N.Y.: Cornell University Press.

Elliott, Delbert S. 1994. "1993 Presidential Address—Serious Violent Offenders: Onset, Developmental Course, and Termination." *Criminology* 32:1–22.

Elliott, Delbert S., Suzanne S. Ageton, David Huizinga, Barbara Knowles, and Rachelle Canter. 1983. *The Prevalence and Incidence of Delinquent Behavior: 1976–1980*. National Youth Survey, Report no. 26. Boulder, Colo.: Behavioral Research Institute.

Elliott, Delbert S., and David Huizinga. 1984. *The Relationship between Delinquent Behavior and ADM Problems*. National Youth Survey Project Report no. 28. Boulder, Colo.: Behavioral Research Institute.

Elliott, Delbert S., David Huizinga, and Suzanne S. Ageton. 1985. *Explaining Delinquency and Drug Use*. Beverly Hills, Calif.: Sage.

Elliott, Delbert S., David Huizinga, and Scott Menard. 1989. *Multiple Problem Youth: Delinquency, Substance Use, and Mental Health Problems*. New York: Springer.

Elliott, Delbert S., David Huizinga, and Barbara Morse. 1987. "Self-Reported Violent Offending: A Descriptive Analysis of Juvenile Violent Offenders and Their Offending Careers." *Journal of Interpersonal Violence* 1:472–514.

English, Kim. 1993. "Self-Reported Crime Rates of Women Prisoners." *Journal of Quantitative Criminology* 9:357–82.

English, Kim, and Mary J. Mande. 1992. *Measuring Crime Rates of Prisoners*. Final report to National Institute of Justice. Washington, D.C.: National Institute of Justice.

Espiritu, Rachele C., David Huizinga, Anne M. Crawford, and Rolf Loeber. 2001. "Epidemiology of Self-Reported Delinquency." In *Child Delinquents:*

Development, Intervention, and Service Needs, edited by Rolf Loeber and David P. Farrington. Thousand Oaks, Calif.: Sage.

Fagan, Jeffrey. 1989. "Cessation of Family Violence: Deterrence and Dissuasion." In *Family Violence,* edited by Lloyd Ohlin and Michael Tonry. Vol. 11 of *Crime and Justice: A Review of Research,* edited by Michael Tonry and Norval Morris. Chicago: University of Chicago Press.

Farrington, David P. 1977. "The Effects of Public Labeling." *British Journal of Criminology* 17:122–35.

———. 1979. "Longitudinal Research on Crime and Delinquency." In *Crime and Justice: An Annual Review of Research,* vol. 1, edited by Norval Morris and Michael Tonry. Chicago: University of Chicago Press.

———. 1986. "Age and Crime." In *Crime and Justice: An Annual Review of Research,* vol. 7, edited by Michael Tonry and Norval Morris. Chicago: University of Chicago Press.

———. 1987. "Predicting Individual Crime Rates." In *Prediction and Classification: Criminal Justice Decision Making,* edited by Don Gottfredson and Michael Tonry. Vol. 9 of *Crime and Justice: A Review of Research,* edited by Michael Tonry and Norval Morris. Chicago: University of Chicago Press.

———. 1989. "Self-Reported and Official Offending from Adolescence to Adulthood." In *Cross-National Research in Self-Reported Crime and Delinquency,* edited by Malcolm W. Klein. Dordrecht: Kluwer.

———. 1991. "Childhood Aggression and Adult Violence: Early Precursors and Later Life Outcomes." In *The Development and Treatment of Childhood Aggression,* edited by Debra J. Pepler and Kenneth H. Rubin. Hillsdale, N.J.: Lawrence Erlbaum.

———. 1994. "Early Developmental Prevention of Juvenile Delinquency." *Criminal Behaviour and Mental Health* 4:209–27.

———. 2000. "Explaining and Preventing Crime: The Globalization of Knowledge—the American Society of Criminology 1999 Presidential Address." *Criminology* 38:1–24.

———. 2001. "Key Results from the First Forty Years of the Cambridge Study in Delinquent Development." In *Taking Stock of Delinquency: An Overview of Findings from Contemporary Longitudinal Studies,* edited by Terence P. Thornberry and Marvin D. Krohn. New York: Kluwer/Plenum.

Farrington, David P., Bernard Gallagher, Lynda Morley, Raymond St. Ledger, and Donald J. West. 1990. "Minimizing Attrition in Longitudinal Research: Methods of Tracing and Securing Cooperation in a 24-Year Follow-Up Study." In *Data Quality in Longitudinal Research,* edited by David Magnusson and Lars R. Bergman. Cambridge: Cambridge University Press.

Farrington, David P., and J. David Hawkins. 1991. "Predicting Participation, Early Onset, and Later Persistence in Officially Recorded Offending." *Criminal Behaviour and Mental Health* 1:1–33.

Farrington, David P., Darrick Jolliffe, J. David Hawkins, Richard F. Catalano, Karl G. Hill, and Rick Kosterman. Forthcoming. "Comparing Delinquency Careers in Court Records and Self-Reports." *Criminology.*

Farrington, David P., Sandra Lambert, and Donald J. West. 1998. "Criminal Careers of Two Generations of Family Members in the Cambridge Study in Delinquent Development." *Studies on Crime and Crime Prevention* 7:85–106.

Farrington, David P., and Rolf Loeber. 1998. "Major Aims of This Book." In *Serious and Violent Juvenile Offenders: Risk Factors and Successful Interventions*, edited by Rolf Loeber and David P. Farrington. Thousand Oaks, Calif.: Sage.

Farrington, David P., Rolf Loeber, Delbert S. Elliott, J. David Hawkins, Denise Kandel, Malcolm Klein, Joan McCord, David C. Rowe, and Richard E. Tremblay. 1990. "Advancing Knowledge about the Onset of Delinquency and Crime." In *Advances in Clinical and Child Psychology*, vol. 13, edited by Benjamin B. Lahey and Alan E. Kazdin. New York: Plenum.

Farrington, David P., and Barbara Maughan. 1999. "Criminal Careers of Two London Cohorts." *Criminal Behaviour and Mental Health* 9:91–106.

Farrington, David P., Lloyd E. Ohlin, and James Q. Wilson. 1986. *Understanding and Controlling Crime: Toward a New Research Strategy*. New York: Springer.

Farrington, David P., Howard N. Snyder, and Terence A. Finnegan. 1988. "Specialization in Juvenile Court Careers." *Criminology* 26:461–87.

Farrington, David P., and Per-Olof H. Wikström. 1994. "Criminal Careers in London and Stockholm: A Cross-National Comparative Study." In *Cross-National Longitudinal Research on Human Development and Criminal Behavior*, edited by Elmar G. M. Weitekamp and Hans-Jürgen Kerner. Dordrecht: Kluwer.

Fergusson, David M., and L. John Horwood. 2002. "Male and Female Offending Trajectories." *Development and Psychopathology* 14:159–77.

Fergusson, David M., L. John Horwood, and Daniel S. Nagin. 2000. "Offending Trajectories in a New Zealand Birth Cohort." *Criminology* 38:525–52.

Fox, James Alan, and Paul E. Tracy. 1988. "A Measure of Skewness in Offense Distributions." *Journal of Quantitative Criminology* 4:259–73.

Frazier, Charles E. 1976. *Theoretical Approaches to Deviance: An Evaluation*. Columbus, Ohio: Merrill.

Garfinkel, Harold. 1965. "Conditions of Successful Degradation Ceremonies." *American Journal of Sociology* 61:420–24.

Giordano, Peggy C., Stephen A. Cernkovich, and Jennifer L. Rudolph. 2002. "Gender, Crime, and Desistance: Toward a Theory of Cognitive Transformation." *American Journal of Sociology* 107:990–1064.

Glueck, Sheldon, and Eleanor Glueck. 1940. *Juvenile Delinquents Grown Up*. New York: Commonwealth Fund.

———. 1950. *Unraveling Juvenile Delinquency*. New York: Commonwealth Fund.

Gottfredson, Don M. 1999. *Effects of Judges' Sentencing Decisions on Criminal Careers*. Research in Brief. Washington, D.C.: National Institute of Justice.

Gottfredson, Michael R., and Travis Hirschi. 1986. "The True Value of Lambda Would Appear to Be Zero: An Essay on Career Criminals, Criminal Careers, Selective Incapacitation, Cohort Studies, and Related Topics." *Criminology* 24:213–34.

———. 1987. "The Methodological Adequacy of Longitudinal Research on Crime." *Criminology* 25:581–614.

———. 1988. "Science, Public Policy, and the Career Paradigm." *Criminology* 26:37–55.

———. 1990. *A General Theory of Crime.* Stanford, Calif.: Stanford University Press.

Gottfredson, Stephen D., and Don M. Gottfredson. 1994. "Behavioral Prediction and the Problem of Incapacitation." *Criminology* 32:441–74.

Greenberg, David F. 1975. "The Incapacitative Effect of Imprisonment: Some Estimates." *Law and Society Review* 9:541–80.

———. 1977. "Delinquency and the Age Structure of Society." *Contemporary Crisis* 1:189–223.

———. 1991. "Modeling Criminal Careers." *Criminology* 29:17–46.

Greene, M. A. 1977. *The Incapacitative Effect of Imprisonment on Policies of Crime.* Ph.D. thesis, School of Urban and Public Affairs, Carnegie-Mellon University, Pittsburgh. Ann Arbor, Mich.: University Microfilms.

Greenwood, Peter W., and Allan Abrahamse. 1982. *Selective Incapacitation.* Rand Report no. R-2815-NIJ. Santa Monica, Calif.: Rand.

Greenwood, Peter W., C. Peter Rydell, Allan F. Abrahamse, Jonathan P. Caulkins, James Chiesa, Karyn E. Model, and Stephen P. Klein. 1994. *Three Strikes and You're Out: Estimated Benefits and Costs of California's New Mandatory-Sentencing Law.* Rand Report no. MR-509-RC. Santa Monica, Calif.: Rand.

Greenwood, Peter W., and Susan Turner. 1987. *Selective Incapacitation Revisited: Why the High-Rate Offenders Are Hard to Predict.* Rand Report no. R-3397-NIJ. Santa Monica, Calif.: Rand.

Guerra, Nancy G. 1998. "Serious and Violent Juvenile Offenders: Gaps in Knowledge and Research Priorities." In *Serious and Violent Juvenile Offenders: Risk Factors and Successful Interventions,* edited by Rolf Loeber and David P. Farrington. Thousand Oaks, Calif.: Sage.

Guttridge, Patricia, William F. Gabrielli, Jr., Sarnoff A. Mednick, and Katherine T. Van Dusen. 1983. "Criminal Violence in a Birth Cohort." In *Prospective Studies of Crime and Delinquency,* edited by Katherine T. Van Dusen and Sarnoff A. Mednick. Boston: Kluwer-Nijhoff.

Haapanen, Rudy. 1990. *Selective Incapacitation and the Serious Offender: A Longitudinal Study of Criminal Career Patterns.* New York: Springer.

Hagan, John, and Alberto Palloni. 1988. "Crimes as Social Events in the Life Course: Reconceiving a Criminological Controversy. *Criminology* 26:87–100.

Hamparian, Donna M., Richard Schuster, Simon Dinitz, and John Conrad. 1978. *The Violent Few: A Study of Dangerous Juvenile Offenders.* Lexington, Mass.: Lexington Books.

Hawkins, J. David, and Richard F. Catalano, Jr. 1992. *Communities That Care: Action for Drug Abuse Prevention.* San Francisco: Jossey-Bass.

Haynie, Dana L. 2001. "Delinquent Peers Revisited: Does Network Structure Matter?" *American Journal of Sociology* 106:1013–57.

Henry, Bill, Terrie E. Moffitt, Avshalom Caspi, John Langley, and Phil A.

Silva. 1994. "On the 'Remembrance of Things Past': A Longitudinal Evaluation of the Retrospective Method." *Psychological Assessment* 6:92–101.

Hindelang, Michael, Travis Hirschi, and Joseph Weis. 1981. *Measuring Delinquency.* Beverly Hills, Calif.: Sage.

Hirschi, Travis. 1969. *Causes of Delinquency.* Berkeley: University of California Press.

Hirschi, Travis, and Michael G. Gottfredson. 1983. "Age and the Explanation of Crime." *American Journal of Sociology* 89:552–84.

Home Office Statistical Bulletin. 1995. *Criminal Careers of Those Born between 1953 and 1973.* London: Home Office.

Horney, Julie, and Ineke Haen Marshall. 1991. "Measuring Lambda through Self-Reports." *Criminology* 29:471–96.

Horney, Julie, D. Wayne Osgood, and Ineke Haen Marshall. 1995. "Criminal Careers in the Short-Term: Intra-individual Variability in Crime and Its Relation to Local Life Circumstances." *American Sociological Review* 60:655–73.

Hsiao, Cheng. 1986. *Analysis of Panel Data.* Cambridge: Cambridge University Press.

Huizinga, David, and Delbert S. Elliott. 1986. "Re-assessing the Reliability and Validity of Self-Report Delinquency Measures." *Journal of Quantitative Criminology* 2:293–327.

Huizinga, David, Finn-Aage Esbensen, and Anne Wylie Weiher. 1991. "Are There Multiple Paths to Delinquency?" *Journal of Criminal Law and Criminology* 82:83–118.

Huizinga, David, Rolf Loeber, and Terence P. Thornberry. 1993. "Longitudinal Study of Delinquency, Drug Use, Sexual Activity, and Pregnancy among Children and Youth in Three Cities." *Public Health Reports: Journal of the U.S. Public Health Service* 108(suppl. 1):90–96.

Hurrell, Karen T. 1993. "Modeling the Relationship between Crime Count and Observation Period in Prison Inmates' Self-Report Data." *Applied Statistics* 42:355–67.

Johnston, Lloyd D., Jerald G. Bachman, and Patrick M. O'Malley. 1994. *Monitoring the Future.* Ann Arbor, Mich.: Institute for Social Research.

Johnston, Lloyd D., Patrick M. O'Malley, and Jerald G. Bachman. 2000. *The Monitoring the Future National Results on Adolescent Drug Use: Overview of Key Findings, 1999.* Bethesda, Md.: National Institute on Drug Abuse, Public Health Service, National Institute of Health, U.S. Department of Health and Human Services.

Junger-Tas, Josine, and Ineke Haen Marshall. 1999. "The Self-Report Methodology in Crime Research." In *Crime and Justice: An Annual Review of Research*, vol. 25, edited by Michael Tonry. Chicago: University of Chicago Press.

Kann, Laura, Steven A. Kinchen, Barbara I. Williams, James G. Ross, Richard Lowry, Jo Anne Grunbaum, and Lloyd J. Kolbe. 2000. "Youth Risk Behavior Surveillance—United States, 1999." CDC Surveillance Summaries, *Morbidity and Mortality Weekly Report 49* no. SS-5. Washington, D.C.: United States Government Printing Office.

Kazdin, Alan E., Helena C. Kraemer, Ronald C. Kessler, David J. Kupfer, and David R. Offord. 1997. "Contributions of Risk-Factor Research to Developmental Psychopathology." *Clinical Psychology Review* 17:375–406.

Kelley, Barbara Tatem, David Huizinga, Terence P. Thornberry, and Rolf Loeber. 1997. *Epidemiology of Serious Violence.* Office of Juvenile Justice Bulletin. Washington, D.C.: Office of Juvenile Justice and Delinquency Prevention, U.S. Department of Justice.

Kempf-Leonard, Kimberly, Paul E. Tracy, and James C. Howell. 2001. "Serious, Violent, and Chronic Juvenile Offenders: The Relationship of Delinquency Career Types to Adult Criminality." *Justice Quarterly* 18:449–78.

Klein, Malcolm. 1984. "Offense Specialization and Versatility among Juveniles." *British Journal of Criminology* 24:185–94.

Kobner, O. 1893. "Die methode einer wissenschaftlichen ruckfallsstatistik als grundlage einer reform der kriminalstatistik." *Zeitschrift gesamter strafrechtswissenschaft* 13:670–89.

Kratzer, Lynn, and Sheilagh Hodgins. 1999. "A Typology of Offenders: A Test of Moffitt's Theory among Males and Females from Childhood to Age 30." *Criminal Behaviour and Mental Health* 9:57–73.

Krohn, Marvin D., Terence P. Thornberry, Craig Rivera, and Marc Le Blanc. 2001. "Later Delinquency Careers." In *Child Delinquents: Development, Intervention, and Service Needs,* edited by Rolf Loeber and David P. Farrington. Thousand Oaks, Calif.: Sage.

Kruttschnitt, Candace, Christopher Uggen, and Kelly Shelton. 2000. "Predictors of Desistance among Sex Offenders: The Interaction of Formal and Informal Social Controls." *Justice Quarterly* 17:61–87.

Lanctôt, Nadine, and Marc Le Blanc. 2002. "Explaining Deviance by Adolescent Females." In *Crime and Justice: An Annual Review of Research,* vol. 29, edited by Michael Tonry. Chicago: University of Chicago Press.

Land, Kenneth C., Patricia L. McCall, and Daniel S. Nagin. 1996. "A Comparison of Poisson, Negative Binomial, and Semiparametric Mixed Poisson Regression Models: With Empirical Applications to Criminal Careers Data." *Sociological Methods and Research* 24:387–442.

Land, Kenneth C., and Daniel S. Nagin. 1996. "Micro-Models of Criminal Careers: A Synthesis of the Criminal Careers and Life-Course Approaches via Semiparametric Mixed Poisson Regression Models with Empirical Applications." *Journal of Quantitative Criminology* 12:163–91.

Lattimore, Pamela K., Richard L. Linster, and John M. MacDonald. 1997. "Risk of Death among Serious Young Offenders." *Journal of Research in Crime and Delinquency* 34:187–209.

Lattimore, Pamela K., John MacDonald, Alex R. Piquero, Richard Linster, and Christy A. Visher. Forthcoming. "Frequency and Variation in Criminal Offending." *Journal of Research in Crime and Delinquency* 40.

Lattimore, Pamela K., Christy A. Visher, and Richard Linster. 1994. "Specialization in Juvenile Careers: Markov Results for a California Cohort." *Journal of Quantitative Criminology* 10:291–316.

Laub, John H., Daniel S. Nagin, and Robert J. Sampson. 1998. "Good Marriages and Trajectories of Change in Criminal Offending." *American Sociological Review* 63:225–38.

Laub, John H., and Robert J. Sampson. 2001. "Understanding Desistance from Crime." In *Crime and Justice: An Annual Review of Research*, vol. 28, edited by Michael Tonry. Chicago: University of Chicago Press.

Laub, John H., Robert J. Sampson, and Elaine Eggleston. 2001. "Examining Long-Term Trajectories of Criminal Offending: The Glueck Delinquents from Age 7 to 70." Paper presented at the annual meeting of the American Society of Criminology, Atlanta.

Laub, John H., and George E. Vaillant. 2000. "Delinquency and Mortality: A 50-Year Follow-Up Study of 1,000 Delinquent and Nondelinquent Boys." *American Journal of Psychiatry* 157:96–102.

Lauritsen, Janet. 1998. "The Age-Crime Debate: Assessing the Limits of Longitudinal Self-Report Data." *Social Forces* 77:127–55.

Le Blanc, Marc. 1998. "Screening of Serious and Violent Juvenile Offenders: Identification, Classification, and Prediction." In *Serious and Violent Juvenile Offenders: Risk Factors and Successful Interventions*, edited by Rolf Loeber and David P. Farrington. Thousand Oaks, Calif.: Sage.

———. Forthcoming. "The Offending Cycle, Escalation, and De-escalation in Delinquent Behavior: A Challenge for Criminology." *International Journal of Comparative and Applied Criminal Justice* vol. 26.

Le Blanc, Marc, G. Côté, and Rolf Loeber. 1991. "Temporal Paths in Delinquency: Stability, Regression, and Progression Analyzed with Panel Data from an Adolescent and a Delinquent Sample." *Canadian Journal of Criminology* 33:23–44.

Le Blanc, Marc, and Marcel Fréchette. 1989. *Male Criminal Activity from Childhood through Youth: Multilevel and Developmental Perspectives*. New York: Springer.

Le Blanc, Marc, and Nathalie Kaspy. 1998. "Trajectories of Delinquency and Problem Behavior: Comparison of Synchronous Paths on Social and Personal Control Characteristics of Adolescents." *Journal of Quantitative Criminology* 14:181–214.

Le Blanc, Marc, and Rolf Loeber. 1998. "Developmental Criminology Updated." In *Crime and Justice: An Annual Review of Research*, vol. 23, edited by Michael Tonry. Chicago: University of Chicago Press.

Lemert, Edwin M. 1951. *Social Pathology: A Systematic Approach to the Theory of Sociopathic Behavior*. New York: McGraw-Hill.

Loeber, Rolf, and David P. Farrington, eds. 1998. *Serious and Violent Juvenile Offenders: Risk Factors and Successful Interventions*. Thousand Oaks, Calif.: Sage.

Loeber, Rolf, David P. Farrington, Magda Stouthamer-Loeber, Terrie E. Moffitt, and Avshalom Caspi. 1998. "The Development of Male Offending: Key Findings from the First Decade of the Pittsburgh Youth Study." *Studies on Crime and Crime Prevention* 7:141–72.

Loeber, Rolf, and Marc Le Blanc. 1990. "Toward a Developmental Criminology." In *Crime and Justice: An Annual Review of Research*, vol. 12, edited by Michael Tonry and Norval Morris. Chicago: University of Chicago Press.

Loeber, Rolf, and Howard N. Snyder. 1990. "Rate of Offending in Juvenile Careers: Findings of Constancy and Change in Lambda." *Criminology* 28: 97–110.

Loeber, Rolf, Magda Stouthamer-Loeber, Welmoet B. Van Kammen, and David P. Farrington. 1991. "Initiation, Escalation, and Desistance in Juvenile Offending and Their Correlates." *Journal of Criminal Law and Criminology* 82:36–82.

Loeber, Rolf, Evelyn Wei, Magda Stouthamer-Loeber, David Huizinga, and Terence P. Thornberry. 1999. "Behavioral Antecedents to Serious and Violent Offending: Joint Analyses from the Denver Youth Survey, Pittsburgh Youth Study, and the Rochester Youth Development Study." *Studies on Crime and Crime Prevention* 8:245–64.

Lynam, Donald R., Avshalom Caspi, Terrie E. Moffitt, Per-Olof H. Wikström, Rolf Loeber, and Steven P. Novak. 2000. "The Interaction between Impulsivity and Neighborhood Context on Offending: The Effects of Impulsivity Are Stronger in Poorer Neighborhoods." *Journal of Abnormal Psychology* 109:563–74.

Lynam, Donald, Alex R. Piquero, and Terrie E. Moffitt. 2002. "Specialization Observed from Self-Reports but Not Official Records." Unpublished manuscript. Lexington: University of Kentucky.

Maltz, Michael D., and Jacqueline M. Mullany. 2000. "Visualizing Lives: New Pathways for Analyzing Life Course Trajectories." *Journal of Quantitative Criminology* 16:237–54.

Manski, Charles F., and Daniel S. Nagin. 1998. "Bounding Disagreements about Treatment Effects: A Case Study of Sentencing and Recidivism." *Sociological Methodology* 28:99–137.

Maruna, Shadd. 2001. *Making Good: How Ex-convicts Reform and Rebuild Their Lives.* Washington, D.C.: American Psychological Association.

Mazerolle, Paul. 1997. "Delinquent Definitions and Participation Age: Assessing the Invariance Hypothesis." *Studies on Crime and Crime Prevention* 6: 151–68.

Mazerolle, Paul, Robert Brame, Raymond Paternoster, Alex Piquero, and Charles Dean. 2000. "Onset Age, Persistence, and Offending Versatility: Comparisons across Gender." *Criminology* 38:1143–72.

McCord, Joan. 1978. "A Thirty-Year Follow-Up of Treatment Effects." *American Psychologist* 33:284–89.

———. 1991. "Family Relationships, Juvenile Delinquency, and Adult Criminality." *Criminology* 29:397–418.

———. 1992. "The Cambridge-Somerville Study: A Pioneering Longitudinal-Experimental Study of Delinquency Prevention." In *Preventing Antisocial Behavior: Interventions from Birth through Adolescence,* edited by Joan McCord and Richard E. Tremblay. New York: Guilford.

———. 1999. "Alcoholism and Crime across Generations." *Criminal Behaviour and Mental Health* 9:107–17.

———. 2000. "Developmental Trajectories and Intentional Actions." *Journal of Quantitative Criminology* 16:237–53.

Mednick, Sarnoff A., William F. Gabrielli, Jr., and Barry Hutchings. 1984.

"Genetic Influences in Criminal Convictions: Evidence from an Adoption Cohort." *Science* 224:891–94.

Miller, Frederick J. W., S. D. M. Court, E. A. Knox, and S. Brandon. 1974. *The School Years in Newcastle-upon-Tyne, 1952–1962.* London: Oxford University Press.

Miranne, Alfred C., and Michael R. Geerken. 1991. "The New Orleans Inmate Survey: A Test of Greenwood's Predictive Scale." *Criminology* 29:497–518.

Moffitt, Terrie E. 1993. "'Life-Course-Persistent' and 'Adolescence-Limited' Antisocial Behavior: A Developmental Taxonomy." *Psychological Review* 100: 674–701.

Moffitt, Terrie E., and Avshalom Caspi. 2001. "Childhood Predictors Differentiate Life-Course-Persistent and Adolescence-Limited Antisocial Pathways, among Males and Females." *Development and Psychopathology* 13:355–75.

Moffitt, Terrie E., Avshalom Caspi, Nigel Dickson, Phil A. Silva, and Warren Stanton. 1996. "Childhood-Onset versus Adolescent-Onset Antisocial Conduct in Males: Natural History from Age 3 to 18." *Development and Psychopathology* 8:399–424.

Moffitt, Terrie E., Avshalom Caspi, Michael Rutter, and Phil A. Silva. 2001. *Sex Differences in Antisocial Behaviour: Conduct Disorder, Delinquency, and Violence in the Dunedin Longitudinal Study.* Cambridge: Cambridge University Press.

Moffitt, Terrie E., Donald R. Lynam, and Phil A. Silva. 1994. "Neuropsychological Tests Predicting Persistent Male Delinquency." *Criminology* 32:277–300.

Morris, Norval. 1972. Foreword to *Delinquency in a Birth Cohort*, by Marvin E. Wolfgang, Robert M. Figlio, and Thorsten Sellin. Chicago: University of Chicago Press.

Mulvey, Edward P., and J. F. Larosa. 1986. "Delinquency Cessation and Adolescent Development: Preliminary Data." *American Journal of Orthopsychiatry* 56:212–24.

Muthen, Bengt, and Linda K. Muthen. 2000. "Integrating Person-Centered and Variable-Centered Analyses: Growth Mixture Modeling with Latent Trajectory Classes." *Alcoholism: Clinical and Experimental Research* 24:882–91.

Nagin, Daniel S. 1999. "Analyzing Developmental Trajectories: A Semi-parametric, Group-Based Approach." *Psychological Methods* 4:139–77.

Nagin, Daniel S., and David P. Farrington. 1992*a*. "The Onset and Persistence of Offending." *Criminology* 30:501–23.

———. 1992*b*. "The Stability of Criminal Potential from Childhood to Adulthood." *Criminology* 30:235–60.

Nagin, Daniel S., David P. Farrington, and Terrie E. Moffitt. 1995. "Life-Course Trajectories of Different Types of Offenders." *Criminology* 33:111–39.

Nagin, Daniel S., and Kenneth C. Land. 1993. "Age, Criminal Careers, and Population Heterogeneity: Specification and Estimation of a Nonparametric, Mixed Poisson Model." *Criminology* 31:327–62.

Nagin, Daniel S., and Raymond Paternoster. 1991. "On the Relationship of Past and Future Participation in Delinquency." *Criminology* 29:163–90.

———. 2000. "Population Heterogeneity and State Dependence: State of the Evidence and Directions for Future Research." *Journal of Quantitative Criminology* 16:117–44.

Nagin, Daniel S., and Douglas A. Smith. 1990. "Participation in and Frequency of Delinquent Behavior: A Test for Structural Differences." *Journal of Quantitative Criminology* 6:335–56.

Nagin, Daniel S., and Richard E. Tremblay. 1999. "Trajectories of Boys' Physical Aggression, Opposition, and Hyperactivity on the Path to Physically Violent and Nonviolent Juvenile Delinquency." *Child Development* 70: 1181–96.

Nagin, Daniel S., and Joel Waldfogel. 1995. "The Effects of Criminality and Conviction on the Labor Market Status of Young British Offenders." *International Review of Law and Economics* 15:109–26.

Nevares, Dora, Marvin E. Wolfgang, and Paul E. Tracy. 1990. *Delinquency in Puerto Rico: The 1970 Birth Cohort Study.* New York: Greenwood.

Office of Juvenile Justice and Delinquency Prevention (OJJDP). 1998. *Serious and Violent Juvenile Offenders.* Washington, D.C.: U.S. Department of Justice.

Osgood, D. Wayne, Patrick M. O'Malley, Jerald G. Bachman, and Lloyd D. Johnston. 1989. "Time Trends and Age Trends in Arrests and Self-Reported Illegal Behavior." *Criminology* 27:389–418.

Osgood, D. Wayne, and David C. Rowe. 1994. "Bridging Criminal Careers, Theory, and Policy through Latent Variable Models of Individual Offending." *Criminology* 32:517–54.

Ouimet, Marc, and Marc Le Blanc. 1995. "The Role of Life Experiences in the Continuation of the Adult Criminal Career." *Criminal Behaviour and Mental Health* 6:73–97.

Ouston, Janet. 1984. "Delinquency, Family Background, and Educational Attainment." *British Journal of Criminology* 24:120–33.

Paternoster, Raymond. 1989. "Absolute and Restrictive Deterrence in a Panel of Youth: Explaining the Onset, Persistence/Desistance, and Frequency of Delinquent Offending." *Social Problems* 36:289–309.

Paternoster, Raymond, and Robert Brame. 1997. "Multiple Routes to Delinquency? A Test of Developmental and General Theories of Crime." *Criminology* 35:49–84.

Paternoster, Raymond, Robert Brame, and David P. Farrington. 2001. "On the Relationship between Adolescent and Adult Conviction Frequencies." *Journal of Quantitative Criminology* 17:201–26.

Paternoster, Raymond, Robert Brame, Alex Piquero, Paul Mazerolle, and Charles W. Dean. 1998. "The Forward Specialization Coefficient: Distributional Properties and Subgroup Differences." *Journal of Quantitative Criminology* 14:133–54.

Paternoster, Raymond, Charles W. Dean, Alex Piquero, Paul Mazerolle, and Robert Brame. 1997. "Generality, Continuity, and Change in Offending." *Journal of Quantitative Criminology* 13:231–66.

Paternoster, Raymond, and Ruth Triplett. 1988. "Disaggregating Self-Reported Delinquency and Its Implications for Theory." *Criminology* 26: 591–625.

Patterson, Gerald R. 1993. "Orderly Change in a Stable World: The Antisocial Trait as a Chimera." *Journal of Consulting and Clinical Psychology* 61:911–19.

Patterson, Gerald R., L. Crosby, and S. Vuchinich. 1992. "Predicting Risk for Early Police Contact." *Journal of Quantitative Criminology* 8:335–55.

Patterson, Gerald R., and Karen Yoerger. 1999. "Intraindividual Growth in Covert Antisocial Behaviour: A Necessary Precursor to Chronic Juvenile and Adult Arrests?" *Criminal Behaviour and Mental Health* 9:24–38.

Petersilia, Joan. 1980. "Criminal Career Research: A Review of Recent Evidence." In *Crime and Justice: An Annual Review of Research*, vol. 2, edited by Norval Morris and Michael Tonry. Chicago: University of Chicago Press.

Petersilia, Joan, Peter W. Greenwood, and Marvin Lavin. 1978. *Criminal Careers of Habitual Felons*. Washington, D.C.: National Institute of Law Enforcement and Criminal Justice, Law Enforcement Assistance Administration; Washington, D.C.: U.S. Government Printing Office.

Peterson, Mark A., and Harriet B. Braiker. 1980. *Doing Crime: A Survey of California Prison Inmates*. Report no. R-2200-DOJ. Santa Monica, Calif.: Rand.

Piper, Elizabeth. 1983. "Patterns of Violent Recidivism." Ph.D. dissertation, University of Pennsylvania, Sellin Center for Criminology.

———. 1985. "Violent Recidivism and Chronicity in the 1958 Philadelphia Cohort." *Journal of Quantitative Criminology* 1:319–44.

Piquero, Alex R. 2000. "Assessing the Relationships between Gender, Chronicity, Seriousness, and Offense Skewness in Criminal Offending." *Journal of Criminal Justice* 28:103–16.

———. 2001. "Testing Moffitt's Neuropsychological Variation Hypothesis for the Prediction of Life-Course Persistent Offending." *Psychology, Crime and Law* 7:193–216.

———. Forthcoming. "The Intermittency of Criminal Careers." In *Ex-offender Reintegration: Pathways to Desistance from Crime*, edited by Shadd Maruna and Russ Immarigeon. Albany: State University of New York Press.

Piquero, Alex R., Alfred Blumstein, Robert Brame, Rudy Haapanen, Edward P. Mulvey, and Daniel S. Nagin. 2001. "Assessing the Impact of Exposure Time and Incapacitation on Longitudinal Trajectories of Criminal Offending." *Journal of Adolescent Research* 16:54–74.

Piquero, Alex R., Robert Brame, and Donald Lynam. 2002. "Do the Factors Associated with Life-Course-Persistent Offending Relate to Career Length?" Unpublished manuscript. Gainesville: University of Florida.

Piquero, Alex R., Robert Brame, Paul Mazerolle, and Rudy Haapanen. 2002. "Crime in Emerging Adulthood." *Criminology* 40:137–70.

Piquero, Alex R., and Timothy Brezina. 2001. "Testing Moffitt's Account of Adolescence-Limited Delinquency." *Criminology* 39:353–70.

Piquero, Alex R., and Stephen L. Buka. 2002. "Linking Juvenile and Adult Patterns of Criminal Activity in the Providence Cohort of the National Collaborative Perinatal Project." *Journal of Criminal Justice* 30:1–14.

Piquero, Alex R., and He Len Chung. 2001. "On the Relationships between Gender, Early Onset, and the Seriousness of Offending." *Journal of Criminal Justice* 29:189–206.

Piquero, Alex R., John MacDonald, and Karen F. Parker. 2002. "Race, Local Life Circumstances, and Criminal Activity over the Life-Course." *Social Science Quarterly* 83:654–70.

Piquero, Alex R., Randall MacIntosh, and Matthew Hickman. 2002. "The Validity of a Delinquency Scale." *Sociological Methods and Research* 30:492–529.

Piquero, Alex R., and Paul Mazerolle, eds. 2001. *Life-Course Criminology: Contemporary and Classic Readings.* Belmont, Calif.: Wadsworth.

Piquero, Alex R., Raymond Paternoster, Paul Mazerolle, Robert Brame, and Charles W. Dean. 1999. "Onset Age and Offense Specialization." *Journal of Research in Crime and Delinquency* 36:275–99.

Polk, Kenneth, Christine Alder, Gordon Basemore, G. Blake, S. Cordray, G. Coventry, J. Galvin, and M. Temple. 1981. *Becoming Adult: An Analysis of Maturational Development from Age 16 to 30.* Final Report, grant MH 14806, Center for Studies of Crime and Delinquency, National Institute of Mental Health. Washington, D.C.: U.S. Department of Health and Human Services.

PRIDE Surveys. 2000. *1999–2000 National Summary, Grades 6 through 12.* Bowling Green, Ky.: PRIDE Surveys.

Pulkkinen, Lea. 1988. "Delinquent Development: Theoretical and Empirical Considerations." In *Studies of Psychosocial Risk: The Power of Longitudinal Data,* edited by Michael Rutter. Cambridge: Cambridge University Press.

Puzzanchera, Charles M. 2000. *Self-Reported Delinquency by 12-Year-Olds, 1997.* Office of Juvenile Justice and Delinquency Prevention Fact Sheet no. 03. Washington, D.C.: Office of Juvenile Justice and Delinquency Prevention, U.S. Department of Justice.

Quetelet, Adolphe. [1831] 1984. *Research on the Propensity for Crime at Different Ages.* Translated by Sawyer F. Sylvester. Cincinnati, Ohio: Anderson.

Rand, Alicia. 1987. "Transitional Life Events and Desistance from Delinquency and Crime." In *From Boy to Man, from Delinquency to Crime,* edited by Marvin E. Wolfgang, Terence P. Thornberry, and Robert M. Figlio. Chicago: University of Chicago Press.

Raudenbush, Stephen W. 2001. "Toward a Coherent Framework for Comparing Trajectories of Individual Change." In *New Methods for the Analysis of Change,* edited by Linda M. Collins and Aline G. Sayers. Washington, D.C.: American Psychological Association.

Reiss, Albert J., Jr. 1986a. "Co-offender Influences on Criminal Careers." In *Criminal Careers and "Career Criminals,"* vol. 2, edited by Alfred Blumstein, Jacqueline Cohen, Jeffrey A. Roth, and Christy A. Visher. Washington, D.C.: National Academy Press.

———. 1986b. "Why Are Communities Important in Understanding Crime?" In *Communities and Crime,* edited by Albert J. Reiss, Jr., and Michael Tonry. Vol. 8 of *Crime and Justice: A Review of Research,* edited by Michael Tonry and Norval Morris. Chicago: University of Chicago Press.

Reiss, Albert J., Jr., and David P. Farrington. 1991. "Advancing Knowledge about Co-offending: Results from a Prospective Longitudinal Survey of London Males." *Journal of Criminal Law and Criminology* 82:360–95.

Robins, Lee N. 1966. *Deviant Children Grown Up.* Baltimore: Williams & Wilkins.

Roeder, Kathryn, Kevin G. Lynch, and Daniel S. Nagin. 1999. "Modeling Uncertainty in Latent Class Membership: A Case Study in Criminology." *Journal of the American Statistical Association* 94:766–76.

Rojek, Dean G., and Maynard L. Erickson. 1982. "Delinquent Careers: A Test of the Career Escalation Model." *Criminology* 20:5–28.

Rolph, John E., and Jan M. Chaiken. 1987. *Identifying High-Rate Serious Criminals from Official Records.* Rand Report no. R-3433-NIJ. Santa Monica, Calif.: Rand.

Rowe, Alan R., and Charles R. Tittle. 1977. "Life Cycle Changes and Criminal Propensity." *Sociological Quarterly* 18:223–36.

Rutter, Michael. 1985. "Resilience in the Face of Adversity: Protective Factors and Resistance to Psychiatric Disorder." *British Journal of Psychiatry* 147: 598–611.

Sampson, Robert J., and John H. Laub. 1992. "Crime and Deviance in the Life Course." *Annual Review of Sociology* 18:63–84.

———. 1993. *Crime in the Making: Pathways and Turning Points through Life.* Cambridge, Mass.: Harvard University Press.

———. 1997. "A Life-Course Theory of Cumulative Disadvantage and the Stability of Delinquency." In *Developmental Theories of Crime and Delinquency,* vol. 7 of *Advances in Criminological Theory,* edited by Terence P. Thornberry. New Brunswick, N.J.: Transaction.

Sampson, Robert J., Stephen W. Raudenbush, and Felton Earls. 1997. "Neighborhoods and Violent Crime: A Multilevel Study of Collective Efficacy." *Science* 277:918–24.

Sarnecki, Jerzy. 1990. "Delinquent Networks in Sweden." *Journal of Quantitative Criminology* 6:31–51.

———. 2001. *Delinquent Networks: Youth Co-offending in Stockholm.* Cambridge: Cambridge University Press.

Schmertmann, Carl P., Adansi A. Amankwaa, and Robert D. Long. 1998. "Three Strikes and You're Out: Demographic Analysis of Mandatory Prison Sentencing." *Demography* 35:445–63.

Shannon, Lyle. 1978. "A Longitudinal Study of Delinquency and Crime." In *Quantitative Studies in Criminology,* edited by Charles F. Wellford. Papers presented at the 1977 meetings of the American Society of Criminology. Beverly Hills, Calif.: Sage.

———. 1980. "Assessing the Relationship of Adult Criminal Careers to Juvenile Careers." In *Problems in American Social Policy Research,* edited by Clark C. Abt. Cambridge, Mass.: Abt Books.

———. 1982. *Assessing the Relationship of Adult Criminal Careers to Juvenile Careers.* Washington, D.C.: Office of Juvenile Justice and Delinquency Prevention, U.S. Department of Justice.

Shaw, Clifford R. 1930. *The Jack-Roller: A Delinquent Boy's Own Story.* Chicago: University of Chicago Press.

Shelden, Randall G., John A. Horvath, and Sharon Tracy. 1987. "Do Status Offenders Get Worse? Some Clarifications on the Question of Escalation." *Crime and Delinquency* 35:202–16.

Sherman, Lawrence, David P. Farrington, Brandon C. Welsh, and Doris L. MacKenzie, eds. 2002. *Evidence-Based Crime Prevention.* London: Routledge.

Shinnar, Shlomo, and Reuel Shinnar. 1975. "The Effects of the Criminal Justice System on the Control of Crime: A Quantitative Approach." *Law and Society Review* 9:581–611.

Shover, Neal. 1996. *Great Pretenders: Pursuits and Careers of Persistent Thieves.* Boulder, Colo.: Westview.

Silva, Phil A., and Warren Stanton, eds. 1996. *From Child to Adult: The Dunedin Multidisciplinary Health and Development Study.* Oxford: Oxford University Press.

Silverthorn, Persephanie, and Paul J. Frick. 1999. "Developmental Pathways to Antisocial Behavior: The Delayed-Onset Pathway in Girls." *Development and Psychopathology* 11:101–26.

Simons, Ronald L., Christine Johnson, Rand D. Conger, and Glen Elder, Jr. 1998. "A Test of Latent Trait versus Life-Course Perspectives on the Stability of Adolescent Antisocial Behavior." *Criminology* 36:217–43.

Simons, Ronald L., Eric A. Stewart, Leslie C. Gordon, Rand D. Conger, and Glen H. Elder, Jr. 2002. "A Test of Life Course Explanations for Stability and Change in Antisocial Behavior from Adolescence to Young Adulthood." *Criminology* 40:401–34.

Simons, Ronald L., Chyi-In Wu, Rand D. Conger, and Frederick O. Lorenz. 1994. "Two Routes to Delinquency: Differences between Early and Late Starters in the Impact of Parenting and Deviant Peers." *Criminology* 32: 247–76.

Smith, D. Randall, and William R. Smith. 1984. "Patterns of Delinquent Careers: An Assessment of Three Perspectives." *Social Science Research* 13:129–58.

Smith, D. Randall, William R. Smith, and Elliot Noma. 1984. "Delinquent Career-Lines: A Conceptual Link between Theory and Juvenile Offenses." *Sociological Quarterly* 25:155–72.

Smith, Douglas A., and Robert Brame. 1994. "On the Initiation and Continuation of Delinquency." *Criminology* 32:607–30.

Smith, Douglas A., and Patrick R. Gartin. 1989. "Specifying Specific Deterrence: The Influence of Arrest on Future Criminal Activity." *American Sociological Review* 54:94–106.

Smith, Douglas A., and Raymond Paternoster. 1990. "Formal Processing and Future Delinquency: Deviance Amplification as Selection Artifact." *Law and Society Review* 24:1109–31.

Smith, Douglas A., Christy A. Visher, and G. Roger Jarjoura. 1991. "Dimensions of Delinquency: Exploring the Correlates of Participation, Frequency, and Persistence of Delinquent Behavior." *Journal of Research in Crime and Delinquency* 28:6–32.

Soothill, Keith, Brian Francis, and Rachel Fligelstone. 2002. "Patterns of Offending Behaviour: A New Approach." Final report presented to the British

Home Office. London: Research Development and Statistics Directorate, Home Office.

Spelman, William. 1994. *Criminal Incapacitation.* New York: Plenum.

———. 1995. "Criminal Careers of Public Places." In *Crime and Place*, edited by John E. Eck and David Weisburd. Monsey, N.Y.: Criminal Justice Press and Police Executive Research Forum.

Stander, Julian, David P. Farrington, Gillian Hill, and Patricia M. E. Altham. 1989. "Markov Chain Analysis and Specialization in Criminal Careers." *British Journal of Criminology* 29:317–35.

Stattin, Håkan, and David Magnusson. 1991. "Stability and Change in Criminal Behaviour Up to Age 30." *British Journal of Criminology* 31:327–46.

Stattin, Håkan, David Magnusson, and Howard Reichel. 1989. "Criminal Activity at Different Ages: A Study Based on a Swedish Longitudinal Research Population." *British Journal of Criminology* 29:368–85.

Steffensmeier, Darrell J., Emilie Andersen Allan, Miles D. Harer, and Cathy Streifel. 1989. "Age and the Distribution of Crime." *American Journal of Sociology* 94:803–31.

Stolzenberg, Lisa, and Stewart J. D'Alessio. 1997. "'Three Strikes and You're Out': The Impact of California's New Mandatory Sentencing Law on Serious Crime Rates." *Crime and Delinquency* 43:457–69.

Stouthamer-Loeber, Magda, Rolf Loeber, David P. Farrington, Quanwu Zhang, Welmoet Van Kammen, and Eugene Maguin. 1993. "The Double Edge of Protective and Risk Factors for Delinquency: Interrelations and Developmental Patterns." *Development and Psychopathology* 5:683–701.

Sutherland, Edwin. 1937. *The Professional Thief.* Chicago: University of Chicago Press.

———. 1947. *Principles of Criminology.* 4th ed. Philadelphia: Lippincott.

Tarling, Roger. 1993. *Analyzing Offending: Data, Models and Interpretations.* London: Her Majesty's Stationery Office.

Thornberry, Terence P. 1989. "Panel Effects and the Use of Self-Reported Measures of Delinquency in Longitudinal Studies." In *Cross-National Research in Self-Reported Crime and Delinquency*, edited by Malcolm W. Klein. Dordrecht: Kluwer Academic.

———. 1997. "Introduction: Some Advantages of Developmental and Life-Course Perspectives for the Study of Crime and Delinquency." In *Developmental Theories of Crime and Delinquency*, vol. 7 of *Advances in Criminological Theory*, edited by Terence P. Thornberry. New Brunswick, N.J.: Transaction.

Thornberry, Terence P., and Marvin D. Krohn. 2000. "The Self-Report Method for Measuring Delinquency and Crime." In *Measurement and Analysis of Crime and Justice*, vol. 4 of *Criminal Justice 2000*. Washington, D.C.: National Institute of Justice, Office of Justice Programs, U.S. Department of Justice.

Tibbetts, Stephen G., and Alex R. Piquero. 1999. "The Influence of Gender, Low Birth Weight, and Disadvantaged Environment in Predicting Early Onset of Offending: A Test of Moffitt's Interactional Hypothesis." *Criminology* 37:843–78.

Tittle, Charles R. 1988. "Two Empirical Regularities (Maybe) in Search of an Explanation: Commentary on the Age/Crime Debate." *Criminology* 26:75–85.

Tittle, Charles R., and Harold G. Grasmick. 1997. "Criminal Behavior and Age: A Test of Three Provocative Hypotheses." *Journal of Criminal Law and Criminology* 88:309–42.

Tolan, Patrick H. 1987. "Implications of Age of Onset for Delinquency Risk." *Journal of Abnormal Child Psychology* 15:47–65.

Tolan, Patrick H., and Deborah Gorman-Smith. 1998. "Development of Serious and Violent Offending Careers." In *Serious and Violent Juvenile Offenders: Risk Factors and Successful Interventions*, edited by Rolf Loeber and David P. Farrington. Thousand Oaks, Calif.: Sage.

Tonry, Michael, and David P. Farrington, eds. 1995. *Building a Safer Society: Strategic Approaches to Crime Prevention*. Vol. 19 of *Crime and Justice: A Review of Research*, edited by Michael Tonry. Chicago: University of Chicago Press.

Tonry, Michael, Lloyd E. Ohlin, and David P. Farrington. 1991. *Human Development and Criminal Behavior: New Ways of Advancing Knowledge*. New York: Springer.

Tracy, Paul E., and Kimberly Kempf-Leonard. 1996. *Continuity and Discontinuity in Criminal Careers*. New York: Plenum.

Tracy, Paul E., Marvin E. Wolfgang, and Robert M. Figlio. 1990. *Delinquency Careers in Two Birth Cohorts*. New York: Plenum.

Tremblay, Pierre. 1993. "Searching for Suitable Co-offenders." In *Routine Activity and Rational Choice*, vol. 5 of *Advances in Criminological Theory*, edited by Ronald V. Clarke and Marcus Felson. New Brunswick, N.J.: Plenum.

Tremblay, Richard E., and Wendy M. Craig. 1995. "Developmental Crime Prevention." In *Building a Safer Society: Strategic Approaches to Crime Prevention*, edited by Michael Tonry and David P. Farrington. Vol. 19 of *Crime and Justice: A Review of Research*, edited by Michael Tonry. Chicago: University of Chicago Press.

Tremblay, Richard E., Robert O. Pihl, Frank Vitaro, and Patricia L. Dobkin. 1994. "Predicting Early Onset of Male Antisocial Behavior from Preschool Behavior." *Archives of General Psychiatry* 51:732–39.

Triplett, Ruth A. and G. Roger Jarjoura. 1994. "Theoretical and Empirical Specification of a Model of Informal Labeling." *Journal of Quantitative Criminology* 10:241–76.

Uggen, Christopher, and Irving Piliavin. 1998. "Asymmetrical Causation and Criminal Desistance." *Journal of Criminal Law and Criminology* 88:1399–1422.

U.S. Department of Health and Human Services, Centers for Disease Control and Prevention. 2000. "Fact Sheet: Youth Risk Behavior Trends." Available on-line at http://www.cdc.gov/nccdphp/dash/yrbs/trend.htm (visited February 2002).

Visher, Christy A. 1986. "The Rand Inmate Survey: A Re-analysis." In *Criminal Careers and "Career Criminals,"* vol. 2, edited by Alfred Blumstein, Jacqueline Cohen, Jeffrey A. Roth, and Christy A. Visher. Washington, D.C.: National Academy Press.

———. 1987. "Incapacitation and Crime Control: Does a 'Lock 'em Up' Strategy Reduce Crime?" *Justice Quarterly* 4:513–43.

———. 2000. "Career Criminals and Crime Control." In *Criminology: A Contemporary Handbook*, edited by Joseph F. Sheley. 3d ed. Belmont, Calif.: Wadsworth.

Visher, Christy A., and Jeffrey A. Roth. 1986. "Participation in Criminal Careers." In *Criminal Careers and "Career Criminals,"* vol. 1, edited by Alfred Blumstein, Jacqueline Cohen, Jeffrey A. Roth, and Christy A. Visher. Washington, D.C.: National Academy Press.

von Mayr, Georg. 1917. "Statistics and Gesellschaftslehre." *Kriminalstatistik* 3: 425–26.

von Scheel, H. 1890. "Zur einfuhrung in die kriminalstatistik insbesondere diegenige des deutschen reichs." *Allgemeines Statistisches Archiv* 1:183–94.

Walker, Nigel D., David P. Farrington, and Gillian Tucker. 1981. "Reconviction Rates of Adult Males after Different Sentences." *British Journal of Criminology* 21:357–60.

Warr, Mark. 1996. "Organization and Instigation in Delinquent Groups." *Criminology* 34:11–38.

———. 1998. "Life-Course Transitions and Desistance from Crime." *Criminology* 36:183–216.

———. 2002. *Companions in Crime: The Social Aspects of Criminal Conduct.* Cambridge: Cambridge University Press.

Warren, Marguerite Q., and Jill Leslie Rosenbaum. 1987. "Criminal Careers of Female Offenders." *Criminal Justice and Behavior* 13:393–418.

Weiner, Neil Alan. 1989. "Violent Criminal Careers and 'Violent Career Criminals.'" In *Violent Crime, Violent Criminals*, edited by Neil Alan Weiner and Marvin E. Wolfgang. Newbury Park, Calif.: Sage.

Weis, Joseph G. 1986. "Issues in the Measurement of Criminal Careers." In *Criminal Careers and "Career Criminals,"* vol. 2, edited by Alfred Blumstein, Jacqueline Cohen, Jeffrey A. Roth, and Christy A. Visher. Washington, D.C.: National Academy Press.

Weisburd, David, and Elin Waring. 2001. *White-Collar Crime and Criminal Careers.* Cambridge: Cambridge University Press.

Werner, Emmy E., and Ruth S. Smith. 1982. *Vulnerable but Invincible: A Longitudinal Study of Resilient Children and Youth.* New York: McGraw-Hill.

Wikström, Per-Olof H. 1985. *Everyday Violence in Contemporary Sweden: Situational and Ecological Aspects.* Stockholm: National Council for Crime Prevention, Sweden, Research Division.

———. 1990. "Age and Crime in a Stockholm Cohort." *Journal of Quantitative Criminology* 6:61–84.

Wikström, Per-Olof H., and Rolf Loeber. 2000. "Do Disadvantaged Neighborhoods Cause Well-Adjusted Children to Become Adolescent Delinquents?" *Criminology* 38:1109–42.

Wikström, Per-Olof H., and Robert J. Sampson. Forthcoming. "Social Mechanisms of Community Influences on Crime and Pathways in Criminality."

In *The Causes of Conduct Disorder and Serious Juvenile Delinquency*, edited by Benjamin B. Lahey, Terrie E. Moffitt, and Avshalom Caspi. New York: Guilford.

Wilson, James Q., and Richard J. Herrnstein. 1985. *Crime and Human Nature.* New York: Simon & Schuster.

Wilson, James Q., and Joan Petersilia, eds. 2001. *Crime: Public Policies for Crime Control.* 2d ed. Oakland, Calif.: ICS Press.

Wolfgang, Marvin E., Robert M. Figlio, and Thorsten Sellin. 1972. *Delinquency in a Birth Cohort.* Chicago: University of Chicago Press.

Zimring, Franklin E. 1981. "Kids, Groups, and Crime: Some Implications of a Well-Known Secret." *Journal of Criminal Law and Criminology* 72:867–85.

Zimring, Franklin E., Sam Kamin, and Gordon Hawkins. 1999. *Crime and Punishment in California: The Impact of Three Strikes and You're Out.* Berkeley: Institute of Governmental Studies Press, University of California.

Author Index—Volumes 1–30*

* The number in parentheses indicates the volume in which the author's essay is
published.

Subject Index—Volumes 1–30*

* The number in parentheses indicates the volume in which the essay is published.

Population: growth in U.S. prisons, 1980–1996, (26):17; trends, and prison policy, understanding, (26): 63

Prediction: causal inference as a problem of, (9):183; and classification in criminal justice decision making, (9):1; in criminal justice policy development, (9):103; of dangerousness, (6):1; of individual crime rates, (9):53; legal and ethical issues of classification and, (9):367; and racial minorities and use of guidelines in, (9):151; selected methodological issues in, (9):21

Predictors, of male youth violence, (24):421

Preventing crime (*see* Crime prevention)

Prison management trends, 1975–2025, (26):163

Prison policy and population trends, understanding, (26):63

Prison suicide and prisoner coping, (26):283

Prisoner reentry, and parole, in the United States, (26):479

Prisoners' rights movement, 1960–1980, (2):429

Prisons: adjusting to, (16):275; American, at the beginning of the twenty-first century, (26):1; as a crime control strategy, (5):1; cross-national comparisons of, (17):1; industry and labor in, (5):85; interpersonal violence and social order in, (26):205; medical care in, (26):427; in Northern Ireland, (17):51; overcrowding in, (6):95; populations of, (10):231; private, (28):265; private institutions, (16):361; supermax, purposes, practices, and problems of, (28):385; for women, 1790–1980, (5):129; U.S., population growth in, 1980–1996, (26):17

Private security, growth and implications of, (3):193

Probation in the United States, (22):149

Procedural justice, legitimacy, and the effective rule of law (30):283

Psychopathy, construct of, (28):197

Public opinion on crime, (16):99; about punishment and corrections, (27):1

Public transport, and crime, (27):169

Punishment: and corrections, public opinion about, (27):1; penal communications and the philosophy of, (20):1; proportionality in the philosophy of, (16):55; recent social histories of, (3):153; sociological perspectives on, (14):115

Race: and ethnicity, and criminal justice in Canada, (21):469; and gender and sentencing, (22):201; and guidelines (*see* Prediction; Sentencing)

Race relations and the prisoner subculture, (1):1

Racial and ethnic disparities in crime and criminal justice in the United States, (21):311

Racketeering, labor, (30):229

Restorative community justice in the United States, (27):235

Restorative justice, (25):1

Robbery, motivation for and persistence of, (14):277

Savings and loan crisis, (18):247

Savings and loan industry, (18):203

School violence (*see also* Youth violence): curriculum, culture, and community, the challenge of, (24):317

Self-report methodology, in crime research, (25):291

Sentence severity and crime, (30):143

Title Index—Volumes 1–30*

* The number in parentheses indicates the volume in which the essay is published.

Volume Index—Volumes 1–30